Encyclopedia of the

Hundred Years War

Encyclopedia of the
Hundred Years War

John A. Wagner

GREENWOOD PRESS
Westport, Connecticut • London

Library of Congress Cataloging-in-Publication Data

Wagner, J. A. (John A.)
    Encyclopedia of the Hundred Years War / John A. Wagner.
        p. cm.
    Includes bibliographical references and index.
    ISBN 0-313-32736-X (alk. paper)
    1. Hundred Years' War, 1337–1453—Encyclopedias.   I. Title.
DC96.W34   2006
944'.02503—dc22   2006009761

British Library Cataloguing in Publication Data is available.

Library of Congress Catalog Card Number: 2006009761
ISBN: 0-313-32736-X

First published in 2006

Greenwood Press, 88 Post Road West, Westport, CT 06881
An imprint of Greenwood Publishing Group, Inc.
www.greenwood.com

Printed in the United States of America

The paper used in this book complies with the
Permanent Paper Standard issued by the National
Information Standards Organization (Z39.48-1984).

10 9 8 7 6 5 4 3 2 1

To my father,
Joseph L. Wagner,
who encouraged me to be whatever I wanted to be and worked ceaselessly
to give me opportunities to do so.

I have begun [this book] in such a way that all who see it,
read it, or hear it read may take delight and pleasure in it,
and that I may earn their regard.

—Jean Froissart, prologue to *Chronicles*

Contents

List of Entries

Guide to Related Topics

FLANDERS

FRENCH CIVIL WAR (1410s)

Thomas of Woodstock, Duke of
Gloucester

NOBILITY, FRENCH/CONTINENTAL
Albret, Arnaud-Amanieu, Lord of
Albret, Bernard-Aiz, Lord of
Albret, Charles, Lord of
Anne of Burgundy, Duchess of Bedford
Arthur III, Duke of Brittany
Bernard, Count of Armagnac
Charles, Duke of Orléans
Charles of Blois, Duke of Brittany
Charles the Bad, King of Navarre
Grailly, Jean de, Captal de Buch
Harcourt, Godfrey of
John, Count of Dunois and Longueville
John, Duke of Alençon
John, Duke of Berry
John IV, Duke of Brittany
John V, Duke of Brittany
John the Fearless, Duke of Burgundy
Louis, Duke of Anjou
Louis, Duke of Guienne
Louis, Duke of Orléans
Louis de Male, Count of Flanders
Louis de Nevers, Count of Flanders
Marguerite de Flanders, Duchess of
Burgundy
Montfort, John de
Philip the Bold, Duke of Burgundy
Philip the Good, Duke of Burgundy
Robert of Artois

POLITICAL MATTERS
Appanage
Appeal of the Gascon Lords
Armagnacs
Arras, Congress of
Avignon Peace Conference
Burghersh, Henry, Bishop of Lincoln
Burgundians
Cabochiens
Christine de Pizan
Crisis of 1340–1341
Diplomacy
Estates, General and Provincial
Hostages, Treaty of the
Isabella, Queen of England (c. 1292–1358)
Isabella, Queen of England (1388–1409)

Maine, Surrender of
Marcel, Étienne
Margaret of Anjou, Queen of England
Marmousets
National Consciousness, Growth of
Papacy and the Hundred Years War
Process
Propaganda and War Publicity
Stratford, John, Archbishop of Canterbury

PROVINCES, REGIONS, TERRITORIES, AND APPANAGES
Appanage
Aquitaine
Brittany
Burgundy
Estates, General and Provincial
Flanders
Gascony
Maine, Surrender of
Normandy

REVOLUTIONARIES, REBELLIONS, UPRISINGS, AND USURPATIONS
Anglo-Flemish Alliance
Artevelde, James van
Artevelde, Philip van
Cabochiens
Charles the Bad, King of Navarre
Cocherel, Battle of
Edward II, King of England
Harcourt, Godfrey of
Henry IV, King of England
Isabella, Queen of England (c. 1292–1358)
Jack Cade's Rebellion
Jacquerie
Lancaster, House of
Marcel, Étienne
Peasant's Revolt of 1381
Richard II, King of England
Robert of Artois

ROUTIERS
Aquitaine
Badefol, Séguin de
Bernard, Count of Armagnac
Brignais, Battle of
Calveley, Sir Hugh
Cervole, Arnaud de
Great Company

Edward I, King of England
Edward II, King of England
French Civil War
Margaret of France, Queen of England
Paris, Treaty of
Philip IV, King of France
Saint-Sardos, War of

WOMEN
Anne of Burgundy, Duchess of Bedford
Catherine of Valois, Queen of England

Christian de Pizan
Isabeau of Bavaria, Queen of France
Isabella, Queen of England
  (c. 1292–1358)
Isabella, Queen of England (1388–1409)
Joan of Arc
Margaret of Anjou, Queen of England
Margaret of France, Queen of England
Marguerite de Flanders, Duchess of
  Burgundy
Philippa of Hainault, Queen of England

Preface

The *Encyclopedia of the Hundred Years War* provides its users with clear, concise, and basic descriptions and definitions of people, events, and terms relating in some significant way to the series of intermittent conflicts that occurred between France and England in the fourteenth and fifteenth centuries and that later came to be known collectively as the Hundred Years War. Because this volume focuses exclusively on the war itself—what caused it, how it was fought, and what effects it had on the political, social, economic, and cultural life of England and France—it is not a general overview of fourteenth- and fifteenth-century history in either country, but a specialized treatment of the Anglo-French warfare that occurred during those centuries.

The *Encyclopedia* was written primarily for students and other nonspecialists who have an interest—but little background—in this period of European history. Besides providing a highly usable resource for quickly looking up names and terms encountered in reading or during study, the *Encyclopedia* offers an excellent starting point for classroom or personal research on subjects relating to the course, causes, and consequences of the Hundred Years War. The entries provide the basic information needed to choose or hone a research topic, to answer small but vital questions of fact, and to identify further and more extensive information resources. The *Encyclopedia* also serves as a handy guide for those interested in recreating the military and social aspects of the Anglo-French wars, as well as a useful reader's companion for those whose reading on the period—whether fiction or nonfiction—is more for enjoyment than for study.

SCOPE OF THE BOOK

In chronological terms, the *Encyclopedia of the Hundred Years War* concerns itself mainly with the period 1337 to 1453, the traditional dates for the start and end of the Hundred Years War. As discussed in the entry "Hundred Years War, Phases of," actual fighting was intermittent across this period, which many historians divide into different wars conducted by different leaders but for largely the same reasons. Some entries, such as those on the Treaty of Paris of 1259 or the Anglo-French War of 1294–1303, examine topics and events that led up to the Hundred Years War, while others, such as those on Aquitaine or the Salic Law of Succession, cover broader topics or issues related to the long-term causes of the Hundred Years War.

In geographical terms, the *Encyclopedia* is concerned not only with the course of political and military events in France and England, but also with how the Anglo-French wars both affected and were influenced by people and happenings in other countries and states. Because of its length and intensity, the Hundred Years War spilled over into neighboring states and affected the whole of Western

Europe. Readers will thus find entries on various of those states, including Brittany, Flanders, and Scotland; on various rulers of those states, such as David II of Scotland and Duke Philip the Good of Burgundy; and on important related events in those states, such as the Castilian War of Succession and the Anglo-Scottish Battle of Neville's Cross.

CRITERIA FOR INCLUSION

To be included in the *Encyclopedia*, a topic, event, or person had to have a role in some significant aspect of the Hundred Years War. Nonbiographical entries relate mainly to military issues—for example, the raising of armies, the nature of combat, and the use of naval forces—to political terms and events—for example, truces and treaties, legislative and judicial bodies, and peace conferences and alliances—to the major battles of the Hundred Years War—for example, Poitiers, Agincourt, and Verneuil—and to the chief political and military leaders of the war—for example, Edward III, Bertrand du Guesclin, and Joan of Arc.

Because medieval warfare was the domain of kings and magnates, the great majority of biographical entries cover members of the French and English royal families and the most important noblemen to command armies, conduct diplomacy, or govern provinces. Besides the kings of both countries, such as Charles V and Richard II, and the leading noblemen of both realms, such as John of Gaunt, duke of Lancaster, and Louis, duke of Anjou, the *Encyclopedia* also includes entries on the royal families themselves, such as the Houses of Plantagenet, Valois, and Lancaster, and on non-noble figures of importance in both realms, such as Étienne Marcel, Sir Thomas Dagworth, Christine de Pizan, and William de la Pole.

STRUCTURE OF ENTRIES

The *Encyclopedia*'s 256 entries, 104 of which are biographical, average about 750 words in length. Each entry opens with a sentence or brief paragraph that carefully places its subject, whether a person, event, or term, within the context of the Hundred Years War, explaining the subject's significance for the emergence, course, or impact of the conflict. Each entry also contains numerous cross-references to related entries (which appear in SMALL CAPITALS) and concludes with one or more recommendations for additional reading. These reading recommendations include both scholarly works and popular treatments. In a few cases, older books have been included if no more recent study has been published or if the older work remains the accepted scholarly standard on the subject, as is the case, for instance, with biographies of some lesser-known figures. Also included in the readings are some important essays and papers published in journals or collections of articles. All works appearing at the ends of entries as further reading are listed in the general bibliography, which also contains numerous other worthwhile books not found among the entry recommendations. A reader interested in further reading on a particular person or topic should check both the general bibliography and the further reading listings at the ends of relevant entries.

All biographical entries provide the person's title or office. For titles of nobility, only the highest title attained is given; thus, Louis, younger brother of Charles VI, is noted as duke of Orléans, the title he acquired in 1392 and is best known by, and not as duke of Touraine, the title he had held previously. In a few cases, such as John, the Bastard of Orléans, who is best known as count of Dunois and only later became count of Longueville, both titles are given. Except in cases where birth dates are unknown, as is often the case with medieval figures, life dates are also supplied for all biographical entries. When exact birth or death years are uncertain, the *c.* notation, meaning "circa" or "at about that time," precedes the date to indicate that the year given is approximate. When a single year is preceded by *d.*, the year given is the death date, and the birth date is totally unknown. The date ranges supplied for ruling monarchs are birth and death dates, not the years of their reign, which are given in the text of the entry. Because this volume is meant for English-speaking readers, French men and women are noted by the name that is most commonly employed in English historiography, thus Joan of Arc, rather than Jeanne d'Arc, and John II, rather than Jean II, but Jean Froissart, rather than John Froissart.

ADDITIONAL FEATURES

The entries are augmented by maps of battlefield sites, French provinces, and the English position in France at various stages of the war. A detailed chronology and six genealogical tables depicting the royal houses and important noble families are also provided. Appendixes include a chronological listing of major battles, sieges, and campaigns, as well as listings of European rulers and monarchs from the 1250s to the 1450s; popes from the 1290s to the 1450s; holders of important titles among the higher nobility of each country; and the constables and marshals of both realms. Other appendixes offer brief annotations describing important provinces and regions and selected chronicles and sources for the war. Besides an extensive general bibliography, which is divided by broad topics, the *Encyclopedia* also includes various illustrations and a detailed subject index. When used with the cross-references in the entries, the "Guide to Related Topics" will allow readers to trace broad themes, such as diplomacy, Scotland, or women through all their most important events, ideas, and personalities and so help provide users with a sound, basic understanding of the Hundred Years War.

Acknowledgments

I wish to thank the staffs at Arizona State University's Hayden Library and at the Scottsdale, Arizona, Public Library for assisting me in finding important research materials, particularly those relating to French medieval history. At Greenwood Publishing, I want to thank Gary Kuris and Kevin Ohe for their willingness to sign a work of medieval history, Mike Hermann for his development and oversight of history projects, Liz Kincaid for advice on the gathering of illustrations, and Tom Brennan for the preparation of maps and genealogical charts. My thanks also to Mark Kane at Greenwood and to Sheryl Rowe at Bytheway Publishing Services for smoothly guiding me through the production process. Although their assistance was of a less technical nature, I must mention my little button-nosed friends, Kirby, Midnight, and Snuffle, three shih tzus who kept me company through long hours of reading and writing. Finally, as usual, nothing would have been possible without the love and support of my wife, Donna.

Chronology:
The Hundred Years War

1066	*14 October* William, duke of Normandy, wins Battle of Hastings and becomes king of England as William I
1152	*18 May* Henry, count of Anjou and great-grandson of William I, marries Eleanor, heiress to the duchy of Aquitaine
1154	*25 October* Henry, count of Anjou and duke of Normandy, becomes Henry II, first Plantagenet king of England
1204	King John loses most of Plantagenet empire in France to Philip II
1224	Poitou falls to French
1239	*18 June* Birth of Prince Edward, son of Henry III and future king of England as Edward I
1259	*13 October* Treaty of Paris is concluded by Henry III and Louis IX; the agreement recognizes the king of England as duke of Aquitaine, but requires the king-duke to render homage to the king of France
	4 December Henry III of England renders homage to Louis IX of France for Aquitaine
1267	Birth of Philip, grandson of Louis IX, son of Philip III, and future king of France as Philip IV (some authorities date Philip's birth to 1268)
1272	*16 November* Death of Henry III; accession of Edward I to the English throne
1273	*August* Edward I pays homage for his lands in France to Philip III
1284	*25 April* Birth of Prince Edward, son of Edward I and future king of England as Edward II
1285	*5 October* Death of Philip III; accession of Philip IV to French throne
1286	*18 March* Death Alexander III of Scotland; accession of his three-year-old granddaughter, Margaret, the Maid of Norway
	5 June Edward I pays homage for his lands in France to Philip IV
	July Edward I begins a three-year stay in Aquitaine
1289	Birth of Louis, son of Philip IV and future king of France as Louis X
	12 August Edward I returns to England after three years in Aquitaine
1290	Birth of Philip, son of Philip IV and future king of France as Philip V (some authorities date Philip's birth to 1291)
	18 July Conclusion of the Anglo-Scottish Treaty of Birgham which arranges a marriage between Prince Edward of England and Queen Margaret of Scotland

26 September Death of seven-year-old Queen Margaret of Scotland

28 November Death of Queen Eleanor of England

1291 *May* Edward I of England declares himself rightful overlord of Scotland

13 June Guardians and nobles of Scotland swear fealty to Edward I as overlord of the kingdom

1292 *17 November* Court of claims presided over by Edward I awards Scottish Crown to John Balliol

30 November John Balliol crowned king of Scotland under the auspices of Edward I

1293 Birth of Philip of Valois, son of Charles, count of Valois; Philip is the nephew of Philip IV, and future king of France as Philip VI

15 May Gascon seamen, in furtherance of a dispute with Norman sailors, sack the town of La Rochelle, thus initiating a series of events leading to war between England and France

October Philip IV summons Edward I to appear at the French court as duke of Aquitaine and vassal of France to answer charges of breaking his feudal oath by interfering in the affairs of his feudal overlord

1294 Birth of Charles, son of Philip IV and future king of France as Charles IV

January Edward I summoned to appear before the Parlement in Paris to answer appeals against his administration in Aquitaine

March Edward I is again summoned to appear at the court of his feudal suzerain Philip IV

19 May The French Parlement, noting Edward I's failure to answer the summons of his feudal overlord, confiscates all his property in France

July Edward I formally renounces his allegiance to Philip IV as his feudal overlord and sends troops to Aquitaine, thus beginning a nine-year Anglo-French war

1295 *22 October* Conclusion of Franco-Scottish alliance, eventually known as the "Auld Alliance"

1296 *March* War erupts between Edward I and King John Balliol of Scotland

27 April Edward I defeats a Scottish army at the Battle of Dunbar

10 July John Balliol abdicates the Scottish throne

1297 *May* William Wallace kills the sheriff of Lanarkshire, initiating Scottish rebellion against Edward I

11 September Scots army led by William Wallace defeats English force at Battle of Sterling Bridge

October Wallace invades northern England

1298 *27 June* Pope Boniface VIII, empowered by both sides to settle their dispute, declares perpetual peace between England and France and imposes the prewar status quo on Aquitaine

1 July Edward I invades Scotland

	22 July Edward I defeats Scottish army under William Wallace at Battle of Falkirk
1299	*June* Treaty of Montreuil restores Edward I's French fiefs
	10 September Edward I marries Margaret of France, half sister of Philip IV, as part of settlement ending the Anglo-French war
1300	*30 October* Edward I agrees to a truce with the Scots
1302	*11 July* Army of French knights is defeated by Flemish rebels at Battle of Courtrai
1303	*May* Final peace agreement ending the Anglo-French war is signed
1305	*3 August* English capture William Wallace
	23 August Execution of William Wallace in London
1306	*25 March* Robert Bruce crowned king of Scotland
	19 June English destroy Scottish army under Robert Bruce at Battle of Methven
1307	*10 May* Robert Bruce of Scotland defeats a larger English army at Battle of Loudon Hill
	7 July Death of Edward I; accession of Edward II to the English throne
1308	*c. 25 January* Edward II marries Isabella, daughter of Philip IV of France
	25 February Edward II is crowned king of England
1312	*January* Beginning of civil war in England between Edward II and dissident barons led by Thomas, earl of Lancaster
	13 November Birth of Prince Edward, son of Edward II and future king of England as Edward III
1313	Robert Bruce captures most English strongholds in Scotland
1314	*23–24 June* Scots under Robert Bruce win major victory over English at Battle of Bannockburn
	November Death of Philip IV; accession of Louis X to French throne
1315	*May* Edward Bruce, brother of King Robert Bruce of Scotland, invades Ireland
1316	*May* Edward Bruce is crowned king of Ireland, thereby challenging English rule there
	5 June Death of Louis X of France precipitates a succession crisis; Philip, count of Poitiers, brother of Louis X, seizes regency pending outcome of queen's pregnancy
	13 November Son is born posthumously to Louis X; he becomes king as John I
	18 November Death of John I; French succession is disputed between the regent, Philip, count of Poitiers and brother of Louis X, and Jeanne, the minor daughter of Louis X
1317	*9 January* Philip, count of Poitiers, is crowned king of France as Philip V

2 February   Assembly of French nobles meets in Paris to ratify coronation of Philip V and affirm that "a woman cannot succeed to the throne and kingdom of France," thereby overthrowing the claim of Jeanne, daughter of Louis X

April   Roger Mortimer, a Welsh nobleman, checks the Scottish advance in Ireland

1318   *14 February*   Death of Margaret of France, widow of Edward I and sister of Philip IV

2 April   Scots capture town of Berwick on Anglo-Scottish border

14 October   Death of Edward Bruce in Ireland

1319   Birth of John of Valois, son of Philip, count of Maine (the future Philip VI), and future king of France as John II

June   Edward II pays homage by proxy to Philip V for the Plantagenet lands in France

20 September   Scots raiders defeat an English army in northern England at the Battle of Myton, thereby helping lift the English siege of Berwick

1320   *June*   Edward II does homage to Philip V for duchy of Aquitaine

1321   England drifts toward civil war as a coalition of barons opposes Edward II and his powerful favorites, the Despensers

1322   *2 January*   Death of Philip V; accession of his brother, Charles, count of La Marche, to the French throne as Charles IV

16 March   Edward II and the Dispensers defeat baronial opposition at the Battle of Boroughbridge

22 March   Execution of Thomas, duke of Lancaster, the leading opponent of Edward II

1323   *March*   Roger Mortimer, an imprisoned opponent of Edward II, escapes to France

15 October   Raymond-Bernard, lord of Montpezat, precipitates the War of Saint-Sardos by destroying the *bastide* at Saint-Sardos and hanging the French official in charge

1324   *July*   Start of the War of Saint Sardos—Charles IV confiscates the duchy of Aquitaine

August   French armies invade Gascony

22 September   Gascon town of La Réole in Aquitaine falls to armies of Charles IV

1325   *March*   Queen Isabella of England arrives in France to arrange a settlement of the War of Saint-Sardos; while at the French court, the queen becomes the lover and ally of Roger Mortimer, an exiled opponent of her husband, Edward II

May   Charles IV restores Edward II's French fiefs under settlement brokered by his sister, Queen Isabella

14 August   Peace is proclaimed ending the Anglo-French War of Saint Sardos

10 September Prince Edward leaves England to join his mother in France

24 September Prince Edward (the future Edward III), now duke of Aquitaine, pays homage for his duchy to Charles IV

December Death of Charles, count of Valois, brother of Philip IV and father of the future Philip VI

1326 *23 September* Determined to overthrow Edward II and the Dispensers, Queen Isabella and Roger Mortimer land in England with a force of mercenaries

26 October Barons of England declare Prince Edward keeper of the realm

27 October Execution of Hugh Despenser the Elder

16 November Edward II is captured by his opponents

24 November Execution of Hugh Despenser the Younger

1327 *20 January* Deposition of Edward II

21 January Accession of Edward III to the English throne

1 February Coronation of Edward III

21 September Probable date of murder of Edward II

1328 *30 January* Edward III marries Philippa of Hainault

1 February Death of Charles IV; Charles's cousin, Philip of Valois, count of Maine and Anjou, becomes regent of France pending outcome of queen's pregnancy

17 March Conclusion of Anglo-Scottish Treaty of Edinburgh, which, when ratified by English on 4 May, recognizes Robert Bruce as king of Scotland as Robert I

1 April Queen Jeanne, widow of Charles IV, gives birth to a daughter

2 April Acting as regent, Philip of Valois convenes an assembly of notables that declares him rightful king of France

20 May English deputation arrives in France to present Edward III's claim to the French throne; the French nobility largely ignore Edward's claim

29 May Philip of Valois is crowned king of France as Philip VI

23 August Battle of Cassel—French royal army defeats the rebel towns of Flanders

1329 *14 April* Edward III writes to Philip VI promising to come to France and do homage for his duchy of Aquitaine

6 June Edward III pays homage to Philip VI for the duchy of Aquitaine

7 June Death of Robert I (Robert Bruce), king of Scotland; accession of David II to Scottish throne

1330 *4 March* Coronation of Philippa of Hainault as queen of England

8 May Convention of Bois de Vincennes is ratified; the agreement calls for the creation of joint commissions of inquiry to investigate and settle all disputes between Edward III and Philip VI over Aquitaine

15 June   Birth of Prince Edward, later known as the Black Prince, eldest son and heir of Edward III

28 July   Edward III is summoned to French court to confirm that the homage done for Aquitaine in the previous year was liege homage

19 October   Edward III arrests Roger Mortimer, earl of March, and overthrows the regime led by Mortimer and Queen Isabella

29 November   Execution of Roger Mortimer, earl of March; Queen Isabella is forced to retire to Castle Rising in Norfolk

1331   *March*   Edward III travels to France in disguise to confirm that his earlier homage to Philip VI for Aquitaine was liege homage

24 March   Coronation of David II of Scotland

1332   *April*   Robert of Artois is banished from France

24 September   Edward Balliol is crowned king of Scotland

1333   *19 July*   BATTLE OF HALIDON HILL—English defeat Scottish army

1334   *May*   David II of Scotland flees to France

June   Edward Balliol recognizes Edward III as suzerain of Scotland

1335   *July–August*   Edward III campaigns in Scotland

November   Conclusion of an Anglo-Scottish truce

1336   *July*   Edward III resumes campaigning in Scotland

August   French fleet threatens intervention in Scotland; English government embargos exports of wool to Flanders

September   Parliament votes taxation for war with France

1337   *16 March*   Edward III creates six new earls, thereby enlarging the English military command in preparation for war with France

30 April   Philip VI proclaims the *arrière-ban* throughout France in preparation for war with England

May   Edward III seeks allies against France in the Low Countries and Germany

24 May   Philip VI seizes Edward III's duchy of Aquitaine; the act is usually taken as the start of the Hundred Years War

October   Edward III denies Philip VI's right to the French throne and repudiates his homage to Philip for the duchy of Aquitaine

1338   French raid Portsmouth and Southampton

January   Flanders rises in rebellion against its pro-French count, Louis de Nevers

3 January   James van Artevelde elected captain of Ghent

21 January   Birth of Charles, grandson of Philip VI, son of John II, and future king of France as Charles V

February   English government begins buying up wool as part of the war funding scheme that leads eventually to issuance of the Dordrecht Bonds

May   Edward III's formal declaration of war is delivered in Paris

July   Holy Roman Emperor Ludwig of Bavaria appoints Edward III deputy vicar of the Empire

August   Holy Roman Emperor Ludwig of Bavaria joins Edward III's anti-French coalition

1339   French raid Dover and Folkestone

February   Louis de Nevers, count of Flanders, flees to French court after rebellion sweeps his county

July   French unsuccessfully besiege Bordeaux

20 September–24 October   THIÉRACHE CAMPAIGN is fought in northern France

3 December   Anglo-Flemish alliance is concluded

1340   *January*   Bernard-Aiz V, lord of Albret, named royal lieutenant in Aquitaine by Edward III

6 February   Edward III officially assumes the Crown of France at a ceremony in Ghent

April   Acting at the request of Philip VI, the pope places Flanders under an interdict

24 June   BATTLE OF SLUYS—English fleet under Edward III destroys a French fleet assembling at Sluys

18 July–25 September   SIEGE OF TOURNAI—English fail to capture northern French town of Tournai; Edward's anti-French coalition begins to dissolve

26 July   BATTLE OF SAINT-OMER—French defeat Anglo-Flemish army under Robert of Artois

25 September   Truce of Esplechin halts the war for almost a year

30 November   Edward III returns to England and orders arrest and dismissal of ministers he believes did not support the war effort, including William de la Pole; commencement of the English political Crisis of 1340–41

29 December   Archbishop John Stratford excommunicates royal servants as part of his dispute with Edward III

1341   *February*   During the Crisis of 1340–41, Edward III publishes his list of charges against his former minister, Archbishop John Stratford, who calls the accusations a *libellus formosus* (infamous libel)

March   Archbishop Stratford responds to Edward III's charges against his administration with his *Excusiones*, a document justifying his actions

April   Servants of Edward III prevent Archbishop John Stratford from attending Parliament

30 April   Death of Duke John III of Brittany initiates a succession dispute and the long Breton civil war

3 May   Archbishop John Stratford is readmitted to royal favor, ending the Crisis of 1340–41

June   David II returns to Scotland

7 September Parlement of Paris settles Breton succession dispute in favor of Charles of Blois

October Edward III annuls the reform statutes of the spring Parliament

2 November John de Montfort, English-backed claimant to the duchy of Brittany, surrenders to the French at Nantes

1342 *17 January* Birth of Philip the Bold, the fourth son of John II and the first Valois duke of Burgundy

April English army lands in Brittany

20 July William de Bohun, earl of Northampton, becomes English lieutenant in Brittany

30 September BATTLE OF MORLAIX—First pitched battle of the war; English army in Brittany uses tactics developed in Scotland and soon to be employed elsewhere in France to fight off larger French force under Charles of Blois, the French-backed claimant to the duchy of Brittany

October John de Montfort, claimant to the duchy of Brittany, concludes an agreement with Edward III, whereby the former recognizes the latter as king of France

26 October Edward III lands in Brittany and overruns most of the duchy's western districts

1343 *19 January* Truce of Malestroit—Negotiated cessation of hostilities designed to allow England and France time to pursue papal-mediated talks for a permanent peace

1344 *30 January* Death of William Montagu, earl of Salisbury, friend and confidant of Edward III

October Anglo-French peace talks open in Avignon under the auspices of Pope Clement VI

1345 *February* Collapse of peace talks at Avignon

June Edward III renounces the Truce of Malestroit, more than a year before its official expiration

17 July James van Artevelde is murdered by a mob in Ghent

late August CAPTURE OF BERGERAC—English capture Gascon town of Bergerac

26 September Death of John de Montfort, the English-backed claim to the duchy of Brittany; cause of Montfort's children now championed by Edward III

21 October BATTLE OF AUBEROCHE—English force under Henry, earl of Derby, defeats a larger French army attempting to besiege English fortresses in Aquitaine

1346 *January* Henry of Grosmont, duke of Lancaster, captures La Réole in Gascony

April French forces invade Aquitaine

1 April–20 August SIEGE OF AIGUILLON—John, duke of Normandy (the future John II), fails to capture the Gascon town of Aiguillon

9 June Sir Thomas Dagworth wins encounter at Saint-Pol de Léon in Brittany

12 July Upon landing in Normandy, Edward III knights his son Edward, the Black Prince

26 August BATTLE OF CRÉCY—Edward III wins great victory in first major battle of the war

4 September SIEGE OF CALAIS—English siege of French port of Calais begins

17 October 1346 BATTLE OF NEVILLE'S CROSS—English defeat and capture David II of Scotland

1347   *10 January* Sir Thomas Dagworth becomes Edward III's lieutenant in Brittany

20 June BATTLE OF LA ROCHE-DERRIEN—Anglo-Montfortist forces defeat and capture Charles of Blois, the French-backed duke of Brittany

3 August Calais falls to the English; Edward III fills the town with English settlers

28 September Truce of Calais is concluded

Autumn Black Death reaches southern France

30 November Estates-General condemns the Truce of Calais

1348   *23 April* This St. George's Day is the likely founding date of the Order of the Garter at Windsor

July Black Death arrives in Rouen in Normandy; first English case of the plague is reported in Dorset

August–September Black Death reaches Paris

November Black Death reaches London

December Conclusion of the Treaties of Dunkirk between Edward III and Louis de Male, count of Flanders

1349   *January* Louis de Male, count of Flanders, regains control of his county, thus ending the pro-English revolutionary regime that had been in power in Flanders since 1338

31 December Edward III personally foils a French attempt to retake Calais by stealth

1350   *20 July* Sir Thomas Dagworth is ambushed and slain in Brittany

22 August Death of Philip VI; accession of John II to the French throne

29 August BATTLE OF WINCHELSEA (LES ESPAGNOLS-SUR-MER)—English defeat a Castilian fleet allied with France

8 September Sir Walter Bentley succeeds Sir Thomas Dagworth as English lieutenant in Brittany

1351   *26 March* COMBAT OF THE THIRTY—Famous staged encounter between thirty-man groups of knights drawn from nearby French and English garrisons in Brittany

1 April BATTLE OF SAINTES—English victory in Saintonge that is notable for the French commander's use of the English tactic of fighting on foot

November   John II founds a new order of chivalry, the Order of the Star

1352   *6 January*   Inauguration ceremony for French Order of the Star is held at royal manor of Saint-Ouen

14 August   BATTLE OF MAURON—major English victory in the Breton civil war

October   John II transforms the Order of the Star from an order of chivalry to a confraternity for common worship

1353   *1 March*   Charles of Blois, the French-backed duke of Brittany, concludes an agreement for his release from English captivity

1354   *January*   Charles the Bad, king of Navarre, arranges the murder of Charles of Spain, constable of France

February   John II concludes the Treaty of Mantes with Charles the Bad, king of Navarre, who is pardoned for the murder of Charles of Spain

6 April   Anglo-French Treaty of Guines is concluded

10 April   Anglo-French encounter at castle of Tinténiac in Brittany

September   John II repudiates the Treaty of Guines

1355   *May*   John II retrieves the *Oriflamme* from Saint-Denis, thus ending the series of Calais truces and indicating his intention to resume the war

September   John II imposes Treaty of Valognes on Charles the Bad, king of Navarre; Henry of Grosmont, duke of Lancaster, is made king's lieutenant in Brittany

21 September   Edward, the Black Prince, is officially installed in Bordeaux as king's lieutenant in Aquitaine

5 October–9 December   CHEVAUCHÉE OF 1355—Edward, the Black Prince, leads a highly destructive *chevauchée* across southern France

1356   *5 April*   John II arrests Charles the Bad, king of Navarre, during a banquet given by the dauphin at Rouen

August   Charles of Blois, French-backed duke of Brittany, is released from English captivity

19 September   BATTLE OF POITIERS—English army under Edward, the Black Prince, defeats and captures John II of France

1357   *23 March*   Truce of Bordeaux is concluded between Edward, the Black Prince, and his captive, John II

5 May   John II lands in England with his captor, Edward, the Black Prince

October   David II of Scotland is released from English captivity

9 November   Charles the Bad, king of Navarre, escapes from prison

1358   *22 February*   Parisian rebels led by Etienne Marcel slay two marshals in the presence of Dauphin Charles, who soon after flees Paris; the *routier* army known as the Great Company sacks the town of Sainte-Maximin

May-June   Peasant uprising known as the *Jacquerie* erupts in northern France

8 May   First Treaty of London is concluded

31 July   Étienne Marcel is murdered by a Paris mob

2 August   Dauphin Charles reenters Paris after overthrow of Marcel regime

23 August   Death of Queen Isabella, wife of Edward II and mother of Edward III

November   Edward III abandons First Treaty of London

1359   *24 March*   Conclusion of the Second Treaty of London

23 June   BATTLE OF NOGENT-SUR-SEINE—French forces defeat *routier* army in Champagne

4 November   RHEIMS CAMPAIGN—Edward III launches large campaign that aims to take Rheims and have him crowned king of France

1360   *11 January*   Edward III abandons his siege of Rheims

10 March   During Rheims Campaign, Edward III concludes Treaty of Guillon with Burgundy

13 April   Sudden severe weather causes many deaths from exposure in English army, causing day to be known as "Black Monday"

8 May   Preliminaries of Anglo-French peace agreed at Brétigny

10 May   News of the acceptance of the Brétigny agreement by Dauphin Charles ends the long English Rheims Campaign

July   John II is sent to Calais from England in preparation for his release

16 September   Death of the English captain William de Bohun, earl of Northampton

24 October   Modified Brétigny peace agreement is ratified at Calais; John II is released from English captivity

December   John II obtains regular indirect taxes, including the *gabelle*, from the Estates-General

1361   *23 March*   Death of Henry of Grosmont, duke of Lancaster, a prominent English captain and royal kinsman

November   John II annexes the duchy of Burgundy to the Crown of France

1362   *6 April*   BATTLE OF BRIGNAIS—Large *routier* force defeats a French royal army

19 July   Edward, the Black Prince, is made Duke of Aquitaine

November   Treaty of the Hostages in concluded between Edward III and the French hostages being held to ensure payment of John II's ransom

1363   *13 March*   John II reluctantly confirms the Treaty of the Hostages

27 June   John II invests his fourth son, Philip the Bold, with the duchy of Burgundy

September   Louis, duke of Anjou, breaks parole and refuses to return to English captivity; duke's dishonorable act leads John II to voluntarily return to captivity in 1364

13 September   Great Company seizes the town of Brioude

December   John II secures a hearth tax—the *fouage*—from the Estates General

1364   *3 January*   John II of France voluntarily returns to captivity in London

April   Breton civil war resumes

8 April   Death of John II; accession of Charles V to the French throne

16 May   BATTLE OF COCHEREL—French royal army defeats the forces of Charles the Bad, king of Navarre

29 September   BATTLE OF AURAY—Anglo-Montfortist army defeats and kills Charles of Blois

1 November   Great Company seizes the town of Anse as a base

1365   *12 April*   Treaty of Guérande is signed, officially ending the Breton civil war

September   Great Company is paid to withdraw from the town of Anse, which the *routier* army has been using as a base

1366   *January*   Charles the Bad, king of Navarre, poisons the *routier* captain Séguin de Badefol

c. April   Birth of Henry, son of John of Gaunt, duke of Lancaster and future king of England as Henry IV (some authorities date Henry's birth to 1367)

25 May   Death of the *routier* captain Arnaud de Cervole

21 June   Death of William de la Pole, war financier to Edward III

1367   *6 January*   Birth of Richard, son of Edward, the Black Prince and future king of England as Richard II

3 April   BATTLE OF NÁJERA (NAVARRETTE)—Anglo-Gascon army under Edward, the Black Prince, defeats the French-backed forces of Henry of Trastámare and thereby restores King Pedro to the throne of Castile

1368   *May*   John, count of Armagnac, lodges a secret appeal against Edward, the Black Prince, with the Paris Parlement

30 June   At a meeting of the royal council, Charles V decides to accept the appeals of Armagnac and the other Gascon lords

November   Charles V signs a treaty with Henry of Trastámare, pretender to the throne of Castile

3 December   Birth of Charles, son of Charles V and future king of France as Charles VI; Charles V announces acceptance of the "Appeal of the Gascon Lords"

1369   *January*   Edward, the Black Prince, is summoned to appear before the Parlement in Paris to answer appeals against his administration in Aquitaine

14 March   Henry of Trastámare regains Castilian throne by defeating and killing Pedro I at the Battle of Montiel; Castile now becomes an ally of France

2 May   Parlement of Paris declares Edward, the Black Prince, contumacious

3 June   Edward III resumes title of king of France

19 June   Philip the Bold, duke of Burgundy, marries Marguerite, daughter of Louis de Male, count of Flanders

15 August   Death of Philippa of Hainault, queen of England and wife of Edward III

13 November   Death of the English captain Thomas Beauchamp, earl of Warwick

30 November   Charles V confiscates the Duchy of Aquitaine

1370   *1 January*   Death of the English captain Sir John Chandos

19 September   SACK OF LIMOGES—Edward, the Black Prince, recaptures and destroys Limoges, a town in Aquitaine that had surrendered to the French

4 December   After the *chevauchée* led by Sir Robert Knolles breaks up, part of this English force is defeated at Pontvallain

1371   *January*   Edward, the Black Prince returns to England, leaving Aquitaine to his brother, John of Gaunt, duke of Lancaster

22 February   Death of David II of Scotland; accession of Robert II, first king of the House of Stewart

28 May   Birth of John the Fearless, the second Valois duke of Burgundy

1372   *January*   Death of the English captain Walter Mauny, Lord Mauny

23 June   BATTLE OF LA ROCHELLE—Castilian fleet destroys an English fleet sent to restore English authority in Poitou

23 August   French capture famed Gascon captain Jean de Grailly, captal de Buch

September   La Rochelle falls to the French

1373   *August–January 1374*   CHEVAUCHÉE OF 1373—John of Gaunt, duke of Lancaster, leads one of the largest English *chevauchées* of the war

1375   *March*   Bruges Peace Conference opens

1376   *28 April*   So-called Good Parliament opens; Commons impeaches several royal ministers and removes the king's rapacious mistress, Alice Perrers

8 June   Death of Edward, the Black Prince

1377   *February*   Parliament passes first poll tax to support the English war effort

21 June   Death of Edward III; accession of Richard II to the English throne

Summer   French warships raid the south coast of England

1 September   Battle of Eymet—French defeat an Anglo-Gascon army, taking prisoner Thomas Felton, the English seneschal of Gascony

1378   Charles V precipitates the Great Schism by supporting the election of the Avignon pope Clement VII

20 October   English Parliament endorses the Roman pope Urban VI

18 December Charles V, angered by the pro-English stance of Duke John IV, confiscates the duchy of Brittany

1379 *April* Parliament enacts the second English poll tax to fund the war

1380 *13 July* Death of Bertrand du Guesclin, constable of France

Summer Thomas of Woodstock, duke of Gloucester, launches the last great English *chevauchée* of the century

16 September Death of Charles V; accession of Charles VI to French throne

November Parliament enacts the third English poll tax, resistance to which precipitates the Peasants' Revolt in 1381

1381 *4 April* Second Treaty of Guérande restores John IV to power in Brittany as a Valois vassal

May-June Spurred by resistance to the poll tax, the Peasants' Revolt erupts in England

15 June Richard II meets Wat Tyler and the Kentish rebels at Smithfield

November Parliament issues a pardon to those involved in the Peasants' Revolt

1382 *20 January* Richard II marries Anne of Bohemia

24 January Philip van Artevelde is elected captain of Ghent

3 May Philip van Artevelde launches a successful surprise attack on Bruges, which is held by Count Louis de Male

27 November Battle of Roosebeke—French army crushes Flemish rebel forces

1384 *January* Death of Louis, duke of Anjou, brother of Charles V and eldest uncle of Charles VI

30 January Death of Louis de Male, count of Flanders; control of Flanders now passes to Louis's daughter Marguerite and her husband, Philip the Bold, duke of Burgundy

1385 French forces arrive in Scotland

17 July Charles VI marries Isabeau of Bavaria

1386 *16 September* Likely birth date of Henry of Monmouth, son of Henry of Bolingbroke (the future Henry IV) and future king of England as Henry V (some authorities date Henry's birth to 1387)

October Wonderful Parliament impeaches royal ministers and establishes a commission to reform royal household and limit authority of Richard II

1387 *1 January* Death of Charles the Bad, king of Navarre

24 March BATTLE OF CADZAND (MARGATE)—Richard Fitzalan, earl of Arundel, defeats and captures a Franco-Castilian wine fleet

August Royal judges declare parliamentary commission in violation of royal prerogative

14 November Lords Appellant, led by Thomas of Woodstock, duke of Gloucester, gather troops and demand arrest of royal favorites

20 December   Appellant force defeats royalist army at Radcot Bridge, putting Thomas of Woodstock, duke of Gloucester, in control of English government

1388   *February*   Under leadership of Lords Appellant, the Merciless Parliament condemns and exiles Richard II's favorites

3 November   Charles VI declares himself of full age and dismisses his uncles; Marmouset regime takes power in Paris

1389   *May*   Richard II declares himself of full age and assumes personal control of the English government

18 June   Anglo-French Truce of Leulinghen is concluded

1390   *February*   John of Gaunt, duke of Lancaster, is created duke of Aquitaine by his nephew Richard II

19 April   Death of Robert II of Scotland; accession of Robert III

1392   *5 August*   Charles VI experiences his first schizophrenic episode; the king's incapacity allows his uncles to reassert control and overthrow the Marmouset regime

1393   *28 January*   Charles VI narrowly escapes death when a torch sets alight the masque costumes of the king and others at the so-called *Bal des Ardents* (Burning Men's Ball)

1394   *16 March*   Death in Italy of the great English *routier* captain Sir John Hawkwood

23 April   Death of the English *routier* captain, Sir Hugh Calveley

7 June   Death of Anne of Bohemia, queen of England and wife of Richard II

1396   Birth of Philip the Good, the third Valois duke of Burgundy

4 November   Richard II marries Isabella, the daughter of Charles VI

1397   *10 July*   Richard II arrests his uncle Thomas of Woodstock, duke of Gloucester, who later dies in custody in Calais

September   Richard II appeals the former Lords Appellant before Parliament for treason

1398   *16 September*   Richard II exiles his cousin Henry of Bolingbroke, son of John of Gaunt, duke of Lancaster

1399   *3 February*   Death of John of Gaunt, duke of Lancaster; Richard II subsequently makes Bolingbroke's banishment permanent and confiscates the Lancastrian estates

1 June   Richard II leaves to campaign in Ireland

4 July   Henry of Bolingbroke, son of John of Gaunt, duke of Lancaster, lands in England to reclaim his father's estates

19 August   Richard II is taken prisoner

29–30 September   Abdication of Richard II; accession of Henry IV to the English throne

November   Death of John IV, duke of Brittany

1400   Henry IV sends Richard II's queen, Isabella of Valois, daughter of Charles VI, back to France

	c. February Murder of Richard II
1402	*14 September* Anglo-Scottish Battle of Homildon Hill
1403	*22 February* Birth of Charles, son of Charles VI and future king of France as Charles VII
1404	*27 April* Death of Philip the Bold, duke of Burgundy; John the Fearless succeeds as new duke of Burgundy
1405	*21 March* Death of Marguerite de Flanders, duchess of Burgundy; her lands in the Low Countries and the Empire are inherited by her son, John the Fearless, duke of Burgundy
	5 October Christine de Pizan writes letter to Queen Isabeau urging her to intervene in political struggle between dukes of Burgundy and Orléans
1406	*22 March* James, heir to the Scottish throne, is captured at sea by the English
	4 April Death of Robert III of Scotland; accession of James I, whose imprisonment in England necessitates a regency government
1407	*23 April* Death of the former French constable Olivier de Clisson
	15 August Death of English *routier* captain Sir Robert Knolles
	23 November Louis, duke of Orléans, the brother of Charles VI, is assassinated in Paris
	25 November John the Fearless, duke of Burgundy, confesses that he ordered the murder of Orléans through "the intervention of the devil"
	26 November Barred from the royal council, John the Fearless, duke of Burgundy, flees Paris
1408	*February* John the Fearless, duke of Burgundy, returns to Paris
	8 March John the Fearless, duke of Burgundy, presents his written *Justification* for the murder of Louis, duke of Orléans, to Charles VI and the royal council; the *Justification* legitimizes the murder by accusing Orléans of numerous acts of tyranny
	September Charles, duke of Orléans issues his own manifesto answering the changes leveled against his father by John the Fearless, duke of Burgundy, in his *Justification*
1409	*9 March* Charles VI presides over a formal ceremony of reconciliation at Chartres; all French princes of the blood swear friendship for one another and promise to keep the peace
	13 September Death of Isabella, former queen of Richard II
1410	*April* Anti-Burgundian League of Gien is created by leading Armagnac princes
	November Peace of Bicêtre temporarily ends the French civil war
1411	*July* Charles, duke of Orléans, demands that the king punish John the Fearless, duke of Burgundy, for the murder of Orléans' father, Louis, duke of Orléans
	October English army lands in Calais to assist John the Fearless, duke of Burgundy, against the Armagnacs; Burgundy breaks the Armagnac siege of Paris

30 November   Henry IV dismisses Prince Henry and his supporters from the government

1412   *c. 6 January*   Joan of Arc is born in Domremy

18 May   Anglo-Armagnac Treaty of Bourges is concluded

11 July   Thomas, duke of Clarence, lands in France with an English army, thereby fulfilling the terms of the Treaty of Bourges

August   Treaty of Auxerre is concluded, temporarily ending the French civil war

14 November   Anglo-Armagnac Treaty of Buzançais is concluded, providing payment for Thomas, duke of Clarence, to withdraw to Gascony

1413   *January*   John the Fearless, duke of Burgundy, summons Estates-General to convene in Paris to vote new taxation

20 March   Death of Henry IV; accession of Henry V to the English throne

27–28 April   Cabochien uprisings occur in Paris

26–27 May   Charles VI promulgates the *Ordonnance Cabochienne*, the great reform measure demanded by the Cabochiens

July   Louis, duke of Guienne, dauphin of France, negotiates Peace of Pontoise in an attempt to settle the French civil war

4 August   Louis, duke of Guienne, dauphin of France, re-enters Paris in triumph

23 August   John the Fearless, duke of Burgundy, after trying unsuccessfully to kidnap the king, flees Paris

1 September   Armagnacs enter Paris

5 September   *Ordonnance Cabochienne* is annulled

1414   *January*   John V, duke of Brittany, concludes a ten-year truce with England

1415   *February*   Anglo-Armagnac talks collapse, making resumption of the Hundred Years War inevitable; Peace of Arras is arranged between parties to French civil war

August   Southampton Plot against Henry V is uncovered

11 August   Henry V sails for France

18 August–22 September   SIEGE OF HARFLEUR—Henry V besieges and captures the port of Harfleur

25 October   BATTLE OF AGINCOURT—In one of the major battles of the war, Henry V wins unexpected victory over superior French forces

December   Death of Louis, duke of Guienne, dauphin of France

1416   *March*   BATTLE OF VALMONT—Thomas Beaufort, earl of Dorset, wins a series of encounters with French forces while on a foraging mission to resupply the besieged English garrison of Harfleur

June   Death of John, duke of Berry, uncle of Charles VI

15 August BATTLE OF THE SEINE—John, duke of Bedford, wins naval victory that breaks the French siege of Harfleur; Treaty of Canterbury is concluded between Henry V and Emperor Sigismund

1417 *5 April* Death of John, duke of Touraine, dauphin of France; later in the month, the new dauphin, Charles, exiles his mother, Queen Isabeau, from Paris

1 August NORMAN CAMPAIGN (1417–19)—Henry V launches his campaign to conquer Normandy

September Caen in Normandy falls to the English

8 November Queen Isabeau escapes from confinement in Tours and joins with John the Fearless, duke of Burgundy, against the Armagnac regime

1418 *29 May* Pro-Burgundian riots erupt in Paris; Dauphin Charles flees the capital

29 June Dauphin assumes title of lieutenant-general of France on his own authority

12 July Armagnac leader Bernard, count of Armagnac, is slain by a Burgundian mob in Paris

14 July John the Fearless, duke of Burgundy, re-enters Paris

29 July SIEGE OF ROUEN—Henry V lays siege to the Norman capital of Rouen

September John the Fearless, duke of Burgundy, imposes the Treaty of Saint-Maur on the Dauphin Charles

1419 *19 January* Rouen surrenders to the English; Henry V formally enters the town next day, thus effectively completing his Norman Campaign

July Henry V captures Pontoise, putting the English within striking distance of Paris; Dauphin Charles and John the Fearless, duke of Burgundy, meet at Corbeil to discuss ending the French civil war

10 September Duke John the Fearless is murdered by partisans of Dauphin Charles while meeting with Charles to discuss peace on the bridge at Montereau; Philip the Good succeeds his father as duke of Burgundy

19 December Philip the Good, duke of Burgundy, responds to his father's murder by the Armagnacs by formally allying with the English

1420 *January* Henry V sends representatives to Troyes to begin peace talks with the French court

3 March BATTLE OF FRESNEY—English army defeats large Franco-Scottish force attempting to besiege Fresnay-le-Vicomte

21 May Treaty of Troyes, making Henry V heir to Charles VI, is signed

2 June Henry V marries Catherine of Valois, daughter of Charles VI

9 July–18 November SIEGE OF MELUN—Henry V besieges and ultimately captures French town of Melun

1 December Henry V enters Paris

1421 *January* Parlement of Paris declares Dauphin Charles incapable of succeeding to the French throne and banished from the realm; Thomas Beaufort, duke of Exeter, becomes English military governor of Paris

February Henry V returns to England with his new bride, Catherine of Valois

22 March BATTLE OF BAUGÉ—Thomas, duke of Clarence, brother and heir of Henry V, is slain by a Franco-Scottish army

6 October–2 May 1422 SIEGE OF MEAUX—Henry V besieges town of Meaux; long winter siege undermines English morale and the king's health

6 December Birth of Prince Henry, son of Henry V and future king of England as Henry VI

1422 *31 August* Death of Henry V; accession of Henry VI to the English throne

21 October Death of Charles VI leaves disputed succession to the French throne between his son, Charles (later crowned as Charles VII) and Henry VI of England

1423 *13 April* Tripartite Treaty of Amiens signed by John, duke of Bedford; Philip the Good, duke of Burgundy; and John V, duke of Brittany

18 April Burgundy and Brittany sign a secret agreement to remain allies even if one reconciles with the dauphin, thereby in effect negating the Treaty of Amiens

13 May John, duke of Bedford, marries Anne, the sister of Philip the Good, duke of Burgundy

31 July BATTLE OF CRAVANT—English victory in eastern France

1424 *March* Archibald Douglas, earl of Douglas, lands at La Rochelle with a large Scottish army sent to assist the dauphin

April English government releases James I, king of Scotland

17 August BATTLE OF VERNEUIL—Major English victory over Franco-Scottish army; often called "the second Agincourt"

1425 *March* Dauphin appoints Arthur de Richemont, brother of Duke John V of Brittany, constable of France

December Conclusion of Franco-Breton Treaty of Saumur

1427 *15 July–5 September* SIEGE OF MONTARGIS—John, Bastard of Orléans, breaks English siege of Montargis

September Duke John V of Brittany repudiates the Treaty of Saumur with France and reaffirms his support for the Treaty of Troyes

1428 *12 October* SIEGE OF ORLÉANS—English forces lay siege to Orléans on the Loire

c. 24 October Thomas Montagu, earl of Salisbury, is mortally wounded by cannon fire while conducting surveillance at the Siege of Orléans

3 November Death of Thomas Montagu, earl of Salisbury, the English commander at Orléans

1429   *12 February*   BATTLE OF THE HERRINGS (ROUVRAY)—French army surprises but fails to stop an English supply convoy bound for Orléans

6 March   Joan of Arc arrives at dauphin's court at Chinon

22 March   Joan of Arc dictates her "Letter to the English"

29 April   Joan of Arc enters Orléans

8 May   French forces, led by Joan of Arc, lift the siege of Orléans

10 June–18 June   LOIRE CAMPAIGN—French army led by Joan of Arc takes Jargeau, Beaugency, and Meung, clearing the Loire of English garrisons

18 June   BATTLE OF PATAY—French army concludes Loire Campaign with major victory over English forces under Sir John Fastolf

17 July   Dauphin Charles is crowned at Rheims as Charles VII of France

8 September   Joan of Arc leads an unsuccessful attack on Paris

November   English coronation of Henry VI at Westminster

1430   *23 May*   Joan of Arc is captured by Burgundians at Compiègne

December   Joan of Arc is transferred to an English military prison in Rouen

1431   *21 February*   Joan of Arc's trial begins in Rouen

24 May   Joan of Arc recants her voices

30 May   Joan of Arc is burned to death for heresy in Rouen

11 August   Battle of the Shepherd, named for presence of a French shepherd boy who is touted as the successor to Joan of Arc

16 December   Henry VI is crowned king of France in Paris

1432   *14 November*   Death of Anne, duchess of Bedford, wife of John, duke of Bedford, and sister of Philip the Good, duke of Burgundy

1434   English suppress a series of revolts in Normandy

1435   *September*   Death of Isabeau of Bavaria, queen of France and widow of Charles VI

1 September   English withdraw from the Congress of Arras

14 September   Death of John, duke of Bedford

20 September   Franco-Burgundian Treaty of Arras is signed, thereby ending the Anglo-Burgundian alliance

1436   *13 April*   French retake Paris

1437   *3 January*   Death of Catherine of Valois, widow of Henry V and mother of Henry VI

13 February   John Talbot retakes Pontoise for the English

21 February   Murder of James I, king of Scotland; accession of James II

12 November   Henry VI is declared of full age and assumes control of the English government

1439   *30 April*   Death of Richard Beauchamp, earl of Warwick, the English lieutenant in France

November Charles VII declares military recruiting a Crown monopoly

1440 *July* Richard, duke of York, is reappointed king's lieutenant in France

1441 *6 June–19 September* Siege of Pontoise—French army besieges and captures Pontoise

1443 *March* John Beaufort, duke of Somerset, is made lieutenant-general and captain-general of Aquitaine in preparation for leading a major campaign against the French

July–August Somerset's campaign is a complete failure; duke returns to England in disgrace

1444 *February* William de la Pole, earl of Suffolk, sails to France to begin talks that will lead to conclusion of the Truce of Tours

27 May Death of John, duke of Somerset, possibly by his own hand

28 May Anglo-French Truce of Tours is concluded

1445 *23 April* Henry VI marries Margaret of Anjou, niece of Charles VII

22 December Henry VI secretly agrees to surrender Maine to the French

1447 *23 February* Death in royal custody of Humphrey, duke of Gloucester, uncle of Henry VI and leader of pro-war faction at English court

11 April Death of Cardinal Henry Beaufort, bishop of Winchester, leader of the peace party at the English court

December Edmund Beaufort, earl of Somerset, becomes king's lieutenant in France

1448 *February* Charles VII lays siege to Le Mans in Maine

15 March Le Mans in Maine surrenders to the French

28 April Charles VII issues *ordonnance* creating the *franc-archers*

1449 *24 March* SACK OF FOUGÈRES—English attack on the Breton fortress of Fougères breaks the Truce of Tours and leads to resumption of active warfare

31 July Charles VII orders a French invasion of Normandy

12 August NORMAN CAMPAIGN (1449–50)—French armies begin campaign for reconquest of Normandy

29 October French capture Rouen, the capital of Normandy

2 November Charles VII enters Rouen

1450 *28 January* Parliament impeaches William de la Pole, duke of Suffolk, leader of Henry VI's government

15 April BATTLE OF FORMIGNY—French defeat the last major English field force in Normandy

May–July Jack Cade's Rebellion erupts in southeastern England

2 May William de la Pole, duke of Suffolk, is seized and beheaded by unknown parties as he attempts to sail into exile

1 July Edmund Beaufort, duke of Somerset, surrenders Caen in Normandy to the French

12 August Cherbourg falls to the French, thus ending the Norman Campaign

1451 *30 June* Bordeaux surrenders to the French

1452 *23 October* John Talbot, earl of Shrewsbury, recaptures Bordeaux

1453 *17 July* BATTLE OF CASTILLON—French force under Jean Bureau defeats English force under John Talbot, earl of Shrewsbury, in Gascony, thus effectively ending the Hundred Years War

19 October French recapture Bordeaux—the subsequent fall of all English Aquitaine is usually taken as the end of the Hundred Years War

1455 *21 May* First Battle of St Albans is usually taken as the start of the series of English civil conflicts known as the Wars of the Roses

1461 *March* Henry VI is deposed and driven into exile in Scotland by his cousin, Edward, duke of York, who becomes king of England as Edward IV

22 July Death of Charles VII; accession of Louis XI as king of France

1467 *15 June* Death of Philip the Good, duke of Burgundy

1471 *21 May* Murder of Henry VI in the Tower of London

1475 *4 July* Edward IV launches the first English invasion of France since the end of the Hundred Years War

29 August Conclusion of the Treaty of Picquigny, whereby Edward IV of England agrees to withdraw from France in return for an annual pension from Louis XI

1558 *January* Calais, the last English holding in France, falls to the French

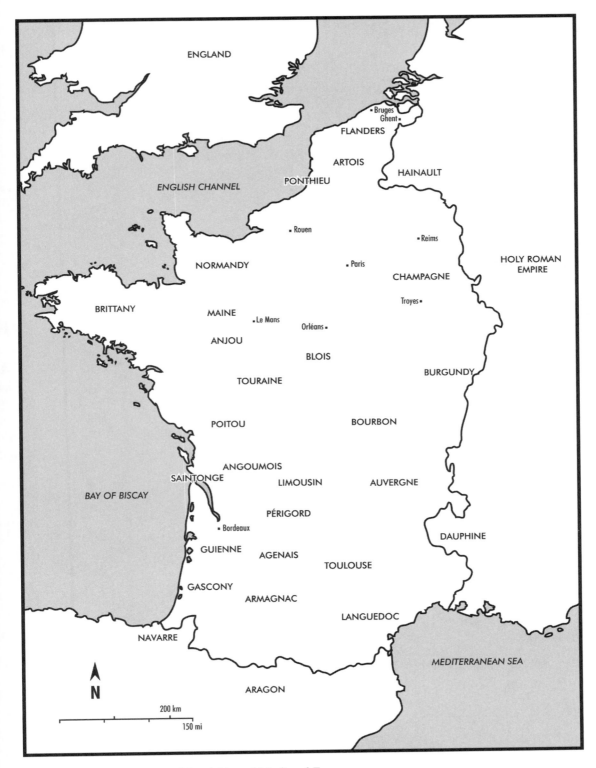

ENGLAND

Bruges
Ghent

FLANDERS

ARTOIS

HAINAULT

PONTHIEU

ENGLISH CHANNEL

Rouen

Reims

HOLY ROMAN
EMPIRE

NORMANDY

Paris

CHAMPAGNE

BRITTANY

MAINE

Le Mans

Orléans

Troyes

ANJOU

BLOIS

BURGUNDY

TOURAINE

POITOU

BOURBON

ANGOUMOIS

SAINTONGE

LIMOUSIN

AUVERGNE

BAY OF BISCAY

PÉRIGORD

Bordeaux

DAUPHINE

GUIENNE

AGENAIS

TOULOUSE

GASCONY

ARMAGNAC

LANGUEDOC

NAVARRE

MEDITERRANEAN SEA

N

200 km

150 mi

ARAGON

Major Duchies, Counties, and Lordships of Medieval France

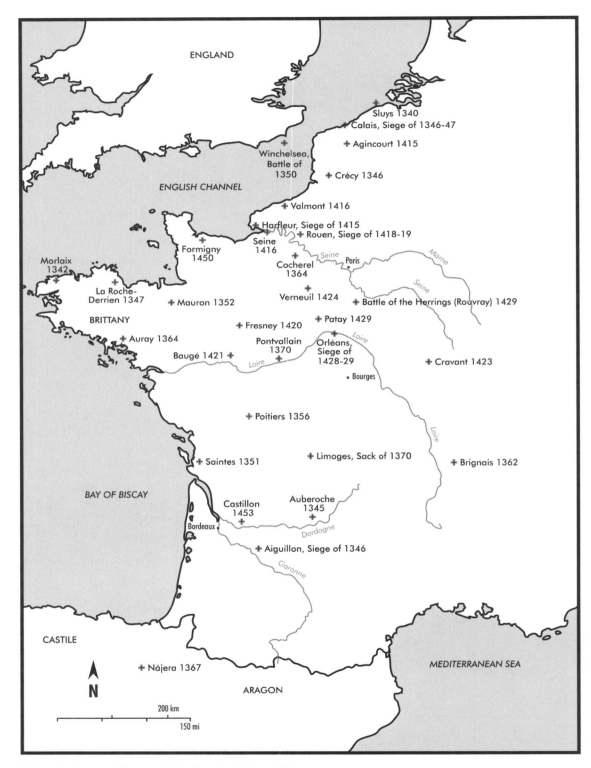

ENGLAND

Sluys 1340
Calais, Siege of 1346-47
Agincourt 1415
Winchelsea, Battle of 1350
Crécy 1346

ENGLISH CHANNEL

Valmont 1416
Harfleur, Siege of 1415
Rouen, Siege of 1418-19
Formigny 1450
Seine 1416
Cocherel 1364
Morlaix 1342
Paris
La Roche-Derrien 1347
Verneuil 1424
Battle of the Herrings (Rouvray) 1429
Mauron 1352
BRITTANY
Patay 1429
Fresney 1420
Auray 1364
Pontvallain 1370
Orléans, Siege of 1428-29
Cravant 1423
Baugé 1421
Loire
Bourges
Poitiers 1356
BAY OF BISCAY
Saintes 1351
Limoges, Sack of 1370
Brignais 1362
Loire
Castillon 1453
Auberoche 1345
Bordeaux
Dordogne
Aiguillon, Siege of 1346
Garonne
CASTILE
Nájera 1367
N
ARAGON
MEDITERRANEAN SEA
200 km
150 mi

Seine
Marne
Seine
Loire

Major Battles and Sieges of the Hundred Years War

lii

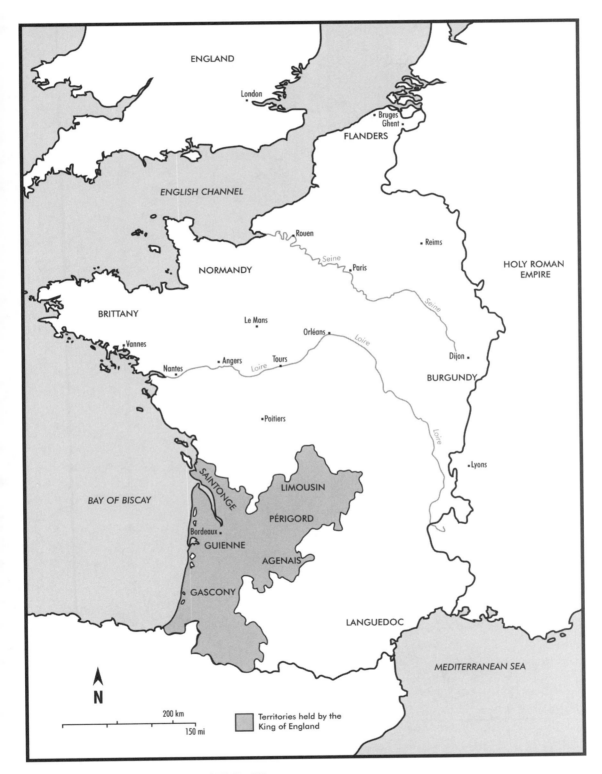

ENGLAND

London

Bruges
Ghent

FLANDERS

ENGLISH CHANNEL

HOLY ROMAN
EMPIRE

Rouen

Seine

Reims

NORMANDY

Paris

Seine

BRITTANY

Le Mans

Orléans

Loire

Dijon

Vannes

Angers

Loire

Tours

Nantes

BURGUNDY

Poitiers

BAY OF BISCAY

SAINTONGE

LIMOUSIN

Loire

PÉRIGORD

Lyons

Bordeaux

GUIENNE

AGENAIS

GASCONY

LANGUEDOC

N

MEDITERRANEAN SEA

200 km

150 mi

Territories held by the
King of England

France in 1328, at the Accession of Philip VI

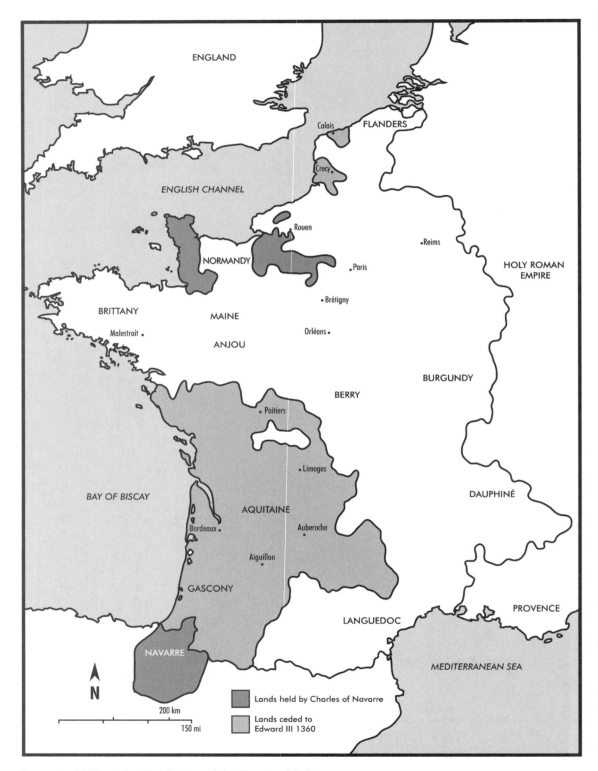

France in 1360, at the Conclusion of the Treaty of Brétigny

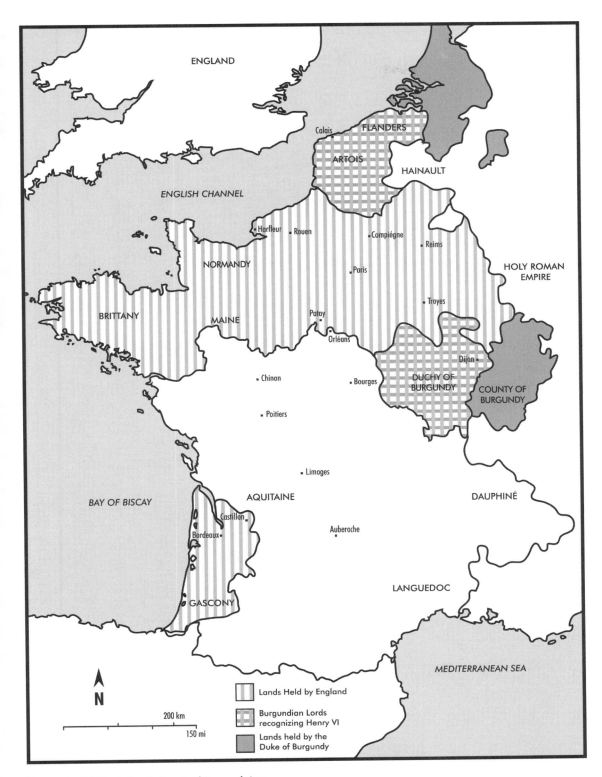

ENGLAND

ENGLISH CHANNEL

Calais

FLANDERS

ARTOIS

HAINAULT

HOLY ROMAN EMPIRE

Harfleur • Rouen

NORMANDY

Compiégne

Reims

Paris

Troyes

BRITTANY

MAINE

Patay

Orléans

Dijon

Chinon

Bourges

DUCHY OF BURGUNDY

COUNTY OF BURGUNDY

Poitiers

Limoges

BAY OF BISCAY

AQUITAINE

DAUPHINÉ

Castillon

Auberoche

Bordeaux

LANGUEDOC

GASCONY

MEDITERRANEAN SEA

N

200 km

150 mi

Lands Held by England

Burgundian Lords recognizing Henry VI

Lands held by the Duke of Burgundy

France in 1429, at the Advent of Joan of Arc

AGEN, PROCESS OF. *See* PROCESS

AGINCOURT, BATTLE OF (1415)

One of the greatest English victories of the HUNDRED YEARS WAR, the Battle of Agincourt was fought on St. Crispin's Day, 25 October 1415, near the village of Agincourt in western Artois. Although militarily indecisive—being basically the successful culmination of an English *CHEVAUCHÉE*—the totally unexpected victory was an incalculable moral and psychological triumph for HENRY V, who thereby won enormous popularity for himself and the war in England and greatly improved his diplomatic standing in Europe. In France, which was already divided by civil war, the battle devastated the nobility and discredited the ARMAGNAC government, leaving the country without the strong leadership required to effectively resist the English.

When he landed in France in August 1415, Henry intended to quickly seize HARFLEUR and then march down the Seine past ROUEN and PARIS before turning south for BORDEAUX. However, taking Harfleur, which did not fall until 22 September, proved unexpectedly long and difficult, costing the king six weeks and one-third of his army and rendering the planned *chevauchée* to GASCONY impossible. Rejecting advice to withdraw to England, Henry decided to march to English-held CALAIS, about 160 miles northeast. Much criticized by later historians as an unnecessary risk, the decision was based upon the belief that the English would be unopposed and was meant perhaps as a demonstration of the king's ability to march unhindered through NORMANDY, thus indicating to all God's approval of Henry's claims to the duchy. Abandoning their ARTILLERY and taking only eight days' provisions, the English left Harfleur on 6 October. The army, which contained many men still weakened by dysentery, numbered about six thousand men—one thousand men-at-arms and the rest ARCHERS. Intending to cross the Somme at EDWARD III's ford at Blanchetaque, Henry found the crossing held against him by John Boucicaut, marshal of France, whose men were part of a larger force shadowing the English all along the Somme. Forced to turn southeast, away from Calais, the English, now desperately short of supplies and pelted daily by cold rain, marched sixty miles upriver before finding and crossing two undefended fords on 19 October.

During a day of rest on 20 October, heralds informed the king of the French intention to bring him to battle, the very thing Henry had hoped to avoid. Marching northwest through continuing rain, the English finally encountered the enemy on the evening of 24 October, when scouts reported "an innumerable host" (Seward, 162) blocking the road to Calais. Camped near the village of Maisoncelles, the English were stunned by the size of the French army, which was conservatively put at about twenty thousand. Nominally commanded by Boucicaut and Constable Charles d'ALBRET, the French force comprised contingents of men-at-arms supplied by the Dauphin LOUIS, duke of Guienne (who was not allowed to fight), and the leading Armagnac lords. JOHN THE FEARLESS, duke of BURGUNDY, refused to participate, although he allowed his two younger

A depiction from the *Chronique d'Angleterre* of the Battle of Agincourt, 1415. *HIP/Art Resource, New York.*

brothers to join the royal army. Despite its weak leadership, the French force was large and confident, a marked contrast to the small, tired, and hungry English army, whose lack of confidence was demonstrated by Henry's offer to restore Harfleur in exchange for safe passage to Calais. When this was rejected, the English had no choice but to fight.

Next morning, the two armies deployed on a wet, muddy field flanked on both sides by woods and lying between the villages of Agincourt and Tramecourt. The English, with Henry commanding the center, formed into three battalions of dismounted men-at-arms with bodies of archers projecting slightly forward at the wings and in the gaps between the battalions. The French formed in two long lines of dismounted men-at-arms supported on the flanks and in the rear by mounted cavalry. With neither army willing to attack, the two forces faced each other for several hours until Henry ordered his flanking archers forward. Entrenching themselves behind lines of sharpened stakes, they opened fire, causing great disorder in the enemy lines and forcing the French cavalry to charge. However, the mud, arrows, and stakes broke up this attack before the first wave of dismounted men-at-arms could strike the English lines, thereby allowing the archers to disrupt the French column with a devastating flanking fire. Forced into a tight

mass and immobilized by the thick mud, the French knights were then set upon by the archers, who, being unarmored and therefore able to move more quickly, did great execution with their knives, axes, and swords. Once a French knight was knocked down, he was dead, either from a dagger thrust through a visor or from suffocation in the mud under the bodies of fallen comrades.

When the second French column attacked, it fell into similar disorder and met a similar fate, the English now fighting from atop piles of French dead. As this second wave receded, the English began gathering prisoners and arranging RAN-SOMS, a process that was suddenly interrupted by a French assault on the English baggage train and by the rumored arrival of French reinforcements. Fearing a new attack, Henry ordered the immediate execution of all prisoners except those of the highest rank. This act, despite the circumstances that prompted it, was a serious breech of the rules of medieval warfare, especially since the third attack never materialized. The remaining French, although still outnumbering their enemy, had seen enough; they withdrew from the field without striking another blow.

French casualties were enormous, with some estimates putting the number of dead at ten thousand. Among the slain were Constable Charles d'Albret; three dukes, including John, duke of Alençon, who at one point had actually beaten Henry to his knees; six counts; both brothers of Burgundy; 120 barons; and over 1,500 knights. The 1,500 French prisoners included Marshal Boucicaut. The English dead barely exceeded three hundred, although among them were the king's cousin Edward, duke of York, and Michael de la Pole, earl of Suffolk. Reaching Calais on 29 October, Henry was joyously received, although his men were forced to pay exorbitant prices for food and drink and were soon relieved of their booty and captives. Arriving in LON-

DON on 23 November, Henry was acclaimed a national hero and enthusiasm to both fight and pay for new campaigns was unbounded. *See also* FRENCH CIVIL WAR.

Further Reading: Burne, Alfred H. *The Agincourt War*. Ware, England: Wordsworth Editions Ltd., 1999; Curry, Anne. *Agincourt: A New History*. Stroud, England: Tempus Publishing Limited, 2005; Hibbert, Christopher. *Agincourt*. London: Phoenix, 1995; Seward, Desmond. *The Hundred Years War*. New York: Penguin, 1999.

AIDES. *See* TAXATION AND WAR FINANCE

AIGUILLON, SIEGE OF (1346)

Running from April to August 1346, the unsuccessful French siege of the Gascon town of Aiguillon seriously weakened the French military position throughout southwestern France.

In late 1345, Ralph STAFFORD, Lord Stafford, captured Aiguillon after a brief siege. Situated at the confluence of the Lot and the Garonne, the town commanded the approaches to La Réole and BORDEAUX; control of Aiguillon was therefore vital to the security of English GASCONY. An arrangement seems to have been made in advance with confederates within the town, who attacked the French garrison and opened the gates shortly after Stafford's arrival. Determined to restore French fortunes in the southwest after the recent successful campaigns there of HENRY OF GROSMONT, earl of Lancaster, PHILIP VI dispatched a large army to the region in March 1346. Commanded by the king's son, John, duke of Normandy (*see* JOHN II), and numbering almost twenty thousand, the army arrived at Aiguillon on 1 April. After proclaiming the ARRIÈRE-BAN for southern France, the duke settled down for a long siege, vowing that he would not withdraw until the town fell.

To prevent the kind of surprise attack from a relieving force that had recently destroyed an army of French besiegers at AUBEROCHE, the duke ordered that defensive trenches be dug behind the French siege lines. However, Lancaster, whose army was far inferior in numbers, withdrew to Bordeaux to regroup, waiting for an opportunity to disrupt the French lines of supply and communication. Commanded by Stafford and by the captain of the town, Sir Hugh Menil, the garrison numbered about nine hundred men—six hundred archers and three hundred men-at-arms, with the latter including the famous captains Walter MAUNY and Alexander de Caumont. In the early weeks of the siege, the garrison made frequent sorties on foot and by barge to prevent the French from bridging the rivers and completely encircling the town. By June, the French had cut off communication to the west, although, on 16 June, a daring sortie by Caumont captured two French supply barges.

In July, a contingent of Lancaster's army fought its way into the town with more supplies, while Normandy found it increasingly difficult to feed his huge force from the surrounding area. Lancaster also harassed the besiegers by killing foragers, seizing supply trains, and attacking isolated units. In late July, a force two thousand strong, which the duke had detached to check raids on his supply lines, was attacked and defeated by the Anglo-Gascon garrison from Bajamont. With the siege stalemated and the CRÉCY campaign developing in the north, Philip recalled his son. On 20 August, after failing to persuade Lancaster to accept a local truce, Normandy abandoned the siege of Aiguillon and marched east along the Garonne. With the duke's departure, Lancaster moved quickly to clear the Lot Valley of French garrisons and to secure English control of most of Gascony. *See also* SIEGE WARFARE.

Further Reading: Burne, Alfred H. *The Crécy War*. Ware, England: Wordsworth Editions Ltd., 1999; Sumption, Jonathan. *The Hundred Years War*. Vol. 1, *Trial by Battle*. Philadelphia: University of Pennsylvania Press, 1991.

ALBRET, ARNAUD-AMANIEU, LORD OF (d. 1401)

Arnaud-Amanieu VIII, lord of Albret, was one of the Gascon nobles who in 1368 lodged the APPEAL OF THE GASCON LORDS, the eventual acceptance of which by CHARLES V overthrew the Treaty of BRÉTIGNY and restarted the HUNDRED YEARS WAR.

The son of Bernard-Aiz V, lord of ALBRET, Arnaud-Amanieu was heir to one of the wealthiest lordships in GASCONY. Although Bernard-Aiz had fought for EDWARD III since the 1340s, the Albret family, which was large and well-connected to the southwestern nobility, had a history of switching allegiances when their interests called for it. Arnaud-Amanieu's grandfather had fought for EDWARD I and against EDWARD II, while his father had briefly supported the VALOIS. Arnaud-Amanieu first appears in the 1350s as leader of the ROUTIER bands maintained by his family. With Sir John Cheverston, the English seneschal of Gascony, he led the Anglo-Gascon force that defeated the French at SAINTES in April 1351. In the late 1350s, his bands overran Quercy and Auvergne, two provinces devastated by routiers in the years after POITIERS. Pressure from his father and from the English government of AQUITAINE, which was now directed by a resident duke, EDWARD, THE BLACK PRINCE, forced Arnaud-Amanieu to gradually curtail his activities and allow himself to be bought out of the fortresses his men had captured.

Succeeding his father as lord of Albret in 1359, Arnaud-Amanieu maintained the family's English allegiance. The Black Prince nominated him as one of the conservators of the Truce of BORDEAUX in 1357, and received his homage as a PLANTAGENET vassal in 1363. In 1362, Albret and many of his relatives were captured at the Battle of Launac, the latest encounter in the long feud between the counts of Armagnac and Foix. The high RANSOMS demanded by Foix left Albret deeply in debt. In 1364, during the civil war between Charles V and CHARLES THE BAD, king of Navarre, Albret sent troops north to fight with the royalist forces under Bertrand du GUESCLIN at the Battle of COCHEREL. He did not go himself because he wished to avoid fighting against his brother-in-law, Jean de GRAILLY, the captal de Buch, who commanded the Navarrese army. However, in 1365, Albret switched sides, agreeing to

command Navarre's routiers in central France for a fee of 60,000 florins. In 1367, hoping to further improve his financial situation, Albret accompanied the Black Prince to Castile, where he fought at the Battle of NÁJERA.

The failure of Pedro I of Castile to pay as promised for the Anglo-Gascon army that restored him frustrated these hopes, and added to Albret's growing discontent with the prince's lordship in an enlarged Aquitaine, where an influx of English administrators and French nobility from newly acquired provinces diluted Albret influence. When the prince instituted a new hearth tax to pay for the Castilian campaign, both Albret and John, count of Armagnac, refused to allow its collection in their lordships. In May 1368, Albret married the sister of the French queen in PARIS. While attending the festivities, Armagnac, later joined by Albret, presented an appeal against the prince to Charles V, whom they thereby recognized as overlord of Aquitaine. In July, Albret joined Armagnac and other Gascon lords in an agreement with Charles V whereby each party agreed to support the other if attacked by the English. When war resumed in 1369, Albret, now in receipt of a French pension, joined the Valois campaigns that reconquered much of Aquitaine over the next decade. Eventually becoming grand chamberlain of France, Albret died in 1401. His son, Charles of ALBRET, was raised at the French court with CHARLES VI and became constable of France in 1403. See also CASTILIAN WAR OF SUCCESSION.

Further Reading: Sumption, Jonathan. *The Hundred Years War.* Vol. 2, *Trial by Fire.* Philadelphia: University of Pennsylvania Press, 2001.

ALBRET, BERNARD-AIZ, LORD OF (d. 1359)

At the start of the HUNDRED YEARS WAR, Bernard-Aiz V, lord of Albret, was head of one of the wealthiest and most influential noble families of GASCONY. Assiduously courted by both PLANTAGENET and VALOIS, Albret eventually supported the former, although his allegiance to EDWARD III was, like that of many Gascon lords, always tempered by personal and familial interests.

The Albret family controlled one of the largest and most important lordships in English Gascony. A tradition of loyalty to the English Crown—Albret's father had undertaken diplomatic missions for EDWARD I—was severed during the War of SAINT-SARDOS in the 1320s, when Albret, after a series of quarrels with EDWARD II and the calculated patronage of CHARLES IV and PHILIP VI, had allied himself with the French. At the start of war in 1337, Albret, thanks to the unwillingness of either side to provoke him, maintained a careful neutrality. In 1338, the expected arrival in Gascony of an English army allowed the ducal seneschal, Oliver Ingham, to threaten Albret with military force if he did not declare for Edward. When cancellation of the expedition removed the threat, Philip sent emissaries promising extensive rewards in return for Albret's allegiance. Philip even had various French lords write personal letters asking for Albret's support. In his, John, duke of NORMANDY (see JOHN II), frankly acknowledged how vital was Albret's adherence: "We know that you have it in your power to do more damage to our interests than any other man in those parts" (Sumption, 1:330).

Despite these appeals, Albret joined the English in 1339. Although his brothers had been fighting for Edward since the start of the war, Albret's decision rested on his assessment of his family's best interests. His chief rivals for territory and influence, Roger-Bernard, count of Périgord, and Gaston de Foix, count of Foix, had declared for Philip and, unlike Albret, had made little attempt to improve their personal position by playing one side against the other. Thus, increasing French support for his rivals led Albret to back Edward. This support proved vital in 1340, when Albret virtually financed the English campaign in Gascony, supplying the government in BORDEAUX with over £9,000, almost three-quarters of the normal annual revenue of the duchy of AQUITAINE. The extensive connections of Albret and his

family also provided much of the manpower for the campaign.

Named king's lieutenant in Aquitaine in January 1340, Albret came to England in the following year. At a December 1341 council meeting, he outlined military plans for the reconquest of the duchy, but his personal ambition was distrusted and his plans were rejected as tending more to the aggrandizement of his family than to the benefit of the English cause. Nonetheless, Albret maintained his English allegiance, recapturing Saint-Jean-d'Angély in 1344 and, on orders of HENRY, earl of Lancaster, clearing the French from the Bazadais region in 1346. In the 1350s, Albret was a chief councilor of EDWARD, THE BLACK PRINCE, for whom he fought at the Battle of POITIERS in 1356. After Albret's death in 1359, his son, Arnaud-Amanieu, lord of ALBRET, maintained the English allegiance until 1368, when failure to continue his pension and marriage to a sister-in-law of CHARLES V led Albret to join the French (see APPEAL OF THE GASCON LORDS).

Further Reading: Sumption, Jonathan. *The Hundred Years War.* Vol. 1, *Trial by Battle.* Philadelphia: University of Pennsylvania Press, 1991; Sumption, Jonathan. *The Hundred Years War.* Vol. 2, *Trial by Fire.* Philadelphia: University of Pennsylvania Press, 2001.

ALBRET, CHARLES, LORD OF, CONSTABLE OF FRANCE (d. 1415)

Charles, lord of Albret and count of Dreux, was constable of France and commander-in-chief of the French army at the Battle of AGINCOURT. Although the Albrets were one of the most important noble families of GASCONY, and thus vassals of the PLANTAGENET dukes of AQUITAINE, Charles was a firm adherent of the House of VALOIS and a prominent figure in the FRENCH CIVIL WAR.

Although Charles's grandfather, Bernard-Aiz V d'ALBRET, had been EDWARD III's lieutenant in Aquitaine, and his father, Arnaud-Amanieu d'ALBRET, had fought for EDWARD, the Black Prince, at NÁJERA, Charles had been raised at the French court as a companion of CHARLES VI. He succeeded his father as lord of Albret in 1401, was named constable of France in 1403, and made count of Dreux in 1407. A supporter of the king's brother, LOUIS, DUKE OF ORLÉANS, the constable took part in the duke's 1405 campaign in Aquitaine, where he cleared the borders of Saintonge and Périgord of English garrisons. With the outbreak of civil war in the years following Orléans's murder in 1407, Albret became a leader of the ARMAGNAC (Orléanist) party. For this allegiance, he was dismissed as constable in 1411, when JOHN THE FEARLESS, duke of BURGUNDY, took power in PARIS. Albret withdrew from the capital with CHARLES, DUKE OF ORLÉANS; JOHN, DUKE OF BERRY; BERNARD, COUNT OF ARMAGNAC; and the other leaders of the Armagnac faction. In 1412, he was party to the Treaty of BOURGES, whereby the Armagnacs made territorial concessions to HENRY IV in return for English assistance against the BURGUNDIANS. In 1413, when Burgundy's flight left the Armagnacs in control of the king and the royal government, Albret was reappointed constable.

In 1415, the constable, acting as chief lieutenant to the dauphin, LOUIS, DUKE OF GUIENNE, took charge of preparations to meet the threatened English invasion. He began collecting an army in NORMANDY and stationed himself with fifteen hundred men on the coast at Honfleur. When HENRY V landed in August 1415, Albret was unable to prevent the English capture of HARFLEUR, but, by October, he and Marshal John Boucicaut had gathered a sizable army at ROUEN. Albret played a leading role in the subsequent campaign, being responsible for the destruction of bridges and the defense of fords along the Somme, and for harassing the English along their line of march. Although, as constable, Albret was nominal commander of the army, the decision to meet the English in pitched battle was made jointly with Boucicaut and the dukes of Orléans and Bourbon. On 25 October, the constable was slain at Agincourt; his office passed to the count of Armagnac, and his lands fell to his son Charles II, lord of Albret.

Further Reading: Burne, Alfred H. *The Agincourt War.* Ware, England: Wordsworth Editions Ltd., 1999; Perroy, Edouard. *The Hundred Years War.* Trans. W. B. Wells. New York: Capricorn Books, 1965; Vaughan, Richard. *John the Fearless.* London: Longman, 1979.

ALBRET, FAMILY. *See* ALBRET, ARNAUD-AMANIEU, LORD OF; ALBRET, BERNARD-AIZ V, LORD OF; ALBRET, CHARLES, LORD OF, CONSTABLE OF FRANCE

ALENÇON, DUKE OF. *See* JOHN, DUKE OF ALENÇON

ALEXANDER V. *See* PAPACY AND THE HUNDRED YEARS WAR

AMIENS, TREATY OF (1423)
Signed at Amiens on 13 April 1423, the Treaty of Amiens was a defensive agreement by which JOHN, DUKE OF BEDFORD; PHILIP THE GOOD, duke of BURGUNDY; and JOHN V, duke of BRITTANY, recognized HENRY VI as king of France and pledged to aid one another against the dauphin (*see* CHARLES VII). Although Burgundian and Breton adherence to the treaty wavered with the self-interest of each duke, the agreement initially strengthened the position of Bedford as English regent of France and created a marriage connection between Bedford and Burgundy that helped maintain the ANGLO-BURGUNDIAN ALLIANCE until 1435.

HENRY V made the first overtures toward Brittany by releasing the duke's brother, Arthur de Richemont (*see* ARTHUR III), who had been captured at AGINCOURT in 1415. Brittany had several times shifted between alliance with Henry and support of the dauphin, depending upon which side seemed most likely to win. A more forceful personality than his brother, Richemont convinced the duke to swear to the Treaty of TROYES, which recognized Henry as heir to the throne of France.

After Henry's death in August 1422, Bedford, acting as regent for Henry VI, sought to bind both Brittany and Burgundy more closely to his young nephew's interest. In December 1422, Bedford concluded a marriage contract that called for him to wed ANNE, a younger sister of the duke of Burgundy, while Richemont wed Margaret, Philip's older sister and widow of the late dauphin, LOUIS, DUKE OF GUIENNE. In February 1423, Bedford proposed a formal alliance, suggesting that all three dukes come to Amiens for negotiations. These talks concluded in April with the signing of a personal alliance that was to lapse on the death of any of the signatories.

The military commitments entailed in the treaty were negligible; each duke agreed to send a force of five hundred ARCHERS and men-at-arms to assist the others in time of need. The real significance of the agreement was the signatories' commitment to work for "the good of our lord the king and his kingdom of France and England" (Williams, 101), a clause that recognized Henry VI's title to the French throne and rejected the authority of the dauphin. The treaty also included a most unusual clause committing the dukes to provide relief for the poor and suffering of the kingdom. On 13 May, Bedford married Anne of Burgundy. Although undertaken for political reasons, the union soon became a love match, with Anne effectively serving as mediator between her equally beloved brother and husband.

The Amiens alliance was almost immediately undermined. On 18 April 1423, Burgundy and Brittany signed a secret agreement to remain friends with each other should either one become reconciled with the dauphin. In 1424, a quarrel between Bedford and Richemont caused the latter to offer his services to the dauphin and led the duke of Brittany to resume his policy of favoring the strongest party. In 1432, Duchess Anne's death seriously weakened the bond between Burgundy and Bedford and was a factor in Burgundy's abandonment of the English cause three years later.

Further Reading: Williams, E. Carleton. *My Lord of Bedford, 1389–1435.* London: Longmans, 1963.

ANGLO-BURGUNDIAN ALLIANCE (1420–1435)

Made possible by the murder of JOHN THE FEARLESS, duke of BURGUNDY, in 1419, and formalized by the Treaty of TROYES in 1420, the Anglo-Burgundian alliance established a joint administration in PARIS, recognized Lancastrian succession to the French throne, permitted the growth and maintenance of a Lancastrian state in northern France, and fostered the development of an independent polity in territories controlled by PHILIP THE GOOD, duke of Burgundy. Created by HENRY V's claim to rule France and by Burgundy's desire to avenge his father's murder, the alliance was maintained after Henry's death by the personal relationship of Burgundy and JOHN, DUKE OF BEDFORD, who were linked by the latter's marriage to the former's sister, ANNE OF BURGUNDY, duchess of Bedford. The alliance ended in 1435, when Burgundy realized that his desire to exercise paramount influence in the French government was better served by recognizing a VALOIS rather than a Lancastrian monarch.

Although uncomfortable with an English king of France, Burgundy could not acknowledge the dauphin as such after the dauphin's servants treacherously slew Burgundy's father during a peace conference at MONTEREAU in September 1419. The duke thus became party to the Troyes agreement, whereby he recognized Henry V as heir to the French throne and regent of France for the remainder of CHARLES VI's reign. Henry agreed to exercise his authority in consultation with the duke, and Burgundian officials, who had controlled the royal administration since 1418, were retained in office. Henry also promised not to interfere in those French provinces ruled directly by the duke, including FLANDERS, Artois, Rethel, Nevers, Charolais, Boulogne, and the duchy of Burgundy. By thus transforming one party in the FRENCH CIVIL WAR from a potential foe into an active ally, Henry was able to win power and territory in a divided France. Although, in practice, the duke took little direct part in the ongoing war between the English and the dauphinists, his alliance with the House of LANCASTER denied the dauphin access to Paris and to the allegiance, wealth, and manpower of a significant part of France. The alliance thus became vital to the maintenance of Lancastrian rule, especially after 1422 when the infant HENRY VI succeeded his father and grandfather on the English and French thrones.

Upon his brother's death, Bedford became regent of France when Burgundy, still unwilling to be too closely associated with a Lancastrian regime, refused the office. In 1423, Bedford fortified the Anglo-Burgundian alliance by concluding the Treaty of AMIENS, a tripartite defensive agreement whereby Bedford, Burgundy, and JOHN V, duke of BRITTANY, recognized Henry VI as king of France and pledged to aid one another against the dauphin. The treaty also arranged Bedford's marriage to Burgundy's sister, whose influence over both men became vital to the maintenance of good relations. Anne's mediation was particularly important in the mid-1420s, when HUMPHREY, DUKE OF GLOUCESTER, Bedford's brother, made an impolitic attempt to enforce his wife's rights in Holland, Zeeland, and Hainault, thus threatening Burgundy's ambitions in the Low Countries. In 1432, Anne's death snapped the personal link between the dukes, and Bedford's remarriage to Jacquetta of Luxembourg five months later offended Burgundy, whose interests were, in any event, beginning to diverge from those of his ally.

By 1433, Burgundy, whose contacts with the dauphin (now crowned as CHARLES VII) were never completely broken, began exploring the possibility of a Franco-Burgundian reconciliation. While the Lancastrians, particularly since the advent of JOAN OF ARC in 1429, were becoming increasingly dependent on the Burgundian alliance, Burgundy was becoming increasingly disillusioned by his inability to dominate the French administration and fearful that continuance of the war would diminish his popularity in Paris. Believing that Charles was weak and controllable, the duke sought honorable means to end the English alliance. Such means were provided by Nicholas Rolin, the Burgundian

chancellor, who argued that since Henry V had predeceased Charles VI and had thus not actually assumed the French Crown, Henry VI could not inherit something his father had never held. With Charles eager for reconciliation, Burgundy agreed to the convening of the Congress of ARRAS, an all-party peace conference from which the English withdrew when they realized that its true purpose was the conclusion of a Franco-Burgundian accord. Under the Treaty of Arras, signed on 20 September 1435, one week after Bedford's death, Charles recognized all grants of territory made to Burgundy by the English, exempted Burgundy from paying homage for his French lands during Charles's lifetime, and humbly apologized for the murder of Burgundy's father. With this agreement, the Anglo-Burgundian alliance was terminated.

Further Reading: Vaughan, Richard. *Philip the Good: The Apogee of Burgundy*. Woodbridge, England: Boydell Press, 2002; Williams, E. Carleton. *My Lord of Bedford, 1389–1435*. London: Longmans, 1963.

ANGLO-FLEMISH ALLIANCE (1339)

Concluded on 3 December 1339 between the English Crown and the revolutionary regime of James van ARTEVELDE, the Anglo-Flemish alliance attached FLANDERS to the PLANTAGENET cause and led EDWARD III to lay formal claim to the throne of France.

During the 1330s, the incompetent administration of the pro-French count, LOUIS DE NEVERS, and the constant interference of VALOIS officials in municipal affairs fostered a growing discontent among the Flemish people. At the start of the Anglo-French war in 1337, PHILIP VI, to prevent the county's defection, allowed the Flemings to remain neutral and to continue trading with the English. However, Edward III undercut this effort by halting English wool exports to Flanders, thereby causing widespread unemployment among Flemish clothworkers. Provoked by English agents, demonstrations against the count and his Valois overlord erupted throughout the province. On 3 January 1338, the people of Ghent elected van

Artevelde *hooftman*, or captain, of the city, a position that he used to form an anti-French alliance with Bruges and Ypres that eventually encompassed most of the Flemish towns. In February 1339, the count fled to France, leaving the van Artevelde regime in control of the county.

Although van Artevelde had advocated closer ties with England, he refused to be rushed into any formal alliance, despite intense pressure from Edward, who was then constructing his grand ANTI-FRENCH COALITION among the provinces of the Low Countries and northwestern Germany. Anxious to avoid another French invasion, such as the 1328 campaign that had culminated in the disastrous Flemish defeat at Cassel, Artevelde offered Edward only friendly neutrality, which was sufficient to achieve a partial lifting of the English wool embargo. When the THIÉRACHE CAMPAIGN ended in failure for the English, Edward put new pressure for an alliance on van Artevelde, who was now more willing to negotiate thanks to the presence of a large French army on the Flemish frontier. Nonetheless, English eagerness for Flemish military support allowed van Artevelde to win highly favorable terms in the agreement concluded in December. Edward permitted the Flemings free access to English wool and agreed to transfer the wool staple, that is, the center of Continental wool export, from Antwerp to Bruges. He also promised to restore to Flanders the three castellanies of Lille, Douai, and Orchies, which had been seized by PHILIP IV. Finally, the king promised a subsidy of 140,000 livres to outfit the Flemish militia and put the county on a war footing, and English military assistance on land and sea should the French attack the province. In return, the Flemish promised troops for the next English campaign in France and, most importantly, recognized Edward as rightful king of France. In accordance with this recognition, Edward, in a ceremony in Ghent on 6 February 1340, formally assumed the title "King of France and England."

In the late summer of 1340, Edward, leading an allied army that included a Flemish contingent under van Artevelde, besieged TOURNAI. When the city held out and the French refused battle, the king's allies, some of whom felt their interests threatened by the new Anglo-Flemish compact, began to desert. On 25 September, Edward reluctantly accepted the Truce of ESPLECHIN, despite the objections of van Artevelde, who feared French retribution, Philip having already prevailed upon the pope to excommunicate the Flemings as oath breakers. From 1342, the count began to regain support in the province, making van Artevelde's regime increasingly dependent on the English alliance. In 1345, rumors that EDWARD, the future Black Prince, was to be made count of Flanders allowed van Artevelde's enemies to assassinate him and overthrow his regime. Although Flanders remained allied with Edward until LOUIS DE MALE, son of the late count, regained power with French support in 1349, the Anglo-Flemish alliance ceased to be militarily effective even before van Artevelde's death.

Further Reading: Carson, Patricia. *James van Artevelde: The Man from Ghent*. Ghent: Story, 1980; Lucas, Henry Stephen. *The Low Countries and the Hundred Years' War, 1326–1347*. Ann Arbor: University of Michigan Press, 1929; Perroy, Edouard. *The Hundred Years War*. Trans. W. B. Wells. New York: Capricorn Books, 1965.

ANGLO-FRENCH WAR OF 1294–1303

The war of 1294–1303, the first Anglo-French conflict since the signing of the Treaty of PARIS in 1259, foreshadowed the HUNDRED YEARS WAR both in its course and its cause.

The war arose from a series of violent encounters between Gascon seamen from Bayonne and their French counterparts from the ports of NORMANDY. In 1292–93, Normans were assaulted on the streets of BORDEAUX and four French customs officers were murdered at Fronsac. Pressed by his brother, Charles of Valois, who led a court faction demanding stricter enforcement of Capetian overlordship in AQUITAINE, PHILIP IV ordered the seneschal of GASCONY, a ducal official, to surrender the offenders to French authorities. When the seneschal refused, the PARLEMENT pronounced the sequestration of the duchy and ordered the surrender of key fortresses to royal officers. When the ducal administration refused to comply, Philip summoned EDWARD I to appear before the Parlement by January 1294. Accustomed to the more cooperative attitude of Philip III, with whom he had negotiated compromises on most disputes involving Aquitaine, Edward, who was heavily engaged in SCOTLAND and unprepared for war on the Continent, suggested that each monarch punish the guilty parties within his own domains, or, failing that, submit the matter to arbitration. Because such proposals would have required him to deal with Edward on equal terms, Philip, who had been seeking a pretext for war, refused. He was interested in enforcing his lordship over his vassal, the duke of Aquitaine, not in compromising with his fellow monarch, the king of England.

Eager to resolve the matter, Edward sent his brother, Edmund, earl of Lancaster, to PARIS. Philip suggested that the English surrender certain towns and fortresses for forty days, thus technically allowing implementation of the sequestration order. At the end of that time, a treaty would be concluded and the duchy restored. Lancaster accepted this arrangement, and, in February 1294, ordered ducal officers to yield the required strongpoints. However, on 19 May, with his officials still in place, Philip suddenly ordered the confiscation of Aquitaine. Hampered by the need to transport men and supplies across the sea, while the French merely crossed their borders, Edward was unable to send an army to Aquitaine until October, by which time most of the duchy had been overrun. Although the English regained a foothold in southern Gascony, Bordeaux and most of the towns remained in French hands. When Valois invaded the duchy with a large army in March 1295, many of the English gains were lost.

When another English army led by Lancaster failed to retake Bordeaux in 1296, Edward adopted a new strategy, one that his grandson, EDWARD III, was to emulate in the 1330s. Since 1294, English agents had been busy in the Low Countries constructing an ANTI-FRENCH COALITION that could menace Philip's northwestern frontier and thus take pressure off Aquitaine. In 1297, Edward, in another move later copied by his grandson, concluded an alliance with FLANDERS, whose count, Guy de Dampierre, renounced his homage to the French king in return for English money and military assistance. However, the English were again unable to move as quickly as the French, who invaded the county in June before English troops could arrive. By 1300, the count was in custody and Flanders was under French control. In Gascony, little fighting occurred after 1298, when Edward requested arbitration of the dispute by Pope Boniface VIII, who was told that Gascony was an allod, that is, a province whose lord had never owed feudal allegiance to the House of CAPET. Although anti-French and convinced that Philip intended to expel the PLANTAGENETS from Aquitaine, the pope rendered a mild verdict: Edward was to do homage to Philip for any lands Philip would restore to him.

Even though Edward had married his sister MARGARET in 1299, Philip saw no reason to restore anything until June 1302, when a poorly armed force of Flemish rebels destroyed a French army at Courtrai. With over twenty thousand Frenchmen dead on the field and his treasury bankrupt, Philip could not afford a renewal of the war in Aquitaine, where the citizens of Bordeaux promptly expelled the French upon hearing of the battle. In May 1303, the two monarchs signed a treaty whereby Philip agreed to restore the duchy in return for Edward's agreement to pay homage for it. To seal the treaty, a marriage was arranged between Edward's son, Prince Edward (see EDWARD II), and Philip's daughter, Isabella (see ISABELLA, QUEEN OF ENGLAND [c. 1292–1358]), a match that was to have momentous future consequences by giving the Plantagenets an eventual claim to the French throne. Despite the treaty, Edward never did homage and Philip never returned all Edward's prewar holdings. The war also hardened attitudes in both kingdoms, persuading each Crown that the Treaty of Paris must ultimately be overturned in its favor. *See also* ANGLO-FLEMISH ALLIANCE.

Further Reading: Curry, Anne. *The Hundred Years War.* 2nd ed. Houndmills, England: Palgrave Macmillan, 2003; Vale, Malcolm. *The Origins of the Hundred Years War.* Oxford: Clarendon Press, 2000.

ANGLO-FRENCH WAR OF 1323–1325. *See* SAINT-SARDOS, WAR OF

ANJOU, DUKE OF. *See* LOUIS, DUKE OF ANJOU

ANNE OF BURGUNDY, DUCHESS OF BEDFORD (1404–1432)

Anne was the fifth daughter of JOHN THE FEARLESS, duke of BURGUNDY, and wife of JOHN, DUKE OF BEDFORD, brother of HENRY V and regent of France for HENRY VI. Through her intelligence, charm, and tact, Anne helped maintain the ANGLO-BURGUNDIAN ALLIANCE by mediating disputes between her husband and her brother, PHILIP THE GOOD, duke of Burgundy.

Born at Arras in September 1404, Anne grew into an intelligent young woman with interests in art, music, and court pageantry. Although not physically attractive—the citizens of PARIS found Burgundy's sisters "plain as owls"—Anne was high-spirited, understanding, and compassionate, with one contemporary describing her as "livelier than all the other ladies of her day" (Williams, 102). In 1414, her father, negotiating for English support, offered her as wife to Henry V, but nothing came of the proposal and she was still unmarried at her father's death in 1419. After his brother's death in August 1422, Bedford, who was anxious to cement the Anglo-Burgundian connection forged by the Treaty of TROYES, resolved to take Philip's favorite sister as his bride. As a preliminary to the 1423 Treaty of AMIENS, which created a formal alliance between England and the dukes of Burgundy and BRITTANY, Bedford ratified his marriage contract with Anne on 12 December 1422. The agreement promised the duke a dowry

of 150,000 gold crowns and the county of Artois should Burgundy die without heirs.

Married on 13 May 1423 in the Church of St. John in Troyes, the same church in which Henry V had wed CATHERINE OF VALOIS in 1420, Bedford and his new duchess took up residence at the Hôtel des Tournelles in Paris. Although fifteen years younger than her more reserved husband, who had married her for political reasons, Anne quickly captured the duke's affection. Bedford depended upon her kindness and companionship, which lightened his burdens and encouraged him in his endeavors; he also relied on her intelligence and judgment, especially in dealing with her brother, who, like Bedford, trusted her completely. The duke's devotion to his wife even evoked contemporary comment; Guillaume Benoit claimed that Bedford never traveled anywhere without her and the Bourgeois of Paris complained that Bedford spent more time in towns with his wife than in the field with his armies.

During the 1420s, Anne's mediation several times resolved quarrels that threatened continuation of the Anglo-Burgundian alliance. Among the most serious was the crisis raised by the precipitate marriage of Bedford's brother, HUMPHREY, DUKE OF GLOUCESTER, to Jacqueline of Hainault in 1423. The union allowed Gloucester to claim the rule of his wife's lands in the Low Countries—Holland, Zeeland, and Hainault—provinces that stood at the heart of the compact block of territories Philip sought to weld into the Burgundian state. Anne used her influence with Philip to keep the angry duke from taking rash action when Gloucester marched into Hainault in late 1424. She also accompanied her husband to a meeting with Philip in FLANDERS in June 1425, when, following Gloucester's return to England, she convinced her brother to reconcile with Bedford and maintain the English connection.

In March 1427, the duke and duchess of Bedford, after residing in England for sixteen months, returned to Paris, where Anne's popularity with the citizens did much to invigorate the English cause. In 1429, Anne helped dissuade her brother from continuing talks with the dauphin, and, in 1430, she tried to temper the imprisonment of JOAN OF ARC, insisting that the guards not molest their prisoner and ordering her tailor to make Joan women's clothes, the Maid's wearing of male attire being one of the most serious charges against her. Anne died on 14 November 1432, having contracted fever when she cared for victims of an epidemic that swept Paris that autumn. Broken, according to Enguerrand de Monstrelet, by a "very great sorrow" (Williams, 222), Bedford lost his personal link to Burgundy, who, in 1435, ended the Anglo-Burgundian alliance by reconciling with CHARLES VII at the Congress of ARRAS.

Further Reading: Williams, E. Carleton. *My Lord of Bedford, 1389–1435.* London: Longmans, 1963.

ANTI-FRENCH COALITION (1337–1340)

Like his grandfather, EDWARD I, who pursued a similar policy during the ANGLO-FRENCH WAR OF 1294–1303, EDWARD III began the HUNDRED YEARS WAR by constructing a network of anti-French alliances with princes of Germany and the Low Countries. Such a coalition relieved French pressure on AQUITAINE by promising Edward the opportunity and resources to invade the VALOIS domains in northern France. However, because the allies' commitment to the coalition was based on money, not principle, maintenance of the alliance proved to be well beyond the king's financial resources. Edward was soon deeply in debt and the payment of subsidies to his allies was soon far in arrears. Thus, by late 1340, the anti-French coalition had proved a costly failure.

In late 1336, months before the confiscation of Aquitaine officially initiated the war, Edward was in communication with the princes of the Low Countries, to whom he complained of Philip's unjust retention of "my hereditary property" (Perroy, 96), meaning those parts of Aquitaine occupied by the French since the War of SAINT-SARDOS. By spring 1337, Henry BURGHERSH, bishop

of Lincoln; William MONTAGU, earl of Salisbury; and William Clinton, earl of Huntingdon, were in the Low Countries purchasing alliances with hard currency borrowed from merchants and bankers. By the end of the year, Edward's anti-French coalition included John, duke of Brabant; William, count of Juliers; and Dietrich, count of Cleves, as well as the duke of Guelders; the counts of Berg, Limburg, and Marck; and Queen PHILIPPA's brother, William, count of Hainault. In August, Edward purchased the alliance of Holy Roman Emperor Ludwig, who spurned French overtures for English gold. In July 1338, the emperor, for a further subsidy, appointed Edward deputy vicar of the empire, by which office the English king was empowered to exercise imperial authority in northwestern Germany. In this way, Edward had more than a monetary hold over his allies, and, in late 1338, he summoned all vassals within his deputyship to swear homage to him and the PLANTAGENET cause.

From the start, the coalition was ruinously expensive; its maintenance made it virtually impossible to pay for the men and supplies needed to launch an actual campaign. An English landing in France planned for autumn 1337 was cancelled for lack of funds, and a truce had to be arranged for the first half of 1338, since no campaign could be contemplated for the same reason. To raise additional funds, the king embarked on the ultimately ill-fated DORDRECHT BOND scheme, whereby his agents bought up cheap wool in England and attempted to sell it at a profit in the Low Countries, where an English wool embargo aimed at LOUIS DE NEVERS, the pro-French count of FLANDERS, had starved clothmakers of their vital raw material. Heavily engaged in alliance DIPLOMACY, and desperately short of cash, Edward waited until September 1339 for his allies to send their promised forces. Exasperated by their failure to send more than a few ill-disciplined mercenaries, Edward advanced with his own army, but the THIÉRACHE CAMPAIGN, bedeviled by PHILIP VI's refusal to fight, ended in failure after only a month.

In December 1339, Edward concluded an ANGLO-FLEMISH ALLIANCE with James van ARTEVELDE, leader of the revolutionary regime that had recently overthrown the count. To provide the Flemings with political cover for their acceptance of Plantagenet overlordship, Edward officially claimed the French Crown on 6 February 1340. The Flemish connection promised to strengthen the anti-French coalition with a new infusion of men and the acquisition of a useful base from which to attack France. It also increased Edward's already crushing expenses, for the Flemish military effort required English financial support. In February 1340, Edward had to obtain the permission of his creditors to sail for England to seek new TAXATION from PARLIAMENT. Queen Philippa and her young children remained in Flanders as hostages guaranteeing the king's return.

Despite a naval victory at SLUYS in June, the English campaign of 1340 was as disappointing as that of the previous year. ROBERT OF ARTOIS and the Flemings were defeated at SAINT-OMER in July, and the large coalition army with which Edward besieged TOURNAI in August was broken up by disputes among the allies. The chief defectors were Brabant and Hainault, whose interests were adversely affected by the Flemish alliance. By the end of 1340, most of the allies were reconciling with Philip. Frustrated by his failure to bring the French to battle, Edward reluctantly accepted the Truce of ES-PLECHIN on 25 September. In November, when Edward returned to England enraged at what he perceived as the failure of his ministers to support his armies (see CRISIS OF 1340–1341), the grand anti-French coalition had largely dissolved.

Further Reading: Perroy, Edouard. *The Hundred Years War*. Trans. W. B. Wells. New York: Capricorn Books, 1965; Sumption, Jonathan. *The Hundred Years War*. Vol. 1, *Trial by Battle*. Philadelphia: University of Pennsylvania Press, 1991.

APPANAGE

Deriving from *apaner*, meaning to endow with a living, the term appanage (also spelled apanage or appannage) refers to a province, territory, or jurisdiction granted out of Crown lands to younger children of the monarch. Although appanages were hereditary grants, with women able to inherit in the absence of a male heir, such territories automatically reverted to the Crown upon the death of their holders without issue. Under the VALOIS, the practice of granting appanages led eventually to the creation within France of great semi-independent states ruled by powerful and wealthy princes of the blood whose rivalries precipitated the FRENCH CIVIL WAR and facilitated the English reopening of the HUNDRED YEARS WAR after 1412.

The Frankish kings had divided their kingdoms among their sons, but the early Capetian kings crowned their eldest sons during their lifetimes and married younger sons to wealthy heiresses in an effort to endow them with their wives' inheritances rather than with parts of the royal domain. In the thirteenth century, the giving of appanages to younger sons and brothers of the House of CAPET became more commonplace. For instance, in 1285, Charles, the younger brother of Philip IV, received the county of Valois, an appanage that returned to the Crown in 1328 when Charles's son became king as PHILIP VI. In the fourteenth century, when the heir to the throne (beginning with Charles, eldest son of JOHN II) began receiving the Dauphiné (with the title of dauphin) as an appanage, younger royal princes became peers of the realm, thereby enhancing their status. LOUIS, JOHN, and PHILIP THE BOLD, the brothers of CHARLES V (the first dauphin) became, respectively, the dukes of Anjou, Berry, and BURGUNDY.

By 1400, when the frequent granting of appanages had significantly reduced the royal domain, the nature of the relationship between the Crown and the great appanage holders had changed. The latter were no longer feudal lords seeking local autonomy and resisting the encroachment of Crown officials, but peers of France who ruled as virtual monarchs in their appanages and who sought, especially under weak kings like CHARLES VI, to control the royal government for their personal benefit. The prime examples of such princes were Philip the Bold and his heirs, the dukes of Burgundy, who, besides their appanage, came to control FLANDERS and various other portions of the Low Countries. Although technically owing homage to both the king of France and the Holy Roman Emperor, the dukes of Burgundy were in the fifteenth century independent of either and, until the end of the century, a serious threat to the French Crown.

The rivalry of Philip the Bold and his son JOHN THE FEARLESS with their nephew and cousin LOUIS, DUKE OF ORLÉANS, brother of Charles VI, was the cause of the civil war between ARMAGNACS (Orléans's faction) and BURGUNDIANS that erupted after 1407. A dispute over which appanage prince would exercise the powers of the Crown as regent for the mad king, the civil war offered the English a golden opportunity to intervene. French internal quarrels, culminating in 1419 with the murder of John the Fearless by supporters of the Dauphin Charles, then the Armagnac leader, allowed HENRY V to invade France, conquer NORMANDY, and impose the Treaty of TROYES on the French Crown. Conclusion of the latter and the maintenance of Lancastrian France thereafter were made possible by the formal alliance of PHILIP THE GOOD, the new duke of Burgundy, with the English. Although that alliance ended in 1435, the policy of the French Crown thereafter was to reduce the independence of appanage princes. Much of Burgundy was reabsorbed by the Crown after the death of the last Valois duke in 1477 and Bourbon, the last great appanage, was seized by the Crown in 1520, thereby ending all threats to the unity of France from appanage princes.

Further Reading: Lewis, Andrew. *Royal Succession in Capetian France.* Cambridge, MA: Harvard University Press, 1981; Wood, Charles T. *The French Apanages and the Capetian Monarchy, 1224–1328.* Cambridge, MA: Harvard University Press, 1966; Vaughan, Richard. *Valois Burgundy.* London: Archon, 1975.

APPEAL OF THE GASCON LORDS (1368–1369)

The term "appeal of the Gascon lords" refers to the petitions that various Gascon nobles sent to CHARLES V in 1368 and 1369 asking the king, whom they thereby recognized as suzerain of AQUITAINE, to resolve their dispute over taxation with their feudal lord, EDWARD, THE BLACK PRINCE, duke of Aquitaine. Because the Treaty of BRÉTIGNY gave sovereignty over Aquitaine to EDWARD III, accepting the appeals, which Charles did in December 1368, violated the agreement and became the mechanism for renewal of the HUNDRED YEARS WAR.

In early 1368, Prince Edward, in need of funds to pay for his intervention in the CASTILIAN WAR OF SUCCESSION in 1367, persuaded the estates of Aquitaine to grant him a *fouage*, or hearth tax, of 10 sous per hearth for five years. The nobility of GASCONY, accustomed to the lax administration of a distant king, balked at the invasive rule of a resident duke, and several of the most powerful, including John, count of Armagnac, and Arnaud-Amanieu, lord of ALBRET, refused to allow collection of the tax in their domains. These lords appealed to Edward III, but, before the English king could respond, Armagnac, in PARIS for the wedding of Albret to the French queen's sister, lodged a secret appeal against the duke with the king of France, who was addressed as "the sovereign lord of the Duke and whole duchy of Aquitaine" (Sumption, 574).

Although Charles V had heretofore scrupulously observed the Brétigny agreement, he had been seeking a means of eventually undermining it, and Armagnac's appeal, if it could be legally justified, presented such an opportunity. On 30 June 1368, Charles held a meeting of an enlarged royal council to discuss whether or not the appeal should be received. Although lawyers were asked to debate such legal questions as "Did the failure of each king to make the renunciations required by the treaty mean Charles still held sovereignty over Aquitaine?" and "Did Edward's failure to prevent English ROUTIERS from continuing to wage war invalidate the agreement?'' Charles decided the issue on politics. If he rejected the appeal, he would be acknowledging the loss of VALOIS sovereignty in the duchy and losing an opportunity to act against the prince with the support of the prince's own vassals. Because such a chance would likely not come again, Charles accepted the appeal, knowing that to do so meant resumption of the war.

However, before this secret decision was formally announced on 3 December and the prince was summoned to Paris in January (he replied by promising to come at the head of an army), Charles undertook a number of diplomatic initiatives to strengthen his position. In November, he signed a formal treaty with Henry of Trastámare, the Castilian pretender, who, with the resulting French aid, defeated and killed Pedro I in March 1369, thereby turning Castile into a firm French ally. Charles also pushed forward discussions that led to agreement in April 1369 on a marriage between his brother PHILIP THE BOLD, duke of BURGUNDY, and MARGUERITE DE FLANDERS, the daughter of LOUIS DE MALE, count of FLANDERS, thereby ending any possibility of an Anglo-Flemish marriage that would have made Flanders an English APPANAGE. He also instructed his brother, LOUIS, DUKE OF ANJOU, to encourage discontent among the Gascon nobility, so that by the time the PARLEMENT declared the prince contumacious (i.e., in rebellion) on 2 May 1369, almost nine hundred separate appeals had been lodged against him in Paris. Despite attempts by Edward III to avert war, Charles officially confiscated Aquitaine on 30 November, thereby repeating the action by which PHILIP VI had begun the war in 1337. Aided by the disaffection of the Gascon nobility, French armies entered the duchy in 1369, and by 1374 had reduced PLANTAGENET Aquitaine to little more than BORDEAUX and its environs.

Further Reading: Perroy, Edouard. *The Hundred Years War.* Trans. W. B. Wells. New York: Capricorn Books, 1965; Sumption, Jonathan. *The Hundred Years War.* Vol. 2, *Trial by Fire.* Philadelphia: University of Pennsylvania Press, 2001.

AQUITAINE

The duchy of Aquitaine (also known as Guienne) was one of the largest and most important feudal territories of medieval France. Comprising, at its greatest extent, most of southwestern France, Aquitaine was held by the English royal family for three hundred years. Because they were both sovereign rulers and vassals of the Crown of France, the PLANTAGENET dukes of Aquitaine were caught in a political dilemma that, for them, could be satisfactorily resolved only by achieving full sovereignty over the province. Through the Plantagenets' pursuit of this goal, Aquitaine became both a primary cause and a chief battleground of the HUNDRED YEARS WAR.

Although its boundaries, which were always ill-defined, shifted dramatically with the course of events, Aquitaine comprised at it broadest more than a dozen counties, including Poitou, Berry, La Marche, Limousin, Angoumois, Saintonge, Périgord, Agenais, Quercy, Rouergue, and Auvergne. In the eleventh century, the dukes of Aquitaine also incorporated the duchy of GASCONY into their domains, thus extending their authority from the Loire to the Pyrénées. Wealthy and semi-independent, Aquitaine fell under foreign rule in the twelfth century, when Eleanor, daughter and sole heir of Duke William X (d. 1137), married Louis VII of France, thus bringing the duchy to the House of CAPET. In 1152, Eleanor divorced Louis and married Henry, count of Anjou, who in 1154 became Henry II of England. Under Henry, Aquitaine was part of the vast Angevin Empire, a conglomeration of English feudal holdings that comprised most of western France. Henry granted Aquitaine to his son, who, after his accession to the English throne as Richard I in 1189, restored the duchy to Eleanor. After her death in 1204, Eleanor's son John, king since 1199, lost most of the Angevin holdings to the French Crown. The Plantagenets retained only a greatly reduced Aquitaine, their possession of which was disputed by the Capetian kings of France for over fifty years.

In 1259, this unsatisfactory situation was resolved by the Treaty of PARIS, by which Louis IX of France recognized Henry III of England as duke of Aquitaine in return for Henry's renunciation of claims to all other former Plantagenet provinces. Although the duchy now comprised little more than a strip of Gascon territory running along the coast from BORDEAUX to the Pyrénées, English authority in the region was generally accepted by the people, who found distant and often indifferent Plantagenet rule preferable to French taxes and bureaucracy. Also, the booming Anglo-Gascon wine trade, which developed in the thirteenth century, became vital to the local economy.

Because the treaty made the king-duke of Aquitaine subordinate to the king of France, the Gascon nobility could appeal any disputes with their feudal overlord to his overlord. The resulting French interference in the rule of the duchy proved intolerable to the Plantagenets and led twice to open conflict. During the ANGLO-FRENCH WAR OF 1294–1303 and the War of SAINT-SARDOS in the 1320s, French monarchs confiscated Aquitaine after English king-dukes refused to appear before the PARLEMENT in PARIS to answer charges arising out of their administration of the duchy. Both wars ended with negotiated settlements that restored Aquitaine to the Plantagenets. However, in the 1330s, EDWARD III, in an effort to end continual French encroachments on his ducal authority, went to war with France to win full sovereignty over Aquitaine. Thanks to a marriage arranged as part of the 1303 peace agreement, Edward was the grandson of PHILIP IV. After the House of VALOIS replaced the Capetian line on the French throne in 1328, Edward used this family connection to pursue a more radical solution to the Aquitaine question—Plantagenet acquisition of the French Crown. If Edward became his own overlord, all sovereignty issues would fade away.

After capturing JOHN II at the Battle of POITIERS in 1356, Edward wrung the Treaty of BRÉTIGNY from the French in 1360. The agreement gave a greatly enlarged Aquitaine, amounting to almost one-third of France, to Edward in full sovereignty. The king's heir, EDWARD, THE BLACK PRINCE, ruled over the new principality, but the harshness of his rule alienated the Gascon nobility and by 1368 CHARLES V was again accepting appeals against the duke, thereby overthrowing the treaty (see APPEAL OF THE GASCON LORDS). By 1380, the French had reconquered much of the duchy and English authority was again largely restricted to coastal Gascony. In the 1390s, RICHARD II granted the duchy to his uncle, JOHN OF GAUNT, duke of Lancaster, an attempt to create a new ducal line that was unpopular with the Gascons. The problem resolved itself in 1399 when Lancaster's son became king of England as HENRY IV, thus reuniting the duchy to the Crown.

When HENRY V renewed the war with France in 1415, his efforts focused mainly on NORMANDY and northern France, and Aquitaine saw less fighting than it had in the previous century, when the duchy was devastated by frequent military campaigns and destructive ROUTIER bands. In 1450, CHARLES VII, having expelled the English from northern France, launched a new campaign against Aquitaine. Bordeaux fell in 1451, but the Gascons appealed to HENRY VI, who dispatched John TALBOT, earl of Shrewsbury, with an expeditionary force that recaptured much of the duchy by late 1452. However, in July 1453 at the Battle of CASTILLON, the French slew Shrewsbury and destroyed his army, thus ending the Hundred Years War and English rule in Aquitaine.

Further Reading: Labarge, Margaret Wade. *Gascony, England's First Colony: 1204–1453*. London: Hamish Hamilton, 1980; Vale, Malcolm. *English Gascony, 1399–1453*. London: Oxford University Press, 1970; Vale, Malcolm. *The Origins of the Hundred Years War*. Oxford: Clarendon Press, 2000.

ARCHERS

Archers were specialized troops who fired the two main types of missile weapons used during the HUNDRED YEARS WAR, the crossbow and the longbow. The increasing use of archers, particularly mounted archers, revolutionized medieval warfare, for the ability of massed archers to disrupt a cavalry charge increased the use and importance of dismounted infantry. English longbowmen frequently affected the outcome of battles, particularly during the war's earlier phases (*see* HUNDRED YEARS WAR, PHASES OF).

The favorite missile weapon of the French was the crossbow, a complicated device consisting of a bow, or lath, mounted crosswise on a wooden stock, or tiller. To draw the bow, the crossbowman placed his foot in an iron stirrup on the front of the stock and, while crouching down, attached the string to a hook and pulley on his belt; by standing up, he could then draw back the string sufficiently to attach it to the trigger mechanism. The overall length of the stock was about two and a half feet, while the bow span was just over two feet. The crossbow had sights and fired short, heavy wooden arrows known as quarrels, which were about 15 inches in length. The flights, or vanes, were made of leather, horn, or wood, rather than feather. The tip of the quarrel was iron and the rear end was tapered to allow it to fit into the revolving nut mechanism that was released to fire the quarrel. The quarrel sat atop the stock in a grooved rest made of antler. The bow was a composite of wood, horn, and sinew, which gave it greater flexibility. Although the crossbow possessed greater velocity than the longbow, it had a shorter range and was heavier, weighing up to 20 pounds. Because of its complicated firing process, the crossbow's most serious disadvantage was its slow rate of fire. At best, an experienced crossbowman could fire four quarrels per minute, while a longbowman could fire three times as many arrows in the same time. This slower rate made the crossbow far more useful for SIEGE WARFARE than for pitched battles, as was clearly illustrated by the devastation wrought by English archers on PHILIP VI's crossbowmen at CRÉCY. Because proper use of the crossbow required specialized skills, the

French often employed hired Genoese crossbowmen, who were known for their proficiency with the weapon.

The favorite missile weapon of the English, the longbow, had an incalculable impact on the course of the war. Made of yew wood that was frequently imported from Spain or AQUITAINE, the typical longbow of the war period was about six feet long. Yew was the best bow wood because it contained two layers, the white sapwood that could withstand high tension and the red heartwood that could resist compression and thus give the bow its power. A skilled bow maker, or bowyer, had to fashion the weapon to leave a thin layer of sapwood over the heartwood, a requirement that usually left some irregularity in the curve of the bow. The bowstring was looped to horn tips, called notches or nocks, at the ends of better bows or simply to grooves cut into the wood of lesser ones. The string was made of good quality flax or linen and, when strung, coated with beeswax to repel moisture. The center of the string had thread wound tightly about it to protect it from the arrow nock and the shooting hand, on which the archer wore a leather shooting glove. The longbow fired wooden arrows that were about 30 inches long, fledged with goose or peacock feathers, and tipped with an iron barb. Although there were many types of arrowheads, the most common military head was the bodkin, a deadly, four-sided steel spike. The longbow had a range of 150–200 yards, a draw-weight of 80–100 pounds, and the ability to pierce plate ARMOR at up to 60 yards. A skilled longbowman could fire ten to twelve arrows per minute and waves of arrows fired simultaneously by hundreds of bowmen could darken the sky and terrorize an enemy with their dramatic sound and impact. Each archer carried a sheaf of twenty-four arrows, and common practice during combat was to retrieve and reuse arrows whenever possible.

The English first encountered the longbow in Wales in the twelfth century and adopted it for their own use in the thirteenth century, especially during the reign of EDWARD I, who commanded Sunday archery practice in every village. During their campaigns in SCOTLAND in the early fourteenth century, the English used archers in combination with dismounted men-at-arms, placing the former on the wings or interspersed in wedges set between and slightly before the latter. Properly integrated and coordinated, each force gave protection to the other. The archers could disrupt a cavalry charge long before it reached the men-at-arms, who could then advance on foot or remount to fall upon the disordered enemy. This powerful defensive combination, which was unknown on the Continent before the 1340s, proved its effectiveness in numerous battles, including MORLAIX, Crécy, and AGINCOURT. The ability of these two groups to fight in concert was one of the most important tactical developments of the period. Another important innovation was the appearance of mounted archers during EDWARD III's Scottish campaigns in the early 1330s. Although the longbow was a defensive weapon—mounted archers had to dismount to shoot—horse archers were a devastating combination of mobility and firepower, and became mainstays of the swift-moving English CHEVAUCHÉES of the fourteenth century. However, foot archers outnumbered mounted archers in English armies until the fifteenth century, when HENRY V recruited more of the latter for the Agincourt campaign. Although better plate armor for men and horses somewhat limited the effectiveness of the longbow later in the war, the advantage in missile weapons did not shift until the mid-fifteenth century when technical improvements allowed ARTILLERY to dominate the battlefield. *See also* BATTLE, NATURE OF; STRATEGY AND TACTICS.

Further Reading: Bradbury, Jim. *The Medieval Archer.* Woodbridge, England: Boydell Press, 2002; Featherstone, Donald. *The Bowman of England.* Barnsley, England: Pen and Sword Books, 2003; Hardy, Robert. *Longbow: A Social and Military History.* 3rd ed. Sparkford, England: Patrick Stephens, 1992; Prestwich, Michael. *Armies and Warfare in the Middle Ages: The English Experience.*

New Haven, CT: Yale University Press, 1996; Seward, Desmond. *The Hundred Years War.* New York: Penguin, 1999.

"ARCHPRIEST." *See* CERVOLE, ARNAUD DE

ARMAGNAC, COUNT OF. *See* BERNARD, COUNT OF ARMAGNAC

ARMAGNACS

"Armagnac" was the name given to one of the political factions that fought the FRENCH CIVIL WAR, thereby allowing HENRY V to successfully resume the HUNDRED YEARS WAR. The term was first used by Parisians in 1411 for supporters of CHARLES, DUKE OF ORLÉANS, and his allies in their struggle for control of the French government with JOHN THE FEARLESS, duke of BURGUNDY. The name arose because of the growing influence within the Orléanist party of Duke Charles's father-in-law, BERNARD, COUNT OF ARMAGNAC.

The Armagnac party originated among the supporters of LOUIS, DUKE OF ORLÉANS and brother of CHARLES VI, who, before he was murdered by his rival's agents in November 1407, waged a bitter feud for political dominance with his cousin Burgundy. On Orléans's death, leadership of the anti-Burgundian party fell nominally on the duke's young sons, Charles and Philip, whose following swelled in 1410–11, when Burgundy's exclusion of all rivals from court and council drove most princes of royal blood into alliance with the Orléanists. Besides Armagnac, whose daughter Bonne married Charles of Orléans in 1410, the Armagnac leadership eventually included JOHN, DUKE OF BERRY, last surviving brother of CHARLES V; Louis, duke of Anjou; John, duke of Bourbon; John, duke of Alençon; JOHN V, duke of BRITTANY; Charles, lord of ALBRET and constable of France; and John, count of Clermont.

The king averted civil war in 1410 by imposing the Peace of Bicêtre on both parties, but the Armagnacs besieged PARIS in 1411, forcing Burgundy to seek assistance from HENRY IV. The English king sent a small force—the first English army to land in France in twenty-eight years—that broke the siege and allowed Burgundy to drive the Armagnacs south of the Loire. Fearing attack by the royal army Burgundy was gathering, the Armagnac leaders also turned to Henry IV; in the Treaty of BOURGES, concluded in May 1412, Henry agreed to send another force in return for territorial concessions. However, before this new English army could take the field, Burgundy forced the Armagnac lords to capitulate and LOUIS of Guienne, the dauphin, helped negotiate a reconciliation that was embodied in the Treaty of Auxerre in August. In 1413, Burgundy overreached himself by inciting his supporters in Paris to riot; called CABOCHIENS after their most prominent leader, the butcher Simon Caboche, the violent Burgundian bands turned the capital against the duke, who fled Paris in August.

Burgundy's fall instituted an Armagnac regime that fell increasingly under the dominance of Armagnac himself. Defeat at the Battle of AGINCOURT in 1415 discredited the Armagnac government as did the subsequent English conquest of NORMANDY and the count's ruthless use of his Gascon retainers to overawe the capital. By 1417, the Armagnac leadership had been decimated and the regime was powerless to halt the English advance. Berry, Anjou, and Albret were dead, as were Charles VI's two eldest sons, the Dauphins Louis and John, both of whom were at least nominally associated with the Armagnac government. Orléans and Bourbon, captured at Agincourt, were prisoners in England. Deeply hated for the excesses of his supporters, Armagnac tried to rule through the king's last son, the weak and sickly Dauphin Charles (see CHARLES VII). When Charles's mother, Queen ISABEAU, began plotting against the regime, the count banished her from Paris in 1417; she responded by allying with Burgundy, whose supporters in the capital rioted in May 1418, murdering Armagnac and many of his party. Burgundy regained power, but the remnants of the Armagnac faction, now led by the dauphin, fled to Bourges.

In September 1419, when the dauphin's Armagnac councilors murdered Burgundy during a peace conference at MONTEREAU, PHILIP THE GOOD, the new duke of Burgundy, accepted transfer of the Crown to Henry V rather than see it pass to the Armagnac-dominated dauphin. In 1420, in the Treaty of TROYES, Charles VI and Burgundy agreed to disinherit the dauphin in favor of the English king. After the deaths of both Charles VI and Henry V in 1422, the Armagnac faction became the dauphinist party, committed to continuing the VALOIS monarchy in the person of the dauphin. Charles was finally crowned in 1429 after the intervention of JOAN OF ARC improved the military situation and made possible his coronation in Rheims. In 1435, at the Congress of ARRAS, the king was reconciled with Burgundy, an event that finally transformed Charles from Armagnac leader to monarch of all France.

Further Reading: Famiglietti, Richard. *Royal Intrigue: Crisis at the Court of Charles VI, 1392–1420.* New York: AMS Press, 1986; Perroy, Edouard. *The Hundred Years War.* Trans. W. B. Wells. New York: Capricorn Books, 1965.

ARMIES, COMMAND OF

Supreme command of all medieval military forces in both France and England was vested in the king, but, because of the temporal length and geographic scope of the HUNDRED YEARS WAR, the royal power of command was often delegated to the Crown's chief military officers, the constables and marshals. Thus, as the war progressed, the powers, authority, and privileges of these officers grew steadily.

In France, the war saw significant expansion in the powers of the constable. This growth was fueled in part by the ability of some of the men who held the office, and in part by the incapacity of some of the kings they served. During much of the reign of CHARLES V, whose fragile constitution did not allow him to lead armies, the constable was the formidable Breton captain, Bertrand du GUESCLIN (1370–80). During the minority of CHARLES VI, the constable was du Guesclin's able comrade, Olivier de CLISSON (1380–92), and during much of the FRENCH

CIVIL WAR, when Charles was enfeebled by madness, the constables were equally strong figures, Charles d'ALBRET (1403–11, 1413–15) and BERNARD, count of Armagnac (1415–18). Under CHARLES VII, another nonmartial king, the vigorous Arthur de Richemont (*see* ARTHUR III) (1425–58) led the campaigns of reconquest and oversaw the vital military reforms of the 1440s (*see* CHARLES VII, MILITARY REFORMS OF). According to the president of the PARLEMENT, by the time the French retook PARIS in 1436, the constable was "the principal and first office of France in honors and prerogatives, coming before that of chancellor and all others" (Fowler, 119). The office became so prestigious that the dauphin, who was anxious to attract more volunteers from SCOTLAND, rewarded John STEWART, the Scottish earl of Buchan, with it after his victory at BAUGÉ in 1421.

In the absence of the king, the constable had power to make treaties and truces and to grant pardons; by the late fourteenth century, he was a member of the royal *conseil privé*, where military policy and strategy were devised. Clisson, for instance, was a strong proponent of avoiding pitched battle, a strategy employed with much success under Charles V. The constable was also entitled to lodging at court and to assist at coronations, where he carried the "Holy Ampule" containing the oil of anointment, and any crimes committed against him were considered crimes against the king's majesty. When the king was not in the field, the constable had supreme command of the armies, making all troop dispositions, tactical arrangements, and personnel decisions. He sent out all messengers and spies and also decided all garrison assignments and troop detachments. The Crown met all his wartime costs, including replacement of horses for himself and his retinue and double pay of 100 livres tournois per day during sieges and battles. Save for gold and prisoner RANSOMS, he was also entitled to share all booty taken during battle or from captured fortresses.

French marshals commanded the cavalry under the constable and also had responsibility for army discipline and administration.

Their chief task was the supervision of troop musters, preparing camps and reviewing troops once in camp. Marshals also dealt with all civilian complaints against soldiers and commanded the army in the absence of the king and constable. They also enjoyed numerous perquisites and were paid 2,000 livres tournois per year. The holders of the marshal's office were less celebrated than the great constables. Jean de Clermont was slain at POITIERS in 1356, John de Boucicaut was captured at AGINCOURT in 1415, and Pierre de Rieux was captured in 1419. One of the most famous French marshals of the war, Arnoul d'AUDREHEM, who was himself captured at NÁJERA in 1367, had previously served in another high military office, the keeper of the ORIFLAMME, the war banner of French kings. The keeper, who was appointed for life, swore to die before surrendering the banner, an oath that Geoffrey de Charny, JOHN II's keeper, fulfilled at Poitiers. Another important French military officer was the master of the crossbowmen, who commanded all infantry and ARTILLERY, although, in the fifteenth century, the latter came under the control of the master of the king's artillery, who, like Jean BUREAU, was more administrator and technician than military man.

In England, the offices of constable and marshal were, unlike in France, hereditary in great noble families, the former residing, up to 1372, with the Bohuns and the latter, after 1385, mostly with the Mowbrays. Even when not held by members of these families, the offices were exercised by great noblemen, never by members of the lesser nobility as occurred in France, for instance, with du Guesclin. During the most active phases of the war, the English had energetic martial kings and princes—EDWARD III, HENRY V, and EDWARD, THE BLACK PRINCE. Their dominance prevented English constables and marshals from attaining the powers and prominence achieved by their French counterparts. Under less martial kings, high military offices were held by relatives; THOMAS OF WOODSTOCK, duke of Gloucester, was constable for his nephew, RICHARD II, and JOHN, DUKE OF BEDFORD, exercised the same office for his nephew, HENRY VI. Other important English military commands usually went to noblemen, such as HENRY OF GROSMONT, duke of Lancaster; WILLIAM DE BOHUN, earl of Northampton; RICHARD BEAUCHAMP, earl of Warwick; THOMAS MONTAGU, earl of Salisbury; and John TALBOT, earl of Shrewsbury. However, command opportunities for talented men of lesser social rank appeared in AQUITAINE and BRITTANY, where virtually constant conflict, particularly during the BRETON CIVIL WAR, allowed such captains as Sir John CHANDOS, Walter MAUNY, Sir Thomas DAGWORTH, Sir Hugh CALVELEY, and Sir Robert KNOLLES to have famous and lucrative military careers. *See also* ARMIES, COMPOSITION OF; ARMIES, RECRUITMENT OF; ARMIES, SIZE OF; ARMIES, SUPPLYING OF; APPENDIX 6: CONSTABLES AND MARSHALS OF FRANCE AND ENGLAND DURING THE HUNDRED YEARS WAR.

Further Reading: Allmand, Christopher. *The Hundred Years War.* Cambridge: Cambridge University Press, 1988; Fowler, Kenneth. *The Age of Plantagenet and Valois: The Struggle for Supremacy, 1328–1498.* New York: G. P. Putnam's Sons, 1967; Prestwich, Michael. *Armies and Warfare in the Middle Ages: The English Experience.* New Haven, CT: Yale University Press, 1996.

ARMIES, COMPOSITION OF

The armies of the HUNDRED YEARS WAR were composed of two types of troops, men who fought on horseback, the cavalry, and men who fought on foot, the infantry. Although the war saw the former fight increasingly on foot and many of the latter ride to the battlefield, the social and military distinctions that defined these two groups remained largely unchanged throughout the conflict. Drawn from the landed classes, the nobility and armigerous gentry, the cavalry was the elite wing of medieval armies. Drawn from townsmen and peasants, both free and unfree, the infantry lacked the social distinctions of their mounted comrades, but it was the infantry, particularly the English ARCHERS, who became increasingly important, both in numbers and employment, during the war.

The mounted knight dominated medieval warfare until the late thirteenth century. In England, Edward I's campaigns in Wales and SCOTLAND, mountainous countries unsuited to the use of cavalry, demonstrated the importance of foot soldiers, while in France, the destruction of French knights by massed Flemish infantry at Courtrai in July 1302 demonstrated how foot soldiers could defeat mounted warriors. Nonetheless, the mounted knight was far from obsolete, as the French, still relying primarily on cavalry, proved with their crushing defeat of later Flemish rebels at Cassel in 1328. However, to subdue the Welsh and defeat the Scots, the English needed to modify their battle tactics in ways that significantly altered the role and importance of cavalry. EDWARD I began recruiting armies composed mainly of infantry; the force he marched into North Wales in 1277 comprised over fifteen thousand foot soldiers, many of them bowmen, and less than one thousand cavalry. Over time, the English devised effective ways to integrate foot with horse, such as at Maes Moydog in 1295, when William Beauchamp, earl of Warwick, defeated the Welsh by employing the novel tactic of interspersing crossbowmen with the cavalry. By July 1333, when EDWARD III defeated the Scots at HALIDON HILL, the English had learned to combine dismounted cavalry with archers to create a defensive formation that could withstand a cavalry charge. When the French experienced the effectiveness of such formations at MORLAIX, CRÉCY, and elsewhere, archers and infantrymen came to comprise increasingly larger percentages of both armies. Cavalry also began to fight more frequently on foot; at POITIERS in 1356, JOHN II took the unprecedented step of ordering the French cavalry to dismount. Meanwhile, infantrymen and archers found themselves increasingly on horseback—not to fight, but to provide mobility for rapid deployment in battle or to maximize destruction during raids. The border raids of the Scottish wars and the swift English CHEVAUCHÉES of the Anglo-French war proved the worth of mounted bowmen and the light horsemen known as hobelars.

Fighting on horseback required wealth to acquire and maintain the necessary equipage, and freedom from other employment to undertake the training. Knighthood also conferred honor and social distinction, and CHIVALRY was its code of conduct. Weapons, ARMOR, and, especially, warhorses were expensive and beyond the reach of anyone not in possession of land or in the paid service of someone in such possession. In previous centuries, all who fought on horseback were called knights (milites), but, by the fourteenth century, gradations of rank began to appear. Bannerets constituted a superior military rank based not only on social status, but also on personal reputation. The rank of banneret was not hereditary, but its holders commanded other knights, from whom they were distinguished by their use of rectangular banners, rather than simple pennants. According to Jean FROISSART, EDWARD, THE BLACK PRINCE, elevated Sir John CHANDOS to the rank of banneret by cutting off the end of his pennant to form a banner. Below bannerets were knights. In France, knighthood was hereditary, but it was not necessarily so in England. The term "knight" could encompass a wide range of men, from substantial landholders to landless men retained as mounted warriors by the king or noblemen. In many cases, the term was simply applied to anyone who had the training and equipage of a mounted soldier, and by the fourteenth century the main qualification for knighthood appears to have been the financial ability to bear the cost of arming oneself as a knight. Below the level of knight were various ill-defined ranks often encompassed in the generic term "men-at-arms," but also broken down into such categories as sergeants, valets, and squires, the last two being virtually synonymous and usually designating men in training for knighthood.

Medieval cavalry was organized around a series of retinues attached to the king and great nobles. The knights, sergeants, and squires of the royal household often formed the core of the army. At the start of the war, Edward III had seventeen bannerets, forty-four knights, and almost ninety squires in his paid service. Such powerful lords as JOHN OF GAUNT, duke of Lancaster, and PHILIP THE BOLD, duke of Burgundy, also maintained large retinues. In combat, the cavalry was often organized into "battles"; Edward III divided his army into three battles at Crécy, as did John II at Poitiers. In the 1440s, the military reforms of CHARLES VII, drawing upon organizational innovations developed by such ROUTIER captains as Sir John HAWKWOOD, organized the French cavalry into lances, a grouping that included one cavalryman, one squire, two archers, and two pages.

Armed with bows, daggers, swords, axes, halberds, and similar weapons, and lightly or totally unarmored, infantrymen were recruited from the towns and rural peasantry. In England, the king sent commissions of array, composed usually of nobles or knights of local influence, into certain counties or districts to raise a certain number of men for royal service. In many cases, the selection of men was made by local officials. Occasionally, townsmen or villagers pooled their resources to hire people to serve on their behalf. The system had great potential for corruption and the troops raised were often of poor quality. Pay was meager, meant only to provide subsistence. In English armies, an ordinary foot soldier received 3d per day, although a mounted archer got twice that amount. The real inducements were the opportunities the war provided for quick wealth through plunder and RANSOMS. In some cases, men fought for the promise of a royal pardon for past crimes. Lacking the coats of arms of the cavalry, the infantry saw the first appearance of uniforms to help men identify friend from foe in battle. French towns often dressed the men they sent in identical attire, while the Welsh bowmen who accompanied the Black Prince on the CHEVAUCHÉE OF 1355 all wore green and white parti-colored hats and tunics. The war probably raised the social status of most infantrymen, since the poorest and least capable of a village or town could not serve as archers or hobelars; most such men were likely free townsmen and peasants. However, stories of men rising through the ranks, such as that of Sir Robert KNOLLES, who supposedly went from being an archer in BRITTANY to command of a campaign, are rare. *See also* ARMIES, COMMAND OF; ARMIES, RECRUITMENT OF; ARMIES, SIZE OF; ARMIES, SUPPLYING OF; CHARLES VII, MILITARY REFORMS OF; INDENTURES; STRATEGY AND TACTICS; TOWNS AND THE HUNDRED YEARS WAR.

Further Reading: Allmand, Christopher. *The Hundred Years War.* Cambridge: Cambridge University Press, 1988; DeVries, Kelly. *Infantry Warfare in the Early Fourteenth Century: Discipline, Tactics, and Technology.* Rochester, NY: Boydell Press, 1996; Prestwich, Michael. *Armies and Warfare in the Middle Ages: The English Experience.* New Haven, CT: Yale University Press, 1996.

ARMIES, RECRUITMENT OF

In both France and England, the HUNDRED YEARS WAR, which required kings to field larger forces for longer periods of time, witnessed a significant change in the way royal governments raised armies. The war accelerated a preexisting trend—by the late fourteenth century, most men fought for the Crown not because they had a feudal obligation to do so, but because the Crown paid them to do so. In both countries, this move to a voluntary system of recruitment also led to the development of a system of national TAXATION to pay for military forces.

By the 1330s, the practice of paying men to serve in the king's army was already well established in England. Although armies were raised by feudal summons for EDWARD III's early campaigns in SCOTLAND, most of the troops sent to France went voluntarily, being persuaded by the promise of steady pay or the possibility of profits derived from RANSOM or plunder. Because the English king wanted men to travel abroad and fight an offensive war, he needed to convince them that it was in their interest to do so. Royal recruiting agents acting through county commissions of array were charged with mustering a certain number of troops from a certain region. Although all able-bodied subjects between the ages of sixteen and sixty were liable for military service, Edward's commissioners were given a set

quota of ARCHERS, infantry, and even cavalry, whom they were to muster into royal service and lead to predetermined mobilization points. The men thus raised were given INDENTURES, which were written contracts spelling out rates of pay, terms of service, ransom arrangements, and such details as the provision of horses and transport. By the 1380s, the use of indentures had largely replaced the feudal levy as the chief means of raising royal armies in England. Although English war aims changed significantly in the fifteenth century, when HENRY V abandoned the *CHEVAUCHÉE* in favor of the conquest and defense of territory, the English system of recruitment by indenture changed little.

In France, where men were being called upon to fight in defense of their homes and country, feudal traditions lasted longer. The *ARRIÈRE-BAN*, by which the king could summon able-bodied men between the ages of eighteen and sixty to provide military service in an emergency, was issued at least seven times during the first two decades of the war. In most cases, the king accepted money in lieu of service. Towns often agreed to raise and pay for a troop of crossbowmen, and the Church, forbidden from active participation in war, often provided money, supplies, or horses. However, this system proved inadequate, being too cumbersome, inefficient, and slow to effectively address the frequent military emergencies caused by English invasions. After the Battle of POITIERS in 1356, the French Crown abandoned the *arrière-ban*. Under CHARLES V, French recruitment practices were thoroughly revised, creating a smaller army of volunteers raised by *letters de retente*, which, like English indentures, spelled out details of pay and service. Conducted by royal officials, the centralized military recruitment of the 1360s was better organized and more efficient. The armies raised were truly royal armies, paid by the king, commanded by officers chosen by the king, and operating under strategies and toward goals devised by the king. Under Charles and his constable, Betrand du GUESCLIN, French armies avoided pitched battle and concentrated on the reconquest of AQUITAINE.

After Charles's death in 1380, French recruitment practices reverted to a feudal basis, as powerful APPANAGE princes, such as PHILIP THE BOLD, duke of BURGUNDY, dominated the royal government, using it to serve their own interests. After 1410, as the FRENCH CIVIL WAR intensified, the *arrière-ban* reappeared, and French armies, such as the one Henry V defeated at AGINCOURT in 1415, became aggregations of magnate retinues lacking a clear organization or unified command. However, in the 1440s, CHARLES VII prepared for a final push against the English by reinstituting many of his grandfather's reforms, thereby creating a permanent national army paid for by the king and led by officers of his choosing (*see* CHARLES VII, MILITARY REFORMS OF). Thus, by the end of the war in 1453, the recruitment of armies by feudal summons had largely disappeared from both kingdoms. *See also* ARMIES, COMMAND, OF; ARMIES; COMPOSITION OF; ARMIES, SIZE OF; ARMIES, SUPPLYING OF.

Further Reading: Allmand, Christopher. *The Hundred Years War*. Cambridge: Cambridge University Press, 1988; Contamine, Philippe. *War in the Middle Ages*. Trans. Michael Jones. Oxford: Basil Blackwell, 1984; Prestwich, Michael. *Armies and Warfare in the Middle Ages: The English Experience*. New Haven, CT: Yale University Press, 1996.

ARMIES, SIZE OF

Realistic calculation of the size of HUNDRED YEARS WAR armies is difficult, since official records are sparse and chronicle estimates notoriously untrustworthy. Yet, since most men were in receipt of the king's wages, having been recruited by INDENTURES or other types of contracts, surviving pay records, particularly in England, allow some plausible estimates of army size to be made for most major battles and campaigns.

Being able, at least in the fourteenth century, to recruit from a larger geographic area with a larger population, the VALOIS kings of France were usually able to field larger armies than their PLANTAGENET and Lancas-

trian rivals. On several occasions, especially earlier in the war, French kings commanded armies numbering 20,000, which was usually about as large a force as could be effectively raised and supplied. In most cases, these large armies were commanded by the king himself or by the heir to the throne. For instance, during the THIÉRACHE CAMPAIGN in 1340, PHILIP VI shadowed EDWARD III with an army of about 20,000, while John, duke of Normandy, the future JOHN II, led a force of about the same size at the siege of AIGUILLON in GASCONY in 1346. Philip commanded an even larger army—some English chroniclers say 100,000—at CRÉCY in 1346 and he also gathered about 20,000 for his abortive attempt to break the siege of CALAIS in 1347. John II had about 11,000 men at POITIERS in 1356. The largest English armies of the war were also usually commanded by the king or the prince of Wales. Edward III, in what was probably the war's largest concentration of English troops, eventually gathered more than 20,000 men to besiege Calais—over 30,000 if one includes the king's allies from FLANDERS. Edward had an army of about 10,000 men during the Thiérache Campaign, although more than half of these were supplied by members of the king's ANTI-FRENCH COALITION. Edward also commanded about 10,000 at Crécy and over 12,000 during the RHEIMS CAMPAIGN in 1359–60, when he tried unsuccessfully to take Rheims and have himself crowned king of France. EDWARD, THE BLACK PRINCE, commanded about 6,000 men at Poitiers, although chronicle estimates vary from about 3,000 to 12,000, and he had over 10,000 at NÁJERA in 1367, when many of his men were Gascon *ROUTIERS*. The one large army of the war not personally commanded by the king was the French force of 20,000 that fought at AGINCOURT in 1415, the mad CHARLES VI being incapable of military command.

The many fourteenth-century English *CHEVAUCHÉES*, campaigns of swift movement intended to devastate countryside rather than fight battles, used smaller armies to increase mobility. The force of over 10,000 with which JOHN OF GAUNT, duke of

Lancaster, swept around PARIS during the *CHEVAUCHÉE* OF 1373 was entirely exceptional, and even the 6,000 men who accompanied the Black Prince on the CHEVAUCHÉE OF 1355 constituted a large force for such a campaign. Because the BRETON CIVIL WAR was largely a sideshow after the 1340s, most of the armies there were smaller. For instance, at LA ROCHE-DERRIEN in 1347, the army of CHARLES OF BLOIS, the French-backed duke, numbered about 3,000, while the English force under Sir Thomas DAGWORTH, numbered scarcely 1,000. At AURAY, in 1364, Blois again had about 3,000 men, while his opponent, the future JOHN IV, commanded about 2,000.

The military reforms of two nonmartial kings—CHARLES V in the 1370s and CHARLES VII in the 1440s—promoted creation of smaller but more professional French armies paid by the king and led by his hand-picked officers. Thus, French armies at most of the major encounters of the fifteenth century, when French kings almost never took the field themselves, were smaller than fourteenth-century forces. For instance, at BAUGÉ in 1421, the French force numbered about 5,000; at CRAVANT in 1423, about 8,000; and at CASTILLON in 1453, about 9,000. The huge French force at Agincourt was due mainly to the collapse of Charles V's reforms during the FRENCH CIVIL WAR, which meant that the Agincourt army was drawn largely from the retinues of great ARMAGNAC lords. During the early 1420s, the French relied heavily on troops from SCOTLAND, who comprised a great part of the unusually large 15,000-man French force at VERNEUIL in 1424. Even JOAN OF ARC, whose activity in 1429 greatly enhanced dauphinist recruitment, brought only about 4,000 to ORLÉANS and had no more than 8,000 with her on the LOIRE CAMPAIGN and at the Battle of PATAY.

English armies had always been smaller, so fifteenth-century English forces did not shrink as much in comparison to their fourteenth-century counterparts, although the large armies of the Calais siege or the Rheims Campaign did not reappear. HENRY

V's abandonment of the *chevauchée* for campaigns of siege and conquest meant that many men were on garrison duty while others formed smaller forces besieging various castles and strongpoints (*see* SIEGE WARFARE). The 9,000 men Henry took to France in 1415 comprised one of the largest English expeditions of the century, although he had only about 6,000 with him at Agincourt. JOHN, DUKE OF BEDFORD, had almost 10,000 men, gathered from numerous garrisons, at Verneuil, but that was one of the largest encounters of the century; most English armies of the period were well under that number. THOMAS, DUKE OF CLARENCE, led only about 1,500 men at Baugé, while the English armies at Cravant, Patay, FORMIGNY, and Castillon were all between about 3,000 and 5,000 men. Thomas MONTAGU, earl of Salisbury, besieged Orléans in 1428 with 5,000 men, which was a sizable English force for the time. *See also* ARMIES, COMMAND OF; ARMIES, RECRUITMENT OF; ARMIES, SUPPLYING OF; CHARLES VII, MILITARY REFORMS OF; LANCASTER, HOUSE OF.

Further Reading: Allmand, Christopher. *The Hundred Years War*. Cambridge: Cambridge University Press, 1988; Prestwich, Michael. *Armies and Warfare in the Middle Ages: The English Experience*. New Haven, CT: Yale University Press, 1996.

ARMIES, SUPPLYING OF

Few factors had a greater impact on the length, course, and outcome of a military campaign during the HUNDRED YEARS WAR than a ruler's ability to feed and supply his armies. Operating in a preindustrial age, late medieval governments faced no more difficult problem than that of maintaining an army in the field.

To be effective, all military forces, whether field armies, castle or town garrisons, or ships' crews had to be regularly fed and supplied. In 1359–60, EDWARD III's RHEIMS CAMPAIGN achieved less than intended in part because it was difficult to keep such a large force fed during a harsh winter. In 1416, the series of encounters known as the Battle of VALMONT occurred primarily because Thomas BEAUFORT, earl of Dorset, desperately needed to collect supplies for his starving garrison at HARFLEUR. In 1421–22, during the siege of MEAUX, HENRY V was obliged to send away his horses for lack of forage and to organize convoys to maintain the flow of supplies from PARIS. Because most men, at least after the mid-fourteenth century, fought for wages (see ARMIES, RECRUITMENT OF; INDENTURES), the Crown was under no obligation to also provide food. However, leaving soldiers to provision themselves while on campaign was to invite disaster, for discipline could collapse as men spent more time acquiring food than making war. Foraging troops were also not usually particular about how or where they obtained supplies and the hostility they bred among local populations could hamper military operations. During the BRETON CIVIL WAR, English soldiers in BRITTANY were so hated for levying PÂTIS on the regions they controlled that furious peasants used sticks and stones to attack the garrison of LA ROCHE-DERRIEN when it was besieged in 1347. During the NORMAN CAMPAIGN OF 1417–19, Henry V was so concerned with the ill effects of uncontrolled foraging on both the local people and food supplies that he ordered full and immediate payment for all food obtained by his men in NORMANDY.

Problems of supply differed for the two Crowns. The French had a certain advantage in that they were fighting in their own country and were more likely to obtain cooperation and less likely to meet resistance in the collection of provisions. They could more easily anticipate the needs of their armies by sending agents in advance into areas of operation to collect and distribute food, and they had greater opportunity to organize local merchants in the collection and stockpiling of food. Thus, the French usually had less necessity to live off the land and less need to bring vital supplies over long distances. Being the invaders, the English received less cooperation from local populations and often had to bring supplies from far away. Edward III arranged supply from England to maintain his siege of Calais in 1347 (see CALAIS, SIEGE OF), and thereafter

the town and garrison of CALAIS had also to be supplied from England. During the siege of ROUEN in 1418–19, Henry V also had supplies ferried across the Channel, thus necessitating his creation of a royal navy (see NAVAL WARFARE).

In France, the *prise* constituted the usual system of raising provisions from both individuals and such corporate entities as towns and monasteries. A royal household officer known as the *panetier du roi* oversaw the collection of supplies, often delegating his authority to local officials and commanders, who sent out agents to gather the required provisions in the required quantities. Under PHILIP VI, the collection officers were divided into three groups: those gathering cereal products, those collecting wine, and those obtaining fodder for horses. Because many people obtained exemption from the *prise*, and many others were or believed themselves abused by *prise* officers, the system generated many disputes that eventually ended in the courts. In England, where the system of supply collection was known as purveyance, the gathering of food for royal armies generated even more friction, largely because, as one commentator put it, the king's purveyors "were sent to act in this world as the devil acts in Hell" (Allmand, 98). Having already paid taxes voted by PARLIAMENT for support of the war, many people resented the additional obligation of providing cheap food for the army. Purveyance allowed the sheriff to compel people or institutions like monasteries to accept deferred payment at below-market rates for their contributions to a general supply requisition.

The provision of nonfood items, such as weapons, clothing, and horses was also to some degree borne by the Crown. A knight was expected to provide himself with arms, ARMOR, and a horse, although he might expect the Crown to reimburse him if the animal was killed or injured in combat. For this purpose, all horses were appraised by the king's experts before the campaign began. English soldiers raised by commissions of array were to be armed at the expense of their locality, which provided bows, arrows, and other smaller weapons and supplies, including, according to a royal order of 1417, six wing feathers from every goose in the district. Nonetheless, the need for weaponry was enormous, forcing both Crowns to provide some of what was needed. In England, the keeper of the king's arms worked from the Tower of London, purchasing, storing, and delivering weapons to armies, garrisons, and ships. The demands of a long war are illustrated by the following figures from the Tower armory: in 1360, the keeper reported having on hand over 23,000 sheaves of arrows (24 arrows to a sheaf), but by 1381, a decade after resumption of the war, that number had dropped to less than 1,000 sheaves. Finally, Hundred Years War armies did not have uniforms in the modern sense, and, for the most part, soldiers were expected to provide their own clothing, making no doubt for a great variety of attire. However, some effort was made, particularly by local communities, to standardize what solders wore. For instance, the town of Tournai outfitted the men it sent to the French royal army in 1340 in identical uniforms, while archers sent to the English army from Wales and Cheshire after 1350 usually appeared in green and white. *See also* ARMIES, COMMAND OF; ARMIES, COMPOSITION OF; ARMIES, SIZE OF.

Further Reading: Allmand, Christopher. *The Hundred Years War*. Cambridge: Cambridge University Press, 1988; Prestwich, Michael. *Armies and Warfare in the Middle Ages: The English Experience*. New Haven, CT: Yale University Press, 1996.

ARMOR AND NONMISSILE WEAPONRY

During the HUNDRED YEARS WAR, the increasing use of the longbow, of mounted ARCHERS, and of dismounted cavalry led to new developments in metal armor, the defensive body covering for men and horses designed to deflect blows from heavy weapons in close combat and to ward off arrows, crossbow quarrels, or other projectiles shot from a distance. These trends also fostered the development and employment of various types of nonmissile weapons for use in hand-to-hand combat.

In the mid-fourteenth century, most English men-at-arms still wore chainmail, which was made of interlinked metal rings. The typical English man-at-arms had a mail shirt, running from neck to knees, that covered a thick padded tunic and was laced to a conical, open-faced helmet, although visors were becoming more common. His chest was protected by steel breastplates, his arms by steel plates with articulated elbow pieces, and his feet by metal footguards worn over mail stockings. Covering all this, he wore a short linen surcoat. Most French knights of the period wore less old-fashioned protection—plate armor for shoulders and limbs topped by a bascinet, a metal helmet with projecting hinged visors and air holes. Instead of the surcoat, they wore a shorter leather jupon, and their warhorses were also armored, with plate covering their heads and mail or leather their flanks. In both armies, the basic weapon was a long straight sword, worn usually on the left side and balanced on the right by a short dagger called a *misericord*, because it was often used to grant the "mercy" of death to the mortally wounded. On horseback, the principal weapon was a 10-foot-long wooden lance carried with a small wedge-shaped shield and sometimes a short, steel-handled battleaxe. On foot, especially among the English, the primary weapon was a halberd, which carried a spiked axe head and had to be swung at an opponent to be most effective.

By the fifteenth century, the making of plate armor had become a fine art, and new methods of forging iron allowed for the production of lighter, stronger, more flexible suits of armor that could better protect a larger portion of the body and allowed for greater mobility and endurance. Although a complete set of armor was expensive, and might only be available to wealthy nobles and knights, most men went into combat at least partially armored, even if with older, lower-quality pieces. The finest armor had curved and fluted design elements, which

27

gave it strength and allowed it to deflect blows more easily. Totally encased in metal, a knight in full armor had greater confidence in battle, and, by the mid-fifteenth century, many discarded the shields and opted instead to wield heavier two-handed weapons designed to crush the new fluted armor. More lightly armored men-at-arms continued to carry a small, round shield known as a buckler, which could be easily slung from a belt or strap worn around the waist.

Full armor was worn over a heavy padded doublet that was slit for ventilation. Gussets (i.e., metal or mail inserts) were sewn to the doublet to protect vulnerable areas such as the arms, elbows, and armpits, where metal joints would have been too restrictive of movement. Wax cords (arming points) were attached to the doublet to allow the plate armor to be secured to the body. Other undergarments included heavy, padded hose and leather shoes. The main body armor comprised upper and lower breastplates, which were hinged vertically on one side, and backplates, a metal skirt, and tassets, which hung from straps on the skirt and protected the lower body. The feet were encased in plate shoes called sabatons, which were attached to lower leg coverings called greaves. The greaves and the upper leg coverings, known as cuisses, had two halves that hinged on the side and were secured by buckles and straps. A special knee piece, attached by rivets or pins, protected the gap between greaves and cuisses. Arms were protected by two similar coverings, the vambraces (lower arm) and rerebraces (upper arm), with special pieces called cowters and pauldrons attached by straps to protect, respectively, the elbows and shoulders. Gauntlets fitted over the vambrace protected the hands and wrists. The sallet, a visored metal helmet worn over a padded arming cap, protected the head, while the bevor, a triangular metal plate worn below the sallet, protected the neck.

Fourteenth-century battles like Crécy showed how vulnerable unarmored or inadequately armored horses were to archers. The heavier horse armor involved protective plates for the head, neck, chest, rump, and flank, and might even include armor-plated reins to prevent an enemy from cutting them and depriving the rider of control. Nonetheless, the weight and expense of horse armor limited its use to the wealthiest combatants, who, by the fifteenth century, generally used their mounts only to ride to or escape from the battlefield.

For close-quarter combat, the fifteenth-century knight usually carried a sword that could be used for both cutting and thrusting. Such weapons varied greatly in length and width, from a broad, single-handed sword that was about two and a half feet in length to a narrower, two-handed version that was almost three and a half feet long. Swords meant solely for thrusting tended to have longer, narrower blades and longer hilts. When not in use, a sword fit into a scabbard that hung from a hip belt in such a way as to position the point a little to the rear where it could not trip its owner. From the other hip many men hung a rondel dagger, which was used to exploit gaps in an opponent's armor or to pry open the visor of a downed enemy, who was then dispatched by a thrust to the eye or throat. The rondel was characterized by a disk- or conical-shaped guard between hilt and blade and a similarly shaped pommel at the other end of the hilt. Because it was used for stabbing, the rondel had a straight, slender blade that was triangular in shape and up to fifteen inches in length to allow for maximum penetration of an enemy's body.

Because the stronger, fluted armor used in the fifteenth century could deflect sword and spear thrusts, many knights began carrying new types of heavy weapons, often with hooks or spikes, which were designed to crush or puncture plate armor. Perhaps the most deadly of these weapons was the pollaxe, which consisted of a wooden shaft, four to six feet long, topped by a long spike that was flanked on one side by an axe head and on the other by a spiked hammer or fluke (a curved, beaklike extension for hooking an opponent to the ground). The spike could puncture plate or damage armored joints and rob a man of mobility. The axe and hammer could crush both armor and the flesh it covered. Against unarmored opponents, a skillfully wielded pollaxe was devastating.

While the pollaxe was used only for combat on foot, such other battering weapons as the battle-axe, the mace, and the war hammer were carried primarily by horsemen, who swung their weapon with one hand and held their reins with the other. Weighing from two to five pounds, the war hammer was serrated and usually carried a fluke opposite the hammer head. Of a similar weight, the mace had a head composed of six interlocking serrated edges or some similarly formidable configuration of spikes and points. Like the pollaxe, these weapons were used to deliver crushing blows to armored opponents.

Further Reading: DeVries, Kelly. *Medieval Military Technology*. Peterborough, Ontario: Broadview Press, 1992; Prestwich, Michael. *Armies and Warfare in the Middle Ages: The English Experience*. New Haven, CT: Yale University Press, 1996.

ARRAS, CONGRESS OF (1435)

Held in the Burgundian town of Arras in August and September 1435, the Congress of Arras was the largest, most comprehensive diplomatic gathering of the HUNDRED YEARS WAR. Mediated by cardinals appointed by the pope, the Congress brought together delegations from England, France, BURGUNDY, and other interested parties, such as various towns, princes, and the University of Paris. The first Anglo-French negotiation since the talks that resulted in the Treaty of TROYES in 1420, the Congress made no peace between the two Crowns, but, as intended by its host, PHILIP THE GOOD, duke of Burgundy, replaced the fifteen-year-old Anglo-Burgundian alliance with the Treaty of Arras, a reconciliation between Philip and CHARLES VII that changed the nature of the war and led eventually to the English expulsion from France.

By 1431, interest in a negotiated settlement was growing at both the French and Burgundian courts. Despite the victories in-

spired by JOAN OF ARC in 1429–30, Charles VII, who preferred negotiation to combat, was financially unable to raise the armies required to carry the war into Anglo-Burgundian France. Although he personally detested Charles, the man he held responsible for the murder of his father, JOHN THE FEARLESS, Philip had come to believe that he could more easily dominate a French government headed by the weak and indolent Charles than one controlled by the forceful English regent, JOHN, DUKE OF BEDFORD. When death removed the mediation of ANNE OF BURGUNDY, Philip's sister and Bedford's wife, in November 1432, relations between the two men deteriorated. Also, with the French blockading PARIS, the growing hardship of life in the capital was turning many citizens against the English and threatening to erode Burgundy's great popularity within the city. With the pope also advocating peace, primarily as a means of strengthening his authority within the antipapal Council of Basle, the desire for some agreement was strong among all parties except the English.

Although Franco-Burgundian talks regarding a reconciliation began in 1432, an agreement that resulted in the calling of an all-party congress was not achieved until early 1435. Philip's desire to avoid the appearance of betraying his ally was satisfied by his chancellor, Nicholas Rolin, who declared that HENRY VI had no valid claim to the French Crown since the Treaty of Troyes passed the Crown only to HENRY V, who had died before actually inheriting it and so could not pass it on to his son. That the Troyes agreement also disinherited Charles VII was conveniently ignored. Under Rolin's interpretation, Philip could abandon the English alliance while remaining technically faithful to the treaty that created it.

When the Congress opened in August, the French delegation, led by Arthur de Richemont (*see* ARTHUR III) the brother of JOHN V of BRITTANY, and Regnault of Chartres, archbishop of Rheims, demanded that Henry VI renounce his claim to the French Crown as a preliminary to any further talks. The English delegation, led by Henry BEAUFORT, cardinal of Winchester, refused to even discuss Henry's claim and proposed instead that Charles could retain those parts of the kingdom under his control if he paid homage for them to Henry as his king. The French found this offer as ridiculous as the English found the renunciation demand. With no compromise possible, the English left the Congress on 1 September.

With the English gone, the French and Burgundians quickly came to terms, concluding the Treaty of Arras on 20 September. In the agreement, Charles confirmed almost all the territorial concessions made to Philip by the English, including the Somme towns, which constituted a line of fortresses that protected Burgundian Artois and threatened Paris. A special clause exempted Philip from making homage for his lifetime to Charles for all the duke's French fiefs. Finally, Philip exacted a measure of revenge for his father's death. Charles was forced to deny any personal involvement in the murder, to agree to punish the guilty parties (who were named), to erect an expiatory monument, and to pay for Masses for the late duke's soul. Charles also sent a councilor, who, on the king's behalf, made humble apology on his knees before Philip.

Although humiliating for Charles, the treaty, combined with the death of Bedford on 14 September, brought the king great rewards. The treaty immediately returned Burgundian France to its VALOIS allegiance and, through its implied renunciation of the ARMAGNAC party, finally transformed Charles from faction leader to king of all France. In April 1436, French forces retook Paris and revolts erupted in English NORMANDY. Although it took almost another twenty years to expel the English entirely, the Treaty of Arras initiated the process by undercutting English authority in the occupied territories and depriving Lancastrian France of vital Burgundian support.

Further Reading: Dickinson, Jocelyne G. *The Congress of Arras: A Study in Medieval Diplomacy.* Oxford: Clarendon Press, 1955; Griffiths, Ralph A. *The Reign of Henry VI.* Berkeley: University of California Press, 1981.

ARRAS, PEACE OF. *See* FRENCH CIVIL WAR

ARRAS, TREATY OF. *See* ARRAS, CONGRESS OF

ARRIÈRE-BAN

The *arrière-ban* was a military summons employed by the French Crown to call into service all men able to bear arms. The term derived from the Latin *retrobannum*, and meant literally the summoning of the king's back-vassals, who owed military service to an intermediate lord rather than directly to the monarch. As employed during the HUNDRED YEARS WAR, the *arrière-ban* was a device for impressing upon the people the seriousness of the military situation and thereby facilitating the mustering of men and the payment of money in lieu of service.

Although the *arrière-ban* was employed since at least the twelfth century to summon the king's feudal vassals, its scope was expanded following the defeat of a French army by Flemish rebels at Courtrai in 1302. Thereafter, PHILIP IV and his successors claimed the right to summon all men of military age and capacity. However, beyond the cavalry supplied by the nobility and the contingents of ARCHERS and infantrymen supplied by the towns, the king neither expected nor wanted a mustering of all those fit to bear arms. Thus, one of the main components of the *arrière-ban* was the expectation that many of those called would not actually serve, but would instead purchase an exemption. Like the ORIFLAMME, the *arrière-ban* was employed in times of national emergency and served to convey the urgent need for men or money.

The *arrière-ban* was used most frequently during the early decades of the Hundred Years War. PHILIP VI proclaimed it throughout the kingdom on 30 April 1337 prior to implementing his decision to confiscate EDWARD III's duchy of AQUITAINE, the act that initiated the Anglo-French war. The *arrière-ban* of 1339, called to meet a threatened English invasion, raised large sums of money, which Philip agreed to place with representatives of the local communities for disbursal upon confirmation that the king or his eldest son had actually taken the field. The *arrière-ban* of 4 July 1340, which was proclaimed in northern France to meet the Anglo-Flemish campaigns of that year, resulted in the mustering of an army of over twenty thousand at Arras (*see* SAINT-OMER, BATTLE OF).

In 1341, the *arrière-ban* was issued twice—in June to prosecute the war in GASCONY, where the Truce of ESPLECHIN had never taken hold; and in August for the whole kingdom to respond to English intervention in BRITTANY. Multiple proclamations were also made in 1345—to meet English threats in both the north and Languedoc—and in 1346—to support the operations of John, duke of Normandy (*see* JOHN II), in the southwest, and to gather the northern army that fought at CRÉCY.

Use of the *arrière-ban* declined after 1356 and particularly during the reign of CHARLES V, when institution of the hearth tax (*fouage*) provided a larger and more assured source of revenue. Charles's policy of refusing to meet the English in battle also reduced the government's need to summon large masses of common people to arms. Henceforth, the Crown sought to maintain smaller more professional armies. Although use of the *arrière-ban* revived in the decade after 1410 during the FRENCH CIVIL WAR, the summons was considered archaic and ineffective by the 1440s, when, under the military reforms of CHARLES VII, the term reacquired its original meaning as a formal summoning of the king's feudal tenants-in-chief. *See also* CHARLES VII, MILITARY REFORMS OF.

Further Reading: Contamine, Philippe. *War in the Middle Ages*. Trans. Michael Jones. Oxford: Basil Blackwell, 1984; Henneman, John Bell. *Royal Taxation in Fourteenth-Century France: The Development of War Financing, 1322–1356*. Princeton, NJ: Princeton University Press, 1971.

ARTEVELDE, JAMES VAN (c. 1290–1345)

James van Artevelde, a wealthy merchant of Ghent who became leader of a Flemish revolution, was the effective ruler of FLANDERS from 1338 to 1345. An architect of the ANGLO-FLEMISH ALLIANCE, van Artevelde, by his willingness to recognize EDWARD III's right to the French Crown, played a key role in the first campaigns of the HUNDRED YEARS WAR.

Little is known of van Artevelde before his appointment on 3 January 1338 as one of five captains in the emergency government of Ghent, the revolutionary regime established in the city at the start of the uprising against the pro-French count, LOUIS DE NEVERS. A prosperous broker and trader in foodstuffs, van Artevelde had held no other office prior to his election as captain. Combining a fierce determination and an autocratic temperament with a flair for politics and PROPAGANDA, van Artevelde quickly brought Bruges, Ypres, and the smaller Flemish towns into a union governed from Ghent by a commission under his presidency. Convinced that the future of Flanders depended on the friendship of England, from which came the wool required to fuel the Flemish cloth industry, but fearful of the wrath of PHILIP VI, to whose court Louis de Nevers fled in 1339, van Artevelde offered Edward III a benevolent neutrality, which was sufficient to obtain partial restoration of the Anglo-Flemish wool trade in July 1338.

Following the inconclusive ending of the THIÉRACHE CAMPAIGN, a large French army remained massed upon the Flemish border. Under threat of this army and the probable imposition on Flanders of a papal interdict (officially declared in April 1340), van Artevelde at last gave way to English pressure and, after much hard bargaining, concluded a formal alliance with Edward. Signed on 3 December 1339, the Anglo-Flemish compact gave Flanders free access to English wool, a subsidy of 140,000 livres to purchase military equipment, and the promise of English assistance in repelling any attack by Philip. In return, the Flemings recognized Edward as king of France and promised men for his campaigns. In 1340, van Artevelde, who had become a personal friend of the English king, led the Flemish contingents that participated in the inconclusive siege of TOURNAI. He argued strongly against the Truce of ESPLECHIN, which ended the campaign, believing that it left Flanders open to French attack, and he demanded and got assurances from Philip that no exiled opponents of the revolutionary regime would be allowed to return to the province.

However, the truce, which was extended in 1342, reduced fears of a French attack and thereby reopened political and social divisions within Flanders. The weavers' guild, which supported van Artevelde and dominated the municipal governments, was soon at odds with the Flemish landowners and with the other guilds, particularly the fullers. In 1344–45, van Artevelde lost popularity by associating himself with the weavers' suppression of demands by the fullers for a wage increase. Often portrayed as a democratic reformer for his initial success in uniting rival classes and factions, van Artevelde became in fact dictator of Ghent, maintaining himself in power through the violence and intimidation of his large personal bodyguard. He survived a coup attempt in 1343, but in early 1345 his opponents deprived him of his captaincy. Believing him to be too ambitious and too willing to use Edward III's friendship to bolster his personal position, van Artevelde's enemies in Ghent spread rumors that he planned to recognize Prince EDWARD (the future Black Prince) as count of Flanders. On 17 July 1345, a Ghent mob murdered van Artevelde. Shortly thereafter, the new municipal regime confiscated his property and banished his family. *See also* ARTEVELDE, PHILIP VAN.

Further Reading: Carson, Patricia. *James van Artevelde: The Man from Ghent*. Ghent: Story, 1980; Nicholas, David. *The van Arteveldes of Ghent: The Varieties of Vendetta and the Hero in History*. Ithaca, NY: Cornell University Press, 1988.

ARTEVELDE, PHILIP VAN (1340–1382)

Philip van Artevelde, the youngest son of James van ARTEVELDE, was, like his father, captain of Ghent and leader of a Flemish uprising. Attempting, again like his father, to overthrow the Dampierre counts of FLANDERS and end VALOIS influence over the province, van Artevelde sought an alliance with the English Crown, thus briefly reinvolving Flanders in the HUNDRED YEARS WAR.

Little is known of van Artevelde before his appointment as confiscation commissioner of Ghent in December 1381, more than two years after Flanders rose in rebellion against Count LOUIS DE MALE. On 24 January 1382, van Artevelde, largely with the support of the weavers' guild, won election as captain of Ghent, which was then under a blockade organized by the count with the cooperation of neighboring towns and provinces. Declaring himself *rewaert*, or regent, of Flanders, van Artevelde assumed the wider powers exercised by his father in the 1340s, which he used initially to destroy the descendents of men who had been implicated in his father's assassination in 1345. On 3 May, with Ghent near starvation, van Artevelde launched a successful surprise attack on Bruges. Within weeks, most of the Flemish towns recognized van Artevelde's authority. Forced to flee Bruges by swimming the moat, the count appealed for aid to his overlord CHARLES VI, whose minority government was dominated by his uncle PHILIP THE BOLD, duke of BURGUNDY. As Louis's son-in-law and thus the future ruler of Flanders, Burgundy swiftly secured royal intervention on the count's behalf.

On 9 June, after destroying most of the fortifications of Bruges, van Artevelde laid siege to Oudenaarde, one of the few Flemish towns still loyal to the count. The growing threat from France and the failure of the Oudenaarde siege, which, according to the chronicler Jean FROISSART, was due to the regent's military inexperience, led van Artevelde to pursue an alliance with the government of RICHARD II. Talks continued over the summer, but the Flemish demands, which included repayment of the 200,000 crowns van Artevelde claimed his father had loaned to EDWARD III and removal of the wool staple from CALAIS to Bruges and then to a town of Ghent's choosing, proved too high for the English. Thanks to the PEASANTS' REVOLT of the previous year, they were hesitant to make common cause with men in rebellion against their lawful lord.

With Anglo-Flemish talks stalled, van Artevelde entered into an equally fruitless correspondence with Charles VI in October. On 3 November, the king left PARIS to join Burgundy, who was gathering forces on the Flemish frontier. Formally led by the constable, Olivier de CLISSON, but accompanied by the king, Burgundy, and the other royal uncle, JOHN, DUKE OF BERRY, a French army of perhaps ten thousand entered Flanders in mid-November and quickly forced the capitulation of Ypres and other towns. Leading an army drawn from the militia of Ghent and allied towns and implausibly estimated at forty thousand men, van Artevelde moved to intercept the French before they reached Bruges. On 27 November 1382, van Artevelde was slain at the Battle of Roosebeke.

Further Reading: Nicholas, David. *The van Arteveldes of Ghent: The Varieties of Vendetta and the Hero in History.* Ithaca, NY: Cornell University Press, 1988.

ARTHUR DE RICHEMONT. *See* ARTHUR III, DUKE OF BRITTANY

ARTHUR III, DUKE OF BRITTANY (1393–1458)

Constable of France and one of the leading French commanders of the fifteenth century, Arthur III, duke of BRITTANY, reformed the French army in the 1440s and led the reconquest of NORMANDY in 1449–50.

The third son of JOHN IV, duke of Brittany, Arthur inherited his father's English earldom of Richmond in 1399 and was thus known for most of his life by the French form of that title, comte de Richemont. A strong-willed and combative man, Richemont became a close friend of CHARLES VI's son, LOUIS, DUKE OF GUIENNE, and an adherent of the ARMAGNAC party during the FRENCH CIVIL WAR. He was captured at AGINCOURT in 1415 and remained a prisoner until 1420, when HENRY V released him in return for help in persuading his brother, JOHN V, duke of Brittany, to accept the Treaty of TROYES. In the early 1420s, Richemont supported the House of LANCASTER and the ANGLO-BURGUNDIAN ALLIANCE, having personal ties to both. His mother, Joan,

the daughter of CHARLES THE BAD, king of Navarre, had taken HENRY IV of England as her second husband in 1403, and, in 1423, Richemont had himself married Margaret, the sister of PHILIP THE GOOD, duke of BURGUNDY; the sister-in-law of JOHN, DUKE OF BEDFORD; and the widow of Guienne. In June 1424, Bedford, perhaps distrusting Richemont's loyalty, refused his request to be given command of an Anglo-Breton force to defend PARIS from dauphinist raiders. The resulting rift between the two stubborn, self-righteous men caused Richemont to abandon HENRY VI and offer his services to the dauphin, who appointed him constable of France in March 1425.

Now eager to harm the English, Richemont persuaded his brother to abandon the tripartite alliance with Burgundy and Bedford created by the Treaty of AMIENS. However, his efforts at spurring the dauphin to military action were frustrated by the factionalism the riddled the dauphinist court. Influenced by the royal favorite, Georges de La Trémoïlle, whom Richemont had helped bring to power, the dauphin banished the constable from court in 1428. In June 1429, the constable, acting on his own initiative, joined the French army led by JOHN, DUKE OF ALENÇON, and JOAN OF ARC, and thus took part in the LOIRE CAMPAIGN and the Battle of PATAY. Although the disgraced constable should not have been received, Joan, ignoring the reluctance of her companions, welcomed Richemont and his men. Despite this, the constable, who should have carried the sword of state before the king, was excluded from the coronation of CHARLES VII in July 1429.

Finally returned to favor in June 1433, Richemont urged the king to make peace with Burgundy and was present at the Congress of ARRAS in 1435 when Charles did so. On 13 April 1436, the constable led a French army into Paris, where he purged the royal administration of Anglo-Burgundian officials. In 1439–40, he helped suppress the Praguerie, an uprising of disaffected French noblemen that included Alençon and La Trémoïlle, and, by late 1441, he cleared the environs of Paris of English garrisons and *écorcheurs* (see ROUTIERS). Following conclusion of the Truce of TOURS in 1444, Richemont worked with the king to reform the French army, transforming it into a professional force that was well trained, paid, and led. During the NORMAN CAMPAIGN that began in 1449, Richemont was instrumental in achieving decisive victory at the Battle of FORMIGNY in April 1450 and was present at the successful sieges of Caen and Cherbourg that concluded the campaign in the following summer. On the unexpected death of his nephew, Peter II, in September 1457, Arthur became duke of Brittany, but ruled only a short time, dying childless on 26 December 1458. *See also* CHARLES VII, MILITARY REFORMS OF.

Further Reading: Jones, Michael. *Between France and England: Politics, Power and Society in Late Medieval Brittany.* Burlington, VT: Ashgate Publishing Company, 2003; Jones, Michael. *The Creation of Brittany: A Late Medieval State.* London: Hambledon Press, 1988; Vale, M. G. A. *Charles VII.* Berkeley: University of California Press, 1974.

ARTILLERY

The evolution of modern artillery, large guns capable of firing heavy stones or metal pellets, was one of the most important developments in military technology to occur during the HUNDRED YEARS WAR.

Artillery made its first appearance in European warfare in the early fourteenth century. Although cannon never supplanted the longbow or crossbow (*see* ARCHERS) during the course of the war, firearms eventually altered SIEGE WARFARE by replacing the wooden siege engines used since antiquity to assault towns and fortresses. The war also saw the beginning of changes in NAVAL WARFARE that were not complete until the sixteenth century, when ships became floating artillery platforms. Small guns projecting quarrels (like crossbow bolts) or lead pellets were used at the naval battle of SLUYS in June 1340 and at the French defense of TOURNAI in the following August. EDWARD III employed similar weapons at CRÉCY in 1346 and to guard the approaches to CALAIS during the

siege of 1347. The effect of these weapons, especially on the battlefield, was primarily psychological; their noise and smoke frightened men and horses and caused confusion among attackers.

The resumption of war in 1369 following collapse of the Treaty of BRÉTIGNY coincided with important breakthroughs in the production and use of artillery. Prior to 1370, most guns were made of copper or brass and weighed between 20 and 40 pounds; however, during the last decades of the century, increasingly larger guns of wrought and cast iron began to appear. In 1375, the French besieged Saint-Sauveur-le-Vicomte in AQUITAINE with guns that weighed over a ton and were capable of firing 100-pound stone balls. Although the English captain defending Cherbourg in 1379 had several guns capable of firing large stones, the English before 1400 had few weapons to match the size of the Saint-Sauveur cannon. The end of the century also saw the appearance of various small mortars, different types of handguns, and the ribaudequin, a large multibarreled weapon that could shoot stone balls and lead pellets or quarrels.

By the early fifteenth century, artillery of varying sizes and increasing effectiveness were common in both armies. The largest guns, known as bombardes, could weigh over 5 tons and fire stone balls weighing up to 300 pounds; bombardes were probably more common among the French than the English until the early 1420s. Veuglaires or fowlers could be up to 8 feet long and ranged in weight from 300 pounds to several tons, while crapaudaux or crapaudins were 4 to 8 feet long and generally lighter than veuglaires. Many other types of much smaller and lighter guns, such as serpentines and culverins, also came into common use in the fifteenth century.

Intending a war of siege and conquest, rather than one of *CHEVAUCHÉES*, HENRY V arrived in France in 1415 with a large artillery train that immediately proved its effectiveness at the siege of HARFLEUR. English artillery was vital to the success of the NORMAN CAMPAIGN of 1417–19, and especially to the campaign's culminating triumph, the siege of ROUEN. French cannon killed Thomas MONTAGU, earl of Salisbury, at ORLÉANS in 1428 and were used effectively by JOAN OF ARC's army during the LOIRE CAMPAIGN of 1429. From the mid-1430s to the end of the war, CHARLES VII's artillery was collected, maintained, and deployed by the king's capable master gunner, Jean BUREAU, whose handling of the artillery was key to the success of French sieges at Meaux in 1439, PONTOISE in 1441, and Caen and other strongholds in NORMANDY during the NORMAN CAMPAIGN of 1449–50. Although they had no one to match Bureau, the English had long collected artillery in the Tower of London, where succeeding members of the Byker family had stored and maintained the king's cannon since the time of Edward III. The last encounter of the war, the Battle of CASTILLON in GASCONY in 1453, was the first in which artillery played a significant role. This success was due largely to the placement of the guns, which Bureau sited in an entrenched artillery park. The concentrated firepower of this formation decimated the attacking English army and slew its famous commander, John TALBOT, earl of Shrewsbury.

As cannon came into common use in fifteenth-century siege warfare, military architecture also evolved. Walls became thicker and lower and many were scarped to deflect cannonballs. Angular towers gave way to round towers provided with loops for small cannon and handguns. Because artillery could not be fired long within a tower, where smoke and the restrictive angles of the loops were problems, the guns were moved to the tops of towers, and gun platforms were built into all existing castles and fortresses where such modifications were possible. Gunports were particularly important for coastal fortifications, and many appeared after 1380 at such fortresses as Cherbourg, Brest, Calais, and Dover.

Further Reading: Allmand, Christopher. *The Hundred Years War*. Cambridge: Cambridge University Press, 1988; DeVries, Kelly. *Medieval Military Technology*. Peterborough, Ontario: Broad-

view Press, 1992; Smith, Robert D. "Artillery and the Hundred Years War: Myth and Interpretation" in *Arms, Armies and Fortifications in the Hundred Years War*, ed. Anne Curry and Michael Hughes, 151–60. Woodbridge, England: Boydell Press, 1994.

ARTOIS. *See* ROBERT OF ARTOIS

AUBEROCHE, BATTLE OF (1345)

On 21 October 1345, a numerically inferior English force destroyed a French army besieging the castle of Auberoche in GASCONY. Besides yielding a host of important HOSTAGES, the victory cemented recent English gains in Gascony and disrupted French military efforts in the southwest for the next year.

In mid-October 1345, an army of some seven thousand men commanded by Louis of Poitiers, count of Valentinois, left La Réole to begin the process of clearing Gascony of English garrisons. Moving up the narrow valley of the Auvezère, the French invested the fortress of Auberoche, which sat on a rocky height commanding the river. The castle garrison was commanded by Sir Frank Halle, who managed to get word of his plight to Henry, earl of Derby, in Bordeaux (*see* HENRY OF GROSMONT). Ordering Lawrence Hastings, earl of Pembroke, to rendezvous with him somewhere en route, Derby set out for Auberoche with a force of twelve hundred to fourteen hundred men-at-arms and eight hundred ARCHERS.

On the evening of 20 October, the English reached Auberoche without being detected by the besieging army. That night and most of the next morning, Derby kept his men hidden in a nearby wood to await the arrival of Pembroke. When the earl failed to appear, Derby decided to attack before his presence was discovered and the advantage of surprise lost. At a signal from Derby, the English cavalry charged from the wood into the rear of the French camp while the archers opened fire from a position directly in front of the camp. Taken completely unawares, the French suffered heavy casualties before most of their men could struggle into their ARMOR. As the English cavalry drove deeper into the camp, the archers were forced to hold their fire until knots of French soldiers, attempting to rally on the edges of the camp, again offered them clear targets.

When Halle led a mounted sortie out of the castle, French resistance collapsed. As always happened when one army was put to flight, the pursuers inflicted heavy casualties and seized large numbers of prisoners. Valentinois died of his wounds and his second in command, Bertrand de l'Isle, was taken hostage. Other prisoners included seven viscounts, three barons, twelve bannerets, the seneschals of Toulouse and Clermont, numerous knights, and the nephew of Pope CLEMENT VI. The defeat convinced the French to immediately lift three other sieges of Anglo-Gascon garrisons and to delay a planned campaign in the region by John, duke of Normandy (*see* JOHN II). Although fought by relatively small numbers of men, the battle of Auberoche was one of the most important encounters of the war in Gascony, establishing English military dominance in the region for the next two decades.

Further Reading: Burne, Alfred H. *The Crécy War*. Ware, England: Wordsworth Editions Ltd., 1999; Sumption, Jonathan. *The Hundred Years War*. Vol. 1, *Trial by Battle*. Philadelphia: University of Pennsylvania Press, 1991.

AUDLEY, SIR JAMES (d. 1369)

Celebrated in the *Chronicles* of Jean FROISSART as a hero of the Battle of POITIERS, Sir James Audley was a companion-in-arms of ED-WARD, THE BLACK PRINCE, and a contemporary model of knightly CHIVALRY.

The son of Sir James Audley of Stratton Audley in Oxfordshire, Audley began his military career in 1346, when, as a knight in the prince's retinue, he witnessed EDWARD III conferring knighthood on the prince upon landing in NORMANDY on 12 July. He fought at CRÉCY on 26 August and then participated in the siege of CALAIS, which concluded successfully in August 1347. At about this same time, he became a founding member of the Order of the GARTER. He probably also fought at the naval battle of WINCHELSEA in 1350 and at the relief of the Anglo-Gascon garrison of St.-Jean-d'Angély in 1351. He was with the prince in LONDON in June 1351 and was rewarded with ARMOR for his presence at a tournament with his frequent companion, Sir John CHANDOS, in December 1353. For his past service, he also received at about this time a generous pension of £80 per year.

In 1355, Audley accompanied the prince to AQUITAINE, and participated in the *CHE-VAUCHÉE* OF 1355, during which Audley and Chandos conducted a separate raid against the lands of John, count of Armagnac, in the region of Toulouse. In early 1356, Audley and Chandos raided the Agenais, using the fortress at Moissac as a base, and on 28 August, the two knights routed a French force near Vierzon. In September, Audley participated in negotiations conducted with JOHN II on the eve of Poitiers, through which the prince attempted to avoid battle. However, when fighting began, Audley was in the forefront, having supposedly vowed to strike the first blow. Several accounts of the battle confirm that Audley was later found on the field severely wounded and only revived when carried to the prince, who interrupted his supper with the captive French king to praise and comfort the injured knight. Audley was later rewarded for his service at Poitiers with a grant of £400 a year for life and the lordship of Oléron.

In 1359–60, Audley and Chandos were members of the prince's retinue during the RHEIMS CAMPAIGN, and Audley witnessed the signing of the Treaty of BRÉTIGNY in 1360. After a brief visit to England, he accompanied the prince to Aquitaine in 1362. In 1367, Audley remained in BORDEAUX as governor of Aquitaine when the prince intervened in the CASTILIAN WAR OF SUCCESSION and led an army into Spain for the campaign that culminated at NÁJERA. In 1369, Audley was the prince's lieutenant in Poitou and the Limousin and besieged La Roche-sur-Yon with Edward III's son, EDMUND OF LANGLEY, earl of Cambridge. After the town fell, Audley withdrew to Fontenay-le-Comte, where he died on 23 August. Much praised by both friends and foes as a gallant and chivalrous knight, he was buried with honors at Poitiers.

Further Reading: Barber, Richard. *Edward, Prince of Wales and Aquitaine.* New York: Charles Scribner's Sons, 1978; Harvey, John. *The Black Prince and His Age.* London: Rowman and Littlefield, 1976; Hewitt, Herbert J. *The Black Prince's Expeditions of 1355–1357.* Manchester: Manchester University Press, 1958.

AUDREHEM, ARNOUL D', MARSHAL OF FRANCE (c. 1300–1370)

Arnoul d'Audrehem, marshal of France under JOHN II and CHARLES V, was a loyal and experienced French commander who led VALOIS armies against the English in BRITTANY and GASCONY, and against *ROUTIERS* in Languedoc and Provence.

Born near CALAIS in the Ardres region of northern France, Audrehem, a protégé of Constable Charles of Spain, was appointed marshal in September 1351. During the HUNDRED YEARS WAR, the marshals—PHILIP VI had appointed two—were second in command of the French army under the constable; they had responsibility for recruitment, inspection, and payment of troops, as well as for the maintenance of discipline. Prior to his appointment, Audrehem commanded French garrisons in AQUITAINE, being captain of Angoulême when he was captured by the English at the Battle of SAINTES in April 1351. Ransomed within a month, Audrehem conducted operations against Ralph STAFFORD, earl of Stafford, in Gascony in 1352 and against Anglo-Gascon *routiers* in the Limousin in 1353. In 1354, he was in Brittany, where he captured Sir Hugh CALVELEY in a sharp encounter at the castle of Tinténiac near Montmuran on April 10. After the battle, the marshal knighted a young Bertrand du GUESCLIN, who had distinguished himself in the battle.

In 1355, as John II prepared to resume the war, Audrehem was one of the king's key military advisers. In November, with EDWARD III marching through Picardy, the marshal suggested that the two kings meet in single combat, a common proposal that accorded with contemporary notions of CHIVALRY but that invariably came to naught. In March 1356, Audrehem ruthlessly suppressed a tax revolt in Arras, and, in April, he participated in the king's surprise descent on ROUEN to arrest CHARLES THE BAD, king of Navarre. In September at POITIERS, Audrehem commanded one of the cavalry contingents charged with dispersing the English ARCHERS. Scoffing at attempts to persuade the king to avoid battle and wait for EDWARD, THE BLACK PRINCE, to be starved out of his strong defensive position, Audrehem attacked prematurely and was captured when his force was flanked by the English. He spent the next four years in captivity, being unable to pay the sum demanded by the prince, who had purchased the marshal's RANSOM. Audrehem was released on parole in May 1359 to carry news of the conclusion of the Second Treaty of LONDON to PARIS, but returned within weeks with the Estates-General's rejection of the agreement (*see* ESTATES, GENERAL AND PROVINCIAL).

Released with the king in late 1360, Audrehem became royal lieutenant in Languedoc in 1362, and spent most of that year fighting *routiers*. To remove the companies from France, he negotiated the ultimately unsuccessful Treaty of Clermont with Henry of Trastámare, who agreed to lead *routier* bands into Spain. In 1365, he accompanied du Guesclin to Castile, where their *routier* army put Trastámare on the throne. In 1367, he was again in Castile, where he was captured with du Guesclin at NÁJERA. Because his Poitiers ransom was still unpaid, Audrehem was personally accused by the prince of breaking his oath not to fight against the English. The marshal defended himself by saying that he had taken arms against Pedro I of Castile, not against the prince. Now over sixty, and well known to most of the Anglo-Gascon captains, the marshal elicited much sympathy and was acquitted of the charge by a jury of English, Gascon, and Breton knights. Audrehem resigned as marshal on 20 June 1368 and died in 1370.

Further Reading: Sumption, Jonathan. *The Hundred Years War.* Vol. 2, *Trial by Fire.* Philadelphia: University of Pennsylvania Press, 2001.

AULD ALLIANCE. *See* FRANCO-SCOTTISH ALLIANCE; SCOTLAND

AURAY, BATTLE OF (1364)

Fought on 29 September 1364 outside the Breton port of the same name, the decisive Battle of Auray ended the long BRETON CIVIL WAR.

In 1363, after twenty-three years of war, the two rivals for the ducal title agreed to divide the Duchy of BRITTANY between them, with John de Montfort, the English-backed claimant, taking the southwest, and CHARLES OF BLOIS, the French-backed claimant, holding the northeast. Official conferral of the title and the peerage of duke of Brittany was to be decided by the kings of England and France, EDWARD III and JOHN II, who were both technically neutral in the dispute. However, the question remained unanswered when civil war resumed in April 1364. In July, de Montfort laid siege to Auray, one of the few south coast towns under his rival's control. With the help of Bertrand du GUESCLIN, a Breton then serving CHARLES V, the new French king, Charles of Blois raised an army of over three thousand men. Although backed by royal officials in NORMANDY, Charles of Blois received no official support from Charles V, who even stripped du Guesclin of his Norman captaincy for intervening in Brittany.

De Montfort received no assistance from LONDON but vital aid from such local English captains as Sir Robert KNOLLES and Sir Hugh CALVELEY. Sir John CHANDOS also joined de Montfort with a small English force from GASCONY. By September, de Montfort's army numbered over two thousand, with most drawn from the local English companies. Thus, although the Crowns of England and France remained neutral, their agents in Brittany were actively involved in the war.

Arriving at Auray on 29 September, Charles of Blois prepared for immediate battle. Commanding de Montfort's forces, which he positioned on the heights beyond the river, Chandos deployed his army in three divisions, with himself and Sir Matthew Gourney commanding the right, Knolles the left, and de Montfort the center. Calveley, much to his chagrin, was sent behind the lines to lead the reserves. Deploying his army in similar fashion, Charles of Blois gave command of its three divisions to du Guesclin; Jean de Chalon, son of the Count of Auxerre; and himself. During the negotiations that preceded the battle, the Bretons in each party displayed a greater willingness to compromise than either their English or French allies. The English threatened to kill Charles's representatives if they prolonged the talks and du Guesclin urged Charles to win the entire duchy for himself, a belligerence that convinced some of Charles's Bretons to quit the field.

Fought on foot, which limited the effectiveness of the English ARCHERS, the battle opened with the Anglo-Breton army capturing Jean de Chalon and driving his men into du Guesclin's force. Chandos then focused his attack on Charles of Blois, whose position was made vulnerable by further desertions from his division. When Charles's division was overwhelmed, he was slain and his army dissolved. The battle now became a rout. De Montfort's men killed nearly eight hundred and took over fifteen hundred captives, including du Guesclin, who brought Chandos almost £20,000 in RANSOM.

With Charles of Blois dead and his sons either dead or captive, his cause collapsed and his supporters submitted to de Montfort. Although he had won the duchy with English aid, de Montfort, now freed of the need for allies, quickly offered his allegiance to Charles V. The French king accepted the outcome of Auray and brokered the favorable Treaty of GUÉRANDE, whereby Jeanne de Penthièvre, Charles of Blois's widow, in whose right he had claimed the duchy, acknowledged de Montfort as Duke JOHN IV in April 1365.

Further Reading: Sumption, Jonathan. *The Hundred Years War.* Vol. 2, *Trial by Fire.* Philadelphia: University of Pennsylvania Press, 2001.

AUXERRE, TREATY OF. *See* FRENCH CIVIL WAR

AVIGNON PEACE CONFERENCE (1344)

The Anglo-French conference convened by Pope CLEMENT VI in Avignon in 1344 was the most ambitious papal attempt to achieve a negotiated settlement of the HUNDRED YEARS WAR. During the talks, the differences between the parties proved irreconcilable and neither EDWARD III nor PHILIP VI displayed any willingness to modify his demands. Doomed by this intransigence, the conference collapsed within weeks and war resumed in 1345.

On 19 January 1343, papal representatives negotiated the Anglo-French Truce of MALESTROIT, which was to run until 29 September 1346. The stated purpose of the truce was to allow the warring parties to send representatives to Avignon to discuss a permanent end to the war. English distrust of papal intentions, manifested through a series of procedural objections, delayed the conference until 22 October 1344. When the delegations finally arrived, Clement kept them separated and himself acted as go-between. The English began by demanding recognition of Edward's claim to the French Crown, which the French refused to even discuss. Having proclaimed himself rightful king of France, Edward could not accept any possibility of VALOIS overlordship in AQUITAINE. When, after four sessions, neither side would budge from its original position, Clement withdrew from the conference, leaving its conduct to a commission of two cardinals.

The cardinals attempted to shift the focus to Aquitaine, asking if the English would accept restitution of the duchy as it had existed before the War of SAINT-SARDOS. Although they again reiterated their refusal to discuss Aquitaine separately from the rest of Edward's French kingdom, the English eventually admitted the possibility of a settlement based on an Aquitaine defined by the borders specified in the Treaty of PARIS and held in full sovereignty by the PLANTAGENETS. The French flatly rejected this suggestion, declaring that Philip could not dismember his kingdom. The cardinals now proposed that Edward renounce GASCONY in exchange for all lands in England held by the Hospitallers and by foreign religious houses, a suggestion that the English denounced as an unequal and dishonorable bargain. The cardinals next proposed that Edward renounce Gascony in exchange for the Crown of SCOTLAND, which Philip would convince DAVID II to surrender in return for lands in France. Since Edward already considered Scotland to be his by right, the English ambassadors declared this plan acceptable. Finally, the cardinals suggested that Edward grant Gascony as an APPANAGE to one of his sons, who could thus accept Valois overlordship without any diminution of status or honor. The English also rejected this proposal and on 10 November declined to consider any plan for surrendering Gascony in return for territorial compensation outside France. When the French confirmed their refusal to consider any plan that extinguished Valois sovereignty over the duchy, the English refused to continue the talks.

Although Clement tried to persuade the English to remain in Avignon, their money was short and the mood in the city was distinctly anti-English, leading several delegates to leave for England by mid-December. A papal suggestion that Edward replace his largely clerical delegation with a new embassy led by influential noblemen, such as HENRY OF GROSMONT, earl of Derby, and William de BOHUN, earl of Northampton, also came to naught. In February 1345, the last English delegate in Avignon, Bishop John Offord, whom Clement had not allowed to depart, fled the city without leave, thus effectively ending the conference. On 15 June, more then a year before the truce's expiration, Edward renounced the Malestroit agreement and resumed the war.

Further Reading: Sumption, Jonathan. *The Hundred Years War.* Vol. 1, *Trial by Battle.* Philadelphia: University of Pennsylvania Press, 1999.

AVIGNON PAPACY. *See* PAPACY AND THE HUNDRED YEARS WAR

B

BABYLONIAN CAPTIVITY. *See* PAPACY AND THE HUNDRED YEARS WAR

BADEFOL, SÉGUIN DE (c. 1331–1366)

Séguin de Badefol was a famous soldier of fortune and a notorious captain of ROUTIERS. His company was widely known and feared and was one of the largest components of the GREAT COMPANY, a powerful army of *routiers* that terrorized southeastern France in the 1360s.

Badefol was the second son of the lord of Badefol-sur-Dordogne, a small castle on the frontier of GASCONY in territory that had long been in dispute between the kings of England and France. He fought for the French at POITIERS in 1356, but the capture there of JOHN II and the resulting truce ended payments from the French Crown and led Badefol to form his own *route*, or company of men, which, with other similar bands, took to pillage to support themselves. Nicknamed "le Margot," and numbering almost two thousand men, Badefol's company was part of the Great Company that attacked Pont-Saint-Esprit in the spring of 1361. Bought off by Pope Innocent VI and Robert Fiennes, constable of France, the companies were promised employment in Italy or Spain but the cessation of wars in those lands largely frustrated the plan and Badefol remained in command of a large force of brigands that continued to plague the southern provinces.

In November 1361, Badefol abandoned his leadership of the companies as part of a deal whereby the local administrations in Toulouse, Carcassonne, and Beaucaire paid the Great Company to leave their territories.

Remaining quiet until the summer of 1363, Badefol resumed command of the Great Company and on 13 September seized and looted the town of Brioude on the borders of Auvergne. Making Brioude their base, the companies devastated the surrounding countryside. News of Badefol's success drew many other captains and their companies to Brioude, and by the late autumn of 1363 the town was said to contain almost ten thousand *routiers*. Needing to expand his area of operations to keep his men supplied, Badefol soon launched raids eastward into the wealthy duchy of BURGUNDY. In April 1364, the Estates of Auvergne purchased Badefol's withdrawal from Brioude for a royal pardon, a papal absolution, and 40,000 florins, the largest RANSOM ever recorded.

Ostensibly accepting employment with CHARLES THE BAD, king of Navarre, who was then at odds with the French Crown, Badefol and his *routiers* seized the town of Anse near Lyon on 1 November 1364. Although calling himself one of Navarre's captains, Badefol turned Anse into a second Brioude and again became the scourge of the surrounding region. Pope Urban V excommunicated Badefol and his associates, and even offered a crusade indulgence to anyone who expelled them from the town, but the *routiers* did not depart Anse until they were paid another 40,000 florins in September 1365. Leaving the companies, Badefol withdrew to Navarre where he demanded the payment promised him by Charles the Bad. Unhappy with the services rendered and offended by Badefol's importunity, Charles, in January 1366, invited the *routier* to dine and offered him a poisoned pear, from which Badefol died after six days of agony.

Further Reading: Henneman, John Bell. *Royal Taxation in Fourteenth Century France: The Captivity and Ransom of John II.* Philadelphia: American Philosophical Society, 1976 (see particularly chap. 5); Sumption, Jonathan. *The Hundred Years War.* Vol. 2, *Trial by Fire.* Philadelphia: University of Pennsylvania Press, 2001.

BASTIDES

Bastides were fortified settlements established in western France in the thirteenth and early fourteenth centuries by kings or nobles for mainly economic purposes. In a period of population growth, a *bastide* generated for its lord an increased income from land that had been previously underutilized or uncultivated. In AQUITAINE, where *bastides* were founded by both Capetian kings (*see* CAPET, HOUSE OF) and PLANTAGENET king-dukes, the settlements also served to define spheres of influence within contested regions. As such, local frictions generated by *bastides* often aggravated the larger Anglo-French jurisdictional dispute over Aquitaine, and thus contributed to the coming of the HUNDRED YEARS WAR.

Although *bastide* creation had occurred in southwestern France since the 1240s, the first new settlement in Plantagenet Aquitaine was Monségur, established in 1263. Until conclusion of the Treaty of PARIS in 1259, the uncertain status of English rule within the duchy had inhibited *bastide* foundation, and proliferation of *bastides* within the Plantagenet domains only followed EDWARD I's acquisition of the Agenais in 1279. However, by 1287, the seneschal of Gascony, acting under the king-duke's authority, founded two dozen *bastides*, particularly within newly acquired or weakly administered territories, where the settlements did not so much defend frontiers as define jurisdictional and administrative boundaries. Such attempts at demarcation often caused disputes that wound up in ducal or royal courts. *Bastides* also tended to disrupt established economic and social patterns, thus creating further jurisdictional friction. Because their founders

granted charters of settlement (*pariage*) that conferred attractive and valuable rights and franchises on settlers, *bastides* came into conflict with neighboring towns, villages, or lords, who were often adversely affected by the activities of the new community. Since *bastides* were settlements of free peasants, serfs from neighboring manors were drawn to the new communities, and economic privileges granted to settlers frequently harmed the trade of local merchants.

Bastide disputes gradually increased in number over the three decades that preceded EDWARD III's accession in 1327. Typical of such cases were the complaints that ducal officials lodged with Edward I in the early 1290s regarding Jean Archier, administrator of the new French *bastide* of Grenade, who frequently heard cases that were clearly within the king-duke's jurisdiction. Two decades later, EDWARD II asked PHILIP IV to ensure that all French foundations in Aquitaine observed the same law enforced by the ducal administration in existing communities. By the eve of the War of SAINT-SARDOS in March 1324, at least five Gascon cases involving *bastides* were pending before the PARLEMENT in PARIS. Because it was the immediate cause of the Anglo-French war of the same name, the *bastide* at Saint-Sardos was the most famous of the disputed Gascon communities. In October 1323, a ducal vassal, Raymond-Bernard, lord of Montpezat, protested the construction of a French *bastide* at Saint-Sardos by burning the village and hanging the royal official in charge. When CHARLES IV intruded on ducal jurisdiction by ordering Montpezat's arrest, the resulting dispute led eventually to confiscation of the duchy and a French invasion that overran most of Plantagenet GASCONY. Although the conflict ended in 1325 with the restoration of Aquitaine, which Edward II then granted to his son, who did homage for it to the French king, the war effectively halted *bastide* creation in southwestern France, and the political crises of the 1330s and constant warfare of the following decades destroyed the economic climate that had earlier favored their foundation.

Further Reading: Beresford, Maurice. *New Towns of the Middle Ages: Town Plantation in England, Wales, and Gascony.* New York: Praeger, 1967; Vale, Malcolm. *The Origins of the Hundred Years War.* Oxford: Clarendon Press, 2000.

BATTLE OF THE THIRTY. *See* COMBAT OF THE THIRTY

BATTLE, NATURE OF

Although the battles of the HUNDRED YEARS WAR varied as to the reasons they were fought, the ground they were fought over, the tactics they displayed, and the length of time they lasted, most comprised at least some of the basic elements of a medieval military encounter, including an exchange of missile weapons, a cavalry charge, a hand-to-hand mêlée, and a final rout.

Prior to the outbreak of the Anglo-French conflict, full-scale battles were uncommon and many warriors had surprisingly little experience of them. Although the length of the war gave such men as Sir Walter MAUNY and Bertrand du GUESCLIN considerable experience in skirmishes, ambushes, and other small-scale encounters, major battles were still infrequent. Even such a seasoned campaigner as EDWARD III was present at only two large battles—HALIDON HILL in 1333 and CRÉCY in 1346. The king's other expeditions, such as the THIÉRACHE CAMPAIGN in 1339 and the RHEIMS CAMPAIGN in 1359–60, resulted in no great battle. Such encounters were often considered a matter of seeking judgment from God, who sent victory only to the righteous. Battle was therefore a large risk, and kings and commanders would avoid combat if they believed themselves able to win in another way. PHILIP VI did not fight in 1339 and 1340 because he knew that Edward III could not hold together his ANTI-FRENCH COALITION if he did not fight and win a battle. The future CHARLES V did not fight in 1359–60 because he did not want to risk another Crécy or POITIERS and because he believed the English could not long maintain an army in the field if unable to live off the land or win a battle. Although some historians argue that the largest such campaigns

also sought to draw the French into battle, English CHEVAUCHÉES focused on ravaging the countryside, destroying property and morale. The great battles of the war—Crécy, Poitiers, and AGINCOURT—can all be seen either as *chevauchées* during which the English were trapped and forced to fight against their will or campaigns by which the English all along intended to bring the enemy to battle. In some instances, men were eager for combat. At AURAY in 1364, poor English knights in need of booty and RANSOMS begged Sir John CHANDOS, commander of the Montfortist army, to forego negotiations.

Battles could take many forms. At AUBEROCHE in 1345, HENRY OF GROSMONT, earl of Derby, won by means of a sudden cavalry charge on an unprepared enemy. At the Battle of the HERRINGS in 1429, the French came suddenly upon an English force under Sir John FASTOLF, who repelled his attackers by quickly forming his men behind a laager of wagons. In most cases, however, both armies had time to prepare for combat. These preparations could take different forms depending on circumstances. For instance, at Agincourt in 1415, the overconfident French spent the night gambling for prisoners to be won next day, while the English took confession and silently contemplated their probable demise. Hearing Mass and taking communion, as Edward III and EDWARD, THE BLACK PRINCE, did before Crécy, was common in most armies. Also common were stirring speeches delivered by king or commander to encourage the men. The prince of Wales supposedly gave two before Poitiers in 1356, and HENRY V famously reminded his men before Agincourt of the justice of their cause and earlier English triumphs. Henry also told his ARCHERS of a French threat to cut off three fingers of their right hands so they would never draw bow again. Sometimes battle was preceded by challenges to single combat—one of Edward III's household knights defeated a Scottish champion prior to Halidon Hill—or to a joust between groups of knights from both armies.

Actual combat was a confusing affair with commanders often uncertain about what was happening on other parts of the field. Chroniclers who were able to interview participants often got good accounts of preparations and aftermaths, but few informative details about the fighting itself. The start of a battle was often extremely noisy, in part to instill fear in the enemy. Trumpets, drums, and ARTILLERY opened the fighting at Crécy, while the noise of Poitiers was said to have reverberated off the walls of the town seven miles away. Battle cries from thousands of men—"Montjoie St. Denis" for the French and "St. George for Guienne" for the English—added to the din. Although long-distance archery duels were rare, many battles began with an exchange of archer fire. Artillery made its presence increasingly felt in the fifteenth century, although big guns were a major factor on the battlefield only at CASTILLON in 1453. After English bowmen devastated French horsemen at Crécy, the coordinated cavalry charge, which is traditionally considered the classic tactic of medieval warfare, was rarely used to start battles. However, cavalry charges still had their place. Derby's knights launched a surprise charge to good effect at Auberoche, while the Black Prince remounted some of his men to ride down groups of dismounted French knights at Poitiers. The hardest part of the battle to comprehend is the mêlée, the confused press of horses and men engaged in combat at close quarters. Friends advancing from the rear could cause as much harm as enemies to the front. At Agincourt, men in later waves could only engage the enemy by climbing onto piles of dead from the initial clash. Many men in heavy ARMOR, such as Edward, duke of York, died when they suffocated under piles of corpses six feet high. The mêlée usually ended when one side could no longer hold a line or maintain an attack, or when a new force, such as that led around the flank at Poitiers by Jean de GRAILLY, captal de Buch, tipped the balance.

Often, most of the CASUALTIES sustained during a battle occurred at the end during the rout, when the beaten army fled and its members were run down and slain. At NÁJERA in 1367, more than half the Franco-Castilian army was slain fleeing the field. Many battles fought near a river ended with a great slaughter of men trying to cross the water. The rout often took longer than the battle itself. At Poitiers, the battle was fought in the morning, but the pursuit continued through the afternoon and into the evening. The duration of battles could vary greatly. Agincourt was over in a few hours as was Crécy, which began in the late afternoon and ended at dusk, but NEVILLE'S CROSS lasted from about nine in the morning until evening and MORLAIX in 1343 was lengthened by the repeated need for exhausted combatants to stop and refresh themselves. *See also* CHIVALRY; SIEGE WARFARE; STRATEGY AND TACTICS.

Further Reading: Burne, Alfred H. *The Agincourt War*. Ware, England: Wordsworth Editions Ltd., 1999; Burne, Alfred H. *The Crécy War*. Ware, England: Wordsworth Editions Ltd., 1999; Prestwich, Michael. *Armies and Warfare in the Middle Ages: The English Experience*. New Haven, CT: Yale University Press, 1996.

BAUGÉ, BATTLE OF (1421)

On 22 March 1421, a Franco-Scottish army overwhelmed a smaller English force near the village of Baugé, some twenty miles east of the Angevin capital of Angers. The Battle of Baugé, a rare English defeat in pitched battle, resulted in the death of the heir presumptive to the English throne and a great boost in morale for supporters of the dauphinist cause.

When HENRY V returned to England in February 1421, he left his brother and heir, THOMAS, DUKE OF CLARENCE, in command in PARIS. Following the king's instructions, Clarence led four thousand men on a largely unopposed raid through Maine and Anjou, which culminated with the duke basing himself at the castle of Beaufort, roughly halfway between Angers and Baugé. On Good Friday, 21 March, a dauphinist army of five thousand, composed of newly arrived Scottish troops under John STEWART, earl of Buchan, and a sprinkling of local French levies under Marshal Lafayette, reached

Baugé. The allies dispatched reconnaissance patrols, one of which fell into English hands, thereby alerting Clarence of the enemy's presence at Baugé.

Although his troops were widely dispersed, the duke, who had missed AGINCOURT, was eager to fight. Ordering his second-in-command, Thomas MONTAGU, earl of Salisbury, to collect the ARCHERS and follow as quickly as possible, Clarence rode off at once with a force of no more than fifteen hundred men-at-arms. Although several of his captains counseled caution, urging the duke to wait until the entire army could be gathered, Clarence would brook no delay. To enter Baugé, which he reached shortly before dusk, Clarence had to cross the River Couosnon, which was narrow but marshy along its banks. The Scots held the bridge, forcing the English to dismount and wade across the water in full ARMOR. Thus flanked, the bridge defenders fled into the village church, where they were quickly besieged. However, the bridge fight and the river crossing had scattered and disordered the English forces, and Clarence had no more than a few hundred men under effective command when the bulk of the allied army appeared on the ridge above the village.

Undaunted by his foe's advantage in numbers and ground, Clarence led a charge uphill into the enemy, initiating a desperate melée. The allies rapidly enveloped Clarence's men, and, in less than an hour, the duke, many of his captains, and most of his men were dead. John Holland, earl of Huntingdon, and John BEAUFORT, earl of Somerset, were taken for RANSOM. Salisbury reached the field either just before sunset or early the next day and was able by some means to retrieve the bodies of Clarence and his leading officers, which were eventually shipped back to England. The Battle of Baugé temporarily jeopardized the English position in France and spurred both Henry V and the dauphin (see CHARLES VII) to immediate action. The English king began preparing a new army, while the dauphin, who honored Buchan with appointment as constable of France, announced his intention to invade English-held NORMANDY. Although the battle ultimately caused little change in the military situation, it had great if opposite effects on the morale of both sides. *See also* SCOTLAND.

Further Reading: Allmand, Christopher. *Henry V.* Berkeley: University of California Press, 1993; Burne, Alfred H. *The Agincourt War.* Ware, England: Wordsworth Editions Ltd., 1999.

BEAUCHAMP, RICHARD, EARL OF WARWICK (1382–1439)

Richard Beauchamp, thirteenth earl of Warwick, was a councilor and companion-in-arms of HENRY V, and governor and tutor of HENRY VI. Like such other nobles as Thomas MONTAGU, earl of Salisbury, and John TALBOT, earl of Shrewsbury, Warwick was one of the chief English captains of the fifteenth century.

Richard was the grandson of Thomas BEAUCHAMP, the eleventh earl, who fought in France under EDWARD III, and the godson of RICHARD II, who, in 1397, imprisoned Richard's father, Thomas Beauchamp, the twelfth earl, for treason. However, when HENRY IV deposed his cousin in 1399, he restored the Beauchamps to favor by releasing the earl and knighting his son. Richard inherited his father's lands and titles in April 1401. In 1403, he fought for the House of LANCASTER at the Battle of Shrewsbury, for which he was rewarded with admittance to the Order of the GARTER. The earl also fought with Prince Henry in Wales until about 1407, after which he spent some years visiting Rome and the Holy Land and winning a reputation as a jouster in continental tournaments. Although Warwick joined the royal council in 1410, when the prince dominated the government in place of his ailing father, the earl was dismissed in 1411 when the king resumed control.

The accession of the prince as Henry V in 1413 saw Warwick achieve immediate political prominence. He became captain of CALAIS in February 1414 and by 1415 had served on diplomatic missions to France, BURGUNDY, and the Holy Roman Empire. Warwick fought at the siege of HARFLEUR in

1415, but was then ordered to convey prisoners to Calais and so missed the Battle of AGINCOURT. The earl participated in the conquest of NORMANDY after 1417, including the sieges of Caen and ROUEN, and played a major role in the negotiations surrounding conclusion of the Treaty of TROYES in 1420. He was deputy steward at the coronation of Queen CATHERINE OF VALOIS in February 1421, but was back in France with the king by May to conclude the siege of MEAUX, and then to lead independent expeditions that captured Gamaches and St. Valéry-sur-Somme. At Henry V's death in August 1422, Warwick was named an executor of the royal will, and, in December, he joined Henry VI's minority council.

Although one of the wealthiest men in England and politically dominant in the west Midlands, Warwick's influence declined during the early years of the new reign, when the earl became associated with the council faction led by Cardinal Henry BEAUFORT. This connection persuaded Beaufort's rival, HUMPHREY, DUKE OF GLOUCESTER, to support Warwick's political opponents and so diminish his local standing. Warwick returned to France in late 1425, when he was made custodian of Normandy by the regent, JOHN, DUKE OF BEDFORD. In early 1427, the earl captured Pontorson in BRITTANY, but, in September, he was defeated at the siege of MONTARGIS by a dauphinist force under JOHN, the Bastard of Orléans.

In 1428, Warwick returned to England to become governor of seven-year-old Henry VI, whom, in a famous episode, the earl carried to his coronation in November 1429. Except for accompanying the king to his French coronation in PARIS in 1431, Warwick remained in England until 1436, when he served with Gloucester's expeditions to Calais and FLANDERS. In July 1437, the king named Warwick lieutenant-general and governor of France and Normandy, but inadequate manpower and funding allowed him to do no more than maintain the status quo against both CHARLES VII and PHILIP THE GOOD, duke of Burgundy, who had abandoned his English alliance at the Congress of ARRAS in 1435. Warwick died in Rouen on 30 April 1439.

Further Reading: Allmand, Christopher. *Henry V.* Berkeley: University of California Press, 1993; Carpenter, Christine. *Locality and Polity: A Study of Warwickshire Landed Society, 1401–1499.* Cambridge: Cambridge University Press, 1992; Harriss, G. L. *Cardinal Beaufort: A Study of Lancastrian Ascendency and Decline.* Oxford: Clarendon Press, 1988.

BEAUCHAMP, THOMAS, EARL OF WARWICK (c. 1314–1369)

Thomas Beauchamp, eleventh earl of Warwick and one of EDWARD III's most important and distinguished companions-in-arms, participated in most of the early battles and campaigns of the HUNDRED YEARS WAR.

Beauchamp was only a child when his father, Guy de Beauchamp, tenth earl of Warwick, died in 1315. EDWARD II gave custody of the Warwick lands to his favorite, Hugh Despenser the Elder, but the young earl's person and marriage were entrusted to Roger Mortimer, the future earl of March, whose daughter Warwick married in about 1327. In February 1329, the minority regime of his father-in-law and Queen Isabella (*see* ISABELLA, QUEEN OF ENGLAND [c. 1292–1358]) allowed Warwick to be knighted and to take possession of his lands, even though he was still under age. In the 1330s, Warwick fought in SCOTLAND, where he was appointed commander of the army in 1337. In 1339, he accompanied Edward III to France and in 1340 was present at the siege of TOURNAI and took part in the talks leading to the Truce of ESPLECHIN. From September 1340 until May 1341, the earl was imprisoned in Malines as surety for payment of the king's debts.

In 1342, Warwick served at the siege of Vannes in BRITTANY and in 1346 fought alongside EDWARD, THE BLACK PRINCE, at CRÉCY, where the earl's already considerable military reputation was enhanced. Warwick was present at the siege of CALAIS in 1347 and accompanied the Black Prince on his *CHEVAUCHÉE* through southern France in 1355. The chronicler Geoffrey Baker wrote that Warwick and his comrades fought "like lions" at POITIERS in September 1356, and, in 1359–60, the earl participated in the RHEIMS CAMPAIGN and was a witness at the signing of the Treaty of BRÉTIGNY.

Warwick was handsomely rewarded for his service, being appointed earl marshal of England in 1344 and receiving a gift of over £1,300 in 1347. In 1348, the king granted Warwick an annuity of 1,000 marks and also chose him to become a founding member of the Order of the GARTER, taking precedence after Prince Edward and HENRY OF GROS-MONT, duke of Lancaster. In the 1360s, the earl served with the Black Prince in AQUI-TAINE, went crusading in Prussia, and led a diplomatic mission to Scotland. On the resumption of war in 1369, Warwick accompanied JOHN OF GAUNT, duke of Lancaster, to Calais, where news of the earl's arrival allegedly convinced PHILIP THE BOLD, duke of BURGUNDY, to withdraw his army from the area. Warwick then participated in Gaunt's *chevauchée* into NORMANDY; upon his return to Calais, the earl contracted the plague and died on 13 November 1369. See also CHE-VAUCHÉE OF 1355.

Further Reading: Fowler, Kenneth. *The King's Lieutenant: Henry of Grosmont, First Duke of Lancaster, 1310–1361.* London: Elek, 1969; Ormrod, W. M. *The Reign of Edward III: Crown and Political Society in England, 1327–1377.* New Haven, CT: Yale University Press, 1990.

BEAUFORT, EDMUND, DUKE OF SOMERSET (c. 1406–1455)

As king's lieutenant in France when NOR-MANDY fell to the French in 1450, Edmund Beaufort, duke of Somerset, was blamed both by contemporaries and later historians for causing the final English defeat in the HUNDRED YEARS WAR.

Edmund Beaufort was the third son of John, marquis of Dorset, and thus a grandson of JOHN OF GAUNT, duke of Lancaster, and a cousin of HENRY V. Beaufort was in his teens when he went to war in France, being captured with his elder brother John BEAUFORT at BAUGÉ in 1421. Released in about 1427, Beaufort received his first independent command in 1431 and was a member of the

English embassy at the Congress of ARRAS in 1435. In 1436, Beaufort successfully defended CALAIS and was rewarded with admission to the Order of the GARTER. He relieved Avranches in 1439 and distinguished himself at the recapture of HARFLEUR in 1440. In August 1442, HENRY VI ennobled his kinsman as earl of Dorset and in 1443 raised him to a marquisate. Upon his brother's death in May 1444, Dorset became earl of Somerset.

In about 1427, Beaufort conducted a brief affair with CATHERINE OF VALOIS, the widow of Henry V and mother of Henry VI. Although little is known about the liaison, it led to passage of a parliamentary statute controlling the remarriage of former queens and may also have resulted in the birth of Catherine's son Edmund, who is usually considered the child of Owen Tudor and thus an ancestor of the royal House of Tudor. While it is unlikely that Beaufort fathered Catherine's son, it is not impossible, since the dates of Catherine's secret marriage to Tudor and of Edmund Tudor's birth are unknown.

In the 1440s, Somerset became associated with the court faction led by William de la POLE, duke of Suffolk, a protégé of Somerset's uncle, Cardinal Henry BEAUFORT, bishop of Winchester. In December 1447, the king, influenced by Suffolk, appointed Somerset lieutenant of France and governor-general of the duchies of Normandy and AQUITAINE. Succeeding Suffolk's opponent, RICHARD, DUKE OF YORK, Somerset, who was himself raised to a dukedom on 31 March 1448, was thus responsible for the defense of Lancastrian France when CHARLES VII ended the Truce of TOURS by invading Normandy in July 1449. The French resumption of the war, which caught the English unprepared to defend Normandy, was triggered in March 1449 by the English seizure of the Breton town of FOUGÈRES, an ill-advised venture for which Somerset was partially responsible. Somerset was also involved in the unpopular English surrender of MAINE in 1448. Although ceding the province was the king's idea, Somerset, as captain-general of Maine since 1438, had held up the transaction, not out of opposition to the voluntary surrender of territory, but out of unwillingness to yield the revenues of his office without compensation from the Crown. Unable to properly fund Norman defense needs, the government found itself compelled to pay Somerset a huge annual sum out of the duchy's revenues before he would undertake the French lieutenancy.

Charles VII's NORMAN CAMPAIGN lasted barely a year, with many towns offering the French no resistance. Although not present at the decisive English defeat at FORMIGNY in April 1450, Somerset personally surrendered ROUEN on 29 October 1449 and Caen on 1 July 1450. Returning to England, where the loss of Normandy had already driven Suffolk from power, Somerset found himself blamed for the disaster. York considered Somerset's feeble defense of the duchy to be treasonous, but the king and his wife, MARGARET OF ANJOU, protected the duke, who became effective head of the government and captain of Calais in 1451. In 1453, the defeat at CASTILLON and the final loss of GASCONY triggered Henry VI's first bout of mental illness and made York protector of the realm. Committed to the Tower by the protector in November, Somerset remained there until Christmas 1454 when a newly recovered Henry VI released him. In the spring of 1455, Somerset was officially exonerated of all charges brought by York. Fearing that a conference called by Somerset to discuss threats to the king was aimed at them, York and his allies, the earls of Salisbury and Warwick, intercepted the royal army at St. Albans on 21 May 1455. At what became the first armed encounter of the Wars of the Roses, the partisans of York slew Somerset and other political opponents in the streets of St. Albans.

Further Reading: Allmand, C. T. *Lancastrian Normandy, 1415–1450: The History of a Medieval Occupation.* Oxford: Clarendon Press, 1983; Griffiths, Ralph A. *The Reign of Henry VI.* Berkeley: University of California Press, 1981.

BEAUFORT, HENRY, CARDINAL-BISHOP OF WINCHESTER (c. 1375–1447)

Henry Beaufort, Cardinal-Bishop of Winchester, was the most powerful and influential clerical politician in Lancastrian England. A skilled diplomat who was three times chancellor of England, Beaufort played leading roles in both domestic and foreign affairs. A wealthy prelate who provided the Crown with large loans to fund the war, Beaufort in the 1430s led the court party that favored a negotiated settlement of the HUNDRED YEARS WAR.

The second of four children born to JOHN OF GAUNT, duke of Lancaster, by his mistress Katherine Swynford, Beaufort and his siblings were legitimated by RICHARD II in 1397, a year after Lancaster married their mother as his third wife. Named bishop of Lincoln in February 1399, Beaufort played no part later in the year when his half-brother deposed Richard and took the Crown as HENRY IV, first king of the House of LANCASTER. Little interested in ecclesiastical affairs, Beaufort began an active political career in 1402 when he joined the royal council. In February 1403, he became chancellor, holding the post until March 1405; in November 1404, he was elevated to the bishopric of Winchester, the wealthiest see in England. He began a diplomatic career in 1408–09 by negotiating a renewal of the Anglo-French truce. In 1410, Prince Henry, assuming control of the government for his ailing father, placed Beaufort and his young brother, Thomas BEAUFORT, future duke of Exeter, at the head of the royal administration. At the prince's direction, the Beauforts pursued a pro-BURGUNDIAN foreign policy, providing military support to JOHN THE FEARLESS, duke of Burgundy, in his struggle with the ARMAGNACS (*see* FRENCH CIVIL WAR). Opposed to this policy, the king resumed the government in 1412 and the Beauforts were dismissed from office.

At HENRY V's accession in March 1413, Beaufort again became chancellor, his main task being to persuade PARLIAMENT to financially support the king's campaign to secure the French Crown. In July 1415, he rejected, on the king's behalf, the final French offers to avert war, and, on the following 29 October, he announced the victory of AGINCOURT to the citizens of LONDON.

Involved in securing new funding for the war, Beaufort also participated in negotiations with Emperor Sigismund for the Treaty of CANTERBURY and with Burgundy for a possible alliance against the Armagnac government that controlled PARIS and CHARLES VI. In 1417, the bishop resigned the chancellorship and made his first substantial loan to the Crown, providing £14,000 for the forthcoming NORMAN CAMPAIGN. In 1418, he attended the Council of Constance, where the king directed him to secure election of a pope sympathetic to the English cause. Although Beaufort was himself considered a candidate, the council chose Martin V, who, while allowing him to retain the see of Winchester, rewarded the bishop with elevation to the cardinalate, appointment as legate *a latere*, and exemption from the authority of Canterbury. Upon hearing of these appointments, Henry V, who was unhappy with Martin's selection, accused the bishop of conspiring with the pope for his own enrichment, and forbade Beaufort to accept any rewards. Having lost Henry's trust, Beaufort spent the rest of the reign out of favor and office.

On the king's death in 1422, Beaufort became a prominent member of HENRY VI's minority council, where he made a lasting enemy of HUMPHREY, DUKE OF GLOUCESTER, by leading the successful opposition to the duke's attempt to have himself named regent. In 1424, shortly before being named chancellor for the third time, Beaufort loaned the Crown £9,300, which financed the army with which JOHN, DUKE OF BEDFORD, won the Battle of VERNEUIL. In 1425, the bishop's rivalry with Gloucester turned violent, as Beaufort's retinue forcibly prevented the duke's men from taking custody of the king. When Bedford returned from France in 1426, he enforced a settlement whereby Beaufort resigned the chancellorship and left the council, although the duke did allow Beaufort to finally accept a cardinal's hat. Commissioned by the pope to raise an army for a crusade against the Hussite heretics, Beaufort, in the wake of the disasters at ORLÉANS and PATAY in 1429, instead led the army to Bedford's assistance, thus earning the duke's gratitude and the pope's enmity. The cardinal witnessed the burning of JOAN OF ARC at ROUEN in May 1431 and crowned Henry VI in Paris in the following December. In 1432, further efforts by Gloucester to deprive the cardinal of his wealth and see compelled Beaufort to return and defend himself before Parliament. Thanks to Bedford's support and his own indispensability as a source of loans, Beaufort weathered the storm and in 1435 represented the English at the Congress of ARRAS where he made an unsuccessful plea to PHILIP THE GOOD to maintain the ANGLO-BURGUNDIAN ALLIANCE.

Convinced of the need for a negotiated settlement that secured Lancastrian control of NORMANDY, Beaufort tried unsuccessfully to arrange such an agreement in 1439. Although Gloucester, who favored vigorous prosecution of the war, continued his efforts to undermine the bishop, Beaufort's peace policy was supported by the king, who assumed personal control of the government in 1437. After 1440, Beaufort, old and ill, gradually withdrew from government, his place being taken by William de la POLE, earl of Suffolk. In the mid-1440s, Beaufort used his money and influence to advance the careers of his nephews, John BEAUFORT and Edmund BEAUFORT, successively dukes of Somerset. The cardinal died on 11 April 1447.

Further Reading: Griffiths, Ralph A. *The Reign of King Henry VI*. Berkeley: University of California Press, 1981; Harriss, G. L. *Cardinal Beaufort: A Study of Lancastrian Ascendency and Decline*. Oxford: Clarendon Press, 1988.

BEAUFORT, JOHN, DUKE OF SOMERSET (1403–1444)

In 1443, John Beaufort, first duke of Somerset, organized and led a costly and spectacularly unsuccessful campaign in northern France. Somerset's incompetent leadership destroyed his career, impoverished and embarrassed the English Crown, and seriously damaged relations between England and BRITTANY.

Beaufort's father, John Beaufort, earl of Somerset (d. 1409), was a half-brother of HENRY IV, being the eldest son of JOHN OF GAUNT, duke of Lancaster, by his mistress (and future wife) Katherine Swynford. Succeeding to the earldom of Somerset upon the death of his brother Henry in 1419, Beaufort gained his first military experience in 1420, when, at the age of seventeen, he accompanied his cousin HENRY V on campaign in France. In 1421, Somerset fought with the king's brother, THOMAS, DUKE OF CLARENCE, at the disastrous Battle of BAUGÉ, where Clarence was slain and Somerset captured. Eventually ransomed, Somerset continued his military career in France, holding various commands and captaincies demanded by his rank, but otherwise doing little to distinguish himself.

In March 1443, HENRY VI made Somerset a duke and named him lieutenant and captain-general of Aquitaine. Somerset was also given authority to act outside his province, including in Anjou and Maine, where his powers conflicted with those of RICHARD, DUKE OF YORK, another royal cousin serving as lieutenant-general of France. Somerset's appointment was clearly political, designed by his uncle, Henry BEAUFORT, cardinal of Winchester, to undercut the standing and influence of York. Provided with an annual income of 600 marks and given authority to engage the French in GASCONY and in all lands in which "my said Lord of York cometh not" (Griffiths, 466), Somerset was in effect the political and military successor to JOHN, DUKE OF BEDFORD, in all areas of English activity outside NORMANDY. This broad brief drew strong protests both from York and from the military establishment in Lancastrian France.

Although much was expected of Somerset's campaign, the duke proved a poor planner, failing twice to appear on the appointed muster date and offering the king and council only delays, excuses, and demands for money. Deficient as they were, his preparations absorbed an increasingly larger share of the government's scarce resources—the council even had to tell York to be patient and "forbear . . . for a time" when the duke asked about reimbursement of his expenses (Seward, 241). In early July, an exasperated council ordered Somerset to sail at once for Normandy. Landing with a force of over four thousand, and keeping his plans secret from even his chief subordinates, Somerset launched an ineffective and disorganized CHEVAUCHÉE into Maine, which turned into complete disaster when the duke inexplicably entered Brittany, where he pillaged the countryside and seized the town of La Guerche. As an ally of England, Duke Francis I complained bitterly to an embarrassed council in LONDON, which in turn sternly rebuked Somerset. After only a few weeks of campaigning, the duke returned to England to find himself disgraced and banished from court. The entire episode demoralized the Lancastrian war effort and boosted the confidence of CHARLES VII, who had witnessed the English inability to find proper funding or leadership for an effective campaign. Although Charles acceded to the English desire for a temporary end to the fighting, agreeing to the Truce of TOURS in 1444, it was only to strengthen his position against Burgundy and to complete the military reforms that would prepare his armies for the final push against the English. On 27 May 1444, Somerset died, a probable suicide. His only child, Margaret Beaufort (1443–1509), later transmitted the Lancastrian claim to the Crown to her only child, Henry Tudor, earl of Richmond, the future Henry VII. *See also* CHARLES VII, MILITARY REFORMS OF.

Further Reading: Griffiths, Ralph A. *The Reign of Henry VI.* Berkeley: University of California Press, 1981; Seward, Desmond. *The Hundred Years War.* New York: Penguin, 1999.

BEAUFORT, THOMAS, DUKE OF EXETER (c. 1377–1426)

Thomas Beaufort, duke of Exeter, was a staunch supporter of the House of LANCASTER and a leading lieutenant of HENRY V, who entrusted Exeter with guardianship of the most important English conquests in France.

The third son of JOHN OF GAUNT, duke of Lancaster, by his mistress Katherine Swynford, Thomas and his siblings were officially legitimated in 1397. In 1399, Beaufort, although a member of RICHARD II's retinue, abandoned the king to support his half-brother, who seized the Crown as HENRY IV. Named captain of Ludlow on the Welsh marches in 1402, Beaufort fought with Prince Henry at the Battle of Shrewsbury in 1403 and commanded a series of garrisons in Wales between 1404 and 1407. Named admiral of the north in November 1403, Beaufort thwarted a French attempt to blockade CALAIS in 1404. Because he supported the prince's pro-BURGUNDIAN policy, Beaufort became chancellor of England in January 1410 when the king's illness allowed the prince to dominate the council. A soldier who was ill-suited to such an administrative position, Beaufort nonetheless retained the king's favor when Henry dismissed the prince's council in the following December. Created earl of Dorset in July 1411 and admiral of England for life in March 1412, Beaufort participated in the expedition of THOMAS, DUKE OF CLARENCE, which was sent to France in July 1412 under the terms of the Anglo-ARMAGNAC Treaty of BOURGES.

On his accession in March 1413, Henry V appointed Dorset lieutenant of AQUITAINE and in 1415 named him to the embassy charged with presenting the king's demands in PARIS. Dorset organized and commanded the fleet that transported the English army to France in August 1415 and in the following month took charge of the garrison of newly captured HARFLEUR. In March 1416, in an effort to supply the besieged town, Dorset launched a foray into NORMANDY that was ambushed at VALMONT, although the earl was able, after a series of skirmishes, to return with most of his force to Harfleur. Nonetheless, the town was near to starvation when it was finally relieved by JOHN, DUKE OF BEDFORD, at the Battle of the SEINE in August 1416. In November, Dorset was rewarded for the discipline and resolve he displayed at Harfleur with elevation to the dukedom of Exeter.

In 1418, Exeter returned to France to take part in the siege of ROUEN, which was placed in his custody after its fall in January 1419. He then besieged and captured various important enemy strongholds, including Château Gaillard in September. After participating in the negotiations that led to the Treaty of TROYES in 1420, Exeter was entrusted with the captaincies of Conches and Melun, and, in January 1421, with the military governorship of Paris, a position that made him custodian of CHARLES VI. In 1422, the duke served at the siege of MEAUX and was present when Henry V died at Vincennes in August. In his will, the king named Exeter governor of the person of his infant son HENRY VI. Returning to England with the king's body, Exeter joined his brother, Henry BEAUFORT, cardinal-bishop of Winchester, in opposing the claim of HUMPHREY, DUKE OF GLOUCESTER, to the regency. Although he returned to France in 1423, Exeter's service was limited by illness and he died childless at Greenwich on 31 December 1426.

Further Reading: Allmand, Christopher. *Henry V.* Berkeley: University of California Press, 1993; Harriss, G. L. *Cardinal Beaufort: A Study of Lancastrian Ascendency and Decline.* Oxford: Clarendon Press, 1988.

BEDFORD, DUCHESS OF. *See* ANNE OF BURGUNDY, DUCHESS OF BEDFORD

BEDFORD, DUKE OF. *See* JOHN, DUKE OF BEDFORD

BENEDICT XII. *See* PAPACY AND THE HUNDRED YEARS WAR

BENTLEY, SIR WALTER (c. 1310–1359)
Through military prowess and a fortuitous marriage, Walter Bentley, an obscure Yorkshire knight and soldier of fortune, achieved a meteoric rise in wealth and position.

Bentley fought in SCOTLAND in the early 1330s and served as king's sergeant in France in 1339. He arrived in BRITTANY in 1342 as a member of the retinue of William de BOHUN, earl of Northampton. In the mid-1340s, Bentley formed his own mercenary band and by 1346 controlled two castles in western Brittany, including the island fortress of Tristan, from which his men levied tolls on passing ships. In about 1348, Bentley married Jeanne de Belleville, the widow of Olivier de Clisson, head of a powerful Breton family. For consorting with the English, Clisson was executed in PARIS in 1343, but his widow, with the aid of English soldiers, saved most of the family lands from confiscation.

In 1349, Bentley began feuding with Raoul de Caours, the English lieutenant of Bas-Poitou, over the possession of certain Clisson fortresses that Caours had seized from the French. The quarrel divided the English command in the duchy and drove Caours to intrigue with the French, who promised him the disputed fortresses in return for his change of allegiance. The scheme collapsed when EDWARD III took the strongholds and their loyal English garrisons into his possession before Caours could act. In October 1349, Edward granted these fortresses to Bentley, who thereafter carved a personal military fiefdom out of his wife's lands.

On 8 September 1350, Bentley succeeded Sir Thomas DAGWORTH as king's lieutenant in Brittany. In June 1351, when the French laid siege to Ploermel, Bentley relieved the Breton town by gathering a force from the English garrisons and raiding into Maine and along the Loire. In a memorandum written in early 1352, Bentley complained that many of the frontier captains supported themselves and their men through the exaction of PÂTIS and thus were effectively beyond his control and that of the king. The memorandum, which was a fair description of Bentley's own career, caused much consternation in LONDON but changed little in Brittany.

Bentley was in England in May 1352, when a French army under Guy de Nesle invaded Brittany. Given a special subsidy and the right to recruit men in the West Country, the lieutenant returned to the duchy in late July and on 14 August defeated de Nesle at the Battle of MAURON, a victory that secured English dominance in Brittany for the next decade. Dismissed from his lieutenancy in early 1353, Bentley resumed his mercenary career. Later in the year, when the king demanded that he surrender the Clisson fortresses in accordance with a treaty concluded with the captive CHARLES OF BLOIS, Bentley refused and sailed to England to plead his case. Imprisoned in the Tower of London, Bentley was eventually released and allowed to return to Brittany, where, in January 1357, he and his wife were granted the barony of La Roche-Moisan. Bentley died in December 1359 still possessed of most of his wife's Breton lordships. *See also* BRETON CIVIL WAR.

Further Reading: Jones, Michael. "Edward III's Captains in Brittany." In *Between France and England: Politics, Power and Society in Late Medieval Brittany*, 98–118. Burlington, VT: Ashgate Publishing Company, 2003; Sumption, Jonathan. *The Hundred Years War*. Vol. 2, *Trial by Fire*. Philadelphia: University of Pennsylvania Press, 2001.

BERGERAC, CAPTURE OF (1345)

In late August 1345, HENRY OF GROSMONT, earl of Derby, captured Bergerac, a French garrison town on the Dordogne about sixty miles east of BORDEAUX in southern Périgord. The sudden seizure of the town disrupted French operations in southwestern France, opened Périgord to English penetration, and initiated an English campaign that eventually cleared GASCONY of enemy garrisons.

On 9 August 1345, Derby, newly appointed king's lieutenant in AQUITAINE, landed at Bordeaux with two thousand men. Accompanied by such veteran captains as Sir Walter MAUNY and Sir James AUDLEY, Derby was to do "whatever could be done" (Sumption, 455) to drive the French from the duchy. Although Derby's expedition was originally planned as part of a dual operation involving a simultaneous campaign in northern France by EDWARD III, the king's expedition, delayed by the overthrow of James van ARTEVELDE in FLANDERS and violent storms in the Channel, was cancelled in late July. With PHILIP VI now free to send men and resources to the southwest, Derby decided to strike quickly before the scattered French forces in the region could be concentrated against him. Accordingly, he lifted sieges being conducted against Blaye and Langon by Ralph STAFFORD, seneschal of Aquitaine, and marched their combined forces, perhaps five thousand men, against the VALOIS garrison at Bergerac, a town ideally located to serve as a base of operations against French-held Poitou.

The attack on Bergerac was strongly endorsed by Bernard-Aiz V, lord of ALBRET, whose castle of Montcuq, standing only three miles from Bergerac, was under siege by the French. Derby's swiftly moving force reached Montcuq before the besiegers received word of their coming. Panicked by the sudden arrival of a large Anglo-Gascon army, the French fled northward toward the village of La Madeleine, which stood on the south end of a fortified bridge across the Dordogne that led to Bergerac on the north bank. Derby's cavalry reached the bridge just as the Montcuq besiegers, now reduced to a disorderly mob, were flooding through the barbican that defended the bridge's southern end. Dismounted English men-at-arms assaulted the barbican, which they carried with the help of ARCHERS on the south bank, who did great execution among the Montcuq troops and a force from the Bergerac garrison that sortied out onto the bridge. As frightened men and horses crowded into the town, preventing the garrison from dropping the portcullis that defended the bridge's northern end, Derby's men rushed into Bergerac, which fell shortly thereafter. Besides significant amounts of war material and large numbers of horses, the fall of the town gave the English the largest haul of RANSOM-worthy prisoners yet seen in the HUNDRED YEARS WAR, including the seneschal of Périgord and ten French nobles.

The capture of Bergerac and Derby's subsequent victory at AUBEROCHE revived the PLANTAGENET position in southwestern France, freeing Gascony of French garrisons and opening Poitou to English invasion. Alarmed at the deterioration of the French position in Aquitaine, Philip dispatched his son, John, duke of NORMANDY (*see* JOHN II) to the southwest, but the duke was unable to keep his army in the field, which allowed Derby to take La Réole in January 1346. Although Normandy returned in March, the English kept him occupied at AIGUILLON until it was too late for him or his men to take part in the CRÉCY campaign, then underway in northern France.

Further Reading: Sumption, Jonathan. *The Hundred Years War*. Vol. 1, *Trial by Battle*. Philadelphia: University of Pennsylvania Press, 1999.

BERNARD, COUNT OF ARMAGNAC (1391–1418)

Bernard VII, count of Armagnac, was constable of France and a central figure in the FRENCH CIVIL WAR. His leadership of the Orléanist party caused its members to become known as "ARMAGNACS." After the faction came to power in 1413, the count's Gascon supporters ruthlessly enforced the authority of the regime, thereby helping to make Armagnac the most powerful figure in the royal government and the most hated man in PARIS.

The counts of Armagnac, a county in southwestern France that formed part of the province of GASCONY, had long been allies of the French Crown against the PLANTAGENET dukes of AQUITAINE. In 1410, Armagnac's daughter Bonne married CHARLES, DUKE OF ORLÉANS, the son of LOUIS, DUKE OF ORLÉANS, whose murder by Burgundian assassins in 1407 had ignited civil war. The marriage sealed Armagnac's adherence to the Orléanist faction, which he had joined in April 1410 by entering the League of Gien, an anti-Burgundian alliance that included Orléans and Armagnac's father-in-law, JOHN, DUKE OF BERRY, as well as JOHN V, duke of BRITTANY, and the counts of Alençon and Clermont. A stronger personality and more vigorous leader than either Orléans or Berry, Armagnac soon became the dominating member of the Orléanist alliance. The count also commanded numerous bands of armed Gascons, whose clashes with the supporters of JOHN THE FEARLESS, duke of BURGUNDY, frustrated royal attempts to end the feud.

These bands, whose emblem was a white shoulder sash, became so identified with the Orléanist cause that by the summer of 1411 the name "Armagnacs" was being used in Paris to describe all partisans of Orléans and his allies.

In 1412, Armagnac was party to the Treaty of BOURGES, a compact with HENRY IV whereby the Armagnacs agreed to surrender territory in return for English military assistance against Burgundy, who then controlled the royal government and the person of CHARLES VI. Although the English sent an expedition, the dauphin, LOUIS, DUKE OF GUIENNE, negotiated a formal reconciliation at Auxerre in August 1412. In August 1413, Burgundy, having eroded his popularity through his incitement of the CARBOCHIEN riots in Paris, fled the capital, allowing the Armagnacs to take power. Acting under the nominal leadership of Guienne, who tried to distance himself from the count and the Armagnac leaders, the new government negotiated with HENRY V, but talks broke off over the English king's territorial demands and the HUNDRED YEARS WAR resumed in August 1415.

In the following October, the battle of AGINCOURT decimated the ranks of the Armagnac leadership; Constable Charles d'ALBRET was slain and the dukes of Orléans and Bourbon were captured. These losses, when coupled with the deaths of Guienne in December 1415 and Berry in June 1416, made Armagnac virtual ruler of France. Named constable at the end of 1415, the count moved quickly to expel the English from HARFLEUR, an effort that was frustrated at VALMONT in March 1416 and completely defeated at the Battle of the SEINE in the following August. In April 1416, dissatisfaction with the regime led to an uprising in Paris, which the count ruthlessly suppressed. In April 1417, Armagnac, now acting in the name of fourteen-year-old Dauphin Charles (see CHARLES VII), removed another rival for power by exiling Queen ISABEAU from Paris for plotting against the regime. The queen escaped to Troyes, where she set up a rival government in alliance with Burgundy. On 29 May 1418, a new uprising erupted in Paris. Although the count's supporters spirited the dauphin out of the capital, violent mobs slew any Armagnac official they caught, including the count, who was murdered on 12 July, two days before Burgundy and the queen reentered Paris.

Further Reading: Burne, Alfred H. *The Agincourt War*. Ware, England: Wordsworth Editions Ltd., 1999; Famiglietti, Richard C. *Royal Intrigue: Crisis at the Court of Charles VI, 1392–1420*. New York: AMS Press, 1986; Perroy, Edouard. *The Hundred Years War*. Trans. W. B. Wells. New York: Capricorn Books, 1965.

BERRY, DUKE OF. *See* JOHN, DUKE OF BERRY

BICÊTRE, PEACE OF. *See* FRENCH CIVIL WAR

BLACK DEATH

Black Death was the name given to the bubonic plague, which struck Western Europe with unprecedented virulence between 1347 and 1350. This fourteenth-century epidemic was the greatest natural disaster in European history. At its height in France and England, the Black Death destroyed about one-third of the population; damaged commerce and agriculture; disrupted the functioning of the Church and national and local governments; and brought the HUNDRED YEARS WAR to a virtual standstill.

Carried by flea-infested rats, the disease, which had been endemic in the east for centuries, appeared in Italy in late 1347. Over the winter, it followed the trade routes into southern France and GASCONY; by July 1348, it reached ROUEN in NORMANDY and was in PARIS by September. In England, the first case was reported in July 1348 in Dorset, from where the disease moved north to Bristol by August and east to LONDON by November. Winter brought a slackening of the initial outbreak, but also saw the first appearance of an even deadlier form of the disease, the pneumonic plague, which spread rapidly from person to person by exhalation. The epidemic was most intense in the summer of 1349 before finally fading away in 1350. In France, mortality rates were especially high in the south, where a warmer climate and war-ravaged populations fostered the spread of the disease. Perhaps half the population of BORDEAUX succumbed, while Paris and Rheims in the north lost about one-quarter of their residents. In England, where a cooler climate may have promoted spread of the pneumonic form, the mortality rates were generally higher than in France. Over 40 percent of the rural population of southern England may have died, and rates were likely higher in London and the larger towns.

The war largely ceased during the height of the plague in 1348 and 1349. EDWARD III, who likely could not have afforded a new campaign, proposed that the Truce of CALAIS be extended and PHILIP VI dropped plans for an invasion of England and for a resumption of the war in BRITTANY and AQUITAINE. As royal courts fled to country air and ministers or officials either dispersed or died, government ceased to function and taxes went uncollected. In terms of the war, the most serious consequence of the plague in France was the disruption of royal finances. The Black Death caused the demand for land and food to fall and for agricultural labor to rise. Since the Crown was the premier landowner and financed the war through taxes imposed on other landowners, the plague-related declines in noble and ecclesiastical incomes precipitated a severe fiscal crisis in France in the 1350s. To compensate for a shrinking tax base, the government raised rates and devised new taxes, actions that only provoked taxpayer resistance, especially during the period of political instability that followed the defeat and capture of JOHN II at POITIERS in 1356 (see JACQUERIE). In England, where the systems of assessment and collection were more efficient, and the country free of armies, ROU-TIERS, and political turmoil, taxes continued to be gathered at preplague rates and taxpayer discontent was suppressed until the 1380s by close cooperation between Crown and nobility (see PEASANTS' REVOLT OF 1381).

War recruitment was only slightly affected by the plague. The high mortality rates in French towns made them more difficult to defend, since manning the walls was the citizens' duty, and the English had some difficulty recruiting ARCHERS in the early 1350s. However, the nobility and gentry—the men who comprised the bulk of the armies in both countries—were better fed, clothed, and housed than the lower classes and so suffered lower death rates. The high mortality among the young in the 1340s may have caused a shortage of recruits in the mid-1360s, but there were no major recruiting problems in either kingdom in the 1350s. For instance, the army Edward III raised for the RHEIMS CAMPAIGN of 1359 was one of the largest of the war. Thus, once the plague passed and campaigning resumed in the mid-1350s, lack of finance and supply, rather than plague-induced manpower shortages, had the greatest impact on the size and frequency of campaigns.

Further Reading: Gottfried, Robert S. *The Black Death: Natural and Human Disaster in Medieval Europe.* New York: Free Press, 1985; Herlihy, David. *The Black Death and the Transformation of the West.* Cambridge, MA: Harvard University Press, 1997; Twigg, Graham. *The Black Death: A Biological Reappraisal.* London: Batsford, 1984; Ziegler, Philip. *The Black Death.* New York: Harper and Row, 1969.

"BLACK MONDAY." *See* RHEIMS CAMPAIGN

BLACK PRINCE. *See* EDWARD, THE BLACK PRINCE

BOHUN, WILLIAM DE, EARL OF NORTHAMPTON (c. 1312–1360)
William de Bohun, first earl of Northampton, a cousin and confidant of EDWARD III, was twice king's lieutenant in BRITTANY during the BRETON CIVIL WAR and a leading English commander during the first phase of the HUNDRED YEARS WAR.

The fifth son of Humphrey de Bohun, earl of Hereford and Essex, and Elizabeth, the daughter of EDWARD I, Bohun was one of the royal favorites who, in October 1330, seized Roger Mortimer, earl of March, at Nottingham Castle, thereby initiating the personal rule of Edward III. Bohun fought in SCOTLAND in the early 1330s, and in 1336 negotiated an Anglo-Scottish truce. In 1332, Bohun received lands formerly held by the king's uncle, Thomas of Brotherton, earl of Norfolk, and in 1335 married Elizabeth, the widow of March's heir, who thereby brought Bohun not only a portion of her father's estates but also her Mortimer dower lands. On 16 March 1337, Bohun was ennobled as earl of Northampton, one of six new earls created to enlarge the number of English aristocrats capable of providing military leadership in the coming war with France. To support this new dignity, the earl received future rights in various lordships and an annuity from the customs revenue of LONDON and Essex to maintain himself until these properties came into his possession.

Northampton negotiated for Edward with the French and with prospective allies in the Low Countries in 1337–38, and, in the latter year, was the king's liaison to the council in England. He fought in the 1339 campaigns in northern France (see THIÉRACHE CAMPAIGN) and in the June 1340 naval battle at SLUYS, for which campaign he loaned the king £800. In July 1340, he was briefly detained in Brussels as a hostage for the king's extensive debts and only avoided further confinement by absconding for England with Edward in November. Northampton spoke on the king's behalf with John STRATFORD, archbishop of Canterbury, during the political CRISIS OF 1340–1341, and was one of the peers named to hear the royal charges leveled against Stratford's administration.

Appointed king's lieutenant in Brittany on 20 July 1342, Northampton raised the siege of Brest and defeated CHARLES OF BLOIS, the French-backed candidate for the ducal title, at MORLAIX on 30 September. He then laid siege to Nantes before resigning the lieutenancy on 2 April 1343 to take part in peace talks proposed by CLEMENT VI as part of the Truce of MALESTROIT (see AVIGNON PEACE CONFERENCE). With the collapse of these negotiations, Northampton was reappointed lieutenant in Brittany on 24 April 1345. He fought at CRÉCY in August 1346 and served at the siege of CALAIS until January 1347, when he again resigned the Breton lieutenancy to conduct negotiations with the French and Flemings. Admitted to the Order of the GARTER in September 1349, Northampton returned to Scotland in the 1350s, serving as warden of the marches, admiral of the northern fleet, and commander of Carlisle. In 1359–60, the earl returned to France, serving in the RHEIMS CAMPAIGN and witnessing the signing of the Treaty of BRÉTIGNY. He died on 16 September 1360.

Further Reading: Jones, Michael. ''Edward III's Captains in Brittany.'' In *Between France and England: Politics, Power and Society in Late Medieval Brittany*, 98–118. Burlington, VT: Ashgate Publishing Company, 2003; Sumption, Jonathan. *The Hundred Years War*. Vol. 1, *Trial by Battle*. Philadelphia: University of Pennsylvania Press, 1999.

BONIFACE VIII. *See* PAPACY AND THE HUNDRED YEARS WAR

BORDEAUX

Located on the Gironde River in southwestern France, the city of Bordeaux was the seat of PLANTAGENET government in AQUITAINE. Although the frequent objective of French campaigns in the fourteenth century, Bordeaux remained under English control until 1453, when its fall to the French signaled the end of the HUNDRED YEARS WAR.

Originally a Gallic settlement that evolved into a major commercial center of Roman Gaul, Bordeaux became the capital of Aquitaine in about 630. The city and duchy came to the Plantagenets in 1152, when Eleanor, duchess of Aquitaine, married Henry, count of Anjou, the future Henry II of England. Although much of Henry's continental empire was lost to the House of CAPET after 1204, Bordeaux remained under English rule as the capital of GASCONY, the portion of Aquitaine never retaken by the French Crown. In the thirteenth century, increasing English importation of the red wine of

Bordeaux created a strong economic link between the town and the merchant community of LONDON. Bordeaux was briefly seized by PHILIP IV during the ANGLO-FRENCH WAR OF 1294–1303, but its citizens had little taste for French rule and the town held out for EDWARD II during the War of SAINT-SARDOS in the 1320s.

With the start of the Hundred Years War in 1337, Aquitaine became a main theater of conflict and Bordeaux an important staging center for English campaigns in the southwest. In July 1339, Jean d'Marigny, bishop Beauvais, attacked Bordeaux with a force of almost fifteen thousand. The French were admitted by sympathizers within the walls and the town seemed about to fall when Oliver Ingham, the English commander, organized a counterattack and drove the French out. Unprepared for a long siege, while the town and garrison could be readily supplied by water, the bishop abandoned the siege on 19 July.

In the 1340s, Bordeaux was the base of operations for the Gascon campaigns of HENRY OF GROSMONT, duke of Lancaster, and in the winter of 1347–48, the BLACK DEATH devastated Bordeaux, which may have suffered a mortality rate of nearly 70 percent. In the 1360s, EDWARD, THE BLACK PRINCE, established his court at Bordeaux, from where he ruled the enlarged duchy of Aquitaine created by the Treaty of BRÉTIGNY. The prince's son, the future RICHARD II, was born at Bordeaux in January 1367. Although the French retook much of the duchy after 1369, when CHARLES V resumed the war by accepting the APPEAL OF THE GASCON LORDS, Bordeaux remained English, withstanding even Bertrand du GUESCLIN's 1377 campaign, which brought VALOIS forces within a day's march of the city.

In the fifteenth century, the war shifted to NORMANDY and northern France; Bordeaux was unsuccessfully besieged in 1438, but otherwise saw little military activity until 30 June 1451, when the city fell to the armies of CHARLES VII. Preferring distant English rule to the more invasive authority of the French Crown, the citizens of Bordeaux cooperated with John TALBOT, earl of Shrewsbury, when he retook the town in October 1452. However, Shrewsbury's defeat at CASTILLON in the following July led to the surrender of Bordeaux on 19 October 1453, an act that effectively ended English Aquitaine and the Hundred Years War.

Further Reading: Labarge, Margaret Wade. *Gascony, England's First Colony, 1204–1453.* London: H. Hamilton, 1980.

BORDEAUX, TRUCE OF (1357)

Concluded in BORDEAUX on 23 March 1357 by representatives of the captive French king, JOHN II, and those of his captor, EDWARD, THE BLACK PRINCE, the Truce of Bordeaux ended Anglo-French hostilities for two years. The purpose of the truce was to preserve the territorial status quo until a secret peace agreement negotiated by the prince and his royal captive could be ratified by EDWARD III. Because this agreement represented John's repudiation of the reformist regime that had seized power in PARIS since his captivity, neither the truce nor the accompanying treaty ever took effect.

Following John's capture at POITIERS in September 1356, discontent with the Crown's conduct of the war led many in France to demand a thoroughgoing reform of the royal administration. Led by Robert le Coq, bishop of Laon, a royal opponent and associate of CHARLES THE BAD, king of Navarre, and by Étienne MARCEL, provost of the merchants in Paris, the Estates-General demanded reform of the government and more vigorous prosecution of the war. By early 1357, the assembly forced the dauphin (see CHARLES V) to accept a sweeping reform ordinance, which removed the government from the control of professional administrators and jurists and placed it in the hands of noblemen primarily interested in winning the war and friends of Charles of Navarre primarily interested in bringing him to power.

Frightened by news of events in Paris, where the new regime seemed uninterested in negotiating for his RANSOM and release, John, convinced that his son was no longer a free agent, decided to take matters into his own hands. In early March 1357, a new peace conference opened in Bordeaux, where John was being held in honorable confinement. Ignoring the Paris government, the king nominated his own ambassadors. Eight of the eleven men selected were fellow prisoners, while the other three were royal ministers dismissed by the new regime. After brief negotiations, a peace treaty was concluded with the prince's representatives on 18 March. Because no copy of the agreement has survived, its exact terms are unknown, but given John's desire for a quick release and the prince's ready acceptance, the treaty likely contained substantial territorial concessions to the House of PLANTAGENET. Fearing an adverse reaction in Paris, the parties were anxious to keep the agreement secret until Edward could approve it. To protect the treaty from any changes in the military situation that might occur in the meantime, the parties, on 23 March, also agreed to a truce, which was to hold for all of France until Easter 1359. The agreement also declared that neither party would be deemed to have broken the truce if any of their partisans continued to fight, provided that the Crowns gave no support to such disobedient subordinates.

Three of John's ambassadors were immediately paroled and sent to Paris with royal letters-patent announcing the truce (but not the treaty) and commanding all subjects to observe it. The king also issued an odd directive commanding all French taxpayers to refuse payment of the war tax recently approved by the Estates-General. All contrary ordinances or declarations of either the Estates or the dauphin were to be ignored. News of the truce threw Paris into turmoil. Led by le Coq and Marcel, the Estates forced the dauphin to officially countermand his father's orders on 10 April. By the time John landed in England on 5 May, the treaty concluded in Bordeaux was effectively dead and the truce, while officially in effect, went largely unobserved throughout much of France. In LONDON, the two kings reopened negotiations, producing two more failed agreements by 1359 (*see* LON-

DON, FIRST TREATY OF; LONDON, SECOND TREATY OF). *See also* ESTATES, GENERAL AND PROVINCIAL.

Further Reading: Sumption, Jonathan. *The Hundred Years War.* Vol. 2, *Trial by Fire.* Philadelphia: University of Pennsylvania Press, 2001.

BOURGES, KINGDOM OF. *See* CHARLES VII

BOURGES, TREATY OF (1412)

Concluded on 18 May 1412, during a period of formal truce between England and France, the Treaty of Bourges allied HENRY IV of England with a French political faction then contending for control of the French king and government. Although the agreement promised substantial territorial concessions, it failed to bring the English immediate gains. It did, however, whet English appetites for French RANSOMS and convince the English leadership that advantage could be won by exploiting French disunity and reopening the HUNDRED YEARS WAR.

In November 1407, shortly after arranging the murder of his rival and cousin, LOUIS, DUKE OF ORLÉANS, brother of CHARLES VI, JOHN THE FEARLESS, duke of BURGUNDY, fled PARIS. Popular with the Parisians, Burgundy returned to the capital in 1408 and won the king's pardon. By 1411, he controlled the royal administration. The leaders of the Orléans faction—now known as ARMAGNACS, a name derived from BERNARD, COUNT OF ARMAGNAC, the father-in-law of the murdered duke's son—assembled an army and besieged the capital. Turning to Henry IV for help, Burgundy agreed to wed his daughter to the prince of Wales, to surrender four FLANDERS towns to the English, and to assist in the eventual conquest of NORMANDY in return for twenty-eight hundred English ARCHERS and men-at-arms. With this English force and three thousand Parisian militia, Burgundy captured the fortress at Saint-Cloud and broke the Armagnac blockade in October 1411.

Now totally excluded from the royal government, the leading Armagnac princes—JOHN, DUKE OF BERRY, the sole surviving brother of CHARLES V; CHARLES, DUKE OF OR-LÉANS, the son of Burgundy's slain rival; Charles D'ALBRET, the constable of France; John, Duke of Bourbon; John, Duke of Alençon; and Armagnac himself—approached Henry IV with even more attractive terms than those conceded by Burgundy. The princes offered to recognize the English king's right to the duchy of AQUITAINE and promised to support his efforts to recover the duchy. They also agreed to hold certain of their lands as fiefs of the king of England and to cede twenty Gascon towns and castles (not in their possession) to Henry. In return for these concessions, Henry promised to make no agreements with Burgundy and to send four thousand archers and men-at-arms to assist his allies against the duke. In July 1412, two months after the conclusion of the Treaty of Bourges, Henry's second son, THOMAS, DUKE OF CLARENCE, led the agreed-upon force to France.

Burgundy reacted to the treaty by sending a royal and Burgundian army to besiege Bourges, the capital of the duchy of Berry. The success of this campaign and Burgundy's issuance of a royal letter ordering all French princes (including Burgundy) to disavow any agreements with the English overthrew the Bourges alliance and isolated Clarence in Normandy. With the Treaty of Auxerre, the VALOIS princes effected a solemn reconciliation within the royal family and the FRENCH CIVIL WAR seemed at last to be over.

Before leading his army on a destructive CHEVAUCHÉE to English-held BORDEAUX, Clarence extracted ransom from the French princes, including handsome individual payments for himself and the other English leaders. By the Treaty of BUZANÇAIS, the Armagnac leaders bought off Clarence for the sum of 150,000 écus, with 66,000 écus paid immediately by Berry and the rest guaranteed by the surrender of seven hostages, including Orléans's younger brother. Although the Bourges agreement had not brought the English the rewards it promised, the treaty had revealed to the ambitious prince of Wales, who was soon to rule

as HENRY V, that the French princes were murderously divided against themselves and willing to make almost any concession for aid in defeating their rivals. *See also* GASCONY.

Further Reading: Allmand, Christopher. *Henry V.* Berkeley: University of California Press, 1993; Perroy, Edouard. *The Hundred Years War.* Trans. W. B. Wells. New York: Capricorn Books, 1965; Seward, Desmond. *The Hundred Years War.* New York: Penguin, 1999; Vaughan, Richard. *John the Fearless.* London: Longman, 1979.

BOWMEN. *See* ARCHERS

BRÉTIGNY, TREATY OF (1360)

Concluded on 8 May 1360 at the village of Brétigny near Chartres, the Anglo-French Treaty of Brétigny ended the first phase of the HUNDRED YEARS WAR. Considered at the time and by later historians to be a victory for EDWARD III and a disaster for VALOIS France, the treaty was never fully implemented and war resumed within a decade of its signing.

Since the capture of JOHN II at POITIERS in 1356, Edward III had negotiated two abortive treaties with the French, the First and Second Treaties of LONDON. Both agreements foundered on the French inability to meet Edward's RANSOM demands for John's release and on their unwillingness to accept Edward's territorial demands for almost half of France in full sovereignty. To force the French to accept a settlement on his terms, Edward launched the RHEIMS CAMPAIGN in October 1359. One of the largest campaigns of the war, the march on Rheims aimed at having Edward crowned king of France at the traditional coronation site of French monarchs. However, the English were unable to take Rheims and the campaign, bedeviled by bad weather, lack of supply, and the French refusal to fight a pitched battle, ended in failure in April 1360, forcing Edward to modify his demands and seek the best settlement he could get. As a result, an English delegation, led by EDWARD, THE BLACK PRINCE, and HENRY OF GROSMONT, duke of Lancaster, met John's representatives at Brétigny on 1 May.

Although Dauphin Charles, believing the English could no longer continue their campaign, was reluctant to treat with them, John was eager to win his release and the final agreement was largely the work of his advisors, not the dauphin's. With both sides desiring a quick settlement, the main terms of the treaty were agreed by 3 May. In return for renouncing his claim to the French throne, Edward received territory amounting to one-third of France in full sovereignty. In the southwest, an enlarged AQUITAINE included Poitou, Saintonge, Quercy, Rouergue, and the Agenais; and in the north, the PLANTAGENET holdings included Ponthieu, Montreuil, and CALAIS. Although a significant concession by the French, these territories also represented a significant reduction in Edward's demands, which had earlier included the former Plantagenet possessions of NORMANDY, BRITTANY, Maine, Anjou, and Touraine. Edward also agreed to surrender all English-held castles and fortresses in areas remaining under Valois control and to forego any alliance with FLANDERS while the French agreed to end the "Auld Alliance" with SCOTLAND (see FRANCO-SCOTTISH ALLIANCE).

John's ransom was set at 3 million écus (about £500,000), another reduction of English demands, and was to include sixteen prominent French prisoners taken at Poitiers. The French were to pay 600,000 écus before the king's release and the rest in six annual installments, payment of which was to be secured by the giving of hostages, including John's sons LOUIS, DUKE OF ANJOU, and JOHN, DUKE OF BERRY. The two kings ratified the treaty at Calais (thus the settlement is sometimes called the Treaty of Calais) on 24 October, after which John was released. The two most important provisions of the agreement—the French renunciations of sovereignty over the ceded territories and the English renunciation of the French Crown—were embodied in a separate charter known, from its opening words, as the C'est Assavoir. This document was to be ratified upon completion of the territorial transfers or by November 1361. In fact, the ratification never occurred and the chief terms of the treaty were thus nullified. The reasons for this failure to ratify the charter are unclear. Edward may have wanted legal grounds to resume the war and the French Crown, should he decide to do so, and John may have been simply unwilling to part forever with the ceded lands. In January 1364, John returned to LONDON, ostensibly to expunge the dishonor brought upon him when Anjou broke parole, but perhaps also to personally negotiate a reduction of his ransom, which had fallen seriously in arrears. When John died in London in April, implementation of the Brétigny settlement fell to the dauphin, now CHARLES V, who had never supported it. In 1369, Charles resumed the war and effectively renounced the treaty by accepting the APPEAL OF THE GASCON LORDS and thereby declaring Valois sovereignty over Aquitaine.

Further Reading: Allmand, Christopher. *The Hundred Years War*. Cambridge: Cambridge University Press, 1988; Curry, Anne. *The Hundred Years War*. 2nd ed. Houndmills, England: Palgrave Macmillan, 2003; Le Patourel, John. "The Treaty of Brétigny, 1360." *Transactions of the Royal Historical Society*, 5th ser., 10 (1960): 19–39; Sumption, Jonathan. *The Hundred Years War*. Vol. 2, *Trial by Fire*. Philadelphia: University of Pennsylvania Press, 2001.

BRETON CIVIL WAR (1341–1365)

Initiated by the death of Duke John III in 1341 and ended by conclusion of the Treaty of GUÉRANDE in 1365, the Breton civil war, the result of a bitter succession dispute in the duchy of BRITTANY, was prolonged and intensified by its incorporation into the HUNDRED YEARS WAR. By intervening in the Breton conflict on behalf of one of the claimants, EDWARD III gained a new front upon which to attack the VALOIS.

John III died childless on 30 April 1341, leaving two possible candidates for the ducal title—his niece, Jeanne de Penthièvre, who was married to CHARLES OF BLOIS, a nephew of PHILIP VI of France, and his half brother, John de MONTFORT. In May, Montfort, who was not well known in Brittany,

The English, on the left with their leopard standard, and the French, on the right with their fleur-de-lys standard, fight a battle during the Breton civil war in this illustration from the *Chronicles* of Jean Froissart. *Erich Lessing/Art Resource, New York.*

nephew secure his new duchy. In October, Montfort concluded a treaty of alliance with Edward, agreeing to accept PLANTAGENET overlordship in return for military aid. However, before English troops could arrive, a French army commanded by John, duke of NORMANDY (*see* JOHN II), invaded Brittany and defeated Montfort, who surrendered Nantes on 2 November.

With her husband imprisoned in Paris, and Blois installed as duke, Montfort's wife, Jeanne de FLANDERS, assumed leadership of the Montfortist cause, holding various strongpoints until the landing, in April 1342, of an English army commanded by ROBERT OF ARTOIS and William de BOHUN, earl of Northampton. Known as the "war of the two Joans," because of the leading roles played by Jeanne de Penthièvre and Jeanne de Flanders, this period of conflict split Brittany between the factions, opened the door to outside intervention, and ended any hope of a quick settlement. When Montfort died in 1345, Edward assumed guardianship of his son and leadership of his cause. Thus, the Breton war, now an extension of the Anglo-French war, became an endless, bloody affair. Most of Breton-speaking western Brittany, many of the towns, and a majority of the gentry supported Montfort, while the French-speaking eastern districts, the clergy, and most of the nobility backed Blois.

On 30 September 1342, Northampton fought Blois to a standstill at MORLAIX, thereby establishing an English foothold in the duchy and denying Blois a quick victory. In January 1343, with the Breton conflict stalemated, Edward and Philip accepted the papal-mediated Truce of MALESTROIT, which allowed Pope CLEMENT VI to convene the AVIGNON PEACE CONFERENCE in 1344. Because neither king had firm control over his Breton

arrived at Nantes, the ducal capital, and proclaimed himself duke. He received only qualified acceptance from the Breton nobility, especially in the pro-French eastern region, where a military campaign was required to enforce his authority. Blois appealed to his uncle for help, but received no response until August, when rumors that Montfort was negotiating with the English led Philip to summon him to PARIS. Ordered not to leave the capital, Montfort fled to Brittany, where he immediately sought English assistance. On 7 September, the PARLEMENT declared in favor of Blois and Philip began gathering an army to help his allies, fighting between the factions continued throughout the conference, which ended in failure in 1345. On 20 June 1347, an Anglo-Breton force under Sir Thomas DAGWORTH, the English governor in Brittany, defeated and captured Blois at LA ROCHE-DERRIEN. Because Blois's partisans refused to capitulate or accept any agreement made by him for his release, the civil war continued. In March 1351, the COMBAT OF THE THIRTY, one of the most famous episodes of the Hundred Years War, was fought between members of nearby English and French garrisons in Brittany, and included such noted warriors as Sir Robert KNOLLES and Sir Hugh CALVELEY. On 14 August 1352, Sir Walter BENTLEY, Dagworth's successor, won at major victory at MAURON, which largely ended direct French involvement in the civil war, but not the war itself. The reason for this was explained in a memorandum Bentley had sent to LONDON earlier in the year. By the 1350s, the English were fighting the Breton war mainly through hired ROUTIER captains who were ostensibly under the authority of the English governor. In his memo, Bentley complained that most of these captains supported themselves and their men through the exaction of PÂTIS and thus were effectively beyond his control and that of the king. Although the English were largely in the ascendant in Brittany in the late 1350s, the civil war between the supporters of Blois and Montfort continued unabated.

In 1360, Brittany was excluded from the provisions of the Treaty of BRÉTIGNY and both Crowns now proclaimed neutrality in the ongoing civil war. Finally released in August 1356, Blois kept his promise not to take up arms against Edward until 1362, when the English king terminated his guardianship and allowed Montfort's son to return to Brittany. Assisted by Bertrand du GUESCLIN, Blois launched a series of campaigns that culminated in September 1364 with an attempt to relieve the besieged town of AURAY. In the resulting battle, an Anglo-Breton force led by Sir John CHANDOS slew Blois and captured du Guesclin. With Blois dead, most of his supporters submitted to Montfort, who in April 1365 concluded the

Treaty of Guérande with Jeanne de Penthièvre, thus ending the war. Now recognized as Duke JOHN IV by his rival and by CHARLES V of France, Montfort did homage to the latter while maintaining friendly relations with England. For the remainder of the Anglo-French war, the Breton dukes strove to maintain military neutrality and political independence.

Further Reading: Jones, Michael. *Between France and England: Politics, Power and Society in Late Medieval Brittany.* Burlington, VT: Ashgate Publishing Company, 2003; Jones, Michael. *The Creation of Brittany: A Late Medieval State.* London: Hambledon Press, 1988; Sumption, Jonathan. *The Hundred Years War.* Vol. 2, *Trial by Fire.* Philadelphia: University of Pennsylvania Press, 2001.

BRIGNAIS, BATTLE OF (1362)

The Battle of Brignais, a shocking defeat of French royal forces by a *ROUTIER* army temporarily formed by the free companies of southeastern France, was fought on 6 April 1362 outside the castle of Brignais near Lyon. Although a terrible blow to the authority and confidence of JOHN II's government, and a cause of great panic in eastern France, the battle was quickly followed by the break-up of the *routier* force and was thus of little political consequence. However, the defeat forced the French Crown to continue military reforms leading to the creation of a salaried standing army that proved more effective against both the *routiers* and the English.

When Philip de Rouvre, the fifteen-year-old duke of BURGUNDY, died without heirs in November 1361, John II annexed the wealthy duchy to the French Crown. The king's announcement was greeted with gloom in the duchy, where the plague was rife, the nobility were suspicious of their new overlord, and elements of the GREAT COMPANY, a constantly shifting combination of *routier* bands, were threatening the southern border. In January 1362, the king ordered local peasants to bring themselves and their goods inside the nearest walled town or fortress and placed Burgundy and the eastern provinces under the military command of Jean de

Melun, count of Tancarville, who by mid-March had gathered an army of about four thousand men comprising the military strength of Burgundy and the surrounding provinces. Tancarville marched south and laid siege to the small castle of Brignais, which was held by a detachment from the company of Hélie (or Petit) Meschin, who, with Garciot du Châtel, an associate of the brigand leader Séguin de BADEFOL; Perrin Boias; and other *routier* captains, was a leader of the Great Company. Although Brignais was of little importance, the brigand leaders could not ignore the threat from Tancarville, especially since another royal army under Arnoul d'AUDREHEM was advancing on them from the south. By early April, Meschin and other *routier* leaders had collected a force of about five thousand north of Lyon.

Early on the morning of 6 April, the Great Company caught the royal army totally unawares. Being contemptuous of the companies, Tancarville and his fellow commander, Jacques de Bourbon, count of La Marche, had made no reconnaissance of the area or taken few precautions to defend the camp. The royal forces were overrun before they could fully arm; over a thousand were captured, including Tancarville, and most of the rest were slain, including La Marche, who died of his wounds after the battle.

The royal government was stunned by news of the defeat and eastern France was thrown into turmoil, with all localities daily expecting the arrival of the Great Company. However, the *routier* commanders could not hold their forces together once the battle was won. They paroled Tancarville and agreed to a truce to last until 26 May. By then, talks between the *routiers* and the government having broken down, and the Great Company having dissolved into its constituent parts, the immediate danger had passed without further consequences to the government, although Burgundy and its neighbors continued to be plagued by bands of *routiers*. However, the shock of Brignais helped spur reforms that resulted in new taxes to fund new standing armies during the reign of CHARLES V. By Charles's death in

1380, these new armies had regained much of AQUITAINE from the English and largely suppressed the *routiers*.

Further Reading: Sumption, Jonathan. *The Hundred Years War*. Vol. 2, *Trial by Fire*. Philadelphia: University of Pennsylvania Press, 2001.

BRITTANY

Occupying a long peninsula with an extensive Channel coastline lying opposite western Britain, the duchy of Brittany was one of the most politically and culturally distinctive regions of medieval France. During the Edwardian phase of the HUNDRED YEARS WAR, Brittany experienced a long and bloody succession struggle that made it a major theater of Anglo-French conflict. For over a century thereafter, Breton dukes preserved the independence of their duchy by carefully maintaining ties with England and France without firmly adhering to either one.

In the fifth and sixth centuries, migrants from Cornwall and Wales settled the western portion of the old Roman province of Armorica, thus giving rise to the name "Brittany," which first appears in the late sixth century in the writings of Gregory of Tours. With strong similarities to Welsh and Cornish, the Breton language, as well as the survival of British religious and social traditions, differentiated the Bretons from their Frankish-Latin neighbors throughout the Middle Ages. In the late ninth century, a Breton ruler illustrated his independence from the Carolingian kings to the east by calling himself *rex* (king) in his charters and by creating an autonomous Breton archbishopric for the Breton Church. By the late eleventh century, much of Brittany acknowledged Norman overlordship, and in the twelfth century, Henry II, first English king of the House of PLANTAGENET and duke of NORMANDY, brought the duchy into his family by marrying his son Geoffrey to Constance, the daughter and heiress of Henry's vassal Conan IV, duke of Brittany. On Conan's death in 1166, Henry assumed control of the duchy on behalf of his young son. In 1203, Henry's son John murdered his nephew Arthur, who, as the son of John's elder brother, had claims to both Brittany and England. In 1212, Philip II of France brought Brittany under Capetian overlordship (see CAPET, HOUSE OF) by marrying his kinsman, Peter Mauclerc, to Arthur's maternal half sister, Alix. Thus, over the next century, the penetration into Brittany of French language and culture gradually increased.

The death of Duke John III in April 1341, five years after the start of the Hundred Years War, initiated the BRETON CIVIL WAR (1341–1365), a bitter succession dispute between John's niece, Jeanne de Penthièvre, and his half brother, John de MONTFORT. When PHILIP VI, as feudal suzerain, decided the question in favor of Jeanne and her husband, CHARLES OF BLOIS, who was Philip's nephew, Montfort allied himself with EDWARD III, who, after Montfort's death in 1345, assumed guardianship of Montfort's son and leadership of his cause. In 1362, Edward terminated his guardianship and allowed young Montfort to return to Brittany and press his own claims. After defeating and killing Blois at AURAY in September 1364, Montfort concluded the Treaty of GUÉRANDE with his cousin. Jeanne recognized Montfort as Duke JOHN IV, while the new duke rendered homage to CHARLES V of France. Although John maintained generally good relations with England, with which Brittany had strong economic ties, the Breton nobility developed a strong pro-French element, with such Breton noblemen as Bertrand du GUESCLIN, Olivier de CLISSON, and Arthur de Richemont (see ARTHUR III) entering French service. However, after the accession of CHARLES VI in 1380 and the start of the FRENCH CIVIL WAR after 1407, John IV and his son JOHN V took advantage of increasing French weakness to strengthen Breton independence and national identity. Refusing liege homage to the VALOIS, the Breton dukes established an elaborate court ceremonial to enhance their own prestige, while collecting taxes, administering justice, and conducting foreign policy independent of the French Crown. The Breton Church was also independent; any agreement between

French kings and the papacy did not apply to Brittany.

In the fifteenth century, John V remained aloof from the Anglo-French war, shifting allegiance from one party to the other as circumstances dictated. In 1422, he acknowledged the Treaty of TROYES making HENRY V heir to the French throne. In 1423, he joined with JOHN, DUKE OF BEDFORD, and PHILIP THE GOOD, duke of BURGUNDY, in the anti-French Treaty of AMIENS, but later repudiated that agreement and thereafter gradually increased Breton neutrality. After his accession in 1458, as England descended into civil war, Duke Francis II came under increasing pressure to submit to French overlordship. In 1488, only months before the duke's death, Charles VIII attacked Brittany. Now ruled by Francis's daughter Anne, Brittany capitulated in 1491, when Anne, despite English objections, agreed to marry Charles and accept gradual incorporation of Brittany into the French state. In 1532, in return for the Crown's promise to protect the duchy's ancient liberties, the Breton estates voted for perpetual union with France.

Further Reading: Galliou, Patrick, and Michael C. E. Jones. *The Bretons*. Oxford: Blackwell, 1991; Jones, Michael. *Between France and England: Politics, Power and Society in Late Medieval Brittany*. Burlington, VT: Ashgate Publishing Company, 2003; Jones, Michael. *The Creation of Brittany: A Late Medieval State*. London: Hambledon Press, 1988; Jones, Michael. *Ducal Brittany, 1364–1399*. London: Oxford University Press, 1970.

BRITTANY, DUKE OF. See ARTHUR III, DUKE OF BRITTANY; CHARLES OF BLOIS, DUKE OF BRITTANY; JOHN IV, DUKE OF BRITTANY; JOHN V, DUKE OF BRITTANY

BRUGES PEACE CONFERENCE (1375–1377)

Encouraged by the papacy and by their own financial exhaustion, EDWARD III and CHARLES V sent representatives to a peace conference that opened in Bruges in March 1375. Although the negotiators came close to a final settlement of the HUNDRED YEARS WAR, the old issue of sovereignty in AQUI-

TAINE proved insoluble, causing the talks to end without agreement in 1377.

Upon becoming pope in 1370, Gregory XI, the nephew of CLEMENT VI, who had sponsored the abortive AVIGNON PEACE CONFERENCE in 1344, sought to effect an Anglo-French reconciliation as a prelude to his plan for returning the papacy to Rome. Gregory's initial contacts with LONDON and PARIS, and with EDWARD, THE BLACK PRINCE, in BORDEAUX, and LOUIS, DUKE OF ANJOU, the royal lieutenant of Languedoc in Toulouse, were largely unsuccessful. Edward believed the Avignon popes had conspired with the French to restart the war and Charles was unwilling to halt the successful French campaigns in GASCONY. Brief talks were held in CALAIS in 1372 and in Bruges in 1373, but English demands for the French Crown or for restoration of the Treaty of BRÉTIGNY could not be reconciled with French demands that Edward first surrender Calais and the remainder of PLANTAGENET Gascony. However, by 1375, the French campaign in the southwest had stalled and neither monarch had the economic resources to continue a long war, making some type of negotiated settlement more attractive to both parties.

With LOUIS DE MALE, count of FLANDERS, acting as mediator and the archbishop of Ravenna as president, a full peace conference opened at Bruges in March. Charles's brother, PHILIP THE BOLD, duke of BURGUNDY, led the French delegation, while Edward's son, JOHN OF GAUNT, duke of Lancaster, headed the English deputation. On 27 June, the parties concluded a one-year truce, which was subsequently extended to 1377. To obtain a final peace, the English were willing to retreat from the Brétigny agreement and accept a partition of the enlarged Aquitaine created in 1360, while the French were willing to return some of their recent conquests in the southwest. Either the Aquitaine of 1360 could be divided equally between Plantagenet and VALOIS, or Charles could grant half his conquests as a fief to an English prince, with Edward retaining the unconquered portion of Gascony. Charles was also willing to concede Calais in return

for the English willingness to reduce the remaining balance of JOHN II's RANSOM.

However, despite agreement on all these issues, the question of sovereignty could not be resolved. The English insisted that Edward's territories, whatever their size, be held in full sovereignty, while Charles was equally insistent that the Valois retain overlordship of any Plantagenet provinces. Although the pope proposed a temporary sovereignty, whereby Aquitaine be wholly English during the lifetimes of Edward and the Black Prince and then revert to Valois overlordship, neither side would agree. For Charles, such a plan would undermine his justification for restarting the war, and for the English, with the king in his sixties and the prince in poor health, their period of sovereignty seemed likely to be brief. Although talks continued for some time at Bruges and elsewhere, agreement on the sovereignty issue could not be reached and the war resumed in 1377. *See also* PAPACY AND THE HUNDRED YEARS WAR.

Further Reading: Perroy, Edouard. *The Hundred Years War*. Trans. W. B. Wells. New York: Capricorn Books, 1965.

BUCH, CAPTAL DE. *See* GRAILLY, JEAN DE, CAPTAL DE BUCH

BUCHAN, EARL OF. *See* STEWART, JOHN, EARL OF BUCHAN

BUREAU, JOHN (d. 1463)
Although a lawyer and administrator rather than a military man, John Bureau, master of the king's ARTILLERY, played a major role in the last campaigns of the HUNDRED YEARS WAR. By modernizing and enlarging the French supply of siege and field ordnance, and by expertly overseeing its deployment and use, Bureau helped ensure the final expulsion of the English from NORMANDY and GASCONY.

Born in Champagne, Bureau came to PARIS, where he studied law and became a legal officer in the city's Lancastrian administration. In 1434, Bureau left the capital and entered the service of CHARLES VII, who appointed him receiver of Paris in 1436 and treasurer of France in 1443. Although he had no training as a soldier, Bureau had served as a gunner for the English under JOHN, DUKE OF BEDFORD. Perhaps sensing a financial opportunity, Bureau and his brother Gaspard soon made themselves experts in the use of artillery, a branch of fifteenth-century military science that was largely in the hands of civilian specialists. Described as a small man with a precise and practical mind, Bureau may also have been naturally drawn to a field that required technical imagination and a willingness to adapt to changing technology. Recognizing the importance of the brothers' expertise, Charles placed them in charge of the royal artillery, the quality and use of which they significantly improved over the last two decades of the war.

Deftly handled by Bureau, the royal guns quickly proved their worth at the sieges of numerous English-held towns—at Montereau in October 1437; at Meaux in the summer of 1439; and at PONTOISE, which capitulated in September 1441 after Bureau's guns destroyed the fortified bridge that protected the southern end of the town. Bureau's handling of the artillery was particularly important during the NORMAN CAMPAIGN of 1449–50, when conquest of the duchy became largely a matter of reducing enemy strongholds. At the siege of Caen, Edmund BEAUFORT, duke of Somerset, surrendered the town after one of Bureau's cannonballs smashed into the room occupied by the duke's wife and children. At Cherbourg, Bureau determined that the most advantageous placement of his guns was on the beach, which would be submerged each day by high tide. To solve the problem, he had the weapons covered in tallow and hides, in effect waterproofing them so that the bombardment could resume as soon as the tide receded.

In 1451, Bureau, overseeing an artillery train that was said to contain three hundred guns of all sizes, accompanied JOHN, COUNT OF DUNOIS, on campaign in Gascony. The French artillery helped quickly reduce the remaining English towns and fortresses, including BORDEAUX, which fell on 30 June. When John TALBOT, earl of Shrewsbury, retook the town for HENRY VI in the following year, Bureau returned in 1453 with an army over which he shared command. It was Bureau who laid out the fortified camp and directed the artillery that destroyed Shrewsbury and his army at CASTILLON in July 1453 and thereby effectively ended the Hundred Years War. As a reward for Bureau's services, the king appointed him mayor of Bordeaux for life. Until his death in Paris on 5 July 1463, Bureau continued to serve both Charles and his son Louis XI in various administrative capacities.

Further Reading: Seward, Desmond. *The Hundred Years War.* New York: Penguin, 1999; Vale, M. G. A. *Charles VII.* Berkeley: University of California Press, 1974.

BURGHERSH, HENRY, BISHOP OF LINCOLN (1292–1340)

Henry Burghersh, bishop of Lincoln, was EDWARD III's chief foreign policy advisor during the opening years of the HUNDRED YEARS WAR. Burghersh conducted Edward's policy of negotiating alliances with princes in Germany and the Low Countries and was therefore primarily responsible for creation of the extensive ANTI-FRENCH COALITION of 1337–38.

The third son of a noble Sussex family, Burghersh opted for an ecclesiastical career and undertook the study of civil and canon law. In 1320, EDWARD II named him bishop of Lincoln, an appointment that owed much to the influence of Burghersh's uncle, Bartholomew, Lord Badlesmere. However, in 1322, Badlesmere's involvement in the unsuccessful rebellion against the king and his favorites led to confiscation of the bishop's temporalities. Although eventually restored to Edward's favor, Burghersh was among the first to join Queen Isabella (*see* ISABELLA, QUEEN OF ENGLAND [c. 1292–1358]) in September 1326, when she returned from the

Continent to overthrow her husband. In January 1327, Burghersh was one of the commissioners sent to Kenilworth to secure Edward's surrender of the Crown, and, in 1328, the bishop was appointed treasurer and then chancellor of England. In June 1329, Burghersh accompanied Edward III to Amiens, where the sixteen-year-old king did homage to PHILIP VI for the duchy of AQUITAINE. When disputes arose over the form of homage required, Burghersh, acting for the king, delivered a brief speech protesting the French demands and outlining the English position. When Edward seized power from his mother in October 1330, Burghersh, being too closely associated with the previous regime, was imprisoned in the Tower of London and deprived of the chancellorship.

Being a capable administrator and diplomat, Burghersh was soon restored to favor, winning reappointment as treasurer in 1334. By 1337, Burghersh, whom a contemporary described as "an ingenious advisor, audacious and smooth" (Sumption, 194), became one of Edward's most influential councilors, assuming prime responsibility for the implementation of foreign policy. Having decided upon war with France and the creation of a grand anti-French alliance, Edward left negotiation of the necessary agreements largely to Burghersh, who, being an ambitious man with few scruples, promised whatever was necessary to carry out the royal will. In March 1338, the bishop negotiated a favorable treaty with the new revolutionary government of FLANDERS; the agreement effectively committed the province to neutrality in the coming Anglo-French war and thereby deprived Philip of Flemish manpower and ports. In May 1338, Burghersh delivered Edward's formal declaration of war to Philip in PARIS.

Throughout 1337 and 1338, Burghersh negotiated a series of agreements with various princes, including the German emperor, Ludwig of Bavaria; the duke of Brabant; the margrave of Juliers; and the counts of Hainault and Guelders. Although theoretically creating a large anti-French army, the agreements also bound Edward to pay some £160,000 in fees as well as the usual costs of war. Because these commitments were far beyond the king's means, payments fell into arrears, leading inevitably to desperate financing schemes, such as the DORDRECHT BONDS, and to the eventual collapse of the alliance. In 1339, as Edward realized the impossibility of meeting the financial obligations to which he was committed, the bishop's influence declined. By the time of Burghersh's death in Ghent on 2 December 1340, many of Edward's long unpaid allies had opened negotiations with France. *See also* ANGLO-FLEMISH ALLIANCE.

Further Reading: Sumption, Jonathan. *The Hundred Years War.* Vol. 1, *Trial by Battle.* Philadelphia: University of Pennsylvania Press, 1999.

BURGUNDIANS

One of the political factions that fought the FRENCH CIVIL WAR, the Burgundian party comprised adherents of the dukes of BURGUNDY, particularly those supporting the political supremacy of JOHN THE FEARLESS between 1404 and 1419. The Burgundians were opposed by the ARMAGNACS, a faction derived from supporters of LOUIS, DUKE OF ORLÉANS, chief rival of the dukes of Burgundy for paramount influence within the royal government. After 1420, the ANGLO-BURGUNDIAN ALLIANCE created by the Treaty of TROYES fostered development of an independent Burgundy and maintained Lancastrian rule in NORMANDY and northern France for two decades.

PHILIP THE BOLD, first VALOIS duke of Burgundy, became a dominant figure in the royal government in 1380, when his nephew CHARLES VI ascended the throne. Following the onset of the king's schizophrenia in 1392, the duke filled the royal administration with men devoted to his interests. Although Burgundy's position was increasingly challenged by LOUIS, DUKE OF ORLÉANS, Charles's younger brother, the dukes' rivalry did not become violent until after Burgundy's death in 1404. Because John, the new duke of Burgundy, lacked his father's experience and authority, Orléans, in alliance with

Queen ISABEAU, was able to frustrate many of his rival's plans and ambitions. In consequence, Burgundy arranged Orléans's murder in November 1407. In early 1408, Burgundy, taking advantage of the king's mental instability, returned to court, where he issued the *JUSTIFICATION OF THE DUKE OF BURGUNDY*, a document that, by way of condoning Burgundy's action, brazenly detailed the many alleged crimes and enormities of Orléans. When public opinion largely accepted the *Justification*, Burgundy quickly established his dominance over the court, and, by 1409, the Burgundians enjoyed a near monopoly of power.

Civil war began in 1410, as the Armagnacs—the name given to supporters of CHARLES, DUKE OF ORLÉANS, and his father-in-law, BERNARD, COUNT OF ARMAGNAC—besieged the capital. Because he controlled the royal person, Burgundy was able to portray himself as the king's lieutenant and his opponents as rebels and traitors. In 1411–12, both Burgundy and the Armagnacs sought military assistance from HENRY IV of England. Although an expedition led by THOMAS, DUKE OF CLARENCE, landed in 1412 in accordance with the Anglo-Armagnac Treaty of BOURGES, Burgundy used his control of the government to raise an army under royal authority and force the Armagnacs to repudiate the agreement. In 1413, the dauphin, LOUIS, DUKE OF GUIENNE, attempted to form a royalist party capable of reconciling the factions, while members of the ESTATES-GENERAL leveled charges of corruption against the Burgundian administration. In response, Burgundy, who was popular in PARIS, instigated a riot by his supporters in the city. Led by a member of the butchers' guild named Simon Caboche, the rioters, who thus became known as CABOCHIENS, rampaged through Paris on 28 April, seizing or killing the dauphin's officers. Moving quickly beyond the duke's control, the Cabochien uprising became a reign of terror that alienated many Parisians, who turned to the dauphin and the Armagnacs for deliverance. In August, Burgundy fled the capital, leaving the king and the government to his rivals.

Excluded from power, Burgundy withdrew to his domains until 1418, taking no part in the interval in negotiations with HENRY V, in the AGINCOURT campaign, or in the defense of Normandy and ROUEN (*see* NORMAN CAMPAIGN [1417–1419]). Anxious only to regain power in Paris, Burgundy supported the queen when she fled the capital in 1417 after quarreling with her surviving son Charles, who was now dauphin and nominal leader of the Armagnacs. In May 1418, an uprising in Paris overthrew the Armagnac regime, forcing the dauphin to flee and allowing Burgundy and his adherents to resume control of both king and government. Believing he could dominate the dauphin, who was young and inexperienced, Burgundy sought some accommodation whereby he could eliminate the Armagnacs, unite the kingdom, and expel the English. However, when the two parties met at MONTEREAU in September 1419, old servants of Orléans in the dauphin's entourage avenged their late master by murdering Burgundy.

Since no accommodation was possible with his father's killer, PHILIP THE GOOD, the new duke of Burgundy, allied himself with Henry V in 1420. By accepting the Treaty of Troyes, Philip recognized Henry as regent and heir to the French throne. Although the royal administration remained largely in Burgundian hands, the Crown itself was pledged to the House of LANCASTER. After the deaths of Henry V and Charles VI in 1422, Burgundy took little direct part in English efforts to defend HENRY VI's rights against the dauphin and his party, which was now essentially an amalgam of Armagnacs and others who supported the continuance of Valois rule. Rather than pursue his father's dream of ruling in Paris, Burgundy concentrated on consolidating his holdings in France and on expanding his territory in the Low Countries, efforts that made the state of Burgundy a power in northwestern Europe and turned the one-time Burgundian faction into the administration of an independent principality. In 1435, the duke abandoned the Anglo-Burgundian alliance at the

Congress of ARRAS, thus allowing the dauphin, now CHARLES VII, to enter Paris in 1436 and finally end the factional divisions of the civil war.

Further Reading: Perroy, Edouard. *The Hundred Years War.* Trans. W. B. Wells. New York: Capricorn Books, 1965; Vaughan, Richard. *John the Fearless.* London: Longman, 1979; Vaughan, Richard. *Philip the Good: The Apogee of Burgundy.* Woodbridge, England: Boydell Press, 2002.

BURGUNDY

In the fourteenth century, the term "Burgundy" referred both to a duchy of eastern France owing homage to the French king and to a county across the Saône owing homage to the German emperor. In 1363, the duchy of Burgundy became a VALOIS APPANAGE, which, in the fifteenth century, became the center of an autonomous principality that also encompassed the county of Burgundy, other lordships in northern and eastern France, and most of the Low Countries. This accumulation of territory allowed the fifteenth-century dukes of Burgundy to play a central role in both the FRENCH CIVIL WAR and the HUNDRED YEARS WAR.

Until 1361, the duchy of Burgundy was ruled by a cadet branch of the House of CAPET. Upon the death in that year of Philip de Rouvre, the last Capetian duke, the duchy passed to JOHN II, who granted it to his youngest son, PHILIP THE BOLD, in 1363. CHARLES V enabled his brother to expand his holdings by arranging for Philip to marry MARGUERITE DE FLANDERS, the only child of LOUIS DE MALE, count of FLANDERS. Besides her father's provinces of Flanders, Nevers, and Rethel, which she inherited in 1384, Marguerite was her grandmother's heir to Artois and to the county of Burgundy (the Franche-Comté), which she inherited in 1382. Through her mother, Marguerite also had a claim to Brabant, although this duchy did not come to the dukes of Burgundy until 1430. Ruling both his own and his wife's territories, Philip, thanks to the mental illness of his nephew, CHARLES VI, also dominated the French government after 1392. Following Philip's death in 1404 and Marguerite's in

1405, their eldest son, JOHN THE FEARLESS, inherited his parents' lands and his father's political rivalry with LOUIS, DUKE OF ORLÉANS, the king's brother. Descending to violence, this rivalry led in 1407 to the murder of Orléans by assassins hired by Burgundy and to the development of the BURGUNDIAN and ARMAGNAC (Orléanist) factions, whose struggle for political dominance in PARIS led after 1410 to eruption of the French civil war.

Expelled from Paris in 1413, Burgundy did not fight at AGINCOURT in 1415 and took no part in defending NORMANDY against HENRY V (*see* NORMAN CAMPAIGN [1417–1419]), preferring to concentrate on overthrowing the Armagnac regime in Paris, which he did in 1418. On 10 September 1419, partisans of the dauphin, who was nominal head of the Armagnacs, murdered Burgundy during a peace conference on the bridge at MONTEREAU. Rejecting any agreement with his father's murderers, the new duke, PHILIP THE GOOD, allied himself with Henry V, whom, through acceptance of the Treaty of TROYES, he recognized as heir to the French throne. Establishment of an Anglo-Burgundian government in Paris allowed Philip to consolidate his holdings in France and to enlarge his territories in the Low Countries. By 1440, Namur, Brabant, Luxembourg, Holland, Zeeland, and Hainault had all been incorporated into the Burgundian state, which, thanks to the weakness of the French monarchy, was now effectively independent.

However, despite the ANGLO-BURGUNDIAN ALLIANCE, Philip provided little military assistance to the English, and in 1435 abandoned his allies at the Congress of ARRAS, where the dauphin, now CHARLES VII, agreed to exempt the duke from paying homage for his French fiefs and to send a courtier to apologize on the king's behalf for the murder at Montereau. Although Burgundy remained a culturally influential state, particularly in terms of music, art, and literature, the reconciliation effectively ended Burgundian involvement in the Hundred Years War or in royal administration. The expulsion of the English from France in 1453 and the subsequent revival of

French royal authority gradually reduced the ability of the dukes to thwart French designs on Burgundy. After Philip's son, Charles the Bold, died without male heirs in 1477, the duchy of Burgundy was eventually reincorporated into the kingdom of France.

Further Reading: Vaughan, Richard. *John the Fearless.* London: Longman, 1979; Vaughan, Richard. *Philip the Bold: The Formation of the Burgundian State.* Woodbridge, England: Boydell Press, 2002; Vaughan, Richard. *Philip the Good: The Apogee of Burgundy.* Woodbridge, England: Boydell Press, 2002; Vaughan, Richard. *Valois Burgundy.* London: Archon, 1975.

BURGUNDY, DUCHESS OF

See MARGUERITE DE FLANDERS, DUCHESS OF BURGUNDY

BURGUNDY, DUKE OF

See JOHN THE FEARLESS, DUKE OF BURGUNDY; PHILIP THE BOLD, DUKE OF BURGUNDY; PHILIP THE GOOD, DUKE OF BURGUNDY

BUZANÇAIS, TREATY OF (1412)

Concluded on 14 November 1412, the Treaty of Buzançais was an agreement whereby the leaders of the ARMAGNAC faction in the FRENCH CIVIL WAR bought off THOMAS, DUKE OF CLARENCE, the leader of an English military expedition sent to France to assist the Armagnacs under the Treaty of BOURGES. Although the settlement ended English intervention in France without any political or military benefit being derived from Clarence's expedition, the French willingness to pay handsomely for Clarence's withdrawal revealed the bitter divisions within the French nobility and rekindled an appetite for plunder within the English nobility.

Under the Bourges agreement of May 1412, HENRY IV undertook to send a force of four thousand men to support the Armagnac princes in their struggle for power with JOHN THE FEARLESS, duke of BURGUNDY, who controlled the person of CHARLES VI and thus the royal government. In return, the Armagnac leaders—JOHN, DUKE OF BERRY,

the brother of CHARLES V; CHARLES, DUKE OF ORLÉANS; Charles d'ALBRET, constable of France; John, Duke of Bourbon; John, Duke of Alençon; and BERNARD, COUNT OF ARMAGNAC—swore homage to Henry, whom they recognized as ruler of AQUITAINE. On 11 July, Clarence, Henry's second son, landed in NORMANDY and marched south toward Blois. On 21 July, Burgundy, acting in the king's name, ordered all princes, including himself, to disavow any agreements with England. Unwilling to disobey the king, and facing a Burgundian invasion of Berry's territories, the Armagnac leaders capitulated and wrote to Henry on 22 July repudiating the Bourges agreement.

In August, the Treaty of Auxerre effected a reconciliation within the royal family (*see* VALOIS) and seemed to end the civil war. Now facing a France ostensibly united against him, an angry Clarence led a CHEVAUCHÉE across the Loire and into the Indre Valley, where, at the village of Buzançais, he concluded a financial settlement with his erstwhile allies. The duke agreed to withdraw to GASCONY for a promise of 150,000 écus (over £30,000), with two-thirds to be paid by the end of the month and the balance by Christmas. Clarence and his noble lieutenants also demanded personal gifts that eventually amounted, in money and treasure, to over 66,000 écus. For himself, the duke received 40,000 écus (he had demanded 120,000), mainly in the form of jewels and precious artifacts supplied by Berry. To ensure fulfillment of the terms, Clarence took seven hostages, including John, count of Angoulême, the younger brother of Orléans. Because payment of the settlement's final installment was long delayed, Angoulême spent over thirty years in captivity.

Further Reading: Allmand, Christopher. *Henry V.* New Haven, CT: Yale University Press, 1997; Seward, Desmond. *The Hundred Years War.* New York: Penguin, 1999; Tuck, Anthony. *Crown and Nobility: England, 1272–1461.* 2nd ed. Oxford: Blackwell, 1999.

C

CABOCHE, SIMON. *See* CABOCHIENS

CABOCHIENS (1413)

Named for one of their leaders, the butcher Simon Caboche, whose fellow butchers and flayers represented a leading element in the movement, the Cabochiens were pro-BUR-GUNDIAN tradesmen and burgesses of PARIS who were used by JOHN THE FEARLESS, duke of BURGUNDY, to overawe the royal court and destroy his ARMAGNAC rivals. For three months in 1413, the Cabochiens imposed a reign of terror on the city, thwarting efforts by the dauphin, LOUIS, DUKE OF GUIENNE, to end the FRENCH CIVIL WAR and reunite the country on the eve of HENRY V's renewal of the HUNDRED YEARS WAR.

Fearing an English invasion, Burgundy, who had controlled the royal government since 1409, summoned the Estates-General to Paris in January 1413 to grant new war TAX-ATION. However, the assembly refused to discuss supply until the government under-took a series of administrative and financial reforms. The Estates also charged the Bur-gundian administration with corruption, de-manding the dismissal of some thirty royal officials accused of misappropriation of gov-ernment funds. The action of the Estates heartened the Armagnac partisans in the households of the dauphin and Queen ISA-BEAU. Under the leadership of the dauphin, talks for ending the civil war were begun with CHARLES, DUKE OF ORLÉANS; JOHN, DUKE OF BERRY; BERNARD, COUNT OF ARMAGNAC; and other self-exiled Armagnac leaders. Because the dauphin's efforts, if successful, would end Burgundy's dictatorship, the duke struck at his enemies by inciting the Parisians, who

had always favored him, to rise in defense of the regime. On 27 April, rioters, led by Ca-boche, besieged the Bastille, invaded the dauphin's palace, and seized or murdered suspected Armagnacs across the city. Many of the dauphin's officers were arrested and de-nounced as traitors, and many anti-Burgun-dian courtiers, such as the queen's brother, Ludwig of Bavaria, were also seized.

Riots occurred almost daily for the next month, with the Cabochiens several times entering the Hôtel Saint-Pol, where they terrorized the court by demanding that all opponents of Burgundy be turned over to them. Ill and frightened, CHARLES VI took no action against the Cabochiens, who de-manded that the king act upon the reforms earlier proposed by the Estates-General. On 26 and 27 May, Charles presided over a *lit de justice* (i.e., a royally attended session of the PARLEMENT of Paris) at which was promul-gated a massive reform ordinance of 258 articles that became known as the *Ordon-nance Cabochienne*. Reviving many of the administrative reforms earlier advocated by the MARMOUSETS, the *Ordonnance* did not seek to control the Crown, but merely to make royal administration more economical and efficient. Offices were eliminated, the pay of royal officials was reduced, the pro-vision of services was consolidated, and stricter supervision, especially of financial affairs, was mandated. To fund the war with England, a special treasury was established in Paris to receive half of any taxes collected.

Once he had unleashed insurrection, Burgundy found he could not control it, and Cabochien violence continued throughout the summer. By August, the excesses of the rioters had alienated many Parisians, who turned to the dauphin and the Armagnac leaders to save them from anarchy. In late July, the dauphin, having secured a royal order freeing those imprisoned by the Cabochiens, concluded the peace of Pontoise with the Armagnac princes. On 4 August, the dauphin was cheered as he rode through Paris, a welcome that incited a failed Cabochien attack on the Town Hall. Realizing he had lost the support of the city, Burgundy made an unsuccessful attempt to kidnap the king and then fled the capital on 23 August. The Armagnac leaders entered Paris on 1 September, and the Gascon bands of the count of Armagnac immediately imposed order by arresting or killing leading Cabochiens. On 5 September, the king formally annulled the *Ordonnance Cabochienne* at a new *lit de justice*. Rather than ending the civil war and securing Burgundian rule, the Cabochien insurrection aggravated civil strife and handed power to the Armagnacs. *See also* ESTATES, GENERAL AND PROVINCIAL.

Further Reading: Famiglietti, Richard C. *Royal Intrigue: Crisis at the Court of Charles VI, 1392–1420.* New York: AMS Press, 1986; Perroy, Edouard. *The Hundred Years War.* Trans. W. B. Wells. New York: Capricorn Books, 1965.

CADORET, BATTLE OF. *See* DAGWORTH, SIR THOMAS

CADZAND, BATTLE OF (1387)

Fought off Margate on 24 March 1387, the Battle of Cadzand (or Margate) was a naval engagement between an English flotilla under Richard Fitzalan, earl of Arundel, and a Franco-Flemish wine fleet. Besides lowering the cost of wine in LONDON and thereby winning much popularity for Arundel, the victory gave the English temporary command of the Channel and allowed the earl to raid the Flemish coast, although he failed to achieve the ultimate goal of his enterprise, the incitement of an anti-BURGUNDIAN uprising in FLANDERS.

In October 1386, the so-called Wonderful PARLIAMENT, angered by the financial excesses of RICHARD II and his court, and concerned by the government's failure to respond to a threatened French invasion, established a commission to reform the royal household and administration and re-invigorate the English war effort. With Parliament's approval, the commission began gathering men and ships for a descent on Flanders, which was aimed at provoking an insurrection that would replace the government of PHILIP THE BOLD, duke of BURGUNDY, with a pro-English regime. On 10 December, Arundel, a member of the commission, was appointed admiral; a week later, the earl indented (*see* INDENTURES) with the Crown to serve with twenty-five hundred men for three months beginning on 1 March 1387.

On 16 March, Arundel arrived at Sandwich, where he took command of a fleet of sixty ships. Intending to invade England, the French had gathered an army of thirty thousand men and a fleet of twelve hundred vessels at Sluys in the previous autumn, but when Burgundy, who was the driving force in CHARLES VI's minority government, fell ill, the expedition was cancelled and the fleet dispersed. The ships that Arundel engaged on 24 March 1387 were part of a 250-vessel fleet carrying wine from La Rochelle to Sluys. Although significantly larger than Arundel's flotilla, the French fleet, which included contingents of Flemish, German, and Castilian vessels, was inferior in both manpower and armaments, having an inadequate complement of soldiers to defend it from the English attack. After some German and Flemish vessels deserted to them, the English were eventually able to overcome the enemy, capturing some fifty ships and the fleet's Flemish commander. Over a dozen ships were sunk or burned, and almost nine thousand tuns of wine were captured and carried to London, where they sold for a fraction of the normal price.

Arundel, meanwhile, pursued remnants of the enemy fleet to Sluys, which was virtually undefended. However, instead of seizing the port, which might have initiated the Flemish uprising he was seeking, the earl pillaged the surrounding countryside, thereby capturing much booty but setting off no rebellion. On 14 April, with supplies running low and his men falling ill, Arundel returned to England. After refitting, the earl sailed to BRITTANY, where he resupplied the besieged garrison at Brest, but failed to effect a reconciliation with Duke JOHN IV. Although Arundel won a major victory, damaged French naval capabilities, and ended the threat of French invasion for the next decade, he had failed to achieve his main goal—the destruction of Burgundian rule in Flanders. When Arundel's term of service ended in June, the military initiative again passed to the French.

Further Reading: Goodman, Anthony. *The Loyal Conspiracy: The Lords Appellant under Richard II.* London: Routledge and Kegan Paul, 1971; Palmer, J.J.N. *England, France, and Christendom, 1377–99.* Chapel Hill: University of North Carolina Press, 1972; Saul, Nigel. *Richard II.* New Haven, CT: Yale University Press, 1997; Tuck, Anthony. *Richard II and the English Nobility.* London: Edward Arnold, 1973.

CALAIS

Located on the English Channel only twenty-three miles from Dover, the French town of Calais was the closest continental port to the English coast and thus of great strategic importance during the HUNDRED YEARS WAR. Captured by EDWARD III in 1347, Calais rapidly became vital to the economy and security of England, and was the only French possession to remain in English hands after 1453.

On 4 September 1346, only a week after his victory at CRÉCY, Edward laid siege to Calais. Besides its proximity to English allies in FLANDERS and the Low Countries, the town was ideally situated to serve as a supply depot and base of operations for English armies in France. After a long and difficult siege, Calais surrendered on 3 August 1347, thus beginning over two hundred years of English possession. After expelling most of the inhabitants, Edward resettled the town and its surrounding pale with English citizens, who were granted tax exemptions and other privileges for taking up property abandoned by the French. The town immediately became an important base for English military operations, being, for instance, the staging point for the RHEIMS CAMPAIGN in 1359. In 1363, when Edward established the wool staple in Calais, the town took on a new economic significance. By concentrating the export of English wool in Calais, Edward made easier the Crown's collection of export duties on wool, England's largest and most profitable trade commodity. Besides expanding royal revenue, placing the staple in English territory allowed the profits of the trade to flow into the hands of a small group of English merchants, known as the Company of the Staple, whose resulting wealth allowed them to make regular loans to the Crown.

Calais also became vital to English defense. The Calais garrison was the Crown's only standing army, numbering, by the early fifteenth century, eight hundred men in peacetime and a thousand in war. Divided equally between men-at-arms and ARCHERS, the garrison was paid out of the customs duties collected on the wool exported to Calais. By 1400, the wages and expenses of the garrison came to over £10,000 per year, and more in time of war, sums that consumed almost one-quarter of the Crown's annual income. In the fifteenth century, and especially during the reign of HENRY VI, when the Crown was chronically short of funds, the profits of the Calais wool trade were often diverted to meet other royal expenses, causing the unpaid garrison to rebel, as happened in 1407 and 1454. After the latter uprising, the government instituted a new system of payment, whereby the merchants of the staple collected the customs and paid the garrison, accounting for any surplus to the Crown.

The king entrusted Calais to a lieutenant or captain, who was usually a military man. Besides commanding the garrison of Calais, the captain had authority over the captains and garrisons of Guisnes, Hammes, Newnham Bridge, Rysbank, and the other fortresses defending the approaches to the town. The Calais captaincy was thus an important and coveted position. During the Wars of the Roses in the late fifteenth century, control of Calais and its garrison was of vital importance. By the sixteenth century, Calais was an English town and was considered English territory. In the 1530s, its citizens were even allowed to send representatives to PARLIAMENT.

The French made numerous attempts to regain the town. In the 1390s, the government of CHARLES VI demanded Calais as part of the price for signing a peace treaty. Although RICHARD II was eager for a final settlement, he declined to surrender Calais. In 1406–7, JOHN THE FEARLESS, duke of BURGUNDY, launched an unsuccessful attack on Calais, and in 1435–36, his son, PHILIP THE GOOD, having just abandoned the ANGLO-BURGUNDIAN ALLIANCE, conducted a long and equally fruitless siege of the town. Despite various other French efforts over the years, Calais remained English until captured by Francis, duke of Guise, in January 1558. *See also* CALAIS, SIEGE OF.

Further Reading: Perroy, Edouard. *The Hundred Years War*. Trans. W. B. Wells. New York: Capricorn Books, 1965; Sumption, Jonathan. *The Hundred Years War*. Vol. 1, *Trial by Battle*. Philadelphia: University of Pennsylvania Press, 1999.

CALAIS, SIEGE OF (1346–1347)

The eleven-month siege of CALAIS, a small port in the county of Boulogne, led to the English capture of a secure base in northern France.

Following his victory at the Battle of CRÉCY on 26 August 1346, EDWARD III marched north seeking a port from which to embark his army. Believing Calais could be taken quickly, Edward demanded the town's surrender. When the citizens refused, the king laid siege on 4 September. PHILIP VI quickly began gathering relief forces, but, thanks to the loss of confidence engendered by Crécy, found himself unable to raise either money or troops. Edward, meanwhile, was enabled to undertake what ultimately became one of the longest and costliest campaigns of the HUNDRED YEARS WAR by a wave of public support stemming from his victory. Regular cross-Channel convoys of men and supplies were quickly established and within weeks Edward had over twelve thousand men in the rapidly growing siege works outside Calais. However, the success of French convoys in carrying supplies into the port prolonged the town's resistance and forced the English, much to the dismay of Edward's men, to continue the siege through the winter, a most unusual occurrence in medieval warfare.

The town contained a strong garrison commanded by Jean de Vienne, but in April 1347 the English completed their encirclement of the port, thereby ending any hope of further resupply by sea. English victories elsewhere, including over France's ally DAVID II of SCOTLAND at the Battle of NEVILLE'S CROSS in October 1346, and over France's client in the BRETON CIVIL WAR, CHARLES OF BLOIS, at the Battle of LA ROCHE-DERRIEN in June 1347, sapped the willingness of the French nobility to fight for the VALOIS. Although Philip took the ORIFLAMME from St.-Denis in March, intending to have an army at Calais by the end of April, it was not until July that he had sufficient forces to engage the English. On 27 July, Philip brought an army of twenty thousand to within six miles of Calais. Before the town, he found English forces numbering over thirty-two thousand and allied Flemish contingents numbering almost twenty thousand. Reconnaissance patrols showed that the swampy ground was not suited to cavalry and all possible approaches to the town were heavily guarded. Philip concluded that relieving Calais was impossible, but he held his position for several days to pursue negotiation. When none of the French proposals proved acceptable to Edward, Philip abandoned his camp and the town surrendered the next day, 3 August.

Angered by the length and cost of the siege, Edward declared that all lives and property within Calais were at his disposal, a harshness that shocked his nobles and councilors. After much entreaty, they persuaded him to spare the lives of the garrison and citizens, although Edward demanded that six of the wealthiest burgesses appear before him wearing halters and bearing the keys of the town. In one of the most famous episodes of the war, Edward's wife, Queen PHILIPPA, interceded for the captives and convinced the king to rescind his order for their immediate execution. Nonetheless, Edward expelled most of Calais's inhabitants and repopulated the town with Englishmen. In September, Edward, financially exhausted by the siege, concluded the Truce of CALAIS with the French. Later an important entrepôt for English trade, Calais came to be considered English soil and key to the realm's defense. The town remained English until 1558, well beyond the end of the war.

Further Reading: DeVries, Kelly. ''Hunger, Flemish Participation and the Flight of Philip VI: Contemporary Accounts of the Siege of Calais, 1346–47.'' *Studies in Medieval and Renaissance History* 12 (1991): 129–81; Perroy, Edouard. *The Hundred Years War.* Trans. W. B. Wells. New York: Capricorn Books, 1965; Sumption, Jonathan. *The Hundred Years War.* Vol. 1, *Trial by Battle.* Philadelphia: University of Pennsylvania Press, 1999.

CALAIS, TREATY OF. *See* BRÉTIGNY, TREATY OF

CALAIS, TRUCE OF (1347)

Concluded on 28 September 1347, the Anglo-French Truce of Calais was the first of a series of truces that limited fighting until 1355. Although mutual financial exhaustion provided the initial impetus for a truce, the onset of the BLACK DEATH was largely responsible for its repeated extension.

Like the earlier Truce of MALESTROIT, the Truce of Calais was mediated by representatives of Pope CLEMENT VI. Although eager to continue the war after his victories at CRÉCY and the siege of CALAIS, EDWARD III found himself unable to fund new campaigns or even to pay the men already under arms. PHILIP VI faced a depletion of both money and morale; the recent defeats bred an unwillingness to join royal armies or pay royal taxes. As a result, both monarchs agreed to a truce to last until 8 July 1348.

Under the agreement, each side maintained its present positions, terms which favored the English, who retained Calais and held the upper hand in BRITTANY, GASCONY, and SCOTLAND. Each king also swore not to threaten or intrigue with the other's allies during the truce period.

When the Estates-General convened in PARIS on 30 November, members condemned the truce as a shameful capitulation and demanded that a large army be raised in 1348 to undertake an invasion of England. French preparations were well underway in May, when Edward proposed extending the truce. Since he was having difficulty raising money for a new campaign, the continuing cessation of hostilities suited him. Philip, buoyed by a general willingness to support the invasion plan, rejected the proposal and the truce lapsed. However, by August, the Black Death, which had been ravaging southern France since the winter, struck Paris; by November, the plague was in LONDON, and military plans in both kingdoms ground to a halt. The truce was therefore renewed in November 1348 and in the following year was extended to May 1350.

However, neither truce nor plague ended the fighting in the southwest, where local garrison commanders attacked each other and recently discharged English troops, now turned to brigandage, seized French strongholds (see ROUTIERS). Angered by these losses, the French repudiated the truce in August 1349, and the war in Gascony resumed its course. On 13 June 1350, the two governments renewed the truce until August 1351. But when Philip died on 22 August 1350, the new French king, JOHN II, repudiated his father's agreement, and war resumed in the southwest, with the Battle of SAINTES occurring in April 1351. At sea, the truce was never effective, and the English engaged a Castilian fleet at the Battle of WINCHELSEA in late August 1350. In Brittany, the fighting also continued, neither Crown being able to effectively control its clients in the BRETON CIVIL WAR.

However, the aftereffects of plague and continuing financial weakness convinced both monarchs to renew the truce for one year on 11 September 1351; the agreement largely held in the north, but fighting continued in the southwest. Despite frequent breaches of the peace in Brittany and Gascony, the truce was extended again in March 1353 and once more in the following December. On 6 April 1354, as part of the newly concluded Treaty of GUINES, the truce was extended to 1 April 1355. But by that date, the French had repudiated the treaty and both kingdoms were preparing for full-scale resumption of war. Any possibility of continuing the series of truces ended in May 1355, when John retrieved the ORIFLAMME from Saint-Denis and proclaimed the ARRIÈRE-BAN to summon a new army for operations against the English. *See also* ESTATES, GENERAL AND PROVINCIAL.

Further Reading: Barber, Richard. *Edward, Prince of Wales and Aquitaine.* New York: Charles Scribner's Sons, 1978; Sumption, Jonathan. *The Hundred Years War.* Vol. 2, *Trial by Fire.* Philadelphia: University of Pennsylvania Press, 2001.

CALVELEY, SIR HUGH (d. 1394)

Sir Hugh Calveley was one of the most prominent English captains and ROUTIER leaders of the HUNDRED YEARS WAR. Serving on the Continent for almost forty years, he was particularly active in BRITTANY during the BRETON CIVIL WAR and in Spain during the CASTILIAN WAR OF SUCCESSION.

Born into a Cheshire gentry family, Calveley was closely associated with his fellow Cheshire captain, Sir Robert KNOLLES, who is often portrayed as his close kinsman, although no familial relationship can be proven. Calveley's military career began in Brittany, where he fought under the English lieutenant, Sir Thomas DAGWORTH, at the Battle of LA ROCHE-DERRIEN in 1347. In 1351, he and Knolles were among the English knights who participated in the famous COMBAT OF THE THIRTY, which ended with their capture. In 1354, Calveley was captured again at Bécherel, a Breton town under his command. He fought for EDWARD, THE BLACK PRINCE, at POITIERS in 1356, but thereafter took service with CHARLES THE

BAD, king of Navarre, for whom he commanded a large company in NORMANDY and central France in 1358–59.

Following conclusion of the Treaty of BRÉTIGNY in 1360, Calveley led his own band of *routiers*, capturing Bertrand du GUESCLIN at Juigné-sur-Sarthe in about 1360 and fighting for Pedro the Cruel of Castile in a campaign against the Moors in 1362. By 1364, he was back in Brittany, where he fought for JOHN IV at AURAY. In 1365, Calveley joined the *routier* army that du Guesclin was recruiting for service in Spain. Since the ultimate aim of this French-backed expedition was the replacement of Pedro the Cruel with his pro-French half brother Henry of Trastámare, EDWARD III ordered Calveley and all other English captains to keep English soldiers out of Spain. This order arrived too late to prevent Calveley from contracting to provide troops for the campaign in return for wages and an interest in the territorial grants promised to du Guesclin by Trastamare and Pedro IV of Aragon. Although the contract allowed him to withdraw if the English actively intervened in the Castilian war, Calveley commanded a company of a thousand men in the campaign that placed Trastámare on the Castilian throne.

In 1367, Calveley returned to AQUITAINE and joined the Anglo-Gascon army that the Black Prince was recruiting to restore Pedro, an objective that was accomplished at NÁJERA on 3 April. In 1368, Calveley married an Aragonese lady who brought him lands and wealth in that kingdom. However, if his intention was to settle in Spain, his plans changed in 1369, when the Black Prince recalled him to Aquitaine to lead raids into Armagnac and the lordship of ALBRET. In 1370, Calveley joined the CHEVAUCHÉE led by Knolles, and, in 1371, he was retained by JOHN OF GAUNT, duke of Lancaster, whom he accompanied on the great CHEVAUCHÉE OF 1373. In 1374, when LOUIS, DUKE OF ANJOU, besieged La Réole in GASCONY, Calveley vigorously but unsuccessfully defended the town. In 1375, Calveley returned to England, where he was appointed captain of CALAIS and admiral of the western fleet. Over the next decade, he participated in several naval campaigns and oversaw English coastal defenses during the invasion scare of 1385–86; his last major expedition was the *chevauchée* led by THOMAS OF WOODSTOCK, earl of Buckingham, in 1380. Calveley died on 23 April 1394.

Further Reading: Sumption, Jonathan. *The Hundred Years War*. Vol. 2, *Trial by Fire*. Philadelphia: University of Pennsylvania Press, 2001.

CAMBRAI, SIEGE OF. *See* THIÉRACHE CAMPAIGN

CAMPAIGN OF 1339. *See* THIÉRACHE CAMPAIGN

CANTERBURY, ARCHBISHOP OF. *See* STRATFORD, JOHN, ARCHBISHOP OF CANTERBURY

CANTERBURY, TREATY OF (1416)

Concluded on 15 August 1416, the Treaty of Canterbury created an alliance between HENRY V and Holy Roman Emperor Sigismund (1368–1437). For Henry, the treaty meant acceptance by a major European ruler of the Lancastrian right to the French Crown and recognition of the justice of Henry's war against France, as well as the promise of Imperial assistance in prosecuting that war.

In 1414, Sigismund helped convene the Council of Constance to heal the schism in the Church. Since 1378, two lines of popes had claimed the obedience of different national churches, with politics generally determining which countries gave allegiance to which popes. Convinced that Anglo-French hostility was a major obstacle to ecclesiastical unity, the emperor came west in 1416 to reconcile the two kingdoms. In Paris, he found the ARMAGNAC-controlled government divided, with BERNARD, COUNT OF ARMAGNAC, determined to maintain the blockade of HARFLEUR and deny the English a base in NORMANDY.

Rebuffed by the French, Sigismund sailed to England in May, where Henry provided him with every comfort and courtesy, making him a knight of the GARTER, awarding him the Lancastrian S.S. collar, and arranging for him to witness a session of PARLIAMENT. Although Henry impressed upon his guest the righteousness of his cause and the duplicity of the French, Sigismund continued to work for a peace settlement. However, in July, Armagnac, embarrassed by his recent defeat at VALMONT and believing that truce talks were merely a device to save Harfleur, convinced the French government to refuse reception of an English embassy. This decision persuaded Sigismund to conclude an alliance with Henry.

The Treaty of Canterbury, which was signed on the same day the English victory at the Battle of the SEINE relieved Harfleur, pledged each signatory to support the other in recovering by any means necessary any rights or territories currently withheld by the French. Subjects of one ruler were also given free access to the lands and trade of the other, and neither side was to shelter the traitors or rebels of the other. A perpetual agreement that also bound the emperor to Henry's heirs, the treaty completed the encirclement of France that English diplomacy had sought and bound the allies to assist one another against attack from any quarter, saving only the pope.

Although Henry now viewed the emperor as committed to the English cause, Sigismund still saw himself as a mediator and his main interests remained the Council of Constance and the cementing of his authority in his kingdom of Bohemia, both of which absorbed his attention and his political and financial resources. As a result, Imperial military assistance never materialized and the subsequent English abandonment of Sigismund's policies at Constance made the Treaty of Canterbury a dead letter before the end of Henry's reign.

Further Reading: Allmand, Christopher. *Henry V*. New Haven, CT: Yale University Press, 1997; Jacob, E. F. *The Fifteenth Century, 1399–1485*. Oxford: Oxford University Press, 1993.

CAOURS, RAOUL LE. *See* BENTLEY, SIR WALTER; BRETON CIVIL WAR; DAGWORTH, SIR THOMAS

CAPET, HOUSE OF

The House of Capet was the ruling dynasty of France from 987 to 1328, although the kings of the succeeding House of VALOIS and all later monarchs down to the French Revolution were descendents in the male line of the first Capetian king. Initially little more than rulers of PARIS and its environs, the Capetians gradually expanded their territory and succeeded in enforcing their suzerainty over their vassals. This process brought the later Capetians into conflict with the House of PLANTAGENET, the royal dynasty of England since 1154, and, as lords of various territories in western France, vassals of the French Crown. Because the English kings found this feudal subordination to be incompatible with their status as sovereign monarchs, Capetian overlordship of the Plantagenet provinces became a root cause of the HUNDRED YEARS WAR.

Although the term "Capetian" first came into use during the French Revolution, the name "Capet," meaning cap or cape, had been applied to Hugh, the founder of the dynasty, since the thirteenth century. Hugh Capet and his immediate successors exercised little authority outside Paris, but the dynasty enjoyed important advantages over all other ducal and comital families and thus gradually made effective its claim to overlordship. First, the Capetians were seen as heirs of Charlemagne and the Carolingian kings, and thus attained a sacred aura that prevented any other family from claiming royal authority after the tenth century. In the eleventh century, Robert II extended this quasi-religious status by claiming the ability to heal by his touch the disease scrofula, which became known as "the king's evil." Second, the Capetians produced a male heir to the Crown in every generation for over three hundred years. Until the twelfth century, the dynasty practiced anticipatory succession—crowning eldest sons before the deaths of their fathers. Third, several Capetians had only one son, thus eliminating the kinds of sibling quarrels that disrupted twelfth-century England. The Capetians always passed the original family patrimony intact to the eldest son, finding endowments for younger brothers in newly acquired lands or through advantageous marriages. This practice established cadet branches of the family in important provinces and became the basis of the APPANAGE system, which developed in the thirteenth century.

In the early twelfth century, Louis VI married his son, the future Louis VII, to Eleanor, heiress of the duchy of AQUITAINE. However, Capetian control of Aquitaine ended in 1152, when Eleanor divorced Louis and married Henry, count of Anjou, who became Henry II, the first Plantagenet king of England, in 1154. Although the other French territories held in virtual sovereignty by Henry, including NORMANDY, Maine, and Anjou, were conquered and annexed to the French Crown by Louis's son, Philip II, in the early thirteenth century, GASCONY, the southern portion of Aquitaine, remained under English control. In 1259, Philip's grandson, Louis IX (St. Louis), regularized the status of Gascony by signing the Treaty of PARIS, which recognized Henry III of England as duke of Aquitaine in return for Henry's renunciation of all other former Plantagenet provinces. This formal subordination of the Plantagenet king-dukes to the Capetians, and the growing tendency of the royal bureaucracy to interfere in the administration of the great feudal territories, caused numerous jurisdictional disputes in Aquitaine and led to the ANGLO-FRENCH WAR OF 1294–1303 and the War of SAINT-SARDOS in the 1320s. Because the former was settled in part by arrangement of a marriage between Isabella, the daughter of PHILIP IV of France (see ISABELLA, QUEEN OF ENGLAND [c. 1292–1358]), and Edward (see EDWARD II), the son of EDWARD I of England, their son EDWARD III, who assumed the English Crown in 1327, had a strong claim to the Capetian throne. When the direct Capetian line ended with the death of CHARLES IV in 1328, Edward's claim was set aside in favor of Philip, count of Valois, who, as eldest nephew of Philip IV, was the Capetian heir in the male line. As PHILIP VI, the count became first king of the House of Valois. In his reign, the continuing dispute over Aquitaine and the Plantagenet claim to be rightful heirs of the House of Capet became the underlying causes of the Hundred Years War.

Further Reading: Dunbabin, Jean. *France in the Making, 843–1180.* Oxford: Oxford University Press, 1985; Fawtier, Robert. *The Capetian Kings of France: Monarchy and Nation, 987–1328.* Trans. Lionel Butler and R. J. Adam. New York: St. Martin's Press, 1960; Hallam, Elizabeth M. *Capetian France, 987–1328.* London: Longman, 1980.

CASSEL, BATTLE OF. *See* FLANDERS; LOUIS DE NEVERS, COUNT OF FLANDERS

CASTILE
See CASTILIAN WAR OF SUCCESSION; JOHN OF GAUNT, DUKE OF LANCASTER

CASTILIAN WAR OF SUCCESSION (1362–1369)

Occurring during the nominal peace created by the Treaty of BRÉTIGNY, the disputed succession in the central Spanish kingdom of Castile provided the French and English Crowns with an opportunity to strike indirectly at each other's interests. War in Spain also offered the governments of France and AQUITAINE a way to employ the bands of ROUTIERS ravaging their territories.

On the death of Alfonso XI in 1350, the Castilian Crown passed to his son, Pedro I (1334–69), who quickly acquired the epithet "the Cruel" by executing his father's mistress, Leonor de Guzman. Leonor was the mother of ten children by the late king, and her death drove her eldest son, Henry of Trastámare (1333–79), to declare himself king and raise an unsuccessful rebellion against his half brother. Although Henry fled Castile, Pedro revived his rival's cause by executing several of Henry's brothers and by quarreling with the Castilian Church, actions which won Henry support from the pope and the king of Aragon. In 1361, the mysterious death of Pedro's French queen, Blanche of Bourbon, soured Castilian relations with France, where Pedro was suspected of poisoning his wife.

Fearful of the coalition building against him, Pedro sought an alliance with EDWARD III's son, EDWARD, THE BLACK PRINCE, the ruler of English Aquitaine. To honor the Brétigny settlement, the prince agreed to provide military assistance solely as duke of Aquitaine and not as a representative of the English Crown. Besides a large sum of money, Pedro offered the prince a Castilian dukedom, tax exemptions for English merchants, and the hereditary right to lead armies into Castile. Henry, meanwhile, concluded a similar agreement with LOUIS, DUKE OF ANJOU, the brother of CHARLES V and king's lieutenant in Languedoc. Largely comprised of *routier* bands from southern France, an army bearing the flag of Castile but led by the French constable Bertrand du GUESCLIN entered Castile in late 1365. Pedro immediately appealed to the prince, but the king's support quickly dissolved and by April 1366 Pedro was in exile in Aquitaine and his rival was king of Castile as Henry II.

Although opposed by many of his advisors, the prince honored his agreement with Pedro and led an Anglo-Gascon army into Spain. After Edward's attempts at mediation failed, the two sides met on 3 April 1367 at NÁJERA, where the prince won a major victory. Although Pedro was restored to power, his half brother eluded capture and immediately renewed his alliance with Anjou, who hoped a friendly Castile would assist the French reconquest of Aquitaine. Unable to raise the money he owed, Pedro soon quarreled with the prince, who, ill and despairing of payment, withdrew to Aquitaine. With the increasingly open assistance of France, Henry of Trastámare launched a second invasion that concluded with Pedro's death after the battle of Montiel in March 1369. Firmly allied with France, the new Castilian regime thereafter provided valuable naval support for French campaigns against Aquitaine and England. *See also* LA ROCHELLE, BATTLE OF.

Further Reading: Harvey, John. *The Black Prince and His Age.* London: Rowman and Littlefield, 1976; Hillgarth, J. N. *The Spanish Kingdoms, 1250–1516.* 2 vols. Oxford: Oxford University

Press, 1976–78; O'Callaghan, James F. *A History of Medieval Spain*. Ithaca, NY: Cornell University Press, 1992; Russell, P. E. *The English Intervention in Spain and Portugal in the Time of Edward III and Richard II*. Oxford: Oxford University Press, 1955.

CASTILLON, BATTLE OF (1453)

Fought on 17 July 1453 near the town of Castillon in eastern GASCONY, the Battle of Castillon ended the HUNDRED YEARS WAR and stripped the English of all French holdings except the town of CALAIS.

After the French conquest of NORMANDY in 1450, CHARLES VII focused his military resources on Gascony, the last English-held province in France. As an army of seven thousand entered the province, other French forces besieged the fortresses protecting BORDEAUX, the Gascon capital, while a joint French, Spanish, and Breton fleet blockaded the mouth of the Gironde to prevent the English from relieving the city. Isolated and outnumbered, the English garrison in Bordeaux surrendered on 30 June 1451. A severe blow to English national pride, the loss of Bordeaux was reversed in 1452, thanks to the English sympathies of the Gascon people and the military skill of John TALBOT, earl of Shrewsbury, who led an army of three thousand ashore on 17 October. Within months of reentering Bordeaux on 23 October, Shrewsbury had largely restored Gascony to English control.

Respected and feared in France, Shrewsbury was the most famous English commander of the war's last decades. By the summer of 1453, three French armies were converging on Gascony. Although reinforcements brought by his son raised his strength to over five thousand, Shrewsbury was still heavily outnumbered by the combined French forces, and his only option was to wait in Bordeaux until an opportunity arose to fall upon one army before the others could support it. However, when a French force of nine thousand laid siege to Castillon about thirty miles east of Bordeaux, Shrewsbury, against his better judgment, yielded to the pleas of representatives from both Castillon and Bordeaux and marched to the relief of the town on 16 July.

Early next morning, Shrewsbury arrived at Castillon with his mounted contingents, and led an immediate and successful assault on the French ARCHERS holding the Priory of St. Laurent. The surviving archers fled to the fortified French camp east of the priory, thereby alerting the main army of Shrewsbury's arrival. Although the French army was commanded by committee, the camp and been laid out by Charles VII's ordinance officer, Jean BUREAU. Designed to maximize the opportunity for oblique and enfilading fire from the French ARTILLERY, which may have numbered almost three hundred guns of all sizes, Bureau's camp was protected on three sides by a ditch and palisaded rampart and on the fourth side by the steep bank of the River Lidoire.

Upon receiving reports that the enemy was retreating, Shrewsbury reversed an earlier decision to wait for the rest of his army to arrive and attacked immediately with the twelve hundred men he had at hand. The reports proved inaccurate, and when the French guns opened fire, the dismounted English suffered severe casualties. Shrewsbury, who wore no ARMOR to honor the pledge he had made when last released from French custody, pressed the attack, believing the arrival of his remaining troops would secure victory. However, as reinforcements came up, they suffered the same fate as the initial attackers, and the eventual arrival of French reserves broke the English attack and sent the survivors streaming back to Bordeaux.

With both Shrewsbury and his son dead on the field, the English position in Gascony quickly collapsed and the French entered Bordeaux to stay on 19 October 1453. After three hundred years, English rule in Gascony, like the Hundred Years War itself, was over. In England, news of the battle may have triggered HENRY VI's mental collapse, for the king's illness descended upon him in early August, about the time he would have learned of the disaster.

Further Reading: Pollard, A. J. *John Talbot and the War in France, 1427–1453*. London: Royal Historical Society, 1983.

CASUALTIES

As with the overall size of armies during the HUNDRED YEARS WAR, casualty figures, even for major battles, are difficult to calculate and often seriously inflated by contemporary commentators. Also, most contemporary tallies of men killed took account only of noble and knightly dead; slain ARCHERS and infantrymen were rarely counted.

The size of the armies involved and the increasing bitterness engendered between the two peoples by the long conflict led to a sharp rise in casualty levels during the war, especially when compared to European battles of the previous two centuries. Contemporary casualty figures for twelfth- and thirteenth-century battles were usually small. Orderic Vitalis claimed that only three knights were slain at Brémule in 1119, while only one French lord died at Lincoln in 1217. Even at the vicious Battle of Evesham in 1265, when Prince Edward's men mutilated the body of Simon de Montfort, earl of Leicester, only about thirty knights were killed, and the deaths of sixteen knights and many common soldiers in Anglesey in 1282 during EDWARD I's Welsh war were considered shocking losses. With such figures common before the Anglo-French war, counting the thousands who lay dead on the field after one of the war's major encounters must have been difficult, and the temptation to exaggerate great. At CRÉCY in 1346, EDWARD III ordered Sir Reginald Cobham to organize the heralds (who could recognize coats of arms) and make a careful tally of dead knights and nobles. So long and difficult was their task that the spot on the battlefield where they worked is still known as the "valley of the clerks." Cobham's clerks counted 1,542 French dead, although contemporary chroniclers offered much different figures. JEAN LE BEL put the French losses at 12,000 knights and over 15,000 others, but claimed that the English lost only three knights. Although Geoffrey le Baker's number—4,000 knightly dead—seems more realistic, one modern historian, by reckoning three kills for every English archer, estimates the total French dead at over 10,000.

It might be expected that as RANSOM amounts rose during the course of the war, the emphasis placed on capturing men for profit would reduce casualties among the warrior class; however, this does not appear to be the case. In 1356 at POITIERS, which degenerated into a mad scramble for prisoners after the capture of JOHN II, the official English tally of enemy dead was 2,345, with casualties among ordinary foot soldiers uncounted. One modern historian estimates that the French lost 40 percent of their cavalry at both Poitiers and AGINCOURT. The latter battle was particularly bloody, with HENRY V's chaplain putting the French dead at almost 100 nobles and up to 6,500 knights and other gentlemen. Some modern estimates put the number of French dead at Agincourt near 10,000. Support is given to these figures by the fact that five grave pits containing over 1,200 men each were dug near Agincourt field. As to English dead, the chaplain numbered them at less than twenty, with the king's cousin, Edward, duke of York, being the most prominent. No effort was made to count the number of English archers and common infantrymen who were slain.

Part of the reason for these high figures may be that at most major engagements, such as Crécy, Poitiers, and Agincourt, the victorious English found themselves heavily outnumbered and thus were less willing to give quarter than they might have been had their numbers been larger. At Agincourt, the process of rounding up prisoners was well underway when the French threatened a new assault. Faced with the possibility of many abandoned French prisoners regrouping and attacking his men from the rear, Henry V ordered no quarter, and a large but unknown number of captives had their throats cut before the new French attack dissolved. At VERNEUIL in 1424, the large Scottish contingent in the dauphinist army was virtually annihilated because the Scottish leaders, Archibald DOUGLAS, earl of Douglas, and John STEWART, earl of Buchan, informed JOHN, DUKE OF BEDFORD, that they would neither give nor expect quarter. Thus, while many smaller battles, sieges, and skirmishes, especially in GASCONY and in BRITTANY during the BRETON CIVIL WAR, saw small numbers engaged and few killed, casualties in the great battles numbered in the thousands, far beyond the figures seen in such earlier conflicts as the ANGLO-FRENCH WAR OF 1294–1303, the War of SAINT-SARDOS, and the English wars in Wales and SCOTLAND. *See also* ARMIES, COMPOSITION OF; ARMIES, SIZE OF.

Further Reading: Burne, Alfred H. *The Agincourt War*. Ware, England: Wordsworth Editions Ltd., 1999; Burne, Alfred H. *The Crécy War*. Ware, England: Wordsworth Editions Ltd., 1999; Prestwich, Michael. *Armies and Warfare in the Middle Ages: The English Experience*. New Haven, CT: Yale University Press, 1996.

CATHERINE OF VALOIS, QUEEN OF ENGLAND (1401–1437)

The youngest daughter of CHARLES VI, Catherine of VALOIS became, as part of the Treaty of TROYES, the wife of HENRY V. Through her children born of a later liaison with one of her household officers, the widowed queen also became an ancestor of the royal House of Tudor.

HENRY IV tried several times to arrange a marriage for his eldest son with a daughter of Charles VI. Negotiations focusing on Catherine opened in 1413 and continued until 1415, when Henry V, king since 1413, collapsed the talks by demanding a dowry of two million crowns and the surrender of most of western France. By 1419, Henry had conquered NORMANDY, and the French, still distracted by civil war, were eager to reopen negotiations. Concluded in 1420, the Treaty of Troyes made Henry regent of France during Charles's lifetime and arranged a marriage between Henry and Catherine, who had charmed her prospective husband during a meeting set up by Catherine's mother, Queen ISABEAU. Betrothed on 21 May and married at Troyes on 2 June 1420, Catherine accompanied her husband to England in February 1421. The new queen was crowned at Westminster on 24 February and went on progress with the king later

that year. On 6 December 1421, Catherine gave birth to the future HENRY VI at Windsor. In the following spring, she returned to France with her husband and was at Senlis with her parents when Henry died on 31 August 1422.

Returning to England, Catherine lived for a time with her son at Windsor. In 1424, she took up residence at Baynard's Castle, which had been granted to her by PARLIAMENT. In response to rumors that the young widow might marry, and fearful of the influence a stepfather might have on the boy king, the council, led by the king's uncle HUMPHREY, DUKE OF GLOUCESTER, persuaded Parliament to enact a statute prohibiting anyone from marrying the queen dowager without the consent of the king and his council. Since the king's consent could not be given until he reached full age, Catherine was effectively barred from remarrying for almost a decade. However, by about 1429, Catherine became sexually involved with Owen Tudor, a minor Welsh gentleman who was master of the queen's wardrobe. The couple may have secretly married in 1430 when Catherine became pregnant, although this is uncertain. She eventually bore Tudor four children. Edmund, the eldest, and Jasper, the second brother, were raised to the English peerage by Henry VI, becoming the earls of Richmond and Pembroke, respectively. Owen became a monk at Westminster and the daughter, Tacina, married Lord Grey de Wilton.

Catherine retired to Bermondsy Abbey in 1436, dying there on 3 January 1437 after a long but unknown illness. Although briefly imprisoned, Tudor was eventually taken into royal favor and lived the life of an English gentleman until his execution by the Yorkists following the Battle of Mortimer's Cross in 1461. By his marriage to Margaret Beaufort, daughter of John BEAUFORT, duke of Somerset, the king's cousin, Catherine's son Edmund became the father of Henry Tudor, earl of Richmond, who was born posthumously in 1457. In 1485, Richmond became Henry VII, first king of the House of Tudor. *See also* FRENCH CIVIL WAR.

Further Reading: Allmand, Christopher. *Henry V.* New Haven, CT: Yale University Press, 1997; Griffiths, Ralph A., and Roger S. Thomas. *The Making of the Tudor Dynasty.* New York: St. Martin's Press, 1985; Wolffe, Bertram. *Henry VI.* London: Eyre Methuen, 1981.

CAUCHON, PIERRE. *See* JOAN OF ARC

CAVALRY. *See* ARMIES, COMPOSITION OF

CERVOLE, ARNAUD DE (c. 1320–1366)

Arnaud de Cervole, known as "the Archpriest," was the creator of the GREAT COMPANY and one of the most feared *ROUTIER* captains of the HUNDRED YEARS WAR.

The younger son of minor Périgord nobility, Cervole joined the clergy, becoming archpriest of Vélines, the position from which his later sobriquet derived. Eschewing his clerical duties for the company of brigands, Cervole soon showed himself to be more suited to warfare than to the Church, which eventually deprived him of all his benefices. His first recorded military action, undertaken in VALOIS service, was the capture of the Gascon fortress of Montravel in April 1351. An associate of the French constable, Charles of Spain, Cervole received the lordship of Chateauneuf-sur-Charente and served as king's lieutenant in the region between the Dordogne and Loire Rivers. After the constable's murder by henchmen of CHARLES THE BAD, king of Navarre, in 1354, Cervole raised his own company of men and undertook military operations on his own account, seizing three castles in Angoulême and, later, while serving under JOHN II at the siege of Breteuil, another fortress in NORMANDY.

In September 1356, Cervole was captured by the English at POITIERS. In March 1357, Cervole, who had acquired several lordships in the region through marriage to a rich widow, was named in the Truce of BORDEAUX as one of the French conservators for Berry. Upon regaining his freedom, Cervole became the first *routier* leader to understand the opportunities for enrichment offered to men of arms by the capture of the king at Poitiers and the resulting breakdown of French royal authority. From the bands of Gascon freebooters left unemployed after Poitiers, Cervole formed the Great Company, the name given to a succession of large *routier* armies that terrorized Provence and southern France after 1357. The ease with which Cervole and his brigands gathered plunder and RANSOMS soon encouraged other *routier* leaders to follow the Archpriest's example.

Beginning in July 1357, Cervole led his army, which eventually numbered almost three thousand men, down the Rhône to Provence, where the *routiers* maintained themselves through pillage and extortion. The Great Company even threatened Marseille, but the town proved too strong and in April 1358 Cervole departed for the north, where revolutionary disorders in PARIS and the intrigues of Charles of Navarre seemed to promise easier pickings. Although the Great Company began to disband, many *routiers* were still active in Provence and the vicinity of Avignon when Cervole returned in September 1358 to strike a bargain with Pope Innocent VI. In return for withdrawing the companies from Provence and restoring all captured papal properties, Cervole received a payment of 20,000 gold florins. From 1358 to 1361, Cervole was in the pay of LOUIS DE MÂLE, count of FLANDERS, who commissioned the *routier* leader to defend Berry and the Nivernais from other brigands, an unfortunate decision that left both provinces open to the depredations of *routier* bands.

In 1362, Cervole fought for the Crown against the Great Company at the Battle of BRIGNAIS, where he was captured, and, in 1364, he served under Bertrand du GUESCLIN in the royal army that defeated the forces of Charles of Navarre at COCHEREL. In 1365, the Archpriest received payment to lead remnants of the Great Company out of eastern France and into the Holy Roman Empire, where it was hoped most would join a crusade against the Turks. However, delays in arranging passage and payment made his men restive, and, on 25 May 1366, Cervole was killed while arguing with some malcontents.

Further Reading: Sumption, Jonathan. *The Hundred Years War.* Vol. 2, *Trial by Fire.* Philadelphia: University of Pennsylvania Press, 2001.

C'EST ASSAVOIR. See BRÉTIGNY, TREATY OF

CHANDOS, SIR JOHN (d. 1370)

A friend and comrade-in-arms of EDWARD, THE BLACK PRINCE, Sir John Chandos, like Sir Thomas DAGWORTH and Sir Robert KNOLLES, was among the circle of well-known and respected nonnoble commanders who served EDWARD III during the first decades of the HUNDRED YEARS WAR. For his wartime exploits, Chandos, like Walter MAUNY, earned a European reputation for CHIVALRY and valor.

The son of Sir Edward Chandos, a knight of Derbyshire, Chandos traced his ancestry back to a companion of William the Conqueror. Chandos participated in many of the major campaigns of the fourteenth century. He is first mentioned at the siege of Cambrai in 1337, distinguished himself at the Battles of CRÉCY in 1346 and WINCHELSEA in 1350, and took a prominent part in the prince's CHEVAUCHÉE to the Mediterranean in 1355 and the RHEIMS CAMPAIGN of 1359–60. At POITIERS in 1356, Chandos fought alongside the prince, whom he advised during the battle, a service for which he received a substantial annuity and the Lincolnshire manor of Kirkton. In 1360, Chandos was a member of the English commission that negotiated the Treaty of BRÉTIGNY and, as constable of Guienne from 1362, helped oversee the transfer of lands called for in the agreement.

He was one of the prince's closest advisors in the government of AQUITAINE until 1364, when Chandos took command of the English-backed Montfortist forces in BRITTANY. In October, he won the Battle of AURAY, where John de Montfort's rival, CHARLES OF BLOIS, was killed and the great pro-French captain, Bertrand du GUESCLIN, was captured. The battle ended the BRETON CIVIL WAR and made de Montfort duke as

JOHN IV, while du Guesclin's capture brought Chandos a huge RANSOM. Returning to Aquitaine, Chandos opposed the prince's plan to intervene in the CASTILIAN WAR OF SUCCESSION, but recruited large numbers of *ROUTIERS* from the GREAT COMPANY when the prince decided on the campaign. At the resulting battle of NÁJERA in April 1367, Chandos further distinguished himself by again capturing du Guesclin.

In May 1368, after failing to convince the prince to remit the highly unpopular hearth tax, Chandos retired to the estates in NORMANDY given to him by Edward III. However, the prince sorely missed his counsel and in December 1368 Chandos returned to Aquitaine at the prince's request. Named seneschal of Poitou in March 1369, Chandos vigorously defended the frontier of the duchy from renewed French incursions. Wounded while, typically, fighting in an avoidable skirmish against superior numbers, Chandos died on 1 January 1370. One of the founding members of the Order of the GARTER, Chandos had an unparalleled reputation for courage and gallantry, and his death was mourned even by his enemies, including du Guesclin and CHARLES V of France.

Chandos's officer of arms, the Chandos Herald, an unknown native of Hainault, wrote the French poem *La Vie du Prince Noir* (*Life of the Black Prince*) in about 1385. The work is an important source for the life and career of the prince as well as for the major English campaigns of the mid-fourteenth century. *See also CHEVAUCHÉE OF 1355.*

Further Reading: Barber, Richard. *Edward, Prince of Wales and Aquitaine.* New York: Charles Scribner's Sons, 1978; Harvey, John. *The Black Prince and His Age.* London: Rowman and Littlefield, 1976.

CHARLES, DUKE OF ORLÉANS (1394–1465)

The son of LOUIS, DUKE OF ORLÉANS, and a nephew of CHARLES VI, Charles of Orléans was leader of the ARMAGNAC faction and thus a central figure in the FRENCH CIVIL WAR. Considered largely ineffective as a politician, Orléans is today best remembered as a talented and prolific poet.

In June 1406, Charles, then eleven, married his cousin Isabella, the daughter of Charles VI and widow of RICHARD II of England (*see* ISABELLA, QUEEN OF ENGLAND [1388–1409]). Charles was only thirteen in November 1407 when his father was murdered by agents of JOHN THE FEARLESS, duke of BURGUNDY. The death of his mother, Valentine Visconti, in December 1408, left the fourteen-year-old boy as nominal head of his father's political faction, which, in the previous year, had been excluded from power by Burgundy and his supporters. To curb the growing violence between adherents of the two parties, the king ordered all royal princes, including Orléans and Burgundy, to participate in a ceremony of reconciliation at Chartres on 9 March 1409.

However, the Chartres agreement proved unworkable and, in April 1410, Orléans joined the League of Gien, an alliance of anti-Burgundian nobles that included JOHN, DUKE OF BERRY, Orléans's great-uncle, and JOHN V, duke of BRITTANY. Another member of the alliance, and, with Orléans, a driving force in its formation, was BERNARD, COUNT OF ARMAGNAC, who became the duke's father-in-law in 1410, when Orléans married his daughter Bonne, Duchess Isabella having died in September 1409. Because of the count's growing influence within the alliance and the escalating violence that his Gascon supporters perpetrated on its behalf, the Orléanist faction soon became known as the Armagnac party.

The Gien agreement created an army of nine thousand men to be used "for the good of the kingdom" (Vaughan, 82), which, in a September manifesto, the allies defined as rescuing the king and the dauphin (*see* LOUIS, DUKE OF GUIENNE) from Burgundy. Orléans led the alliance army on PARIS, but open war was avoided by the conclusion of the peace of Bicêtre in November 1410. In July 1411, Orléans, having superceded Berry as effective leader of the Armagnacs, reopened the struggle by sending a defiant letter to the king demanding punishment of his father's murderers.

In 1412, both factions sought military aid from England. In May, Orléans, with his Gien allies, signed the Treaty of BOURGES, whereby the Armagnac leaders, in return for such assistance, swore homage to HENRY IV and recognized him as ruler of AQUITAINE. Controlling both the royal army and royal person, Burgundy forced the Armagnacs to disavow the Bourges agreement. By the Treaty of BUZANÇAIS, concluded in November, Orléans and his allies bribed THOMAS, DUKE OF CLARENCE, leader of the English expedition, to withdraw. The settlement was guaranteed by the giving of hostages, who included Orléans's younger brother, John, count of Angoulême.

In 1413, Burgundy's high-handed rule and, in particular, his fomenting of the CABOCHIEN uprising in Paris turned the king and dauphin against him. The latter negotiated the peace of Pontoise with Orléans and his allies in July and, in late August, Burgundy, sensing his loss of support in the capital, fled Paris. On 1 September, Orléans and the Armagnac princes entered the city and took control of both king and government. In October 1415, the English captured Orléans at AGINCOURT. Unable to pay his RANSOM, the duke remained a prisoner in England for twenty-five years.

During most of the duke's captivity, his estates were administered by officials of the dauphin, Charles, who won the allegiance of Orléans's half brother, JOHN, COUNT OF DUNOIS, the leader, with JOAN OF ARC, of the 1429 campaign that drove the English from the town of Orléans and allowed the dauphin to be crowned as CHARLES VII. Ironically, the duke's freedom was finally secured by PHILIP THE GOOD, duke of Burgundy, the son of Orléans's old enemy. Seeking allies against Charles VII, Burgundy formed an alliance with the duke and arranged his marriage to a kinswoman, although Orléans took little part in politics after his release, preferring instead to preside over a court of poets at Blois. Orléans's son by his third wife became king of France as Louis XII in 1498. The duke died at Amboise on 4 January 1465.

Orléans wrote poetry all his life; the first poem attributed to him dates from about 1405, when he was ten. His surviving works include over 120 ballades, over 400 rondeaux, 4 carols, and almost 90 chansons. Many of his poems, such as the "Complainte de France" (1433), were written in England during his captivity, and about 125 of them are in English. Although traditionally dismissed as conventional and superficial, the last examples of medieval court poetry, the duke's poems have found more favor among modern literary scholars, who now consider Orléans a precursor of the romantic and symbolist poets of the nineteenth century.

Further Reading: Arn, Mary-Jo, ed. *Charles d'Orléans in England, 1415–1440.* Woodbridge, England: D. S. Brewer, 2000; Fein, David A. *Charles d'Orléans.* Boston: Twayne Publishers, 1983; Fox, John. *The Lyric Poetry of Charles d'Orléans.* Oxford: Clarendon, 1969; Goodrich, Norma Lorre. *Charles, Duke of Orleans: A Literary Biography.* New York: Macmillan, 1963; Steele, Robert, and Mabel Day. *The English Poems of Charles d'Orléans.* London: Oxford University Press, 1941; Vaughan, Richard. *John the Fearless.* London: Longman, 1979.

CHARLES IV, KING OF FRANCE (1294–1328)

Known as "the Fair," Charles IV was the last king of the House of CAPET. His death without male heirs threw the succession into doubt and left his nephew, EDWARD III of England, as one of the leading candidates for the French throne, a claim that was to complicate the history of the HUNDRED YEARS WAR.

The youngest son of PHILIP IV, Charles ascended the throne in January 1322 on the death of his brother, PHILIP V. Charles's supersession of his nieces, Philip's daughters, aroused no opposition, for Philip had himself taken the throne in 1317 by overriding the rights of another niece, the daughter of Philip IV's eldest son, LOUIS X. In February 1317, as confirmation of Philip's actions, an assembly of notables declared women incapable of succeeding to the throne of France.

Much influenced by his uncle, Charles, count of VALOIS, Charles took strong steps to improve his finances, employing such unpopular and questionable methods as selling offices, manipulating the coinage, and demanding payment to the Crown of debts owed to exiled Jews by Christian debtors. Charles also vigorously enforced obedience to his authority throughout the realm, dispatching an army to disaffected FLANDERS and making a long progress through the south after executing a rebellious southern noble, Count Jourdain de l'Isle.

Charles also reversed the more tolerant policy of his brothers toward EDWARD II of England, who, as duke of AQUITAINE, had been lax in recognizing the authority of his feudal suzerain, the king of France. In 1323, violence against royal officials arising from a dispute over a Gascon *BASTIDE* initiated the War of SAINT-SARDOS and led Charles to confiscate Aquitaine in July 1324. A campaign by Valois quickly overran the entire duchy except for BORDEAUX and a few other strongholds. In May 1325, Charles agreed to restore the duchy under a settlement proposed by his sister Isabella, the wife of Edward II (*see* ISABELLA, QUEEN OF ENGLAND [c. 1292–1358]), with whom she was increasingly at odds. Under Isabella's plan, Edward granted the duchy to his twelve-year-old son, Prince Edward, who joined his mother at the French court, where, on 24 September, he did homage to Charles for Aquitaine. This arrangement collapsed in January 1327, when Isabella and her lover Roger Mortimer deposed Edward and crowned her son as Edward III.

Charles died at Vincennes on 1 February 1328. Although he left no sons, his wife, Jeanne of Évreux, was pregnant, and an assembly of nobles vested the regency in the late king's cousin, Philip of Valois. When Jeanne gave birth to a girl on 1 April, Valois convened another assembly to decide between the two strongest claims to the throne, his own, and that of Charles's nephew, Edward III, whose claim came through his mother. The chief legal issue—whether or not a woman, who, under the 1317 decision, was herself barred from the throne, could pass her claim to her male heirs—carried less weight than practical considerations. The assembly rejected the young foreign prince dominated by his mother for the mature French prince already ruling the kingdom. Although Edward was to resurrect his claim when it suited his purposes, Valois was crowned as PHILIP VI in May. *See also* SALIC LAW OF SUCCESSION.

Further Reading: Brown, Elizabeth A. R. *The Monarchy of Capetian France and Royal Ceremonial.* London: Variorum, 1991; Jordan, William Chester. *The French Monarchy and the Jews from Philip Augustus to the Last Capetians.* Philadelphia: University of Pennsylvania Press, 1989.

CHARLES V, KING OF FRANCE (1338–1380)

Known as *le Sage*, ''the Wise,'' Charles V, the son of JOHN II, was the third VALOIS king of France. Because his reign, in stark contrast to those of his predecessor and successor, witnessed a strengthening of royal authority and the triumph of French arms, Charles has traditionally been considered the most able of the early Valois kings, an assessment that has been questioned by some modern historians.

In 1349, Charles, by acquiring Vienne from its last count, or dauphin, became the first heir to the French throne to bear the title ''dauphin.'' In 1355, Charles was implicated in the St. Cloud plot, which was hatched against his father by his kinsman, CHARLES THE BAD, king of Navarre. Although the extent of the dauphin's involvement is unclear, Charles appeared willing to countenance a significant limitation of John's authority, although likely not any harm to his person. The king uncovered the plot and regained his son's support by granting Charles the APPANAGE of NORMANDY and by paying off his debts. In September 1356, Charles was in nominal command of the first French division at POITIERS, where his retirement from the field following the repulse of his attack may have unwittingly initiated the withdrawal of the unengaged second division, a retreat that left the king's division unsup-

ported. John's subsequent capture thrust the inexperienced dauphin into the political arena, where, as regent for his father, he faced a host of crises, including Étienne MARCEL's PARIS revolution, the JACQUERIE uprising, growing noble defiance of royal authority, a severely disordered currency, the depredations of ROUTIERS, and the rebellion of Navarre. By 1359, Charles, through skill and good fortune, saw his position improve, as the nobility, alienated by Marcel's radicalism, the *Jacques'* violence, and Navarre's ambition, rallied to the Crown. In 1360, the failure of EDWARD III's RHEIMS CAMPAIGN, due mainly to bad weather and Charles's avoidance of pitched battle, forced the English king to conclude the Treaty of BRÉTIGNY on terms more favorable to the French.

During the four years between John's release in 1360 and his death in 1364, royal authority revived, as the Crown secured new and regular TAXATION that stabilized the currency, met the king's RANSOM payments, and rebuilt a royal army capable of suppressing *routiers* and defeating the English. Historians are divided on the question of who deserves the most credit for this recovery—Charles or his father. On 6 May 1364, one month after Charles's accession, a royal army defeated the forces of Navarre at COCHEREL, thereby ending his rebellion. The new king was unlike his father in that poor health and personal inclination prevented him from leading armies. An obscure chronic illness contracted in the late 1350s eventually left him unable to carry a weapon or ride a horse. Nonetheless, Charles possessed a keen mind and a shrewd judgment, which allowed him to choose capable advisors and to view political and military issues in clear and realistic terms. Despite these talents, Charles's favorable reputation rests in large part upon the writings of CHRISTINE DE PIZAN, who depicted him as an exceptionally wise and skilled ruler, a fact that has led some historians to attribute his successes more to luck and PROPAGANDA than to ability.

The heart of Charles's policy from the start of his reign was to avenge the defeats at

CRÉCY and Poitiers and to regain AQUITAINE and the other provinces lost to the PLANTAGENETS through the Brétigny agreement. To this end, Charles made his capable brother, LOUIS, DUKE OF ANJOU, royal lieutenant in Languedoc, where he arranged an ultimately successful French intervention in the CASTILIAN WAR OF SUCCESSION, thereby placing a pro-French king on the Castilian throne by 1369. Charles secured another important ally by convincing the pope to forbid a proposed marriage between MARGUERITE, the daughter of LOUIS DE MALE, count of FLANDERS, and EDMUND OF LANGLEY, a son of Edward III. In place of that match, which would have created a dangerous English appanage on France's northern frontier, he arranged for his brother, PHILIP THE BOLD, duke of BURGUNDY, to marry Marguerite, thus turning Flanders and, eventually, much of northwestern Europe, into a Valois appanage. Although the resulting state of Burgundy ultimately threatened the French Crown, it was in the short-term important in helping to overthrow the Brétigny settlement.

Charles also used money and DIPLOMACY to cultivate the Gascon nobility, thereby inducing key southwestern noblemen to ignore the treaty and appeal to the PARLEMENT against taxes imposed in Aquitaine by EDWARD, THE BLACK PRINCE. Accepted by Charles in 1369, this APPEAL OF THE GASCON LORDS restarted the HUNDRED YEARS WAR. Led by such experienced Breton warriors as Bertrand du GUESCLIN, whom Charles made constable, and Olivier de CLISSON, who promoted the policy of avoiding battle, the royal armies, now effectively paid and supplied, restored much of Aquitaine to French control by 1380. Despite this success, Charles, in 1378, made two misjudgments in foreign policy. He confiscated BRITTANY from Duke JOHN IV, thereby alienating the Breton nobility and losing their valuable military service, and he recognized the questionable election of Clement VII as pope, thereby initiating the great schism that split the Church for almost four decades. On his deathbed, Charles, who was a pious man

much concerned with the rightness of his actions, cancelled the *fouage* (hearth tax), which had financed his armies. Although this impolitic act eased the king's conscience, it created problems for his successor. Charles died on 16 September 1380 at the age of 42; he was succeeded by his son, CHARLES VI. *See also* MARMOUSETS.

Further Reading: Perroy, Edouard. *The Hundred Years War*. Trans. W. B. Wells. New York: Capricorn Books, 1965; Sumption, Jonathan. *The Hundred Years War*. Vol. 2, *Trial by Fire*. Philadelphia: University of Pennsylvania Press, 2001.

CHARLES VI, KING OF FRANCE (1368–1422)

Afflicted by recurring mental illness, Charles VI, the son of CHARLES V and fourth VALOIS king of France, presided over the near dissolution of his country and his dynasty. Unable to govern effectively, Charles was for much of his reign a mere figurehead, while other members of the royal family sought to control his person and government.

Charles was eleven when he succeeded his father in September 1380. Charles V had appointed his eldest brother, LOUIS, DUKE OF ANJOU, as regent, but, under pressure from the young king's other uncles, JOHN, DUKE OF BERRY; PHILIP THE BOLD, duke of BURGUNDY; and Louis, duke of Bourbon, Anjou agreed to share power. After Anjou's death in 1384, power largely fell to Burgundy, who used it to promote his personal interests, and to Berry, who used it to finance his passion for collecting. In July 1385, Charles, in fulfillment of a match promoted by Burgundy, married ISABEAU OF BAVARIA, the sixteen-year-old king being so smitten that he accepted her without dowry.

In November 1388, one month short of the king's twentieth birthday, Charles's younger brother, Louis, duke of Touraine, persuaded the king to dismiss his uncles and take power into his own hands. Weak and immature, the king, taking his brother's lead, gave himself over to a continuous round of court festivities, while real power lay in the hands of a group of ministers allied with

Touraine. Led by Constable Olivier de CLIS- SON and Cardinal Pierre Aycelin, the king's new councilors, who became known as MARMOUSETS, were former servants of Charles V who sought to reform royal government by making it more rational and efficient. In June 1389, the Marmousets, following what they believed to be the policy of their late master, concluded the Truce of LEULINGHEN with the government of RICHARD II. The agreement provided for a three-year cessation of hostilities and the initiation of talks for a permanent settlement. Although no peace treaty resulted, Charles married his daughter Isabella (see ISABELLA, QUEEN OF ENGLAND [1388–1409]) to Richard in 1396.

The Marmouset regime collapsed in August 1392 when the king suffered his first schizophrenic episode. On 5 August, while leading an army into BRITTANY, the king was accosted by a madman, whose sudden appearance, in concert with the heat and noise, threw Charles into a fit of violent madness, during which he attacked members of his entourage. This eruption was followed by a stupefied daze in which the king babbled nonsense and recognized no one. With their nephew incapacitated, the uncles resumed power. By mid-September, Charles seemed fully recovered, although he relapsed in the following year, only to recover again. During the episodes, the king exhibited schizophrenic delusions of persecution, believing that all around him sought to harm him. He also refused to let anyone touch or tend him, believing himself to be made of glass. For the rest of the reign, occasional periods of lucidity were invariably followed by periods of madness, with the former growing shorter and less frequent and the latter longer and more intense.

On 28 January 1393, the king barely escaped death at the so-called *Bal des Ardents* (Burning Men's Ball), during which Charles and a group of courtiers, dressed as wild animals for a court masquerade, caught fire when their costumes of pitch and flax were ignited by a torch. Such excesses of court life robbed the king of any sense of duty or responsibility and overwhelmed his fragile

sanity. Although Charles remained the source of power, he could not exercise it, and the royal family began to fragment as its more ambitious members sought to do so in the king's stead. After Burgundy's death in 1404, a bitter rivalry developed between the king's brother, now duke of Orléans, and the king's cousin, JOHN THE FEARLESS, the new duke of Burgundy. In November 1407, Burgundy had Orléans assassinated. Unable to deal either consistently or rationally with his brother's murder, Charles allowed Burgundy to return to court (see JUSTIFICATION OF THE DUKE OF BURGUNDY) and seize power. The refusal of the ARMAGNACS (the Orléanist faction) to accept Burgundy's rule initiated the FRENCH CIVIL WAR, during which the king was largely the pawn of the party in power—Burgundy from 1409 to 1413, the Armagnacs from 1413 to 1418, and Burgundy again in 1418–19.

In 1413, the dauphin, LOUIS, DUKE OF GUIENNE, tried to end civil strife by forming a royalist party, but this effort was frustrated by HENRY V's victory at AGINCOURT in October 1415 and by the dauphin's death two months later. When his second son, John, duke of Touraine, died in April 1417, Charles's only remaining male heir was fourteen-year-old Charles, who was largely a tool of BERNARD, COUNT OF ARMAGNAC, leader of the unpopular Armagnac regime then ruling in PARIS. In May 1418, with Paris about to fall to the BURGUNDIANS, the dauphin fled. Efforts to reconcile Charles, now the nominal head of a Burgundian government, with his son, now the nominal head of the Armagnac opposition, collapsed after the dauphin approved the murder of Burgundy at the MONTEREAU CONFERENCE in September 1419. In 1420, after the dauphin committed technical treason by declaring himself regent, Charles disinherited his son by accepting the Treaty of TROYES, whereby Henry V became regent and heir to the French Crown. By also marrying his daughter, CATHERINE OF VALOIS, to Henry, Charles accepted the eventual accession of a PLANTAGENET to the Valois throne. However, Charles unexpectedly outlived his son-in-law by two months, dying on 21 October 1422. He was eventually succeeded by his son, who was crowned as CHARLES VII in 1429. In the 1450s, Charles's English grandson, HENRY VI, also suffered bouts of recurring mental illness.

Further Reading: Famiglietti, Richard. *Royal Intrigue: Crisis at the Court of Charles VI, 1392–1420.* New York: AMS Press, 1986; Perroy, Edouard. *The Hundred Years War.* Trans. W. B. Wells. New York: Capricorn Books, 1965; Seward, Desmond. *The Hundred Years War.* New York: Penguin, 1999.

CHARLES VII, KING OF FRANCE (1403–1461)

Charles VII, the fifth VALOIS king of France, is often known as "the Victorious" or "the Well-Served" because his reign witnessed the final defeat of the English and the end of the HUNDRED YEARS WAR. Although condemned by both contemporaries and later historians for his abandonment of JOAN OF ARC, his ingratitude toward long-time servants, and his avoidance of combat, Charles, during the course of his reign, brought France and the Valois Crown from weakness, disorder, and dismemberment to strength, peace, and unity.

The eleventh child and fifth son of CHARLES VI and ISABEAU OF BAVARIA, Charles, in his youth, had no expectation of the Crown. He became dauphin in 1417 at the age of fourteen following the deaths of his older brothers, LOUIS, DUKE OF GUIENNE, and John, duke of Touraine. His political career began at a dark moment in French history, with HENRY V, the recent victor of AGINCOURT, poised to begin the conquest of NORMANDY (*see* NORMAN CAMPAIGN [1417–1419]), while the BURGUNDIAN and ARMAGNAC factions continued to fight one another for control of the schizophrenic king and his government. As dauphin, Charles became nominal head of the Armagnacs, whose in-

Jean Fouquet's portrait of Charles VII. *Erich Lessing/Art Resource, New York.*

creasingly unpopular regime held PARIS. Dominated by the regime's true leader, BERNARD, COUNT OF ARMAGNAC, Charles quarreled with his mother, whom he banished from the capital. In May 1418, an uprising in Paris delivered the city to JOHN THE FEARLESS, duke of BURGUNDY, whose supporters massacred the count and nearly two thousand other Armagnacs. Spirited out of Paris at night by his servants Tanguy du Châtel and Guillaume d'Avaugour, Charles fled south of the Loire, where he became the center of an alternative court dominated by Armagnacs. On 29 June, with his addled father now under the influence of Burgundy, Charles, on his own initiative, assumed the title of lieutenant-general of France.

Believing the dauphin to be weak and easily led, Burgundy sought a reconciliation that would end the civil war and allow united action against the English. On 10 September 1419, at a conference arranged by the dauphin's officers, Charles met the duke at MONTEREAU. During the meeting, Charles's servants, acting to avenge the murder of their former master, LOUIS, DUKE OF ORLÉANS, slew Burgundy. Although the extent of Charles's involvement in the killing is unclear, it appears likely that he condoned the act. Condemned by PHILIP THE GOOD, the new duke of Burgundy, as a murderer, and repudiated by his estranged mother as a bastard unfit to rule, Charles was formally disinherited by the Treaty of TROYES, which made Henry V heir to the French throne. Concluded in May 1420, the treaty also created an ANGLO-BURGUNDIAN ALLIANCE and arranged a marriage between Henry and the dauphin's sister, CATHERINE OF VALOIS. Although the unexpected death of the English king in August 1422, two months before the death of Charles VI, heartened the dauphin's supporters, Charles controlled only the southern third of France, which was contemptuously referred to as the "kingdom of Bourges." Even though his rival for the throne was his infant nephew, HENRY VI, Charles, who had a weak constitution, odd appearance, and disinclination to lead armies himself, generated little enthusiasm in Anglo-Burgundian France, where his association with the Armagnacs and the murder of Burgundy also worked against him. Victories at CRAVANT in 1423 and VERNEUIL in 1424 allowed the English to advance to the Loire, where they laid siege to ORLÉANS in 1428. Uncrowned and unsuccessful in battle, the dauphin faced the possibility of never ruling the whole kingdom.

This gloomy situation was radically transformed in the spring of 1429 by the advent of Joan of Arc, whose claim that God supported the dauphinist cause made possible the relief of Orléans in May, the victory at PATAY in June (see LOIRE CAMPAIGN), and Charles's coronation at Rheims in July. Confirmed by her military success, Joan's mission was accepted by the public as divinely inspired and Charles's association with her legitimated his authority and restored the prestige of his dynasty. However, the king, who favored DIPLOMACY to battle, was always uncomfortable with Joan's insistence on vigorous offensive warfare. After the failure of her attack on Paris in September, he negotiated a truce and disbanded the army. When Joan was captured by the Burgundians in 1430, and then tried and executed by the English in 1431, Charles made no attempt to help her, an inaction for which he has ever since been condemned by Joan's friends and admirers. Nonetheless, the victories of 1429 turned the tide of the war. In 1435, Charles reconciled with Burgundy at the Congress of ARRAS. Although the settlement was personally humiliating, requiring Charles to apologize, through a representative, for the murder at Montereau, it ended the divisions of the civil war and finally won Charles widespread recognition as king.

In 1436, Charles entered Paris for the first time in nineteen years, and, by 1440, Lancastrian France had been largely reduced to Normandy (see LANCASTER, HOUSE OF). In preparation for a final push against the English, Charles undertook to reform his government, reorganize his army, and rebuild his authority. Once much influenced by ambitious favorites, Charles dismissed the worst of them, Georges de la Trémoïlle, in 1433, and turned to more prudent advisors, such as Arthur de Richemont (see ARTHUR III), who led the successful campaigns of the 1430s and the army reform of the 1440s, and Jacques Coeur, a merchant who financed the final campaigns against the English. In 1438, Charles issued the Pragmatic Sanction, whereby the Crown claimed control from the papacy of ecclesiastical appointments and revenues. In 1439, the king won new taxes from the Estates-General and issued the first of his ordinances reforming the army (see CHARLES VII, MILITARY REFORMS OF), although these attempts to enlarge royal power led to a revolt of the dauphin and the nobility known as the Praguerie. Charles defeated the rebels in 1440, but was forced to delay army reform until after 1444, when the Truce of TOURS temporarily ended the Anglo-French war.

Now possessing a smaller but better trained army led by hand-picked commanders and supported by excellent ARTILLERY, Charles reopened the war in 1449 with a campaign of successful sieges that culminated in August 1450 with the reconquest of Normandy (*see* FORMIGNY, BATTLE OF; NORMAN CAMPAIGN [1449–50]). In 1451, a campaign led by JOHN, COUNT OF DUNOIS, overran GASCONY, which passed finally to French control after the Battle of CASTILLON in July 1453. With the end of the Anglo-French war, Charles continued the consolidation of royal authority, beginning a process that eventually culminated with the French reabsorption of much of Burgundy. In 1450, Charles convened a nullification trial that in 1456 overturned the original verdict against Joan of Arc. Undertaken perhaps to clear the king of association with a condemned heretic, the trial transcripts have provided historians with much information on Joan. Charles died on 22 July 1461 and was succeeded by his son, Louis XI. *See also* ESTATES, GENERAL AND PROVINCIAL.

Further Reading: Vale, M. G. A. *Charles VII.* Berkeley: University of California Press, 1974.

CHARLES VII, MILITARY REFORMS OF

During the five-year cessation of hostilities that followed conclusion of the Truce of TOURS in 1444, the government of CHARLES VII undertook a series of military reforms designed to create a professional standing army paid and controlled by the French Crown, and capable of rapid and flexible deployment against both *écorcheur* bands (see *ROUTIERS*) and English garrisons. When fighting resumed in 1449, this new French army drove the English out of NORMANDY and GASCONY within four years and thus ended the HUNDRED YEARS WAR.

Unlike previous truces and treaties, the proclamation of which had disbanded armies and thereby unleashed thousands of unemployed soldiers to prey upon the

French countryside, the Truce of Tours witnessed the first attempt by any royal government to maintain troops under arms during peacetime. To prepare for the final expulsion of the English, and to resolve rather than aggravate the *écorcheur* problem created in 1435 by the Franco-Burgundian reconciliation at the Congress of ARRAS, Charles VII attempted, even before conclusion of the truce, to reinstitute some of the military reforms carried out in the 1360s by his grandfather, CHARLES V. In November 1439, the king declared military recruiting a royal monopoly, limited the strength of royal companies to one hundred men, and established permanent regular garrisons around the country. When accompanied by more regular pay and stricter attention to discipline, these efforts reduced brigandage and strengthened royal control over French military resources.

When the Truce of Tours took effect in 1444, the government did not automatically disband its forces, but, under the supervision of Constable Arthur de Richemont (*see* ARTHUR III), purged the army of its most unruly elements and formed the rest into some twenty standing cavalry units known as "companies of the king's ordinance" or *companies d'ordonnance*, which contained one hundred "lances" consisting of a man-at-arms and five more lightly armed attendants. In 1446, this organization was also applied to Languedoc in southern France, which was required to raise five more companies. Each town and province had to house and maintain a certain number of lances, a special tax being levied for that purpose. Through these reforms, the French Crown succeeded in doing what had not been done before in Western Europe—raise and maintain an army in time of peace.

On 28 April 1448, in an effort to raise a similar body of infantry, the king issued an *ordonnance* requiring every parish to pay for the maintenance of one ARCHER. To entice men to volunteer, the Crown granted an exemption from all taxes to anyone who participated, thus giving rise to the name "franc-archers" or "free-archers" for the resulting militia units. Paid 9 livres tournois per year and up to 4 livres tournois per month when called into active service, the franc-archers trained once a week and stood ready to join their companies should war erupt. The *ordonnance* called for companies of 500 men formed into four divisions 4,000 strong, thus theoretically providing the Crown with an infantry force of 16,000. Although never fully mobilized, the franc-archers, like the professional cavalry units, played an important role in the final campaigns of the Hundred Years War, and in the eventual suppression of the *écorcheurs*. *See also* ARTILLERY; NORMAN CAMPAIGN (1449–1450).

Further Reading: Contamine, Philippe. *War in the Middle Ages*. Trans. Michael Jones. London: Blackwell, 1984; Perroy, Edouard. *The Hundred Years War*. Trans. W. B. Wells. New York: Capricorn Books, 1965; Vale, M. G. A. *Charles VII*. Berkeley: University of California Press, 1974.

CHARLES OF BLOIS, DUKE OF BRITTANY (c. 1319–1364)

Charles of Blois was the French-backed claimant to the duchy of BRITTANY during the BRETON CIVIL WAR.

Charles was the second son of Guy de Châtillon, count of Blois, and Margaret of VALOIS, the sister of PHILIP VI of France. In 1337, Charles married Jeanne, countess of Penthièvre, the niece of John III, duke of Brittany, who, being childless, promised the ducal succession to Jeanne in preference to his half brother, John de MONTFORT. However, upon the duke's death in April 1341, both Charles, by right of his wife, and Montfort claimed the duchy, leaving Philip VI, as feudal overlord, to decide between them. When Philip declared for Charles, Montfort refused to renounce his claims and the king imprisoned him in the Louvre. Montfort died in 1345. Charles, who was supported by a majority of the Breton nobility, quickly reduced most of the Montfortist strongholds with the assistance of a French army led by Philip's son, John, duke of NORMANDY.

Besieged in Brest, Montfort's wife, Jeanne of Flanders, appealed to EDWARD III, who, in 1342, seized the opportunity to open a new front against France and intervened militarily in Brittany. Faced with a growing English presence, Charles was unable to secure the duchy, which now lapsed into civil war. In 1347, an English force under Sir Thomas DAGWORTH defeated and captured Charles at the Battle of LA ROCHE-DERRIEN. After four years of captivity in Vannes and LONDON, Charles was paroled in late 1351 and returned to PARIS where JOHN II agreed to pay his RANSOM. When the king could not meet the first payment, Charles, a rigidly upright man, surrendered himself and was again confined in the Tower of London.

Disheartened by news of the English victory at MAURON in 1352, Charles agreed to Breton neutrality in the Anglo-French war in return for his freedom (for a ransom of £50,000) and English recognition of his right to the ducal title. This agreement was concluded on 1 March 1353 and Charles returned to the duchy on parole, but his supporters continued the war, slaughtering the English garrison of Tristan Castle in September and forcing Charles to return again to English custody. Finally released in August 1356, Charles, who had pledged not to take arms against Edward, had to watch while a campaign led by HENRY OF GROSMONT, duke of Lancaster, brought much of Brittany under English control.

In 1360, Brittany, its succession still in dispute, was largely excepted from the Treaty of BRÉTIGNY, and civil war flared anew in 1362, when Edward III surrendered the duchy to Montfort's son, John, who was now old enough to lead his own cause. With the assistance of Bertrand du GUESCLIN, Charles launched a series of campaigns that culminated in September 1364 with his attempt to relieve the besieged port of AURAY. Overwhelmed by an Anglo-Breton force under Sir John CHANDOS, Charles was slain and his cause overthrown. In April 1365, the long civil war finally ended when Charles's widow signed the Treaty of GUÉRANDE recognizing young John de Montfort as Duke JOHN IV.

Further Reading: Jones, Michael. *The Creation of Brittany: A Late Medieval State*. London: Hambledon Press, 1988.

CHARLES THE BAD, KING OF NAVARRE (1332–1387)

Like EDWARD III of England, Charles II, ruler of the small Spanish kingdom of Navarre, had a claim to the Crown of France that descended through his mother. In the 1350s, Navarre, in furtherance of that claim, tried to wrest the throne for his VALOIS kinsmen by exploiting the economic distress and social unrest fostered by military failure in the HUNDRED YEARS WAR. Because his quest for power seriously weakened the authority of the Crown, Navarre became known in the sixteenth century as "El Malo," "the Bad," a sobriquet later adopted by French historians.

The son of Philip, count of Évreux, and Jeanne, the daughter of LOUIS X, Charles succeeded to his father's title in 1343 and to his mother's kingdom of Navarre in 1349. When PHILIP V displaced Jeanne as heir to the French throne in 1316, an action that led to the formal prohibition of female royal succession, he promised her possession of the rest of her inheritance—Navarre, where a woman could succeed, and the counties of Champagne and Brie. However, neither Philip nor his Valois successors relinquished the latter two territories. When other lands and revenues promised as compensation for Champagne and Brie were also withheld or delayed, the disgruntled House of Évreux quickly became the focus of magnate discontent in northwestern France. Royal attempts at pacifying the family included PHILIP VI's marriage to Navarre's sister in 1350 and Navarre's marriage to JOHN II's daughter in 1352. However, John's failure to promptly pay his daughter's dowry and his decision to grant Angoulême, a county to which Navarre had claim, to Charles of Spain, a royal favorite recently made constable, led Navarre to arrange the constable's murder in January 1354. With this act, and his subsequent attempts to negotiate for English aid, Navarre initiated a decade-long rebellion against his father-in-law.

Because of the support Navarre enjoyed among the French nobility, particularly in the northwest, John was forced, in February 1354, to conclude the Treaty of Mantes, whereby Navarre agreed to renounce Champagne and Brie in return for a pardon and a substantial grant of lands in NORMANDY. However, Navarre continued to intrigue with Edward III, whose failed attempt to invade Normandy in concert with Navarre allowed John to force the more favorable Treaty of Valognes on his son-in-law in September 1355. But Navarre continued to foment rebellion and even plotted to kidnap the king and turn the dauphin against his father. On 5 April 1356, Navarre was a guest at a banquet hosted by the dauphin in ROUEN. Leading a large body of armed men, the king burst in and, seizing Navarre by the throat, denounced him as a traitor. With Navarre in prison and his chief supporters executed, Normandy erupted in civil war between royalists and Navarrese partisans.

When the English captured John at POITIERS in the following September, criticism of the Crown and its policies overwhelmed the inexperienced dauphin, who faced a host of discontented factions demanding Navarre's release. On 9 November 1357, he escaped from prison. Hailed as the savior of France by those who sought governmental reform, Navarre quickly eroded his popularity by cooperating with the Parisian revolutionaries led by Étienne MARCEL, whose excesses alienated the nobility, and by negotiating with the English, an act that seemed motivated more by personal ambition than by an interest in reform. Following John's release in 1360, Navarre began recruiting troops among the bands of ROUTIERS left unemployed by the Treaty of BRÉTIGNY. In 1363, when the king gave BURGUNDY as an APPANAGE to his son PHILIP THE BOLD, Navarre claimed the duchy, thereby initiating a new civil war. In May 1364, only days before the dauphin was crowned as CHARLES V, a royal army commanded by Bertrand du GUESCLIN crushed Navarre's forces at COCHEREL, thereby destroying Navarrese power in Normandy and around PARIS. Forced to accept a treaty relinquishing his Norman strongholds, Navarre's political importance rapidly diminished, although he continued to intrigue against the Crown until his death on 1 January 1387.

Further Reading: Sumption, Jonathan. *The Hundred Years War.* Vol. 2, *Trial by Fire.* Philadelphia: University of Pennsylvania Press, 2001.

CHARTRES, PEACE OF. *See* FRENCH CIVIL WAR

CHÂTEL, TANGUY DU. *See* CHARLES VII; MONTEREAU CONFERENCE

CHEVALIERS DE L'ÉTOILE. See STAR, ORDER OF THE

CHEVAUCHÉE

The *chevauchée*, a swift and highly destructive raid through enemy territory, was a military tactic frequently employed by English forces during the HUNDRED YEARS WAR, especially in campaigns before 1380. Such raids sought to destroy the authority and legitimacy of the VALOIS monarchy and to win profit and honor for the English Crown and soldiery.

Derived from strategies used both by and against the English in the Anglo-Scottish wars of the early fourteenth century, the *chevauchée* was employed in France as early as 1339, when English burning and looting of the rich French countryside shocked all Europe (*see* THIÉRACHE CAMPAIGN). However, the tactic offered the English many advantages and was highly effective in the early stages of the war. The goal of the *chevauchée* was to challenge the authority and military effectiveness of the French king by demonstrating his inability to defend his lands and people. A long sweeping raid into the heart of Valois territory also illustrated EDWARD III's superior military might and therefore his superior claim to be king of France. A campaign against noncombatants was also

easier and cheaper to plan and organize, less hazardous to English troops, and very damaging to the defender's economic ability to make war. Scarce resources were tied up building and maintaining town walls and other fortifications for subjects whose ability to pay taxes had been significantly reduced. Frequent repetition of such attacks over wide areas could also stimulate a popular demand for peace that could not be ignored by the defenders and that would allow the attackers to dictate terms.

Although historians have traditionally argued that the English *chevauchée* was also intended to force the French to give battle, more recent theories suggest that this was not always the case. Leading a mobile force that rarely numbered more than a few thousand, English commanders needed to move quickly through enemy lands, doing as much damage as possible and collecting sufficient plunder and prisoners to make the whole venture profitable. Seeking battle was, especially for outnumbered English forces in enemy territory, a risky tactic. To the medieval mind, such a plan was to invite the intervention of God, who often seemed willing to bring defeat upon the issuer of the invitation. Thus, the early raids, such as those of HENRY OF GROSMONT, duke of Lancaster, in 1345, and EDWARD, THE BLACK PRINCE, in 1355 and 1356, were, despite the culmination of the 1356 campaign in the Battle of POITIERS, aimed mainly at destroying the authority and not the armies of the French king (see *CHEVAUCHÉE* OF 1355).

By the 1360s, the immense scale of destruction and the frequency of the raids reduced their effectiveness. Also, any attempt to invite battle failed completely of its purpose after 1364, when CHARLES V refused to fight. This strategy left the countryside open to plunder but also avoided the repetition of defeats like CRÉCY and Poitiers, which proved even more damaging to morale than the *chevauchées*. The RHEIMS CAMPAIGN of 1359–60, essentially a grand *chevauchée* designed to have Edward III crowned at Rheims, failed due to bad weather and the ironic inability of the English-devastated countryside to supply the army. When war resumed in 1369, the English initiated a series of overly ambitious *chevauchées*, with JOHN OF GAUNT, duke of Lancaster, looting Artois, Picardy, and NORMANDY in 1369; Sir Robert KNOLLES raiding around PARIS and into BRITTANY and Poitou in 1370; and Gaunt, in one of the longest *chevauchées* ever attempted, plundering in a wide arc around Paris from CALAIS to BORDEAUX in 1373 (see *CHEVAUCHÉE* OF 1373). The failure of these raids to produce any concrete results made English use of the *chevauchée* far less frequent thereafter, although occasional plundering campaigns, such as those of THOMAS, DUKE OF CLARENCE, in 1412 and John BEAUFORT, duke of Somerset, in 1443, continued to be undertaken. *See also* STRATEGY AND TACTICS.

Further Reading: Allmand, Christopher. *The Hundred Years War*. Cambridge: Cambridge University Press, 1988; Curry, Anne. *The Hundred Years War*. 2nd ed. Houndmills, England: Palgrave Macmillan, 2003; Seward, Desmond. *The Hundred Years War*. New York: Penguin, 1999.

CHEVAUCHÉE OF 1355

Led by EDWARD, THE BLACK PRINCE, the two-month-long English *CHEVAUCHÉE* of 1355 covered over six hundred miles on a route that ran across southern France from BORDEAUX to the Mediterranean and back again. Although the campaign precipitated neither pitched battles nor territorial conquests, it significantly reduced the economic ability of the region to support the VALOIS war effort, and severely shook French confidence in JOHN II's ability to defend his subjects.

On 21 September, the day after his arrival in Bordeaux, the prince was officially installed as royal lieutenant in AQUITAINE. Anxious to strike at the Valois lieutenant of Languedoc, John, count of Armagnac, who had been raiding PLANTAGENET territories since the spring, the prince called upon his Gascon vassals to provide troops for an autumn campaign. On 5 October, he left Bordeaux with an Anglo-Gascon force numbering over six thousand, of which twenty-two hundred had come with the

prince from England. Among the army's captains were Sir John CHANDOS; Thomas BEAUCHAMP, earl of Warwick; and the Gascon nobles Jean de GRAILLY, Captal de Buch, and Bernard-Aiz V, lord of ALBRET. On 12 October, the army left Aquitaine and entered the county of Armagnac. Moving quickly in three columns across a broad front so as to maximize opportunities for both forage and destruction, the army marched southeast through a rich, undefended country, destroying everything in its path.

The French commanders in the region—Armagnac, Marshal Jean de Clermont, and Constable John of Bourbon—fearing a repeat of the disasters at AUBEROCHE and CRÉCY, refused to give battle and instead prepared to defend the wealthy town of Toulouse, to which the prince appeared to be heading. However, having neither time nor equipment for a long siege, the prince bypassed Toulouse in late October. On 3 November, the raiders reached Carcassonne, where, after rejecting an offer of payment to be left alone, the prince destroyed the lower town but bypassed the walled fortress. On 8 November, the army reached Narbonne, where it came within sight of the Mediterranean. After dismissing papal representatives attempting to negotiate a truce, the prince learned that the French commanders were at last on the move, attempting to block his return. He therefore left Narbonne on 10 November, as soldiers and townsmen in the fortress, which was again unmolested, began bombarding his men with catapults and burning arrows.

Taking a more southerly return route to avoid the enemy, the army passed through a region of difficult terrain and few towns; the men suffered much from lack of food and water, and from cold and freezing rain when the weather turned. The French harassed stragglers and foragers, but made no attempt to give battle until 20 November, when an English contingent captured more than thirty prisoners in a clash with a French detachment. The two armies spent the night watching each other across the River Save, and then, on 21 November, Armagnac, having destroyed all the bridges, withdrew northward. The prince resumed his march and continued unhindered to Bordeaux, which he reached on 9 December. Returning with hundreds of carts of booty and many prisoners for RANSOM, the expedition was a great success, having destroyed almost five hundred villages, more than twenty walled towns, and the trade and residential centers of three large cities. What's more, the outcry across France against the inactivity of the French commanders embarrassed the royal government and forced the king, who was focused on EDWARD III's activities in northern France, to devote more time and resources to the defense of Languedoc.

Further Reading: Burne, Alfred H. *The Crécy War.* Ware, England: Wordsworth Editions Ltd., 1999; Sumption, Jonathan. *The Hundred Years War.* Vol. 2, *Trial by Fire.* Philadelphia: University of Pennsylvania Press, 2001.

CHEVAUCHÉE OF 1373

The largest and longest English CHEVAUCHÉE of the HUNDRED YEARS WAR, the five-month campaign led by JOHN OF GAUNT, duke of Lancaster, in 1373 brought great destruction to eastern and central France but accomplished little for the flagging PLANTAGENET war effort and was considered a failure in England.

With the resumption of war in 1369, the English response to CHARLES V's policy of avoiding pitched battles was a series of *chevauchées* designed to cripple the French economy and force Charles to fight. In 1369, Lancaster led a brief raid from CALAIS to HARFLEUR, and in 1370, Sir Robert KNOLLES led a *chevauchée* across northern France to BRITTANY. That expedition ended in failure when Knolles was deserted by his cocommanders, one of whom was subsequently defeated by the French at Pontvallain. For the 1373 campaign, Lancaster left Calais in August with a force of between ten and fifteen thousand men, over half of whom were ARCHERS. Instead of striking south toward AQUITAINE, which was under increasing enemy pressure, the duke moved east and

then south, ravaging Picardy, Champagne, and BURGUNDY, perhaps in an effort to draw Charles out of PARIS. The English inflicted tremendous damage on the provinces they entered, but the French king forbade direct confrontations and urged people to flee to the fortified towns.

In late autumn, Lancaster turned south, moving through the Bourbonnais into mountainous, lightly populated Auvergne, where the French constable, Bertrand du GUESCLIN, subjected the English to the same harassing attacks and ambushes they had suffered earlier from the forces of PHILIP THE BOLD, duke of Burgundy. As winter arrived in November and December, horses and men died for lack of shelter, while du Guesclin's attacks, which continued almost to BORDEAUX, became bolder and more frequent. Hungry, tired, and increasingly on foot, the English army finally stumbled into the Gascon capital at the beginning of January 1374. About half the army had been lost to exposure, starvation, and enemy action.

The raid had covered almost a thousand miles and had severely damaged the economies of the regions through which it passed; it also relieved French pressure on Brittany, from which du Guesclin was recalled to defend France, and brought reinforcements to the shrinking remnant of Plantagenet Aquitaine, which also experienced relief while the French were focused on Lancaster. However, no battles had been won and no towns had been taken and the raid's disastrous ending precluded the securing of sufficient plunder to compensate for its high cost in money and men. The English subsequently conducted two more such campaigns—EDMUND OF LANGLEY, earl of Cambridge, raided in Brittany in 1375, and THOMAS OF WOODSTOCK, earl of Buckingham, plundered northern France in 1380—but neither was successful, and no further *chevauchées* were undertaken in the fourteenth century. By 1380, the only parts of Aquitaine still in English hands were Bordeaux and its environs.

Further Reading: Burne, Alfred H. *The Agincourt War.* Ware, England: Wordsworth Editions

Ltd., 1999; Packe, Michael. *King Edward III*. Ed. L. C. B. Seaman. London: Routledge and Kegan Paul, 1983; Seward, Desmond. *The Hundred Years War*. New York: Penguin, 1999.

CHIVALRY

Related to the French word for knight—*chevalier*, from *cheval*, "horse"—chivalry is a complex term referring both to a class of knights or armed horsemen, and to a set of values, qualities, and behaviors that became, between the eleventh and fifteenth centuries, an internationally recognized code of conduct for those who belonged or aspired to the European aristocracy of mounted warriors. Because war justified the existence and privileged status of knights, the HUNDRED YEARS WAR was the perfect stage for the promotion of chivalrous ideals and the display of chivalrous conduct. Many contemporaries saw the war primarily in chivalric terms, such as the chroniclers JEAN LE BEL and JEAN FROISSART, who, in the words of the latter, wrote so that "the honourable enterprises, noble adventures, and deeds of arms which took place during the wars waged by France and England should be fittingly related and preserved for posterity" (Froissart, 37).

Medieval chivalry had its greatest flowering in France, where much of the literature of chivalry, whether ecclesiastical, instructional, or literary/romantic, was written and disseminated. Although notions of chivalry varied by time and place, certain virtues and values were near universal attributes of the chivalrous knight. The most prominent were loyalty, which grew out of the feudal concept of faithfulness to one's lord, to whom one owed military service in return for land, and military prowess, which meant not only the ability to handle arms, but to do so with courage and style in battle. During the course of the war, the feudal duty of loyalty to one's lord evolved into an obligation of loyalty to one's king. As kings came increasingly to be seen as the embodiment of the state, disloyalty came to be treated as treason, as betrayal of one's king and country. Thus, in 1350, when Constable Raoul de Brienne, count of

Eu, surrendered his castle of Guines, an important strongpoint on the CALAIS march, to EDWARD III to pay Eu's RANSOM, JOHN II interpreted the transfer, which the constable saw as a private arrangement to meet a just obligation, as treason and had Eu executed. The virtue of prowess in battle was particularly recognized by the great orders of chivalry established during the war—the Order of the GARTER in England and of the STAR in France. At annual meetings of the latter, a special table was set aside for those members who were judged to have performed the most valiant feats of arms during the previous year.

Other key chivalric qualities included largess, courtesy, honor, and nobility. Deriving probably from the need for equitable distribution of booty among a war band, largess came to encompass the economic dimension of chivalry, for medieval knighthood was expensive, requiring a man to equip himself with a warhorse and much costly ARMOR and weaponry. Without land, a man could not acquire a knight's training or equipage unless helped by his lord. Thus, after many French knights were captured at AUBEROCHE in 1345, PHILIP VI demonstrated chivalrous lordship by paying to reequip those who had to sell their horses and armor to meet their ransoms. Beyond this, the quality of largess was much lauded by troubadours, whose livelihood depended upon the generosity of the nobility.

Although later associated mainly with the proper treatment of women, courtesy originally encompassed protection of the weak and defenseless, punishment of those who broke the code of chivalry, and the expectation of being rewarded for chivalrous behavior with land, office, or the hand of an heiress. In 1346, during the CRÉCY campaign, Sir John CHANDOS famously escorted two French ladies safely away from the battle zone. In 1357, Jean de GRAILLY, the Captal de Buch, a famous companion of EDWARD, THE BLACK PRINCE, assisted a band of French knights in defending the wife and children of the future CHARLES V from the violence of the *JACQUERIE* rebels.

Honor, the esteem of one's peers and others, was particularly important during wartime, for it could best be won and maintained on the battlefield. The war is replete with stories of men who took unnecessary risks to be the first into a besieged castle or to raid an enemy encampment. In 1342, for instance, Sir Walter MAUNY, rather than evade a party of French horsemen by retiring, vowed to unhorse one of them and was nearly captured as a result. One of the most famous episodes of the war, the COMBAT OF THE THIRTY, which occurred in 1351 during the BRETON CIVIL WAR, was an entirely unnecessary encounter between members of two Breton garrisons; nonetheless, participants on both sides won everlasting renown throughout both kingdoms. Because one could not win honor if one was not in the forefront of battle, Sir Hugh CALVELEY, in what was considered an act of chivalry rather than one of insubordination, refused to command the rearguard at AURAY in 1364, while Edward, duke of York, lost his life when HENRY V granted the duke's request to lead the van at AGINCOURT. The maintenance of honor also demanded that prisoners not take up arms against their captors until their ransoms had been honorably met. Thus, John II returned voluntarily to captivity in 1364 when his son, LOUIS, DUKE OF ANJOU, broke parole, and CHARLES OF BLOIS, the French-backed duke of BRITTANY, twice returned to English captivity when he could not honor the terms of his parole.

The final attribute, nobility, encompassed the social aspect of chivalry. By the fourteenth century, many nonnobles, particularly among the royal bureaucracy in France and the urban merchant elites of both realms, had grown wealthy and were no longer economically inferior to the aristocracy. This trend placed a new emphasis on high birth and aristocratic heritage as a qualification for membership in the chivalrous class. Thus, in 1369, John Hastings, earl of Pembroke, considered it socially demeaning to serve under the command of even so experienced and chivalrous a figure as Chandos.

Further Reading: Barber, Richard. *The Reign of Chivalry*. New York: St. Martin's Press, 1980; Froissart, Jean. *Chronicles*. Trans. Geoffrey Brereton. New York: Penguin Books, 1978; Keen, Maurice. *Chivalry*. New Haven, CT: Yale University Press, 1984; Painter, Sidney. *French Chivalry: Chivalric Ideas and Practices*. Ithaca, NY: Cornell University Press, 1940; Vale, Malcolm. *War and Chivalry: Warfare and Aristocratic Culture in England, France, and Burgundy at the End of the Middle Ages*. London: Duckworth, 1981.

CHRISTINE DE PIZAN (c. 1364–c. 1430)

Christine de Pizan was the first European woman of letters to earn her living by writing. Influenced by the FRENCH CIVIL WAR and the renewal of the HUNDRED YEARS WAR, and by the tastes of her patrons, Christine wrote a host of popular commentaries on monarchy, CHIVALRY, war, and contemporary politics, focusing particularly on the need for a leader to save France from itself and from the English.

Italian by birth, Christine came to France as a child, when her father won appointment as CHARLES V's astrologer. Through her father's position, Christine was able to indulge a studious nature and indirectly benefit from the cultural and educational opportunities made possible by contact with the VALOIS court. She married Étienne du Castel, a royal clerk, in 1380, the year the king's death ended her father's association with the court. When her husband died unexpectedly in 1390, Christine found herself responsible for supporting three children and a widowed mother. To express her grief, she wrote poetry, which soon attracted the attention of LOUIS, DUKE OF ORLÉANS, the brother of CHARLES VI. Christine dedicated a series of poems to the duke, including the *Épistre au Dieu d'Amour* (1399), a narrative poem that pokes fun at the literary pretensions of young courtiers; the *Épistre Othea* (c. 1400), a partly prose commentary on classical mythology that also offers advice to young knights; the *Chemin de long estude* (1402–3), a partly autobiographical work that proposes creation of an international monarchy to cure society's ills; and the

Mutacion de Fortune (1403), an examination of the role of Fortune in history. Although Christine continued to favor the Orléanist (ARMAGNAC) party in the subsequent civil war, she ceased dedicating works to the duke in 1404, when Orléans declined to employ her son.

Christine also wrote a number of works that examined the condition of women in contemporary society. In about 1402, she was drawn into the debate over Jean de Meun's (c. 1235–1305) completion of the *Roman de la Rose*, a long narrative poem that was considered the first masterwork of French literature. By criticizing Meun's misogynistic tone and the unfortunate affect it had on general attitudes toward women, Christine countered the acclaim accorded the poem by male commentators. She brought the debate into the public consciousness by giving copies of the letters it generated to Queen ISABEAU, an act that bolstered Christine's own literary reputation. The debate also inspired her to write three other works that commented on the place of women in contemporary French society: the *Dit de la Rose* (c. 1403), the *Cité des dames* (c. 1405), and the *Livre des trios vertus* (1405).

In 1404, PHILIP THE BOLD, duke of BURGUNDY, commissioned Christine to write a biography of his late brother, Charles V; the result was her first entirely prose work, the *Livre des fais et bonnes meurs du sage roy Charles V*. The laudatory nature of this work is today considered to have had an important role in creating Charles's posthumous reputation as a wise and skillful ruler. After 1405, as the country slid into anarchy, Christine's writing began focusing on politics and public affairs. On 5 October 1405, Christine addressed a letter to the queen, begging her to intervene in the increasingly violent feud between Orléans and Burgundy. In 1410, she wrote a letter to JOHN, DUKE OF BERRY, last surviving brother of Charles V, asking him to save the country from civil war. When these efforts failed, she turned to the dauphin, LOUIS, DUKE OF GUIENNE, to whom she dedicated the *Livre du corps de policie* (1407), which described the ideal prince; the *Livre des fais d'armes et de chevalerie* (c. 1410), which explored military leadership and called for international laws to govern warfare; and the *Livre de la paix* (1412–14), which was a reaction to the CABOCHIEN uprising in PARIS. When the dauphin died in December 1415, two months after the Battle of AGINCOURT, Christine dedicated the *Épistre de la prison de vie humaine* to Berry's daughter. The work addressed the suffering of women who had lost loved ones in the battle or to war in general.

As the armies of HENRY V spread across northern France and violence increased in Paris, Christine took refuge in the abbey of Poissy, where her daughter was a nun. The savior she had sought finally appeared in 1429 in the unlikely person of JOAN OF ARC, of whom Christine wrote her last poem, the *Ditié de Jehanne d'Arc*, which was completed shortly after the coronation of CHARLES VII. Although the exact date of Christine's death is unknown, it appears likely that she died before she could have heard of Joan's capture on 23 May 1430.

Further Reading: Richards, J. E. *Reinterpreting Christine de Pizan.* Athens: University of Georgia Press, 1991; Willard, Charity Cannon. *Christine de Pizan: Her Life and Works.* New York: Persea, 1984.

CLARENCE, DUKE OF. *See* THOMAS, DUKE OF CLARENCE

CLEMENT V. *See* PAPACY AND THE HUNDRED YEARS WAR

CLEMENT VI (1291–1352)

As a prominent former servant of the French Crown, Pierre Roger, elected in 1342 as Clement VI, the fourth of the Avignon popes, aroused the mistrust of the English and failed to broker an end to the HUNDRED YEARS WAR.

Born at Maumont in the Limousin in 1291, Roger was by birth a subject of the English Crown. He entered the Benedictine monastery of La Chaise-Dieu around 1301 and later studied theology in PARIS, receiving his doctorate in May 1323. Trusted by Pope John XXII and King PHILIP VI, Roger advanced rapidly in both his ecclesiastical and secular careers. By 1330, he was archbishop of Rouen, having served previously as abbot of Fécamp, bishop of Arras, and archbishop of Sens, as well as chancellor of France, having distinguished himself as a diplomat and orator. In 1328, Philip sent Roger to England to summon EDWARD III to pay homage for his duchy of AQUITAINE. Harshly rebuffed by Queen Isabella, Edward's mother (see ISABELLA, QUEEN OF ENGLAND [c. 1292–1358]), Roger upon his return served on a commission charged with sequestering Edward's ducal revenues. In 1334, Roger helped negotiate a treaty with English commissioners at Senlis, although the agreement dissolved when Philip insisted on including the Scots in the peace. In July 1335, Roger announced Philip's decision to intervene in the Anglo-Scottish war on behalf of the exiled DAVID II of SCOTLAND. The archbishop declared the new policy during the course of an official sermon preached in the palace courtyard in Paris. After being created a cardinal in December 1338, Roger served on another unsuccessful peace commission, meeting at Arras and Paris with such high-ranking English representatives as Archbishop John STRATFORD.

Because he was well known to the English as a favored VALOIS minister, Roger's election as pope in May 1342 was as unwelcome to them as it was heartening to Philip, who had sent his son John, duke of Normandy (see JOHN II), to Avignon to secure Roger's election. The trip was unnecessary, for the cardinals—largely French in nationality—were happy to replace the rigid Benedict XII with the more worldly and pliable Roger, who chose the name Clement to emphasize his belief that power should be exercised with clemency. Although he viewed the war as a French courtier and politician, seeing Edward III as a contumacious feudal vassal, Clement sincerely desired peace for Europe. Within weeks of his coronation, he ap-

pointed two cardinals to mediate the Anglo-French dispute, but then undercut their effectiveness by granting Philip's request to lift the longstanding papal interdict imposed through French influence on rebellious FLANDERS. Although the action did not break the ANGLO-FLEMISH ALLIANCE, it made the Flemings reluctant to actively support the English cause and led such other English allies as the duke of Brabant to conclude a separate peace with France.

Clement was instrumental in arranging the 1343 Truce of MALESTROIT, which charged the pope to act as a "mutual friend not a judge" (Sumption, 437). English distrust of papal impartiality delayed peace talks until October 1344, when commissioners for the two realms met in Avignon. Although the pope himself initially acted as go-between, the AVIGNON PEACE CONFERENCE collapsed in early 1345. The English blamed papal bias, but neither Edward nor Philip had been seriously interested in peace. The English believed that papal fees and taxes collected in England were supporting the French war effort and that papal provision of vacant English benefices (ecclesiastical offices) to foreigners supported anti-English clerics in Avignon and France. The latter belief provided the stimulus for the 1351 passage by PARLIAMENT of the Statute of Provisors, an act that confirmed the Crown's right to reject papal appointees to English livings.

Although the increasing vehemence of their hostility to the pope provoked some of Clement's pro-French actions, the English had legitimate complaints. Clement had allowed Philip to annually levy a tax of a tenth on French ecclesiastical incomes—something Edward was not similarly authorized to do in England—and the pope had relieved Philip of the duty to repay the money previously collected in France for the aborted crusade, something Benedict XII had never allowed. In 1343, Clement loaned Philip 50,000 florins (£7,500), and in 1345 and 1346 the pope agreed to secret loans of 42,000 and 330,000 florins (£6,300 and

£49,500, respectively). Money from these taxes and loans was used to supply French troops and hire Genoese mercenaries. Clement also irritated the English king by withholding the dispensation for EDWARD, THE BLACK PRINCE, to marry the daughter of the duke of Brabant. Although the granting of such documents was normally a formality, Clement had privately assured Philip that he would never permit the politically sensitive union. Thus, when Clement arranged another truce in 1347 following Edward's capture of CALAIS, the English rejected the pope's mediation as biased and the new peace effort collapsed (see CALAIS, TRUCE OF).

Clement also ensured that the papacy remained under French influence in Avignon, which he purchased in 1348 and where he built the sumptuous Palais Neuf as a new papal residence. He refused to return the papal court to Rome, but granted that city's request to reduce the hundred-year interval between jubilees, thus allowing Rome to reap the economic benefits derived from the hordes of pilgrims who came to celebrate the jubilee of 1350. By also defining the "treasury of merit" earned by Christ and the saints, *Unigenitus*, the bull announcing the jubilee decision, had far-reaching consequences. Over the next two centuries, the Church began dispensing this reservoir of merit to sinners through a system of indulgences; by the sixteenth century, the growing abuse surrounding the sale of indulgences helped precipitate the Reformation.

Although he maintained a lavish and worldly court, engaged in nepotism, and stood accused of sexual misconduct, Clement distinguished himself during the devastating appearance of the BLACK DEATH in Avignon in 1348–49. He defended the Jews against charges that they were responsible for the pestilence and he took vigorous steps to relieve the suffering of the city's poor and afflicted. Clement died on 6 December 1352 and was buried at La Chaise-Dieu. In 1562, Huguenots (French Protestants) destroyed

his tomb and burned his remains. *See also* PAPACY AND THE HUNDRED YEARS WAR.

Further Reading: Kelly, J. N. D. *The Oxford Dictionary of Popes.* Oxford: Oxford University Press, 1988, s.v. "Clement VI"; McBrien, Richard P. *Lives of the Popes.* New York: HarperCollins, 1997, s.v. "Clement VI"; Renouard, Yves. *Avignon Papacy, 1305–1403.* Trans. Denis Bethell. London: Faber, 1970 (especially pp. 42–49); Sumption, Jonathan. *The Hundred Years War.* Vol. 1, *Trial by Battle.* Philadelphia: University of Pennsylvania Press, 1999; Wood, Diana. *Pope Clement VI: The Pontificate and Ideas of an Avignon Pope.* Cambridge: Cambridge University Press, 1989.

CLEMENT VII. *See* PAPACY AND THE HUNDRED YEARS WAR

CLISSON, OLIVIER, CONSTABLE OF FRANCE (1336–1407)

Originally a supporter of the English-backed Montfort faction in the BRETON CIVIL WAR, the Breton nobleman Olivier IV de Clisson supported the VALOIS cause after 1370, leading French armies in the reconquest of AQUITAINE and eventually becoming constable of France. In the 1380s, Clisson became leader of the MARMOUSETS, a political faction that controlled the government of CHARLES VI for four years. Although eventually driven from power and deprived of office, Clisson remained a political force in France and BRITTANY until his death.

The son of Olivier III de Clisson, a Montfort partisan who was executed for treason by PHILIP VI in 1343, Olivier IV was raised in England, where he fled with his mother after the French Crown confiscated the family's estates. Clisson's mother later married Sir Walter BENTLEY, an English ROUTIER captain, who helped her regain some of the Clisson lands. By the early 1360s, Clisson had inherited the Breton estates given to his mother by the English and had regained the original family lands seized by the French. In 1364, he fought at AURAY, the battle that made John de Montfort duke of Brittany as JOHN IV. In 1367, Clisson fought with

EDWARD, THE BLACK PRINCE, at the Battle of NÁJERA.

In 1370, Clisson, increasingly at odds with John IV, threw off his English allegiance and brought his Breton supporters into the service of CHARLES V by concluding a private compact with the French constable, Bertrand du GUESCLIN. Clisson played a leading role in the French reconquest of Saintonge and Poitou in 1371–72 and in the invasion of Brittany that expelled the pro-English duke in 1373. An effective commander and fierce warrior who strongly promoted the policy of refusing pitched battle, Clisson became one of the most renowned of Charles V's commanders. In 1380, the king named Clisson constable in succession to du Guesclin.

In the 1380s, the constable became leader of the Marmousets, a political faction comprising the leading financial and military advisors of Charles V. The Marmousets opposed the minority government of Charles VI's uncles, JOHN, DUKE OF BERRY, and PHILIP THE BOLD, duke of BURGUNDY. In 1388, the Marmousets, acting with the support of the king's brother, LOUIS, DUKE OF ORLÉANS, declared the king of full age and took control of the government in his name. In August 1392, the king, while on campaign to punish the duke of Brittany for an attempt on Clisson's life, experienced a psychotic episode, which allowed the uncles to resume power. Made the scapegoat for the discredited regime, Clisson fled to Brittany, but was eventually captured and brought to trial. Stripped of the constableship, Clisson was also fined and banished from court.

Returning to Brittany, Clisson reactivated his long and bitter feud with John IV, who had briefly held Clisson for RANSOM in 1387 and who may have instigated Pierre Craon's murderous attack on Clisson in 1392. Although married to the duke's cousin, Béatrix de Laval, Clisson was also father-in-law to John of Blois, count of Penthièvre, heir to the rival Penthièvre claim to the Breton ducal title. In consort with his son-in-law, Clisson waged open war against the duke until 1395, when Burgundy arranged a settlement that brought Clisson back into ducal favor. When

Clisson died on 23 April 1407, he left his daughters a large landed estate, which his Penthièvre grandsons forfeited in 1420 by kidnapping Duke JOHN V.

Further Reading: Henneman, John Bell. "Reassessing the Career of Olivier de Clisson, Constable of France." In *Law, Custom, and the Social Fabric in Medieval Europe: Essays in Honor of Bruce Lyon*, ed. Bernard Bachrach and David Nicholas, 211–33. Kalamazoo, MI: Medieval Institute, 1990; Perroy, Edouard. *The Hundred Years War*. Trans. W. B. Wells. New York: Capricorn Books, 1965.

COCHEREL, BATTLE OF (1364)

Fought on 16 May 1364 near the village of Cocherel in NORMANDY, the Battle of Cocherel pitted the forces of the French Crown against those of CHARLES THE BAD, king of Navarre. A crushing Navarrese defeat, Cocherel destroyed Navarre's military capability and significantly diminished his ability to dominate the French government.

In late 1363, Navarre, who had been at odds with the Crown since 1354, used JOHN II's captivity in LONDON and the political weakness of the dauphin to try again to seize power. Angered by the denial of his claim to the duchy of BURGUNDY, which John gave to his youngest son, PHILIP THE BOLD, Navarre raised two armies—one to invade Burgundy and the other to menace PARIS from the Navarrese strongholds in Normandy. Swayed perhaps by old friends and comrades-in-arms, such as the Gascon lord, Jean de GRAILLY, Captal de Buch, who was now one of Navarre's chief advisors, and Sir John CHANDOS, who held land of Navarre in Normandy, EDWARD, THE BLACK PRINCE, agreed in January 1364 to allow Navarre's forces free passage from Navarre through AQUITAINE. In March, the captal de Buch led advance contingents of his army through the duchy toward Normandy.

Unfortunately for Navarre, the dauphin had a force of a thousand men already in Normandy preparing to besiege the fortress of Rolleboise, which had been captured by a company of English ROUTIERS in the previous autumn. Upon learning of the captal's movements, the dauphin ordered this army, which was nominally commanded by the son of the count of Auxerre but actually led by the Breton captain Bertrand du GUESCLIN, to strike Navarre's forces in Normandy. By the time the captal arrived in the duchy in late April, most of Navarre's strongholds, apart from Évreux and a few isolated hold-outs, had capitulated. Basing himself at Évreux, the captal raised an army of almost two thousand by mid-May, mainly by collecting the scattered remnants of Navarrese garrisons and by pulling together companies of English and Gascon *routiers* operating in BRITTANY and western France.

Leaving Évreux on 14 May, the captal marched east until his path was blocked by du Guesclin, who had twelve hundred men on foot in a defensive line before the River Eure—his numbers augmented by companies of Breton and Gascon *routiers*. For two days, the armies faced each other, neither commander wishing to take the offensive. On 16 May, with his food running out, de Guesclin mounted his troops and began to withdraw. Unwilling to see his enemy escape, the captal sent a band of cavalry to flank the French and block their access to the Eure bridge. The rest of the Navarrese cavalry then charged into du Guesclin's men, initiating one of the bloodiest battles of the fourteenth century. Being the larger force, the Navarrese prevailed until they were outflanked and forced to retreat by du Guesclin's Breton reserves. The retreat quickly became a rout, with the French surrounding the captal and about fifty companions. The former was wounded and captured, and most of the latter were slain.

The battle, which occurred three days before the dauphin's coronation as CHARLES V, broke Navarre's military dominance in Normandy and northern France and overthrew his political influence throughout the kingdom. Although he continued to intrigue until his death in 1387, Navarre never again seriously threatened the authority of the French Crown.

Further Reading: Sumption, Jonathan. *The Hundred Years War.* Vol. 2, *Trial by Fire.* Philadelphia: University of Pennsylvania Press, 2001.

COEUR, JACQUES. *See* CHARLES VII

COMBAT OF THE THIRTY (1351)
Fought on 26 March 1351 at a site midway between the Breton castles of Josselin and Ploermel, the Combat (or Battle) of the Thirty was an armed melee arranged by the garrison commanders of the two fortresses between two thirty-man groups of knights. Although of little military significance for either party in the BRETON CIVIL WAR, the Combat is important because it became one of the most celebrated episodes of the HUNDRED YEARS WAR and because it illustrates the increasingly chaotic nature of the war in the mid-fourteenth century.

Accounts of why and how the Combat was initiated differ. What is known is that Jean de Beaumanoir, the pro-French Breton commander of Josselin, and Robert (or Richard) of Bamborough, the English commander of Ploermel, each agreed to select teams of thirty knights to fight against each other according to a set of agreed-upon rules. The combatants fought with any weapons they chose, including swords, maces, and battle-axes, but the battle was supervised by referees who signaled the start of combat and oversaw truces for the provision of refreshments and medical care. The English force, which included Sir Hugh CALVELEY and Sir Robert KNOLLES, also contained Breton and German knights.

The teams fought on foot for several hours and were apparently watched by local peasants. Although tradition states that one or more of Beaumanoir's men mounted a cavalry charge at some point, this is uncertain. The Combat ended with Bamborough and eight of his men slain and the surviving English combatants, who eschewed flight as dishonorable, taken captive. Beaumanoir's team lost four (or perhaps six) knights, and all participants on both sides suffered wounds of varying severity.

The Combat inspired a long and famous Breton ballad that was translated into several dialects and made heroes of the victors. In 1373, the chronicler Jean FROISSART witnessed firsthand the honor accorded to a survivor of Beaumanoir's thirty when he displayed his scars at a feast given by CHARLES V. Although some contemporaries criticized such melees as foolish, the Combat of the Thirty, and similar battles arranged at various times during the war, reflected the joy of combat and the desire for fame and profit that characterized much fourteenth-century fighting. Also, the Combat, which was clearly in breach of the Truce of CALAIS of 1347, indicates how little centralized control either government exercised over the fighting, especially after 1350, when local captains often conducted local operations as they saw fit. *See also* BRITTANY; CHIVALRY.

Further Reading: Burne, Alfred H. *The Crécy War*. Ware, England: Wordsworth Editions Ltd., 1999; Seward, Desmond. *The Hundred Years War*. New York: Penguin, 1999; Sumption, Jonathan. *The Hundred Years War*. Vol. 2, *Trial by Fire*. Philadelphia: University of Pennsylvania Press, 2001.

COMPAGNIES D'ORDONNANCE. *See* CHARLES VII, MILITARY REFORMS OF

CONSTABLE OF FRANCE. *See* ARMIES, COMMAND OF; CLISSON, OLIVIER, CONSTABLE OF FRANCE; GUESCLIN, BERTRAND DU, CONSTABLE OF FRANCE; APPENDIX 6: "CONSTABLES AND MARSHALS OF FRANCE AND ENGLAND"

COUNTER-JACQUERIE. *See* JACQUERIE

COURTRAI, BATTLE OF. *See* FLANDERS

CRAVANT, BATTLE OF (1423)
The Battle of Cravant was fought on 31 July 1423 outside the besieged Burgundian town of Cravant, which lay on the River Yonne, some ninety miles southeast of PARIS. Won by an Anglo-Burgundian force commanded by Thomas MONTAGU, earl of Salisbury, the battle resulted in the destruction of a French army, the strengthening of Anglo-Burgundian cooperation, and the thwarting of French efforts to menace Paris.

Since the death of HENRY V in 1422, the English war effort had been directed by JOHN, DUKE OF BEDFORD, eldest uncle of HENRY VI. In preparation for further advances, the duke attempted to consolidate the English position by eliminating enemy enclaves within Anglo-Burgundian territory. To this end, Bedford ordered Salisbury to capture Montaiguillon, a dauphinist stronghold about fifty miles southeast of Paris. At Montaiguillon, the earl was well placed to meet a new French offensive in the summer of 1423. The dauphin (*see* CHARLES VII) sent a large army into the duchy of Burgundy to disrupt the domains of Duke PHILIP THE GOOD, to relieve pressure on Montaiguillon and other besieged dauphinist strongholds, and to threaten Paris. Marching with about four thousand men, Salisbury reached Auxerre on 29 July. Auxerre was nine miles from Cravant, the capture of which was the first goal of the French commanders, Sir John Stewart of Darnley, constable of SCOTLAND, and Louis, count of Vendôme. Although Salisbury was met at Auxerre by a hastily raised Burgundian force, his army was still half or less the size of the dauphinist army, which probably numbered eight to ten thousand men, including a large contingent of Scots and even some Spaniards and Italians.

Maneuvering to circumvent an impregnable French position on the heights northwest of the town, Salisbury crossed to the west bank of the Yonne and marched south to Cravant, arriving opposite the town and its French besiegers on 31 July. The river in front of Cravant was swift and shallow, 40–60 yards wide and knee-to-waist deep. For several hours, the English held their position, waiting in extreme summer heat for the French to make a move. Finally, Salisbury led the left wing of the army across the river, precipitating a fierce fight along the narrow strip of land between the water and the town. On the right, Robert Willoughby, Lord Willoughby, led his men against the town's main bridge, which was stoutly defended by a large contingent of Scots.

As the French on the bridge slowly gave way, the Burgundian garrison of Cravant, although weak from hunger, attacked the French from behind, thereby causing sufficient panic to throw the dauphinists into disordered flight. Escape proved difficult, with the only line of retreat running southward between Salisbury's men and the garrison of the town. The French lost perhaps two thousand dead, with CASUALTIES being particularly high among the Scots, and another two thousand captured, with both Stewart and Vendôme among the prisoners. The rest of the dauphinist army disintegrated, allowing the allies to drive the French from Burgundy in the following months.

Further Reading: Burne, Alfred H. *The Agincourt War*. Ware, England: Wordsworth Editions Ltd., 1999; Waurin, Jean. *Recueil des croniques et anchiennes istories de la Grant Bretaigne, a present nomme Engleterre* (*A Collection of the Chronicles and Ancient Histories of Great Britain, Now Called England*). 5 vols. London: Longman, Green, Longman, Roberts, and Green, 1864–91.

This illustration from *Les Grandes Chroniques de France* depicts the English victory at the Battle of Crécy, 1346. *Erich Lessing/ Art Resource, New York.*

CRÉCY, BATTLE OF (1346)

The Battle of Crécy was fought on 26 August 1346 near the village of Crécy in Ponthieu, a PLANTAGENET possession in northern France. The first great land battle of the HUNDRED YEARS WAR, Crécy was also the only time during the conflict when a king of England and a king of France faced each other across the battlefield. Like POITIERS and AGINCOURT, Crécy was a major English victory, and the battle that introduced the French to a new and devastatingly effective defensive tactic—coordinated formations of longbowmen and dismounted knights protected by pit-traps and baggage lines.

During the first months of 1346, EDWARD III collected a fleet of over seven hundred ships and an army of almost ten thousand men. Although both BRITTANY and GASCONY were considered as landing sites, the king finally brought his army ashore near Saint-Vaast-la-Hogue in NORMANDY on 12 July. During the next month, Edward led a destructive CHEVAUCHÉE across Normandy and then southeastward toward PARIS, which was thrown into an uproar by the sight of nearby villages in flames. After spending three days at Poissy, Edward turned north on 16 August, hoping to cross the Somme and reach FLANDERS before the French concentrated their forces. As Edward withdrew, PHILIP VI, who had so far done little more than shadow the English, suddenly gathered his troops and marched for the Somme. Finding all bridges broken and the line of the river strongly defended, Edward finally got his men across the Somme at the ford of Blanchetaque, which he reached after midnight on 24 August. Although the French held the opposite bank in force, English

ARCHERS drove them back, thereby allowing a small body of infantry to establish a bridgehead and permit the rest of the army to cross and eventually disperse the enemy.

With the French closing rapidly, Edward marched into Ponthieu, where, on 26 August, he deployed his army along a low ridge between the villages of Crécy and Wadicourt. Although there is much debate over the exact nature of Edward's dispositions, it appears that EDWARD, THE BLACK PRINCE; William de BOHUN, earl of Northampton; Thomas BEAUCHAMP, earl of Warwick; and the rest of the nobility formed the front line while the king commanded the reserve to the rear. The archers, numbering half the army, deployed on each flank and slightly forward, with lines of baggage carts and shallow pit-traps protecting their flanks and front. ARTILLERY pieces, being deployed on a battlefield for the first time, were placed along the baggage lines. The entire army was dismounted.

At noon, French scouts discovered the English. Philip hurried his men forward, arranging them in three divisions, with Genoese crossbowmen in the front, the elite French cavalry in the second line, and a cavalry reserve under royal command in the third battalion. At about five o'clock, as rain began to fall, the crossbowmen advanced. Since the longbow had a greater range, English arrows began doing great execution among the Italians well before they came within crossbow range of the English. When English artillery also opened fire, the Italians broke and ran for their own lines. Having no experience of the longbow, Philip and his commanders misinterpreted the flight of the crossbowmen as cowardice, an assumption that caused Charles, count of Alençon, commander of the French cavalry, to charge forward without orders. The French knights rode down their own crossbowmen and then drove for the English center. As the horsemen came within range of the archers, a storm of arrows disrupted their advance—downed men obstructed the path of those behind and horses bolted in terror to escape arrows and artillery. Some French knights reached the English line, where Prince Edward, only sixteen and experiencing his first combat, was hard-pressed. However, the prince fought manfully and the line held. The French continued to reform and charge, perhaps as many as fifteen times, but each assault was broken up by the archers. Nightfall ended the fighting as remounted English knights began attacking surviving clusters of French horsemen.

English CASUALTIES were slight, but the French had lost more than fifteen hundred knights, including John, the blind king of Bohemia; LOUIS DE NEVERS, count of Flanders; and the brother of CHARLES OF BLOIS, the French-backed claimant in the BRETON CIVIL WAR. Although the English army was smaller, it had won because it fought on the defensive and because the longbow was far superior in range and rate of fire to the crossbow. English archers had proven that if properly protected they could decimate charging cavalry, a lesson that the French nobles, who initially blamed their defeat on the cowardice of the crossbowmen, took some time to learn.

Further Reading: Burne, Alfred H. *The Crécy War.* Ware, England: Wordsworth Editions Ltd., 1999; DeVries, Kelly. *Infantry Warfare in the Early Fourteenth Century: Discipline, Tactics, and Technology.* Rochester, NY: Boydell Press, 1996; Sumption, Jonathan. *The Hundred Years War.* Vol. 1, *Trial by Battle.* Philadelphia: University of Pennsylvania Press, 1991.

CRISIS OF 1340–1341

Caused primarily by the financial strains and military failures that characterized the first English campaigns of the HUNDRED YEARS WAR, the crisis of 1340–41 was the most serious political confrontation to occur in England during the reign of EDWARD III. Although the crisis resulted in few permanent reforms, it raised important constitutional issues and demonstrated the ability of clergy, lords, and commons to cooperate in curbing arbitrary royal action.

Forced by bankruptcy and military stalemate to conclude the ignominious Truce of ESPLECHIN in September 1340, Edward III precipitated the crisis in November by publicly blaming his ministers for his financial problems. Edward's increasingly unreasonable demands for money had strained relations with his regency council in England and with PARLIAMENT, which in the spring of 1340 granted new TAXATION only on condition that royal tax collectors be made responsible to Parliament and that all money collected be used only for war costs. Believing that Archbishop John STRATFORD, the president of his council, covertly opposed his policies and was convincing other ministers to do the same, Edward landed unannounced at the Tower of London on 30 November and issued orders for the dismissal or arrest of various officials, including the chancellor, treasurer, and several judges and financiers. Carried out in secret by a small group of followers, these actions frightened Stratford, who retired to Canterbury and refused all summonses to appear before the king. On 29 December, the feast of St. Thomas Becket, Stratford delivered an emotional address in Canterbury Cathedral, the site of Becket's murder. Declaring that the king's supporters had arrested men in contravention of the Magna Carta, had falsely accused him of treason, and might do even worse in the future, the archbishop solemnly pronounced their excommunication.

A bitter pamphlet war now ensued. On 31 December, Stratford circulated a letter, *Sacrosancta ecclesia*, which stoutly defended the liberty of the church. The archbishop also wrote to the king, declaring him the victim of ill counsel and reminding him of his coronation oath. A new royal demand that the archbishop appear at court elicited only a series of letters denouncing the clerical exactions of 1340 and lamenting the king's disregard of the law. In February 1341, Edward published his accusations against the archbishop, angrily declaring him guilty of insubordination, treason, and misappropriation of royal funds. Calling the document a *libellus famosus* (infamous libel), Stratford responded in March with his *Excusaciones*, a

detailed and reasoned rebuttal of all the king's charges and a firm refusal to answer those charges anywhere but in Parliament. By standing on the constitutional principle of a peer's right to trial in Parliament and by tapping into the commons' frustration over exorbitant taxation for an unsuccessful war, Stratford fostered development of a dangerous coalition of domestic opposition that included not only the nobility and bishops, but also the commons and lower clergy. When the king's household knights denied the archbishop admittance to the Parliament summoned to Westminster in April 1341, the outraged assembly named a delegation of bishops and lords to intercede for Stratford, who, although never again appointed to high office, was formally readmitted to royal favor on 3 May.

Politically isolated and desperately in need of supply, Edward, in return for a new grant of taxation, reluctantly assented to a series of parliamentary petitions. The lords declared that no peer could be arrested, tried, or imprisoned except in full Parliament, and both houses demanded a public audit of the king's finances and the appointment of all high officers of state in Parliament. Although Edward annulled these statutes in October, declaring that they had been forced upon him against his will, he never again acted so arbitrarily, and an improvement in English military fortunes, highlighted by the victory at CRÉCY in 1346, rekindled public enthusiasm for the war and strengthened cooperation between the Crown and its subjects.

Further Reading: McKisack, May. *The Fourteenth Century, 1307–1399.* Oxford: Clarendon Press, 1976; Ormrod, W. M. *The Reign of Edward III: Crown and Political Society in England, 1327–1377.* New Haven, CT: Yale University Press, 1990; Waugh, Scott L. *England in the Reign of Edward III.* Cambridge: Cambridge University Press, 1991.

CROSSBOW. *See* ARCHERS

D

DAGWORTH, SIR THOMAS
(c. 1310–1350)

The Suffolk knight Sir Thomas Dagworth was one of EDWARD III's chief lieutenants in BRITTANY during the 1340s. Although a soldier of fortune contracted to serve the English cause in the BRETON CIVIL WAR, Dagworth was a capable administrator and a brave and resourceful soldier who maintained a fundamental loyalty to the PLANTAGENET Crown. Dagworth is a prime example of a nonnoble English commander of obscure origins who won wealth, position, and a high military reputation through service in the HUNDRED YEARS WAR.

Dagworth began his rise to prominence by marrying Eleanor de Bohun, the sister of William de BOHUN, earl of Northampton, in whose retinue Dagworth sailed to Brittany in June 1345. Dagworth immediately demonstrated his military prowess by leading a detachment of Northumberland's troops on a raid into central Brittany, where he caught and defeated CHARLES OF BLOIS, the French-backed duke of Brittany, in a sharp encounter at Cadoret. On 9 June 1346, Dagworth won a second victory over Blois at Saint-Pol de Léon, where Dagworth's force of less than two hundred men was surprised by Blois's much larger army. Deploying his ARCHERS and men-at-arms in the traditional English manner in a hastily fortified hilltop position, Dagworth fought off successive attacks until nightfall, when Blois, appalled at his losses, withdrew.

On 10 January 1347, Dagworth replaced his brother-in-law as king's lieutenant in Brittany. Focused on the war in northern France and always short of money, Edward III left conduct of the war in Brittany to independent captains who were nominally subject to the royal government, but who, in fact, fought the war with their own retainers, at their own expense, and in their own way. Although able, in an emergency, to summon troops from the local English garrisons and from pro-English Breton nobles, Dagworth relied mainly on his army of about five hundred personal retainers and such Flemish and German mercenaries as he could hire.

On 20 June 1347, Dagworth, after quickly gathering a force of about seven hundred men from the dispersed garrisons under his command, won a major victory at LA ROCHE-DERRIEN, where he defeated and captured Charles of Blois and slew many of his noble Breton supporters. In 1348, Dagworth sent his prisoner to LONDON, selling Blois's RANSOM to the king for £3,500. While lack of men and resources prevented Dagworth from extending English authority throughout the duchy, La Roche-Derrien forced the French to divert vital supplies and manpower to the Breton war to shore up the cause of Blois.

Besides lack of men, Dagworth's main problem, which was later succinctly described in a memo to the English government by his successor as lieutenant, Sir Walter BENTLEY, was the nominal nature of his control over the English-contracted captains. In the La Roche-Derrien campaign, for example, the de Spinefort brothers, commanders of the Hennebont garrison, refused Dagworth's summons to join his army. After the battle, Dagworth, to reinforce his authority, stormed Hennebont and hanged the brothers. Dagworth died on 20 July 1350, when he was ambushed by Raoul de

Caours, a former English captain who had switched sides.

Further Reading: Sumption, Jonathan. *The Hundred Years War.* Vol. 1, *Trial by Battle.* Philadelphia: University of Pennsylvania Press, 1999; Sumption, Jonathan. *The Hundred Years War.* Vol. 2, *Trial by Fire.* Philadelphia: University of Pennsylvania Press, 2001.

DAUPHIN. *See* CHARLES V; CHARLES VI; CHARLES VII; LOUIS, DUKE OF GUIENNE

DAVID II, KING OF SCOTLAND (1324–1371)

David II, the son of Robert I and second king of the House of Bruce, maintained the FRANCO-SCOTTISH ALLIANCE that had existed since the 1290s, making Anglo-Scottish relations an important factor in the coming and course of the HUNDRED YEARS WAR.

David was only five when he succeeded his father on 7 June 1329, and only seven when he was crowned at Scone on 24 March 1331. Although England had recognized Scottish independence in the 1328 Treaty of Northampton, EDWARD III, seeking to overturn the agreement, backed an invasion launched in August 1332 by the Bruces' rival, John Balliol, who was supported by nobles who had been dispossessed for supporting the English against Robert I. On 11 August, the invaders defeated a Scottish army at Dupplin Muir, killing the king's guardian, Donald, earl of Mar, and enabling Balliol to be crowned on 24 September. When Sir Andrew Moray, David's new guardian, drove him into England, Balliol paid homage for SCOTLAND to Edward III, thereby allowing the English king to invade Scotland on the pretext of defending his vassal. On 19 July 1333, the English won a major victory at HALIDON HILL, which allowed Balliol and his allies to secure much of the kingdom under English overlordship.

In May 1334, David fled to France, leaving defense of the Bruce cause in the hands of Moray and Robert Stewart, David's cousin and heir apparent. The king's arrival in France derailed a nearly completed Anglo-French agreement over AQUITAINE, which might have prevented or at least delayed the Hundred Years War. Realizing that he could not diplomatically abandon a king to whom he had granted physical asylum, PHILIP VI stunned the English ambassadors by telling them that the proposed treaty had to include David. Since Edward considered Balliol the Scottish king and could in no way countenance an independent, pro-French Scotland, the talks collapsed. David remained in France until June 1341, by which time the Bruce forces, helped after 1337 by the English preoccupation with France, had recaptured most of the strongpoints held by Balliol and the English, with Edinburgh falling in 1341.

During the 1340s, as Edward became more heavily committed in France, David secured his throne and drove the English across the border. In October 1346, only weeks after the English victory at CRÉCY, David invaded England on behalf of his French ally, but suffered a devastating defeat at NEVILLE'S CROSS, where the king was captured and the Scots nobility decimated. Imprisoned in the Tower of London, David became friends with Edward and was attracted by the chivalrous aura of the English court, an atmosphere that he tried to recreate at his own court after his release in October 1357. Negotiations for David's RANSOM were long and complicated. Although the king was willing to compromise with his captor, the Scottish government, led by Stewart as guardian, rejected Edward's exorbitant ransom demands and his insistence that an English prince be recognized as David's heir. No settlement was possible until 1356, when the English capture of JOHN II at POITIERS robbed the Scots of all hope of French assistance. Under the Treaty of Berwick, the Scots agreed to a ransom of 100,000 marks, the surrender of twenty-three noble hostages, and a promise to remain at peace with England until the ransom was paid in full. Because the ransom was so large, the last clause in effect created an indefinite truce that removed Scotland from active participation in the Anglo-French war for the rest of the century.

DIPLOMACY

Because peace revived trade, the economy improved after 1360. Accused of spending some of the money raised for the ransom on luxuries required to maintain his English lifestyle, David had to suppress a rebellion led by Stewart in 1363. Thereafter, David's throne was secure, although his failure to secure a final peace with England led him to delay ransom payments. Although the childless king seemed amenable to English proposals that he be succeeded by a PLANTAGENET prince, the Scottish PARLIAMENT rejected the notion and reaffirmed Stewart as heir. In 1362, David's queen, Joan, the sister of Edward III, died, thus ending their loveless and barren marriage and allowing David to marry his mistress in hopes of an heir. David was in the process of annulling this equally barren match when he died unexpectedly on 22 February 1371 at the age of forty-six. His death ended the Bruce line and passed the Scottish Crown to the House of Stewart. *See also* CHIVALRY.

Further Reading: Nicholson, Ranald. *Scotland: The Later Middle Ages*. New York: Barnes and Noble, 1974; Penman, Michael A. *David II, 1329–71*. East Linton, Scotland: Tuckwell Press, 2004.

DIPLOMACY

The HUNDRED YEARS WAR generated much diplomatic activity, not only between France and England, but also among the courts of Western Europe, including SCOTLAND, BRITTANY, BURGUNDY, and the states of Spain, Italy, Germany, and the Low Countries. Also involved, usually in terms of mediation, were the two supranational rulers of Europe, the pope and the Holy Roman emperor (*see* PAPACY AND THE HUNDRED YEARS WAR). This expansion of diplomatic business encouraged the development of internationally accepted conventions of diplomatic practice; of better training in the law for men who specialized in the conduct of diplomacy; and of archives for the collection, preservation, and organization of diplomatic documents. The war also promoted a trend toward greater royal participation in the conduct of diplomacy and a change in the selection criteria for ambassadors, with men

no longer being chosen solely for their social status, but also for their diplomatic experience, geographic knowledge, and linguistic and oratorical skills.

The sending of permanent representatives to the court of another ruler began in the late fifteenth century in Italy and only became common practice in Western Europe in the sixteenth century. During the Hundred Years War, neither kingdom had a separate department of state responsible for foreign affairs, and diplomacy was still conducted on an ad hoc basis, with embassies returning home on the conclusion of their particular mission. Diplomacy was also viewed to some degree as an extension of military activity. In 1337 and 1415, respectively, EDWARD III and HENRY V put forward diplomatic proposals that they knew would not be accepted, and then used the subsequent French rejections as justifications for war (*see* PROPAGANDA AND WAR PUBLICITY). Truces that were ostensibly arranged to facilitate peace negotiations, such as the 1343 Truce of MALESTROIT that allowed CLEMENT VI to convene the AVIGNON PEACE CONFERENCE, were in fact used by both parties as respites to prepare for the renewal of war. The Truce of TOURS, concluded in 1444, gave CHARLES VII time to implement the administrative and military reforms that allowed his armies to expel the English from NORMANDY and GASCONY in the 1450s and thus effectively end the war (*see* CHARLES VII, MILITARY REFORMS OF). Governments also used manufactured disputes over documents or procedures to buy time or gain tactical advantages during negotiations. At the BRUGES PEACE CONFERENCE in the 1370s, the parties jockeyed for position by quarrelling over the seating order for PHILIP THE BOLD, duke of Burgundy, and JOHN OF GAUNT, duke of Lancaster. In 1418, during preliminary talks for the Treaty of TROYES, the English ambassadors suddenly objected to discussions in French, claiming that they could not understand the language. During the course of the war, such aggressive diplomacy clearly fostered the growth of NATIONAL CONSCIOUSNESS in both realms.

In England, the long dispute over AQUI-TAINE and the many issues arising from the Treaty of PARIS, led in the late thirteenth century to creation of a diplomatic archive and to development of personnel who specialized in diplomacy. This process of diplomatic specialization and record-keeping was far advanced in England by the mid-fifteenth century, when Bishop Jean Juvénal des Ursins recommended that Charles VII institute a similar system for the French Crown. About the time of the ANGLO-FRENCH WAR OF 1294–1303, EDWARD I appointed a keeper of the PROCESSES, who not only archived the records of those Anglo-French commissions, but also organized all records pertaining to the duchy of Aquitaine. In the 1320s, prior to the War of SAINT-SARDOS, these documents were calendared "thus providing a fuller memory thereof in the future" (Allmand, 117) to all English embassies handling matters relating to Aquitaine. As war continued, the personnel of both English and French embassies became more professional, although specialization in the affairs of a particular country or the history of a particular issue was more common among the English. A new emphasis was also placed upon legal training for diplomats, and most English embassies contained at least one legal expert who had trained at EDWARD II's foundation of King's Hall, Cambridge, which became known for preparing men for royal service. Other specialized knowledge and skills were also increasingly valued, such as familiarity with past agreements or the ability to speak well. Thomas Bekynton, one of HENRY VI's ambassadors, was well known for his ability to speak Latin (the English distrusted the use of French), while Henry V's envoys complained during the Troyes discussions of the French ignorance of geography and the terms of the 1360 Treaty of BRÉTIGNY.

In both kingdoms, the importance of the war increased the importance of diplomacy and fostered a growing respect for diplomats and their work. Envoys were accorded a growing number of immunities and privileges, although some commentators complained that these were frequently abused and that ambassadors were often little more than spies. In most cases, however, safe-conducts were respected and ambassadors were allowed to come and go without harm or hindrance, even when traveling across enemy territory. Envoys to foreign courts were often well treated and many were given gifts in hopes that it would induce them to give favorable reports of their host to their own and other rulers. International agreements were also couched in more ritualistic terms to give them a more sacred and binding character. The Treaty of Troyes, for instance, was proclaimed in an elaborate ceremony before the high altar of St. Peter's Cathedral, with Henry V using the same seal with which Edward III had sealed the Brétigny agreement in 1360. At the Congress of ARRAS in 1435, PHILIP THE GOOD could only withdraw from the ANGLO-BURGUNDIAN ALLIANCE created at Troyes by obtaining a papal dispensation.

The need for alliances, military and political, also fostered the professionalization of diplomacy during the war. The French, at various times, concluded agreements with Castile (especially during the CASTILIAN WAR OF SUCCESSION), FLANDERS, and Brittany, and frequently renewed the longstanding FRANCO-SCOTTISH ALLIANCE, while the English forged various agreements with Flanders, Brittany, and rulers in the Low Countries and Germany, including the Treaty of CANTERBURY with the emperor. To make the closest connection between those who formulated foreign policy and those who implemented it, royal direction and oversight increased during the war, with more diplomatic documents being stored in the royal household and more diplomats being selected from among trained royal servants with access to the king. Thus, CHARLES V was closely involved in the diplomatic efforts that preceded acceptance of the APPEAL OF THE GASCON LORDS and the resumption of war in 1369, and Henry V kept close direction of English diplomacy prior to the AGINCOURT campaign of 1415 and during negotiations for the Troyes agreement. In this manner was military and diplomatic effort more effectively coordinated in both kingdoms.

Further Reading: Allmand, Christopher. *The Hundred Years War.* Cambridge: Cambridge University Press, 1988; Curry, Anne. *The Hundred Years War.* 2nd ed. Houndmills, England: Palgrave Macmillan, 2003.

DORDRECHT BONDS (1337–1338)

In February 1338, EDWARD III, as part of a plan to fund the war by exploiting the sale of wool, bought up ten thousand sacks of wool awaiting sale to continental purchasers at the Dutch city of Dordrecht. The king paid the English owners of this wool with notes of acknowledgment that entitled the holders to remission of customs duties owed to the Crown on future wool exports. Known as "Dordrecht bonds," these notes and other dubious financing schemes were made necessary by the severe financial strain placed on the English economy by the enormous cost of the HUNDRED YEARS WAR.

By 1337, Edward, having promised more that £120,000 in payments to his allies in the Low Countries, found himself increasingly unable to meet his war-related obligations. Despite resorting more frequently to loans and direct TAXATION authorized by PARLIAMENT, Edward needed large additional sums to fund his aggressive military plans and maintain his ANTI-FRENCH COALITION (*see also* ANGLO-FLEMISH ALLIANCE). Because wool was England's chief export, Edward hoped to raise significant new revenue by splitting the profits derived from the sale of wool with a syndicate of merchants led by William de la POLE. The merchants agreed to purchase thirty thousand sacks of wool for the king's use. Recent government embargos on wool exports ensured a plentiful supply in England and an eager demand on the Continent. The king set the domestic price of wool at the minimum fair market value, which allowed the syndicate to buy on favorable terms, while wool hunger on the Continent allowed them to sell high. Secured by assignments on the wool customs, the king's half of the expected profits was estimated at £200,000.

However, cooperation between the syndicate and royal officials quickly broke down when Henry BURGHERSH, bishop of Lincoln, demanded even greater sums from the merchants to meet the subsidies he had promised to Edward's allies. When Pole and his associates balked at the amount, the king seized all the wool gathered at Dordrecht by giving the owners bonds that could be used to pay future customs duties. Upon issuance of these Dordrecht bonds, the monopoly initiative collapsed, and the syndicate agreed that the government should dispose of the wool in its possession as it saw fit. To facilitate this sale and to assist the collection of wool in England, Edward temporarily banned wool exports, thereby reducing the usefulness of the bonds to their holders. Many smaller merchants lost heavily and were soon forced to sell their Dordrecht bonds at steep discounts. The Crown eventually authorized various domestic and foreign merchants—including a new syndicate organized by Pole—to buy the bonds, which they obtained for shillings on the pound but redeemed at the Exchequer for full value in remission of customs duties.

Edward, meanwhile, tried other ways to raise ready cash. In 1338, he persuaded Parliament to authorize Crown preemption of half the kingdom's wool production in return for assurances that private traders could dispose of the other half without royal interference. On the strength of this grant, Edward raised new loans from his Italian bankers. In 1343, the king permitted a group of financiers headed by Pole to collect the wool customs in return for cash. However, despite these efforts, the collapse of the original monopoly scheme was a financial disaster for Edward, who was forced into bankruptcy in the early 1340s largely as a result of it.

Further Reading: Fryde, E. B. *William de la Pole: Merchant and King's Banker.* London: Hambledon and London, 2003; Lloyd, T. H. *The English Wool Trade in the Middle Ages.* Cambridge: Cambridge University Press, 1977; McKisack, May. *The Fourteenth Century, 1307–1399.* Oxford: Clarendon Press, 1976.

DOUGLAS, ARCHIBALD, EARL OF DOUGLAS (c. 1369–1424)

Archibald Douglas, fourth earl of Douglas, was the most famous Scottish noble to enter French service during the HUNDRED YEARS WAR. As commander of the Scottish contingent in the dauphinist army, Douglas was richly rewarded for his support, receiving grants of lands, titles, and money that were unprecedented for a nonroyal foreigner.

The son and heir of Archibald Douglas, third earl of Douglas, the younger Archibald married Margaret, the daughter of the future Robert III, in about 1387. Archibald first entered politics in the late 1390s, when, as master of Douglas, he supported his father's efforts to improve the family's fortunes by intervening in the power struggle between the son and brother of Robert III, respectively, David, duke of Rothesay, and Robert, duke of Albany. Allied with Rothesay, the master launched a series of raids into England that provoked an invasion by HENRY IV in the summer of 1400. Succeeding his father as earl in the following December, Douglas routed an English force in eastern Lothian in 1401, and thereafter became the most powerful magnate in southern SCOTLAND and the leading exponent of war with England. After Albany arrested Rothesay, Douglas agreed to the latter's death in return for the former's commitment to the English war. Douglas thereupon led a large army into England, but was defeated and captured at Homildon Hill in September 1402.

Seeking to profit from a growing conflict between his captor, Henry Percy (known as "Hotspur"), son of the earl of Northumberland, and Henry IV, Douglas sided with Hotspur and, in July 1403, fought against the king at Shrewsbury, where he was again captured. Now taken to LONDON, the earl eventually shared his confinement with such other important Scottish captives as Albany's son, Murdoch, earl of Fife, who was also taken at Homildon Hill, and Robert III's son, James, who was seized on his way to France in 1406. Paroled several times to serve as a destabilizing force in Scotland, where

Albany was regent after 1406, Douglas pledged allegiance to Henry IV before breaking parole and returning to Scotland for good in about 1408. Douglas thereafter concluded an agreement—subsequently sealed by the marriage of the earl's daughter to Albany's son, John STEWART, earl of Buchan—that left Douglas in effective control of southern Scotland. Based on Douglas's extensive political connections, his monopoly of local offices, and his appropriation of royal revenues, the earl's power was widely recognized outside the kingdom, where he was considered the real ruler of much of Scotland. Thanks to French attempts to secure his release, Douglas was well known in France, when he traveled in 1412 to negotiate an agreement with JOHN THE FEARLESS, duke of BURGUNDY and regent for CHARLES VI. Anxious for assistance against the ARMAGNACS in the FRENCH CIVIL WAR, Burgundy promised to support Douglas in Scotland in return for a Scottish force of four thousand men. Although the agreement was never implemented, it set a precedent for the dauphin (see CHARLES VII), who in 1419 appealed directly to Douglas, Albany, and other Scottish magnates for military assistance.

The Scottish lords responded by sending an army of six thousand to France under the command of Buchan and Douglas's son. In 1421, Douglas, continuing to play one side against the other, received an annuity of £200 in return for agreeing to serve HENRY V for life. The move forged links with the English court, pressured the dauphin to sweeten his bid for Douglas support, and improved relations with Douglas's brother-in-law, James I, who was still a captive in England. However, English rewards soon paled compared to those showered by the dauphin on Buchan following the earl's victory at BAUGÉ. In October 1423, Douglas, at Buchan's urging, entered dauphinist service. Landing at La Rochelle in March 1424 with an army of sixty-five hundred, Douglas was created duke of Touraine. A former APPANAGE of VALOIS princes, Touraine was an extensive and wealthy lordship, which

Douglas quickly took into his possession. For three months, Douglas and his men lived off his new lands, where they quickly became highly unpopular. In August, Douglas marched to NORMANDY and captured the town of VERNEUIL, which provoked JOHN, DUKE OF BEDFORD, to offer battle. Against the advice of the French nobles, Douglas and Buchan accepted the challenge, and both men died in the subsequent battle, which also resulted in the virtual destruction of the Scottish army in France.

Further Reading: Boardman, Stephen I. *The Early Stewart Kings: Robert II and Robert III, 1371–1406*. East Linton, Scotland: Tuckwell Press, 1996; Brown, Michael. *The Black Douglases: War and Lordship in Late Medieval Scotland, 1300–1455*. East Linton, Scotland: Tuckwell Press, 1998.

DOUGLAS, EARL OF. *See* DOUGLAS, ARCHIBALD, EARL OF DOUGLAS

DUAL MONARCHY. *See* TROYES, TREATY OF

DUNKIRK, TREATIES OF. *See* FLANDERS; LOUIS DE MALE, COUNT OF FLANDERS

DUNOIS, COUNT OF. *See* JOHN, COUNT OF DUNOIS AND LONGUEVILLE

E

ÉCORCHEURS. See ROUTIERS

EDMUND OF LANGLEY, DUKE OF YORK (1341–1402)

The fifth surviving son of EDWARD III and PHILIPPA OF HAINAULT, Edmund of Langley, first duke of York, participated in the last military campaigns of his father's reign and exercised significant political influence during the reign of his nephew, RICHARD II. Although a supporter of HENRY IV and the House of LANCASTER, the duke was founder of the House of York, which eventually overthrew the Lancastrian dynasty.

In 1347, the king granted Edmund numerous manors in northern England that came in the fifteenth century to comprise the core of the Yorkist dynasty's landed wealth. In 1359, Edmund accompanied his father on the RHEIMS CAMPAIGN. Elected to the Order of the GARTER in 1361 and created earl of Cambridge in 1362, Edmund in the mid-1360s became the focus of his father's efforts to create an English APPANAGE in the Low Countries by marrying the earl to MARGUERITE, the daughter and heir of LOUIS DE MALE, count of FLANDERS. In combination with CALAIS and other PLANTAGENET holdings in northern France, the possession of Flanders would have made Edmund a powerful prince in northwestern Europe and a serious check on VALOIS ambitions. However, in 1364, the French pope Urban V forbade the match on grounds of consanguinity. The pope's true motives were revealed in 1367 when he readily dispensed with the same impediment for Marguerite's proposed marriage to PHILIP THE BOLD, duke of BURGUNDY, the brother of CHARLES V.

With the resumption of the HUNDRED YEARS WAR in 1369, Edmund joined his brother, EDWARD, THE BLACK PRINCE, at the sack of LIMOGES in 1370, and his father on the abortive attempt to relieve La Rochelle in 1372. He was king's lieutenant in BRITTANY in 1374 and commanded a CHEVAUCHÉE through the duchy in 1375. In 1372, Cambridge, like his brother, JOHN OF GAUNT, duke of Lancaster, married a daughter of the late Pedro I of Castile, and thereby became associated with his brother's ambition to win the Castilian Crown. In 1381, the earl led an English expedition to Portugal, where, with the help of the Portuguese Crown, he planned to join Lancaster's invasion of Castile. However, neither Lancaster nor the Portuguese arrived, and Cambridge, having lost control of his men, was forced to return to England in 1382.

After the accession of Richard II in 1377, Cambridge, who is traditionally portrayed as retiring and unambitious, supported the policies and bolstered the influence of Lancaster. Created duke of York in 1385, Cambridge served on the governing council established by the Wonderful PARLIAMENT in 1386, but otherwise opposed his brother, THOMAS, DUKE OF BUCKINGHAM, and the Lords Appellant in their attempt to control the royal government during the political upheavals of 1387–89. With Lancaster, York exercised a moderating influence in government in the 1390s, and participated in the Anglo-French peace negotiations that followed conclusion of the Truce of LEULINGHEN in 1389.

After his destruction of Buckingham and the other Lords Appellant in 1397, the king granted many of their lands to York, who was appointed custodian of the realm during Richard's Irish campaign in 1399. When Henry of Bolingbroke, Lancaster's son, returned from exile during the king's absence to reclaim the estates Richard seized from him, York abandoned the king and joined the men he raised in Richard's name with Bolingbroke's forces. York's approval of Richard's subsequent deposition placed him in high favor with Bolingbroke, who took the Crown as Henry IV. On the night of 3 January 1400, York, having learned from his son Edward—who was one of the plotters—of a plan to murder Henry and reinstate Richard, rode to Windsor to warn the king, thereby saving his life. York died shortly thereafter on 1 August 1402.

Further Reading: Biggs, Douglas. "'A Wrong Whom Conscience and Kindred Bid Me to Right': A Reassessment of Edmund of Langley, Duke of York, and the Usurpation of Henry IV." *Albion* 26, no. 2 (1994): 253–72; Russell, Peter E. *The English Intervention in Spain and Portugal in the Time of Edward III and Richard II*. Oxford: Clarendon Press, 1955; Saul, Nigel. *Richard II*. New Haven, CT: Yale University Press, 1997.

EDWARD, THE BLACK PRINCE, PRINCE OF WALES (1330–1376)

Edward of Woodstock, prince of Wales and AQUITAINE, was the eldest son of EDWARD III and PHILIPPA of Hainault, and thus heir to the PLANTAGENET throne. Because he was one of the most successful commanders of the HUNDRED YEARS WAR, the prince was regarded by contemporaries as a model of CHIVALRY and the greatest knight of his age.

For reasons that are now lost, Edward has been known since the sixteenth century as "the Black Prince," a sobriquet that is often tied to his alleged use of black ARMOR, but that may actually stem from attempts to distinguish the prince, who was frequently called Edward IV in anticipation of his accession, from the fifteenth-century Yorkist king Edward IV. Born at Woodstock on 15 June 1330, the prince was sixteen when he first accompanied his father to France. Knighted by the king upon landing at Saint-

Vaast-la-Hogue in NORMANDY on 12 July 1346, the prince, acting with the advice of such veteran captains as William de BOHUN, earl of Northampton, and Thomas BEAUCHAMP, earl of Warwick, held nominal command of the English center at the subsequent Battle of CRÉCY, where he distinguished himself in combat and established his reputation as a warrior. In honor of King John of Bohemia, who was slain fighting the English at Crécy, the prince adopted John's badge of ostrich feathers as his own, and may likewise have acquired his motto, *Ich dene* (I serve).

In 1347, the prince participated in the successful siege of CALAIS, and in about 1348 became a founding member of the Order of the GARTER. In 1350, he helped his father defeat a Castilian fleet at the naval Battle of WINCHELSEA. Following expiration of the Truce of CALAIS, the prince received his first independent command, being named king's lieutenant in GASCONY, from which he launched the highly destructive CHEVAUCHÉE of 1355, during which the prince's army pillaged more than five hundred towns and villages in southern France. A second CHEVAUCHÉE in 1356 culminated in the Battle of POITIERS, where the English captured JOHN II and many members of the French nobility. After concluding the Truce of BORDEAUX with his captive, the prince conveyed John to LONDON, where both were rapturously received. In 1359, after the collapse of the First and Second Treaties of LONDON, the prince accompanied his father on the RHEIMS CAMPAIGN, which failed to achieve Edward III's coronation as king of France but did make possible conclusion of the Treaty of BRÉTIGNY. Under the treaty, which the prince negotiated for the English with HENRY OF GROSMONT, duke of Lancaster, the Plantagenets acquired a much enlarged Aquitaine in full sovereignty.

On 19 July 1362, Edward III granted his son the principality of Aquitaine. Before sailing for Bordeaux, the prince married Joan, known as the "Fair Maid of Kent," the widow of Thomas HOLLAND, earl of Kent. They kept a brilliant court at Bordeaux, where their two sons—Edward, who died in 1371, and the future RICHARD II—were born. In 1366, the prince intervened in the CASTILIAN WAR OF SUCCESSION, concluding the Treaty of Libourne with Pedro I of Castile, who had been deposed in favor of his half brother by a French-backed army of ROUTIERS led by Bertrand du GUESCLIN. Leading his own *routier* force into Castile in 1367, the prince defeated and captured du Guesclin at the Battle of NÁJERA, thereby restoring Pedro. However, when the Castilian king reneged on his promises to pay for the campaign, the prince, who had contracted what was likely chronic dysentery, was forced to return to Aquitaine empty-handed. The resulting need for funds compelled the prince to demand a *fouage* (hearth tax), the collection of which caused leading members of the Gascon nobility to appeal to CHARLES V. When the French king accepted this APPEAL OF THE GASCON LORDS by summoning him to PARIS, the prince declared himself willing to come only at the head of an army. Charles thereupon confiscated the principality and the war resumed in 1369.

Increasingly ill, the prince left defense of the principality in the hands of his most loyal lieutenants—Sir John CHANDOS, Sir James AUDLEY, and Jean de GRAILLY, captal de Buch. In 1370, stung by the capitulation of LIMOGES, the prince, although forced to travel by litter, personally led an expedition to effect its recapture. The city was retaken and sacked, although the massacre of civilians described by Jean FROISSART and long considered a stain on the prince's chivalrous record seems unlikely to have occurred. In 1371, the prince sailed to England and returned the government of Aquitaine to his father. The prince's illness thereafter grew so debilitating that little is known of his activities until the meeting of the Good PARLIAMENT in 1376, when it is claimed that he influenced the actions of the Commons. However, his role, if any, in this assembly has probably been exaggerated, and Parliament was still in session when the prince died on 8 June. An orthodox man who fully shared the martial interests of his time and class, the prince was a popular figure around whom legends gathered both during and after his life. Much was written about him, including the French verse biography later titled *La Vie du Prince Noir* (*Life of the Black Prince*), which was completed in about 1385 by Chandos Herald, an unknown native of Hainault who served as Sir John Chandos's officer of arms.

Further Reading: Barber, Richard. *Edward, Prince of Wales and Aquitaine.* New York: Charles Scribner's Sons, 1978; Chandos Herald. *Life of the Black Prince by the Herald of Sir John Chandos.* Ed. and trans. Mildred K. Pope and Eleanor C. Lodge. Oxford: Clarendon, 1910; Harvey, John. *The Black Prince and His Age.* London: Rowman and Littlefield, 1976; Hewitt, Herbert J. *The Black Prince's Expeditions of 1355–1357.* Manchester: Manchester University Press, 1958; Sedgwick, Theodore Dwight. *The Life of Edward, the Black Prince.* New York: Barnes and Noble, 1993.

EDWARD I, KING OF ENGLAND (1239–1307)

The son of Henry III and grandfather of EDWARD III, Edward I was an able and energetic monarch who conquered Wales, restructured royal government, revised the common law, fostered the development of PARLIAMENT, and initiated almost three centuries of Anglo-Scottish hostility. By vigorously resisting French encroachment on his exercise of ducal authority in AQUITAINE, Edward commenced the long quarrel over the duchy that eventually culminated in the outbreak of the HUNDRED YEARS WAR. Edward also inadvertently created one of the prime components of that later war by arranging a dynastic union with the House of CAPET that eventually gave the PLANTAGENETS a claim to the French throne.

Edward first came to political prominence in the 1250s during the ongoing struggle between his father and the barons of England, who had been alienated by Henry's reckless and spendthrift policies. In May 1264, the baronial opposition, led by Simon de Montfort, earl of Leicester, defeated the king at Lewes, where Edward's impetuous charge routed Montfort's Londoners but left the rest of the royalist army unsupported. Surrendering himself as a hostage to ensure the king's compliance with the settlement subsequently imposed by Montfort, Edward escaped a year later and raised an army that slew the earl at Evesham in August 1265. Having led the royalist recovery, Edward now assumed the leading role in his father's government. Taking the crusader's cross in June 1268, Edward arrived in North Africa in November 1270. In June 1272, a Muslim assassin wounded Edward with a poisoned dagger. Narrowly escaping death, he returned to Sicily, where he learned of his father's death on 16 November. Although now king, Edward did not return to England until August 1274, having spent the previous year in Aquitaine, where Anglo-French relations were generally friendly until the 1290s. In PARIS in August 1273, Edward did homage for the duchy to Philip III, and thereafter the two kings conducted a personal DIPLOMACY that resolved most disputes arising from the Treaty of PARIS. In 1279, the Anglo-French Treaty of Amiens gave Edward the Agenais, in which the king authorized the foundation of numerous BASTIDES over the next decade. In 1285, when the French invaded Aragon, the potential conflict between Edward's obligation as duke to support his feudal overlord and his policy as king to avoid continental war was resolved by Philip's death.

During the first two decades of his reign, Edward undertook a sweeping systemization of English government, devising and implementing a series of parliamentary statutes dealing with the royal confirmation of liberties and franchises, the limitation of land grants to the Church, and the prohibition of new feudal tenures. These acts and Edward's later need for funds to wage war in SCOTLAND and Aquitaine greatly accelerated the institutional development of Parliament. In 1277, Edward invaded Wales, which he finally subdued in 1284, when the Statute of Wales attached the principality to the English Crown. In 1290, following the deaths of Alexander III and his young granddaughter, Margaret of Norway, Edward accepted an invitation from the Scottish nobility to act as arbitrator in a succession dispute between John Balliol and Robert Bruce. Edward's decision for Balliol was largely unopposed, but his claim to be Balliol's feudal overlord and his demand that Balliol perform military service and allow Scottish appeals to English courts convinced the Scottish nobility to ally with PHILIP IV, thus initiating a FRANCO-SCOTTISH ALLIANCE that lasted into the sixteenth century.

Already at war in Scotland, where he sought to impose his overlordship, Edward in the 1290s also found himself at war with France, where he sought to deny Capetian overlordship. In 1286, Edward did homage to Philip IV in Paris. From the autumn of 1286 to June 1289, Edward was resident in GASCONY where he tried to limit appeals to the PARLEMENT by making the ducal administration more efficient. However, after 1292, Philip, pressed by a court faction led by his brother, Charles, count of VALOIS, sought means to more strictly enforce his Gascon overlordship, and French policy in Aquitaine shifted from dealing with Edward as a sovereign monarch to dealing with him as a feudal vassal. Following a series of violent encounters between French and Gascon seamen, Philip had Edward summoned before the Parlement in 1294. When the English king failed to appear, Philip suggested a secret compromise involving a temporary surrender of Aquitaine, but once French officials had possession, Philip reneged on the agreement and confiscated the duchy, thereby initiating the ANGLO-FRENCH WAR OF 1294–1303.

Heavily committed in Scotland, Edward had few resources for war in Gascony, and sought to relieve pressure on the duchy by forging alliances in the Low Countries, particularly with the count of FLANDERS. However, this policy foundered on Edward's inability to support his allies militarily. Despite marrying his sister MARGARET to the English king in 1299, Philip did not restore Aquitaine to Edward until 1303, when rebellion in Flanders and BORDEAUX compelled him to do so. As part of the peace settlement, the two kings agreed to a marriage between Edward's son, Prince Edward, and Philip's daughter, Isabella (*see* ISABELLA, QUEEN OF ENGLAND [c. 1292–1358]), a match that eventually gave Edward's grandson a claim to the French Crown. In 1306, Edward granted Aquitaine to his son. Edward died on 7 July 1307 and was succeeded by his son EDWARD II.

Further Reading: Prestwich, Michael. *Edward I.* Berkeley: University of California Press, 1988.

EDWARD II, KING OF ENGLAND (1284–1327)

The sixth king of the House of PLANTAGENET, Edward II was ill suited to rule a kingdom and much of his reign, which ended with his deposition, was spent in open conflict with his barons. Edward's relations with the French Crown, particularly in regard to AQUITAINE, were bedeviled by the king's indecisive personality, by his reliance on royal favorites, by ongoing baronial opposition, and by the rapid turnover of French monarchs during the last years of the House of CAPET. By the 1320s, these factors led to another confiscation of the duchy of Aquitaine and to another ANGLO-FRENCH WAR.

Born at Caernarvon, the fourth but only surviving son of EDWARD I, Edward was the first heir to the English throne to be called prince of Wales. Although he was named titular regent of England during his father's absence in GASCONY in 1297, and made duke of Aquitaine at his knighting in May 1306, the prince's relations with his father were strained during the king's last years. In June 1305, the king banished his son from court and ordered the Exchequer to refuse him any financial support. The prince was restored to favor in October, following interventions on his behalf by his sisters and stepmother, MARGARET OF FRANCE. The exact cause of the quarrel is unknown, but likely involved the prince's friend Piers Gaveston, a young Gascon knight, whom the king finally banished from England in February 1307. Historians have long speculated on the nature of the prince's relationship with Gaveston, debating whether it was based on a

homosexual liaison or, as one writer has suggested, on an oath of adoptive brotherhood. On his accession in July 1307, Edward II immediately recalled Gaveston, whom he also created earl of Cornwall and betrothed to his niece. In 1308, when Edward traveled to France to marry Isabella, the daughter of PHILIP IV (*see* ISABELLA, QUEEN OF ENGLAND [c. 1292–1358]), he named Gaveston regent during his absence. A haughty man with a sarcastic wit, Gaveston antagonized both the nobility, who considered him an arrogant upstart wielding inappropriate influence, and the new queen, who complained that the king preferred Gaveston's company to her own. Banished several times at the insistence of the barons, Gaveston was seized and executed in 1312 by a coalition of opposition magnates led by Thomas, earl of Lancaster.

In 1311, Lancaster and his allies forced the king to accept the Ordinances, a reform program that limited royal authority. A series of military reverses in SCOTLAND, particularly the defeat at Bannockburn in 1314, weakened Edward's position and allowed Lancaster to dominate the government during the late 1310s. The king, however, turned to a new favorite, his chamberlain, Hugh Despenser the Younger. Although there is no evidence of a sexual relationship between Edward and Despenser, the latter used his influence with the king to enrich himself and his family. In 1321, the barons forced Despenser's banishment, but the king, in an uncharacteristic burst of energy, routed his opponents at Boroughbridge in March 1322. Following Lancaster's execution, Edward and Despenser began four years of unchallenged rule.

While Edward struggled with his baronial opponents, the English position in France deteriorated. Having been invested with Aquitaine prior to his accession, Edward paid homage for the duchy to Philip IV on the day before marrying Philip's daughter in January 1308. Although the Anglo-French commissions known as the PROCESS of Montreuil (1306) and the Process of Périgueux (1311) attempted to settle issues remaining from the war of the 1290s as well as new issues arising thereafter, little was accomplished, and the question of Gascon appeals to the PARLEMENT in PARIS continued to sour relations between the Crowns. In 1313, Edward stabilized the situation by again doing homage for the duchy in Paris. After Philip's death in 1314, his sons followed one another on the throne in rapid succession, leaving Edward obligated to perform homage anew to each one. LOUIS X died in 1316 without ever receiving Edward's homage, but the English king did perform homage to PHILIP V at Amiens in June 1320. Failure to do the same for Philip's brother, CHARLES IV, who became king in 1322, was a factor in the French confiscation of Aquitaine in 1324. However, the immediate cause of the Anglo-French War of SAINT-SARDOS, which began in 1323, was the violent resistance offered to the foundation of a French royal *BASTIDE* in Aquitaine by one of Edward's Gascon vassals.

When the subsequent French campaign reduced Plantagenet Aquitaine to a coastal strip running south of BORDEAUX, Edward sent his queen to France in March 1325 to negotiate with her brother. The resulting settlement was sealed in September, when thirteen-year-old Prince Edward, the future EDWARD III, did homage for the duchy on his father's behalf. With the prince in her custody, Isabella, who despised Despenser, refused to return, and, in concert with her lover, Roger Mortimer, a royal opponent in exile in Paris, raised an army and invaded England in September 1326. Welcomed by the nobility, who almost universally hated the Despenser regime, Isabella engineered the parliamentary deposition of her husband in favor of her son in January 1327. The deposed king was imprisoned at Berkeley Castle, where he supposedly died on 21 September, the victim of a murder allegedly committed by means of a red-hot poker inserted into his rectum to avoid any outward marks of violence.

Further Reading: Fryde, Natalie B. *The Tyranny and Fall of Edward II, 1321–1326*. Cambridge: Cambridge University Press, 1979; Hutchison, Harold F. *Edward II*. London: Eyre and Spottis-woode, 1971; Maddicott, J. R. *Thomas of Lancaster, 1307–1322: A Study in the Reign of Edward II*. London: Oxford University Press, 1970; Phillips, J.R.S. *Aymer de Valence, Earl of Pembroke, 1307–1324: Baronial Politics in the Reign of Edward II*. Oxford: Clarendon Press, 1972.

EDWARD III, KING OF ENGLAND (1312–1377)

The seventh king of the House of PLANTAGENET, and the grandson of PHILIP IV of the House of CAPET, Edward III was an energetic and opportunistic monarch whose claim to the French Crown and ambition for French territory initiated the HUNDRED YEARS WAR. Although his last years were marked by failure and decline, Edward enjoyed popular support at home and military success abroad for most of his fifty-year reign.

The eldest son of EDWARD II and Isabella of France (*see* ISABELLA, QUEEN OF ENGLAND [c. 1292–1358]), Edward became a pawn in his parents' power struggle during the 1320s. To avoid paying homage in person to his brother-in-law, CHARLES IV, the king made Edward duke of AQUITAINE in 1325. Sent to France, where his mother was already negotiating an end to the War of SAINT-SARDOS, Edward performed homage for his new fief on 24 September. Resentful of the influence exercised over her husband by the royal favorite, Hugh Despenser the Younger, Isabella refused the king's demands to return to England with Edward. In 1326, accompanied by her lover, Roger Mortimer, a royal opponent in exile at the French court, the queen traveled to Hainault, where, in return for military assistance, she negotiated a match with the count's daughter, PHILIPPA, whom Edward married in January 1328. Landing in England in September 1326, the queen, aided by widespread dissatisfaction with the Despenser regime, overthrew her husband. In January 1327, PARLIAMENT deposed Edward II and proclaimed the prince king as Edward III. Crowned on 1 February, Edward, at fourteen, was too young to rule, and real power rested with Isabella and Mortimer, who likely ordered Edward II's murder in September. The regency government was quickly discredited by Mortimer's rapacity and the conclusion of two humiliating treaties—a 1327 agreement that allowed Charles to retain much of Aquitaine, and the 1328 Treaty of Northampton which, after a disastrous military campaign, recognized Scottish independence. Increasingly distrustful of Mortimer, Edward plotted with young courtiers such as William MONTAGU to seize personal control of the government. On 19 October 1330, a month before his eighteenth birthday, Edward struck, arresting and executing Mortimer and sending his mother into retirement.

On the death of Charles IV without male heirs in February 1328, Edward was the closest male relative to the last Capetian kings. However, because Edward's claim came through a woman, the French nobility, unwilling to accept a minor English king dominated by his mother, offered the throne to the count of VALOIS, the late king's adult cousin, who became PHILIP VI. On 6 June 1329, Edward performed simple homage for Aquitaine, thereby implicitly accepting the Valois claim. In April 1331, Edward, disguised as a merchant, returned to France at Philip's insistence to confirm that his earlier homage should be construed as liege homage. In the early 1330s, Edward resumed the war in SCOTLAND, seeking, like his grandfather, EDWARD I, to establish English overlordship over the northern kingdom. An English victory at HALIDON HILL in July 1333 forced the young Scottish king, DAVID II, to flee to France, where his cause was taken up by Philip, who refused any settlement in Aquitaine that did not encompass Scotland. Angered by what he considered interference in his internal affairs, and by continuing jurisdictional disputes in Aquitaine, Edward received the French rebel ROBERT OF ARTOIS, whose welcome in LONDON was used by Philip as grounds for confiscating Aquitaine on 24 May 1337.

Edward began the resulting Anglo-French war by constructing, at great expense, a grand ANTI-FRENCH COALITION among the princes of the Low Countries and Germany.

This alliance was fortified in 1339 by conclusion of an ANGLO-FLEMISH ALLIANCE with the revolutionary regime of James van ARTEVELDE. In February 1340, Edward made formal claim to the French throne, a move designed to transform the Gascon quarrel from a dispute between lord and vassal to one between equals, and to allow Edward's allies in FLANDERS and elsewhere to support his cause without rebelling against the French Crown. However, this network of alliances collapsed after the failed THIÉRACHE and TOURNAI campaigns of 1339 and 1340. Despite a major navel victory at SLUYS in June, Edward was bankrupt by late 1340. The king's frustrations caused the one major domestic upheaval of the reign, the CRISIS OF 1340–1341, during which Edward charged Archbishop John STRATFORD and other ministers with failing to financially support his armies. When the confrontation with Stratford threatened to escalate, Edward backed down and in the process confirmed the right of peers to be tried in Parliament and of Parliament to consent to TAXATION.

Abandoning the alliance strategy, Edward turned to CHEVAUCHÉES, highly mobile campaigns of largely English armies that lived partly off the land. To open a new front against France, he intervened in the BRETON CIVIL WAR in the mid-1340s and sent HENRY OF GROSMONT, duke of Lancaster, to conduct a series of successful campaigns in GASCONY. Between 1342 and 1347, victories at BERGERAC and AUBEROCHE in Aquitaine and at LA ROCHE-DERRIEN in BRITTANY established English ascendancies in those provinces, while an innovative combining of ARCHERS and dismounted cavalry won major victories over the French at CRÉCY and the Scots at NEVILLE'S CROSS, where David II was captured. In 1347, the capture of CALAIS, the conclusion of the TRUCE OF CALAIS, and the founding of the Order of the GARTER ended this period of success. The BLACK DEATH, which devastated both countries between 1347 and 1350, temporarily ended the war until the mid-1350s, when Edward's son, EDWARD, THE BLACK PRINCE, desolated southern France during the CHEVAUCHÉE OF

1355 and captured JOHN II at POITIERS in 1356. When his exorbitant demands for RANSOM and territory overthrew two attempts at a settlement—the First (1358) and Second (1359) Treaties of LONDON—Edward launched the RHEIMS CAMPAIGN in 1359, hoping thereby to have himself crowned king and thus force the French to capitulate. However, in 1360, bad weather and the French refusal to give battle defeated the English and forced Edward to conclude the Treaty of BRÉTIGNY, whereby he renounced the French throne in return for an enlarged Aquitaine in full sovereignty.

Having achieved his objectives, Edward granted Aquitaine to the prince, who, having contracted chronic dysentery during the 1367 NÁJERA campaign, resigned the duchy in 1371. By accepting the APPEAL OF THE GASCON LORDS, CHARLES V reopened the war in 1369 and during the 1370s retook most of Aquitaine. Although Edward prepared to resume the field, the death of the queen prevented him from leading a planned expedition to NORMANDY in 1369, and his last campaign, a 1372 naval expedition intended to reverse a recent defeat at LA ROCHELLE, was aborted due to contrary winds. Now in his sixties, and increasingly under the influence of his mistress, Alice Perrers, Edward grew infirm and lost interest in governing. With the prince incapacitated by illness, and the king slipping into senility, Edward's son, JOHN OF GAUNT, duke of Lancaster, dominated the government. In 1376, the Good Parliament, backed by the prince, who died in June, reacted to defeat and corruption by impeaching royal ministers and dismissing Perrers. Abandoned by most of his court, Edward died at Sheen on 21 June 1377. He was succeeded by his grandson, RICHARD II.

Further Reading: Ormrod, W. M. *The Reign of Edward III: Crown and Political Society in England, 1327–1377.* New Haven, CT: Yale University Press, 1990; Packe, Michael. *King Edward III.* Ed. L. C. B. Seaman. London: Routledge and Kegan Paul, 1983; Waugh, Scott L. *England in the Reign of Edward III.* Cambridge: Cambridge University Press, 1991.

ESPLECHIN, TRUCE OF (1340)

Concluded on 25 September 1340, the nine-month Truce of Esplechin was the first negotiated cessation of combat during the HUNDRED YEARS WAR. The truce acknowledged EDWARD III's financial inability to continue the campaign of 1340 and signaled the failure of the ANGLO-FLEMISH ALLIANCE as an instrument for the rapid overthrow of the VALOIS monarchy.

By the spring of 1340, Edward, through the dispersal of large sums of money, had constructed a grand anti-French alliance that included FLANDERS, Brabant, Hainault, Guelders, and Juliers. Following the triumph of his navy at the Battle of SLUYS in June, Edward and his allies agreed to send two armies into northern France. The first, commanded by ROBERT OF ARTOIS, was to capture the town of SAINT-OMER in Artois and then march against CALAIS. The second, commanded by the king, was to besiege the town of TOURNAI. Commencing on 31 July, the siege of Tournai quickly foundered for want of proper siege equipment and effective cooperation among the allies. As the siege continued, it became increasingly clear that Edward could not make the payments he had promised. This realization, coupled with the defeat of Robert's army at the Battle of Saint-Omer, which opened Flanders to French invasion, quickly destroyed allied enthusiasm for the campaign. When a French army led by PHILIP VI approached Tournai in early September, Edward, knowing his allies would not fight, had no choice but to seek a negotiated settlement.

Eager to exploit the divisions among his enemies, and happy to disrupt the English alliance without giving battle, Philip appointed a commission to meet allied representatives in a chapel outside the village of Esplechin, which stood halfway between the two armies. An agreement was quickly concluded; it called for a truce to run until 24 June 1341 and to include not just northern France, but also GASCONY, SCOTLAND, and the war at sea. All parties would maintain their current territorial holdings, no matter how they had been obtained, and all prisoners were to be paroled with the understanding that they must return to captivity should hostilities resume. By promising to prevent the return of all Flemings who had fled to France, and to seek the lifting of all ecclesiastical sanctions imposed on Flanders, Philip reassured the pro-English regime of James van ARTEVELDE, who had opposed the negotiations.

The truce benefited Philip by achieving the break-up of the allied army and the withdrawal of the English king; it benefited Edward's noble allies by buying them time to repair their relationship with Philip; and it benefited Edward by canceling a planned Scottish attack on Sterling and a developing French campaign against the English garrisons in Gascony. However, believing himself cheated of victory, Edward was bitter and accused his ministers, particularly Archbishop John STRATFORD, of failing to support him, a charge that provoked the English political CRISIS OF 1340–1341. Although the truce raised expectations of talks for a permanent settlement, Edward was uninterested and eager to resume the war. He accepted extension of the truce to 29 August 1341 and then to 24 June 1342, but the eruption of the BRETON CIVIL WAR in the autumn of 1341 and the subsequent Anglo-French intervention in the duchy essentially ended the truce. *See also* ANTI-FRENCH COALITION; NAVAL WARFARE.

Further Reading: Perroy, Edouard. *The Hundred Years War.* Trans. W. B. Wells. New York: Capricorn Books, 1965; Sumption, Jonathan. *The Hundred Years War.* Vol. 1, *Trial by Battle.* Philadelphia: University of Pennsylvania Press, 1999.

ESTATES, GENERAL AND PROVINCIAL

The provincial estates of VALOIS France were assemblies of nobles, clergy, and townsmen—the three "estates" or classes of medieval society—that met in various provinces or feudal jurisdictions to consider local issues and provide financial support to local lords. The Estates-General was a national or regional assembly of the three estates that was summoned by the king to render advice and give consent, primarily in regard to the raising of taxes for war. Although the nobility and higher clergy had long attended royal and local assemblies of various kinds, the term "estates" applies only to those bodies that included representatives of towns among their membership. During the HUNDRED YEARS WAR, when the royal need for funds was especially acute, the Crown consulted both local and national estates more regularly in an effort to fully engage local elites in the war effort.

Many provincial assemblies developed out of the right of a feudal lord to summon his vassals to his court to provide aid and counsel. By the thirteenth century, two new concepts encouraged the development of tripartite assemblies of clergy, townsmen, and feudal nobility. The first was the notion that society was broadly divided into three groups—warriors, priests, and workers. The third group, essentially nonnoble laymen in the towns, was large, diverse, and, by the thirteenth century, growing in wealth, education, and influence. The second concept was the principle of representation, which allowed groups to appoint one or more of their number to represent their corporate interests at the court of the king or local lord. Thus, the clergy and laity developed the practice of electing representatives to act in their name just as it became politically useful to include such groups in local assemblies.

The Crown found provincial estates useful as instruments for obtaining the consent of local communities to the collection of war taxes. Provincial elites used the estates to present grievances to the Crown, to defend local interests at court, and to administer funds collected locally for defense and the maintenance of transportation systems. Estates functioned in more than half the provinces of the realm, including NORMANDY in the north and Languedoc in the south. Although some provincial estates met rarely, others developed permanent bureaucracies, devised clear procedures, kept careful records, and levied taxes for their own maintenance. Because the provincial estates never presented a direct challenge to royal authority, French kings viewed such assemblies as useful means for communicating the royal will to local communities and for transmitting local concerns to the royal court.

On the other hand, national and regional assemblies, the Estates-General or the Estates of Languedoil, proved more threatening to royal interests, especially during periods of political or military turmoil. The Estates-General first appeared in the reign of PHILIP IV, when the king, in the midst of his long dispute with the pope regarding secular jurisdiction over the national clergy, sought support for his controversial policies. Beginning in the 1330s, PHILIP VI several times summoned the Estates-General to approve taxes or deal with war-related crises. From the Crown's point of view, the national assembly was of only limited usefulness, since any grant of TAXATION had to be confirmed by the various provincial estates. After the defeat at CRÉCY in 1346, the Estates-General pressed for governmental reforms until the BLACK DEATH interrupted both the war and the reform movement. Between 1356 and 1360, the years following JOHN II's capture at POITIERS, the Estates-General met frequently and demanded reform of the royal administration in return for large tax grants to fund the war. However, due to the disordered state of the realm and the continuing need for provincial assemblies to ratify tax grants, the Estates-General could not provide the taxes promised, leading CHARLES V to conclude that it was more trouble than it was worth. Although Charles continued to summon the Estates-General in the 1360s, the revival of royal authority made these assemblies more amenable to the royal will.

During the troubled reign of CHARLES VI, meetings of the Estates-General were fewer and more turbulent. In 1381, when the Estates of Languedoil granted a hearth tax in return for the right to control its collection and employment, irate taxpayers revolted in ROUEN and PARIS. In 1413, in the midst of the FRENCH CIVIL WAR, the Estates-General refused taxes until the Burgundian regime undertook reform, thereby convincing JOHN THE FEARLESS, duke of BURGUNDY, to foment the CABOCHIEN insurrection. Between 1422 and 1439, CHARLES VII, in need of money and national support, frequently summoned the Estates of Languedoil to approve taxation. However, as royal authority revived after 1440, the king continued to levy taxes but ceased to call the national assembly. The Estates-General thus did not become a regular part of royal government and the last meetings of the medieval Estates-General occurred in 1468 and 1484. *See also* PARLEMENT; PARLIAMENT.

Further Reading: Bisson, Thomas. *Assemblies and Representation in Languedoc in the Thirteenth Century.* Princeton, NJ: Princeton University Press, 1964; Henneman, John Bell. *Royal Taxation in Fourteenth-Century France: The Development of War Financing, 1322–1356.* Princeton, NJ: Princeton University Press, 1971; Major, J. Russell. *Representative Institutions in Renaissance France, 1421–1559.* Madison: University of Wisconsin Press, 1960; Tyrrell, Joseph M. *A History of the Estates of Poitou.* The Hague: Mouton, 1968.

EUGENIUS IV. *See* PAPACY AND THE HUNDRED YEARS WAR

EXETER, DUKE OF. *See* BEAUFORT, THOMAS, DUKE OF EXETER

EYMET, BATTLE OF. *See* GUESCLIN, BERTRAND DU

F

FASTOLF, SIR JOHN (c. 1378–1459)

One of the chief English military leaders of the fifteenth century, Sir John Fastolf overcame low birth to achieve high-ranking commands in the armies and administration of English-occupied France. Fastolf's military career illustrates the opportunities for economic and social advancement that were available to ambitious and enterprising soldiers during the HUNDRED YEARS WAR.

Born into a gentry family in Norfolk, Fastolf entered the service of HENRY IV's second son, THOMAS, DUKE OF CLARENCE, whom Fastolf accompanied to Ireland in 1401 and to France in 1412. Although only an esquire, Fastolf became deputy constable of BORDEAUX in 1413. He fought with HENRY V at AGINCOURT in 1415 and was knighted in 1416. He served with distinction in the campaigns leading to the conquest of NORMANDY and became constable of Fécamp in 1419 and of the Bastille garrison in PARIS in 1420.

The deaths of Clarence in 1421 and Henry V in 1422 allowed Fastolf to rise from subordinate positions to high military commands. In 1423, JOHN, DUKE OF BEDFORD, now regent of France for HENRY VI, made Fastolf master of his household. Appointments as councilor of France, governor of Maine and Anjou, and king's lieutenant in Normandy followed thereafter. Fastolf captured JOHN, DUKE OF ALENÇON, at VERNEUIL in 1424 and commanded the English forces at the Battle of the HERRINGS in February 1429. As the only English leader to escape capture at PATAY in June 1429, Fastolf was unfairly accused of cowardice and was temporarily stripped of his membership in the prestigious Order of the GARTER. Although he was later restored to favor and continued to serve on the French council and in various military posts, the incident at Patay left a lasting mark on Fastolf's reputation and may account for his later transformation by William Shakespeare into the comedic Sir John Falstaff, one of the most striking characters in English literature.

Fastolf was present at the Congress of ARRAS in 1435 and drafted a report on the future conduct of the war in France. He retired from active campaigning in 1440, and returned to England, where he devoted himself to increasing his wealth. Having acquired a considerable fortune through the profits of war—for example, plunder, RANSOMS, and wages—Fastolf enlarged it through wise business practices. While in France, he regularly sent his earnings home and invested his funds with care. He bought much property in Norfolk, where his fortified manor house at Caister became his most prized possession. He also invested heavily in such valuables as plate, jewels, tapestries, and books, and soon commanded the income of an earl. His later years were spent in endless litigation and were marked by a growing obsession with wealth—he complained constantly of £11,000 owed him by the Crown and bitterly denounced the government's failure to protect his French lands. He also displayed a growing distrust of his closest advisors, such as John Paston, in whose family correspondence, the famous "Paston Letters," Fastolf frequently appears. Having disinherited his stepson, Fastolf died childless in 1459, leaving most of his war-generated wealth to Paston.

Further Reading: Bennett, H. S. "Sir John Fastolf." In *Six Medieval Men and Women.* Cambridge: Cambridge University Press, 1955; McFarlane, K. B. "The Investment of Sir John Fastolf's Profits of War." In *England in the Fifteenth Century.* London: Hambledon, 1981; Smith, A. "Litigation and Politics: Sir John Fastolf's Defence of His English Property." In *Property and Politics: Essays in Later Medieval History,* ed. A. J. Pollard. New York: St. Martin's, 1984.

FITZALAN, RICHARD, EARL OF ARUNDEL.

See CADZAND, BATTLE OF; RICHARD II

FLANDERS

Flanders, a county in northwestern Europe roughly corresponding to modern Belgium, was an important focus of Anglo-French military and diplomatic activity during the first decades of the HUNDRED YEARS WAR. Because Flanders was one of the wealthiest fiefs of the French Crown and the most important market for English wool, as well as ideally located to serve as a base of operations against PARIS and northern France, one of the main aspects of the war in the fourteenth century was the struggle for political control of the county.

Flanders was one of the most highly urbanized regions of medieval Europe, containing such sizable cities as Bruges, Ghent, and Ypres. By the fourteenth century, the economy of most Flemish towns was based on trade and the manufacture of cloth, the raw wool for which came mainly from England. Serfdom had largely disappeared by the thirteenth century and the main social division in Flanders was between the wealthy merchants and landowners, who were generally pro-French, and the rising weavers, artisans, and drapers, who favored Flemish autonomy. Although vassals (for most of their fief) of the French Crown, the counts of Flanders, like their PLANTAGENET counterparts in AQUITAINE, sought greater independence in dealings with their feudal overlord. By the fourteenth century, the counts often found themselves caught between their feudal obligations and the demands of their subjects, whose economic strength gave them political influence.

In the 1290s, PHILIP IV, hoping to annex Flanders to the royal domain, interfered frequently in the county's internal affairs, forcing Count Guy de Dampierre to renounce his allegiance in 1297 and ally with EDWARD I during the ANGLO-FRENCH WAR OF 1294–1303. In July 1302, with the count a prisoner in Paris and Flanders under royal rule, the Flemings defeated a French army at Courtrai in the famous "Battle of the Golden Spurs." Humiliated, the French continued the war and by 1312 had forced the Flemings to pay a huge indemnity; surrender the three castellanies of Lille, Douai, and Orchies; and restore pro-French oligarchies to power in the towns. LOUIS DE NEVERS, who became count in 1322, was strongly pro-French. His interference in municipal affairs precipitated a revolt in Bruges in 1323, which was only suppressed with the help of Ghent and the new VALOIS king of France, PHILIP VI, who defeated the rebels at Cassel in August 1328.

At the start of the Hundred Years War, EDWARD III embargoed English wool shipments in an unsuccessful attempt to detach Louis from his French allegiance. However, the resulting economic distress in the towns sparked a revolt that drove Louis from the county in 1339. The new Flemish regime, led by James van ARTEVELDE, captain of Ghent, allied with Edward (*see* ANGLO-FLEMISH ALLIANCE), who was recognized as king of France. English attempts to use Flanders as a base for invading France ended with the failed siege of TOURNAI in 1340, but the Flemings maintained their rebellion until 1349, when LOUIS DE MALE, who had succeeded his father as count in 1346, was restored to power with French assistance.

Louis installed loyal regimes in the cities and, while making formal homage to the Valois, remained carefully neutral toward the Anglo-French war, thus maintaining the flow of English wool. In 1369, after CHARLES V convinced the pope to prevent a match with EDMUND OF LANGLEY, son of Edward III, Louis reluctantly married his daughter and heir MARGUERITE to Charles's brother, PHILIP

THE BOLD, duke of BURGUNDY. In 1379, Ghent again rebelled against comital authority. The rebel regime, which was eventually led by Philip van ARTEVELDE, son of James, sought a new English alliance, but the minority government of RICHARD II was in no position to assist, and Burgundy, summoned by his father-in-law, crushed the Flemings at Roosebeke in November 1382.

Upon Louis's death in January 1384, Burgundy became count, making Flanders a Valois APPANAGE and ending any English hope of controlling the county. In the fifteenth century, Flanders was part of the Burgundian state constructed by Duke Philip's descendents and, as such, was again allied with England during the ANGLO-BURGUNDIAN ALLIANCE of 1420–35. However, the county itself ceased to be an important war theater.

Further Reading: Lucas, Henry Stephen. *The Low Countries and the Hundred Years' War, 1326–1347.* Ann Arbor: University of Michigan Press, 1929; Nicholas, David. *Town and Countryside: Social, Economic, and Political Tensions in Fourteenth-Century Flanders.* Bruges: De Tempel, 1971; Prevenier, Walter, and Willem Blockmans. *The Burgundian Netherlands.* Cambridge: Cambridge University Press, 1985.

FLANDERS, COUNT OF. *See* JOHN THE FEARLESS, DUKE OF BURGUNDY; LOUIS DE MALE, COUNT OF FLANDERS; LOUIS DE NEVERS, COUNT OF FLANDERS; PHILIP THE BOLD, DUKE OF BURGUNDY; PHILIP THE GOOD, DUKE OF BURGUNDY

FLANDERS, COUNTESS OF. *See* MARGUERITE DE FLANDERS, DUCHESS OF BURGUNDY

FLEURS DE LYS, TREATY OF. *See* HOSTAGES, TREATY OF

FORMIGNY, BATTLE OF (1450)

Fought on 15 April 1450, the battle of Formigny destroyed the last English field force in Lancastrian NORMANDY and thereby ensured the French reconquest of the duchy.

In June 1449, three months after the English sack of FOUGÈRES, CHARLES VII repudiated the Truce of TOURS and reopened the HUNDRED YEARS WAR by invading Normandy. Since the English had no field army in the duchy, the campaign quickly became a series of sieges; ROUEN capitulated in October and HARFLEUR followed in December. To halt the French advance, the government of HENRY VI dispatched an army of twenty-five hundred men to Normandy under Sir Thomas Kyriell. Landing at Cherbourg on 15 March 1450, Kyriell, acting at the request of local officials, deviated from his orders to proceed immediately to the relief of Bayeux. Instead, he asked Edmund BEAUFORT, duke of Somerset, the English governor of Normandy, for reinforcements to recapture Valognes, which fell on 10 April. Now commanding an army of four thousand, Kyriell marched toward Bayeux, reaching the village of Formigny on 14 April.

The French had two forces in western Normandy. John, count of Clermont, commanded three thousand men at Carentan, while Arthur de Richemont, constable of France (*see* ARTHUR III), lay twenty miles to the southwest at Coutances with two thousand Bretons. Unwilling to engage the larger English force alone, Clermont allowed Kyriell to proceed unmolested while Richemont marched north to St. Lô, which he reached on 14 April. At Formigny, the English were only ten miles from the safety of Bayeux, but instead of resuming his march, Kyriell held his position, presumably waiting to catch Clermont, whom he knew to be finally on the move. Unaware of Richemont's march of the previous day, Kyriell probably hoped to engage and defeat Clermont before Richemont arrived.

At mid-afternoon, Clermont encountered the English army drawn up much as HENRY V's had been at AGINCOURT, with a thin line of men-at-arms fortified at intervals by groups of ARCHERS that projected forward from the English front. After a pause that allowed the English to further entrench their position, Clermont's dismounted men-at-arms assaulted the English line. When their first attack collapsed, the French sent cavalry charges against the English flanks, but were again unsuccessful. Clermont now brought up his ARTILLERY, two culverins that were quickly captured by English archers, who, goaded by the galling fire, surged forward to overwhelm the gunners. The French were now in disarray; had Kyriell attacked, he might have driven them from the field.

At this moment, Richemont arrived from the south, his forces ideally positioned to assault the flanks and rear of the English army. Lacking a reserve, Kyriell had to maintain his front against Clermont while shifting part of his army to the left to meet Richemont's attack, the sight of which encouraged Clermont's men to resume their assault. The English line quickly disintegrated under the pressure, with groups of men being surrounded and cut down. Although Sir Matthew Gough, commander of Somerset's reinforcements, led a small force to safety, most of the English army was killed or captured, with Kyriell among the latter. Having disposed of Kyriell's army, the French resumed their campaign of sieges, which concluded on 12 August with the fall of Cherbourg, the last English-held fortress in Normandy. *See also* NORMAN CAMPAIGN (1449–50).

Further Reading: Burne, Alfred H. *The Agincourt War.* Ware, England: Wordsworth Editions Ltd., 1999; Griffiths, Ralph A. *The Reign of King Henry VI.* Berkeley: University of California Press, 1981.

FORTIFICATIONS. *See* SIEGE WARFARE

FOUGÈRES, SACK OF (1449)

On 24 March 1449, François de Surienne, a Spanish *ROUTIER* captain who had long served the English Crown, captured and sacked the Breton town of Fougères in violation of the Truce of TOURS. The attack, which was initiated by the English government as part of a plan to prevent BRITTANY from establishing closer ties with France, had disastrous consequences for HENRY VI and his ministers. The episode undermined English morale, destroyed the credibility of

the Lancastrian regime, and precipitated a successful French campaign against NORMANDY.

Surienne, who was known as "l'Arragonais" (the Arrogonese), had fought for the English since at least 1437, when he commanded the garrison at MONTARGIS. By 1447, he had become a key figure in a plan being developed by Henry's chief minister, William de la POLE, earl of Suffolk, to strengthen English influence over Francis I, duke of Brittany. In June 1446, the duke had imprisoned his younger brother Gilles, who was a personal friend of Henry VI, for his forceful and ambitious advocacy of the English cause. Suffolk believed that a military demonstration along the Breton-Norman border would compel Francis to forego any rapprochement with CHARLES VII and to restore Gilles to favor, thus allowing him to continue exerting a pro-English influence. The plan was given even greater urgency in 1448 when Maine fell to the French (*see* MAINE, SURRENDER OF), thus making a friendly Brittany even more important to the defense of Normandy.

Surienne's choice as the government's agent in this plan was signaled in November 1447 when he was elected to the Order of the GARTER and given possession of Sir John FASTOLF's castle of Condé-sur-Noireau, a fortress on the Norman frontier that was ideally situated to serve as a base for operations against Fougères. In March 1449, Surienne led a force of six thousand on a well-executed raid that quickly carried the surprised town by assault. After thoroughly plundering the wealthy citizens, the *routiers* withdrew to the citadel, where they were soon besieged by the Bretons. When Charles VII protested the attack, the English lieutenant of Normandy, Edmund BEAUFORT, duke of Somerset, who had been involved in planning the venture, replied that the action was not a breach of the truce, since the duke of Brittany was a vassal of the English Crown. This contention was highly debatable. Although the English had surreptitiously included Brittany among their list of allies when the truce was renewed in 1448,

Francis had done formal homage to Charles in 1446.

In June, PARLIAMENT congratulated Surienne on his success, but the English government, finding its military resources stretched thin and Brittany now firmly in league with the French, refused to acknowledge its role in the attack or to send relief to Surienne, who was soon in dire straits. Bitterly disillusioned and angry that he was being denounced as a truce breaker who had acted on his own account, Surienne held out until 5 November. Shortly thereafter, he returned his Garter, renounced his English allegiance, and published a lengthy justification placing responsibility for the attack squarely on the English government. The entire episode reflected poorly on the Lancastrian regime. In Normandy, morale dropped among troops who had seen a colleague abandoned. In England, where Suffolk and Somerset were suspected of concocting the entire scheme for their own benefit, support for the government ebbed. In Brittany, Francis and his uncle, Arthur de Richemont (*see* ARTHUR III), acting in conjunction with the French, invaded western Normandy in November in a campaign that concluded with the recapture of Fougères. In France, Charles, no longer trusting English professions of peace, used Fougères as a pretext for ending the truce and sending an army under JOHN, COUNT OF DUNOIS, into Normandy, which, by the summer of 1450, was lost to England. *See also* NORMAN CAMPAIGN (1449–1450).

Further Reading: Griffiths, Ralph A. *The Reign of King Henry VI.* Berkeley: University of California Press, 1981; Perroy, Edouard. *The Hundred Years War.* Trans. W. B. Wells. New York: Capricorn Books, 1965.

FRANC-ARCHERS. *See* CHARLES VII, MILITARY REFORMS OF

FRANCO-SCOTTISH ALLIANCE

Known as the "Auld Alliance," the military and political connection forged between France and SCOTLAND in the 1290s was initiated and maintained by the parties' mutual hostility toward England. Besides providing both countries with important military and diplomatic assistance throughout the HUNDRED YEARS WAR, the alliance also strengthened social, economic, and cultural connections between Scotland and the Continent.

The Franco-Scottish alliance was created by an agreement concluded in October 1295 between PHILIP IV and a twelve-man council of Scottish nobles. The latter had seized power from John Balliol, whom EDWARD I had placed on the Scottish throne as an English vassal. On the Scottish side, the main impetus for the alliance was Edward's unprecedented demand that Balliol and his chief nobles perform military service for the English Crown in France. On the French side, the agreement, which called for a joint attack on England, provided Philip with valuable assistance in his campaign against PLANTAGENET Aquitaine (*see* ANGLO-FRENCH WAR OF 1294–1303). Although the envisioned attack never materialized, the alliance damaged the English war effort by wasting Edward's limited resources and by offering Scottish exiles a continental refuge. From 1309, Robert I, like all his successors down to Mary, Queen of Scots, maintained the French connection. Rather than providing each other with direct military assistance, the allies used diplomatic cooperation and the threat of joint action to hamper English military activity in either country. In 1326, CHARLES IV and Robert I formally renewed the alliance at Corbeil.

In the 1330s, the alliance made the ongoing Anglo-Scottish war an important cause and component of the Anglo-French conflict. By breaking Scotland's isolation, the alliance ended Scottish fears of unfettered English conquest while giving the French a means of diverting English attention from AQUITAINE. In 1334, a year after EDWARD III's victory at HALIDON HILL gave him effective control of southern Scotland, PHILIP VI granted DAVID II asylum in France. Philip then destroyed a prospective Anglo-French settlement in Aquitaine by suddenly demanding that any agreement include the Scots. With the start of the Hundred Years War, growing English involvement in France allowed the Scots to expel most English garrisons by 1341, when David, who had fought with the French army in 1340, returned to Scotland. Although the Scottish king attempted to repay his ally in 1346 by invading England in the weeks following the English victory at CRÉCY, David was captured at NEVILLE'S CROSS and eventually forced to accept a truce.

In 1371, Robert II sent an embassy to France to formally renew the alliance with CHARLES V. In the 1380s, plans were laid for a joint attack on England. French knights arrived in Scotland, but their condescending manner and unconcealed disdain for a country they considered poor and backward bred resentment among their hosts and eventually frustrated the planned invasion. Nonetheless, Robert III and the MARMOUSET regime that ruled for CHARLES VI renewed the alliance in 1391. In the early fifteenth century, France, divided by the FRENCH CIVIL WAR and hard-pressed by HENRY V, sought Scottish military assistance. Individual Scottish knights, such as William Douglas, earl of Douglas, who was at POITIERS in 1356, had fought with French armies since the start of the war, but, in 1419, the dauphin made a direct appeal for Scottish aid, thus initiating a five-year period during which sizable Scottish armies landed in France. Scottish troops played a large role in the defeat and death of THOMAS, DUKE OF CLARENCE, at BAUGÉ in 1421, and Scottish nobles were highly rewarded for their services to the VALOIS, including John STEWART, earl of Buchan, who became constable of France, and Archibald DOUGLAS, earl of Douglas, who became duke of Touraine. In 1424, Buchan, Douglas, and most of the Scots in the French army were slain at VERNEUIL. Although that battle ended the dispatch of whole armies to France, small groups of Scottish knights continued to serve the dauphin, who, after his coronation as CHARLES VII in 1429, recruited such men for his personal bodyguard, the Garde Écossaise, a force of a hundred Scottish ARCHERS that eventually controlled access to the king.

In 1424, the English sought to break the alliance by releasing James I of Scotland, who had been an English prisoner since 1406. Although James had pledged to halt the flow of Scottish soldiers to France as a condition of his release, he renewed the alliance in 1428. By promising to send a new army to France, James also obtained the county of Saintonge and the marriage of his daughter, Margaret, to Charles's son, Louis. However, the murder of James in 1437 effectively ended Scottish involvement in the war for the next decade. Charles renewed the alliance with James II in 1448, but internal instability prevented the Scots from participating in the final campaigns of the Hundred Years War. The Franco-Scottish alliance continued until 1560. *See also* DIPLOMACY.

Further Reading: Bonner, E. "Scotland's 'Auld Alliance' with France, 1295–1560." *History* 84 (1999): 5–30; Laidlaw, James, ed. *The Auld Alliance: France and Scotland Over 700 Years.* Edinburgh: University of Edinburgh, 1999; Wood, Stephen. *The Auld Alliance, Scotland and France: The Military Connection.* Edinburgh, Mainstream, 1989.

FREE COMPANIES. *See* ROUTIERS

FRENCH CIVIL WAR
The French civil war of the 1410s grew out of a struggle between the duke of Orléans and his kinsmen the dukes of BURGUNDY to control the royal government. Erupting in the years following Orléans's murder by Burgundy's agents in November 1407, the civil war bitterly divided the House of VALOIS and the French nobility, thereby depriving the country of strong leadership. Determined to crush their opponents, both the BURGUNDIANS and the ARMAGNACS sought English assistance and thus allowed HENRY V to successfully resume the HUNDRED YEARS WAR and overrun much of northern France. By taking advantage of the civil war, Henry was eventually able to impose a peace settlement that promised the French Crown to the English House of LANCASTER.

The younger brother of CHARLES VI, Orléans had opposed the political ascendancy of his uncles, JOHN, DUKE OF BERRY, and PHI-LIP THE BOLD, duke of Burgundy, since the late 1380s, when Orléans had supported the MARMOUSETS, who briefly overthrew the uncles' control of the royal administration. In 1392, the king's first psychotic episode allowed Berry and Burgundy to resume power. Being the more ambitious uncle, Burgundy soon dominated the government. Although Orléans resented his exclusion from power, Burgundy's experience and authority prevented the rivalry with his nephew from degenerating into open violence. However, when Burgundy was succeeded by his son, JOHN THE FEARLESS, in April 1404, the advantage shifted to Orléans, who was more personally attractive and politically adept than his cold, imperious cousin. Winning the support of Queen ISABEAU, Orléans dominated the court and became increasingly influential in the royal council. On 23 November 1407, assassins hired by Burgundy slew Orléans on a PARIS street.

After confessing his crime, Burgundy fled the court, but returned to Paris, where he was popular, in February 1408. Numbed by his brother's death and anxious to restore peace to his family, the king ignored the duchess of Orléans's demands for justice and allowed Burgundy to present to the council a document later known as the *JUS-TIFICATION OF THE DUKE OF BURGUNDY* (March 1408), which transformed the murder into an act of lawful tyrannicide by listing in great detail the alleged crimes and treasons of Orléans. Although answered by Orléanist polemics, the *Justification* was largely accepted by public opinion, and in March 1409 the king presided at Chartres over a formal reconciliation of Burgundy and CHARLES, the new duke of Orléans. However, the struggle for control of king and government intensified when Burgundy began posing as leader of a popular movement for administrative reform. By the end of 1409, Burgundian appointees filled the royal administration, while the duke dominated the king and court. In 1410, Orléans and other noblemen excluded from power by Burgundy, including Berry; John, duke of Bourbon; Con-stable Charles d'ALBRET; and Orléans's new father-in-law, BERNARD, COUNT OF ARMA-GNAC, withdrew from Paris and prepared for civil war by forming the anti-Burgundian League of Gien.

When another attempt at reconciliation, the peace of Bicêtre, failed in 1411, the Orléanists, who were now known as Armagnacs due to the count's increasing influence within the party, laid siege to Paris. To win English support, Burgundy opened talks with HENRY IV, to whom he indicated a willingness to make territorial concessions in return for military aid. A small English force—the first to land in France in twenty-eight years—arrived in CALAIS in October 1411. It was enough to persuade the Armagnacs to lift the siege, but otherwise accomplished little and soon returned to England. Retreating south of the Loire, the Armagnacs now sought English assistance. In the Treaty of BOURGES (May 1412), they promised the restoration of lands and fortresses in GASCONY captured by CHARLES V in the 1370s in return for four thousand men to serve for three months. By July, when this force arrived under THOMAS, DUKE OF CLAR-ENCE, Burgundy had successfully invaded the Armagnac territories and compelled Berry and his allies to make peace. The conclusion of the Treaty of Auxerre in August 1412 forced the Armagnacs to buy their way out of the Bourges agreement. Signed in November, the Treaty of BUZANÇAIS bribed Clarence to leave France, which he did by way of a *CHEVAUCHÉE* ending in Gascony.

To provide financial support for halting the English threat he had initiated, Burgundy summoned the Estates of Languedoïl (*see* ESTATES, GENERAL AND PROVINCIAL) to Paris in January 1413. This plan backfired when the Estates criticized the Burgundian regime and demanded reform before granting TAXATION. Under the leadership of the dauphin, LOUIS, DUKE OF GUIENNE, who sought to end the civil war and form a united front against the English, Armagnac partisans in the capital used the Estates to begin negotiations with the Armagnac leaders. Burgundy responded by inciting the pro-Burgundian butchers of Paris, led by Simon Caboche and thus called CABOCHIENS, to riot and attack Armagnacs. For three months, the Cabochien reign of terror gripped the capital, overawing the court, stymieing the dauphin's reconciliation effort, and forcing the proclamation in late May of a great reform measure known as the *Ordonnance Cabochienne*. However, the Cabochien violence frightened the Paris burghers, who in late July assisted the dauphin in negotiating the peace of Pontoise with the Armagnac leaders. With his support in the capital eroding, Burgundy, after a failed attempt to kidnap the king, fled on 23 August. Entering Paris on 1 September, the Armagnacs quickly restored order, with the Gascon bands of the count of Armagnac ruthlessly suppressing the Cabochiens.

Both French factions now turned for aid to Henry V, who had become king of England in March 1413. Burgundy asked for two thousand English troops to join him in overthrowing the Armagnacs, for which the duke offered Henry various Armagnac APPANAGES on the borders of Gascony. When Henry demanded reactivation of the Treaty of BRÉTIGNY and recognition of his right to the French Crown, Burgundy, whose ultimate control of the royal government was thereby threatened, broke off talks. Faced with similar demands, the Armagnacs offered to pay the balance of JOHN II's ransom; to provide a handsome dowry upon Henry's marriage to Charles's daughter, CATHERINE OF VALOIS; and to accept Lancastrian sovereignty over an enlarged AQUITAINE. But when Henry refused to renounce his claim to the French throne without at least the surrender of NORMANDY, Anglo-Armagnac negotiations collapsed in February 1415. The dauphin then negotiated the peace of Arras, which lifted Burgundy's banishment, but did not restore him to power and thus failed to reconcile the factions. In August 1415, Henry invaded France and in the following October won a major victory at AGINCOURT. The battle, in which Burgundy took no part, decimated the Armagnac leadership—Orléans and Bourbon were captured and Albret

slain. With these losses, and with the deaths of the dauphin in December, of Berry in June 1416, and of Charles's next son, John, duke of Touraine, in April 1417, the regime was left under the nominal leadership of the king's last surviving son, the Dauphin Charles, and under the actual dominance of Armagnac. While the English systematically conquered Normandy, and Burgundy threatened Paris, the count made ruthless use of his Gascon bands to suppress disorder and maintain Armagnac authority in the capital. After Armagnac and the dauphin quarreled with the queen, who fled to Burgundy in November 1417, their unpopular government was toppled by a Paris uprising in May 1418. The dauphin fled to safety, but Armagnac and many of his supporters were murdered by the mob, allowing Burgundy to reenter the capital on 14 July.

In September, with the dauphin in control of southern France and Burgundy ruling in Paris, the latter imposed the Treaty of Saint-Maur on the former, but the settlement never took hold, and by January 1419, when Henry captured ROUEN, both sides sought some agreement that would allow them to unite against the English. Hoping to destroy the remaining Armagnacs and rule the country through the dauphin, Burgundy met his rival in July at Corbeil, where a preliminary settlement was reached. However, at a second meeting on the bridge at MONTEREAU on 10 September, former servants of Orléans in the dauphin's entourage murdered Burgundy, an act of vengeance that wrecked any hope of reconciliation. Realizing that he needed English assistance to destroy his father's murderer, PHILIP THE GOOD, the new duke of Burgundy, entered into an ANGLO-BURGUNDIAN ALLIANCE, and in 1420 brokered negotiation of the Anglo-French Treaty of TROYES, whereby the dauphin was disinherited in favor of Henry V and his heirs. The French civil war was now subsumed into the Hundred Years War. After the deaths of Henry V and Charles VI in 1422, a largely Burgundian administration in Paris governed Normandy and much of northern France in the name of HENRY VI, while the remnants of the Armagnac faction governed France south of the Loire for the dauphin, who in 1429 was crowned as CHARLES VII. Always a reluctant English ally, Burgundy abandoned the House of Lancaster in 1435 at the Congress of ARRAS, where he made peace with Charles on extremely favorable terms. Although the reconciliation with Burgundy was humiliating for Charles, it won him Burgundian recognition of his title to the Crown and thereby effectively ended the civil war.

Further Reading: Famiglietti, Richard. *Royal Intrigue: Crisis at the Court of Charles VI, 1392–1420*. New York: AMS Press, 1986; Perroy, Edouard. *The Hundred Years War*. Trans. W. B. Wells. New York: Capricorn Books, 1965; Vaughan, Richard. *John the Fearless*. London: Longman, 1979.

FRENCH SUCCESSION CRISES (1316–1328). *See* SALIC LAW OF SUCCESSION

FRESNAY, BATTLE OF (1420)
Fought on 3 March 1420, the Battle of Fresnay resulted in the defeat of a large Franco-Scottish army attempting to break the siege of Fresnay-le-Vicomte and halt the English advance into Maine. The English victory secured HENRY V's hold on NORMANDY and extended his authority southward to Le Mans.

In the spring of 1420, while Henry V was negotiating the Treaty of TROYES, William MONTAGU, fourth earl of Salisbury, one of the English king's leading commanders, completed the conquest of Normandy. After reducing the last Norman strongholds, including Château Gaillard, the famous castle built by England's Richard I, Salisbury, who was lieutenant of Lower Normandy, led an army into Maine, where the reduction of French-held fortresses continued. By early March, Salisbury laid siege to Fresnay. Assembling a large army at Le Mans, Jean de Rieux, marshal of France, marched north to relieve the fortress. Learning of Rieux's intentions, Salisbury, while maintaining the siege, dispatched a force under John Holland, earl of Huntingdon, to deal with the French marshal. Huntingdon lay in ambush along the Le Mans road about three miles south of Fresnay, where he encountered Rieux's army on 3 March.

The sizes of the two forces engaged at Fresnay are uncertain, but all indications are that the French army was considerably larger, being augmented by a newly arrived contingent of Scotsmen that may have numbered over five thousand. The course of the battle is also unknown, although the outcome may have been in part due to overconfidence on the part of Rieux's army, for the Scots thought so little of the possibility of defeat that they adopted the unusual practice of marching into battle with their treasury. When the fighting ended, the French had lost over three thousand men killed or captured, with Rieux, five hundred men-at-arms, and numerous Scottish knights among the latter. The English also seized 12,000 crowns from the Scottish treasury and the standard of Sir William Douglas, the Scottish commander. The *Vita et Gesta Henrici Quinti*, one of the chief English sources for the period, called the battle a "glorious triumph" (Burne, 146), while another source put the English dead at the unlikely number of three.

Whatever the actual casualty figures, the battle destroyed Rieux's army, strengthened the English position in the talks at Troyes, and ensured the fall of Fresnay. The English victory also opened Maine to Salisbury, who within the following weeks advanced unopposed to Le Mans, the capital of the county. *See also* MAINE, SURRENDER OF; SCOTLAND.

Further Reading: Burne, Alfred H. *The Agincourt War*. Ware, England: Wordsworth Editions Ltd., 1999.

FROISSART, JEAN (c. 1337–c. 1404)
Best known for his *Chroniques de France, d'Angleterre et des pais voisins* (*Chronicles of France, England and the Adjoining Countries*), a detailed narrative of the Anglo-French wars of the fourteenth century, Jean Froissart, a native of Hainault, is the most famous contemporary chronicler of the HUNDRED YEARS WAR.

Jean Froissart, clad in clerical garb, presents a copy of his *Chronicles* to Edward III. *Erich Lessing/Art Resource, New York.*

Born at Valenciennes into what was likely a bourgeois family, Froissart was first recognized for his talent as a poet and writer by John of Hainault, the uncle of EDWARD III's wife, PHILIPPA. Heavily influenced by his fellow Hainaulter, JEAN LE BEL, who had chronicled the chivalrous exploits of John of Hainault at the English court in the 1320s, Froissart began gathering material for his own history in the late 1350s. Interested in feats of arms and deeds of CHIVALRY, Froissart collected information by traveling about and interviewing those who had witnessed the wars he sought to recount. In 1361, he traveled to England, where he entered the service of Queen Philippa, to whom he presented a now-lost rhyming chronicle of events between 1356 and 1360. The queen's patronage gave Froissart access to people who provided information and insights that eventually enabled him to write his own chronicle of the Anglo-French wars.

At the English court in the 1360s, Froissart met the French hostages given to guarantee the Treaty of BRÉTIGNY, including Guy, count of Blois, a future patron, and JOHN, DUKE OF BERRY, for whom Froissart wrote the poem, *Dit dou bleu chevalier*. In 1362, he witnessed the departure of EDWARD, THE BLACK PRINCE, for AQUITAINE, and in 1364, he saw JOHN II return voluntarily to captivity in LONDON. He also interviewed the newly arrived herald bearing news of the Anglo-Breton victory at AURAY in September 1364, and visited DAVID II at Edinburgh during a 1365 tour of SCOTLAND that resulted in the poem *Meliador*, an Arthurian epic of thirty thousand lines. In 1366, while on a diplomatic mission for the queen, he met the duke and duchess of Brabant, who later became his patrons. After visiting the West Country of England and then traveling through BRITTANY, Froissart kept Christmas with the Black Prince and his family in BORDEAUX and witnessed the baptism of the future RICHARD II in January 1367. He joined the prince's expedition to Castile (*see* CASTILIAN WAR OF SUCCESSION), but did not see the Battle of NÁJERA, having been sent back to England before it occurred. In 1368, in a party that included Geoffrey Chaucer, Froissart accompanied Lionel, duke of Clarence, to Italy, where he made an extensive tour of the country. Receiving news of the queen's death in August 1369, Froissart did not return to England but entered the service of the duke and duchess of Brabant.

While there in the early 1370s, Froissart, although continuing to write poetry, also began working on book 1 of a French prose chronicle of the Anglo-French wars. Over the next thirty years, Foissart expanded and revised his chronicle until it encompassed four books that recalled the major events and personalities in Britain, France, Spain, and the Low Countries between 1327 and 1400. Totaling about three million words and existing today in various overlapping versions, Froissart's chronicle is a dramatic and sophisticated narrative, full of vivid characters and descriptions that sometimes sacrifice accuracy for dramatic effect. Completed by 1373 and revised from 1376, book 1 covers the period from 1327 to 1376 and is largely plagiarized from the work of Jean le Bel. Completed in about 1387, book 2, covering the years 1377–85, includes Froissart's famous account of the PEASANTS' REVOLT OF 1381. Completed in the early 1390s, book 3 covers the years 1385–89, while book 4, completed around 1400, takes the narrative up to that year.

Froissart continued to travel into his sixties. He witnessed the coronation of CHARLES VI in 1380, and, after entering the service of Guy de Blois in 1384, visited SLUYS to see the fleet being assembled for an invasion of England and Angers to speak with men who had fought in the BRETON CIVIL WAR in the

1340s. In 1389, he returned to Bordeaux, where he saw a tournament held by JOHN OF GAUNT, duke of Lancaster, and in 1395, he returned to England for the first time in almost thirty years. Disappointed by his reception at Richard II's court, which he believed paled in comparison to the chivalrous court of his grandfather, Froissart nonetheless renewed some old acquaintances and attended the king's marriage to Isabella of VALOIS (see ISABELLA, QUEEN OF ENGLAND [1388–1409]) at Saint-Omer in the autumn of 1396. Retiring to the abbey of Cantimpré in about 1400, Froissart, whose name and chronicles were already widely known in Western Europe, died at some unknown date in about 1404.

Further Reading: Ainsworth, Peter F. *Jean Froissart and the Fabric of History: Truth, Myth, and Fiction in the Chroniques.* Oxford: Clarendon Press, 1990; Diverres, A. "Froissart's Travels in England and Wales." *Fifteenth-Century Studies* 15 (1989): 107–22; Froissart, Jean. *The Chronicle of Froissart.* Trans. Sir John Bourchier. 6 vols. London: D. Nutt, 1901–3; Palmer, J. N. N., ed. *Froissart: Historian.* Totowa, NJ: Rowman and Littlefield, 1981.

G

GABELLE. *See* TAXATION AND WAR FINANCE

GARTER, ORDER OF THE

Founded by EDWARD III in the 1340s and still in existence today, the Order of the Garter is the most prestigious order of English CHIVALRY. Created at the height of English success in the HUNDRED YEARS WAR, the order imbued the PLANTAGENET cause with the ideals of chivalry and justice and linked the greatest military figures in the realm with the king in a brotherhood of honor and duty. Conferring prestige on its members by its exclusiveness and its opportunities for association with a popular and victorious king, the order was soon regarded as the height of chivalric distinction both in England and on the Continent.

Because the earliest extant records of the order date to 1416, the origins of the brotherhood and the exact date of its founding are uncertain. Perhaps inspired by a voluntary association of knights recently formed in Lincoln, Edward, at the conclusion of a great tournament held at Windsor in 1344, swore a solemn oath to create his own brotherhood of knights in the image of King Arthur's Round Table. Although Jean FROISSART dated the formal inauguration of the order to 1344, the most probable date appears to be 23 April 1348, the first St. George's Day after the king's victories at CRÉCY and CALAIS. It is for that day that royal letters patent first order the royal chapel at Windsor to be made ready for the king's use, and it is in the following November that the financial accounts of EDWARD, THE BLACK PRINCE, make note of twenty-four garters given as gifts to members of the Society of the Garter. The

order was dedicated to St. George of Cappadocia and St. Edward the Confessor and was headquartered at Windsor, where the members met in solemn convention every St. George's Day. For the members' use, the king renovated the Chapel of St. Edward at Windsor, which was rededicated as the Chapel of St. Edward and St. George, and the Great Tower at Windsor became the site of annual Garter Day feasts.

The exact reasons for the order's founding and for selection of the blue garter as its symbol are also uncertain. Legend states that the young countess of Salisbury dropped her garter while dancing at a royal ball. The king, who was smitten with the countess, picked up the garter, fastened it to his own leg, and then, in rebuke of the amused company, spoke the words that would become the order's motto: "Honi soit qui mal y pense" (Shame to him who thinks ill of this). Declaring that he would make the garter a symbol of honor, the king used it as the badge for his chivalric society. Other versions of the story claim that the countess herself spoke the famous words of reproof or that the garter belonged to Joan of Kent, future wife of the Black Prince. Although modern research does not totally dismiss this tale, it appears that the garter also had some earlier military associations. In the late twelfth century, Richard I, while on crusade, used the garter as a symbol to rally his men at the sieges of Cyprus and Acré, and Edward III had himself employed it to signal across the battlefield at Crécy.

Whatever its origins, the garter symbolized an unbreakable bond of friendship and honor between the king and the exclusive company of twenty-five knights who joined him as members of the order. Given greater distinction by Edward's military fame and his ongoing quest to secure his just rights in France, the order tapped into the highest and most cherished ideals of fourteenth-century chivalry. Among the founding members were the greatest captains of the Edwardian war, including the Black Prince; HENRY OF GROSMONT, duke of Lancaster; Thomas BEAUCHAMP, earl of Warwick; Sir John CHANDOS; and Jean de GRAILLY, captal de Buch. Among those who filled the first vacancies were Sir Walter MAUNY, William de BOHUN, earl of Northampton; and the king's son, JOHN OF GAUNT, duke of Lancaster. Because Edward proclaimed his society in France, SCOTLAND, BURGUNDY, and elsewhere, the order was soon well known and highly regarded across Western Europe. Over the next century, various foreign rulers founded similar orders, including JOHN II of France, who established his rival Order of the STAR in 1351; JOHN IV, duke of BRITTANY, who founded his Order of the Ermine in 1381; and PHILIP THE GOOD, duke of Burgundy, who created the Order of the Golden Fleece in 1430.

Further Reading: Collins, Hugh E. L. *The Order of the Garter, 1348–1461: Chivalry and Politics in Late Medieval England.* Oxford: Oxford University Press, 2000; Keen, Maurice. *Chivalry.* New Haven, CT: Yale University Press, 1984; Vale, Juliet. *Edward III and Chivalry: Chivalric Society and Its Context, 1270–1350.* Woodbridge, England: Boydell Press, 1982.

GASCONY

A province of southwestern France, Gascony comprised the southern part of the duchy of AQUITAINE, and for most of the HUNDRED YEARS WAR constituted that portion of the duchy under effective PLANTAGENET rule.

Except for the Pyrénées to the south and the Atlantic to the west, Gascony had no clear geographical boundaries. The province was a shifting collection of territories extending southward and eastward from BORDEAUX, the provincial capital, into Lan-

guedoc, and usually comprising such counties and viscounties as Armagnac, ALBRET, Bigorre, Comminges, Fézensac, Lomagne, and Marsan. Settled by Basques in the late sixth century, Gascony became an independent duchy in the ninth century. In the 1050s, Gascony was acquired through marriage by the dukes of Aquitaine, who, although vassals of the French Crown, were largely independent in their dual principality, which they ruled from Poitiers in the north and Bordeaux in the south. Gascony and the whole of Aquitaine came to the English Crown in the twelfth century, when Eleanor, duchess of Aquitaine, married Henry, count of Anjou, who, as Henry II of England, ruled a conglomeration of states comprising most of western France. In the early thirteenth century, most of these Plantagenet holdings, including much of Aquitaine, were conquered by the House of CAPET. Only Gascony remained under Plantagenet rule. With few political, social, or economic connections to northern France, the Gascons, who found the lax rule of a distant king-duke preferable to the more invasive authority of the Capetians, developed firm ties to England, which in the thirteenth century became a profitable market for Gascon wine.

In 1259, the Treaty of PARIS, by recognizing the English king as duke of Aquitaine, clarified Gascony's political status. However, the Plantagenets found their feudal subordination as dukes in Aquitaine-Gascony to be incompatible with their role as sovereign kings in England. As overlords of Aquitaine, French monarchs could readily interfere in how the king-dukes ruled their province, thereby provoking frequent disputes and occasional wars. During the ANGLO-FRENCH WAR of the 1290s and again during the War of SAINT-SARDOS in the 1320s, the French Crown confiscated the province. Thus, the Hundred Years War largely evolved out of EDWARD III's desire to exercise in Aquitaine-Gascony the same sovereign rule he enjoyed in England.

During the fourteenth century, Gascony was a main battleground of the war, serving as a base for English operations and a target for French campaigns. In 1360, the Treaty of BRÉTIGNY recreated the enlarged sovereign Aquitaine of earlier centuries, which was governed from Bordeaux by EDWARD, THE BLACK PRINCE. However, the harsher rule and higher taxes of a resident duke alienated the Gascon nobility, who appealed for aid to CHARLES V. By accepting the APPEAL OF THE GASCON LORDS in 1369, Charles overthrew the treaty and revived the war. By 1380, French campaigns reduced Plantagenet rule to the environs of Bordeaux and coastal Gascony, an area smaller than that held by Edward III at the start of the war.

Despite several VALOIS attempts to take Bordeaux, this reduced Gascony saw little military activity in the fifteenth century and remained under English control until 1451, when the armies of CHARLES VII conquered the province. In 1452, John TALBOT, earl of Shrewsbury, recaptured Bordeaux with the support of the Gascons and briefly reconstituted Plantagenet Gascony. However, on 17 July 1453, Shrewsbury was defeated and killed at the Battle of CASTILLON, which marked the end of both English Gascony and the Hundred Years War.

Further Reading: Labarge, Margaret Wade. *Gascony, England's First Colony: 1204–1453.* London: Hamish Hamilton, 1980; Vale, Malcolm. *English Gascony, 1399–1453.* London: Oxford University Press, 1970.

GIEN, LEAGUE OF. *See* FRENCH CIVIL WAR

GLOUCESTER, DUKE OF. *See* HUMPHREY, DUKE OF GLOUCESTER; THOMAS OF WOODSTOCK, DUKE OF GLOUCESTER

GODFREY OF HARCOURT. *See* HARCOURT, GODFREY OF

GODONS/GODDAMS. *See* PROPAGANDA AND WAR PUBLICITY

GOOD PARLIAMENT. *See* PARLIAMENT

GRAILLY, JEAN DE, CAPTAL DE BUCH (d. 1376)

A confidant and companion-in-arms of EDWARD, THE BLACK PRINCE, Jean de Grailly III, captal de Buch, was the most loyal and consistent supporter of the PLANTAGENET cause among the fourteenth-century Gascon nobility. Recognized by the chronicler Jean FROISSART for his CHIVALRY and daring feats of arms, the captal de Buch had a distinguished military career, serving both the English Crown and CHARLES THE BAD, king of Navarre.

The title of "captal," which Jean de Grailly inherited in 1343, was used by only a few of the most prominent noble families of GASCONY, such as the lords of Buch. Jean's family had been associated with the House of Plantagenet since the mid-thirteenth century, when the captal's great-great-grandfather served Henry III. The lords of Buch controlled an extensive territory around the city of BORDEAUX, and also exercised certain seigniorial rights in the town and its suburbs. De Grailly was related to the highest nobility of southwestern France, being first cousin of Gaston Fébus, count of Foix; second cousin of Charles of Navarre; and son-in-law of Bernard-Aiz V, lord of ALBRET. Although a captal de Buch was one of only three foreign knights to become a founding member of the Order of the GARTER in the 1340s, there is some confusion over the exact identity of this knight. Some sources identify him as Jean III, while others claim the Garter knight was Piers or Pierre de Grailly, Jean's grandfather. Despite his age at the time—he was probably only slightly older than Prince Edward, then in his late teens—Jean seems more likely. De Grailly's military prowess first drew attention in 1351, when he and his band of Gascons surprised the French garrison at Saint-Antonin in southern Quercy. After a thorough pillaging, the captal turned the town into a base for further raids into French-held Quercy and Rouergue.

In early 1355, the captal and other Gascon lords sailed to England to consult with EDWARD III on the war in Gascony. Saying that it would greatly hearten the people, the captal suggested that Prince Edward be sent to the duchy, which he was later in the year. De Grailly accompanied the prince on the CHEVAUCHÉE OF 1355 and a led a series of raids into Poitou in early 1356. In September, the captal distinguished himself at the Battle of POITIERS, where he led a band of sixty knights and a hundred ARCHERS around behind the French army. Raising the banner of St. George as a signal to the prince that he was in position, the captal attacked the rear of JOHN II's division as the Prince's horsemen attacked its front. The ferocity of the captal's attack disguised his small numbers and threw the French into confusion, helping the English to eventually win the day. In 1358, upon returning from crusade in Eastern Europe, the captal gallantly joined a band of French knights in defending the dauphin's family from the JACQUERIE rebels at Meaux. In 1360, the captal joined Edward III's RHEIMS CAMPAIGN, during which he was dispatched by Prince Edward to discuss with Navarre the possibility of a joint attack on PARIS.

In 1361, following conclusion of the Treaty of BRÉTIGNY, de Grailly entered the service of Navarre. In 1364, the captal commanded Navarre's forces at COCHEREL, where he was defeated and captured by Bertrand du GUESCLIN. Released for no RANSOM by the treaty concluded between Navarre and CHARLES V, the captal swore fealty to the VALOIS Crown, but returned to his English allegiance by 1367, when he fought with Prince Edward at NÁJERA. The captal was present at the sack of LIMOGES in 1370 and was appointed constable of AQUITAINE in 1371. On 23 August 1372, the French captured de Grailly in an action near Soubise. Refusing to abandon his English allegiance, the captal spent the remaining years of his life as a prisoner in Paris, where he died in 1376, supposedly of sadness at news of the Black Prince's death.

Further Reading: Barber, Richard. *Edward, Prince of Wales and Aquitaine.* New York: Charles Scribner's Sons, 1978; Sedgwick, Theodore Dwight. *The Life of Edward, the Black Prince.* New York:

Barnes and Noble, 1993; Sumption, Jonathan. *The Hundred Years War.* Vol. 2, *Trial by Fire.* Philadelphia: University of Pennsylvania Press, 2001.

GRANDE CHEVAUCHÉE. See CHEVAUCHÉE OF 1355; CHEVAUCHÉE OF 1373

GREAT COMPANY

"Great Company" was the name given by contemporaries to a succession of large ROUTIER armies that terrorized southern and eastern France in the 1360s. Although largely Gascon at its core (see GASCONY), the Great Company comprised many individual companies of various nationalities operating under the loose overall leadership of one captain or a small group of captains. Encouraged by the breakdown of royal authority that followed the capture of JOHN II at POITIERS in 1356, the Great Company formed, dissolved, and reformed in response to new opportunities for adventure and profit. Both LOUIS, DUKE OF ANJOU, the French lieutenant in Languedoc, and EDWARD, THE BLACK PRINCE, duke of AQUITAINE, worked to rid their domains of the Great Company and its constituent bands.

Arnaud de CERVOLE, the former cleric turned mercenary who became known as the "Archpriest," formed the first Great Company in the summer of 1357. Attracted by the Mediterranean trade of Marseille and the rich papal court at Avignon, Cervole collected more than two thousand men along the Rhône on the Provençal frontier. In July, he marched unopposed through Provence, burning and looting as he went. By September, Cervole's bands had infested almost the whole province, forcing people to flee to the larger TOWNS, which were the only centers of effective resistance. Impressed by the easy success of Cervole's enterprise, other *routier* captains flocked to Provence in the following months. In February 1358, the Great Company captured and sacked the rich pilgrimage town of Sainte-Maximin, but Marseille, which Cervole invested with almost three thousand men in March, proved too large and well defended to be taken by assault. As the Great Company began to dissolve, Cervole led a remnant northward to Avignon, where he accepted a papal offer of 20,000 florins to leave Provence and restore all castles seized by his men. By October, the first Great Company had largely disintegrated.

A new Great Company formed in eastern France in the summer of 1360. Said to number over four thousand men, it was originally led by the Scottish *routier* Sir Walter Leslie, but came eventually under the control of a fluctuating body of captains who directed the army's movements through an administrative staff and command hierarchy copied from the national armies of England and France. Rather than seize strongpoints and live by levying tolls and taxes on the surrounding areas, the Great Company of 1360 marched through open country, holding towns and entire provinces to RANSOM. Lured by the promise of wealth and adventure, men from many backgrounds, including criminals from the towns and displaced monks, flocked to the Great Company, which by early 1361 numbered over twelve thousand men, less than half of whom were professional soldiers. In December 1360, drawn by an ultimately false rumor that money collected for King John's ransom was hidden there, the Great Company seized the Rhône town of Pont-Saint-Esprit, which proved an ideal base for raiding Avignon and the Rhône Valley. Although the pope excommunicated the men of the Great Company and proclaimed a crusade against them, and the French king sent Marshal Arnoul d'AUDREHEM to organize local defenses, the *routiers* only began to disband in March 1361 when their growing numbers made the army too unwieldy to feed or control.

After concluding an agreement with the pope, who promised payment in return for the army's withdrawal, many *routiers*, such as the English captain Sir John HAWKWOOD, crossed the Alps to offer their services to the warring Italian states. However, a remnant of the Great Company, now under the leadership of the Gascon captain Séguin de BA-

DEFOL, invaded Languedoc, where they were reinforced by *routiers* from the north left unemployed by the Treaty of BRÉTIGNY. However, local defenses proved more effective than in Provence, and, by the end of 1361, the Great Company, having been abandoned by Badefol, moved east toward BURGUNDY. Motivated by this threat, the royal government raised an army to defend the province. On 6 April 1362, five thousand men of the Great Company surprised and defeated the royal army at BRIGNAIS. Although news of the battle spread panic across eastern France, the Great Company had again become too large to maintain itself and by early 1363 the *routier* army formed in 1360 finally dissolved.

In the summer of 1363, Badefol reconstituted the Great Company in Languedoc. This new incarnation extracted a huge ransom from Toulouse, before seizing the town of Brioude in Auvergne on 13 September. From Brioude, the Great Company, now swollen to almost ten thousand men, overran the whole of Auvergne. Needing food and forage, the *routiers* then seized the abbey of Savigny, which put them within twelve miles of Lyon and within striking distance of Burgundy. In April 1364, Badefol concluded an agreement with the provincial estates of Auvergne (*see* ESTATES, GENERAL AND PROVINCIAL), promising to surrender Brioude and release his prisoners for a royal pardon, a papal absolution, and 40,000 florins. Badefol and his men next took service with CHARLES THE BAD, king of Navarre, but did little to advance Navarre's cause, preferring instead to seize the town of Anse, near Lyon, which, like Brioude, became a base to pillage the surrounding countryside until the *routiers* were once again paid to withdraw.

From 1365 to 1367, many *routier* bands were employed either by Bertrand du GUESCLIN or the Black Prince during the Anglo-French intervention in the CASTILIAN WAR OF SUCCESSION (*see* NÁJERA, BATTLE OF). When the prince disbanded his army in the autumn of 1367, many of its elements coalesced into a new Great Company. This force did much damage in Auvergne and Burgundy, but was unable to establish a base and soon broke up into smaller groups that moved north and west into Champagne and NORMANDY. The last of these groups, a mainly English force that operated in Normandy and BRITTANY, where Duke JOHN IV had to pay them off, remained in being until early 1369, when it was paid to disband by Sir John CHANDOS. Although *routier* bands remained active in many provinces, the revival of royal authority under CHARLES V and the general improvement in local defenses prevented any new force worthy of the name Great Company from forming thereafter.

Further Reading: Sumption, Jonathan. *The Hundred Years War.* Vol. 2, *Trial by Fire.* Philadelphia: University of Pennsylvania Press, 2001; Wright, Nicholas A. R. "'Pillagers' and 'Brigands' in the Hundred Years War." *Journal of Medieval History* 9 (1983): 15–25.

GREAT SCHISM. *See* PAPACY AND THE HUNDRED YEARS WAR

GREGORY XI. *See* PAPACY AND THE HUNDRED YEARS WAR

GUÉRANDE, TREATY OF (1365)
Ratified on 12 April 1365 in the Church of St. Aubin in Guérande in southern BRITTANY, the Treaty of Guérande ended the long BRETON CIVIL WAR. Since 1341, the two claimants to the duchy had served as surrogates for each side in the Anglo-French war; the Breton conflict frequently provided the kings of France and England with opportunities to attack each other's interests even during periods of formal truce. Although the treaty ended most fighting within the duchy, Brittany's dukes, attempting to maintain their independence by playing one side against the other, thereafter remained important political figures in the HUNDRED YEARS WAR.

With the death of CHARLES OF BLOIS at the Battle of AURAY in September 1364, his cause, which was supported by France, collapsed, and most of the Breton towns and nobility submitted to Charles's English-

backed rival, John de Montfort. Despite his ties to EDWARD III and England, Montfort, within days of the battle, offered his homage for the duchy to CHARLES V of France. Charles, accepting the verdict of Auray and seeking to gain advantage out of the formal peace that followed a lost war, helped mediate a final settlement between Montfort and Charles of Blois's widow, Jeanne de Penthièvre, in whose right Blois had contested the duchy.

By the terms of the Treaty of Guérande, Jeanne de Penthièvre surrendered her claims, as niece of the last duke, to the ducal title and recognized John de Montfort as Duke JOHN IV. In return, Jeanne was allowed to keep the title of duchess for the rest of her life and was granted the county of Penthièvre for herself and her heirs. She could also retain the lands of her father, both inside and outside the duchy, a conglomeration of territories that brought her annual rents in excess of 10,000 livres. John IV also agreed that title to the duchy would revert to Jeanne or her heirs should the Montfort line fail. The Treaty of Guérande was thus highly favorable to France, for, despite his military exertions in the duchy and the victory of his candidate, Edward III saw his influence in Brittany slowly decline after 1365.

Further Reading: Jones, Michael. *Ducal Brittany, 1364–1399.* London: Oxford University Press, 1970; Sumption, Jonathan. *The Hundred Years War.* Vol. 2, *Trial by Fire.* Philadelphia: University of Pennsylvania Press, 2001.

GUESCLIN, BERTRAND DU, CONSTABLE OF FRANCE (c. 1320–1380)
Bertrand du Guesclin was constable of France and the most renowned French captain of the HUNDRED YEARS WAR.

Born into a cadet branch of a noble Breton family, du Guesclin began his military career in the 1340s as a mercenary captain in the service of CHARLES OF BLOIS, the French-backed claimant in the BRETON CIVIL WAR. Du Guesclin entered the service of JOHN II in 1351 and succeeded his father as lord of Broons in 1353. Knighted by Arnoul d'AUDREHEM, marshal of France, in April 1354, du

Guesclin took a leading role in defending Rennes when it was unsuccessfully besieged by HENRY OF GROSMONT, duke of Lancaster, in 1356–57. In December 1357, in recognition of his service at Rennes, Dauphin Charles (*see* CHARLES V) granted du Guesclin a life pension of 200 livres and named him captain of Pontorson, a strategic stronghold on the Breton-Norman frontier. In 1359, he was captured at Pas d'Évran in BRITTANY by the English captain Sir Robert KNOLLES, and in 1360 fell again into English hands at Juigné, where he was captured by Sir Hugh CALVELEY. To pay his RANSOMS, du Guesclin borrowed money from Philip, duke of Orléans, the brother of John II and himself a prisoner in LONDON.

In May 1364, du Guesclin defeated the forces of CHARLES THE BAD, king of NAVARRE, at COCHEREL in NORMANDY, where he had been active in royal service since the Treaty of BRÉTIGNY ended the Anglo-French war in 1360. In September 1364, after returning to Brittany and the service of Blois, du Guesclin was captured again when Blois was slain at AURAY. Ransomed by Charles V, du Guesclin resumed royal service, this time in the southwest, where he assisted the king's brother, LOUIS, duke of Anjou, in ridding the region of *ROUTIERS*. In an effort to install a pro-French regime in Castile and thereby undermine the government of EDWARD, THE BLACK PRINCE, in AQUITAINE, du Guesclin intervened in the CASTILIAN WAR OF SUCCESSION by leading a *routier* army into Spain, where it placed Henry of Trastámare on the Castilian throne in 1365. The deposed king, Pedro the Cruel, appealed to the Black Prince, who restored Pedro by defeating and capturing du Guesclin at NÁJERA in April 1367. Ransomed again by the king, de Guesclin led a new army into Castile and restored Trastámare to power for good in 1369.

In 1370, Charles, having resumed the war by accepting the APPEAL OF THE GASCON LORDS, appointed du Guesclin constable, recognizing in the Breton, who was more skilled at leading *routiers* than fighting pitched battles, the ideal commander for the Fabian

tactics the king planned to employ against the English. Du Guesclin used them successfully against the English *CHEVAUCHÉE* of 1370, which was led in part by Knolles. Ignoring English attempts to draw him into battle, du Guesclin waited until disputes among the expedition's leaders caused them to split up; the constable then fell on the contingent under Sir Thomas Grandison, which he routed at Pontvallain on 4 December. In 1371–72, du Guesclin led the French reconquest of Poitou and Saintonge and in 1373 he overran Brittany, driving out the pro-English duke, JOHN IV. For the next five years, the constable led a series of campaigns that retook much of English Aquitaine. In the highly successful campaign of 1377, which included the defeat and capture of Thomas Felton, the English seneschal of Aquitaine, at the Battle of Eymet on 1 September, du Guesclin came within a day's march of BORDEAUX.

An extremely ugly man who was highly popular with the people, but much less so with the king's political advisors, the constable lost favor in 1378 when he opposed Charles's decision to confiscate Brittany. Dispatched to Auvergne to fight *routiers*, du Guesclin died there of fever on 13 July 1380. He was interred at Saint-Denis on the king's orders. *See also* CHIVALRY.

Further Reading: Vernier, Richard. *The Flower of Chivalry: Bertrand de Guesclin and the Hundred Years War.* Woodbridge, England: Boydell Press, 2003.

GUIENNE. *See* AQUITAINE; GASCONY

GUIENNE, DUKE OF. *See* LOUIS, DUKE OF GUIENNE

GUINES, TREATY OF (1354)

Negotiated at the traditional site of Anglo-French conferences in Guines on the borders of the CALAIS enclave, the 1354 Treaty of Guines gave EDWARD III most of southwestern France in exchange for his renunciation of the French Crown. Although growing resistance to the treaty led JOHN II to repudiate it five months later, the agreement, had it taken effect, would have given Edward more than he was to achieve with the Treaty of BRÉTIGNY in 1360, when the French king was his captive.

In February 1354, John pardoned his kinsman, CHARLES THE BAD, king of Navarre, for his murder of the royal constable Charles of Spain. John thereupon admitted to his favor many of Navarre's friends and advisors, who soon formed a council majority in favor of negotiating a permanent peace with England. Talks began at Guines in March 1354 with the French expressing a willingness to cede territory and Edward a willingness to abandon his right to the French Crown in return for such cessions. As sealed on 6 April, the Treaty of Guines gave Edward the duchy of AQUITAINE, as it had existed on the eve of the War of SAINT-SARDOS in 1323, and the provinces of Poitou, Maine, Anjou, Touraine, and the Limousin, all in full sovereignty. Edward was also to retain the town and enclave of Calais. In return for almost the whole of western France, Edward agreed to make peace and to formally renounce his claims to the throne of France. Accompanying the treaty was an agreement to extend the Truce of CALAIS to 1 April 1355. The terms of the treaty were to be kept secret until published by the pope in Avignon on 1 October 1354, when both sides were to make public renunciation of the specified rights and lands.

Without divulging the terms of the agreement, Edward had it ratified by an enthusiastic PARLIAMENT. In France, all English military operations were halted and vigorous attempts were made to restrain local garrison commanders from committing breaches of the truce. Although John initially endorsed the treaty, opposition to it soon developed. John, count of Armagnac, refused to honor the truce and in May launched a campaign against English garrisons in the Agenais. Within the council, opponents of Charles of Navarre informed the king that many of the treaty's leading advocates had been complicit with Navarre in the murder of the constable, leading John to conclude that the treaty had been urged upon him by men whose first loyalty was to Navarre. John decided to repudiate the treaty in September and did not send representatives to Avignon until January 1355, three months after the agreed-upon date. When the English demanded ratification of the agreement, the French ambassadors rejected the idea that Edward could hold any French territories in full sovereignty, declaring that no king of France could authorize the dismemberment of his kingdom. The Treaty of Guines was thus a dead letter and war resumed in earnest in 1355.

Further Reading: Sumption, Jonathan. *The Hundred Years War*. Vol. 2, *Trial by Fire*. Philadelphia: University of Pennsylvania Press, 2001.

H

HALIDON HILL, BATTLE OF (1333)
Fought on 19 July 1333 near the town of
Berwick on the Anglo-Scottish border, the
Battle of Halidon Hill, an encounter between
the forces of EDWARD III and a Scottish army
under Sir Archibald Douglas, guardian of
SCOTLAND, resulted in a decade-long English
occupation of southern Scotland and the
eventual flight to France of Scotland's DAVID
II. Although not a battle of the HUNDRED
YEARS WAR, Halidon Hill is important to the
subsequent conflict because it made Scotland an important factor in the deterioration
of Anglo-French relations and because it
was among the first battlefield demonstrations of the new defensive tactics the English
were to employ with such success at CRÉCY
and other Hundred Years War engagements.

On 9 May 1333, Edward III joined Edward
Balliol, the English-backed claimant to the
Scottish throne, in besieging Berwick-on-
Tweed. After suffering continual bombardment by both gunpowder ARTILLERY and
traditional siege engines, as well as furious
assaults from both land and sea, the Scottish
garrison negotiated a truce whereby they
agreed to surrender the town if not relieved
by 11 July. Although some supplies and reinforcements entered the town by that date,
Edward rejected Scottish claims that Berwick was thus relieved and began executing
the hostages given him by the defenders.
The garrison then negotiated a second truce
that was to run until 20 July. On 19 July,
Edward, warned of the approach of Douglas's army, prepared to meet the enemy near
Halidon Hill, about two miles northwest of
Berwick.

The exact nature and location of the English formations are uncertain. Some accounts put the English in line of battle along
the top of Halidon Hill, while others say that
they stood at the base of the hill. Edward's
men deployed either in a single body of
men-at-arms supported on each flank by
groups of ARCHERS or into three separate
formations of men-at-arms with each flanked
by bodies of archers. All that is certain is that
the English stood on the defensive and were
dismounted, and that the archers and men-
at-arms worked in concert in some fashion
to disrupt the enemy charge. From contemporary accounts, it appears that the fire of
the archers severely disordered the Scottish
attack, allowing the English knights to remount and do great execution among the
fleeing Scots.

Berwick surrendered the next day, and
Balliol was able to win control of much of
Scotland over the next year. In May 1334,
David II fled to France, and Balliol shortly
thereafter gave Edward eight counties in
southern Scotland. In France, PHILIP VI declared that Scotland had to be included in
any negotiated settlement of the growing
Anglo-French dispute over AQUITAINE, a
demand that angered Edward—who considered Scottish affairs a purely internal
concern—and thus became an important
factor in the coming of the Hundred Years
War. Although Edward launched annual
campaigns in Scotland until 1338, the Scots,
by David's return in 1341, had taken advantage of Edward's preoccupation with the
French war to regain much of the occupied
territory.

Further Reading: DeVries, Kelly. *Infantry Warfare in the Early Fourteenth Century: Discipline, Tactics, and Technology.* Rochester, NY: Boydell Press, 1996; Nicholson, Ranald. *Edward III and the Scots: The Formative Years of a Military Career, 1327–1335.* London: Oxford University Press, 1965.

HARCOURT, GODFREY OF (d. 1356)

A member of one of the oldest noble families of NORMANDY, Godfrey of Harcourt, younger brother of John, first count of Harcourt, was lord of the important Norman fortress of Saint-Sauveur-le-Vicomte. Chronically in rebellion against PHILIP VI and JOHN II, Harcourt swore allegiance to EDWARD III in the 1340s and played an important role during the 1346 CRÉCY campaign. Harcourt's career illustrates how the HUNDRED YEARS WAR and the rival claims of PLANTAGENET and VALOIS allowed disaffected noblemen to play one side against the other as their own interests and ambitions dictated.

In 1341, a quarrel over the marriage of a local heiress led to the outbreak of a private war between Harcourt and his rival, Robert Bertrand, lord of Bricquebec. Philip VI intervened and summoned the two men to court, where, in September 1342, their mutual animosity caused them to draw swords in the king's presence. Ordered, like his rival, to appear before the PARLEMENT, Harcourt instead returned to Normandy and led his supporters in a series of destructive raids on the property of Bertrand's family. The king dispatched an army, which, by March 1343, had captured Saint-Sauveur and crushed the uprising. Having fled to Brabant, Harcourt was convicted in absentia of lese-majesté (i.e., committing an affront to the royal dignity) and punished with banishment and forfeiture of property.

In 1344, rumors that Harcourt had accepted the lordship of Edward III were given substance when three of Harcourt's former supporters were captured fighting for the English in BRITTANY. All three were condemned and executed. Although the rumors were probably untrue, Philip's hostility convinced Harcourt to come to England,

where he performed liege homage for his lands to Edward in May 1345. According to the chroniclers JEAN LE BEL and Jean FROISSART, Harcourt was thereafter instrumental in persuading Edward to change the destination of his 1346 expedition from GASCONY to the Cotentin Peninsula of Normandy. Harcourt supposedly told the king that the Normans were unaccustomed to war and their lands were wealthy, full of "great towns without walls where your men shall have riches to last them twenty years" (Sumption, 1:498). Although Normandy had always been a possible landing site—it was the closest landfall to Edward's embarkation point at Portsmouth—Harcourt's knowledge of conditions in the region and promise of local assistance from his supporters probably influenced the king's thinking. During the resulting campaign, Harcourt was one of Edward's chief advisors, leading destructive raids into the Norman countryside and fighting at Crécy as one of the captains of EDWARD, THE BLACK PRINCE.

After the battle, Edward III's realization that he could not hold Normandy and that CALAIS was a better potential base than any Norman port convinced Harcourt to leave the English army and return to Brabant, from which he negotiated his return to Philip's favor. In December 1346, he appeared before the French king and received his pardon and his lands. However, in the 1350s, Harcourt became a strong supporter of CHARLES THE BAD, the rebellious king of Navarre. Although Harcourt briefly abandoned Navarre after the Treaty of GUINES in 1354, he refused to swear homage to Dauphin Charles (*see* CHARLES V) as duke of Normandy in January 1356 and thereafter, in defiance of the rest of his family, held Saint-Sauveur against the duke. In November 1356, Harcourt was killed in combat with ducal troops. The barony of Saint-Sauveur thereafter passed into the hands of Edward III, to whom Harcourt had deeded it.

Further Reading: Sumption, Jonathan. *The Hundred Years War.* Vol. 1, *Trial by Battle.* Philadelphia: University of Pennsylvania Press,

1991; Sumption, Jonathan. *The Hundred Years War.* Vol. 2, *Trial by Fire.* Philadelphia: University of Pennsylvania Press, 2001.

HARFLEUR, SIEGE OF (1415)

In the late summer of 1415, the six-week English siege of the Norman town of Harfleur initiated HENRY V's campaign to reopen the HUNDRED YEARS WAR. Although the town's eventual capitulation gave the English a valuable base on the Seine, the unexpected length and difficulty of the siege weakened the English army and convinced Henry to withdraw toward CALAIS, a retreat that boosted French confidence of victory and led to the momentous Battle of AGINCOURT.

On 11 August, an invasion force of about ten thousand men sailed from Portsmouth. Landing near Le Chef de Caux at the head of the Seine Estuary on 14 August, Henry made for the nearby town of Harfleur, which promised to be an admirable base from which to launch the conquest of NORMANDY. Henry expected the town to fall quickly, but Raoul, Sieur de Gaucourt, and a force of three hundred men reinforced the garrison before the town was surrounded on 18 August. Although THOMAS, duke of Clarence, the king's brother, turned back a convoy carrying weapons and supplies to the garrison, Harfleur's defenses were formidable. The walls had twenty-six towers and three strong barbicans—fortified gateways with drawbridges and portcullises—a moat, and a garrison of several hundred men commanded by Gaucourt and the tough and experienced Sieur d'Estouteville.

While English ships blockaded the Estuary, the army surrounded Harfleur with a ditch and stockade, thus cutting the town off from any hope of supply or reinforcement. Because attempts to undermine the walls were foiled by skillful countermining, Henry turned to his ARTILLERY, which included twelve-foot-long cannon capable of throwing stones weighing nearly half a ton. Such artillery could batter down any walls provided it could be brought in close enough, for the French also had artillery. Employing heavy wooden screens and awkward wheeled platforms, and suffering heavy losses in the process, the English inched their big guns forward and began inflicting damage on the walls.

However, before further progress could be made, Henry's army was swept by disease, probably dysentery and malaria fostered by summer heat, marshy camps, and contaminated food and water. The contagion slew many of all ranks, although the nobility seemed particularly affected, the dead including Thomas Fitzalan, earl of Arundel; Michael de la Pole, earl of Suffolk; and Richard Courtenay, bishop of Norwich. To conclude the siege quickly, Henry ordered an all-night cannonade that led to the capture of one of the barbicans on 18 September. Forced to parley, Gaucourt agreed to surrender the town if his messages to the dauphin, LOUIS, DUKE OF GUIENNE, did not bring relief within four days. When no help arrived, the garrison opened the gates on 22 September. Angered by Harfleur's resistance, Henry eventually expelled most of the townspeople, replacing them with English merchants and craftsmen who could turn Harfleur into another Calais. Leaving the town on 6 October, Henry and his much reduced force marched northeast, coming before the end of the month to the battlefield at Agincourt. Harfleur remained largely under English control until 1449. *See also* SIEGE WARFARE.

Further Reading: Allmand, Christopher. *Henry V.* New Haven, CT: Yale University Press, 1997; Burne, Alfred H. *The Agincourt War.* Ware, England: Wordsworth Editions Ltd., 1999.

HAWKWOOD, SIR JOHN (c. 1320–1394)

Although most of his career was spent in Italy, Sir John Hawkwood is the best-known English ROUTIER captain to emerge from the HUNDRED YEARS WAR.

John was the second son of Gilbert Hawkwood, a minor landowner in Essex. Although little is known for certain about his life before the 1360s, Hawkwood probably began his military career in France in about 1340, the year of his father's death. He may have served in BRITTANY in the 1340s and is said to have fought at both CRÉCY in 1346 and POITIERS in 1356. However, his first service in France may not have occurred until the RHEIMS CAMPAIGN of 1359–60, by which time he had achieved knighthood. The first reliable information on Hawkwood comes from 1360, when, in the aftermath of the Treaty of BRÉTIGNY, he joined one of the companies of freebooters that formed the *routier* army known as the *Tard-Venus* (Late-comers), which threatened Avignon by seizing the Rhone town of Pont-Saint-Esprit in late December. Bought off by the pope, the *routier* force split up, with Hawkwood joining the group that took service in Italy with the marquis of Montferrat. In 1361, Hawkwood apparently returned to France, where, as a member of one of the brigand bands comprising the GREAT COMPANY, he fought against a French royal army at BRIGNAIS in April 1362.

By 1363, Hawkwood was back in Italy for good, serving in a company of Anglo-German mercenaries (known in Italy as *condottieri*) led by a *routier* named Albert Sterz, who was appointed captain-general of Pisa in July. In December, Hawkwood replaced Sterz as commander of the Pisan bands, which were then reorganized as the English White Company. The White Company was composed of units known as lances, groups of four or five men consisting of two mounted men-at-arms, a page, and one or two mounted ARCHERS. Although Hawkwood's personal force was only a small fraction of the troops under his command, it became the stable and seasoned core of most of his armies. Defeated at Bongard in July 1365, Hawkwood joined the remnants of the White Company with English mercenaries led by the illegitimate son of the duke of Milan to form the Company of Saint George, which he left in 1366. In 1372, upon taking service with Pope Gregory XI, Hawkwood became captain-general of the English Company, an amalgamation of bands that had previously fought under other captains. An effective leader of men and a brilliant tactician, Hawkwood soon found his services in high demand among the warring states of Italy. He fought for the duke of Milan from 1368 to 1372, for the pope from 1372 to 1377, and then largely, but not exclusively, for the Republic of Florence after 1380. Besides being led by Hawkwood, whose military reputation soon spread throughout Italy, the English companies were much prized because they fought dismounted and could operate at night and well into the winter.

Hawkwood amassed great wealth from fees, pensions, and RANSOMS, but, unlike other *condottieri*, did not aspire to become an Italian lord. In the mid-1370s, he began sending money to England, where his agents bought property and even made war loans to the Crown. In 1378, Hawkwood, like another famous *routier* captain, Sir Robert KNOLLES, secured a pardon from PARLIAMENT for all youthful indiscretions. Also in 1378, Hawkwood married an illegitimate daughter of the duke of Milan, thereby acquiring a large dowry and powerful family connections. In 1392–93, Hawkwood began preparing to liquidate his Italian assets for a return to England, but he was still in Italy when he died of a stroke on 16 March 1394. He was given a magnificent funeral by the Florentine Republic and buried in the Cathedral of Santa Maria del Fiore in Florence.

Further Reading: Fowler, Kenneth A. *Medieval Mercenaries*. Vol. 1, *The Great Companies*. Oxford: Blackwell, 2001; Fowler, Kenneth A. ''Sir John Hawkwood and the English *Condottieri* in Trecento, Italy.'' *Renaissance Studies* 12 (1998): 131–48; Mallett, Michael. *Mercenaries and Their Master: Warfare in Renaissance Italy*. Totowa, NJ: Rowman and Littlefield, 1974.

HENRY IV, KING OF ENGLAND (1366–1413)

Although a grandson of EDWARD III, Henry IV, the only son of JOHN OF GAUNT, duke of Lancaster, by his first wife, Blanche, the daughter of HENRY OF GROSMONT, duke of Lancaster, was not the direct heir to the PLANTAGENET throne, and his deposition of his cousin RICHARD II in 1399 broke the natural line of succession. Despite this dubious right to the

English throne and an even more tenuous claim to the French throne, Henry came to power by criticizing his predecessor's peace policy and demanding renewal of the HUN-DRED YEARS WAR. However, years of internal rebellion and physical illness prevented Henry from taking advantage of the FRENCH CIVIL WAR and the mental illness of CHARLES VI to invade France and openly challenge the legitimacy of the House of VALOIS.

Little is known of Henry's childhood, which was probably spent on various Lancastrian estates throughout the kingdom. He assumed the title earl of Derby in 1377 and was knighted by his father in 1378. In about 1381, he married Mary de Bohun, the daughter and heiress of the earl of Hereford, who had extensive land holdings in Wales and the West Country. Derby served with his father in SCOTLAND in 1384 and remained in England to oversee Lancastrian interests when the duke left the realm to pursue his claim to the Castilian Crown in 1386. In 1387–89, Derby became one of the Lords Appellant, a group of five nobles who were so named because they appealed (i.e., accused) the king's favorites of treason. Led by Derby's uncle, THOMAS OF WOODSTOCK, duke of Gloucester, the Lords Appellants used their control of the so-called Merciless PAR-LIAMENT to secure the execution or banishment of most of the king's supporters. Although Derby was more moderate than his older colleagues, he commanded the Appellant forces that defeated a royalist army at Radcot Bridge in December 1387.

Upon his father's return in 1389, Derby withdrew from politics. In July 1390, he joined the Teutonic Knights' crusade in Lithuania and in 1392 he went on pilgrimage to Jerusalem. In 1397, following Richard's destruction of Gloucester and the other senior Appellants, Derby informed the king that Thomas Mowbray, duke of Norfolk, who, like the earl, had been pardoned for his role in the events of 1387–89, had warned him that Richard meant to kill them both. When Mowbray denied this, Richard arranged for the dispute to be settled by trial of battle at Coventry. However, at the last minute, Ri-

chard halted the combat and declared both men guilty; the king then exiled Norfolk for life and Derby for ten years. In February 1399, Lancaster died. With Derby in PARIS, Richard declared the earl banished for life and confiscated all the Lancastrian estates. Announcing that he came only to regain his duchy, Derby landed in Yorkshire on 4 July, while Richard was on campaign in Ireland.

The English nobility, fearful of the precedent set by the king's confiscation of a subject's property, and distrustful of Richard's increasing taste for arbitrary government, rallied to Derby. On 30 September, a month after the king surrendered to his cousin in Wales, Parliament deposed Richard and gave the Crown to Derby, who, as Henry IV, became the first king of the House of LAN-CASTER. Although the new king denounced his predecessor's peace policy and declared his intention of renewing the war, Henry ratified the Truce of LEULINGHEN in May 1400. The suspicious death of Richard in February 1400 and the outbreak of a series of anti-Lancastrian uprisings over the next six years left Henry too insecure to consider campaigning in France. However, he signaled his fundamental hostility to the Valois by refusing to allow Richard's queen, Isabella, daughter of Charles VI (*see* ISABELLA, QUEEN OF ENGLAND [1388–1409]), to return to France. When he finally did so in August 1400, Henry kept her dowry and jewels, declaring them payment toward the arrears of JOHN II's RANSOM.

In France, PHILIP THE BOLD, duke of BUR-GUNDY, and LOUIS, DUKE OF ORLÉANS, disagreed over the best response to Henry's usurpation. The former supported maintenance of the truce while the latter advocated driving the English from GASCONY and CA-LAIS while Henry was distracted by internal rebellion. Half-hearted campaigns were launched against the English holdings, but, following the murder of Orléans by agents of the new duke of Burgundy, JOHN THE FEARLESS, in 1407, the French were themselves distracted by internal division. After 1406, when uprisings in Wales and among the English nobility were at last quelled,

Henry suffered increasingly from ill health. Between 1409 and 1411, England was ruled by Prince Henry, and only suggestions that he abdicate spurred the king to resume control of the government. Henry's illness prevented him from taking any significant advantage of the French civil war, although in 1412 he made agreements with both the BURGUNDIANS and the ARMAGNACS, promising to help each fight the other in return for territorial concessions. The Treaty of BOURGES, concluded with the Armagnacs in May 1412, resulted in the sending to France of an expedition under the king's son, THOMAS, DUKE OF CLARENCE. Although a temporary settlement of the civil war overthrew the agreement, Clarence forced his erstwhile allies to pay him a large ransom in the Treaty of BUZANÇAIS. With a feeble Anglo-French truce still in effect, Henry IV died on 20 March 1413, leaving renewal of the war to his son, HENRY V.

Further Reading: Kirby, John Lavan. *Henry IV of England*. London: Constable, 1970; Wylie, James Hamilton. *The History of England under Henry the Fourth*. 4 vols. Reprint, New York: AMS Press, 1969.

HENRY V, KING OF ENGLAND (1387–1422)

Henry V, the eldest son of HENRY IV and second king of the House of LANCASTER, exploited the FRENCH CIVIL WAR to successfully reopen the HUNDRED YEARS WAR. A brilliant soldier and natural leader, Henry conquered NORMANDY and achieved formal French recognition as heir to the VALOIS throne. Although he has traditionally been portrayed as the most heroic and chivalrous of English monarchs, particularly by William Shakespeare in the play *Henry V*, some modern historians have questioned this view, seeing Henry as cruel, bigoted, and self-righteous.

Thomas Hoccleve presents a book of poetry to Henry V. *HIP/ Art Resource, New York.*

Henry was twelve in 1399 when his father deposed his cousin, RICHARD II. In 1403, Henry was wounded at the Battle of Shrewsbury, where royal forces crushed the Percy Rebellion. After campaigning for his father in Wales, the prince took charge of the government in about 1409 when the king's health began to fail. Although largely fictional, the wild, rebellious prince of Shakespeare's *Henry IV* plays may reflect actual disagreements from this period between father and son. In 1411, the king resumed control of the government, reversing his son's pro-BURGUNDIAN foreign policy by concluding the Treaty of BOURGES with the ARMAGNACS. On the king's death in March 1413, Henry, acting both on a desire to unite the country around the new dynasty and on a firm belief that he was rightful king of

France, began preparing for war. Negotiating both with the Armagnac regime currently in power in PARIS and with the Burgundian leader, JOHN THE FEARLESS, duke of BURGUNDY, Henry purposely made demands he knew neither side could meet, including the surrender of Normandy and AQUITAINE, the payment of 2 million crowns, and the hand of CHARLES VI's youngest daughter, CATHERINE OF VALOIS. When both sides rejected these terms, Henry used the French refusal as justification for war.

Before embarking for France, Henry sought to quell all internal opposition. Staunchly orthodox, he sparked the Oldcastle Rebellion early in 1414 by allowing his former friend, Sir John Oldcastle, to be condemned to death for Lollardy, an English heretical movement. Although the uprising was crushed, Oldcastle remained at large until 1417, when he was captured and burned. In late 1413, the king tried to make peace with his father's opponents by exhuming the body of Richard II and giving it respectful reburial at Westminster Abbey. However, the gesture did not prevent the Southampton Plot, a noble conspiracy to murder the king and replace him with Richard's supplanted heir, Edmund Mortimer, earl of March. Led by Henry, Lord Scrope of Masham, the king's friend, and Richard, earl of Cambridge, the king's cousin, the plot was uncovered on the eve of Henry's departure in 1415, and the conspirators were quickly tried and executed.

Landing in France on 14 August 1415, Henry immediately laid siege to HARFLEUR, which, thanks to illness among the English, held out until 22 September. With his army of ten thousand reduced to about six thousand, Henry set out on 6 October, intending to march northeast through Normandy to CALAIS. Harassed by the enemy, and weakened and demoralized by bad weather and lack of supply, the English army was driven forward by Henry's energy and example. On 25 October, when an encounter with the numerically superior French could not be avoided, Henry fought and won a stunningly unexpected victory at AGINCOURT.

The battle cemented Henry's reputation as a general and generated great enthusiasm for the war in England. Aiming, unlike his great-grandfather, EDWARD III, to secure the whole of France rather than just sovereignty over particular provinces, Henry abandoned the CHEVAUCHÉE for campaigns of siege and occupation (see SIEGE WARFARE). After securing additional funding from PARLIAMENT and concluding the Treaty of CANTERBURY with the Emperor Sigismund in 1416, Henry invaded Normandy in 1417. Considering the Normans his subjects, Henry severely punished any English soldiers who ill treated the local population. The NORMAN CAMPAIGN concluded with the capture of ROUEN, which capitulated in January 1419 after a grueling six-month siege marked by Henry's cruel refusal to allow the poor people expelled from the city to pass safely through his lines. With the onset of winter, most died huddled in a ditch outside the city walls.

The fall of Rouen demoralized the French court, which had been under Burgundian influence since May 1418. In September 1419, servants of the dauphin (see CHARLES VII) murdered Burgundy at MONTEREAU, convincing PHILIP THE GOOD, the new duke of Burgundy, to ally himself with Henry, who imposed the Treaty of TROYES on the French in May 1420. Besides creating an ANGLO-BURGUNDIAN ALLIANCE, the treaty disinherited the dauphin in favor of Henry, who immediately became regent of France, and arranged a marriage between Henry and Catherine, which occurred on 2 June. Henry and his wife returned to England in February 1421, following the successful siege of MELUN. In March, Henry's brother and heir, THOMAS, DUKE OF CLARENCE, was slain at BAUGÉ, the first English defeat since Henry restarted the war in 1415. Returning to France on 10 June, the king visited Paris, which was now under Anglo-Burgundian control. Leaving the capital to his uncle, Thomas BEAUFORT, duke of Exeter, Henry laid siege to MEAUX in October. The difficult winter operation, which was brightened only by news of the birth of Henry's son in December, sapped English morale and weakened the king's constitution. In June 1422, only a month after the surrender of Meaux, Henry contracted what was likely dysentery. He died at Vincennes on 31 August and was succeeded on the English throne by his nine-month-old son, HENRY VI, whose reign saw the eventual loss of all English territory in France except Calais.

Further Reading: Allmand, Christopher, *Henry V*. Berkeley: University of California Press, 1992; Harriss, G. L., ed. *Henry V: The Practice of Kingship*. Oxford: Oxford University Press, 1985; Labarge, Margaret Wade. *Henry V: The Cautious Conqueror*. New York: Stein and Day, 1976; Seward, Desmond. *Henry V: The Scourge of God*. New York: Viking, 1988.

HENRY VI, KING OF ENGLAND (1421–1471)

The only child of HENRY V and CATHERINE OF VALOIS, Henry VI ruled England during the last decades of the HUNDRED YEARS WAR. Although the only English king to be crowned king of France, Henry's mental instability prevented him from functioning effectively as monarch in either kingdom and contributed to the eventual expulsion of the English from France.

Born at Windsor on 6 December 1421, Henry was less than a year old when he succeeded his father as king of England and his maternal grandfather, CHARLES VI, as king of France. Having conquered NORMANDY and northwestern France, Henry V won official recognition as heir to the French throne with the Treaty of TROYES in 1420. However, Henry VI's maternal uncle, the Dauphin Charles, rejected this settlement and maintenance of Henry's French claims and possessions required a continuous military effort. During the king's minority, the longest in English history, Henry's eldest paternal uncle, JOHN, DUKE OF BEDFORD, conducted both the war and the English administration in France, while the King's younger uncle, HUMPHREY, DUKE OF GLOUCESTER, presided in England over a minority council.

Acting in the child king's name, though unable to make any permanent decisions affecting his Crowns, the minority administration, through alliance with PHILIP THE GOOD, duke of BURGUNDY, sought to maintain Henry V's conquests while extending Henry VI's authority into dauphinist France. Despite English victories at CRAVANT in 1423 and VERNEUIL in 1424, the advent of JOAN OF ARC in 1429 inspired the French to break the siege of ORLÉANS and allowed the dauphin to be crowned at Rheims as CHARLES VII. Thus, after 1430, the English were on the defensive, and their efforts focused more on maintaining Henry's French possessions than on securing his French Crown. The death of Bedford and Burgundy's abandonment of the English cause at the Congress of ARRAS in 1435, followed by the loss of PARIS in 1436, severely diminished the ability of the English government to do either.

Crowned at Westminster in 1429 and at Paris in 1431, Henry was declared of full age in 1437. He was eager to exercise his office and to have his will in matters that interested him, such as the royal foundations of Eton College and King's College, Cambridge, which the king planned in minute detail and to which he diverted funds that were urgently needed for the French war. However, he had little understanding of the workings of government, and was easily persuaded by self-interested courtiers to grant titles, lands, offices, pardons, and monetary rewards without any thought to the merits or consequences of the request.

An exceptionally pious man, Henry, unlike his father, had no interest in military affairs. In the 1440s, by ineffectively pursuing a peace policy, Henry allowed England's military position in France to deteriorate. In 1444, following the failure of a *CHEVAUCHÉE* ineptly led by John BEAUFORT, duke of Somerset, Henry opened peace talks, which led to conclusion of the Truce of TOURS and the king's marriage to Charles VII's kinswoman, MARGARET OF ANJOU. Pressed by his wife, and anxious to achieve a final settlement in France, Henry, in 1445, secretly agreed to surrender Maine, although the resistance of his officers in the province delayed the actual handover until 1448. The surrender of Maine and the French resumption of the war bought much ill will in England for the king's chief minister, William de la POLE, duke of Suffolk. When the French overwhelmed a poorly defended Normandy, public outrage drove Suffolk from office in early 1450. The duke's fall was followed by JACK CADE'S REBELLION, which protested military failure in France and the breakdown of royal justice in England, and which gave voice to the frustration of English noblemen who felt themselves excluded from royal patronage by a clique of favored courtiers.

Chief among these disaffected magnates was RICHARD, DUKE OF YORK, who was heir presumptive to the childless king. Especially angered by Henry's support of Edmund BEAUFORT, duke of Somerset, who had his own claim to the throne and whom public opinion blamed for the loss of Normandy, York made several abortive attempts to force his way into the royal circle. He did not succeed until 1453, when Henry suffered a serious mental breakdown that left him completely incapacitated. In early August, Henry fell suddenly into a stupor that rendered him incommunicative. The exact cause and nature of Henry's ailment remain mysterious. One contemporary chronicler claimed that it commenced when the king suffered a sudden shock, a suggestion that has led modern historians to speculate that Henry fell ill when he received the devastating news of the Battle of CASTILLON, the defeat that ended the Hundred Years War. Although rumors that Henry was childish or simple had been whispered about the kingdom before 1453, he showed no signs of mental illness until that date. He may have inherited a genetic predisposition to such illness from his grandfather, Charles VI, whose recurring bouts of violent madness were an important cause of the FRENCH CIVIL WAR and the reopening of the Hundred Years War. Henry displayed none of the frenzy that had characterized his grandfather's illness, but he neither recognized nor understood anyone, could not stand or walk, and required round-the-clock care from his servants. When he finally recovered around Christmas 1454, Henry remembered nothing of the previous seventeen months, including the birth of his son, Prince Edward. Henry was again unwell in 1455, when his presence at the Battle of St. Albans, the first battle of the Wars of the Roses, may have triggered another episode.

From 1456, surviving accounts of Henry's condition depict him as weak-minded, requiring inordinate amounts of sleep, and given almost entirely to a routine of religious devotions. After 1457, the king found seclusion attractive, and the queen, who was then engaged in a power struggle with York, often housed him in monasteries, away from any but loyal courtiers. Although the king had periods of lucid activity, he was largely a cipher during the last fifteen years of his life, a symbol of monarchy rather than a functioning monarch. The political factions that coalesced around the queen and York after 1454, when Parliament appointed the duke to the first of two royal protectorates, became the basis of the Lancastrian and Yorkist parties, branches of the House of PLANTAGENET that fought for control of the English government during the Wars of the Roses, a civil war that was largely a result of Henry's incapacity.

In 1461, Henry was deposed by York's son, who took the Crown as Edward IV. Henry spent the next four years in exile in SCOTLAND, or, after his family left for France, in hiding in northern England, where he was captured in 1465. Imprisoned in the Tower of London until a Lancastrian revival restored him to the throne in October 1470, Henry was a mere figurehead for the new regime. In April 1471, Edward reentered LONDON and returned Henry to the Tower. When the battle death of Henry's son ended any need to keep the ex-king alive, he was murdered in the Tower on 21 May 1471. *See also* FORMIGNY, BATTLE OF; MAINE, SURRENDER OF.

Further Reading: Griffiths, Ralph A. *The Reign of King Henry VI*. Berkeley: University of California Press, 1981; Watts, John. *Henry VI and the Politics of Kingship*. Cambridge: Cambridge University Press, 1996; Wolffe, Bertram. *Henry VI.* London: Eyre Methuen, 1981.

HENRY OF GROSMONT, DUKE OF LANCASTER (c. 1310–1361)

A kinsman of EDWARD III and revered ancestor of the House of LANCASTER, Henry of Grosmont, first duke of Lancaster, was among the most important of England's military and diplomatic leaders during the first decades of the HUNDRED YEARS WAR.

Called Henry of Grosmont to distinguish him from his father, Henry, earl of Lancaster, Grosmont was knighted in 1330 when he was called to PARLIAMENT in place of his blind father. Descendents of Henry III, his family led the baronial opposition to EDWARD II, who executed Grosmont's uncle, Thomas, earl of Lancaster, in 1322. Although Grosmont's father supported the deposition of Edward II in 1327, his relations with the king's supplanters, Queen Isabella (*see* ISABELLA, QUEEN OF ENGLAND [c. 1292–1358]) and her lover, Roger Mortimer, earl of March, were equivocal and may have kept Grosmont from court until Edward III overthrew his mother and March in 1330. Being of similar age, Grosmont quickly won the king's confidence. In April 1331, he accompanied the king to France, where, disguised as a merchant, Edward had a secret meeting with PHILIP VI. Grosmont also served in the Scottish campaigns of the 1330s and in April 1336 was appointed king's lieutenant in SCOTLAND.

In March 1337, Edward ennobled Grosmont as earl of Derby, one of six young noblemen given earldoms to enlarge the English military command in preparation for war with France. In August 1337, Derby led a raid on Cadzand. In 1338, while in the Low Countries with the king, he participated in negotiations that created Edward's ANTI-FRENCH COALITION, and he took part in the brief THIÉRACHE CAMPAIGN. In June 1340, Derby fought at SLUYS and in September was present at the siege of TOURNAI and helped negotiate the Truce of ESPLECHIN. He spent most of the following winter in the Low Countries in the custody of the king's cred-

itors. Beginning in 1343, Derby served as the king's representative in a series of continental negotiations that concluded in 1345 with the failed Anglo-French peace talks held at Avignon under the auspices of Pope CLEMENT VI (*see* AVIGNON PEACE CONFERENCE).

Made lieutenant of AQUITAINE on 13 March 1345, Derby launched a highly successful campaign that culminated in October with the battle of AUBEROCHE, a victory that brought the Agenais and most of Périgord and Quercy under PLANTAGENET control. Auberoche increased both the earl's reputation and his wealth; his great London palace, the Savoy, was built with the RANSOMS taken in this campaign. In 1346, Lancaster—he had succeeded his father in 1345—conducted a successful *CHEVAUCHÉE* that captured Poitiers and extended English authority into Saintonge. In 1347, he laid down his lieutenancy in Aquitaine to participate in the siege of CALAIS and then helped negotiate the Truce of CALAIS on the town's fall. He became a founding member of the Order of the GARTER in 1348 and, in 1351, became, as reward for his services, only the second duke in English history (after EDWARD, THE BLACK PRINCE). In an unprecedented show of favor, Edward III also gave the duke a lifetime grant of palatine powers in the county of Lancaster, thereby making Lancaster virtual ruler of his own APPANAGE.

Lancaster led another *chevauchée* in Aquitaine in 1349, fought at the Battle of WINCHELSEA in 1350, and was involved in negotiation of the abortive Treaty of GUINES in 1354. Appointed royal lieutenant in BRITTANY in September 1355, he oversaw the English war effort in that duchy until 1358 and also conducted a successful *chevauchée* in NORMANDY in 1356. Lancaster also participated in the RHEIMS CAMPAIGN of 1359–60 and was chief English negotiator at the talks that resulted in the Treaty of BRÉTIGNY in 1360. However, he did not live to see the treaty implemented, dying at Leicester Castle on 23 March 1361. Because of the *Livre de seyntz medicines*, a French memoir written by Lancaster in 1354, we know a great deal more about his personality than is common for nonroyal figures of the fourteenth century.

Further Reading: Fowler, Kenneth. *The King's Lieutenant: Henry of Grosmont, First Duke of Lancaster, 1310–1361.* London: Elek, 1969.

HERRINGS, BATTLE OF THE (1429)

Known also as the Battle of Rouvray, for the village near which it was fought, the Battle of the Herrings began with a French attack on an English supply train carrying herrings and other Lenten commodities to the besiegers of Orléans. Deriving its popular name from this circumstance, the English victory greatly heartened the city's attackers and severely discouraged its defenders. The battle initiated talks for the surrender of Orléans and prepared the way for the advent of JOAN OF ARC by intensifying the atmosphere of defeatism that surrounded the dauphin (*see* CHARLES VII) and his supporters.

In October 1428, English forces under Thomas MONTAGU, earl of Salisbury, laid siege to Orléans, an important dauphinist town on the Loire about seventy miles southwest of PARIS. Because Salisbury depended on provisions brought from Paris, the French commander at Orléans, John, the Bastard of Orleans (*see* JOHN, COUNT OF DUNOIS AND LONGUEVILLE), persuaded the dauphin to send an army to disrupt English supply lines. If successful, such an action promised to divert much needed provisions from the besiegers to the besieged and to stem growing criticism within the town of the Bastard's seeming inaction. On 12 February, the French army, commanded by Charles of Bourbon, Count of Clermont, intercepted a large English convoy of three hundred wagons, commanded by Sir John FASTOLF, about twenty-five miles north of Orléans. Clermont's army numbered between three and four thousand men, while Fastolf led a force of five hundred to a thousand archers and a similarly sized body of Parisian militia.

Fastolf formed his wagons into a circle and ordered his archers to ring the laager with sharpened stakes. The French opened the battle with a highly effective ARTILLERY bombardment. However, rather than wait for the guns to decimate the English, who could do nothing but hold their ground or retreat, a contingent of Scotsmen led by Sir John Stewart of Darnley, constable of SCOTLAND, attacked the English laager, thereby silencing the French guns and drawing English longbow fire. The archers killed Stewart and drove back the Scots in disorder. Clermont, perhaps believing that the artillery and the Scots had weakened the enemy, ordered a cavalry charge. When the archers and stakes disrupted the assault, the English slipped out from the wagons and attacked the French knights from the flanks and rear. With Clermont wounded, the French attack collapsed and the dauphinist forces withdrew, thus allowing the siege to continue and causing morale at the dauphin's court, and especially in Orléans, to plummet. *See also* ORLÉANS, SIEGE OF

Further Reading: Burne, Alfred H. *The Agincourt War.* Ware, England: Wordsworth Editions Ltd., 1999; DeVries, Kelly. *Joan of Arc: A Military Leader.* Stroud, England: Sutton Publishing, 2003.

HOLLAND, THOMAS, EARL OF KENT (c. 1315–1360)

Named king's lieutenant in BRITTANY in 1354 and royal lieutenant in France in 1360, Thomas Holland, earl of Kent, was one of EDWARD III's most prominent noble captains during the first decades of the Hundred Years War.

The second son of Robert Holland, Lord Holland, a Lancashire nobleman who died in 1328, Thomas began his military career in SCOTLAND in the early 1330s. As a knight of the royal household, he served in the campaigns in FLANDERS and northern France in 1338–39, and fought at the naval battle of SLUYS in June 1340. Around this time, he contracted marriage with the king's cousin, JOAN of Kent, a mésalliance that may have been approved by the king, but that was overridden by Joan's mother, Margaret, countess of Kent, who arranged a more prestigious and lucrative match in 1341 with the son of William MONTAGU, earl of Salisbury. Not until 1349 was Holland able to obtain a papal decree confirming his marriage and invalidating the Montagu union.

Holland fought in the BRETON CIVIL WAR in the mid-1340s and, in 1346, made a name for himself by capturing the count of Eu, constable of France, at the siege of Caen in NORMANDY. Although he sold the count's RANSOM to the king for 80,000 florins, it is unclear how much of this sum he actually received. Holland also fought in the CRÉCY campaign in 1346 and, in 1348, became a founding member of the Order of the GARTER.

Upon the death of his childless brother-in-law in 1352, Holland inherited, through his wife, an extensive landed estate, and in 1354 was summoned to PARLIAMENT as Lord Holland. He became captain of CALAIS Castle in August 1352, royal lieutenant in Brittany from March 1354 to September 1355, and keeper of the Channel Islands in June 1356. In the late 1350s, he received numerous important military posts in Normandy, including the captaincy of Crocy Castle, the governorship of the lands of Godfrey of HARCOURT, the keepership of Barfleur, and the colieutenancy, with Philip of Navarre, of the duchy itself.

In September 1360, Holland was appointed king's lieutenant in Normandy and France with responsibility for overseeing implementation of the provisions of the Treaty of BRÉTIGNY, an important and difficult task that necessitated Holland's elevation to the earldom of Kent to enhance his prestige and authority. Kent had just begun his new duties when he died at ROUEN on 28 December 1360.

Further Reading: Perroy, Edouard. *The Hundred Years War.* Trans. W. B. Wells. New York: Capricorn Books, 1965; Stansfield, M. M. N. "The Holland Family, Dukes of Exeter, Earls of Kent and Huntingdon, 1352–1475." D.Phil. diss., University of Oxford, 1987.

HOSTAGES, TREATY OF THE (1362)

Concluded in LONDON in November 1362, the Treaty of the Hostages (also known as the Treaty of the Fleurs de Lys) was a private agreement between EDWARD III and the French hostages being held to guarantee full payment of JOHN II's RANSOM. Essentially an undertaking of men willing to surrender money and territory to secure their release, the agreement was reluctantly accepted by King John but rejected by the French Estates-General.

In July 1360, John II, a prisoner since his capture at the Battle of POITIERS in 1356, left London for CALAIS, where he remained in English custody until November, when a sufficient amount of ransom had been paid to permit his release. Since the greater portion of the ransom was still to be paid and various of the territories ceded to England by the Treaty of BRÉTIGNY had still to be surrendered, a group of princely hostages remained in London to ensure that the French Crown fulfilled its undertakings. The hostages included John's brother, Philip of Orléans; John's two sons, LOUIS, DUKE OF ANJOU, and JOHN, DUKE OF BERRY; Pierre, count of Alençon; and Louis, duke of Bourbon. In April 1362, the French government, stretched to its financial limits, dispatched an embassy to Edward, asking him to extend the schedule of ransom payments and to release the hostages. The English king would accede to these requests only if the French surrendered more territory as security and agreed that these lands should be forfeited if the new payment schedule was not strictly met. Although John protested that he could not meet the timetable demanded because of the devastation wrought upon his kingdom by English *ROUTIERS*, Edward was adamant.

As payment of the ransom fell further into arrears, the captive princes, growing weary of their prolonged confinement, opened their own negotiations. Acting without the knowledge of their king, the hostages agreed to obtain immediate payment of 200,000 écus of John's ransom and to surrender to Edward all territories currently in dispute. Edward was also not required to do anything further to rid France of *routiers*, and all renunciations of territory would be mutually made upon fulfillment of these terms. In return, Edward would parole the hostages, who agreed to give as security various important castles and fortresses in their possession.

Although dismayed by the terms of the agreement, John, who was eager to settle with the English and go on crusade, confirmed the treaty on 13 March 1363. The hostages were duly transferred to Calais, but French reluctance to hand over the required security delayed their release. In September, Anjou, who found captivity particularly galling, broke parole and refused to return to Calais after a three-day visit with his wife, whom he had not seen in over two years. When John demanded that his son surrender himself, the duke refused. The duke's flight and the failure of the Estates-General of Languedoil to ratify the agreement at its meeting at Amiens in November killed the Treaty of the Hostages. In early 1364, John returned voluntarily to England, where he died in April. Whether John's decision to return was a matter of honor, or an attempt to conclude his own personal agreement with Edward, the remaining hostages were not released until 1367 when CHARLES V paid a further 400,000 écus and promised the rest of the ransom in regular installments. *See also* ESTATES, GENERAL AND PROVINCIAL.

Further Reading: Perroy, Edouard. *The Hundred Years War.* Trans. W. B. Wells. New York: Capricorn Books, 1965; Sumption, Jonathan. *The Hundred Years War.* Vol. 2, *Trial by Fire.* Philadelphia: University of Pennsylvania Press, 2001.

HUMPHREY, DUKE OF GLOUCESTER (1390–1447)

The youngest son of HENRY IV, Humphrey, duke of Gloucester, played a leading role in the military campaigns of his brother, HENRY V, and in the minority government of his nephew, HENRY VI. A consistent advocate of offensive war, Gloucester won the posthumous sobriquet of "the Good Duke" for his opposition to the ultimately ill-fated peace initiatives of the 1440s. A patron of poets and writers and an avid collector of manuscripts, Gloucester is also recognized as

the first English proponent of Italian humanism.

Humphrey was only nine when his father deposed RICHARD II in September 1399. Although knighted two weeks later and elected to the Order of the GARTER in 1400, Humphrey received no office or title until after his brother's accession in March 1413, becoming chamberlain of England in the following May and duke of Gloucester a year later. Upon Henry V's resumption of the HUNDRED YEARS WAR in 1415, Gloucester served at the siege of HARFLEUR and was wounded at the Battle of AGINCOURT. He received his first independent command in February 1418, when, as royal lieutenant in the marches of NORMANDY, he completed the conquest of the Cotentin Peninsula by successfully besieging Cherbourg. After joining the king at the siege of ROUEN, he participated in the advance on PARIS before returning to LONDON at the end of 1419. Replacing his brother JOHN, DUKE OF BEDFORD, as keeper of the realm, Gloucester presided over the PARLIAMENT that ratified the Treaty of TROYES in 1420.

Before his death in August 1422, Henry V named Gloucester tutor and protector of the infant Henry VI. Gloucester interpreted this as conferring upon him the regency, but the opposition of Bedford and the council forced the duke to accept the title of protector and the titular leadership of a council that assumed corporate responsibility for governing. In 1423, Gloucester married Jacqueline of Hainault, who required a champion to help her recover Holland, Zeeland, and Hainault from her uncle and estranged husband. Because PHILIP THE GOOD, duke of BURGUNDY, sought the eventual incorporation of these provinces into his territory, the marriage seriously jeopardized the ANGLO-BURGUNDIAN ALLIANCE, upon which depended the continuance of Lancastrian rule in France. Despite the opposition of Bedford, Gloucester and his wife landed an army in CALAIS in October 1424. They quickly seized Hainault, but Burgundy's active intervention led Gloucester to abandon his wife's cause in March 1425, when he returned to

England, ostensibly to prepare for meeting Burgundy's challenge to single combat. When Gloucester did not return, Jacqueline was eventually forced to admit defeat and accept papal invalidation of her English marriage.

From the mid-1420s, Gloucester pursued a long and bitter feud with his uncle, Henry BEAUFORT, bishop of Winchester. In 1425, this rivalry erupted into open violence as Beaufort's retainers clashed with the duke's men. The disorder forced Bedford to return from France and impose a settlement whereby Beaufort resigned as chancellor and Gloucester declared himself reconciled with Beaufort. In 1429, when Henry's coronation formally ended Gloucester's protectorship, the duke attempted to prosecute Beaufort, who was now a cardinal, for praemunire, that is, exercising an illegal foreign jurisdiction. In 1431, Gloucester won control of the government by impounding Beaufort's treasure and removing his supporters from the council. However, because the war could not be financed without the cardinal's loans, Bedford restored the cardinal to favor when he returned to England in 1433. In 1435, Bedford died and Burgundy abandoned the English alliance at the Congress of ARRAS, leading Beaufort to advocate a negotiated settlement of the war, a policy adopted by the king after he began his personal rule in 1437. After another unsuccessful attack on Beaufort in 1440, and his second wife's conviction on a charge of treasonable necromancy in 1441 for consulting with astrologers concerning the king's death, Gloucester, who was Henry's heir apparent, found himself increasingly out of favor at court. By 1445, when the duke was dismissed from the council, the government was dominated by Beaufort's protégé, William de la POLE, earl of Suffolk, and the new French queen, MARGARET OF ANJOU, both of whom favored the king's peace policy.

Opposed to negotiations with CHARLES VII; the release of CHARLES, DUKE OF ORLÉANS; and the Truce of TOURS, Gloucester became increasingly popular among the military establishment in France and with opponents of Suffolk, especially after rumors of the possible surrender of Maine began to spread in 1446. To silence Gloucester, the government ordered his arrest, which occurred five days before his death on 23 February 1447. Because he died in custody, foul play was rumored, although the likely cause was stroke. Besides being a patron of men of learning and letters, such as the writers John Lydgate and John Capgrave, Gloucester earned his humanist reputation through a benefaction of more than 260 volumes that became the basis of the oldest part of Oxford's Bodleian Library, which is still known as Duke Humfrey's Library. *See also* LANCASTER, HOUSE OF; MAINE, SURRENDER OF.

Further Reading: Griffiths, Ralph A. *The Reign of King Henry VI.* Berkeley: University of California Press, 1981; Harriss, G. L. *Cardinal Beaufort: A Study of Lancastrian Ascendancy and Decline.* Oxford: Clarendon Press, 1988; Williams, E. Carleton. *My Lord of Bedford, 1389–1435.* London: Longmans, 1963.

HUNDRED YEARS WAR, CAUSES OF

Historians have traditionally found the origins of the HUNDRED YEARS WAR in two key issues. The feudal issue arose from the many frictions generated by the fact that the king of England was duke of AQUITAINE and thus owed liege homage to the king of France. The dynastic issue arose from the claim of English kings to be rightful rulers of France. Intertwined with these main issues were such other factors as French support of Scottish resistance to PLANTAGENET ambitions in SCOTLAND, the extension of Capetian authority throughout all the great feudatories of France; and English support for such French rebels as ROBERT OF ARTOIS.

The immediate cause of the war is generally taken to be PHILIP VI's confiscation of Aquitaine in May 1337, but the roots of the dispute over the duchy, which is considered by some historians to be the key to the entire war, extend back to the eleventh century when William, duke of NORMANDY, became king of England. By the mid-twelfth century, William's great-grandson, Henry II, the first Plantagenet king, controlled western France, including Normandy, Anjou, Maine, BRITTANY, and, though his marriage to Eleanor, daughter and heiress of the last duke, Aquitaine. Stimulated in part by the threat from this great Anglo-Norman empire, the French House of CAPET, beginning in the reign of Philip II in the late twelfth century, sought to extend royal authority into the great feudatories by demanding liege homage from their lords. In 1200, Philip refused to allow Henry's son, John, to take possession of his French holdings until he recognized them as fiefs of the French Crown. By doing this, John opened the door to increased Capetian interference in his domains. The French conquered Normandy and Anjou in 1204 and the remaining Plantagenet provinces, except for GASCONY in Aquitaine, by the 1220s. In 1259, the uncertain feudal status of the duchy was clarified by the Treaty of PARIS, whereby Louis IX recognized Henry III as his vassal and a peer of France in return for Henry's renunciation of his claims to other former Plantagenet lands.

Although the treaty stabilized Anglo-French relations for several decades, it led eventually to conflict because the Plantagenets could not reconcile their sovereign authority as kings of England with their feudal subordination as dukes of Aquitaine. Strict observance of a vassal's duty to support his lord, which PHILIP IV and his successors demanded of their Plantagenet vassals from the 1290s, could undermine the ability of English kings to pursue an independent foreign policy. If, as almost happened in the 1280s when Philip III invaded Aragon, the king of France went to war with a kingdom with which the king of England was allied, the former as lord could insist that the latter as vassal ignore his alliance and support the war. But the real source of friction was the ability of the king of France, as feudal overlord, to interfere in the government of Aquitaine, particularly his right to hear appeals of the duke's decisions made by the

duke's vassals to the Paris PARLEMENT. Such appeals lay at the root of the ANGLO-FRENCH WAR OF 1294–1303 and the War of SAINT-SARDOS in the 1320s. And it was the basic insolubility of this jurisdictional problem, as demonstrated by the failure of several Anglo-French commissions (see PROCESS) in the early fourteenth century, that led to the 1337 confiscation.

By the 1330s, the dispute had also acquired a dynastic dimension. The death of CHARLES IV without male heirs in 1328 ended the Capetian line and left the French nobility to decide between two main claimants to the throne: Philip, count of VALOIS, Charles's cousin through the male line, and EDWARD III of England, Charles's nephew through the female line. Having already decided in 1317 to exclude women from the throne, the French magnates in 1328 extended that prohibition to a woman's male heirs, selecting Valois, a French noble in his thirties who was already acting as regent, over Edward, a fifteen-year-old foreign ruler who was dominated by his mother, Isabella (see ISABELLA, QUEEN OF ENGLAND [c. 1292–1358]). In no position to force the issue, Edward performed homage in 1329, and later agreed that it should be construed as liege homage. However, Edward's unpursued claim remained a magnet for French rebels who sought to discomfit Philip, such as Robert of Artois. One of the main reasons given by Philip for his confiscation of Aquitaine was the reception Robert received at the English court in 1334.

The question of how seriously Edward viewed his claim is much debated. He did not formally proclaim himself king of France until 1340, when it became necessary to give cover to the Flemings and other allies, who could then technically avoid breaking their feudal oaths by recognizing Edward as their rightful lord. While he would no doubt have eagerly assumed the French throne if it had become politically or militarily possible, Edward showed himself willing at BRÉTIGNY in 1360 to renounce his claim for sovereignty over Aquitaine. Ironically, in the fifteenth century, HENRY V, second king of the House of LANCASTER, whose claim to the French Crown was far more tenuous than that of his great-grandfather, nonetheless made that claim his main reason for resuming the war, and, with the Treaty of TROYES in 1420, came closer than Edward ever had to attaining that Crown. Although the dynastic struggle is today the popularly accepted cause of the war, it was, until Henry V, subordinate to the dispute over Aquitaine.

Another contributing cause that has received increased attention from modern historians is Philip VI's intervention in Scotland, an action that Edward III viewed as unwarranted interference in his domestic affairs. Initiated in the 1290s, the FRANCO-SCOTTISH ALLIANCE was a source of friction throughout the war, serving as a means whereby the Valois could forestall English invasions of France by threatening Scottish invasions of England. Because Scottish involvement in the war also threatened the possibility of French attacks on England, the Hundred Years War was different from any earlier Anglo-French conflict, and thus served as a further spur to English efforts to neutralize France. In 1334, Philip VI scuttled a proposed settlement over Gascony by insisting that DAVID II, who had recently fled to France, be included in any agreement. In 1337, Edward III used French intervention in Scotland as a justification for war. In 1346, David, now returned to Scotland, invaded England in support of his French ally, thereby suffering defeat and capture at NE-VILLE'S CROSS only weeks after the French disaster at CRÉCY. In the fifteenth century, large Scottish contingents fought with dauphinist forces at BAUGÉ, CRAVANT, VERNEUIL, and elsewhere. Thus, Scotland was also an important factor in the coming and course of the war.

Further Reading: Allmand, Christopher. *The Hundred Years War*. Cambridge: Cambridge University Press, 1988; Curry, Anne. *The Hundred Years War*. 2nd ed. Houndmills, England: Palgrave Macmillan, 2003; Vale, M. G. A. *The Origins of the Hundred Years War: The Angevin Legacy, 1250–1340*. Oxford: Clarendon Press, 2000.

HUNDRED YEARS WAR, NAMING OF

Use of the term "Hundred Years War" to describe the extended period of Anglo-French conflict in the fourteenth and fifteenth centuries did not occur until the middle of the nineteenth century, although the notion that this ongoing Anglo-French rivalry was characterized by a certain unity and coherence may be much older.

The term *La guerre de cent ans* (the Hundred Years War) was coined in France in the late 1850s, following the 1855 publication of historian Henri Martin's influential *Histoire de France*. Martin divided his discussion of the period into separate chapters that he titled *"Guerres des Anglais"* (Wars of the English), to reflect his view of the distinctive nature of each episode of Anglo-French hostility. However, in 1861, Edgar Boutaric referred to the whole period as *"la guerre de cent ans"* in an article that appeared in the *Bibliothèque de l'École des Chartes*, and Henri Wallon also used it in 1864 in his volume on RICHARD II. In 1869, the term was sufficiently accepted in French historiography for Edward Freeman to suggest in a *Fortnightly Review* article that it also be adopted by English historians. When two widely read histories of the 1870s, François Guizot's *Histoire de France* (1873) and John Richard Green's *Short History of the English People* (1874) employed the term, it quickly became established in the popular consciousness. Over the next two decades, the term appeared in numerous French and English monographs, and it was first used in the *Encyclopaedia Britannica* in 1879. By the early twentieth century, the term was in such common usage that historians of the late medieval period could not avoid employing it in some fashion.

By the late twentieth century, historians, while still obliged to use the term, began to caution that it was misleading, putting too much focus on the dynastic issue and too little on the wartime process of national development that turned an Anglo-French polity into two nation-states. Historians also argued that the period from 1337 to 1453, to which the term had given a certain unity, was really part of a much longer period that ran from the Norman Conquest of England in the eleventh century to the French wars of Henry VIII and the loss of CALAIS in the sixteenth century, and perhaps even later. Anglo-French rivalry extended beyond Europe to America and Asia in the seventeenth and eighteenth centuries and English monarchs did not formally abandon their title to the French Crown until 1802. Other historians pointed out that the Edwardian war of the fourteenth century was in many ways different from the Henrician or Lancastrian war of the fifteenth century, during which HENRY VI's claim to the French Crown came to be based not on his descent from EDWARD III, but on the Treaty of TROYES.

While many historians disagree, arguing that the idea is a modern innovation, it appears likely that some notion of a "hundred years war" did predate the nineteenth century. In the early fifteenth century, French writers seeking to counter the claims of HENRY V began developing a theory of the SALIC LAW OF SUCCESSION by tracing the current Anglo-French war back to the demise of the House of CAPET in 1328. In the 1410s, John of Montreuil, a secretary to CHARLES VI, wrote that hostilities had then been going on for a century, even though by traditional dating he was about twenty years too early. In 1513, the historian Polydore Vergil noted in his *Anglia Historia* that Anglo-French wars had been occurring on and off for what he termed "an eternity." In his *Histoire de France*, published in 1643, François de Mézeray wrote for the first time of an Anglo-French war beginning in 1337 and running for 160 years. In his *History of England* (1762), David Hume found a unity in the Anglo-French wars occurring between 1337 and 1453, as did Henry Hallam in his *View of the State of Europe during the Middle Ages* (1818) and Guizot in his Sorbonne lectures of 1828. It was from this tradition of viewing the late medieval Anglo-French wars as a unified whole that the term *La guerre de cent ans* arose in the 1850s. *See also* HUNDRED YEARS WAR, CAUSES OF; HUNDRED YEARS

WAR, PHASES OF; NATIONAL CONSCIOUSNESS, GROWTH OF.

Further Reading: Curry, Anne. *The Hundred Years War*. 2nd ed. Houndmills, England: Palgrave Macmillan, 2003; Fowler, Kenneth. *The Age of Plantagenet and Valois: The Struggle for Supremacy, 1328–1498*. New York: G. P. Putnam's Sons, 1967.

HUNDRED YEARS WAR, PHASES OF

The "Hundred Years War," a term that first came into use in the nineteenth century, is the name applied by historians to a series of intermittent Anglo-French conflicts that in total spanned a period of almost twelve decades in the fourteenth and fifteenth centuries. Modern historians divide the Hundred Years War into three periods of military activity separated by years of relative peace made possible by various truces and treaties. These wars were also preceded and followed by lesser conflicts and campaigns of varying intensity. Although the fundamental issues in dispute remained largely the same across the period, each of the separate wars was dominated by a different royal personality whose goals and plans dictated the nature of the conflict.

Early Anglo-French Wars
The conflicts comprising the Hundred Years War, which is traditionally dated as running from 1337 to 1453, were preceded by two smaller wars. The ANGLO-FRENCH WAR OF 1294–1303 arose from a series of disputes generated by the English king's dual status as a sovereign monarch in England and a subordinate French vassal in AQUITAINE. The PLANTAGENET kings, beginning with EDWARD I in the 1290s, found the French Crown's ability to interfere in the governance of Aquitaine to be intolerable. When PHILIP IV confiscated the duchy in 1294, he initiated a war that ended with a return to the status quo and the arrangement of a marriage that later gave the Plantagenets a claim to the French Crown. This claim offered a potential solution to the problem of Aquitaine, where a Plantagenet king of France would be his own overlord.

The War of SAINT-SARDOS in the mid-1320s essentially replayed the causes and course of the earlier conflict. The continuing irritation over Aquitaine led to a second confiscation, which was settled by an agreement brokered by Queen Isabella (*see* ISABELLA, QUEEN OF ENGLAND [c. 1292–1358]), who arranged that her husband, EDWARD II, should send their son, Prince Edward, to France to do homage for Aquitaine to her brother, CHARLES IV. This agreement ended the war, but Isabella's deposition of her husband in 1327 and the failure of the House of CAPET with Charles's death in 1328 made EDWARD III, the new king of England, a legitimate claimant to the French Crown and helped set the stage for the Hundred Years War.

Edwardian War, 1337–1360
The first phase of the Hundred Years War, running from 1337 to 1360, is termed the Edwardian War because it was driven by the aims and ambitions of Edward III, who sought sovereign authority in Aquitaine and removal of the House of VALOIS from the French throne. The war began with a third confiscation of Aquitaine in 1337, but acquired a new dimension in 1340 when Edward formally declared himself rightful king of France, a step that was taken mainly to give cover to Edward's allies in the Low Countries, many of whom were vassals of the French Crown. Even though Edward spent huge sums of money constructing his web of alliances (*see* ANGLO-FLEMISH ALLIANCE; ANTI-FRENCH COALITION), and both he and PHILIP VI collected taxes and raised loans to fund large armies, no major land engagement occurred during the war's first campaigns (*see* THIÉRACHE CAMPAIGN; TOURNAI, SIEGE OF).

In 1340, mutual financial exhaustion led to the Truce of ESPLECHIN and a temporary end to hostilities. In 1341, the outbreak of the BRETON CIVIL WAR revived the Anglo-French conflict as each side backed a different claimant to the Breton ducal title. In the late 1340s, following the Truce of MALESTROIT and a failed papal attempt to mediate a settlement (*see* AVIGNON PEACE CONFERENCE),

the English won a rapid succession of major victories—AUBEROCHE (1345) in Aquitaine, CRÉCY (1346) and CALAIS (1347) in northern France, and LA ROCHE-DERRIEN (1347) in BRITTANY. The war was then halted by the Truce of CALAIS, which was effectively extended into the mid-1350s by the intervention of the BLACK DEATH. Another period of English triumph was opened by the CHEVAUCHÉE OF 1355 and the Battle of POITIERS (1356), which resulted in the capture of JOHN II. The 1357 Truce of BORDEAUX created another respite during which Edward tried to impose a treaty on the French, who were thrown into political turmoil and social chaos by the king's captivity; the intrigues of CHARLES THE BAD, king of Navarre; and the widespread discontent caused by high TAXATION and military defeat (*see* JACQUERIE; MARCEL, ÉTIENNE).

The failure of the First (1358) and Second (1359) Treaties of LONDON led Edward to launch the RHEIMS CAMPAIGN of 1359, whereby he sought coronation as king of France as a means to force the French to come to terms. Although militarily unsuccessful, the campaign resulted in the Treaty of BRÉTIGNY, which ended the war by arranging for Edward to renounce his claim to the French Crown in exchange for a greatly enlarged Aquitaine held in full sovereignty. The Edwardian war thus ended in English victory.

Caroline War, 1369–1389
The Caroline War, which ran from 1369 to 1389, is named for CHARLES V, who, through good fortune, more regular taxation, and careful DIPLOMACY, largely reversed the outcome of the Edwardian conflict. After a decade of relative peace (except for the Breton war which ended in 1365 and the Castilian campaign that concluded at NÁJERA in 1367), Charles reignited the Anglo-French struggle by accepting the APPEAL OF THE GASCON LORDS, a series of petitions addressed to Charles as feudal overlord of Aquitaine by the Gascon vassals of EDWARD, THE BLACK PRINCE, who had ruled Aquitaine since 1355. By accepting these petitions, Charles overthrew the Brétigny agreement and reasserted

his claim to sovereignty over the duchy. Hampered by Edward III's senility and the prince's chronic ill health, the English proved unable to defend Aquitaine against a series of highly successful campaigns led by LOUIS, DUKE OF ANJOU, and Bertrand du GUESLIN, constable of France. By 1380, Plantagenet Aquitaine had been reduced to BORDEAUX and coastal Gascony, an area smaller than that held by the English in 1337. The only English response was a series of large CHEVAUCHÉES made ineffective by Charles's refusal to allow his armies to engage in pitched battle.

In the 1380s, both countries were ruled by minors—CHARLES VI in France and RICHARD II in England. Minority regimes dominated by royal uncles and distracted by domestic concerns allowed the war to peter out with the Truce of LEULINGHEN in 1389. Attempts by Richard II to conclude a final peace settlement failed, but in 1396 he sealed a 28-year extension of the truce by marrying Charles's daughter Isabella (see ISABELLA, QUEEN OF ENGLAND [1388–1409]). Although neither side was satisfied with the status quo, the deposition of Richard in 1399 and the outbreak of the FRENCH CIVIL WAR after 1407 prevented the resumption of open hostilities. HENRY IV, first king of the House of LANCASTER, was too insecure to contemplate renewal of the war, and Charles VI, a victim of chronic mental illness, was powerless to stop the escalating struggle between the ARMAGNAC and BURGUNDIAN factions. Thus, the Caroline War, itself a French victory, ended not in an Anglo-French peace but in a period of feeble truce sustained only by the political instability of both realms.

Henrician or Lancastrian War, 1415–1453
The Henrician or Lancastrian War, named for HENRY V of the House of Lancaster, had three main phases—the period of English success running from 1415 to 1429, the period of gradual French recovery running from 1429 to 1444, and the final expulsion of the English from France between 1449 and 1453. In 1415, Henry V, who was unin-

terested in reconstituting a sovereign Aquitaine, invaded France with the intention of seizing the French Crown. With the French divided against themselves, Henry won a major victory at AGINCOURT in 1415 and conquered NORMANDY by 1419 (see NORMAN CAMPAIGN [1417–1419]). In September 1419, French attempts to resolve their differences and unite against the English ended in disaster at MONTEREAU, where servants of Dauphin Charles murdered JOHN THE FEARLESS, duke of BURGUNDY. This act drove John's son, PHILIP THE GOOD, into alliance with England and, in 1420, facilitated conclusion of the Treaty of TROYES, whereby the dauphin was disinherited by his parents and Henry was declared heir to the French throne. Although the treaty technically ended the war between England and France, hostilities continued between the forces of the Anglo-Burgundian government that ruled in PARIS, and those of the dauphin, whose area of control in southern France was contemptuously referred to as the "Kingdom of Bourges."

The unexpected death of Henry V in 1422, two months before that of Charles VI, gave new hope to the dauphinists. However, the English war effort was ably directed by Henry's brother, JOHN, DUKE OF BEDFORD, who was regent in France for his infant nephew HENRY VI. Victories at CRAVANT in 1423 and VERNEUIL in 1424 continued the English advance, which was halted only in May 1429, when the advent of JOAN OF ARC inspired French campaigns that lifted the siege of ORLÉANS and cleared the Loire of English garrisons (see LOIRE CAMPAIGN). In July, the dauphin was crowned king of France as CHARLES VII. Although Joan was captured by the Burgundians in 1430 and executed by the English in 1431, the tide had turned. In 1435, Bedford died and Duke Philip abandoned the ANGLO-BURGUNDIAN ALLIANCE at the Congress of ARRAS. Deprived of Bedford's leadership and Burgundy's support, the English lost Paris in 1436, and a series of other English strongholds fell before the Truce of TOURS ended hostilities in 1444.

Charles VII used the truce to reform his army and strengthen the system of taxation that funded it (*see* CHARLES VII, MILITARY REFORMS OF). In England, Henry VI, weak-minded and pacific, became the tool of noble factions whose attempts to rule through the mentally unstable monarch led in the 1450s to the civil conflict known as the Wars of the Roses. In the 1440s, Henry, urged on by his French wife, MARGARET OF ANJOU, sought to make peace on any terms, even agreeing to the voluntary surrender of Maine, which was vital to the defense of Lancastrian Normandy (*see* MAINE, SURRENDER OF). By 1449, Charles VII was ready to resume the war. His professional, salaried army, accompanied by John BUREAU's outstanding ARTILLERY, which gave the French the kind of military advantage the longbow (*see* ARCHERS) had earlier given the English, retook Normandy in twelve months (*see* NORMAN CAMPAIGN [1449–1450]). In 1451, JOHN, COUNT OF DUNOIS, captured Bordeaux, although John TALBOT, earl of Shrewsbury, retook the town with Gascon assistance in 1452. However, the Henrician and Hundred Years Wars ended in July 1453 when Bureau's guns killed Shrewsbury and destroyed his army at CASTILLON. Although no formal treaty ended the war, the English had finally been expelled from GASCONY and their remaining French holdings comprised only the port of Calais.

Campaign of 1475

Although the Battle of Castillon in 1453 is traditionally taken as the end of the Hundred Years War, no treaty formally ended the conflict and English ambitions in France did not disappear. However, because the English were soon distracted by their own series of civil wars, known as the Wars of the Roses, which eventually pitted the Lancastrian and Yorkist branches of the House of Plantagenet against one another, they did not launch a new French campaign until the summer of 1475. Louis XI, who had succeeded Charles VII as king of France in 1461, had promoted continuance of the English civil wars by backing a Lancastrian revival that restored Henry VI to the Crown in 1470. Nonetheless, by 1475, Henry was dead and his Yorkist cousin, Edward IV, was securely seated on the English throne.

Although a renewal of the war with France was highly popular in England, the French Crown was stronger in 1475 than it had been earlier in the century when it had been significantly weakened by civil war and economic and military exhaustion. Edward IV was thus willing to avoid combat and accept an economic victory in place of a military one. On 29 August 1475, the two kings, meeting on a hastily erected bridge over the Somme River at Amiens, agreed to a treaty negotiated by their representatives at the nearby town of Picquigny. The agreement established an Anglo-French truce that was to run for seven years and created free trade between the two kingdoms. Edward agreed to withdraw his army in return for an initial payment of 75,000 crowns and an annual pension of 50,000 crowns to be paid in two installments at Easter and Michaelmas (29 September). The treaty also called for all disputes between the realms to be settled by an Anglo-French commission, for neither king to make a foreign alliance without the other's knowledge, and for Edward's daughter, Elizabeth of York, to be betrothed to Louis's son, the Dauphin Charles.

Engaged in an effort to reduce the power and influence of Charles, duke of Burgundy, Louis was anxious to secure peace with England. He therefore offered lavish gifts and generous pensions to the English nobility to support the Treaty of Picquigny, which was initially unpopular in England. However, Edward quickly suppressed any anti-treaty disorders and the economic benefits that flowed from the treaty—fewer taxes and lower tariffs—led to widespread acceptance of the agreement and fewer calls for war with France. Although Louis abrogated the treaty in 1483, only three months before Edward's death and eight before his own, the 1475 campaign and the Treaty of Picquigny demonstrated that France, when stable and united, was too large and wealthy for England to successfully renew the Hundred Years War.

Further Reading: Allmand, Christopher. *The Hundred Years War*. Cambridge: Cambridge University Press, 1988; Burne, Alfred H. *The Agincourt War*. Ware, England: Wordsworth Editions Ltd., 1999; Burne, Alfred H. *The Crécy War*. Ware, England: Wordsworth Editions Ltd., 1999; Curry, Anne. *The Hundred Years War*. 2nd ed. Houndmills, England: Palgrave Macmillan, 2003; Perroy, Edouard. *The Hundred Years War*. Trans. W. B. Wells. New York: Capricorn Books, 1965; Seward, Desmond. *The Hundred Years War*. New York: Penguin, 1999; Sumption, Jonathan. *The Hundred Years War*. Vol. 1, *Trial by Battle*. Philadelphia: University of Pennsylvania Press, 1991; Sumption, Jonathan. *The Hundred Years War*. Vol. 2, *Trial by Fire*. Philadelphia: University of Pennsylvania Press, 2001.

I

INDENTURES

The military indenture was a binding written contract that spelled out the terms of service and compensation offered by the English Crown to those captains—usually noblemen—who provided troops for royal armies. Although it first appeared in the thirteenth century, the indenture came into common use and assumed a standard form in the fourteenth century during the HUNDRED YEARS WAR. The indenture was the most important administrative innovation to occur in the recruitment of medieval English armies.

Although the earliest surviving indentures date from 1270, when Prince Edward contracted with several knights for a year's service on crusade in the Holy Land, such agreements may have been used earlier. The Crown did not enter into military contracts with the English nobility until the 1290s, when EDWARD I indented with Edmund, earl of Lancaster, and with the earls of Lincoln and Cornwall, to supply a specified number of men at a specified wage for service in GASCONY during the ANGLO-FRENCH WAR OF 1294–1303. The king also contracted with garrison commanders, who undertook to recruit a certain number of men to hold a certain stronghold for a certain time. In 1301, for instance, John Kingston agreed to keep Edinburgh Castle in SCOTLAND for six months with eighty-four men in return for the sum of £220 to be paid in four installments. Not until 1337 did the English government, in need of men for a Scottish expedition, raise an entire army by military indenture.

A typical indenture consisted of a piece of parchment on which the terms of the agreement were written out twice. The indenture derived its name from the practice of cutting the document in half along an indented or jagged line, with each party receiving one copy of the contract. In case of disagreements, the two halves were fitted back together; if the indentations matched, the agreement was held valid, accusations could be brought, and disputes settled. The first indentures were often vague and imprecise, but in the fourteenth century, as the Crown developed standard rates of pay for various types of soldiers and service, the contracts became more elaborate and specific. Most Hundred Years War agreements specified the size and composition of the force to be supplied (e.g., how many men were to be ARCHERS or men-at-arms), the length and place of service, the wages to be paid, whether a regard (or bonus) was to be offered, the division of spoils and RANSOMS, and details involving provision of transport and horses.

Just as the Crown contracted with them, so did the leading English captains contract with their subordinates. JOHN OF GAUNT, duke of Lancaster, who offered the same financial terms as the Crown, developed an extensive military affinity in the late fourteenth century. A fairly typical indenture is the 1371 contract between Roger Maltravers and William Montagu, earl of Salisbury. Maltravers agreed to serve for one year with two archers, to provide his own horses and equipment, and to give one-third of any booty or ransoms to the earl. Salisbury agreed to provide shipping, wages, and a regard, as well as a fee of £20. Because the indenture system was open to fraud and abuse, the practice of mustering troops to make sure the Crown or contracting noble was getting all the men promised became common in the fifteenth century. *See also* ARMIES, RECRUITMENT OF.

Further Reading: Allmand, Christopher. *The Hundred Years War*. Cambridge: Cambridge University Press, 1988; Prestwich, Michael. *Armies and Warfare in the Middle Ages: The English Experience*. New Haven, CT: Yale University Press, 1996.

INFANTRY. *See* ARMIES, COMPOSITION OF

INNOCENT VI. *See* PAPACY AND THE HUNDRED YEARS WAR

ISABEAU OF BAVARIA, QUEEN OF FRANCE (c. 1370–1435)

Isabeau (Isabelle) of Bavaria, the wife of CHARLES VI and mother of CHARLES VII, was a major political figure in France during the first decades of the fifteenth century, and particularly during negotiation of the Treaty of TROYES in 1420.

The daughter of Stephen, duke of Bavaria, Isabeau wed Charles VI on 17 July 1385, the marriage being promoted by Charles's uncle, PHILIP THE BOLD, duke of BURGUNDY. The sixteen-year-old groom, who first met Isabeau only days earlier, was so smitten with his bride that he married her without a dowry or formal marriage contract. However, after 1392, the king's intermittent bouts of schizophrenia caused his feelings toward his wife to veer between affection and suspicion. Although traditionally depicted as dissolute, promiscuous, and devoted only to her own interests, Isabeau was politically adept and, after the FRENCH CIVIL WAR erupted in 1409, strove to protect the authority of the VALOIS Crown from the consequences of her husband's illness. On 1 July 1402, Charles gave his wife leadership of the council during his periods of illness, although her freedom of action was curtailed in 1403 by a series of royal ordinances designed to create a balance of power among members of the royal family. Isabeau remained initially neutral in the rivalry be-

tween her brother-in-law, LOUIS, DUKE OF ORLÉANS, and his cousin, JOHN THE FEARLESS, duke of Burgundy. In 1405, Burgundy's ambition drove the queen closer to Orléans, with whom she plotted to kidnap the dauphin, LOUIS, DUKE OF GUIENNE, to keep him from Burgundy's influence. The plan failed, and the queen's association with Orléans led to rumors that she and the duke were lovers.

In November 1407, Burgundy's agents assassinated Orléans, initiating a period of civil war that allowed Burgundy to dominate both king and court. Secretly opposed to the duke and anxious to shift power to Dauphin Louis, Isabeau supported her son's efforts to negotiate a settlement with leaders of the ARMAGNAC (Orléanist) party. In 1413, with PARIS turning against him, Burgundy fled the capital, and the Armagnacs took power; because the new government was nominally led, until their deaths, by the dauphin (d. 1415) and then his brother, John, duke of Touraine (d. 1417), Isabeau supported the Armagnacs until 1417, when she quarreled with her third son, Charles. A weak and sickly youth who served as figurehead for an increasingly repressive regime dominated by BERNARD, COUNT OF ARMAGNAC, the new dauphin, responding to his mother's growing reputation for unseemly extravagance and sexual license, cut off her allowance and banished her from Paris. On 8 November 1417, Isabeau escaped from confinement at Tours and, with the support of Burgundy, put herself at the head of a rival government.

Isabeau reconciled with her husband after the Burgundians retook Paris in May 1418, but she remained estranged from her son, especially after his supporters murdered Burgundy at MONTEREAU in 1419. In 1420, Isabeau promoted the marriage of her daughter, CATHERINE OF VALOIS, to HENRY V as part of the Treaty of Troyes, which, through Isabeau's apparent admission of infidelity, disinherited the dauphin by branding him a bastard. Although French historians have condemned her support of the agreement, Isabeau, who viewed the dauphin as a tool of the Armagnacs, probably saw the treaty as the best way to preserve the independence of the monarchy. After Charles VI's death in 1422, Isabeau, unpopular and increasingly corpulent, lived quietly in Paris, where she died at the Hôtel Saint-Pol in September 1435.

Further Reading: Famiglietti, Richard. *Royal Intrigue: Crisis at the Court of Charles VI, 1392–1420.* New York: AMS Press, 1986.

ISABELLA, QUEEN OF ENGLAND (c. 1292–1358)

The daughter of PHILIP IV of France and the wife of EDWARD II of England, Isabella transmitted to her son, EDWARD III, the claim to the Crown of France that he raised during the HUNDRED YEARS WAR. In 1326, Isabella instigated the uprising that led to the deposition and death of her husband, the early enthronement of her son, and her own rule of the kingdom in concert with her lover.

Although discussions concerning Isabella's marriage to Prince Edward had begun in 1298 as part of a proposed settlement of the recent ANGLO-FRENCH WAR, the ceremony did not occur until 25 January 1308 after Edward had become king. Isabella's early years in England were troubled by Edward's relationship with his favorite, Piers Gaveston, who, the queen complained to her father, had usurped her position. Marital relations improved after rebellious barons executed Gaveston in July 1312, four months before Isabella gave birth to her son, Prince Edward. Three other children followed by 1321. In the intervening years, Isabella supported her husband in his ongoing disputes with the baronial opposition led by Thomas, earl of Lancaster, and mediated between the parties in 1313 and 1316. The queen exercised influence with her husband in the issuance of grants and pardons, accompanied him on campaign to SCOTLAND, and received several augmentations to her income, including the revenues of the French county of Ponthieu.

In October 1321, Isabella was refused admittance to Leeds Castle, which was held by a royal opponent. Furious, the queen ordered an assault on the gates that ended with the deaths of six men. This insult to his wife allowed Edward to rally most of the nobility to his side and to reopen the civil war, which the king successfully concluded by executing Lancaster in March 1322. Now dominated by his new favorites, Hugh Despenser and his father, Hugh the Elder, Edward allowed them to systematically humiliate the queen, whom he reputedly declared to have married against his will. Isabella's lands were seized, her household and income were reduced, and her children were taken from her custody; Despenser apparently even approached the pope about annulling Isabella's marriage.

In March 1325, in an attempt to use Isabella's influence with her brother, CHARLES IV, to end the War of SAINT-SARDOS, Edward sent his wife to the French court. When Charles agreed to accept his nephew's homage for AQUITAINE, Prince Edward was allowed to join his mother in PARIS. Anxious for revenge on the Despensers, Isabella refused to return with the prince until the favorites had been removed. By early 1326, she had become the lover of Roger Mortimer, a royal opponent in exile at the French court. The couple then moved to Hainault, where they betrothed the prince to the count's daughter, PHILIPPA, and used the dowry to hire a mercenary force with which they invaded England in September. With the nobility rallying to her cause, Isabella declared her son guardian of the realm, and, after Edward's capture and Despenser's execution, worked though PARLIAMENT to engineer her husband's deposition in January 1327.

For the next three years, Isabella and Mortimer, now earl of March, ruled the kingdom. In September 1327, Edward II was murdered at Berkeley Castle, likely on the couple's orders. The new regime soon showed itself to be as rapacious and tyrannical as that of the Despensers, and as unpopular, as the queen and March followed no clear policy beyond their own self-aggrandizement. Their foreign policy, resulting in an unfavorable treaty with France in 1327 and the recognition of Scottish

In this illustration from the *Chronicles* of Jean Froissart, Charles VI of France gives his daughter in marriage to Richard II of England, 1396. *Erich Lessing/Art Resource, New York.*

August 1358. A strong, beautiful woman whom contemporaries considered tragically misguided, Isabella much later acquired the ferocious epithet "she-wolf of France."

Further Reading: Doherty, Paul. *Isabella and the Strange Death of Edward II.* New York: Carroll & Graf Publishers, 2003; Fryde, Natalie B. *The Tyranny and Fall of Edward II, 1321–1326.* Cambridge: Cambridge University Press, 1979; Mortimer, Ian. *The Greatest Traitor: The Life of Sir Roger Mortimer, Ruler of England, 1327–1330.* London: Pimico, 2004; Weir, Alison. *Queen Isabella: Treachery, Adultery, and Murder in Medieval England.* New York: Ballantine Books, 2005.

ISABELLA, QUEEN OF ENGLAND (1388–1409)

Through her marriage to RICHARD II, Isabella of France, the eldest daughter of CHARLES VI and ISABEAU of Bavaria, sealed an Anglo-French truce that was to have ended the HUNDRED YEARS WAR for almost three decades.

Richard's wife, Anne of Bohemia, died on 7 June 1394. Although devastated by the loss, the childless king began looking almost immediately for a new wife. Since conclusion of the Truce of LEULINGHEN in 1389, Anglo-French diplomacy had ground to a halt, and Richard sought with his new marriage to forge an alliance that would check rising French ambitions. To this end, the English proposed a marriage with Yolande, the daughter of France's southern neighbor, King John of Aragon. The French opposed this match because it threatened Yolande's existing engagement to Louis, duke of Anjou, who needed the Aragonese connection to further his Italian ambitions, and it raised the possibility of a future PLANTAGENET claim to the Crown of Aragon. To persuade Richard to abandon this plan, Charles VI offered his six-year-old daughter Isabella as an alternative. Because this proposal reopened the possibility of

independence in the Treaty of Northampton in 1328, was seen as a national humiliation. In 1330, the execution of Edmund, earl of Kent, the late king's brother, whom Isabella and March entangled in a plot against the government, turned many of the nobility against them. On 19 October 1330, Edward III, finding his own loyalty to the regime questioned, arrested March, who was executed shortly thereafter. Although she appeared at court on important occasions, Isabella took no further part in politics, being sent into retirement in Norfolk. In 1348, when PHILIP VI requested that she act as mediator between them, Edward III ignored the suggestion. Isabella died on 23 concluding an actual peace between the two Crowns, Richard accepted it.

Anxious to end the war, Richard directed his representatives to work for a final peace treaty with the marriage, but the French refused and the best that could be obtained was a 28-year extension of the truce. Richard agreed to surrender Cherbourg and Brest, but was confirmed in his possession of AQUITAINE, while Charles agreed to a dowry of 800,000 francs. The preliminary agreement was signed on 9 March 1396 and Charles personally handed his eight-year-old daughter over to Richard at a splendidly staged meeting near Ardres on the following 30 October. On 4 November, Richard married Isabella in the Church of St. Nicholas in CALAIS.

According to the chronicler Jean FROIS-SART, Isabella, who was twenty-one years younger than Richard, fully understood the importance of her marriage. Although she was too young for carnal relations, Richard grew fond of Isabella, treating her as a beloved daughter, while she became devoted to him. Because Isabella was the embodiment of Anglo-French *entente*, her standing at the English court fluctuated with the state of diplomatic relations; in 1398, for example, complaints were heard about the size and cost of her French entourage. However, the queen's relationship with her husband remained warm and affectionate. Their tearful parting when Richard left for Ireland in 1399 led one chronicler to remark that he had never seen ''so great a lord make so much of, nor show such great affection to, a lady as did King Richard to his Queen'' (Hutchison, 209).

The couple never saw one another again, and the peace policy their bond represented lingered weakly until shattered by the renewal of war in 1415. After Richard's deposition in September 1399, the new king, HENRY IV, sought Isabella's hand for his son, the future HENRY V, even though Richard was still alive. When these talks failed, Isabella was transferred to various royal residences before being returned to France in 1400. Never accepting reports of Richard's death, Isabella made several unsuccessful attempts to return to England. In June 1406, she married her cousin, CHARLES, the son of LOUIS, DUKE OF ORLÉANS, a match to which she consented most unwillingly. Her new husband, however, also grew fond of her and was much affected by her death in childbirth on 13 September 1409.

Further Reading: Hutchison, Harold F. *The Hollow Crown: The Life of Richard II*. London: Eyre and Spottiswoode, 1961; Saul, Nigel. *Richard II*. New Haven, CT: Yale University Press, 1997.

J

JACK CADE'S REBELLION (1450)

In the early summer of 1450, only weeks after the English defeat at FORMIGNY signaled the imminent collapse of Lancastrian rule in NORMANDY, the commons of Kent, led by a man named Jack (or John) Cade, rose in rebellion. Because the uprising reflected popular anger over the government's conduct of the war, and because HENRY VI and his advisors suspected that RICHARD, DUKE OF YORK, had instigated it, Jack Cade's Rebellion is often viewed both as a consequence of the HUNDRED YEARS WAR and as a prelude to the Wars of the Roses.

In late May, only three weeks after the murder of Henry's unpopular chief minister, William de la POLE, duke of Suffolk, a large body of men from the towns and villages of Kent gathered at Blackheath across the Thames from LONDON to demand redress of various grievances. Composed of rural peasants, artisans and tradesmen from the towns, and a small group of clergy and landowning gentry, the Kentish rebels were, at least initially, well organized and disciplined. Their elected leader was the mysterious Jack Cade, who also went by the names John Mortimer and John Amendalle. Although he was probably seeking only to attract the duke's supporters to his cause, Cade's use of the name Mortimer—the family name of York's mother—led the government to seriously consider the possibility that York was somehow involved in the rebellion. The rebels denied any connection with York, but their demand that the king rid himself of all advisors linked to the late Suffolk and turn instead to princes of the blood like York, only heightened the government's suspicions.

Thanks to the obscurity of Cade's background, and perhaps to government attempts to discredit Cade, rumors soon circulated that the rebel leader was an Irishman related to York, that he was a black magician, and that he had once fled the realm after murdering a pregnant woman. Whatever Cade's history, his manner impressed the royal councilors who met him, and the rebel manifesto crafted under his leadership—the "Complaint of the Commons of Kent"—displayed his skill as a propagandist. Comprising fifteen articles, the "Complaint" focused on the corrupt practices of royal officials in Kent, who were charged with extortion, perversion of justice, and election fraud. The commons also demanded an inquiry into the failure by Edmund BEAUFORT, duke of Somerset, to defend Normandy and into the misappropriation of royal funds by the king's household servants. Much of the rebels' discontent was also fueled by high war TAXATION and by economic hardship caused by wartime disruption of the cloth trade.

In early June, after submitting their "Complaint" to the council, the rebels obeyed an order to withdraw from Blackheath. However, when a contingent of royal troops followed them into Kent, the rebels ambushed and destroyed their pursuers. At news of this repulse, a nervous council committed Lord Say, the hated former sheriff of Kent, and William Cromer, the equally unpopular current sheriff, to the Tower of London. The king then withdrew from the capital. On 4 July, the Londoners, who were sympathetic to many of the rebels' grievances, allowed Cade and his followers to enter the city, where they immediately seized and executed Say and Cromer. On the night of 5 July, as the rebels grew more disorderly, the citizens, assisted by the Tower garrison under Thomas SCALES, Lord Scales, drove the insurgents from the city and recaptured London Bridge. This action allowed the council to issue a free pardon on 8 July, and most of the rebels returned home. After invalidating his pardon by attempting to seize Queenborough Castle, Cade was killed on 12 July while resisting arrest. A month later, on 12 August, Cherbourg, the last English-held town in Normandy, surrendered to CHARLES VII, thereby further discrediting an already weakened royal government.

Further Reading: Griffiths, Ralph A. *The Reign of King Henry VI.* Berkeley: University of California Press, 1981; Harvey, I. M. W. *Jack Cade's Rebellion of 1450.* Oxford: Clarendon Press, 1991; Wolffe, Bertram. *Henry VI.* London: Eyre Methuen, 1981.

JACQUERIE (1358)

The *Jacquerie* was the largest and bloodiest peasant rebellion of late medieval France. Involving violent attacks on the persons, property, and families of nobles, the uprising swept the region north of PARIS in May and June 1358. Although traditionally characterized as class warfare between nobles and nonnobles, the *Jacquerie* arose mainly from the political instability and economic distress unleashed by the HUNDRED YEARS WAR.

The *Jacquerie* derived its name from the term *Jacques*, which was popularly used to describe French peasants. The origins of the uprising are obscure, but it seems to have begun in the Oise Valley north of Paris in the village of Saint-Leu d'Esserent, where, on 28 May, a mob of armed peasants attacked a company of soldiers stationed there by the dauphin (*see* CHARLES V). Within hours of this event, much of the Beauvaisis rose in

rebellion, with bands of rioters attacking and destroying noble castles and manors. Because the region was at the center of a political struggle between the dauphin and CHARLES THE BAD, king of Navarre, both of whom were garrisoning local strongholds, the initial cause of the *Jacquerie* was anger over the growing demands of both sides for labor services to repair and strengthen castles and fortifications. Also, Navarre's introduction into the region of English ROU-TIERS may have aroused fears of the pillage and destruction that such troops had been causing elsewhere in France since JOHN II's capture at POITIERS in 1356.

Leadership of the rebellion was quickly assumed by a wealthy peasant named Guillaume Cale. Calling himself ''Captain of the men of Beauvaisis,'' and aided by self-appointed lieutenants who included educated townsmen and a few minor noblemen, Cale formed the rebels into organized units under their own banners. By early June, he led an army of almost five thousand men. Although most towns closed their gates to the rebels, many townsmen were sympathetic and provided the *Jacques* with food, weapons, and recruits. In Paris, Étienne MARCEL, leader of the urban revolution that had driven the dauphin from the capital, received a deputation from Cale and urged the *Jacques* to destroy all fortresses and noble residences surrounding the city. Hoping to frustrate the dauphin's attempt to ring the capital with troops, the Paris revolutionaries tried to foment further rebellion in regions west and south of the city. To the north, the *Jacquerie* spread into Picardy, Brie, Champagne, and parts of NORMANDY, as castles and manors were burned and nobles and their retainers murdered.

In early June, Navarre, sensing political possibilities, assumed leadership of the noble reaction, the so-called counter-*Jacquerie*. Assembling a force of over fifteen hundred that included his own men, a body of English *routiers*, and the nobility of northwestern France, Navarre crushed the main rebel army on 10 June. Cale, who was lured into Navarre's camp under flag of truce, was seized and beheaded. On 9 June at Meaux, a small company of men that included the PLANTAGENET captain, Jean de GRAILLY, captal de Buch, who put aside political differences to fight with his fellow nobles, destroyed the other main rebel force.

These actions ended the uprising, although the counter-*Jacquerie* continued as the nobility slaughtered all peasants who were known or suspected rebels, including three hundred who were burned alive in a monastery near Montdidier and another thirteen hundred who were slain when the nobles surprised their camp at Poix. Politically, the *Jacquerie* proved beneficial to the dauphin, who had done nothing to suppress it, and harmful to Navarre, who had led the counterattack, and especially to Marcel, who had backed the *Jacques*. The rebel violence revived support for the Crown among the nobility, allowing the dauphin to recruit troops for action against both Navarre and the Paris revolutionaries.

Further Reading: Bessen, David M. "The Jacquerie: Class War or Co-opted Rebellion?" *Journal of Medieval History* 11 (1985): 43–59; Mollat, Michel, and Philippe Wolff. *The Popular Revolutions of the Late Middle Ages.* Trans. A. L. Lytton-Sells. London: Allen and Unwin, 1973.

JAMES I. *See* SCOTLAND

JARGEAU, SIEGE OF. *See* LOIRE CAMPAIGN

JEAN LE BEL (d. c. 1370)

The fourteenth-century chronicler Jean le Bel is the author of *Les vrayes chroniques*, one of the most valuable contemporary sources for the first phase of the HUNDRED YEARS WAR.

Born at Liège into a wealthy and influential family, Jean le Bel was, like his fellow chronicler, Jean FROISSART, a native of Hainault. In 1313, he became a canon (i.e., a clerical member of a cathedral staff) at Saint-Lambert in Liège. Although a clergyman, Jean moved easily within noble circles and was deeply imbued with the values and ideals of contemporary CHIVALRY. According to one source, Jean lived the lifestyle of the wealthy nobles with whom he consorted. His patron, John of Hainault, the uncle of Queen PHILIPPA, wife of EDWARD III, accompanied Queen Isabella (*see* ISABELLA, QUEEN OF ENGLAND [c. 1292–1358]) to England in 1326, when she overthrew her husband, EDWARD II. In 1327, when John of Hainault participated in Edward's campaign in SCOTLAND, Jean le Bel was a member of Hainault's retinue, and his chronicle is thus an eyewitness account of that expedition. Because of Jean's connection to England and the English court, his chronicle views the war from an English perspective and its great hero is Edward III, whose military achievements are recounted in detail.

According to his prologue, Jean began writing his chronicle at the request of John of Hainault. Jean's stated goal was to faithfully record the great battles, feats of arms, and chivalrous deeds that occurred during Edward's reign. Eschewing rhyme, which he believed required "too many embellishments and repetitions" (Gransden, 165), Jean wrote in French prose, a practice later followed by Froissart, who also incorporated his predecessor's work down to 1361 into the first draft of his *Chroniques*. Froissart adhered so closely to Jean's text that a manuscript of *Les vrayes chronicles* discovered in the nineteenth century was at first believed to be a copy of Froissart.

Jean began writing in about 1357, when he recorded the major events of the war up to that date. Later additions brought the narrative into the 1360s. Although his writings lack the narrative power of Froissart, Jean le Bel was more careful of his facts. Writing in reaction to what he saw as the false or exaggerated histories related by poets and minstrels, Jean was determined to tell the truth as he saw it. The first chronicler to present the Anglo-French war and the deeds of its participants as things worth recording, Jean, despite his pro-English stance, had little influence on the writing of chronicles in England, where, thanks to the war, the use of French rapidly declined in the late fourteenth century. In France, however, Jean le

Bel, through Froissart, became the impetus for a whole series of important works of chivalrous history. *See also* NATIONAL CONSCIOUSNESS, GROWTH OF.

Further Reading: Gransden, Antonia. *Historical Writing in England.* Vol. 2, *c. 1307 to the Early Sixteenth Century.* Ithaca, NY: Cornell University Press, 1974; Thompson, Peter E., ed. and trans. *Contemporary Chronicles of the Hundred Years War: From the Works of Jean le Bel, Jean Froissart, and Enguerrand de Monstrelet.* London: Folio Society, 1966; Tyson, Diana B. "Jean le Bel: Portrait of a Chronicler." *Journal of Medieval History* 12 (1986): 315–32.

JEANNE, COUNTESS OF PENTHIÈVRE.
See BRETON CIVIL WAR

JEANNE D'ARC. *See* JOAN OF ARC

JOAN OF ARC (c. 1412–1431)
Joan of Arc, a French peasant girl whose improbable military leadership raised the siege of ORLÉANS and enabled the dauphin to be crowned king, is the most enigmatic and compelling figure of the HUNDRED YEARS WAR. Although Joan's intervention did not win the war for the French, it did turn the tide in their favor by restoring the prestige of the House of VALOIS and inspiring its partisans to a renewed effort that ultimately expelled the English.

Joan was born in about 1412 in Domrémy, a village in the northeastern province of Lorraine. Her parents were prosperous peasants and her uncle was a priest. At the age of thirteen, Joan began to hear the voices of Saint Margaret, Saint Catherine, and the archangel Michael, who, with increasing urgency, exhorted her to go to the aid of the king of France. By 1428, when Burgundian raiders forced Joan and her family to flee to Neufchatel, the voices made this seemingly impossible mission more precise—Joan was to break the English siege of Orléans. In February 1429, Joan persuaded Robert de Baudricourt, the dauphinist commander at Vaucouleurs, to provide her with an escort to the dauphin. Advised by her voices to cut her hair and assume male attire, Joan and her

attendants traveled for eleven days through enemy territory to reach the dauphin's court at Chinon on 6 March. After being kept waiting for several days while the dauphin's councilors debated the advisability of receiving her, Joan was summoned to court, where she made a sensation by immediately picking the dauphin, whom she had never seen, out of a crowd. Joan and the dauphin then held an intense private conversation during which Joan, by unknown means, convinced him that she had been sent by God to defeat the English and see him crowned.

However, before he would give her an army to relieve Orléans, the dauphin sent Joan to the University of Poitiers, where, for eleven days, she was interrogated by theologians charged with ensuring her orthodoxy. Asked what language her voices spoke, Joan, who spoke French with a pronounced Limousin accent, answered, "A better tongue than I" (DeVries, 46). Showing no fear or anxiety and offering such simple and direct answers to complex questions, Joan passed the test, convincing her inquisitors that her mission was divinely inspired. A few days later at Tours, Joan also passed a physical test conducted by Yolande of Sicily, the queen's mother, who assured her son-in-law that Joan was a virgin. At the end of these tests, on 22 March, Joan dictated her so-called "Letter to the English," which was a stern and confident ultimatum addressed to HENRY VI; JOHN, DUKE OF BEDFORD; and other English leaders. If the English were willing "to give up France and pay for having occupied her," they could go in peace; but if they refused, "then wherever we find you we will strike at you there, and make a great uproar, greater than any made in France for a thousand years" (DeVries, 64). Dispatched in late April, the letter, not surprisingly, elicited no response from the English, but had an immediate effect in dauphinist France, where men enthusiastically flocked to join the army being raised to convey Joan to Orléans.

Assured of Joan's sincerity and purity, and believing, perhaps, that he had nothing

Although it inaccurately depicts her in female attire, this drawing of Joan of Arc in the margin of the register of the Paris Parlement was done on 10 May 1429, only days after the relief of Orléans, and thus is the only likeness of Joan done during her lifetime. *Reunion des Musees Nationaux/Art Resource, New York.*

across to the English lines to demand that they withdraw and in return receiving insults and abuse. During four days of near-continuous combat, the French, driven by Joan's sense of urgency and inspired by her courage—she refused to leave the field after being wounded by an arrow—seized key English defenses. Shaken by the fervor of the French attacks, the English abandoned their remaining positions and marched away on 8 May, thus lifting the siege and completing the first part of Joan's mission. To accomplish the second part, the dauphin's coronation, Joan, in mid-June, accompanied an army commanded by JOHN, DUKE OF ALENÇON, on a week-long campaign (*see* LOIRE CAMPAIGN) that cleared the Loire Valley of English garrisons and ended with a major victory at PATAY. Inspired by these triumphs, the dauphin marched to Rheims, where, on 17 July, he was crowned king as CHARLES VII in Joan's presence.

Thanks to her military success, Joan was now a political force, a recognized leader of the court faction that favored vigorous prosecution of the war over negotiation. Joan urged the king to attack PARIS, but the failure of her ill-considered assault on the capital on 8 September convinced Charles to arrange a truce and disband the army. In April 1430, PHILIP THE GOOD, duke of BURGUNDY, laid siege to Compiègne. Her influence waning, Joan secretly left court to assist the town's Valois garrison. Captured by the BURGUNDIANS on 23 May, Joan was sold to the English and transferred to a military prison in ROUEN in December. Accused of witchcraft and heresy, Joan, beginning on 21 February 1431, was tried before a tribunal led by Pierre Cauchon, bishop of Beauvais, whose brief from the English was to discredit Charles by associating him and his

to lose, the dauphin ordered that Joan be supplied with a suit of ARMOR and a special standard that she had designed on instruction from her voices. On 29 April, Joan, accompanied by a large relief force, entered Orléans, where she demanded that the commander of the garrison, John, the Bastard of Orléans (*see* JOHN, COUNT OF DUNOIS AND LONGUEVILLE), launch an immediate assault on the English. When the Bastard, believing himself unready, did not attack until 4 May, Joan filled the time by shouting cause with a witch and heretic. Convicted by the court and by theologians from the University of Paris, who were appalled by her use of male attire, Joan was brought on 24 May to the cemetery of Saint-Ouen, where she was to be condemned to death. Before sentence could be read, Joan recanted, denying her voices, confessing to blasphemy and sorcery, and promising to wear women's clothes. Sentenced to life imprisonment, Joan asked to be sent to an ecclesiastical prison, where she could have female attendants. Cauchon, however, returned her to the English military prison, where, four days later, she overthrew her recantation by resuming male attire. Although Joan said that it was more suitable to dress like a man while she was in the keeping of men, historians have surmised that the English, angry that she had escaped the flames, sent soldiers to gang-rape her or ordered her jailers to hide her women's clothes. In any event, her subsequent admission that her voices had returned sealed her fate.

Joan was burned at the stake in Rouen on 30 May 1431. Charles VII made no attempt to help her and for twenty years said nothing about her. In 1456, a new trial, ordered by Charles largely to clear his name of involvement with a condemned heretic, reversed the verdict of 1431 and declared Joan innocent. In 1920, Joan, already a popular French icon and destined to become a symbol of the French resistance during World War II, was canonized by the Roman Catholic Church.

Further Reading: Barstow, Anne Llewellyn. *Joan of Arc, Heretic, Mystic, Shaman.* Lewiston, ME: Edwin Mellen Press, 1986; DeVries, Kelly. *Joan of Arc: A Military Leader.* Stroud, England: Sutton Publishing, 2003; Fraioli, Deborah A. *Joan of Arc and the Hundred Years War.* Westport, CT: Greenwood Press, 2005; Gies, Frances. *Joan of Arc: The Legend and the Reality.* New York: Harper and Row, 1981; Pernoud, Régine. *Joan of Arc: By Herself and Her Witnesses.* London: Scarborough House, 1982; Pernoud, Régine, and Marie-Véronique Clin. *Joan of Arc.* Trans. Jeremy Duquesnay Adams. New York: St. Martin's Press, 1999; Richey, Stephen W. *Joan of Arc: The Warrior*

Saint. Westport, CT: Praeger, 2003; Warner, Marina. *Joan of Arc: The Image of Female Heroism.* New York: Knopf, 1981; Wheeler, Bonnie, and Charles T. Woods, eds. *Fresh Verdicts on Joan of Arc.* London: Garland, 1996.

JOAN OF KENT, PRINCESS OF WALES.
See EDWARD, THE BLACK PRINCE; RICHARD II

JOHN, COUNT OF DUNOIS AND LONGUEVILLE (1402–1468)
The illegitimate son of CHARLES VI's brother, LOUIS, DUKE OF ORLÉANS, John, count of Dunois, was CHARLES VII's most loyal and able commander, and JOAN OF ARC's most famous companion at the siege of ORLÉANS.

After the assassination of his father in 1407, John, known as the Bastard of Orléans, was educated by the duke's wife, Valentine Visconti, who saw the precocious boy as her husband's future avenger. After John's half-brother, CHARLES, DUKE OF ORLÉANS, was captured at AGINCOURT in 1415, leadership of the ARMAGNAC party, the Orléanist faction in the FRENCH CIVIL WAR, passed eventually to the Bastard's childhood companion, Dauphin Charles, whose service he entered in 1417. In about 1418, the Bastard was captured by the Burgundians and remained a prisoner for two years. With the death of his half brother Philip in 1420, John assumed active leadership of the Orléans family and prime responsibility for raising Duke Charles's RANSOM. Among the most active dauphinist captains in the 1420s, the Bastard fought at BAUGÉ in 1421, assisted in the defense of Mont-Saint-Michel in 1425, and made a name for himself by breaking the English siege of MONTARGIS in 1427.

In late 1428, the Bastard was given command of the garrison in besieged Orléans. With the help of captains like Étienne de VIGNOLLES and Poton de XAINTRAILLES, he launched a series of sorties against the besiegers, but these were largely unsuccessful and the Bastard's defense of the city has been criticized by some historians as ineffective and overcautious. In February 1429, his plan to disrupt enemy supply lines was frustrated at the Battle of the HERRINGS. In late April, he met Joan of Arc at Blois, where a strong French relief force was gathering. Despite some doubts about her mission and disagreements with her military tactics, the Bastard accepted Joan's moral leadership and won a great reputation for himself as her most famous captain at the relief of Orléans in May 1429 and during the subsequent LOIRE CAMPAIGN, which ended on 18 June with the victory at PATAY.

Throughout the 1430s, the Bastard led a series of effective campaigns in the Seine Valley that ended with the king's triumphant entry into PARIS in 1436. Named grand chamberlain in 1433 and made count of Dunois in 1439 and count of Longueville in 1444, the Bastard played a major role in the implementation of French military reforms in the 1440s (see CHARLES VII, MILITARY REFORMS OF). He again commanded armies in the NORMANDY CAMPAIGN of 1449–50 and in GASCONY in 1451. He testified extensively at Joan of Arc's rehabilitation hearings in 1456 and held various diplomatic and political posts during the last years of Charles VII. Although dismissed from court on the accession of Louis XI in 1461, he reconciled with the king in 1465 and served as a royal councilor until his death on 23 November 1468.

Further Reading: DeVries, Kelly. *Joan of Arc: A Military Leader*. Stroud, England: Sutton Publishing, 2003; Pernoud, Régine, and Marie-Véronique Clin. *Joan of Arc*. Trans. Jeremy Duquesnay Adams. New York: St. Martin's Press, 1999.

JOHN, DUKE OF ALENÇON
(c. 1407–1476)

A friend and companion of JOAN OF ARC, who referred to him as "my fair duke," John II, duke of Alençon, commanded the dauphinist army during the 1429 LOIRE CAMPAIGN and the culminating Battle of PATAY.

The second son of John I, duke of Alençon, who died at AGINCOURT in 1415, John II grew up at the dauphinist court, where his mother, Mary of BRITTANY, fled after HENRY V granted the duchy of Alençon to his brother JOHN, DUKE OF BEDFORD. In response to this grant, the dauphin named John II lieutenant-general of the duchy in 1420. In 1423, John also received appointment to the dauphin's council. Captured at VERNEUIL in 1424, John, who succeeded his brother Peter as duke of Alençon in 1425, remained a prisoner until February 1429. Burdened with an exorbitant RANSOM of 80,000 gold saluts, the duke was forced to take extreme measures to raise the money. His wife, Joan, the daughter of CHARLES, the captive duke of Orléans, pawned her jewels, while Alençon surrendered several lordships, including the barony of Fougères, which passed to his uncle, JOHN V, duke of Brittany.

On 7 March 1429, the day after her first meeting with the dauphin, Alençon met Joan of Arc at Chinon. After jousting with Joan and offering her a horse, the duke, who was surprised at the ease with which she handled arms, quickly became devoted to the Maid and her cause. Although Alençon was not present at the siege of ORLÉANS, Joan stayed with him afterward, visiting his home at Saint-Laurent between 22 May and 2 June. Introduced to his mother and wife, Joan promised the latter that she would bring the duke back from the coming campaign "in the state he is in now or in a better one" (DeVries, 98). Perhaps to ease the strained relationship between Joan and John, Bastard of Orléans (see JOHN, COUNT OF DUNOIS AND LONGUEVILLE) and leader of the Orléans garrison, the dauphin appointed Alençon, who was a friend to the former and a brother-in-law to the latter, commander of the army. On 17 July, after the success of the Loire Campaign, Alençon was knighted by CHARLES VII at his coronation in Rheims.

The duke participated in Joan's unsuccessful assault on PARIS in early September, but left her when Charles VII disbanded the royal army shortly thereafter. Although he took part in campaigns in Maine, Anjou, and NORMANDY in the 1430s, Alençon did not fight again with Joan, who was captured by the Burgundians in 1430 and burned at the stake by the English in 1431. By 1439, Alençon's friendship with the king had cooled, and the duke joined the Praguerie, an uprising of disaffected nobles that was suppressed by the constable, Arthur de

Richemont (see ARTHUR III). Pardoned and released in 1449, when he took part in the NORMAN CAMPAIGN, Alençon was financially ruined and attempted to repair his fortunes by marrying his daughter to the eldest son (the future Edward IV) of RICHARD, DUKE OF YORK. This communication with an English duke was regarded as treason by Charles VII, who ordered the duke's arrest in the midst of his testimony at Joan of Arc's nullification trial in 1456. Imprisoned in the fortress of Aigues-Mortes, Alençon was released on the accession of his godson, Louis XI, in 1461. However, when he refused Louis's demand for control of three fortresses and the wardship of his children, Alençon was rearrested. Although convicted of treason and condemned to death in July 1474, Alençon was never executed and died a prisoner in the Louvre in 1476.

Further Reading: DeVries, Kelly. *Joan of Arc: A Military Leader.* Stroud, England: Sutton Publishing, 2003; Pernoud, Régine, and Marie-Véronique Clin. *Joan of Arc.* Trans. Jeremy Duquesnay Adams. New York: St. Martin's Press, 1999.

JOHN, DUKE OF BEDFORD (1389–1435)

The third son of HENRY IV, John, duke of Bedford, governed England as lieutenant for his brother HENRY V and France as regent for his nephew HENRY VI. After his brother's death in 1422, Bedford oversaw all phases of the English war effort, maintaining the ANGLO-BURGUNDIAN ALLIANCE, ruling NORMANDY and Lancastrian France, and defending his nephew's right to the French throne.

John was knighted in October 1399, only weeks after his father deposed RICHARD II and established the House of LANCASTER on the English throne. A member of the Order of the GARTER by 1402, John became constable of England and warden of the east march with SCOTLAND in 1403. Henry V made his brother duke of Bedford in May 1414 and entrusted him with the government of England in August 1415, when the king invaded France and reopened the HUNDRED YEARS WAR. In August 1416, Bedford commanded the English fleet at the Battle of the SEINE, a naval victory that broke the French blockade

of HARFLEUR. In 1417–19, Bedford again served as king's lieutenant in England, presiding over PARLIAMENT and raising money and supplies for his brother's conquest of Normandy. In 1420, the duke returned to France to attend the signing of the Treaty of TROYES and to participate in the sieges of Sens and MELUN. Bedford became heir to the throne in March 1421, when his elder brother, THOMAS, DUKE OF CLARENCE, was slain at BAUGÉ. After another term as royal lieutenant, Bedford returned to France in May 1422, and was thus present when Henry V died at Vincennes in the following August.

In accordance with Henry V's wishes, Bedford assumed the French regency in late 1422 upon the refusal of PHILIP THE GOOD, duke of BURGUNDY, to take the office on behalf of the infant Henry VI. In 1423, as part of the Treaty of AMIENS, a defensive agreement binding the regent, Burgundy, and JOHN V, duke of BRITTANY, in a triple alliance in support of Henry VI's French Crown, Bedford married Burgundy's sister, ANNE. Until her death in 1432, the duchess played a vital role in easing relations between her husband and her brother and in maintaining the vital Anglo-Burgundian alliance. Between 1423 and 1429, Bedford expanded the area of Lancastrian rule to include most of non-Burgundian France north of the Loire. Understanding the need to rule through French officers and institutions, Bedford initiated popular reforms in the Anglo-Burgundian administration and took steps to control brigandage. Although he seldom took the field in person, the duke commanded at the greatest English victory of the decade, the Battle of VERNEUIL in August 1424. From December 1425 to March 1427, Bedford resided in England, where he intervened in the bitter feud between his brother, HUMPHREY, DUKE OF GLOUCESTER, and his uncle, Cardinal Henry BEAUFORT, bishop of Winchester, a quarrel that split the English regency council.

In 1429, the tide of war turned against the English. Inspired by JOAN OF ARC, the French broke the siege of ORLÉANS, cleared the Loire of English garrisons (see LOIRE CAMPAIGN), and secured the coronation of the dauphin as CHARLES VII. Bedford's regency was temporarily suspended in 1430–31, when Henry VI, in a move urged by Bedford, came to France for his coronation. Bedford took no part in the 1431 trial and execution of Joan of Arc, whom the duke, a man of strictly orthodox belief, later described as a witch. In April 1433, five months after the death of Duchess Anne, Bedford married Jacquetta of Luxembourg, the seventeen-year-old niece of the Anglo-Burgundian chancellor. The duke's relations with Burgundy, who had been seeking means to honorably detach himself from the English alliance, deteriorated after Anne's death, and the two men met for the last time in May 1433. In June, Bedford returned to England, where he again mediated between Gloucester and Beaufort and successfully defended himself against charges of mismanaging the war, which may have been inspired by Gloucester. Returning to France in July 1434, Bedford's health began to fail and he died at ROUEN on 14 September 1435, only a week before Burgundy made peace with Charles VII at the Congress of ARRAS.

Further Reading: Allmand, C. T. *Lancastrian Normandy, 1415–1450: The History of a Medieval Occupation.* Oxford: Clarendon Press, 1983; Williams, E. Carleton. *My Lord of Bedford, 1389–1435.* London: Longmans, 1963.

JOHN, DUKE OF BERRY (1340–1416)

John, duke of Berry, was the son of JOHN II and the younger brother of CHARLES V. Best known as a patron and collector of art, Berry proved to be an inept soldier and a devious, unreliable politician, who, despite efforts to mediate the political disputes of his brothers and nephews, exacerbated the internal rivalries that led to initiation of the FRENCH CIVIL WAR and resumption of the HUNDRED YEARS WAR.

Born at Vincennes on 30 November 1340, John was made count of Poitou in 1356. When Poitou was ceded to EDWARD III by the Treaty of BRÉTIGNY in 1360, John II created his son duke of Berry and Auvergne. From 1360 to 1364, following the French

king's release from captivity, Berry and his brother, LOUIS, DUKE OF ANJOU, were among the hostages held in England to guarantee payment of their father's ransom. Berry was thus involved in negotiation of the Treaty of the HOSTAGES, an abortive 1362 agreement whereby the hostages, acting on their own authority, attempted to speed their release by making further territorial and monetary concessions to the English.

When war resumed in 1369, Charles V regranted Poitou to his brother as an incentive to retake AQUITAINE from the English. However, the subsequent French reconquest of the county and duchy had more to do with the king's success in persuading Gascon nobles to switch allegiance than with Berry's military ability. In October 1374, Charles excluded Berry from the list of guardians named to govern for the dauphin should he succeed as a minor, an omission that may have proceeded from the king's disapproval of his brother's personal life. A man of culture and taste, Berry was one of the greatest patrons of art in French history. As such, his main interest was not politics or war, but using his lands and offices to increase his wealth and enlarge his collections, which ranged in content from jewels, tapestries, and *objets d'art* to castles, dogs, and books. The duke is today best known for the surviving manuscripts he commissioned, particularly his richly illuminated *Très Riches Heures*, a prayerbook (known as a book of hours) that contains a calendar illustrated with depictions of the duke's seventeen castles.

On the accession of CHARLES VI in 1380, Berry was appointed royal lieutenant in Languedoc, but he rarely visited the province, which he used mainly as a source of revenue to fund his collecting. The resulting overtaxation and maladministration threw the region into disorder and forced the king to dismiss his uncle from office in 1389. In 1392, the onset of Charles's mental illness brought Berry back into government. Lacking political ambition himself, the duke had sought, in the 1380s, to temper the conflicting ambitions of his brothers, Louis, duke of Anjou, and PHILIP THE BOLD, duke of BURGUNDY. After the latter's death in 1404, Berry, as the king's sole surviving uncle, used his prestige and influence to mediate the growing rivalry between his nephews, LOUIS, DUKE OF ORLÉANS, and JOHN THE FEARLESS, duke of Burgundy. However, when Burgundy, having arranged his rival's murder, seized power after 1409, Berry reacted to his exclusion from court by joining the ARMAGNAC (Orléanist) faction and thus became party to the 1412 Treaty of BOURGES, an agreement that surrendered many of Charles V's conquests in return for English assistance against Burgundy. Berry died in PARIS on 15 June 1416, a year after civil war had brought the English back into France; he was succeeded by his daughter, Marie, duchess of Bourbon.

Further Reading: Meiss, Millard. *French Painting in the Time of Jean de Berry: The Late Fourteenth Century and the Patronage of the Duke.* 2. vols. London: Phaidon, 1969; Perroy, Edouard. *The Hundred Years War.* Trans. W. B. Wells. New York: Capricorn Books, 1965.

JOHN I, KING OF FRANCE. *See* SALIC LAW OF SUCCESSION

JOHN II, KING OF FRANCE (1319–1364)
John II was the eldest son of PHILIP VI and the second VALOIS king of France. Although John became known to posterity as "le Bon" (the Good), his reign was marked by military defeat, political instability, economic distress, and social unrest, and reached its nadir when the king, after four years of captivity, agreed to the dismemberment of his kingdom. The last years of the reign, however, saw the initiation of a political and military recovery that came to fruition after John's death.

In July 1332, John married Bonne of Luxembourg, by whom he had nine children. He held several important APPANAGES tied to former PLANTAGENET possessions, becoming duke of NORMANDY and count of Maine and Anjou in 1332, and duke of Guienne in 1345. Normandy received his first military command in May 1340, when he launched an offensive against the chief members of EDWARD III's ANTI-FRENCH COALITION. Attacking Hai-

nault, Brabant, and FLANDERS, the duke secured most of the Scheldt Valley before an English naval victory at SLUYS ended the campaign in late June. In 1341, at the start of the BRETON CIVIL WAR, Normandy invaded BRITTANY on behalf of CHARLES OF BLOIS, the French-backed claimant to the Breton ducal title. Quickly overrunning the duchy, he forced John de MONTFORT, Blois's English-backed rival, to capitulate. In 1345, Normandy commanded an army in GASCONY, but failed to intercept the forces of HENRY OF GROSMONT, duke of Lancaster, and ended the campaign upon receiving news of the French defeat at AUBEROCHE. In 1346, he returned to Gascony and invested AIGUILLON, but abandoned the siege in late August when the developing CRÉCY campaign forced his recall. Frustrated by his failure either to take Aiguillon or reach Crécy in time for the battle, Normandy fell into disagreement with his father. In October 1346, the two quarreled over Philip's refusal to honor a safe-conduct the duke had issued to Sir Walter MAUNY. The estrangement deepened in 1350, when Philip, having recently lost his queen, Jeanne de Burgundy, to plague (*see* BLACK DEATH), angered Normandy, who had been close to his mother, by marrying a much younger woman, Blanche d'Évreux, the sister of CHARLES THE BAD, king of Navarre.

Normandy ascended the throne as John II in August 1350. A brave man and a chivalrous knight, John as king was stubborn, impulsive, and easily swayed by stronger personalities and greater intellects. He was also rash, extravagant, and a poor judge of character, tending to rely for advice on close friends and cronies and allowing his council to become the tool of faction. John's first action was the sudden arrest of a recently paroled English captive, Constable Raoul de Brienne, count of Eu, who was subsequently executed for unspecified treasons. Unable to pay his RANSOM, Eu had surrendered his castle of Guines, which lay on the CALAIS march, to Edward III, an action that John interpreted as treason. Angered by the haste and secrecy that surrounded Eu's death, most of the northwestern nobility attached

John II, known as "The Good." *Scala/Art Resource, New York.*

surrender much of western France in exchange for Edward's renunciation of the French Crown. Widespread opposition to the treaty, and revelations that some of the councilors who had supported it were complicit in the murder of the constable, led John to repudiate the agreement and end the Truce of CALAIS.

By 1355, discontent with John's government was widespread. Although the king imposed a new settlement, the Treaty of Valognes, on Navarre, the Estates-General, led by Parisian deputies demanding reform of a corrupt and incompetent administration, assumed oversight of the collection of war TAXATION. In December, Navarre and John's son, the Dauphin Charles, were implicated in an unsuccessful plot to seize power. Both were pardoned, but on 5 April 1356, the king suddenly arrested Navarre at a banquet hosted by the dauphin in Rouen. Although Navarre was imprisoned, some of his Norman supporters were summarily executed, an action that essentially plunged northwestern France into civil war. Having alienated both the bourgeois reformers of PARIS and much of the nobility, John was defeated and captured at POITIERS on 19 September 1356, by EDWARD, THE BLACK PRINCE.

themselves to John's ambitious son-in-law, Charles of Navarre, who took every opportunity to offer himself as an alternative king. In January 1354, Navarre arranged the murder of the new constable, Charles of Spain, a royal favorite to whom John had granted lands claimed by Navarre. In February, in the Treaty of Mantes, John pardoned Navarre and admitted many of his supporters to the council, where they formed a majority in favor of negotiating peace with England. Anxious to go on crusade, John concluded the Treaty of GUINES, whereby he agreed to

For the next four years, while John was a captive in England, France descended into chaos. *ROUTIER* bands roamed the country, *JACQUERIE* rebels murdered noblemen, and bourgeois revolutionaries led by Étienne MARCEL drove the dauphin from Paris. When Navarre escaped from prison in November 1357, the continuance of Valois rule seemed in doubt. Desperate to win his freedom, John negotiated the First (1358) and Second (1359) Treaties of LONDON, promising to pay a large ransom and surrender large blocks of territory in return for his release. Neither treaty took effect, mainly because the French government could not meet English ransom demands, and because Navarre's ambition alienated his allies and improved the dauphin's political position. In 1360, following the failure of Edward III's RHEIMS CAMPAIGN, John's representatives negotiated the Treaty of BRÉTIGNY, whereby Edward agreed to renounce his claim to the French Crown in return for a ransom of 3 million gold écus and an enlarged AQUITAINE held in full sovereignty. Released at Calais on 24 October 1360, John soon fell behind on his ransom payments, being unable to squeeze taxes from a kingdom ravaged by English *routiers*. Although some historians credit the dauphin, the last years of John's reign witnessed a gradual revival of royal authority. The overthrow of Marcel and the waning of Navarre's influence allowed the Crown to regain the support of Paris and the nobility and to convince the Estates to grant taxes that allowed the eventual creation of a royal army capable of suppressing *routiers*.

On 3 January 1364, John voluntarily returned to LONDON. Although he gave no reason for his action, it was partially related to the flight of his son, LOUIS, DUKE OF ANJOU, who, while one of the hostages held in Calais to ensure prompt ransom payments, broke parole and refused to return to custody. A more important reason was likely John's desire to negotiate directly with Edward for a favorable revision of the Brétigny agreement. Discussions were well underway when John died in London on 8 April. He was succeeded by his eldest son CHARLES V. *See also* ESTATES, GENERAL AND PROVINCIAL.

Further Reading: Perroy, Edouard. *The Hundred Years War.* Trans. W. B. Wells. New York: Capricorn Books, 1965; Sumption, Jonathan. *The Hundred Years War.* Vol. 2, *Trial by Fire.* Philadelphia: University of Pennsylvania Press, 2001.

JOHN IV, DUKE OF BRITTANY
(c. 1340–1399)

John IV, the first Montfort duke of BRITTANY, ended the BRETON CIVIL WAR, strengthened ducal authority, and preserved the independence of the duchy.

John IV was the son of John de MONTFORT, who in 1341 claimed the succession to the ducal title of his late half brother Duke John III. Montfort's claim was opposed by his niece, Joan of Penthièvre, whose cause was championed by her husband, CHARLES OF BLOIS, a nephew of PHILIP VI. The civil war that arose from these rival claims was quickly subsumed into the HUNDRED YEARS WAR, with Philip backing Blois and EDWARD III supporting Montfort. When Montfort died in 1345, Edward assumed direction of the Montfort cause and guardianship of the younger John de Montfort, who had been sent to safety in England by his mother Joan of FLANDERS. In 1356, Montfort accompanied HENRY OF GROSMONT, duke of Lancaster, to Brittany, where the sixteen-year-old boy participated in the English siege of Rennes. Although the Anglo-French Treaty of BRÉTIGNY called upon both parties to work toward a settlement of the Breton succession dispute, both JOHN II and Edward III adhered to their own candidates. In 1362, when Edward terminated his guardianship and allowed Montfort to return to Brittany and assume leadership of his cause, the Breton civil war resumed. In April 1364, Montfort, with the assistance of Sir John CHANDOS and such English ROUTIER captains as Sir Robert KNOLLES and Sir Hugh CALVELEY, defeated and killed Blois at AURAY. That victory led in April 1365 to the signing of the Treaty of GUÉRANDE, whereby Joan of Penthièvre recognized Montfort as Duke John IV.

The new duke paid homage to CHARLES V, but maintained close ties with England. In 1370, he allowed Knolles to shelter in the duchy after his abortive CHEVAUCHÉE in northern France, and in 1372, he formally repudiated VALOIS overlordship, an unpopular action that cost him the support of the Breton nobility and forced him to flee to LONDON in 1373. After the exiled duke accompanied JOHN OF GAUNT, duke of Lancaster, on the grand CHEVAUCHÉE OF 1373, a French army under Bertrand du GUESCLIN overran most of the duchy, save for Brest and three other English-held fortresses in the west. On the advice of Olivier de CLISSON and other pro-French Bretons, Charles V declared John contumacious and confiscated the duchy on 18 December 1378. Although unhappy with John's pro-English stance, the Breton people liked the idea of incorporation into the Valois state even less. They invited John to return, and on 4 April 1381, almost six months after the death of Charles V, a second Treaty of Guérande returned John to power as a Valois vassal. Thereafter, the duke followed a more neutral course in foreign affairs. He assisted the French in the suppression of the Flemish revolt in the 1380s but retained links with England even though the English retention of Brest and of John's English lordships strained Anglo-Breton relations later in the decade.

Domestically, the duke, in an effort to increase ducal authority and thereby strengthen Breton independence, reorganized Brittany's government, reformed its finances, and enhanced the prestige of its court through a more formalized ceremonial, which included the founding of an order of CHIV-ALRY, the Order of the Ermine. The last years of John's reign were marred by a bitter feud with John, count of Penthièvre, who revived his mother's cause. In 1387, the duke captured and ransomed Clisson, Penthièvre's father-in-law and strongest supporter, and, in 1392, John may have been responsible for an attempt on Clisson's life. In the 1390s, the duke moved closer to France, marrying his son, the future JOHN V, to Jeanne, the daughter of CHARLES VI. John died in November 1399.

Further Reading: Jones, Michael. *The Creation of Brittany: A Late Medieval State*. London: Hambledon Press, 1988; Jones, Michael. *Ducal Brittany, 1364–1399*. London: Oxford University Press, 1970.

JOHN V, DUKE OF BRITTANY (1389–1442)

By constantly shifting allegiance to align himself with the stronger party, John V, second Montfort duke of BRITTANY, maintained Breton independence against both France and England during the last decades of the HUNDRED YEARS WAR.

John was nine when he succeeded his father, JOHN IV, in November 1399. His marriage to Jeanne of VALOIS, daughter of CHARLES VI and ISABEAU OF BAVARIA, produced seven children. Although lingering support among the Breton nobility for the rival Penthièvre claim to the ducal title allowed Olivier, count of Penthièvre, to briefly imprison the duke in 1420, Montfort authority was largely unchallenged during John's rule. Acting through such capable officials as Chancellor John de Malestroit, the duke strengthened ducal administration, reformed the military, and initiated diplomatic and trade contacts with most of Western Europe. He also promoted Breton independence by emphasizing the sovereign nature of ducal authority through employment of new coronation rituals, adoption of elaborate Burgundian ceremonial for the ducal household, and issuance of gold coinage.

In foreign affairs, the duke vacillated between French and Anglo-Burgundian alliances. Generally considered a weak man who hated war and sought personal comfort, John was often swayed by stronger personalities, particularly his forceful younger brother Arthur de Richemont (see AR-THUR III). However, the duke was committed to Breton independence and genuinely concerned for the welfare of his people, and his shifting alliances allowed Brittany to avoid the suffering visited on the duchy by its fourteenth-century entanglement in the Anglo-French war (see BRETON CIVIL WAR).

In January 1414, John concluded a ten-year truce with England, thereby ensuring Breton neutrality when HENRY V invaded France in the following year. In March 1419, John concluded a more formal alliance with Henry, then at the height of his military success, but repudiated that agreement after the English defeat at BAUGÉ in March 1421. In the following May, the duke concluded an agreement with the dauphin (see CHARLES VII) at Sablé, which included a Breton undertaking to make war on England. In June 1422, Henry undermined this alliance by releasing Richemont, an English prisoner since AGIN-COURT, who persuaded his brother to abandon the dauphin and adhere to the Treaty of TROYES. In April 1423, John brought Brittany into formal alliance with England and BURGUNDY by signing the Treaty of AMIENS with JOHN, DUKE OF BEDFORD, and PHILIP THE GOOD, duke of Burgundy. However, at Philip's urging, John immediately signed a secret understanding with Burgundy whereby the two dukes agreed to remain friends even if one reconciled with the dauphin.

In December 1425, nine months after Richemont entered the dauphin's service, John concluded the Franco-Breton Treaty of Saumur, whereby the duke did homage to the dauphin and allowed the French to recruit in the duchy. After declaring war on Brittany in January 1426, the English invaded and defeated Richemont. In September 1427, the duke repudiated the Saumur agreement, reaffirmed the Treaty of Troyes, and rejoined the triple alliance. Constant clashes between English and Breton sailors damaged Anglo-Breton relations in the early 1430s, although lengthy negotiations, marked by a growing friendship between HENRY VI and John's younger son Gilles, prevented hostilities. After the ANGLO-BURGUNDIAN ALLIANCE ended with the Treaty of ARRAS in 1435, John maintained a delicate neutrality, allied with England but friendly with France and willing to broker any Anglo-French peace. John died on 29 August 1442 and was succeeded by his son Francis I.

Further Reading: Jones, Michael. *The Creation of Brittany: A Late Medieval State.* London: Hambledon Press, 1988.

JOHN OF GAUNT, DUKE OF LANCASTER (1340–1399)

The third surviving son of EDWARD III and PHILIPPA of Hainault, and ancestor of the royal House of LANCASTER, John of Gaunt, duke of Lancaster, was the wealthiest and most powerful English magnate of the late fourteenth century.

Born in Ghent (a later corruption of which became "Gaunt"), John was created earl of Richmond in September 1342. He was early imbued with the martial traditions of his family, being attached as a youth to the household of his elder brother, EDWARD, THE BLACK PRINCE. Richmond was with his brother at the naval battle of WINCHELSEA in August 1350 and was knighted by his father during the abortive English campaign in NORMANDY in 1355. He accompanied the king on expeditions to SCOTLAND in 1355–56 and commanded his own retinue during the RHEIMS CAMPAIGN of 1359–60. He witnessed the ratification of the Treaty of BRÉTIGNY in October 1360 and was elected a knight of the GARTER in April 1361. Richmond married Blanche, the daughter of HENRY OF GROSMONT, duke of Lancaster, in May 1359, and succeeded to his father-in-law's lands and titles in November 1362, thus becoming the wealthiest nobleman in England. In January 1367, Lancaster sailed to AQUITAINE, where he joined the Black Prince's Castilian campaign (*see* CASTILIAN WAR OF SUCCESSION) and led the van of the Anglo-Gascon army at the Battle of NÁJERA. In 1368, the death of his elder brother, Lionel, duke of Clarence, combined with the deteriorating health of the king and the prince, forced Lancaster to assume increasing responsibility for the conduct of the war.

In June 1369, the king appointed Lancaster lieutenant of the PLANTAGENET realm in France. In 1370, the duke reinforced the prince in Aquitaine, where Lancaster was present at the sack of LIMOGES in September and became his ailing brother's lieutenant in October. He vigorously defended the duchy until July 1371, when his inability to pay his troops led him to resign the lieutenancy. In September, Lancaster, a widower since 1368, married Constanza, the daughter of Pedro I, the late king of Castile. Approved by the king and the prince, who sought means to break the Franco-Castilian alliance, the match gave Lancaster a claim to the Castilian Crown and colored his attitude toward English foreign and domestic policy for the next two decades. Lancaster next commanded the *CHEVAUCHÉE of 1373*, the largest and longest English *CHEVAUCHÉE* of the HUNDRED YEARS WAR. Leaving CALAIS, the duke was forced to range far to the east of PARIS before turning south for Aquitaine, where he stayed until April 1374 organizing the duchy's defenses. In 1375–76, the duke led the English delegation at the BRUGES PEACE CONFERENCE, the ultimate failure of which promoted a rumor that Lancaster, encouraged by the imminent deaths of his father and elder brother, intended to secure the English throne for himself. Acting as the king's representative, Lancaster presided over the Good Parliament of 1376, which defied his authority by impeaching those royal officials believed responsible for the Crown's insolvency and recent military failures. Although he did not oppose the will of PARLIAMENT, Lancaster largely reversed its acts during the following year. Granted palatinate rights in the duchy of Lancaster in February 1377, and having constructed the most extensive political affinity in England, Lancaster dominated the government upon the accession of his nephew, RICHARD II, in the following June.

Suspected of having designs on the throne and blamed for high taxes and an unsuccessful war, Lancaster was highly unpopular, particularly in LONDON, where riots followed his intervention in the 1377 trial of John Wycliffe, who won the duke's support by advocating a strong monarchy to reform a corrupt Church. During the PEASANTS' REVOLT OF 1381, the rebels, unable to harm the duke himself, who was then in Scotland, destroyed his London palace, the Savoy. Although influential in the minority government, Lancaster's relations with his nephew were strained. In 1384, Lancaster, perhaps through the machinations of Richard's favorite, Robert de Vere, earl of Oxford, was accused of plotting treason; however, the king accepted his uncle's protestations of loyalty and the scheme came to naught. In 1385, Lancaster again clashed with the king, this time over the latter's refusal to personally lead an expedition to France. Royalist courtiers hatched an unsuccessful plot to assassinate the duke, which led to an angry confrontation between uncle and nephew and an eventual reconciliation brokered by the king's mother, Joan of Kent. In 1386, Gaunt led an expedition to Castile to enforce his claim to the Castilian throne. The campaign achieved little and the duke, after marrying his daughter by Constanza to the king of Castile, eventually renounced his claim. With the end of his Castilian ambitions, Lancaster no longer favored continuance of the Anglo-French war, and his return to England in 1389 allowed the king to resume personal control of the government, something that he had lost during the duke's absence to a prowar faction led by Lancaster's younger brother, THOMAS, DUKE OF GLOUCESTER.

Supporting the Truce of LEULINGHEN, Lancaster, who was created duke of Aquitaine in February 1390, played a leading role in Anglo-French peace negotiations and the arrangement of a marriage between Richard and Isabella, the daughter of CHARLES VI (see ISABELLA, QUEEN OF ENGLAND [1388–1409]). In 1396, Lancaster married his longtime mistress, Katherine Swynford, by whom he had four children who were later legitimated under the name Beaufort (see BEAUFORT, HENRY; BEAUFORT, THOMAS). Lancaster's death on 3 February 1399 was hastened by the king's banishment of his son, Henry of Bolingbroke, in September 1398. In July 1399, Bolingbroke returned to England, where he overthrew Richard and took the throne as HENRY IV, first king of the House of Lancaster.

Further Reading: Goodman, Anthony. *John of Gaunt: The Exercise of Princely Power in Fourteenth-Century Europe.* London: Longman, 1992.

JOHN OF LUXEMBOURG, KING OF BOHEMIA. *See* CRÉCY, BATTLE OF; EDWARD, THE BLACK PRINCE

JOHN THE FEARLESS, DUKE OF BURGUNDY (1371–1419)

John the Fearless, second VALOIS duke of BURGUNDY, was leader of the BURGUNDIAN faction during the FRENCH CIVIL WAR. Eager to assume his father's dominant role in the government of his mentally ill cousin, CHARLES VI, Burgundy ordered the assassination of his main rival, thereby initiating a period of internal strife that culminated both in his own murder and in the English conquest of NORMANDY.

The eldest son of PHILIP THE BOLD and MARGUERITE DE FLANDERS, John became count of Nevers in 1384. In 1396, Nevers led the Franco-Burgundian contingent that participated in the Crusade of Nicopolis, a largely Burgundian effort to aid the king of Hungary against the Turks. On 25 September, at the Battle of Nicopolis, Nevers won his appellation by leading a series of rash cavalry charges that ultimately destroyed his force and left him captive. Put to RANSOM, Nevers remained in Turkish custody for nine months, not returning to Burgundy until February 1398. Nevers succeeded his father as duke of Burgundy in April 1404, and inherited his mother's provinces in the Low Countries and western Germany in March 1405. A cold, brutal, and ambitious man, Burgundy also inherited his father's increasingly bitter political rivalry with the king's younger brother, LOUIS, DUKE OF ORLÉANS. Lacking his father's authority and experience, Burgundy was frequently outmaneuvered by Orléans, whose more attractive personality won him the support of Queen ISABEAU. Clashing initially over a proposed new tax, the cousins were soon at odds over Burgundy's desire for royal assistance in besieging CALAIS as retaliation for English attacks on FLANDERS. When the council, influenced by Orléans, rejected this request, Burgundy, in an effort to weaken his rival, began posing as a champion of governmental reform, a dangerous policy that won him much support in PARIS but also aroused popular expectations that the duke had no intention of fulfilling. In November 1407, Burgundy, finding his interests threatened and his ambitions thwarted, arranged Orléans's murder.

Upon admitting his crime, which he ascribed to the "intervention of the devil" (Perroy, 227), Burgundy was forbidden the council and forced to flee Paris. However, by taking advantage of the addled king's grief, Burgundy returned to court in February 1408, and on 8 March presented to the council a long document entitled the *JUSTI-*

FICATION OF THE DUKE OF BURGUNDY, which portrayed Orléans as a thief, traitor, and practitioner of black magic, whose murder was a justifiable act of tyrannicide, both "lawful and meritorious" (Perroy, 229). When these brazen claims were largely accepted by public opinion, the king pardoned Burgundy, although the supporters of CHARLES, the new duke of Orléans, continued to demand vengeance. By 1410, Burgundy dominated the king and court, forcing the duke's uncle, JOHN, DUKE OF BERRY; the constable, Charles, lord of ALBRET; and various other princes to protest their exclusion from power by joining the Orléanists, who were now known as ARMAGNACS due to the adherence to their cause of BERNARD, COUNT OF ARMAGNAC. Besieged in Paris in 1411, the duke, promising territorial concessions, sought military assistance from HENRY IV of England, who dispatched a small force to help break the siege. In 1412, when the Armagnacs negotiated a similar compact with Henry (*see* TREATY OF BOURGES), Burgundy defeated his enemies before the English could arrive, thus forcing the Armagnacs to repudiate their agreement and strengthening his hold on Paris.

In 1413, an attempt by his son-in-law, the dauphin, LOUIS, DUKE OF GUIENNE, to negotiate an end to the civil war, led the duke to incite the pro-Burgundian butchers of Paris to riot on behalf of his long promised program of reform. Known as CABOCHIENS, for one of their leaders, Simon Caboche, the rioters murdered opponents and overawed the court, initiating a reign of terror that soon passed beyond the duke's control. By summer, moderate city burgesses, alienated by the Cabochiens' excesses, joined with Guienne in inviting the Armagnacs into Paris. On 23 August, Burgundy, after an unsuccessful attempt to kidnap the king, fled the capital. Formally banished, Burgundy retreated to his domains, while the Armagnacs controlled the government. Like his rivals, Burgundy negotiated with HENRY V, but no agreement resulted and in February 1415 the two French factions concluded the Peace of Arras, which lifted Burgundy's banishment but did not restore him to power in Paris. The duke did not participate in the AGINCOURT campaign in 1415 and took no part in the defense of Normandy (*see* NORMAN CAMPAIGN [1417–1419]), preferring instead to war on the Armagnacs.

In May 1418, Burgundy, now allied with the queen, who, like most Parisians, had been alienated by an Armagnac regime nominally led by her remaining son, Dauphin Charles (*see* CHARLES VII), recaptured Paris. Since repelling the English required an accommodation with the dauphin, whom the duke believed to be weak and easily controlled, Burgundy opened talks with his opponents and reached a preliminary agreement at Corbeil in July 1419. To finalize the reconciliation, the dauphinists organized a new conference to be held in a specially prepared enclosure on the bridge at MONTEREAU on 10 September. During the course of the meeting, old servants of Orléans in the dauphin's entourage murdered Burgundy. Thereafter, the new duke, PHILIP THE GOOD, abandoned all attempts at peace and, as part of the subsequent Treaty of TROYES, concluded a formal ANGLO-BURGUNDIAN ALLIANCE.

Further Reading: Perroy, Edouard. *The Hundred Years War.* Trans. W. B. Wells. New York: Capricorn Books, 1965; Vaughan, Richard. *John the Fearless.* London: Longman, 1979.

JUSTIFICATION OF THE DUKE OF BURGUNDY (1408)

The *Justification of the Duke of Burgundy* (*Justification du duc de Bourgogne*) was a lengthy Latin document that justified the murder of LOUIS, DUKE OF ORLÉANS, as an act of heroic patriotism made necessary by the duke's many crimes and villainies. Presented to the king and council on 8 March 1408, the *Justification* transformed JOHN THE FEARLESS, duke of BURGUNDY and instigator of the murder, from a confessed killer to a selfless royal servant who had recognized and acted upon his duty to rid the state of a ruthless tyrant. Although an astoundingly brazen piece of political PROPAGANDA, the

document was well received by public opinion and thus instrumental in rehabilitating Burgundy and initiating the FRENCH CIVIL WAR.

Assassins murdered Orléans in PARIS on the night of 23 November 1407. On 26 November, Burgundy fled the capital, having confessed to his uncle, JOHN, DUKE OF BERRY, that he ordered the attack. Devastated by his brother's death and in the grip of chronic mental illness, CHARLES VI barred Burgundy from the council, but took no further action, despite the urgings of Orléans's wife and sons. Although sympathetic to the Orléans family, Berry and the other princes of the blood shrank from civil war and remained amenable to the king's desire to reconcile the royal family. Taking advantage of this opportunity, Burgundy negotiated his return to court in late February 1408. Always popular in Paris, Burgundy was welcomed by joyous crowds. Restored to the council, Burgundy now sought to portray himself not as a grateful penitent, but as a defender of the common good who was absolutely justified in his actions.

To this end, the duke commissioned Jean Petit, a University of Paris scholar, to prepare a detailed listing of the many misdeeds that had made the elimination of Orléans imperative for the maintenance of order and good government. Virtually everything ever said or rumored about Orléans was included in the *Justification*, which took Petit four hours to read to the council. The late duke was charged with employing black magic to kill the king by a slow and indetectible disorder that would arouse no suspicion. He also, according to the *Justification*, attempted to kill the king and the dauphin, LOUIS, DUKE OF GUIENNE, by various other means, including through the use of a poisoned apple, a cherry branch dipped in animal blood, and a sword consecrated by two devils and touched by the cadavers of executed criminals. The duke was also accused of plotting against the king with numerous foreign rulers, including the pope; his father-in-law, the duke of Milan; and HENRY IV of England, whom Orléans was to help overthrow

RICHARD II in return for the like service in deposing Charles VI. Among the duke's other alleged crimes were an attempt to kidnap Queen ISABEAU and the royal children, the seizure of royal castles and fortresses, and the levying of war taxes that were in fact used to fund attempts to usurp the Crown. Orléans, concluded Petit, was a godless tyrant whose murder, according to theology and history, was a good and necessary act for which the king should declare "the duke of Burgundy's loyalty and good fame both within and without the kingdom" (Vaughan, 72).

Although it is now impossible to know how much of the *Justification* was true, contemporary opinion, especially in Paris, largely believed it. The day after the document was presented, the king, accepting that his brother had plotted against him, pardoned Burgundy. Although the family and supporters of Orléans issued their own equally vituperative manifesto against Burgundy in September 1408, it received little attention. By the end of 1409, Burgundy controlled Paris, the court, and the government. By 1410, Berry and the other princes, stung more by their exclusion from power than by the murder of Orléans, precipitated civil war by rallying around CHARLES, eldest son of the late duke. *See also* ARMAGNACS; BURGUNDIANS.

Further Reading: Perroy, Edouard. *The Hundred Years War*. Trans. W. B. Wells. New York: Capricorn Books, 1965; Vaughan, Richard. *John the Fearless*. London: Longman, 1979.

K

KENT, EARL OF. *See* HOLLAND, THOMAS, EARL OF KENT

KNIGHTS OF THE STAR. *See* STAR, Order of the

KNOLLES, SIR ROBERT (c. 1325–1407)

A renowned leader of *ROUTIERS* who commanded armies for both EDWARD III and JOHN IV, duke of BRITTANY, Sir Robert Knolles (or Knollys) won land, wealth, and fame through his long service in the HUNDRED YEARS WAR.

Born into a Cheshire yeoman family, Knolles began his military career in 1346 at the Battle of LA ROCHE-DERRIEN in Brittany, where he served as an ARCHER under Sir Hugh CALVELEY. Although Knolles is often described as either the nephew or half brother of Calveley, with whom he was frequently associated during the war, no family relationship between the two men can be proven. In 1351, Knolles and Calveley participated in the famous COMBAT OF THE THIRTY, which led to both being taken captive. Shortly after his release, Knolles, who was beginning to acquire considerable land in Brittany, fought with Sir Walter BENTLEY at the Battle of MAURON in August 1352. In 1356–57, Knolles cemented his reputation as a warrior, serving with HENRY OF GROSMONT, duke of Lancaster, on a long *CHEVAUCHÉE* into NORMANDY and leading a daring attack on Honfleur that culminated in the destruction of a French army under Robert of Clermont, marshal of France.

In 1358–59, Knolles led a destructive raid into the Loire region, where the path of his army was marked by charred ruins known as "Knolles's mitres." In January 1359, after burning the suburbs of Orléans, Knolles took Auxerre, which paid him a huge RANSOM to withdraw in April. By the autumn, Knolles was back in Brittany, where he captured Bertrand du GUESCLIN at Pas d'Évran. When the Treaty of BRÉTIGNY formally ended the war in 1360, Knolles returned to England, where he was confirmed in possession of his French estates and pardoned for any crimes committed during his campaigns. In 1363, he entered the service of Duke John of Brittany, who granted Knolles the Breton lordships of Derval and Rougé. He fought under Sir John CHANDOS at AURAY in 1364, and, after a period of retirement following the signing of the Treaty of GUÉRANDE and the end of the BRETON CIVIL WAR, Knolles joined EDWARD, THE BLACK PRINCE, for the Spanish campaign that ended with the Battle of NÁJERA in April 1367.

In 1370, the English government offered Knolles command of a major expedition. When captains of higher rank refused to serve under the lowborn Knolles, he was forced to share command with three other knights, an arrangement that led to disagreements and divided leadership. Although the English raided in a wide arc across northern France, the French, using the Fabian tactics adopted by CHARLES V, refused to give battle, and in the autumn the quarrelling commanders split up. Knolles reached the safety of his fortresses in Brittany, but the force under Sir Thomas Grandison was decisively defeated by du Guesclin at Pontvallain near Le Mans on 4 December. Blamed for the failure of the campaign, Knolles fell out of favor at the English court and spent the next few years fighting in Brittany, Normandy, and AQUITAINE. He was pardoned for the 1370 campaign in 1374 and in about 1378 was retained by JOHN OF GAUNT, duke of Lancaster. In 1379, Knolles was appointed to defend the Kentish coasts and in 1380 he joined THOMAS OF WOODSTOCK, earl of Buckingham, in a *chevauchée* that largely retraced the route of the 1370 expedition. In 1381, Knolles was back in England, where he helped suppress the PEASANTS' REVOLT. Now an English landowner with increasing mercantile interests, Knolles was sufficiently wealthy to make loans of over £6,000 to RICHARD II. Knolles died in retirement at his Norfolk manor of Sculthorpe on 15 August 1407.

Further Reading: Fowler, Kenneth. *The King's Lieutenant: Henry of Grosmont, First Duke of Lancaster, 1310–1361.* London: Elek, 1969; Goodman, Anthony. *John of Gaunt: The Exercise of Princely Power in Fourteenth-Century Europe.* London: Longman, 1992; Sumption, Jonathan. *The Hundred Years War.* Vol. 2, *Trial by Fire.* Philadelphia: University of Pennsylvania Press, 2001.

L

LA HIRE. **LA HIRE.** *See* VIGNOLLES, ÉTIENNE DE

LANCASTER, DUKE OF. *See* HENRY OF GROSMONT, DUKE OF LANCASTER; JOHN OF GAUNT, DUKE OF LANCASTER

LANCASTER, HOUSE OF

The House of Lancaster, a branch of the English royal House of PLANTAGENET, was the ruling dynasty of England from 1399 to 1461, and then again briefly in 1470–71. The family came to power when Henry, duke of Lancaster, deposed and supplanted his cousin RICHARD II. Although the dynasty's right to the English throne was thus questionable, HENRY V, the second Lancastrian king, was convinced that he was also rightful king of France. This conviction underlay the fifteenth-century resumption of the HUNDRED YEARS WAR, a phase of the struggle sometimes referred to as the Lancastrian war.

The family of Lancaster descended from JOHN OF GAUNT, duke of Lancaster, the third son of EDWARD III. At Gaunt's death in 1399, his son, Henry of Bolingbroke, who had opposed the court in the 1380s, was in temporary exile, having been banished for ten years by Richard II. When the king made his cousin's exile permanent and confiscated the extensive Lancastrian patrimony, his arbitrary actions alienated the English nobility. In July, while Richard was in Ireland, Bolingbroke returned to England and assumed leadership of a growing opposition movement. By September, the king was in custody. Because Richard had no children, and his heir presumptive, Edmund Mortimer, earl of March, great-grandson of

Gaunt's elder brother, Lionel, duke of Clarence, was only eight, Bolingbroke was the obvious choice to replace Richard. Beyond his maturity, experience, and Plantagenet blood, Bolingbroke was already master of the kingdom. Although his usurpation was duly recognized by PARLIAMENT, Bolingbroke, now HENRY IV, sought to justify his actions. He countenanced rumors that the marriage of EDWARD, THE BLACK PRINCE, Richard's father, was irregular, thus throwing doubt on the ex-king's legitimacy. He also publicly declared himself the legitimate king by right of descent from Edmund of Lancaster (known as "Crouchback"), the younger brother of EDWARD I. This proclamation took as true the popular belief that Edmund was actually the elder brother, and had been prevented from ascending the throne because of physical deformity.

By thus repudiating descent from Edward III, these specious attempts to legitimize the family's seizure of the English throne essentially destroyed any claim it had to the French throne. However, Henry ignored this and, like his predecessors, proclaimed himself king of France. Although internal rebellion and illness prevented Henry IV from resuming the war, Henry V, who succeeded his father in 1413, rallied the country behind the dynasty by invading France in 1415. Interested in controlling the entire kingdom, not merely individual provinces, Henry won a major victory at AGINCOURT in 1415, and then, taking advantage of internal divisions caused by the FRENCH CIVIL WAR, conquered NORMANDY by 1420. In the subsequent Treaty of TROYES, CHARLES VI disinherited his son and recognized Henry as his heir.

Thus, the treaty, which also arranged Henry's marriage to Charles's daughter, CATHERINE OF VALOIS, became the legal basis of the Lancastrian claim to the French Crown. When Henry and Charles both died in 1422, the Crown of France passed under the treaty to Henry V's ten-month-old son.

HENRY VI, who may have inherited Charles VI's mental instability, was weak-minded and politically inept. Lacking strong leadership, the English were expelled from France in 1453. Henry, shortly after hearing news of the final defeat at CASTILLON, fell into a prolonged stupor that rendered him unaware of his surroundings and unable to communicate. His inability to function as king split the nobility into rival factions and revived the long dormant Mortimer claim, thereby precipitating the English civil conflict known as the Wars of the Roses. In 1460, RICHARD, DUKE OF YORK, laid claim to the throne as the rightful heir, through his Mortimer mother, of Richard II. In 1461, three months after York's death in battle, his son seized the throne as Edward IV, first king of the House of York. Henry VI was restored in October 1470, but then deposed again in April 1471. He was slain at the Tower of London on 21 May, shortly after his only son died in battle. The Lancastrian claim to the English Crown thereupon passed to Henry's distant kinsman, Henry Tudor, earl of Richmond, who in 1485 became the first king of the House of Tudor. *See also* HUNDRED YEARS WAR, PHASES OF; MARGARET OF ANJOU.

Further Reading: Allmand, Christopher, *Henry V*. Berkeley: University of California Press, 1992; Griffiths, Ralph A., *The Reign of King Henry VI*. Berkeley: University of California Press, 1981; Kirby, John Lavan, *Henry IV of England*. London: Constable, 1970; Wolffe, Bertram, *Henry VI*. London: Eyre Methuen, 1981.

LA ROCHE-DERRIEN, BATTLE OF (1347)

The Battle of La Roche-Derrien was fought on 20 June 1347 outside the north Breton town of the same name. Resulting in the capture of CHARLES OF BLOIS, the French-backed claimant to the duchy of BRITTANY, the battle crippled the Bloisian cause and left the English firmly entrenched in the duchy. La Roche-Derrien also forced PHILIP VI, then seeking to break EDWARD III's siege of CALAIS, to divert men and resources to retrieving the French position in the BRETON CIVIL WAR.

In late May 1347, Charles of Blois laid siege to La Roche-Derrien, which was held by a garrison commanded by Richard Totesham. Because of its ruthless imposition of *PÂTIS*, especially the demand for labor to build and maintain fortifications, the garrison was hated by the peasants of the surrounding countryside, who flocked to Blois's army brandishing homemade weapons. Because his army numbered over three thousand men, a much larger force than was required to take the town, it is likely that Blois's real intent was to compel Sir Thomas DAGWORTH, the English governor in Brittany, to give battle.

Dagworth took three weeks to raise a force of no more than a thousand men, which he marched to a position near La Roche-Derrien on 19 June. When reconnaissance indicated that Blois's force was split into four parts, each covering one section of the wall and each divided from the others by woods and marsh, Dagworth planned a predawn attack on the largest group, which was camped east of town and under Blois's direct command. However, when a diversion against the western camp failed, the eastern assault was quickly repulsed, with Dagworth and some of his men taken captive. The tide turned when the growing light revealed the situation to Totesham; he led his garrison and several hundred hatchet-wielding townsmen in a surprise attack on the rear of the French position, which speedily collapsed, allowing the rescue of Dagworth and his fellows.

Blois, fighting fiercely and covered with wounds, was eventually cornered and forced to surrender, which he did to a Breton knight rather than to the lowborn Dagworth. Each of the remaining French contingents was then attacked and defeated in turn. The darkness made it difficult to take prisoners, so French

This illustration from the *Chronicles* of Jean Froissart depicts the defeat of an English Fleet by a Castilian fleet allied with France in the naval Battle of La Rochelle, 1372. *Erich Lessing/Art Resource, New York.*

CASUALTIES were high, with over six hundred dead, including most of Blois's leading noble supporters. Upon receiving news of the battle, Philip VI assumed direct charge of Brittany, to which he dispatched a force of seven hundred men under Amaury de Craon in early July. In 1348, when he was finally able to travel, Blois, whose RANSOM Dagworth had sold to Edward III, was transported to England, where he joined DAVID II of SCOTLAND and the prisoners of CRÉCY in the Tower of London.

Further Reading: Burne, Alfred H. *The Crécy War.* Ware, England: Wordsworth Editions Ltd., 1999; Sumption, Jonathan. *The Hundred Years War.* Vol. 1, *Trial by Battle.* Philadelphia: University of Pennsylvania Press, 1991.

LA ROCHELLE, BATTLE OF (1372)

The Battle of La Rochelle was an Anglo-Castilian naval engagement fought in the waters off the French port of La Rochelle on 23 June 1372. The battle, which resulted in destruction of the English fleet, accelerated the collapse of English authority in AQUITAINE and facilitated the eventual French capture of La Rochelle.

When CHARLES V, through his acceptance of the APPEAL OF THE GASCON LORDS, reignited the HUNDRED YEARS WAR in 1369, the Aquitinian nobility, carefully cultivated by Charles and deeply discontented with the rule of EDWARD, THE BLACK PRINCE, began defecting to the VALOIS. By 1372, Poitou, Périgord, Quercy, Rouergue, and Agenais were largely lost to the English, and even BORDEAUX was under threat from the armies of LOUIS, DUKE OF ANJOU. Advised by Guichard d'Angle, the marshal of Aquitaine, that many Poitevans would readily resume their English allegiance if supported by sufficient arms and money, the English government, with much travail, gathered a fleet of ships to transport reinforcements to La Rochelle. To further reinvigorate the English cause in Poitou, the expedition also carried £20,000, collected with even more difficulty, for disbursement among the local nobility. The expedition was commanded by d'Angle and by John Hastings, the 26-year-old earl of Pembroke, who was also appointed governor of Aquitaine.

As the English ships approached La Rochelle, they found their path blocked by a waiting Castilian fleet, summoned by Charles V under terms of the Franco-Castilian accord by which the French had helped Henry of Trastámare win the Castilian throne in 1369 (*see* WAR OF CASTILIAN SUCCESSION). The 200-ton Castilian galleons were more maneuverable than the square-rigged English ships, which were mainly transport vessels, not fighting ships. Commanded by professional sailors who were experienced in naval warfare, the Castilian fleet also had an advantage in leadership over the English fleet, whose commanders were more accustomed to fighting on land. Carrying 180 oarsmen apiece, the Castilian galleons rammed the English vessels, while Castilian sailors on deck set fire to the enemy rigging and pelted the English ARCHERS with stones and other missiles. The English fleet was quickly overcome, with many vessels sunk and many others captured, including the ship carrying the £20,000. Pembroke, d'Angle, and many English knights were captured and taken back to Castile, where they were imprisoned for more than a year. Weakened by his confinement, Pembroke, whose RANSOM had been sold to Bertrand du GUESCLIN, died on his way home. In September 1372, du Guesclin, with the help of the mayor, forced the capitulation of the unreinforced garrison at La Rochelle, and by the start of 1374, the enlarged Aquitaine created by the Treaty of BRÉTIGNY had ceased to exist. English authority in southwestern France was thereafter confined to Bordeaux and coastal GASCONY.

Further Reading: Packe, Michael. *King Edward III.* Ed. L. C. B. Seaman. London: Routledge and Kegan Paul, 1983; Seward, Desmond. *The Hundred Years War.* New York: Penguin, 1999.

LA TRÉMOÏLLE, GEORGES DE. *See* CHARLES VII

LAUNAC, BATTLE OF. *See* ALBRET, ARNAUD-AMANIEU, LORD OF

LES-ESPAGNOLS-SUR-MER, BATTLE OF. *See* WINCHELSEA, BATTLE OF

"LETTER TO THE ENGLISH." *See* JOAN OF ARC

LEULINGHEN, TRUCE OF (1389)

Concluded on 18 June 1389 at Leulinghen on the border of English-held CALAIS, the Truce of Leulinghen, while not a final settlement of outstanding issues, stopped the fighting and effectively ended the second phase of the HUNDRED YEARS WAR. Although frequently extended, the truce collapsed before its official expiration because the deposition of the English king and the intensification of the FRENCH CIVIL WAR destroyed support for peace in both countries.

In late 1387, a group of English barons led by RICHARD II's uncle, THOMAS OF WOODSTOCK, duke of Gloucester, seized control of the royal government. Tired of rule by royal favorites and anxious to resume the war, the baronial regime soon found itself too poor and insecure to implement the war policy that had brought it to power. In August 1388, the baronial council, with the reluctant acquiescence of Gloucester, agreed to negotiate, and talks opened in the parish church at Leulinghen in November. In that same month, a coup led by LOUIS, DUKE OF ORLÉANS, brother of CHARLES VI, and backed by the MARMOUSETS, overthrew the government of the royal uncles in France. True to the policy of CHARLES V, the Marmousets welcomed the English peace initiative and the two governments soon agreed to a three-year cessation of hostilities and the initiation of talks for a permanent settlement.

In May 1389, Richard, following Charles's example, declared himself of full age and dismissed his baronial keepers. Thereafter, the intermittent Anglo-French negotiations, and the various extensions of the truce that accompanied them, were largely driven by Richard's desire for peace. Abandoning the policy of EDWARD III, Richard agreed to hold AQUITAINE as a vassal of the French king, so long as the terms of his obligation were clearly defined as requiring no more than simple homage. The French rejected this proposal, insisting on liege homage, which placed the vassal under personal obligation to his overlord. The English also demanded that Aquitaine be reconstituted as it had existed at the time of EDWARD, THE BLACK PRINCE. Such a restoration would have required surrender of most of the gains achieved under Charles V. Surprisingly, the French were willing to partially meet this demand and to pay the remaining balance of

JOHN II's RANSOM, so long as the English withdrew from Calais, a requirement that Richard could not accept.

With the talks at a standstill and the truce set to lapse, a personal tragedy allowed Richard to continue his peace policy. The death of Queen Anne of Bohemia in 1394, although personally devastating to the king, allowed Richard to seek a marriage alliance with the VALOIS. On 9 March 1396, Richard, who was then twenty-nine, was married by proxy to Isabella, the eight-year-old daughter of Charles VI (*see* ISABELLA, QUEEN OF ENGLAND [1388–1409]). Although no final agreement could be reached, the Truce of Leulinghen was extended for almost thirty years, promising peace for the next generation.

However, in England, the peace policy was unpopular and its continuance rested largely on the king's ability to impose it on the nobility. In September 1399, Henry of Bolingbroke, the son of JOHN OF GAUNT, late duke of Lancaster, overthrew his cousin and took the throne as HENRY IV. Although prolonged resistance to his usurpation prevented him from actively implementing it, Henry won the throne in part by promising to pursue a war policy. In France, the growing rivalry between Orléans, who advocated renewal of the war against an insecure Henry IV, and JOHN THE FEARLESS, duke of BURGUNDY, who supported maintenance of the truce, split the French nobility and shifted their attention from the English threat to the pursuit of their own quarrels. Thus, by 1413, the outbreak of civil war in France and the accession of the young and ambitious HENRY V to the English throne rendered the Truce of Leulinghen inoperative and paved the way for the renewal of war with the 1415 English invasion of France.

Further Reading: Neillands, Robin. *The Hundred Years War.* London: Routledge, 1991; Perroy, Edouard. *The Hundred Years War.* Trans. W. B. Wells. New York: Capricorn Books, 1965.

LIBELLUS FAMOSUS. See CRISIS OF 1340–1341; STRATFORD, JOHN, ARCHBISHOP OF CANTERBURY

LIBOURNE, TREATY OF. *See* EDWARD, THE BLACK PRINCE

LIMOGES, SACK OF (1370)

Occurring in September 1370, the sack of Limoges, a city on the Vienne River about one hundred miles northeast of BORDEAUX, was the last major military operation conducted by EDWARD, THE BLACK PRINCE. Although long characterized as a horrific massacre of noncombatants perpetrated by an ill and angry prince, the sack is today considered to have been less destructive of civilian life than is portrayed in the chief source for the period, the *Chronicles* of Jean FROISSART.

On 21 August 1370, an army led by JOHN, DUKE OF BERRY, younger brother of CHARLES V, arrived outside Limoges. The town had two parts. The first, dominated by the castle, was held by a strong English garrison; the second, the *cité*, or administrative center dominated by the cathedral and governed by the bishop, had no English troops. By the 1259 Treaty of PARIS, the fortress and its surrounding town had been ceded to the king-duke of AQUITAINE, but the episcopal *cité* had continued under French control. In 1360, the whole of Limoges had become part of the English-held duchy of Aquitaine under the Treaty of BRÉTIGNY. Ignoring the English garrison in the castle, Berry laid siege to the *cité*, which Bishop Jean de Cros surrendered without a fight on 24 August. Berry then installed a small French garrison and withdrew. News of this defection enraged the Black Prince. The bishop was godfather to the prince's eldest son, and Edward had considered de Cros a trusted friend.

Accompanied by his brothers, JOHN OF GAUNT, duke of Lancaster, and EDMUND OF LANGLEY, the prince, who was forced by illness to travel by litter, left Angoulême on 7 September with an army of over three thousand men. Reaching Limoges on 14 September, the prince ordered that the walls of the *cité* be mined. Because Berry's army was still in the area, and another French force under Constable Bertrand du GUESCLIN was also nearby, the English were anxious to retake the town quickly. The mine was fired early on 19 September and a section of the wall collapsed, allowing the English to pour into the town, overwhelm the garrison, and capture its leaders. Also taken captive, the bishop was threatened with execution, but eventually released, while the French commanders were held to RANSOM.

According to Froissart, the English slaughtered the inhabitants of the town, with more than "three thousand persons, men, women, and children...dragged out to have their throats cut" (Froissart, 178), and the prince angrily rejecting all entreaties to restrain his men. However, other contemporary accounts put the number of dead at three hundred and make no mention of the massacre of civilians. While some noncombatants may have died in the assault, and most of the men under arms were probably slain, Froissart's wholesale destruction of civilians is unlikely to have occurred. What made the fall of Limoges memorable was the virtual razing of the *cité* after it had been thoroughly pillaged. Meant as a warning to other towns thinking about abandoning their English allegiance, the sack of Limoges did little to deter defections and served only to highlight the prince's inability to effectively reassert his authority. Increasingly ill, and disheartened by the recent death of his son and the deterioration of English authority in Aquitaine, the prince returned to England in January 1371.

Further Reading: Barber, Richard. *Edward, Prince of Wales and Aquitaine*. New York: Charles Scribner's Sons, 1978; Froissart, Jean. *Chronicles*. Trans. Geoffrey Brereton. New York: Penguin 1978.

LINCOLN, BISHOP OF. See BURGHERSH, HENRY, BISHOP OF LINCOLN

LOIRE CAMPAIGN (1429)

Led by JOAN OF ARC, the French Loire Campaign of June 1429 followed up the relief of ORLÉANS by freeing the Loire Valley of English garrisons and clearing a path to Rheims, where the dauphin could be crowned as King CHARLES VII.

The French broke the English siege of Orléans on 8 May 1429. However, English garrisons installed in the previous autumn by Thomas MONTAGU, earl of Salisbury, continued to control the nearby Loire towns of Jargeau, Beaugency, and Meung-sur-Loire. Although many possible objectives were considered for a new campaign, Joan insisted that priority be given to completion of the second part of her mission, the crowning of the dauphin at Rheims. The first step toward this goal was the reduction of English garrisons along the Loire, to which the dauphin agreed in early June. Thus, on 10 June, after a month spent reinforcing and resupplying the army, which had been seriously worn down at Orléans, the French, now about six thousand strong, began to move against Jargeau. Although Joan was again accompanied by all the captains of Orléans, including John, the Bastard of Orléans (*see* JOHN, COUNT OF DUNOIS AND LONGUEVILLE); Étienne de VIGNOLLES (La Hire); and Poton de XAINTRAILLES, overall command of the army was given to JOHN, DUKE OF ALENÇON, the dauphin's friend and kinsman.

The attack on Jargeau, which lay east of Orléans, began on 11 June, when the French beat back an English sortie and captured most of the suburbs. On 12 June, French ARTILLERY began battering the walls. The English commander, William de la POLE, earl of Suffolk, tried to arrange surrender talks with La Hire, but the French leadership rejected the overture. At Joan's urging, Alençon followed the bombardment with an assault on the town. The attack finally succeeded when the Maid, who had been in the thick of the battle encouraging the men, was knocked down by a stone thrown from the walls. Upon seeing her rise and urge them forward, the French renewed the assault and carried the town; Suffolk was taken prisoner, and most of his men were killed or captured.

On 15 June, the French marched west of Orléans to assault the fortified bridge at Meung, which they captured and garrisoned. With John TALBOT and his men thus trapped in Meung, the French continued west to Beaugency, where on about 16 June the army was joined by a thousand men under Arthur de Richemont, constable of France (*see* ARTHUR III). Although Richemont was currently out of favor with the dauphin and thus should not have been received, Joan welcomed him and his men when an English relief force under Sir John FASTOLF arrived outside Beaugency on 17 June. While continuing the assault on the town, the French formed line of battle, inviting Fastolf to attack. Perhaps aware of the presence of Richemont and his men, Fastolf refused and withdrew to Meung. The French then returned to Beaugency, which the English commanders, Matthew Gough and Richard Guestin, surrendered that evening.

Next day, 18 June, Fastolf attacked the bridge at Meung, but his assault failed. As elements of the French army arrived from Beaugency, Fastolf decided to abandon Meung and retreat northward with his army and Talbot's garrison. With Joan again demanding speed, the French pursued their foes and that afternoon caught and defeated them at PATAY, thus clearing the Loire Valley of English and opening the road to Rheims.

Further Reading: Burne, Alfred H. *The Agincourt War*. Ware, England: Wordsworth Editions Ltd., 1999; DeVries, Kelly. *Joan of Arc: A Military Leader*. Stroud, England: Sutton Publishing, 2003.

LONDON

By far the largest city in the realm, London was the center of English trade and commerce and thus a major source of Crown revenue. The royal government, headquartered in Westminster two miles west of the city, relied heavily on loans and taxes raised from the merchants and residents of London to pay for the HUNDRED YEARS WAR. As a result, London's wartime relations with the English Crown were generally more volatile than PARIS's relations with the French Crown. Strong and militarily successful kings, such as EDWARD III and HENRY V, had little trouble tapping the city's wealth, while weak or less martial mon-

archs, such as RICHARD II and HENRY VI, found themselves or their governments frequently at odds with Londoners.

London was a magnet for both knightly and peasant immigrants from the countryside; its population in the late fourteenth century is estimated at almost ninety thousand, even though the BLACK DEATH had reduced it by one-third in the late 1340s. Dominated by the great craft guilds, whose members were freemen of the city and thus entitled to vote and hold office, London by the 1330s had enjoyed a century of self-government. The chief municipal officer was the mayor, who, with two sheriffs and a council of aldermen, governed the city and presided over its courts. A legislative body, the Court of Common Council, was established in the fourteenth century. Royal attempts to withdraw or limit the city's rights and liberties along with royal demands for money were the most frequent causes of conflict between London and the Crown. Such hostility had been common in the century before Edward III's accession in 1327. Henry III, EDWARD I, and EDWARD II had each imposed direct royal rule on the city at some point during their reigns. Strong, popular, and victorious, Edward III was able to extract the war funding he needed from the city without doing so, even though he followed policies that often harmed London's economy. Edward's manipulation of the wool trade in the late 1330s (*see* DORDRECHT BONDS) and his selling of special trade licenses to foreign merchants in the 1360s were particularly resented.

In the 1370s, the new vulnerability of English overseas trade, as illustrated by the naval disaster at LA ROCHELLE, and a sharp decline in the aging king's personal authority caused London's relations with the Crown to deteriorate. In 1376, the so-called Good PARLIAMENT impeached various corrupt and incompetent government officials, including three royalist members of the Court of Aldermen. The city was particularly hostile to JOHN OF GAUNT, duke of Lancaster, who dominated the royal government in the last years of Edward III and the first of Richard

II. Already unpopular because of an unsuccessful war and his failure to protect English vessels from French attacks on the high seas, Lancaster further angered Londoners by granting extensive trading rights to Italian merchants, thereby seriously threatening the city's commercial supremacy. The result was city support, at least in its early stages, for the PEASANTS' REVOLT OF 1381, during which Lancaster's magnificent London residence, the Savoy, was destroyed by rebellious Londoners.

Under Richard II, London's relations with the Crown worsened. Alienated by the king's extravagant court, Londoners strongly supported THOMAS OF WOODSTOCK, duke of Gloucester, and the other Appellants when, as part of their attempt to curb Richard's authority, they tried and executed the city's royalist mayor, Nicholas Brembre, in 1388. In 1392, Richard, now back in power, punished the city's refusal to loan him money by revoking London's privileges and liberties, seizing control of its revenues, and imposing an enormous fine of £100,000. Although the king eventually reduced the fine and restored some of the privileges, London warmly welcomed HENRY IV when he deposed Richard in 1399.

Relations with the Crown improved under the House of LANCASTER. The city made frequent loans to the impecunious Henry IV, with three-time mayor Richard Whittington loaning the king almost £25,000 by 1413. Although plague, foreign competition, and French depredations depressed trade and population in the early fifteenth century, the popular Henry V had little trouble obtaining loans and TAXATION from London. In the city, Henry's revival of the war was popular, promising a restoration of national glory, safe sea lanes, and profits from plunder and RANSOMS. The king's clever PROPAGANDA efforts, including much triumphant pageantry surrounding celebrations of his victory at AGINCOURT, his conclusion of the Treaty of TROYES, and his marriage to CATHERINE OF VALOIS, ensured civic support for his campaigns. In 1416, Londoners enthusiastically responded to the

king's call for supplies to relieve besieged HARFLEUR, and, in 1418, when Henry, then besieging ROUEN, requested food and drink "for the refreshing of us and our said host" (Inwood, 82), they readily dispatched conveyances with the needed supplies.

All this changed after Henry's death in 1422. For economic and patriotic reasons, Londoners strongly supported the maintenance of Lancastrian France, and the city invested heavily in the war during its last two decades. Between the late 1420s and the Battle of CASTILLON in 1453, London loaned the Crown an average of £6,000 per year. However, by the 1440s, defeat in France and economic depression at home generated much anger in the city against the royal government, which was seen as dominated by corrupt and incompetent courtiers, such as William de la POLE, duke of Suffolk. In 1450, Londoners were initially sympathetic to JACK CADE'S REBELLION, but when the rebels looted the city, opinion in London turned against them, and on the night of 5 July the citizens joined the Tower garrison in expelling the insurgents. By the end of the war, dissatisfaction with Henry VI was already turning into support for his rival, RICHARD, DUKE OF YORK, whose faction retained the allegiance of London throughout most of the subsequent civil war. *See also* TOWNS AND THE HUNDRED YEARS WAR.

Further Reading: Baker, Timothy. *Medieval London.* New York: Praeger, 1970; Inwood, Stephen. *A History of London.* New York: Carroll and Graf Publishers, 1998; Sheppard, Francis. *London: A History.* Oxford: Oxford University Press, 1998; Williams, Gwyn A. *Medieval London from Commune to Capital.* London: Athlone, 1970.

LONDON, FIRST TREATY OF (1358)
Concluded on 8 May 1358 in a formal ceremony held in the hall of Windsor Castle, the First Treaty of London (also known as the Treaty of Windsor) was the initial Anglo-French accord negotiated after the English capture of JOHN II at POITIERS in 1356. More an agreement as to John's RANSOM terms than a settlement of outstanding issues, the

treaty failed because its financial terms could not be met by a French government weakened by internal disorder.

Negotiations between John II and EDWARD III began in LONDON in September 1357. Little progress was made until November, when news arrived of the escape from prison of CHARLES THE BAD, king of Navarre, an event that greatly increased the likelihood of civil war in France and further weakened the VALOIS hold on the French throne. With John anxious to return to France, and Edward anxious to take advantage of his captive's desperation, a provisional treaty was concluded by the end of the year. The agreement set John's ransom at 4 million écus (£667,000). The sum of 600,000 écus (£100,000) was to be paid by 1 November 1358 to secure John's release, with the rest of the ransom to come in regular installments over a period of years. Edward was also to receive, in full sovereignty, most of southwestern France, about a quarter of the kingdom. In the north, John surrendered CALAIS and its pale, the county of Ponthieu, the town of Montreuil, and the Norman lands left to Edward by Godfrey of HARCOURT. Other clauses called for the restoration of Navarre's brother, Philip, to all his French lands and for an eventual resolution of the BRETON CIVIL WAR. The treaty demanded no concessions of Edward and required John to secure performance of his undertakings with the surrender of numerous hostages, including most of the chief nobles of France and two prominent citizens from each of the 20 largest towns.

While humiliating to John, the terms of the treaty were actually less harsh than those of the abortive Treaty of GUINES of 1354, Edward having dropped his claims to NORMANDY and the western Loire Valley. Nonetheless, in France, the agreement was widely opposed, especially in PARIS. In February 1358, the Estates-General rejected the treaty and sought to limit John's power to conduct negotiations while a prisoner. Although the dauphin (see CHARLES V) gradually strengthened his position as head of the French state, revolution in Paris, the JACQUERIE uprisings, the brigandage of Anglo-Gascon ROUTIERS,

and the intrigues of Navarre left his government weak and distracted and made collection of the first ransom payment impossible. When no money arrived on 1 November, and a French embassy asked Edward for more time, complaining that the depredations of his own subjects were preventing fulfillment of the agreement, Edward angrily declared that the *routiers* were not his responsibility and demanded strict compliance with every treaty provision. With this clearly impossible, Edward informed the dauphin on 20 November that he was no longer bound by the treaty and would resume the war on expiration of the truce. The First Treaty of London was thus dead by late 1358, although Edward and John soon began new talks that led to conclusion of the Second Treaty of London in March 1359. *See also* BRÉTIGNY, TREATY OF; ESTATES, GENERAL AND PROVINCIAL; LONDON, SECOND TREATY OF.

Further Reading: Curry, Anne. *The Hundred Years War.* 2nd ed. Houndmills, England: Palgrave Macmillan, 2003; Sumption, Jonathan. *The Hundred Years War.* Vol. 2, *Trial by Fire.* Philadelphia: University of Pennsylvania Press, 2001.

LONDON, SECOND TREATY OF (1359)

Negotiated in little more than a month between a captive king and his captor, the Second Treaty of London was sealed by the monarchs of England and France in LONDON on 24 March 1359. Desperate to return to France where internal disorder and the rebellion of CHARLES THE BAD, king of Navarre, threatened the continuance of the VALOIS dynasty, JOHN II was willing to make almost any concession to win his release. Even though he had little knowledge of conditions in France, where the political position of his son, the dauphin (*see* CHARLES V), had recently improved, John rapidly concluded an agreement that represented an almost complete surrender to EDWARD III.

When failure to pay the initial installment of John's RANSOM led Edward to abandon the First Treaty of London (*see* LONDON, FIRST TREATY OF) in November 1358, the French king and his advisors, all captives in London, concluded that further territorial concessions were required to end the war and convince Edward to join with John in crushing Navarre's uprising. Thus, while the ransom terms of the new agreement were similar to those of the first treaty—a total of 4 million écus (£667,000), a first installment of 600,000 écus (£100,000) due by 1 August 1359, and the surrender of hostages to guarantee the rest—the territorial concessions were far more extensive. Besides the surrender of southwestern France called for in the first treaty, the second agreement also gave Edward NORMANDY, BRITTANY, Maine, Anjou, and Touraine, all in full sovereignty. In effect, the treaty recreated the twelfth-century Angevin Empire of Henry II. Along with CALAIS and an enlarged pale that included the Boulonnais, Edward would dispossess the Valois of almost half their kingdom and control all the French Atlantic provinces except FLANDERS and Picardy. For his part, Edward agreed to renounce his claim to the French throne, to release John upon delivery of the initial ransom payment, and to join the French king in making war on Navarre should he fail to accept the treaty by 24 June.

Because the agreement was so favorable to Edward, some chroniclers speculated that the English king had never expected it to be ratified by the French, but had instead imposed its impossible terms merely as a means of justifying another invasion of France once the treaty was rejected. Although possible, such a ploy seems unlikely, for both kings sincerely tried to convince their subjects to accept the agreement. In France, despite John's support, the treaty met great resistance. PARIS and other towns were appalled by the prospect of England controlling the mouths of most major French rivers, while taxpayers in the remaining Valois territories, seeing some of the richest provinces handed to the PLANTAGENETS, refused to be saddled with the entire burden of John's ransom. When the Estates-General met in Paris on 19 May 1359, the deputies, after long deliberations, pronounced the treaty unacceptable and urged the dauphin to reject it and prepare for war. When Ed-

ward learned of this decision, he abandoned the treaty and announced his intention of invading France before the end of the year. Recruitment for a campaign aimed at the capture of Rheims, the traditional coronation site of French kings, began in June. Thus, the RHEIMS CAMPAIGN, launched in October 1359, had as its objective the crowning of Edward as king of France. *See also* BRÉTIGNY, TREATY OF; ESTATES, GENERAL AND PROVINCIAL.

Further Reading: Curry, Anne. *The Hundred Years War*. 2nd ed. Houndmills, England: Palgrave Macmillan, 2003; Sumption, Jonathan. *The Hundred Years War*. Vol. 2, *Trial by Fire*. Philadelphia: University of Pennsylvania Press, 2001.

LONGBOW. *See* ARCHERS

LONGUEVILLE, COUNT OF. *See* JOHN, COUNT OF DUNOIS AND LONGUEVILLE

LORDS APPELLANT. *See* RICHARD II; THOMAS OF WOODSTOCK, DUKE OF GLOUCESTER

LOUIS, DUKE OF ANJOU (1339–1384)
Louis, duke of Anjou, was the second son of JOHN II and the brother of CHARLES V. Embittered by his experience as an English hostage, Anjou opposed the Treaty of BRÉTIGNY and sought the conquest of AQUITAINE. As his brother's lieutenant in Languedoc after 1364, he strove to undermine the English position in southwestern France.

In 1354, when Anjou was only fifteen, John II gave his son as a hostage to CHARLES THE BAD, king of Navarre, who required a safe-conduct before traveling to PARIS to receive pardon for murder. Although present at the Battle of POITIERS in September 1356, Anjou did not witness his father's capture, having left the field when his uncle, Philip, duke of Orléans, mistakenly withdrew his men after the initial French attack.

In 1360, Anjou, acting under compulsion, surrendered himself to the English as a hostage for his father's RANSOM. Having recently married for love, Anjou was particularly frustrated by the slow pace of negotiations and the failure of the French government to make sufficient payment to secure his release. He was therefore one of the signatories to the 1362 Treaty of the HOSTAGES, a private agreement negotiated by the captives with EDWARD III. The treaty won the hostages' removal to CALAIS, but otherwise became a dead letter when Anjou broke parole by refusing to return to English custody after a three-day visit to his wife. The English proclaimed his flight shameful and dishonorable, and his father demanded his return, but Anjou refused, and John's voluntary return to captivity was motivated in part by a desire to restore his family's honor.

An intelligent man and an astute politician, Anjou, unlike his brothers, was also a competent soldier. However, his many gifts, as one contemporary writer declared, "were tarnished by his unbounded greed" (Sumption, 527) and his lust for power. The duke harbored designs on the kingdoms of Majorca and Naples, and, as lieutenant of Languedoc, conducted a semi-independent foreign policy that generally supported his brother's goals but always furthered his own ambitions.

Anjou led opposition to the Brétigny settlement and, from his position in Languedoc, worked secretly to obstruct the English administration in Aquitaine. He orchestrated French intervention in the CASTILIAN WAR OF SUCCESSION in 1365 and again two years later after the initial effort collapsed in defeat at NÁJERA in 1367. While the king sought mainly to draw ROUTIERS out of France and to distract EDWARD, THE BLACK PRINCE, Anjou always saw the Castilian venture as a prelude to the conquest of Aquitaine. By 1373, the duke's efforts resulted in a friendly regime in Castile and in a series of campaigns, some of which he led, that recaptured many of the territories surrendered to the English in 1360.

On the accession of twelve-year-old CHARLES VI in 1380, Anjou, as eldest uncle, claimed the regency. He eventually agreed to forego the title of regent, but dominated the government until 1382, when he withdrew to Provence to launch a campaign for the conquest of Naples. Having persuaded the French government to give him an army, Anjou invaded Italy but was defeated by his rival, Charles of Durazzo. The duke died in Italy in 1384.

Further Reading: Perroy, Edouard. *The Hundred Years War.* Trans. W. B. Wells. New York: Capricorn Books, 1965; Sumption, Jonathan. *The Hundred Years War.* Vol. 2, *Trial by Fire.* Philadelphia: University of Pennsylvania Press, 2001.

LOUIS, DUKE OF GUIENNE (1397–1415)

Although only in his teens, Louis, duke of Guienne and dauphin of France, was a major figure in the FRENCH CIVIL WAR, having been forced by his father's mental illness to take an active role in government. Frustrating both ARMAGNAC and BURGUNDIAN attempts to dominate him, the dauphin tried unsuccessfully to reconcile the factions by creating his own moderate royalist party.

The eighth child of CHARLES VI and ISABEAU OF BAVARIA, Louis became dauphin at the death of his brother Charles in 1401. His APPANAGE, the duchy of Guienne, comprised those parts of AQUITAINE not held by the English and constituted a future incentive to overthrow English power throughout the southwest. Entrusted to his mother's guardianship, Guienne quickly became a pawn in the escalating feud between JOHN THE FEARLESS, duke of BURGUNDY, and the dauphin's uncle, CHARLES, DUKE OF ORLÉANS. To prevent him from falling into Burgundy's hands, the queen and Orléans spirited him out of PARIS in August 1405, although the Burgundians quickly overtook the dauphin's party and brought him back to the capital. In December 1409, two years after Orléans's murder by Burgundian assassins, Burgundy assumed guardianship of the twelve-year-old dauphin. Although Guienne was empowered to summon and preside over the council in his parents' absence, real power rested with Burgundy.

By 1412, the dauphin began to assert his independence, overseeing, against Burgundy's advice, the drafting of the Treaty of Auxerre with the Armagnac princes and arranging a public ceremony of reconciliation between his warring relatives. In early 1413, the dauphin, whose entourage inclined toward the Armagnacs, decided to move against Burgundy, but was forestalled by the duke, who fomented the CABOCHIEN insurrection in Paris to overawe the court and secure his control of the government. However, by summer, moderates in Paris, alarmed by the excesses of the Cabochiens, rallied around Guienne, who negotiated the peace of Pontoise with the Armagnac leaders in late July. On 4 August, the dauphin made a triumphal entry into Paris, which, with the continuing Cabochien violence, turned the capital against Burgundy, who fled on 23 August.

In 1414, seeking to avoid domination by the new Armagnac regime, Guienne greatly increased his suite of household retainers in an effort to create a moderate party under his own leadership. After an unsuccessful military campaign against Burgundy, Guienne negotiated the peace of Arras, which was ratified in February 1415. The agreement annulled the decree of banishment against Burgundy, but excluded him from power and led the duke to withdraw to his own domains in sullen neutrality. In 1414–15, the dauphin participated in negotiations with HENRY V, whose escalating demands made renewal of the HUNDRED YEARS WAR inevitable. In preparation, the king appointed Guienne captain-general of the frontiers in April 1415. Unable to prevent the English capture of HARFLEUR in September, Guienne was not allowed to be present at the disastrous Battle of AGINCOURT in October. When the dauphin died childless in the following December, his passing ended efforts at Armagnac-Burgundian reconciliation and led to an intensification of the civil war.

Further Reading: Famiglietti, Richard C. *Royal Intrigue: Crisis at the Court of Charles VI, 1392–1420*. New York: AMS Press, 1986; Perroy, Edouard. *The Hundred Years War*. Trans. W. B. Wells. New York: Capricorn Books, 1965.

LOUIS, DUKE OF ORLÉANS (1372–1407)

Louis, duke of Orléans, was the second surviving son of CHARLES V and the younger brother of CHARLES VI. A clever and determined man, Louis sought to rule for his weak and mentally unstable brother, an ambition that brought him into conflict with his uncle and cousin of BURGUNDY. This rivalry split the French royal family and led eventually to the outbreak of the FRENCH CIVIL WAR, which allowed the English to invade France and reopen the HUNDRED YEARS WAR.

Made count of Valois by his father in 1375, Louis received the Duchy of Touraine from his brother in 1386. Touraine married Valentina Visconti, daughter of the duke of Milan in 1387. Besides the county of Asti, the bride's dowry, the match gave Touraine ambitions in Italy. In the early 1390s, the Avignon pope, Clement VII, proposed an eventually unsuccessful plan to make Touraine ruler of the papal states of central Italy. The duke convinced the French royal council, which he then dominated, to provide military support for his Italian adventures and to ally with Milan, a commitment that benefited Touraine more than the kingdom. However, a council no longer controlled by the duke terminated the alliance in 1395, and Touraine's Italian ambitions came to naught, being eventually consumed by his quest for power in France itself.

Touraine entered French politics in November 1388, when, with the assistance of the MARMOUSETS, he engineered a coup that ended his uncles' control of the royal government. The king, who had been largely under his uncles' tutelage since his accession in 1380, was declared of full age and in personal control of the government, a move that permitted dismissal of the royal uncles from the council and of their supporters from the government. Touraine now filled the royal administration with his followers and controlled both council and court, where he encouraged the weak-minded king and his more politically adept wife, Queen ISABEAU, in their constant balls and revels. In June 1392, the duke exchanged Touraine for the wealthier duchy of Orléans.

The onset of the king's madness in August 1392 ended the duke's political dominance and allowed the royal uncles, particularly

PHILIP THE BOLD, duke of Burgundy, to reassert their influence, and thereafter Orléans and Burgundy, supported by growing and increasingly hostile factions, struggled with one another to control the government. After Burgundy's death in April 1404, the rivalry with Orléans was intensified by the late duke's son, JOHN THE FEARLESS, who, although less influential than his father, was equally ambitious. Each cousin worked continually against the interests of the other and the council became the scene of violent disputes between the two. Having more personal charm and political experience than his rival, Orléans proved generally more successful, winning the support of the queen, who was accused by the BURGUNDIANS of being Orléans's lover. In 1405, when Burgundy threatened to impose his will by force, Orléans and the queen spirited the dauphin, LOUIS, DUKE OF GUIENNE, out of PARIS, and civil war was only narrowly averted.

Although the war with England had been suspended by the Truce of LEULINGHEN, Orléans believed that the deposition of RICHARD II in 1399 and the continuing internal rebellion that plagued his supplanter, HENRY IV, offered France a golden opportunity to expel the English from GASCONY and CALAIS. In 1404, despite Burgundy's opposition, Orléans persuaded the royal council to approve campaigns against both. However, Orléans, more a courtier than a soldier, failed in his 1406 invasion of Gascony, and Burgundy's half-hearted investment of Calais was also unsuccessful. By 1407, the two dukes were more interested in fighting each other than fighting the English.

On 23 November 1407, Orléans, who had spent the evening with the queen, was lured into an ambush in a dark Paris street and murdered by assassins hired by Burgundy. Claiming that he had acted "through the intervention of the devil" (Perroy, 227), Burgundy confessed his crime and fled the capital. Orléans's death therefore became the initiating event of a long struggle between the Burgundians and the ARMAGNACS (as Orléans's faction was eventually called).

And unlike the French failure to take advantage of Henry IV's troubles, HENRY V made the most of the opportunity provided by this civil war. Orléans was succeeded as duke by his thirteen-year-old son Charles (*see* CHARLES, DUKE OF ORLÉANS). *See also Justification of the Duke of Burgundy.*

Further Reading: Famiglietti, Richard. *Royal Intrigue: Crisis at the Court of Charles VI, 1392–1420.* New York: AMS Press, 1986; Perroy, Edouard. *The Hundred Years War.* Trans. W. B. Wells. New York: Capricorn Books, 1965.

LOUIS X, KING OF FRANCE (1289–1316)

Known as *le Hutin*, "the Quarrelsome" Louis X was the eldest son of PHILIP IV and Jeanne of Navarre. Louis's death without male heirs initiated the first succession crisis in the history of the royal House of CAPET and led to acceptance of the notion that women could not inherit the throne of France. This principle proved of prime importance twelve years later when one of the claimants to the French Crown was EDWARD III, king of England.

At the death of his mother on 2 April 1305, Louis inherited her lands, becoming count of Champagne and king of Navarre. Five months later, on 23 September, Louis married Marguerite of BURGUNDY, who in 1312 bore him a daughter, Jeanne. In 1314, Philip IV, possibly on information provided by his daughter, Isabella, the wife of EDWARD II of England (*see* ISABELLA, QUEEN OF ENGLAND [c. 1292–1358]), publicly accused Louis's wife, and the wife of Louis's younger brother, Charles of La Marche (*see* CHARLES IV), of adultery. Although the details of the affair are uncertain, Philip was convinced of the charges and had the women imprisoned and their alleged lovers executed. Louis, therefore, spent the last months of his father's reign attempting to secure a papal annulment of his marriage.

Louis succeeded his father in November 1314, but was not crowned until 3 August 1315. He inherited a monarchy tarnished by the adultery scandal, which threw doubt on the legitimacy of Philip IV's grandchildren, and weakened by widespread discontent over the late king's financial policies and frequent disregard of traditional rights. To placate the leagues of disaffected subjects that had formed in the last months of Philip's reign, Louis undertook a series of reforms and, influenced by his uncle, Charles, count of Valois, executed his father's most unpopular minister, Enguerran de Marigny.

The death of the imprisoned Marguerite in April 1315 allowed Louis to marry Clemence of Hungary on the following 31 July. Clemence was pregnant when Louis died on 5 June 1316, after a reign of less than two years. On his deathbed, the king declared Jeanne, his daughter by Marguerite, legitimate, apparently intending her to succeed should Clemence miscarry or have a girl. Born on 13 November, Clemence's son, John I, died five days after his birth, leaving the succession in dispute between Louis's four-year-old daughter Jeanne and his 26-year-old brother Philip, count of Poitiers, who had acted as regent since Louis's death. Despite much opposition, the count was crowned as PHILIP V in January 1317, and an assembly of notables, faced with an anointed monarch, proclaimed, as a rule of law, that a woman could not succeed to the throne. Jeanne was eventually allowed to inherit the Crown of Navarre, which at her death in 1349 passed to her son, CHARLES THE BAD. *See also* SALIC LAW OF SUCCESSION.

Further Reading: Brown, Elizabeth A.R. "Kings Like Semi-Gods: The Case of Louis X of France." *Majestas* 1 (1993): 5–37; Brown, Elizabeth A. R. *The Monarchy of Capetian France and Royal Ceremonial.* London: Variorum, 1991; Strayer, Joseph R. *The Reign of Philip the Fair.* Princeton, NJ: Princeton University Press, 1980.

LOUIS DE MALE, COUNT OF FLANDERS (1330–1384)

Louis de Male, count of FLANDERS, preserved his authority for most his rule by balancing formal allegiance to VALOIS France and informal alliance with PLANTAGENET England.

Louis succeeded his father, LOUIS DE NEVERS, upon the latter's death at CRÉCY in August 1346. Intent on overthrowing the

English-backed regime of Ghent burghers that had ruled Flanders since driving his father into exile in 1339, Louis, assisted by French troops, led a band of Flemish exiles into the county in August 1348 to support an uprising against the Ghent government in the town of Alost. On 29 August, he promised amnesty to Bruges, where loyalty to the House of Dampierre was strong. Although both Ghent and Bruges sent armies against the count, Louis divided the former with promises of pardon and full restoration of municipal privileges. When the army of Bruges mutinied and declared for the count, the army of Ghent dissolved and Louis marched triumphantly across Flanders, arriving at Bruges on 17 September. When the city opened its gates to him, Louis promptly blockaded both Ghent and Ypres, forcing them to appeal to EDWARD III for aid.

Realizing that he had to placate the militantly pro-English elements within his county, which, in any event, was still economically dependent on English wool, Louis opened negotiations with Edward. In December 1348, these talks resulted in the treaties of Dunkirk, whereby the English king accepted restoration of the count's authority and his formal allegiance to PHILIP VI in return for a promise of friendship and Louis's willingness to allow his subjects to continue recognizing Edward as king of France. A second agreement, which was never put into effect, bound Louis to renounce his French allegiance if Philip did not restore Artois and other territories taken from Flanders. Although the former had to be taken by storm, both Ghent and Ypres were under the count's control by mid-January 1349.

Forced to consult with the larger towns before levying taxation, Louis nevertheless strengthened and professionalized the central administration and won the support of smaller towns by confirming their right to produce certain types of cloth. In 1360, he was a signatory to the Treaty of BRÉTIGNY, thereby officially making peace with England, and, in 1363, Edward III established the wool staple at Calais, thereby stabilizing the flow of English wool into Flanders. In 1368, Louis was the only French vassal to refuse to publish CHARLES V's proclamation announcing his acceptance of the APPEAL OF THE GASCON LORDS, an action that renewed the HUNDRED YEARS WAR. In 1375, the count mediated the Anglo-French talks at the BRUGES PEACE CONFERENCE.

In 1363, Louis negotiated the marriage of MARGUERITE, his daughter and heir, to ED- MUND OF LANGLEY, son of Edward III. Be- cause the match created the possibility of a northern English APPANAGE based on Flan- ders, Charles V persuaded the French pope, Urban V, to forbid the marriage because the parties were within the prohibited degree of kinship. Charles then proposed that Mar- guerite marry his brother, PHILIP THE BOLD, duke of BURGUNDY, for whom the pope readily supplied the dispensation denied Langley. Louis, angry over the failure of the English match, did not approve the mar- riage until 1369, when the French agreed to return various territories taken from Flan- ders by PHILIP IV.

Louis excluded his son-in-law from the government until 1380, when the count's favoring of Bruges caused a new uprising in Ghent and forced him to seek assistance from Burgundy. In November 1382, a French army led by the duke crushed the Ghent militia at Roosebeke, killing the rebel leader Philip van ARTEVELDE. Burgundy was thus effective ruler of Flanders when Louis died on 30 January 1384.

Further Reading: Nicholas, David. *Town and Countryside: Social, Economic, and Political Tensions in Fourteenth-Century Flanders.* Bruges: De Tem- pel, 1971.

LOUIS DE NEVERS, COUNT OF FLANDERS (c. 1304–1346)

Although he spent much of his rule in exile or at war with his people, Louis de Nevers, count of FLANDERS, was a loyal vassal of the French Crown. His firm adherence to the VALOIS complicated efforts by EDWARD III to build a strong ANTI-FRENCH COALITION in the Low Countries during the first decades of the HUNDRED YEARS WAR.

By order of PHILIP IV, Louis had been re- moved from his family as a child and raised at the French court. When he succeeded his grandfather, Robert de Béthune, in 1322, he was French in language and tastes and had little knowledge or experience of his county. In 1323, in a clumsy attempt to limit the priv- ileges of the town of Bruges, Louis ignited a rebellion that eventually engulfed almost the entire county. Unable to subdue his re- bellious subjects, Louis appealed to PHILIP VI, who, being anxious to secure the count's support, crushed the Flemish rebels at Cassel on 23 August 1328, thereby restoring Louis to power. Feeling himself beholden to Philip and unwilling to risk further French inter- ference in his county, Louis now pursued a consistently pro-French policy.

In the 1330s, Louis's continued meddling in municipal affairs again increased political tensions, causing even Ghent, which had not supported the earlier uprising, to oppose him. With the advent of the Hundred Years War, Flanders found itself caught between Louis's Valois allegiance and the great towns' need for English wool, the cloth in- dustry being the basis of the Flemish econ- omy. In August 1336, after Louis rejected a proposed ANGLO-FLEMISH ALLIANCE, the En- glish government forbade wool exports, an action that devastated the Flemish economy. In October, when Philip forbade his vassals to trade with the English, Louis dutifully enforced the ban, thereby completely sever- ing relations with England.

In January 1338, economic unrest result- ing from the English embargo erupted into open rebellion. Under the leadership of James van ARTEVELDE, captain of Ghent, the Flemings forged an alliance with Edward III. When attacks on Ghent and Bruges failed, Louis fled to PARIS in February 1339. He accompanied the French army during the campaigns of 1339–40 (*see* THIÉRACHE CAM- PAIGN; TOURNAI, SIEGE OF), and was a member of the French embassy that negotiated the Truce of ESPLECHIN in September 1340. By 1342, the count's intrigues against the in- creasingly high-handed van Artevelde re- gime slowly gained support, especially in the French-speaking areas of the county. In May 1345, the town of Dendermonde declared for the count and in July van Artevelde was assassinated in Ghent. However, the three great towns—Ghent, Bruges, and Ypres—refused to accept Louis unless he recognized Edward as king of France. When the count refused, the towns concluded new agreements with the English king and Louis returned to the French court. On 26 August 1346, the count was slain fighting for the Valois at the Battle of CRÉCY. He was succeeded as count by his son, LOUIS DE MALE.

Further Reading: Lucas, Henry Stephen. *The Low Countries and the Hundred Years' War, 1326–1347.* Ann Arbor: University of Michigan Press, 1929; Nicholas, David. *Town and Countryside: Social, Economic, and Political Tensions in Fourteenth-Century Flanders.* Bruges: De Tempel, 1971.

M

MAINE, SURRENDER OF (1448)

The evacuation of Maine, a county in west-central France held for over two decades by the English, occurred in 1448, two and a half years after HENRY VI secretly agreed to surrender the province as a means of facilitating an Anglo-French peace. By discrediting the English government at home and demoralizing the English military in France, the abandonment of Maine was instrumental in ending the HUNDRED YEARS WAR.

Buffering English NORMANDY to the north and threatening French Anjou to the south, Maine was a vital part of Lancastrian France. Maine had been English since 1425, when JOHN, DUKE OF BEDFORD, had seized its capital, Le Mans. In 1444, CHARLES VII demanded Maine in return for accepting the Truce of TOURS. Although William de la POLE, earl of Suffolk, who negotiated the truce for the English, was accused of secretly agreeing to the surrender, it is uncertain whether he actually did so. The peace policy that comprehended the surrender of Maine was the king's policy; in the summer of 1445, Henry personally promised a French ambassador that he would restore the county by October. Nothing came of this promise, mainly because no royal councilor wanted to be associated with such an unpopular action. Nonetheless, on 22 December 1445, Henry, assured by Charles that the surrender of Maine would ensure a final peace, and repeatedly urged to relinquish the province by his new wife, MARGARET OF ANJOU, whose father would thereby make good his claims to the county, secretly conveyed to Charles's representatives a letter formally promising to surrender Maine by 30 April 1446.

Although Henry had committed himself and his government, the surrender had no support within the Norman administration or the Maine garrisons, both of which had to cooperate if the evacuation was to occur. As a result, several surrender dates passed without any action being taken. Armed with Henry's letter, Charles made extension of the truce conditional on implementation of the surrender. In England, rumors of the surrender generated much anger against Suffolk, who, in May 1447, solemnly declared in the king's presence that he had never been party to any proposals to relinquish Maine. In July 1447, Henry, in return for an extension of the truce to 1 May 1448, gave the French another written promise to surrender Maine. To implement this undertaking, Edmund BEAUFORT, earl of Somerset, whom Henry had created count of Maine, replaced RICHARD, DUKE OF YORK, a royal opponent, as king's lieutenant in Normandy. In July 1447, Somerset, acting as count of Maine, was ordered to convey the county to the English commanders in Le Mans, Mathew Gough and Fulk Eyton, who were, in turn, to surrender Maine to the French.

Expecting to oversee the surrender, Charles's representatives arrived in Le Mans in October. However, Gough and Eyton, supported by such other English military leaders as Sir John FASTOLF, frustrated the handover with a series of delaying tactics. In February 1448, Charles ignored the truce and laid siege to Le Mans. Unable to resist the new standing army Charles had constructed during the truce, Gough and Eyton surrendered Le Mans on 15 March. By June, the English garrisons of Maine had fallen back on Normandy, which now lay exposed to French attack from the south. Henry had undermined his ministers and demoralized his commanders by voluntarily surrendering a key portion of Lancastrian France for nothing more than Charles's vague agreement to look favorably on the conclusion of peace. The surrender of Maine and the subsequent loss of Normandy had serious political consequences in England, overthrowing Suffolk, tarnishing Somerset, and contributing to the internal strife that led eventually to the Wars of the Roses. *See also* CHARLES VII, MILITARY REFORMS OF.

Further Reading: Griffiths, Ralph A. *The Reign of King Henry VI.* Berkeley: University of California Press, 1981; Wolffe, Bertram. *Henry VI.* London: Eyre Methuen, 1981.

MALESTROIT, TRUCE OF (1343)

Concluded on 19 January 1343 and intended to run until 29 September 1346, the Truce of Malestroit was the first step in a papal effort to mediate a permanent settlement of the HUNDRED YEARS WAR. Although financial exhaustion and military stalemate were the main reasons PHILIP VI and EDWARD III accepted the truce, the stated purpose of the agreement was to permit both monarchs to send representatives to Avignon to treat for peace under the auspices of Pope CLEMENT VI. In fact, the truce served mainly as a respite that allowed both sides, but particularly the English, to renew their will and ability to continue the war.

In October 1342, Edward intervened personally in the BRETON CIVIL WAR to revive the failing cause of John de MONTFORT, then a prisoner in PARIS. Landing in BRITTANY on 26 October with an army of five thousand, Edward joined the Montfortists in a plan to recapture the town of Vannes. When an assault failed on 29 November, Edward was forced to lay siege. With the west of the duchy safely Montfortist, Edward launched a *CHEVAUCHÉE* into eastern Brittany, where CHARLES OF BLOIS, the French-backed ducal claimant, was in control. The rapid capitulation of Rédon, Malestroit, and Ploermel

convinced the French to intervene and a royal army led by John, duke of NORMANDY (*see* JOHN II) entered the duchy in late December. Normandy quickly recaptured all the recent English conquests and by mid-January brought his army, which was significantly larger than the Anglo-Breton force, to within twenty miles of Vannes.

Unwilling to risk battle or reveal the weakness of his army, Edward allowed two cardinals, who had sought to arrange a truce since the previous summer, to begin negotiations for a cessation of hostilities, although he would not allow them to view the size or condition of his army. On 19 January, representatives of the two kings signed a truce in the Church of St. Mary Magdalene in Malestroit. Although the agreement gave Vannes to the pope, who was to hold it for Philip until expiration of the truce, its terms were generally favorable to Edward. Both kings retained their current holdings in Brittany, FLANDERS, AQUITAINE, and SCOTLAND, and Philip agreed to release de Montfort. This meant the English were free to consolidate their position in western Brittany, to maintain their alliance with the regime of James van ARTEVELDE in Flanders, and to strengthen their garrisons in GASCONY. Only in Scotland, where DAVID II had recently driven the English from Roxburgh and Sterling, did Edward sustain losses under the truce.

In 1344, negotiations mediated by the pope opened in Avignon. Because Edward believed Clement was pro-French and Philip believed he had the stronger hand, neither king seriously pursued peace. Each made demands the other could not accept. The French refused to discuss either Edward's claim to the French throne or the granting of full sovereignty to the PLANTAGENETs in Aquitaine. Meanwhile, both sides violated the truce in Brittany and Aquitaine, while the Scots continued raiding England and Philip refused to release de Montfort. When the AVIGNON PEACE CONFERENCE collapsed in February 1345, both parties were already preparing to renew the war. In the following June, more than a year before the truce's intended expiration, Edward formally re-nounced the Malestroit agreement.

Further Reading: Sumption, Jonathan. *The Hundred Years War.* Vol. 1, *Trial by Battle.* Philadelphia: University of Pennsylvania Press, 1999.

MANTES, TREATY OF. *See* CHARLES THE BAD, KING OF NAVARRE

MARCEL, ÉTIENNE (1310–1358)

Étienne Marcel was a prosperous PARIS draper, who, as the city's provost of the merchants, led a rebellion against the French Crown in 1357–58. By giving leadership and focus to Parisians who were angered by the high taxes and military defeats of the HUN-DRED YEARS WAR, Marcel became virtual ruler of Paris, driving the Dauphin Charles (*see* CHARLES V) from the capital and nego-tiating with CHARLES THE BAD, king of Navarre, and with other towns to form an anti-VALOIS alliance.

Born into a cadet branch of a prominent family of Parisian merchants, Marcel, in about 1345, married the daughter of a wealthy banker, and used her dowry and her father's connections to launch a suc-cessful career as a cloth merchant. By the late 1340s, he was a supplier of the royal court and a respected and influential busi-nessman. In 1354, he was elected provost of the merchants, an important municipal ma-gistracy that gave him responsibility for the recruitment of the city's military forces and the maintenance of its defenses. As pro-vost, he was also spokesman for the representatives of the towns in the Estates-General, an office he performed when the assembly met in Paris in December 1355. Marcel helped negotiate an agreement whereby JOHN II undertook to cease his de-basement of the coinage, dismiss certain of his ministers, and accept a series of gov-ernmental reforms in return for a large grant of TAXATION to finance new campaigns against the English.

In May 1356, the king, dissatisfied with the tax so far collected, resumed his ma-nipulation of the currency and recalled his dismissed advisors, actions that caused Marcel to break with the Crown and refuse to recruit Parisian contingents for the com-ing campaign. After the king's defeat and capture at POITIERS in September, Marcel threw his support behind the partisans of the recently imprisoned Charles of Navarre, who controlled the session of the Estates-General that began in October. Before voting further supply, the Estates demanded that the dauphin dismiss and try a number of royal officials, govern only with the advice of a permanent commission appointed by the Estates, and release Charles of Navarre. In December, a month after dismissing the Estates and fleeing Paris, the dauphin or-dered a new manipulation of the currency. Marcel organized a boycott of the new coinage and led a mob to the Louvre, where the dauphin's brother, LOUIS, DUKE OF ANJOU, was compelled to suspend the coin-age ordinance. Fearing that widespread ac-ceptance of the new issue would allow the dauphin to dispense with the Estates, Mar-cel continued to incite demonstrations of his supporters to dominate the city and over-awe the court.

In January 1357, the dauphin returned to Paris, withdrew the new coinage, and re-called the Estates. In March, the Estates, dominated by friends of Navarre and Mar-cel's increasingly radical supporters, forced the dauphin to accept a sweeping reform ordinance. By the end of the year, the pro-vost and his supporters, who had adopted distinctive hoods of crimson and blue as their insignia, controlled the city. On 22 February 1358, Marcel, learning that the dauphin planned to bring troops into Paris to overthrow the revolutionary regime, led a mob to the Louvre, where the Parisians murdered two royal marshals in the dau-phin's presence. In March, having appointed Marcel to his council, the dauphin left Paris and began rallying support against the rev-olutionaries, whose excesses generated sympathy for the dauphin in the provinces. In May, the provost gave support to the JACQUERIE, which alienated most nobles from his cause. By July, Marcel's support was ebbing in Paris. Continuing disorder and fear of the English mercenaries whom Navarre, now Marcel's close ally, had deployed around the city, led a group of influential Parisians to conspire with the dauphin against the regime. On 31 July, a royalist mob murdered Marcel, thereby ending the Paris revolution and allowing the dauphin to enter the capital on 2 August. *See also* ESTATES, GENERAL AND PROVINCIAL.

Further Reading: Sumption, Jonathan. *The Hundred Years War.* Vol. 2, *Trial by Fire.* Philadelphia: University of Pennsylvania Press, 2001.

MARGARET OF ANJOU, QUEEN OF ENGLAND (1430–1482)

Margaret of Anjou was the wife of HENRY VI. Queen by virtue of the peace policy pursued by her husband in the 1440s, Margaret was, through her influence on Henry and her intervention in court politics, a key figure in the formulation of English policy during the last decade of the HUNDRED YEARS WAR. During the subsequent Wars of the Roses, Margaret became effective leader of the House of LANCASTER.

Margaret was the daughter of René, duke of Anjou, a descendant of JOHN II, and the niece of CHARLES VII, who was married to Anjou's sister. In the early 1440s, Cardinal Henry BEAUFORT, bishop of Winchester, and William de la POLE, earl of Suffolk, leaders of the English peace party, sought to further their goals by arranging a French marriage for Henry. Being unwilling to offer his own daughter and thus forge yet another English connection with the House of VALOIS, Charles suggested a match with Margaret. Although Henry's uncle, HUMPHREY, DUKE OF GLOUCESTER, and his cousin, RICHARD, DUKE OF YORK, leaders of the court faction favoring more vigorous prosecution of the war, bitterly opposed a French match, Suffolk sailed to France in February 1444 with instructions to conclude both a peace and a marriage. When negotiations for a permanent peace bogged down over the French refusal to make significant concessions, Suffolk accepted a truce running until 1 April 1446 and agreed to the marriage of

Henry and Margaret. On 24 May, with Suffolk acting as proxy, fifteen-year-old Margaret was formally betrothed to the English king; four days later, the two governments signed the Truce of TOURS.

Married to Henry on 23 April 1445, Margaret was crowned on 30 May. Intelligent, energetic, and strong-willed, the young queen was almost immediately unpopular. French, possessed of no dowry, and closely associated with Suffolk and the peace party, she was to many the symbol of a feeble policy that meant defeat and dishonor in France. Easily dominating her weak, vacillating husband, Margaret soon involved herself in politics, becoming a strong advocate for the peace policy that had made her queen. Already derided as a queen who was "not worth ten marks a year" (Seward, 245), Margaret urged Henry to keep his rash promise to surrender Maine to the French, thereby earning even more popular hostility (*see* MAINE, SURRENDER OF). In 1447, Suffolk, who was rumored to be the queen's lover, engineered the arrest of Gloucester, who died while in custody. Public opinion ascribed the mysterious death to murder, and declared Margaret Suffolk's accomplice.

In 1450, the loss of NORMANDY swept Suffolk from power. Embarrassed by financial weakness and shackled by a king who was unfit to rule, Suffolk's government collapsed amid charges of treason leveled by such opponents as York, who, thanks to Margaret's failure to conceive, was Henry's probable heir. As an increasingly bitter rivalry developed between York and Suffolk's successor, Edmund BEAUFORT, duke of Somerset, the queen, who viewed York as a threat to the throne, closely identified herself with Somerset. In August 1453, Henry suffered a mental collapse that rendered him incapable of ruling; in October, Margaret, amidst rumors that the child was not Henry's, gave birth to a son, Edward, who displaced York as heir. To safeguard the rights of her child, Margaret sought the regency, but her claim was rejected in favor of York, who was named protector by PARLIAMENT in March 1454. Henry's recovery the following

Christmas ended York's regime, but the continuing efforts of Margaret and Somerset to destroy York and his allies led to the eventual outbreak of civil war.

Over the next four years, Henry remained too weak-minded to govern effectively and Margaret assumed leadership of the anti-York faction. Following Henry's overthrow in March 1461, Margaret spent most of the next decade in exile in SCOTLAND and France. She helped engineer Henry's brief restoration in 1470–71, but was captured and imprisoned in the Tower of London in May 1471 after her son's death in battle and her husband's murder. Ransomed and returned to France by Louis XI in 1475, Margaret died on 25 August 1482. *See also* NORMAN CAMPAIGN (1449–50).

Further Reading: Griffiths, Ralph A. *The Reign of King Henry VI.* Berkeley: University of California Press, 1981; Maurer, Helen E. *Margaret of Anjou: Queenship and Power in Late Medieval England.* London: Boydell Press, 2003; Seward, Desmond. *The Hundred Years War.* New York: Penguin, 1999.

MARGARET OF FRANCE, QUEEN OF ENGLAND (1279–1318)

The daughter of Philip III and half-sister of PHILIP IV, Margaret of France became the second wife of EDWARD I as part of the peace process that ended the ANGLO-FRENCH WAR OF 1294–1303. Like her niece, Isabella (*see* ISABELLA, QUEEN OF ENGLAND [c. 1292–1358]), who was married to EDWARD II as part of the same peace process, and such later French princesses as Isabella, the second wife of RICHARD II (*see* ISABELLA, QUEEN OF ENGLAND [1388–1409]), and CATHERINE OF VALOIS, the wife of HENRY V, Margaret was part of a series of attempts to use marriage to create amity between the English royal Houses of PLANTAGENET and LANCASTER and the French royal Houses of CAPET and VALOIS.

The possibility of a marriage between Edward, who had been a widower since the death of Queen Eleanor of Castile in 1290, and Margaret was first raised in 1293–94, although actual discussions regarding the match did not begin until 1298 as part of the

Anglo-French peace negotiations conducted by Pope Boniface VIII. The couple was wed at Canterbury on 10 September 1299, almost four years before the signing of a final peace agreement. Their first child, Thomas of Brotherton, earl of Norfolk, was born in June 1300, with his younger brother, Edmund of Woodstock, earl of Kent, arriving in August 1301, and his sister, Eleanor, in May 1306. Forty years younger than her husband, Margaret exercised little political influence, but frequently interceded with the king on behalf of subjects needing pardons or favors. Her most important effort in this regard was on behalf of Prince Edward, whom she reconciled with his father in 1305. The queen persuaded the king to allow LONDON merchants to resume lending money to the prince and was largely responsible for preventing the break-up of the prince's household.

Margaret may have undertaken such intercessions in part to counter bad feeling aroused by her French birth and her association with an unpopular peace treaty. Although a later story that she passed important political and military information to her brother is highly implausible, it may indicate the existence of suspicion and hostility regarding the French queen. In 1299, for instance, a chronicler criticized Margaret's visit to St. Albans as too long and costly, although at her death most English writers praised her as kind, beautiful, and pure. Margaret enjoyed good relations with Prince Edward and his surviving sisters, and was treated with affection and tenderness by her husband, who several times rescued her from the consequences of her overspending. In 1302, he gave her £4,000 out of the royal revenues from marriages and wardships to meet her debts, and, in 1305, he increased her landed endowment by £500 per year. After Edward's death in July 1307, Margaret remained on good terms with Edward II, although little is known of her life after 1308. She died on 14 February 1318 and was buried in London.

Further Reading: Prestwich, Michael. *Edward I.* Berkeley: University of California Press, 1988.

MARGATE, BATTLE OF. *See* CADZAND, BATTLE OF

MARGUERITE DE FLANDERS, DUCHESS OF BURGUNDY (c. 1349–1405)

Marguerite was the daughter and heir of LOUIS DE MALE, count of FLANDERS. Through her marriage to PHILIP THE BOLD, duke of BURGUNDY and brother of CHARLES V, and through the marriages she and her husband arranged for their children, she helped create the state of Burgundy, which in the fifteenth century played a central role in the HUNDRED YEARS WAR.

Married briefly to Philip de Rouvre, the last Capetian duke of Burgundy (*see* CAPET, HOUSE OF), who died in November 1361, Marguerite thereafter became one of the most coveted heiresses in Europe. Her dowry included not only her father's provinces of Flanders and Rethel, but her paternal grandmother's counties of Artois and Burgundy, and a claim through her mother to the duchy of Brabant. Marriage to Marguerite thus promised a potential husband substantial holdings in the Low Countries and western Germany. Seeking to create a great English APPANAGE on the northern borders of France, EDWARD III, in the early 1360s, proposed a marriage between Marguerite and his son EDMUND OF LANGLEY, earl of Cambridge. By combining Flanders and Marguerite's other inheritances with CALAIS, Ponthieu, and the PLANTAGENET holdings in northern France, Cambridge would be the most powerful prince in northwestern Europe and a significant threat to VALOIS France, which would then be bracketed by Plantagenet Flanders in the north and Plantagenet AQUITAINE in the south. Although Marguerite's father was agreeable to the match, Charles V derailed the marriage in 1364 by prevailing upon the French pope, Urban V, to forbid it on grounds of consanguinity. Like the members of most noble families, the couple was related within the degrees of affinity prohibited by the Church; their marriage could not proceed without a papal dispensation.

Although the pope justified his prohibition by calling the proposed match with Cambridge "a danger to [the couple's] souls, a pernicious example to others and a scandal to many" (Sumption, 577), in 1367, he readily granted a dispensation for Marguerite to marry Burgundy, to whom she was even more closely related. Angered by French interference in his affairs, Flanders drove a hard bargain for his daughter's hand, which Charles won for his brother only by agreeing to return to Flanders the towns and castellancies of Lille, Douai, and Orchies, which had been seized by PHILIP IV in 1305. Marguerite finally wed Burgundy at Ghent on 19 June 1369, and eventually bore him at least eleven children, seven of whom lived to adulthood.

Marguerite succeeded to her grandmother's lands in 1382, and her father's in 1384. In 1385, Marguerite and Philip arranged advantageous marriages for two of their children with members of the Wittelsbach family, thereby ensuring the eventual incorporation of Holland, Zeeland, and Hainault into the Burgundian state. In 1390, Marguerite's maternal aunt Jeanne named her niece and husband co-heirs to Brabant. Although Philip ruled all his wife's lands, Marguerite frequently acted as regent in his absence. Like her husband, she was a great patron of the arts and a collector of books. Marguerite willed her lands to her husband in 1391, but only died a year after Philip, on 21 March 1405. She was succeeded in her territories by her eldest son, JOHN THE FEARLESS, the second Valois duke of Burgundy.

Further Reading: Sumption, Jonathan. *The Hundred Years War.* Vol. 2, *Trial by Fire.* Philadelphia: University of Pennsylvania Press, 2001; Vaughan, Richard. *Philip the Bold: The Formation of the Burgundian State.* Woodbridge, England: Boydell Press, 2002.

MARGUERITE DE MALE. *See* MARGUERITE DE FLANDERS

MARMOUSETS

The term "Marmousets" denotes a French political faction composed of former financial and military servants of CHARLES V who tried to reimpose his ideals of efficient, economical government on the administration of CHARLES VI. Although the Marmousets dominated the royal government for less than four years, many of their ideas remained influential within the ARMAGNAC/dauphinist party during the FRENCH CIVIL WAR and were put into practice during the last years of the HUNDRED YEARS WAR.

"Marmouset," meaning "small boy," and implying a person of no status or consequence, was a term of derision applied to the faction by their political opponents, the supporters of Charles VI's uncles, JOHN, DUKE OF BERRY, and PHILIP THE BOLD, duke of BURGUNDY. On the death of Charles V in 1380, the minority government of his twelve-year-old son fell under the control of the boy's uncles. By 1384, when the eldest uncle, LOUIS, DUKE OF ANJOU, died, most of Charles V's ministers had been dismissed or relegated to minor offices, their places taken by partisans of Berry and Burgundy, who exploited their control of king and council for the financial and political advantage of themselves and their masters.

On 3 November 1388, Pierre Aycelin, cardinal of Laon and a royal councilor, announced the king's intention to assume personal control of the government. Charles dismissed his uncles and filled his council and administration with his father's old ministers, who soon became known as Marmousets. Although the king was nearly twenty, he was still immature and easily led; the driving force behind the change in government was the king's brother, LOUIS, DUKE OF ORLÉANS, who, in likely alliance with Queen ISABEAU, sought the power and profit denied him by his uncles. Besides Aycelin, the leading Marmousets included Olivier de CLISSON, constable of France; Bureau de La Rivière; John le Mercier; John de Montaigu; William Melun, count of Tancarville; and Nicolas de Bosc, bishop of Bayeux.

Although favoring the interests of Orléans, the Marmouset regime sought no revolutionary change, but worked instead for a return of the administrative arrangements that had characterized the reign of Charles V. While Orléans distracted his brother with costly entertainments, the Marmousets ran the kingdom. The council was reduced to a more manageable size and its members were bound by oath to each other and to the welfare of the realm. To avoid the favoritism of the previous regime, appointments to important offices were made by the council, and the financial and judicial departments were reformed and reorganized, with all servants of the royal uncles dismissed or demoted. In late 1389, the Marmousets took the king to Languedoc, where Berry's lieutenancy had impoverished the province. Charles dismissed his uncle and replaced or arrested his supporters in the provincial administration.

Although generally more rational and economical, the new government proved no more popular than the uncles' regime. This unpopularity stemmed largely from the Marmousets' unwillingness to countenance true reform and their insistence on maintaining the high war TAXATION of the previous reign, which, with the conclusion of the Truce of LEULINGHEN in 1389, seemed to fund only court extravagance. Marmouset dominance abruptly ended in August 1392 when the king fell into a fit of violent madness, the first episode in a lifetime of intermittent insanity. The royal uncles quickly resumed control, removing the leading Marmousets from office. La Rivière and Le Mercier were imprisoned; John of Montaigu fled to Avignon; and Clisson was fined, banished, and dismissed as constable. Although some Marmousets eventually returned to office in minor posts, they ceased to exist as a coherent faction; however, many of their ideas and policies were later put into effect by CHARLES VII, the eventual heir of the Marmouset-Armagnac tradition.

Further Reading: Perroy, Edouard. *The Hundred Years War.* Trans. W. B. Wells. New York: Capricorn Books, 1965.

MARSHAL OF FRANCE. *See* ARMIES, COMMAND OF; AUDREHEM, ARNOUL D', MARSHAL OF FRANCE; APPENDIX 6: "CONSTABLES AND MARSHALS OF FRANCE AND ENGLAND"

MARTIN V. *See* PAPACY AND THE HUNDRED YEARS WAR

MAUNY, WALTER, LORD MAUNY
(d. 1372)

Walter Mauny (or Manny), one of the ablest English captains of the HUNDRED YEARS WAR, earned a European reputation for valor and CHIVALRY.

The son of a noble Hainaulter family, Mauny came to England in 1327 in the entourage of his countrywoman, Queen PHILIPPA, wife of EDWARD III. Knighted in 1331, Mauny fought in SCOTLAND in the early 1330s and was appointed admiral of the north in 1337. In the first of many gallant exploits recorded by his fellow Hainaulter, Jean FROISSART, Mauny descended on Cadsand, an island at the mouth of the Scheldt from which French privateers attacked English shipping. During the raid, Mauny single-handedly rescued HENRY OF GROSMONT, earl of Derby, when he was in danger of capture; Mauny also took several prisoners, including the bastard brother of LOUIS DE NEVERS, count of FLANDERS. In 1340, the king, who had already granted Mauny numerous lands and offices, gave him £8,000 for the RANSOM of his Cadsand prisoners.

In 1339, at the start of the THIÉRACHE CAMPAIGN, Mauny, according to Froissart, vowed to be the first to enter France and seize a stronghold, which he did by crossing the Hainault frontier with forty companions and surprising the castle of Thun l'Evêque. In June 1340, Mauny fought at the Battle of SLUYS and was present later in the year at the siege of TOURNAI. In 1342, Mauny landed in BRITTANY, where, among other adventures, he broke the siege of Hennebon, thereby liberating the wife of John de MONTFORT, the English client in the BRETON CIVIL WAR. In 1345–46, Mauny distinguished himself during Derby's first two campaigns in GASCONY. In the latter year, while John, duke of NORMANDY, was besieging the Gascon town of AIGUILLON, Mauny released a Norman knight in his custody without ransom in return for a safe-conduct from the duke to travel through France to join Edward for the developing CRÉCY campaign. Despite this safe-conduct, Mauny was attacked and most of his men were captured, although he escaped, thereby adding to his growing reputation.

In 1347, Mauny served at the siege of CALAIS and was one of the English representatives who negotiated the Truce of Calais after the city's fall (*see* CALAIS, TRUCE OF). On 31 December 1349, he played a key part in foiling a French attempt to retake Calais by treachery. Leading a small party of knights that included the king and EDWARD, THE BLACK PRINCE, traveling incognito, Mauny ambushed the French as they entered Calais Castle. Uttering the war cry "Mauny to the rescue" to preserve his anonymity, the king led Mauny and his comrades in a nightlong fight that saved the town. During the 1350s, Mauny undertook various military and diplomatic assignments; he fought at the naval Battle of WINCHELSEA in 1350, broke the Scottish siege of Berwick Castle in 1355, and negotiated an extension of the Anglo-French truce in 1359. He accompanied the king during the RHEIMS CAMPAIGN of 1359–60, was one of the English guarantors of the Treaty of BRÉTIGNY in 1360, and was one of JOHN II's guardians when the captive French king was transferred to Calais. In the 1360s, Mauny served briefly in Ireland and participated in negotiations for a marriage between the king's son, EDMUND OF LANGLEY, and MARGUERITE, daughter of LOUIS DE MALE, count of Flanders.

Mauny's service in the war made him both wealthy and famous. Summoned to PARLIAMENT as Lord Mauny in 1347, he became a knight of the GARTER in 1359 and received extensive grants of land in England and AQUITAINE. Although likely exaggerated by Froissart, Mauny's chivalric exploits were well known on both sides of the Channel. In 1349, he acquired land near Smithfield outside LONDON where fifty thousand victims of the BLACK DEATH were supposedly buried. Mauny later founded a house of Carthusian monks, the London Charterhouse, on the site and was buried in the monastery on his death in January 1372.

Further Reading: Packe, Michael. *King Edward III*. Ed. L. C. B. Seaman. London: Routledge and Kegan Paul, 1983; Sumption, Jonathan. *The Hundred Years War*. Vol. 1, *Trial by Battle*. Philadelphia: University of Pennsylvania Press, 1999.

MAURON, BATTLE OF (1352)

The Battle of Mauron occurred on 14 August 1352 near the village of Mauron in central BRITTANY. Although the English forces in Brittany were seriously depleted by this costly victory, the French army was shattered, forcing the French Crown to largely abandon its direct involvement in the BRETON CIVIL WAR for the next decade.

Upon his return from England in July 1352, Walter BENTLEY, Thomas DAGWORTH's successor as English governor in Brittany, found that Guy de Nesle, the French commander in the duchy, had reestablished the sieges of English garrisons at Ploermel and Fougeray. Gathering a force that probably numbered fewer than a thousand men, Bentley broke both sieges before the French commander could stop him. Leaving his camps near Rennes on 11 August, de Nesle encountered Bentley a half mile east of Mauron in the late afternoon of 14 August.

The English deployed on high ground in the traditional formation, with bodies of ARCHERS on the wings to cover the dismounted men-at-arms in the center. However, the English line stood on open ground, unprotected by woods or field works and backed by a hedgerow that could hinder retreat. When Bentley refused his invitation to surrender, de Nesle launched his attack, sending his cavalry to disperse the archers on the English right, and his men-at-arms to simultaneously attack on foot in the English fashion. The French cavalry charge was successful; most of the archers fled the field thereby exposing the men-at arms to their left, who were quickly pushed back to the hedgerow. With Bentley wounded, the English were in serious trouble.

However, on the English left, the second body of archers, facing no cavalry charge, quickly broke up the French assault in their front, driving their foes back down the hill. On the English right, the hedgerow anchored the struggling English line and also disrupted any cavalry pursuit of the fleeing archers. As the French right wing collapsed, the English men-at-arms fell on the exposed flank and the entire French line was eventually driven downhill in confusion. On the valley floor and on the steep slopes of the hill opposite the battle site, the English archers did great execution, shooting down hundreds of exhausted French knights who were rendered practically immobile by the heat and the weight of their own ARMOR.

French casualties were horrendous. Over five hundred men-at-arms lay dead on the field, and 160 prisoners were taken for RANSOM. Guy de Nesle was killed, along with many prominent Breton noblemen who supported the cause of CHARLES OF BLOIS, the French-backed claimant in Brittany. Also slain were eighty-nine knights of JOHN II's Order of the STAR, which had only recently been formed to rival EDWARD III's Order of the GARTER. English losses were also heavy, and became even larger after the battle when Bentley had thirty archers beheaded for leaving the field. So desperate was the English manpower shortage at Mauron that Bentley had to send immediately to England for reinforcements. Nonetheless, English dominance in the duchy remained largely unchallenged until the 1360s.

Further Reading: Burne, Alfred H. *The Crécy War*. Ware, England: Wordsworth Editions Ltd., 1999; Sumption, Jonathan. *The Hundred Years War*. Vol. 2, *Trial by Fire*. Philadelphia: University of Pennsylvania Press, 2001.

MEAUX, SIEGE OF (1421–1422)

Lasting from October 1421 to May 1422, the English investment of Meaux, a town on the River Marne about thirty miles east of PARIS, was HENRY V's longest siege and last major campaign. The fall of the city cleared northern France of dauphinist strongholds, secured English communications with BURGUNDY and FLANDERS, and ended all immediate threats to Anglo-Burgundian control of Paris. However, the long and difficult winter operation accelerated English war weariness and may have undermined the health of the king, who died three months later.

Meaux was situated in a horseshoe bend of the Marne, which divided the town from the Marché, a heavily fortified market. The siege began on 6 October 1421, with Henry dividing his twenty-five hundred men into four divisions, which communicated with one another via a bridge of boats across the Marne. The king commanded the northern sector, while Richard BEAUCHAMP, earl of Warwick; Thomas BEAUFORT, duke of Exeter; and Edmund Mortimer, earl of March, led the other divisions. Many ARTILLERY pieces, both gunpowder cannon and traditional wooden siege engines, were deployed about the walls. Because of dauphinist raiders, supplies had to be brought from Paris, necessitating the detailing of troops to protect English convoys. Inside the town, the garrison was led by the Bastard of Vaurus, an experienced soldier with a reputation for brutality, and contained a large number of Scots and some English and Irish deserters, all of whom understood that they would receive no mercy if the town fell.

English attempts to bombard Meaux into surrendering failed, and, in December, heavy rains caused the Marne to overflow its banks and flood the English siege lines. When the bridge of boats was swept away, Warwick's southern division was for a time dangerously isolated from the rest of the army, while the garrison, plentifully supplied with boats, made frequent sorties outside the walls. Dysentery appeared in the cold, wet English camps, which were now even more difficult to supply, the king being obliged to send away most of his horses for lack of forage. As the siege dragged on, demoralization and doubt began to afflict the English soldiery. Upon seeing his son killed by a cannonball, Sir John Cornwall supposedly cried out that he had come to France to conquer NORMANDY, not to deprive the dauphin (see CHARLES VII) of his rightful Crown. Even the king became disheartened by the inactivity of his ally PHILIP THE GOOD,

duke of Burgundy, and by the seeming decline of enthusiasm for the war in England, where recruitment was becoming increasingly difficult. Only news of the birth in early December of Henry's son, the future HENRY VI, gave cause for cheer.

In March, the garrison withdrew to the Marché, which was protected by the river and by a canal that effectively turned the peninsula on which the market lay into an island. With much travail, the English brought up their artillery and repaired the connecting bridge, which had been destroyed by the garrison during its retreat. Realizing that they could expect no help from the dauphin, the garrison decided to negotiate. Henry's terms were harsh. The Bastard of Vaurus; all English deserters; anyone implicated in the murder of JOHN THE FEARLESS, duke of Burgundy; and anyone who had sworn to uphold the Treaty of TROYES were to be surrendered to the king to await his pleasure. Henry even demanded that the man who "blewe and sounded an Horn during the siege" (Burne, 175) be handed over. With no alternative, the garrison accepted these terms on 2 May 1422. The Bastard of Vaurus was hanged and four other men, including the unfortunate horn blower, were also executed. The other prisoners were carried to Paris and then to confinement in England. Northern France was now free of dauphinist garrisons, but, in June, the king, perhaps affected by his exertions at Meaux, fell ill. His condition deteriorated steadily over the following weeks until he died at Vincennes on 31 August.

Further Reading: Allmand, Christopher. *Henry V*. New Haven, CT: Yale University Press, 1997; Burne, Alfred H. *The Agincourt War*. Ware, England: Wordsworth Editions Ltd., 1999.

MELUN, SIEGE OF (1420)

Extending from July to November 1420, the English siege of Melun, a town on the Seine some thirty miles southeast of PARIS, removed an important dauphinist garrison from the environs of the capital, which thereafter submitted to the Anglo-Burgundian regime created by the Treaty of TROYES. Because of its length and difficulty, the siege angered HENRY V, who revealed his implacable resolve to be obeyed as rightful heir and regent by treating the prisoners of Melun with exceptional severity.

Following conclusion of the Troyes agreement in May, and his marriage to CATHERINE OF VALOIS in early June, Henry, accompanied by his new ally, PHILIP THE GOOD, duke of BURGUNDY; his new father-in-law, CHARLES VI; and his brothers, THOMAS, DUKE OF CLARENCE, and JOHN, DUKE OF BEDFORD, left Troyes and marched west with an Anglo-Burgundian force of twenty thousand. Before entering Paris, Henry moved against a string of dauphinist garrisons holding key towns on the Yonne and Seine southeast of the capital. Sens surrendered without a fight on 10 June, but Montereau, site of the recent murder of JOHN THE FEARLESS (see MONTEREAU CONFERENCE), held out until 1 July, not capitulating until Henry had eighteen prisoners hanged in full view of the garrison. On 9 July, the king invested Melun, which, according to the *Chronicle of London*, was "one of the worst [places] that ever he laid siege to" (Allmand, 152). The city was strongly defended, with its center and citadel located on a small island in the Seine that was connected to the rest of the city on each bank by heavily fortified bridges. The experienced 700-man garrison was ably led by Arnaud Guillaume, lord of Barbazan, and enthusiastically assisted by armed townsmen. Although Henry had Charles call upon his subjects to surrender, they refused. When the Scots soldiers in the garrison refused a similar call from their king, James I (see SCOTLAND), who was a prisoner in the English camp, Henry began siege operations, with the English encamped on the west bank and the BURGUNDIANS on the east.

Although English ARTILLERY began an almost constant bombardment, the guns had little effect, causing Henry to begin tunneling under the walls in an effort to undermine them. Because they were close to the river, the miners had to work in knee-deep water and mud. Barbazan, meanwhile,

began a series of counter-tunnels, which allowed his men to attack the English in a series of desperate underground struggles fought by torchlight in stale air and at close quarters. In one such encounter, the king was fiercely engaged by Barbazon, who withdrew when he realized whom he was fighting. As the siege dragged on into the autumn, Henry's position deteriorated. Dysentery struck the English camp, while large numbers of Burgundians deserted and rumors abounded that a dauphinist relief force was coming. However, conditions were even worse inside the city, where the garrison was eating horseflesh by October. Finally, on 18 November, Barbarzan, whose men had eaten nothing for almost a week, negotiated the town's surrender with Richard BEAUCHAMP, earl of Warwick.

Henry spared the lives of most of the garrison and townsmen, although some were summarily executed, such as Bertrand de Chaumont, who, as an English subject from GASCONY, was, despite the pleas of Clarence, beheaded as a traitor. Barbazan and five hundred of his men were taken prisoner, as was anyone in the town connected to the murder of Burgundy's father. Although most of the soldiers were held for RANSOM, Barbazan was imprisoned in a cage in Paris and Château Gaillard for seven years. On 1 December, Henry, Charles, and Philip entered Paris, where English troops quickly secured all strongpoints, and the city authorities, realizing from Melun that Henry "would put to death without mercy" (Seward, 151) all who opposed him, quickly submitted.

Further Reading: Allmand, Christopher. *Henry V.* New Haven, CT: Yale University Press, 1997; Seward, Desmond. *Henry V: The Scourge of God.* New York: Viking, 1988.

MEN-AT-ARMS. *See* ARMIES, COMPOSITION OF

MERCENARIES. *See* ROUTIERS

MERCILESS PARLIAMENT. *See* PARLIAMENT

MONTAGU, THOMAS, EARL OF SALISBURY (1388–1428)

Commander of the besieging army at OR-LÉANS, Thomas Montagu (or Montague), fourth earl of Salisbury, was a friend and companion of HENRY V and among the most capable and effective English leaders of the HUNDRED YEARS WAR.

The son of John Montagu, third earl of Salisbury, who was posthumously attained for treason against HENRY IV in 1401, Thomas, through loyal service to the House of LANCASTER, was officially recognized as fourth earl of Salisbury in 1409 and fully restored to his father's estates by 1421. His military career began in 1412, when he served with THOMAS, DUKE OF CLARENCE, in the French expedition necessitated by the Anglo-ARMAGNAC Treaty of BOURGES. Admitted to the Order of the GARTER in 1414, the earl fought with Henry V at AGINCOURT in 1415 and with JOHN, DUKE OF BEDFORD, in the naval Battle of the SEINE, which relieved HARFLEUR in 1416. In 1417, Salisbury accompanied the king to NORMANDY, where he served at the sieges of Caen, Falaise, and ROUEN. In April 1419, the king named Salisbury lieutenant-general in Normandy, with responsibility for defense of the English marches south of the Seine. As further evidence of royal confidence, Salisbury was given military command in Anjou in November 1420 and made governor of Alençon and other English-held fortresses in the following month. For these services, the earl was rewarded with numerous French land grants and creation as count of Perche in 1419.

In March 1421, Salisbury retrieved Clarence's body from the battlefield of BAUGÉ, after the duke had rushed into combat without waiting for the earl to arrive with the rear guard. In June 1423, Bedford, now regent for HENRY VI, appointed Salisbury governor of Champagne. In the following July, the earl fought at CRAVANT, and, in August 1424, he distinguished himself at the Battle of VERNEUIL. In late 1424, Salisbury and William de la POLE, earl of Suffolk, attempted to clear Champagne of dauphi-nist garrisons. In 1425, Salisbury consolidated the English hold on Anjou and Maine by leading a successful campaign that culminated with the capture Le Mans (*see* MAINE, SURRENDER OF). When Bedford returned to England in 1425, conduct of the war was entrusted to Salisbury, Suffolk, and Richard BEAUCHAMP, earl of Warwick, with Salisbury's special charge being Normandy, Anjou, and Maine.

In February 1426, Salisbury resigned his commands to go on pilgrimage to Jerusalem in fulfillment of a vow made in combat. However, the pope released him from the vow and the earl returned to royal service by the end of the year. In 1427, Salisbury, now a member of the royal council, sailed to England, where he attended PARLIAMENT and raised reinforcements. In 1428, the earl launched a campaign against Orléans, which he invested on 12 October after seizing the neighboring Loire towns of Jargeau, Meung, and Beaugency. Because the Orléans campaign was opposed by England's ally, PHILIP THE GOOD, duke of BURGUNDY, there has been much debate over why it was undertaken and on whose decision. The plan is sometimes ascribed to Salisbury, who was said to hold a grudge against Burgundy for sexual advances made by the duke toward the countess of Salisbury in 1424; however, this is uncertain, and the earl certainly acted with the approval of Bedford, with whom he had also clashed over the extent of his jurisdiction in various of his commands. On about 24 October 1428, the earl, while observing Orléans from the newly captured fortification of Les Tourelles, was severely wounded in the face by a cannon shot from the city. He died on 3 November. *See also* MONTAGU, WILLIAM, EARL OF SALISBURY; NORMAN CAMPAIGN (1417–1419).

Further Reading: Allmand, Christopher. *Henry V.* New Haven, CT: Yale University Press, 1997; Seward, Desmond. *Henry V: The Scourge of God.* New York: Viking, 1988; Warner, M. W. "Chivalry in Action: Thomas Montague and the War in France, 1417–1428." *Nottingham Medieval Studies* 42 (1998): 146–73; Williams, E. Carleton. *My Lord of Bedford, 1389–1435.* London: Longmans, 1963.

MONTAGU, WILLIAM, EARL OF SALISBURY (1301–1344)

William Montagu (or Montague), first earl of Salisbury, was a close friend and advisor of EDWARD III and a leading figure in the diplomatic and military initiatives of the 1330s and early 1340s.

The eldest son of William Montagu, Lord Montagu, the younger William succeeded to his father's title in 1319. In September 1325, Montagu, who was knighted by EDWARD II prior to embarking, accompanied Prince Edward to France. After his father's deposition in 1327, the prince, now Edward III, grew increasingly frustrated with the tight control exercised over him and his government by his mother, Queen Isabella (see ISABELLA, QUEEN OF ENGLAND [c. 1292–1358]), and her lover, Roger Mortimer, earl of March. Taking Montagu and a few other trusted household knights into his confidence, the king plotted to free himself. In September 1329, Edward sent Montagu to Avignon, where, in secret audience, he gave the pope a password ("Pater Sancte"), whereby he could know which letters from England reflected the king's true mind. In October 1330, after being interrogated by the council on suspicion of intriguing with the king, Montagu led a band of armed men into Nottingham Castle and arrested March.

Immediately awarded with lands worth £1,000 a year, Montagu thereafter maintained a special influence with Edward. Over the next decade, his attendance at court was constant and he accompanied the king on all major military and diplomatic expeditions. His advice was sought on all matters of importance, his seal was used to validate royal letters, and he even occasionally conducted official business on his own authority. He was allowed to adopt the eagle crest, a royal symbol, as his own emblem, and he stood godfather to Edward's second son, Lionel of Antwerp.

Montagu accompanied the king to France in April 1331, when Edward traveled in disguise to pay homage to PHILIP VI for AQUITAINE. In 1333, Montagu campaigned with the king in SCOTLAND and was present at the Battle of HALIDON HILL. In 1334, he was part of the English commission that failed to negotiate a settlement of the Aquitaine question. In 1336, he conducted an unsuccessful siege of Dunbar Castle in Scotland. Created earl of Salisbury in 1337 and endowed with extensive lands in WALES and the West Country, Montagu was in the same year appointed lord admiral and commander of a projected expedition to GASCONY. In 1338, Salisbury became earl marshal of England and campaigned again in Scotland. During the winter of 1338–39, the earl again participated in negotiations with the French and was a member of Edward's inner council of advisors at his court in the Low Countries. Although Salisbury opposed the policy of paying continental allies, finding the subsidies demanded shockingly high, he loyally supported efforts to conclude the ANGLO-FLEMISH ALLIANCE and twice stood hostage with the king's creditors to allow Edward to return to England and arrange payment.

In April 1340, Salisbury was captured while leading a reconnaissance of the town of Lille; coming too close to the walls, his party was cut off by a sortie from the town. Sent to PARIS, Salisbury and his comrades were saved from execution by the intervention of John of Bohemia. In October, Salisbury was exchanged for the Scottish earl of Moray as part of the Truce of ESPLECHIN, the earl agreeing to never again take arms against Philip. Salisbury stood with Edward during the CRISIS OF 1340–1341, arresting various treasury officials for incompetence and serving on the commission that investigated the charges against Archbishop John STRATFORD. In 1343, Salisbury campaigned in BRITTANY with ROBERT OF ARTOIS before undertaking a diplomatic mission to Castile. The earl died on 30 January 1344 from wounds received in a tournament held at Windsor. His descendant, Thomas MONTAGU, fourth earl of Salisbury, was the leading English captain in France in the 1420s.

Further Reading: Packe, Michael. *King Edward III.* Ed. L. C. B. Seaman. London: Routledge and Kegan Paul, 1983; Sumption, Jonathan. *The*

Hundred Years War. Vol. 1, *Trial by Battle.* Philadelphia: University of Pennsylvania Press, 1999.

MONTARGIS, SIEGE OF (1427)

Running from July to September 1427, the English siege of Montargis, a town sixty miles southeast of PARIS, resulted in one of the few victories won by dauphinist forces before the appearance of JOAN OF ARC.

Intending to launch an offensive into dauphinist France, JOHN, DUKE OF BEDFORD, in early July 1427, ordered Richard BEAU-CHAMP, earl of Warwick, to capture the fortress town of Montargis, a key point in the region between the rivers Seine and Loire. With a force of about three thousand, Warwick commenced his siege on 15 July. Standing on high ground and encircled by the rivers Loing and Vernisson, Montargis was a formidable stronghold defended by a large, well-supplied garrison. The town was also intersected by various canals, which likewise divided the besieging force. English progress was therefore slow; by early September, despite a vigorous and continuous ARTILLERY bombardment, little headway had been made against the town's defenses.

To reinforce and resupply the garrison, the dauphin (*see* CHARLES VII) dispatched a force of sixteen hundred commanded by John, Bastard of Orléans (*see* JOHN, COUNT OF DUNOIS AND LONGUEVILLE), and by Étienne de VIGNOLLES, an able soldier better known as "La Hire." The Bastard sent a message to Montargis telling the garrison of his impending arrival and laying out a coordinated plan of action. On 5 September, his men appeared suddenly on the road south of town. As the English moved forward to attack, crossing a small wooden bridge over the Loing, the garrison opened the town's sluice-gates, thereby initiating a flood that split the English army in two by sweeping away the bridge and the men on it. Meanwhile, the garrison attacked the English from behind while the Bastard simultaneously pressed his assault across the river. In the ensuing rout, Warwick lost a third of his force, with the survivors abandoning their artillery as they fled in panic.

Besides establishing the military reputation of the Bastard, the victory greatly heartened the dauphin and his supporters and severely disrupted Bedford's plans; the English could ill afford the loss of men, guns, and supplies suffered at Montagis. Nonetheless, Bedford moved to quickly reestablish the siege, even offering a substantial reward to anyone who could take the town. By late 1428, as the English commenced the assault on dauphinist France with the siege of ORLÉANS, Montagis was in English hands.

Further Reading: Seward, Desmond. *The Hundred Years War.* New York: Penguin, 1999; Williams, E. Carleton. *My Lord of Bedford, 1389–1435.* London: Longmans, 1963.

MONTEREAU CONFERENCE (1419)

Held on 10 September 1419 in a specially prepared enclosure on the Yonne River bridge at Montereau, the conference between the dauphin and JOHN THE FEARLESS, duke of BURGUNDY, leaders, respectively, of the ARMAGNAC and BURGUNDIAN factions, was called ostensibly to reconcile the parties and thus end the FRENCH CIVIL WAR. However, rather than unite the French against the English invader, the conference, which resulted in the murder of Burgundy, drove the duke's son into formal alliance with HENRY V, thereby prolonging the HUNDRED YEARS WAR and jeopardizing VALOIS rule.

When the English completed their conquest of NORMANDY by capturing ROUEN in January 1419, Burgundy, who had custody of PARIS and of the king, CHARLES VI, and the dauphin, who controlled the southern third of France, the so-called "Kingdom of Bourges," sought to make peace as a prelude to joint action against the English. The two leaders met at Corbeil in July and drafted a preliminary agreement, but the dauphinists pushed for another meeting to finalize terms, and, after obtaining Burgundy's reluctant consent, arranged the conference at Montereau. The dauphinists also constructed the palisaded enclosure on Montereau Bridge

Partisans of the dauphin Charles (Charles VII) murder John the Fearless, duke of Burgundy, on the bridge at Montereau, 1419. *Snark/Art Resource, New York.*

where the parties would meet and stipulated that no more than ten men attend the conference for each side.

Although much is unclear about the meeting, what is certain is that at some point during the discussion members of the dauphin's entourage attacked and killed Burgundy. The actual murderers—Guillaume Bataille, Robert de Lairé, and the viscount of Narbonne—were old servants of LOUIS, DUKE OF ORLÉANS, who was himself murdered on Burgundy's orders in 1407. The deed was thus an act of revenge. What is uncertain, and the cause of much heated debate among both contemporaries and later historians, is the exact nature of the dauphin's role, if any, in the murder. The best evidence indicates that the dauphin consented to the murder, but did not originate or encourage it. When the attack began, Tanguy du Châtel, the man who had spirited the dauphin out of Paris when the city fell to the Burgundians in 1418, pushed the prince outside the enclosure, thus shielding him from harm and preventing him from witnessing the murder.

Immediately after the assassination, the dauphinists denied that it was in any way premeditated, and that Burgundy died as a result of an argument that came to blows when one of the duke's attendants drew his sword. The dauphin even hinted that Burgundy had intended to abduct him. This version of events is refuted by the fact that after the duke's death all Burgundians on the bridge were taken prisoner, thus suggesting that the dauphinists were prepared for a struggle and had more than ten men in the enclosure. The other contrary evidence is the testimony of Jean de Poitiers, bishop of Valence, who claimed that just before entering the enclosure, the dauphin had an animated discussion with his chancellor, Robert le Maçon, who several times tried to prevent him from leaving. As soon as the dauphin had gone, the bishop approached Maçon, who was visibly upset, and asked what was amiss. The chancellor replied that the dauphin was "badly advised" and that he was preparing to "do something today by which this kingdom and he himself will be lost" (Vale, 30).

Whatever the truth, the events at Montereau transformed the course of the Hundred Years War. Unable to make common cause with the man he held responsible for his father's murder, PHILIP THE GOOD, the new duke of Burgundy, allied himself with Henry V in the Treaty of TROYES in 1420. Although never an enthusiastic supporter of the House of LANCASTER, the duke used the ANGLO-BURGUNDIAN ALLIANCE as a means of securing his French possessions and enlarging his holdings in the Low Countries. In 1435, Burgundy abandoned the English connection and reconciled with the dauphin, now king as CHARLES VII, at the Congress of ARRAS. As part of the settlement, Charles was required to deny any personal involvement in the murder at Montereau, to punish the guilty parties, and to pay for Masses for the late duke's soul. Charles was also required to send a councilor to make humble apology on his knees before Philip on the king's behalf. So momentous were the events at Montereau to future generations, that a monk conducting Francis I through the burial vault of the dukes of Burgundy in the early sixteenth century picked up the shattered skull of Duke John and said, "This is the hole through which the English entered France" (Seward, 180).

Further Reading: Seward, Desmond. *The Hundred Years War*. New York: Penguin, 1999; Vale, M. G. A. *Charles VII*. Berkeley: University of California Press, 1974; Vaughan, Richard. *John the Fearless*. London: Longman, 1979.

MONTFORT, JOHN DE (d. 1345)

John, count of Montfort, was the English-backed claimant to the duchy of BRITTANY at the start of the BRETON CIVIL WAR.

The half brother of Duke John III, Montfort, whose lands were concentrated mainly in northern France, was little known inside the duchy when the duke died in April 1341. In early May, Montfort took possession of Nantes, the ducal capital. After securing the ducal treasury, the count summoned the Breton nobility to Nantes to pay him homage as duke. However, most Breton noblemen stayed away because they expected PHILIP VI to give the duchy to his nephew, CHARLES OF BLOIS, the husband of Montfort's niece and rival, Jeanne de Penthièvre. To improve his position, Montfort tried to secure control of eastern Brittany, the most pro-French region of the duchy. In June and July, he marched through the eastern districts accepting the submission of the most important towns. By mid-August, the bulk of the duchy was in Montfort's possession.

Anxious to avoid civil war in Brittany, Philip might have left Montfort undisturbed had the king not heard rumors that the count planned to ally himself with EDWARD III. To forestall this, Philip summoned Montfort to PARIS, where he was ordered to remain until the PARLEMENT rendered its decision on the Breton succession. Even though Montfort talked to English agents, he had made no commitments and therefore denied any collusion with Edward. However, since it was clear that Philip intended to detain him while Blois secured the duchy, Montfort secretly returned to Brittany in early September to put his garrisons on a war footing. On 7 September, the Parlement declared in favor of Blois.

Montfort now sent representatives to England, where, in early October, Edward agreed to provide military assistance in return for Montfort's recognition of PLANTAGENET overlordship. However, plans to send an English expedition to Brittany were abandoned when word arrived that Montfort had surrendered Nantes on 2 November to a French army commanded by Blois and John, duke of NORMANDY (see JOHN II). In December, Montfort traveled to Paris under a safe-conduct; however, Philip cancelled the safe-conduct and imprisoned the count when he refused to surrender his claim to the duchy in return for a pension and a grant of land in France. While Montfort languished in the Louvre, Brittany fell into civil war. The strong-willed countess of Montfort, Jeanne de FLANDERS, kept her husband's cause alive until it was rescued by English military intervention in 1342.

Under the terms of the Anglo-French Truce of MALESTROIT concluded in January 1343, Philip released Montfort on 1 September, but extracted from him a promise not to return to Brittany. With his wife, who had fallen into madness, and his young children in England, Montfort adhered to this agreement until 1345, when Philip, in an effort to complete the destruction of the Montfortist party, again placed the count in detention. On 25 March, Montfort escaped to England. In July, he returned to Brittany with William de BOHUN, earl of Northampton, who allowed the count to take charge of the siege of Quimper in an effort to revive support for his cause. However, Montfort proved to be a poor general and an uninspiring leader. He was surprised at Quimper by Blois's army and forced to withdraw in disorder. Trapped in a nearby fortress, Montfort escaped only by bribing a sentry. His party in disarray, the count withdrew to Hennebont, where he fell ill and died on 26 September. The Montfortist cause was thereafter maintained by Edward III, who assumed guardianship of Montfort's son. In 1364, the younger Montfort slew Blois at AURAY and thus won recognition as JOHN IV, duke of Brittany.

Further Reading: Jones, Michael. *Between France and England: Politics, Power and Society in Late Medieval Brittany*. Burlington, VT: Ashgate Publishing Company, 2003; Jones, Michael. *The Creation of Brittany: A Late Medieval State*. London: Hambledon Press, 1988; Sumption, Jonathan. *The Hundred Years War*. Vol. 1, *Trial by Battle*. Philadelphia: University of Pennsylvania Press, 1999.

MONTIEL, BATTLE OF. *See* CASTILIAN WAR OF SUCCESSION

MONTREUIL, PROCESS OF. *See* PROCESS

MORLAIX, BATTLE OF (1342)

The Battle of Morlaix, an encounter between an Anglo-Breton army and the forces of CHARLES OF BLOIS, the French-backed claimant to the duchy, was fought on 30 September 1342 near Morlaix in northwestern BRITTANY. The first pitched battle of the BRETON CIVIL WAR, Morlaix was also the first major land battle of the HUNDRED YEARS WAR, and as such was the first demonstration of the English battle tactics—dismounted men-at-arms flanked by ARCHERS in a strong defensive line—that were to win such later fourteenth-century battles as CRÉCY and POITIERS.

The death of childless Duke John III of Brittany in April 1341 initiated a war of succession between his two heirs—his niece Jeanne de Penthièvre, who was Blois's wife, and his half brother John de MONTFORT. Claiming the duchy in right of his wife, Blois, who was declared duke by his uncle PHILIP VI, invaded Brittany and captured Montfort. However, Jeanne de FLANDERS, Montfort's wife, appealed for aid to EDWARD III, who had promised to support her husband in exchange for his recognition of Ed-

ward as king of France. Edward dispatched a small relief force under Sir Walter MAUNY, which landed in May 1342. Although credited by chroniclers with many daring exploits during this period, Mauny was too weak to attack Blois, who ignored the English and laid siege to Monfortist strongholds in southern Brittany. By August, Countess Jeanne was besieged by land and sea at Brest and the future of the Monfortist cause looked bleak. However, on 18 August, an English fleet carrying an army of three thousand under William de BOHUN, earl of Northampton, dispersed the French ships and landed the earl and his men at Brest, forcing Blois to lift the siege.

Reinforced by eight hundred men under ROBERT OF ARTOIS and by contingents of Breton Montfortists, Northampton marched to Morlaix, which he placed under siege in early September. Learning that Blois was approaching with a relieving force several times larger than his own army, Northampton withdrew most of his army from the siege lines and marched toward the enemy. On the morning of 30 September, he deployed his men in a strong defensive position on the slope of a hill that was backed by a thick wood, which gave protection from cavalry attack and served as a baggage park. Northampton's line consisted of dismounted men-at-arms at its center and bodies of archers on the flanks. Remembering the tactics of the Scots at Bannockburn, the English dug a trench in their front and covered it with branches as an unwelcome surprise for enemy horsemen.

Finding the English in his front, Blois divided his force into three divisions and ordered the first, which consisted of dismounted Bretons, to launch a frontal assault. A hail of arrows broke up the attack before Blois's men had even reached the hidden trench. Thus, when the mounted second column attacked, Blois's unsuspecting cavalry plunged into the trench, where the English archers did terrible execution among the downed and tangled men. Although appalled by his losses, Blois ordered his third division to attack the still outnumbered

English. Because his archers were low on ammunition and the trench, battered and filled with corpses, was no longer a barrier, Northampton retreated into the woods at his rear, where his men stood siege for several days until Blois, unable to effectively reach his enemy, withdrew. Having fought a much larger force to a standstill, Northampton returned to the siege of Morlaix. Because the English had now won a foothold in Brittany, the civil war, which had seemed so near its end, would last for another two decades.

Further Reading: Burne, Alfred H. *The Crécy War*. Ware, England: Wordsworth Editions Ltd., 1999.

MORTIMER, ROGER, EARL OF MARCH. *See* ISABELLA, QUEEN OF ENGLAND (1292–1358)

N

NÁJERA, BATTLE OF (1367)

The Battle of Nájera (or Navarrete) was fought in northeastern Castile near the town of Nájera on 3 April 1367 between an Anglo-Gascon army commanded by EDWARD, THE BLACK PRINCE, and a Franco-Castilian force commanded by Bertrand du GUESCLIN, constable of France, and Henry of Trastámare, the pretender to the Castilian throne. A major victory for the Black Prince, Nájera was the result of Anglo-French intervention in the CASTILIAN WAR OF SUCCESSION, a conflict that offered both sides in the HUNDRED YEARS WAR an opportunity to employ the ROUTIERS who were ravaging their lands and a chance to strike at each other's interests without openly jeopardizing the BRÉTIGNY peace settlement. Although a military success, the battle and its aftermath were political disasters for the prince, who in his effort to obtain funds to meet his campaign expenses initiated events that led eventually to resumption of the Hundred Years War.

Suspected of poisoning his French wife and known as "the Cruel" for his harsh rule, Pedro I of Castile was overthrown by his half brother, Henry of Trastámare, in March 1366. Assisted by a *routier* army commanded by du Guesclin and including numerous English captains such as Hugh CALVELEY, Trastámare was crowned king of Castile on 29 March, one day after Pedro fled Burgos, the Castilian capital. By backing Trastámare, CHARLES V and his brother, LOUIS, DUKE OF ANJOU, the royal lieutenant in Languedoc, had emptied southern France of *routiers* and placed a strong French ally on the southern borders of PLANTAGENET Aquitaine. In late July, Pedro landed in AQUITAINE, where, in

an effort to win support for his cause, he opened talks with the prince and CHARLES THE BAD, king of Navarre. On 23 September, these three principals signed the Treaty of Libourne, whereby Pedro promised money and land to his allies in return for their assistance in restoring him to the Castilian throne. Although many in the prince's entourage disliked and distrusted Pedro, EDWARD III and his ministers were alarmed by the threat posed by a pro-French Castile, while the prince, besides being eager for military action, was, like the French, anxious to free his domains of *routiers*. Relying on Pedro to keep his promise to pay for the campaign, the prince gathered an army of ten thousand men and in February 1367 led them through the Pyrénéan passes, which had been opened to the invaders by the king of Navarre, who sent troops but declined to participate himself.

Advised by the French king to avoid battle and wait for hunger and exhaustion to force the prince to withdraw, Trastámare recalled du Guesclin and many of the French captains who had served him in the previous year. With their forces largely deployed in Aragon, the French brought only about a thousand men to augment Trastámare's Castilian troops. As the Anglo-Gascon army advanced, shadowed from a distance by Trastámare, the towns and garrisons in its path quickly declared for Pedro. On 1 April, Trastámare, fearing the imminent collapse of his political support, abandoned the defensive strategy urged by Charles V and deployed his forces on open ground astride the main road from Logroño near the town of Nájera, a spot the prince later called "a good place to wait for us'' (Sumption, 552). On 2 April, the prince left Logroño, advancing to the village of Navarrete, where he formed his army into line of battle. The front line comprised the English ARCHERS and men-at-arms, who were nominally led by JOHN OF GAUNT, duke of Lancaster, the prince's brother, but in fact commanded by the more experienced Sir John CHANDOS. The main body of the army consisted largely of Gascons, who were commanded on the right by Arnaud-Amanieu, lord of ALBRET, and John, count of Armagnac, and on the left by Jean de GRAILLY, the captal de Buch. In the center, the prince commanded various bands of *routiers* and Castilian exiles. Once in formation, the army left the road and advanced upon the enemy overland from the north, a line of march that put them on Trastámare's left flank by dawn on 3 April.

Surprised by the speed and direction of the enemy advance, du Guesclin was forced to quickly wheel his eastward facing army to the north. Amidst the panic and confusion caused by this maneuver, much of the Castilian infantry and cavalry defected to the enemy. Fearing the breakup of his force, du Guesclin ordered his dismounted French and Castilian men-at-arms to attack. They fell upon the division led by Lancaster and Chandos, which was also dismounted. The English held the French attack, allowing the Gascon wings of the prince's army to begin an enveloping movement against du Guesclin's men. Led by Trastámare and his brother, the Castilian heavy cavalry, refusing to demean themselves by fighting on foot, charged the enemy, but were decimated by English arrows, just as the French had been at CRÉCY. The prince now attacked all along the line, with his own command assailing the Castilians along their front while Lancaster and Chandos struck their flank. As Trastámare's army disintegrated, more than half of it was destroyed trying to flee.

While the prince's army suffered few casualties, Trastámare lost more than five thousand men. The pretender himself escaped the field, but du Guesclin, the French marshal Arnoul d'AUDREHEM, and most of Trastámare's leading captains were captured, indicating that Nájera, like POITIERS, had degenerated at the end into a scramble for prisoners and RANSOMS. Although many of his men made a fortune in ransoms, the prince was soon at odds with the newly restored Pedro, who declared himself unable to pay his debt to the prince and unwilling to cede him territory as security. In late August, when Pedro reneged on his promise to pay a first installment on what he owed, the prince, ill with the disease the eventually killed him and unable to maintain his men in the field any longer, withdrew to Aquitaine empty-handed. Forced to raise taxes in Aquitaine to pay for the campaign, the prince thereby alienated such powerful Gascon noblemen as Armagnac and Albret, whose subsequent petition against the prince's actions (*see* APPEAL OF THE GASCON LORDS) gave Charles V the pretext he required to resume the Hundred Years War in 1369.

Further Reading: Barber, Richard. *Edward, Prince of Wales and Aquitaine.* New York: Charles Scribner's Sons, 1978; Sumption, Jonathan. *The Hundred Years War.* Vol. 2, *Trial by Fire.* Philadelphia: University of Pennsylvania Press, 2001.

NATIONAL CONSCIOUSNESS, GROWTH OF

Through its length and intensity, the HUNDRED YEARS WAR gradually broke down regional loyalties and local identities, thereby fostering a growing sense of nationalism within both societies. If the development of national consciousness was more dramatic in France than in England, this was largely because the former, as the kingdom under attack, was in greater need of unity to defend itself, while the latter, being smaller and less populous, already possessed an administrative unity based on highly developed and widely accepted royal institutions.

Since the late twelfth century, the expansion of royal power and prestige under the kings of the House of CAPET had done much to foster French unity. By the early fourteenth century, the personal piety of Louis

IX (St. Louis) and the centralizing policies of his grandson, PHILIP IV, had extended royal authority and prestige well beyond the confines of the royal domain. One of the long-term causes of the Hundred Years War, the ongoing jurisdictional dispute between the kings of France and the PLANTAGENET king-dukes of AQUITAINE, was just the most famous example of what was occurring in all French fiefs—royal authority was slowly undermining the government of local lords. The idea was growing that "France" encompassed more than just the lands ruled directly by the king; it included all lands that had a feudal connection to the Crown, and all the people of these lands belonged to one country under one king, who, through his officials, acted for the common good. After 1337, the long Anglo-French war accelerated this process by increasing the need for a coordinated national defense against the English, and thus became the most important factor in the promotion of French nationhood.

Besides involving the Crown in local affairs, the war stimulated the development of national institutions, such as the army and the fiscal system that supported it. The growth of a national army as the royal instrument for defending all the people began in the last years of JOHN II and was completed by the reforms of CHARLES V. Discarded during the FRENCH CIVIL WAR, the reforms that had created a professional army paid by the Crown and led by the king or his officers were reinstituted in expanded form by CHARLES VII in the 1440s. In 1448, the creation of the franc-archers, raised by having each community provide one man for military service in return for tax exemptions, signaled the transformation of the king's army into a French national army comprising representatives from each community and locality in the realm. Along with development of the army came development of a national system of TAXATION. The nation could not be defended if the army could not be maintained, and the army could not be maintained if it could not be paid for. The need to collect John II's enormous RANSOM,

the imposition of new types of taxes late in John's reign, and the publication of the ordinance of 1383 whereby CHARLES VI established the principle that all people, whether they lived in Crown lands or the territories of Crown vassals, were to pay *aides*, led to a system of royal taxation that was accepted, if grudgingly, because it was required to successfully resist the English. By the end of the fourteenth century, even the nobility and the clergy were paying royal taxes and thus being tied more closely to the wider national community.

In England, the war promoted national feeling in two ways. The long conflict defined the French as the great national enemy, who were derided as weak, effeminate, and deceitful. Through their many battlefield victories, the English developed a sense of superiority and a greater confidence in themselves and their military prowess. The popes might be French, but triumphs like those at CRÉCY, POITIERS, and AGINCOURT clearly indicated that God favored the English. Thus, for the English, hatred of their enemy inspired pride in themselves, their country, and their king. The war accelerated this process by encouraging the replacement of French with English as the official language of government and DIPLOMACY. In 1362, PARLIAMENT opened for the first time with a speech in English, and the Statute of Pleading, passed in the same parliamentary session, allowed English law courts to conduct business in English. The war also promoted the use of English among the nobility, whose members, prior to the war, had displayed their French heritage by speaking French. However, by the 1390s, Geoffrey Chaucer was writing in English, and, by the early fifteenth century, English diplomats were objecting to the use of French at Anglo-French conferences and negotiations. Thus, language, in conjunction with widespread anti-French feeling, blended the various segments of English society into one community of common interests. *See also* ARMIES, COMMAND OF; CHARLES VII, MILITARY REFORMS OF; PAPACY AND THE HUNDRED YEARS WAR; PROPAGANDA AND WAR PUBLICITY.

Further Reading: Allmand, Christopher. *The Hundred Years War.* Cambridge: Cambridge University Press, 1988; Curry, Anne. *The Hundred Years War.* 2nd ed. Houndmills, England: Palgrave Macmillan, 2003; Seward, Desmond. *The Hundred Years War.* New York: Penguin, 1999.

NAVAL WARFARE

Although noblemen were not trained for naval warfare, which, unlike fighting on land, was not considered a noble pursuit, naval operations were an important part of the HUNDRED YEARS WAR. The English, being the aggressors, required ships to transport men, supplies, and equipment, as well as to control sea lanes and defend coasts against raiders. The French, attempting to resist invasion, needed vessels that could intercept enemy fleets and launch swift, destructive raids on enemy shores. While navies only became vital components of European military establishments in the sixteenth century, the Hundred Years War laid the groundwork for that development in both England and France, neither of which had real navies before 1300. During the war, both kingdoms developed ships and fleets suited to their particular needs, as well as the facilities and administrative support required to maintain naval forces.

The Hundred Years War witnessed several large naval battles. The most important of these encounters were the Battle of SLUYS (1340), which was the first major Anglo-French engagement of the war; the Battle of WINCHELSEA (1350), which was an English attempt to clear the Channel of Castilian raiders; the Battle of LA ROCHELLE (1372), which cost the English both a fleet and an important port; the Battle of CADZAND (1387), which gave the English temporary control of the Channel; and the Battle of the SEINE (1416), which broke the French siege of HARFLEUR. Other important naval actions included the English seizure of Brest (1342), which gave EDWARD III a major port in BRITTANY and secured the sea route to AQUITAINE; the French attack on Winchelsea (1360), which destroyed an English town and foreshadowed the damage French raiders would frequently inflict on the English coast in the 1370s; and the Franco-Castilian blockade of BORDEAUX (1451), which helped complete the French reconquest of GASCONY. The naval battles of the Hundred Years War were hand-to-hand encounters that recreated land combat on the decks of ships. Men fought with the same weapons used on land, although sailors might throw soap or stones to impede enemy boarders, or quicklime to blind enemy combatants. The same projectile weapons employed on land were used to bombard enemy ships, including longbows and crossbows—English ARCHERS made effective use of the former against grappled French vessels at Sluys—as well as lances, spears, and darts; ARTILLERY, however, was rarely mounted on ships before the fifteenth century.

Naval needs also affected overall strategy and the course of wartime DIPLOMACY. The VALOIS soon realized that they could not depend on the maritime resources of FLANDERS, the Flemings being too dependent on wool for their cloth industry to make war on the main supplier of that vital commodity. As a result, French kings forged agreements with Castile, Genoa, and even Denmark to supply ships for naval actions against the English. The Anglo-French interventions in the CASTILIAN WAR OF SUCCESSION in the 1360s were based in large part on the desire of both parties to secure for themselves the assistance of the Castilian fleet, the value of which was clearly demonstrated at La Rochelle in 1372. Intervention in Brittany in the 1340s was similarly based on a desire to control the ports and naval resources of that duchy, and Edward III's siege of CALAIS in 1346–47 was undertaken in the hope of securing for England a cross-Channel port for landing men and supplies. In the fifteenth century, HENRY V focused his attention on conquering NORMANDY in part to achieve English control of both sides of the Channel and thus secure his armies' lines of supply and communication.

In the fourteenth century, neither Crown owned many ships, largely because the cost of building them and the facilities required to maintain them were prohibitively expensive. Thus, war fleets were raised as needed by impressing private vessels. Officers working under the admirals were sent to ports to requisition ships for the king's use. In England, the Cinque Ports, a confederation of southeastern towns, had a special responsibility to provide the Crown with ships and sailors; however, the large fleets required to transport Edward III's army to France for the RHEIMS CAMPAIGN in 1359 or Henry V's for the AGINCOURT campaign in 1415 deprived many merchants and fishermen of their vessels during the height of the trading and fishing seasons. Because ship owners received no payment for the use of their vessels, no compensation for lost business, and no reimbursement for vessels destroyed, damaged, or captured in royal service, such impressments were highly unpopular. What's more, requisitioned ships often had to be substantially modified for war service. Ships carrying horses needed special accommodations below decks, while merchant vessels destined for naval combat had to be fitted with high castles fore and aft.

The English need for vessels with carrying capacity meant that high-sided merchant cogs were best suited to royal service, and impressments of such ships continued to be the best way to raise a fleet. In France, where the need was for smaller, faster ships that could engage the enemy at sea and raid his coasts, the ideal vessel was the galley, a flat-bottomed ship powered by oars or sails that could come in close to shore. By the 1360s, the French Crown was building its own galleys at the Clos de Galées, a shipyard in ROUEN. In the fifteenth century, Henry V realized that he needed a permanent fleet to patrol the Channel and regularly ferry men and supplies to France. By the 1420s, the king, through purchase, capture, and construction, had built a royal fleet of thirty-five vessels and given oversight of naval matters to a clerk of the king's ships headquartered in Southampton. However, after Henry's death in 1422, the fleet was gradually disbanded to save money, with ships being sold or allowed to rot. By the 1440s, when the government of

HENRY VI was too poor to rebuild his father's fleet, the English war effort was severely hampered by lack of a navy.

Further Reading: Allmand, Christopher. *The Hundred Years War*. Cambridge: Cambridge University Press, 1988; Rodger, N. A. M. *The Safeguard of the Sea: A Naval History of Britain, 660–1649*. London: HarperCollins, 1997; Sherborne, J. W. "The Hundred Year's War: The English Navy: Shipping and Manpower." *Past and Present* 37 (1967): 163–75.

NAVARRE. *See* CHARLES THE BAD, KING OF NAVARRE

NAVARRETE, BATTLE OF. *See* NÁJERA, BATTLE OF

NEVILLE'S CROSS, BATTLE OF (1346)

Although an Anglo-Scottish battle fought near Durham in northern England, Neville's Cross was an important engagement of the HUNDRED YEARS WAR, being the culmination of a Scottish invasion of England undertaken by DAVID II to relieve English pressure on his ally, PHILIP VI of France. Occurring on 17 October 1346, less than two months after the Battle of CRÉCY, Neville's Cross allowed the victorious English to capture the Scottish king and to neutralize the "Auld Alliance" as a threat to English action in France.

When EDWARD III landed in NORMANDY in July 1346, David II, whom the English had driven into French exile in the 1330s, launched a series of raids into northern England. Upon receiving news of the French defeat at Crécy on 26 August, David assembled the largest Scottish invasion force of the century, which he led into England on 7 October in an effort to disrupt the English siege of CALAIS. After besieging Liddell Castle and sacking the wealthy priory of Hexham, the Scots arrived before the walls of Durham on 16 October. Although the town agreed to pay RANSOM, elements of an English army commanded by William la Zouch, archbishop of York, and the wardens of the Scottish border, Henry Percy, Lord Percy, and Ralph Neville, Lord Neville of Raby, arrived at Durham next day and quickly deployed for battle on a hill known as Ne-ville's Cross. The armies remained immobile for some hours until David's *schiltrons*, the traditional Scottish formations of massed spearmen, advanced on the English position. Although the Scots fought bravely, they were decimated by the English ARCHERS and repulsed by the English infantry. Hit twice by arrows and having lost one-third of his men, King David was compelled to surrender when his army at last began to disintegrate.

Almost fifty Scottish nobles, including John Randolph, earl of Moray, lay dead on the field. Although Robert Stewart, David's nephew and heir apparent, fled to safety while the battle was still in progress, he was appointed guardian of the realm during David's captivity, which lasted until October 1357. In return for David's release, Edward tried to force the Scots to pay an exorbitant ransom and to accept an English prince as heir to the Scottish throne. The Scots rejected these proposals, although David, increasingly desperate to regain his freedom, was more willing to compromise than were his subjects. When the English capture of JOHN II in 1356 ended all hope of French assistance, the Scots agreed to a ransom of 100,000 marks and swore to take no arms against England until it was paid in full. Because this sum was a heavy burden for SCOTLAND, the final result of Neville's Cross was an indefinite truce that ended the Anglo-Scottish war and largely nullified the FRANCO-SCOTTISH ALLIANCE for the rest of the fourteenth century.

Further Reading: Grant, Alexander. *Independence and Nationhood: Scotland, 1306–1469*. London: E. Arnold, 1984; Neillands, Robin. *The Hundred Years War*. London: Routledge, 1991; Nicholson, Ranald. *Scotland: The Later Middle Ages*. New York: Barnes and Noble, 1974.

NEWSLETTERS. *See* PROPAGANDA AND WAR PUBLICITY

NOGENT-SUR-SEINE, BATTLE OF (1359)

The Battle of Nogent-sur-Seine, a clash between a royal army and a force of ROUTIERS captained by Eustache d'Aubricourt, was fought near the town of Nogent in Champagne on 23 June 1359. The battle was a key victory in the first successful campaign to expel brigand companies from a French province.

The first *routier* bands entered the great, open plain of Champagne, a prosperous region east of PARIS, in late 1358. Many of these companies had been in the pay of CHARLES THE BAD, king of Navarre, who in the previous year had employed them to suppress the JACQUERIE in districts around the capital. Comprising men of many states, but primarily English, French, and Hainaulters, the companies found easy pickings in Champagne, a province that heretofore had seen little fighting or brigandage. Besides Aubricourt, a Hainaulter who had fought for the English in GASCONY and whose elder brother was a founding member of the Order of the GARTER, the chief *routier* captains were two Englishmen who had long served Navarre, a mysterious figure known to the French as Rabigot Drury and an adventurer named Robert Scot. Aubricourt also joined forces with two other *routier* leaders, a German known as Albrecht and an Englishman named Peter Audley, the brother of Sir James AUDLEY, one of EDWARD, THE BLACK PRINCE's lieutenants at POITIERS. The three created a *routier* army of more than a thousand men. By March 1359, these and other captains, acting together or separately, had seized castles and strongholds across Champagne, from which they sallied forth to commit further acts of rape, pillage, and murder.

Aubricourt's men captured the town of Nogent on the Seine, which they used as a base to strike northward, plundering villages and castles in the Marne Valley and the vicinity of Rheims. By late April, Aubricourt controlled a string of towns and strongholds in the area between Nogent and Rheims, with Drury, Scot, and other captains exercising similar dominance over western Champagne. While forming large bands allowed the *routiers* to assault sizable towns and fight pitched battles, the companies found their numbers to be a detriment when they tried to base themselves on a small castle, for too many mouths quickly depleted the locally available supplies, especially should the fortress come under siege. This problem dictated the strategy of seizing a chain of nearby castles, thus easing the supply problem but permitting the companies to combine quickly to raise a siege or meet an enemy in battle.

To counter the *routier* threat, the royal lieutenants of Champagne—John of Chalon, lord of Arlay, and Henry, count of Vaudémont—gathered an army in the Seine Valley south of Nogent near Troyes. Drawing infantry from the towns and hiring cavalry from the local nobility, the lieutenants assembled a force of about twenty-five hundred by mid-June, when they marched on Nogent. Unwilling to stand siege, Aubricourt, leading a force of about seven hundred men, retreated about fifteen miles down the Seine to a strong defensive position near Bray. Adopting English tactics, Aubricourt deployed his men on foot along high ground in a vineyard, where the vines would disrupt cavalry charges. Although Aubricourt was confident of victory, the royal lieutenants, unlike PHILIP VI at CRÉCY, did not engage in headlong cavalry assaults, but divided their force into three divisions to attack the *routiers* from several directions at once, thereby maximizing their advantage in numbers. Aubricourt's men were quickly overwhelmed; most were killed, with the leaders, such as Aubricourt himself, taken prisoner and held to RANSOM. After the victory at Nogent, royalist forces attacked the other companies in turn, thereby clearing Champagne of *routier* garrisons by late summer. Although the king's lieutenants allowed some bands to withdraw from the province under safe-conducts, local peasants and townsmen were not so generous, falling upon the retreating *routiers* and killing many.

Further Reading: Sumption, Jonathan. *The Hundred Years War*. Vol. 2, *Trial by Fire*. Philadelphia: University of Pennsylvania Press, 2001.

NORMAN CAMPAIGN (1417–1419)

Launched in August 1417, HENRY V's Norman campaign, unlike the fourteenth-century *CHEVAUCHÉES* of EDWARD III, aimed at conquest and occupation of territory rather than destruction of enemy morale and resources. Henry was interested not in dismembering France, but in possessing its Crown, which he fervently believed was his by right. To achieve that ultimate end, Henry needed to establish effective political and economic control over NORMANDY by systematically seizing all important towns and fortresses. Thus, the Norman campaign was a slow process characterized by carefully prepared sieges, and by treatment of the Norman people as rebellious subjects who received mercy when they submitted to their rightful lord and punishment when they did not.

On 1 August 1417, Henry landed an army of about ten thousand men on the Norman coast near the castle of Touques, which promptly surrendered. The English then marched southwest, investing Caen on the River Orne. The town surrendered on 4 September after a two-week siege that was highlighted by the capture intact of the monastery of St. Étienne, the burial site of William the Conqueror. As he had done at HARFLEUR two years earlier, Henry expelled that part of the town's population that refused to accept his lordship, their places to eventually be taken by settlers from England. To cut off western Normandy, Henry moved south, taking all strongholds between Caen and Alençon, which fell in mid-October. The English then turned east, taking Mortagne and Bellême, before settling down in late December to the siege of Falaise, the Conqueror's birthplace. The town and its formidable castle withstood a prolonged ARTILLERY bombardment before surrendering in mid-February 1418. In March, a new expedition led by Thomas BEAUFORT, duke of Exeter, left LONDON with supplies and two thousand men, who, like the troops already in France, had indented (*see* INDENTURES) to serve for a year. By August, almost the whole of the duchy west of the

Seine had fallen to Henry, with only the port of Cherbourg, which capitulated to HUMPHREY, DUKE OF GLOUCESTER, in September, causing any difficulty.

Thanks to the ongoing FRENCH CIVIL WAR, the English, prior to May 1418, had little reason to fear an attempt to relieve the Norman garrisons. The ARMAGNAC government in PARIS was hard pressed by JOHN THE FEARLESS, duke of BURGUNDY, who was more concerned with blockading the capital than with resisting the English. In May, an uprising in Paris overthrew the Armagnac regime and handed the city to Burgundy, who once again had custody of CHARLES VI and was thus de facto ruler of France. Although now theoretically committed to the defense of Normandy, Burgundy was in no position to do so effectively. All thought of Burgundian opposition to the English advance ended on 20 July, when the English, after a three-week siege, crossed the Seine and captured Pont-de-l'Arche, thus cutting the link between ROUEN and Paris. The river crossing was achieved with the use of pontoons, with which, thanks to Henry's careful planning, the army was well supplied. Using a pontoon bridge to cross by night to an island in the middle of the stream, Sir John Cornwall led a small force that rowed to the north bank under cover of ARCHERS firing from the island. Cornwall was able to surprise the BURGUNDIANS and thus secure and hold a bridgehead. When another English force crossed via two pontoon bridges laid above and below the town, Pont-de-l'Arche was cut off and surrendered, forcing the Burgundians to abandon the line of the Seine.

On 29 July, Henry opened the siege of Rouen, the Norman capital, which held out until 19 January 1419, thus necessitating another winter investment. When the citizens of Rouen appealed to Burgundy for aid, the duke advised the city to look to its own defense. The capture of Rouen led to the capitulation of most of the remaining French strongholds in northern and eastern Normandy. Lillbourne surrendered on 31 January, Mantes on 5 February, and Dieppe and Eu on 8 and 15 February, respectively. By the beginning of March, only five major castles held out, including Château Gaillard, Gisors, and Mont St. Michel, all of which (save for the latter), fell shortly thereafter. For the first time in over two hundred years, Normandy was a possession of the English Crown. *See also* NORMAN CAMPAIGN (1449–1450).

Further Reading: Allmand, Christopher. *Henry V.* New Haven, CT: Yale University Press, 1997; Burne, Alfred H. *The Agincourt War.* Ware, England: Wordsworth Editions Ltd., 1999.

NORMAN CAMPAIGN (1449–1450)

In little more than a year, the French campaign launched against NORMANDY in July 1449 extinguished English rule in the duchy and, with the exception of CALAIS, stripped the House of LANCASTER of its holdings in northern France. Marked by one pitched battle and a series of successful sieges, the Norman Campaign illustrated the effectiveness of the reorganized French army and especially of the new French ARTILLERY train.

On 24 March 1449, an English force under the *ROUTIER* captain François de Surienne seized the Breton town of FOUGÈRES. Undertaken in retaliation for recent French operations in Maine, the ill-advised English attack made an open enemy of Francis I, duke of BRITTANY, and convinced CHARLES VII to abandon the Truce of TOURS. At a council held at Chinon on 17 July 1449, the king ended talks with the English lieutenant, Edmund BEAUFORT, duke of Somerset, and announced formal resumption of the HUNDRED YEARS WAR. Within a month, the French opened a three-pronged attack on Lancastrian Normandy, with overall command given to the veteran soldier, JOHN, COUNT OF DUNOIS, JOAN OF ARC's companion at the siege of ORLÉANS. By the end of the year, the counts of Eu and Saint-Pol had overrun much of eastern Normandy; Dunois, supported by another of the Maid's captains, JOHN, DUKE OF ALENÇON, had captured VERNEUIL and most of central Normandy; and Francis of Brittany, supported by his uncle, Arthur de Richemont, the French constable (*see* ARTHUR III), had retaken most of the west, including Fougères, which fell on 5 November. Everywhere, but especially in the countryside, the French were greeted as liberators. The English, even though they controlled many strongpoints, were thoroughly demoralized by the speed and effectiveness of the French campaign, and many towns and fortresses offered little or no resistance.

On 9 October, an army commanded by the king himself encamped around ROUEN. When the city authorities opened the gates, Beaufort and his men withdrew into the castle, which the duke surrendered on 29 October, thereby allowing Charles to make a triumphal entry into the Norman capital on 20 November. Although winter slowed French operations, and John TALBOT, earl of Shrewsbury, made a futile attempt to disrupt enemy movements with his small force, English strongpoints continued to fall, including HARFLEUR, which capitulated in December.

In England, the increasingly unpopular regime of William de la POLE, duke of Suffolk, collected, with much difficulty, a relieving force of about five thousand men, which was dispatched under Sir Thomas Kyriel in March 1450. Landing at Cherbourg, Kyriel retook several fortresses before his army was destroyed by Richemont and John, count of Clermont, at FORMIGNY on 15 April. In this battle, as well as in all the campaign's important sieges, the artillery of the French master of ordinance, Jean BUREAU, played an important role, giving the French the tactical advantage that the longbow (see ARCHERS) had once given the English at such battles as CRÉCY and AGINCOURT. With no English army in the field, the campaign became simply a matter of reducing the remaining English fortresses, the successful conclusion of which was made almost inevitable by Bureau's guns. While the Bretons cleared the western districts, the royal army forced the capitulation of Caen on 1 July, which Somerset surrendered after a cannonball smashed into a room occupied by his family. Falaise fell on 21 July and Domfront on 2 August, with Cherbourg, the last English stronghold in the duchy, surrendering on 12 August, a year to the day after the commencement of French operations.

The ease of his victory persuaded Charles to attack GASCONY in 1451, a campaign that culminated with the final conquest of that duchy in 1453. In England, the rapid collapse of Lancastrian Normandy overthrew Suffolk, was a factor in the outbreak of JACK CADE'S REBELLION, and aggravated the aristocratic feuds that later helped launch the Wars of the Roses. See also CHARLES VII, MILITARY REFORMS OF; MAINE, SURRENDER OF; NORMAN CAMPAIGN (1417–1419).

Further Reading: Burne, Alfred H. *The Agincourt War*. Ware, England: Wordsworth Editions Ltd., 1999; Perroy, Edouard. *The Hundred Years War*. Trans. W. B. Wells. New York: Capricorn Books, 1965.

NORMANDY

Located across the Channel from England in northwestern France, the duchy of Normandy, a former PLANTAGENET possession held by the French Crown since 1204, became the center of Lancastrian France in the fifteenth century.

In the fourteenth century, English activity in France focused mainly on AQUITAINE, BRITTANY, and FLANDERS, and interest or involvement in Normandy was brief and sporadic. The first English intervention in the duchy began on 12 July 1346, when EDWARD III, encouraged by Norman dissidents led by Godfrey of HARCOURT, opened the CRÉCY campaign by landing at Saint-Vaaste-la-Hogue. Although the culminating battle was fought in Ponthieu, most of the campaign occurred in Normandy, as the English marched eastward through the duchy burning and looting. However, the campaign demonstrated that pro-English sentiment in Normandy was weak and that Edward lacked the manpower to effectively garrison the duchy. In the late 1350s, Edward assumed the title duke of Normandy and included the duchy among the territories to be granted him in full sovereignty in the abortive Second Treaty of LONDON, but the final settlement achieved by the Treaty of BRÉ-TIGNY in 1360 left Normandy to the VALOIS. In 1378, the English acquired the Norman port of Cherbourg from CHARLES THE BAD, KING OF NAVARRE, who had made Normandy a center of revolt against the government of Dauphin Charles (*see* CHARLES V) in the early 1360s (*see* COCHEREL, BATTLE OF). The English used the town as a base for naval raids until 1393, when RICHARD II surrendered it in pursuit of the peace policy he followed after the Truce of LEULINGHEN.

In the fifteenth century, Normandy became vital to the English war effort. HENRY V proclaimed himself duke of Normandy and stressed his Norman ancestry by way of proving his right to hold the duchy in full sovereignty. In 1415, the king opened the AGINCOURT campaign by seizing the Norman port of HARFLEUR at the mouth of the Seine. Beginning in 1417, Henry undertook a systematic conquest of the duchy, which was completed with the fall of ROUEN in January 1419. Each of the main towns and fortresses received an English garrison and English subjects were encouraged to settle in the duchy to eventually make Normandy a self-sustaining English province capable of paying for its own defense. In 1420, the Treaty of TROYES provided for an English-controlled Normandy that was to remain separate from France until Henry or his heirs inherited the French Crown from CHARLES VI.

After his brother's death in 1422, JOHN, DUKE OF BEDFORD, tried to foster Lancastrian rule in the duchy by carefully observing local laws and customs and by frequently consulting the Norman Estates on defense and taxation. Following the Battle of VERNEUIL in 1424, which pushed the war

southward toward the Loire, English rule in Normandy was secure; the duchy was generally peaceful and the English garrisons were reduced. In 1429, English defeats at ORLÉANS and PATAY opened eastern Normandy to French attack. Insecurity increased both taxes and brigandage, making the English administration highly unpopular and leading to a serious revolt in western Normandy in 1435–36. Although the uprising was eventually suppressed, Harfleur was lost until 1441 and Lancastrian rule in the duchy was permanently weakened.

After 1436, when CHARLES VII recovered PARIS, Rouen became the administrative center of Lancastrian France, but the English were now seen as an occupying force and Norman support for the Lancastrian regime declined throughout the 1440s, when Anglo-French hostilities were halted by the Truce of TOURS. In 1449, the French resumed the war with a campaign that retook the duchy within a year. The last English army in Normandy was decisively defeated at FORMIGNY in April 1450 and English rule—and the HUNDRED YEARS WAR—ended in Normandy with the fall of Cherbourg on the following 12 August. *See also* NORMAN CAMPAIGN (1417–1419); NORMAN CAMPAIGN (1449–1450); PONTOISE, SIEGE OF.

Further Reading: Allmand, C. T. *Lancastrian Normandy, 1415–1450: The History of a Medieval Occupation.* Oxford: Clarendon Press, 1983; Curry, Anne. *The Hundred Years War.* 2nd ed. Houndmills, England: Palgrave Macmillan, 2003.

NORTHAMPTON, EARL OF. *See* BOHUN, WILLIAM DE, EARL OF NORTHAMPTON

NORTHAMPTON, PEACE OF. *See* SCOTLAND

ORDER OF THE GARTER. *See* GARTER, ORDER OF THE

ORDER OF THE STAR. *See* STAR, ORDER OF THE

ORDONNANCE CABOCHIENNE. See CABOCHIENS

ORIFLAMME

The Oriflamme, a long forked banner of scarlet embroidered with golden flames and carried from a gilded lance, was the military standard of the VALOIS kings of France during the HUNDRED YEARS WAR.

The origins of the banner are uncertain, although it was believed to be the emblem of Charlemagne, and to represent a sacred flaming lance with which the emperor could defeat the enemies of Christendom. In some of the earliest traditions, the banner is merely ornamentation for the lance on which it hangs, which is the true symbol of importance. In the tenth century, Hugh, the first king of the House of CAPET, entrusted the Oriflamme to the Abbey of Saint-Denis, the monastery near PARIS that became the burial place of French kings. A twelfth-century story also linked the banner to the counts of Vexin and their traditional role as protectors of Saint-Denis, a special relationship that passed with the county to the kings of France in 1077.

Descriptions of the standard's appearance vary, perhaps as a result of worn or damaged banners being occasionally replaced. In general, the Oriflamme was said to be of blood-red silk with green fringe, golden lines or circles of flame, and two or three forked indentations on the free end. The banner was attached either vertically to the lance or to a bar suspended from the lance tip. In later battles, the Oriflamme was carried in association with the French royal standard of golden fleur-de-lis on a blue background, a more familiar emblem to modern eyes.

The banner was first carried into battle in the 1120s, when Louis VI, disregarding the tradition that it only be used against enemies of Christianity, unfurled it against various Christian rulers, including Henry I of England. In the thirteenth century, Louis IX (St. Louis) retrieved the banner from Saint-Denis to carry it on his crusade against the Muslims. In the fourteenth century, French kings raised the Oriflamme whenever the military situation was deemed serious enough to require display of such a potent symbol of royal authority and power. Almost destroyed during the French victory over Flemish militia at Mons-en-Pévèle in 1304, the banner also appeared on the battlefields of Cassel (1328) and Roosebeke (1382), which were victories over Flemish rebels, and at CRÉCY (1346), POITIERS (1356), and AGINCOURT (1415), all major defeats at the hands of the English. Perhaps because of its association with so many military disasters, the Oriflamme was raised less frequently after 1420. It appeared on the battlefield for the last time in the late fifteenth century, and thereafter remained at Saint-Denis until it was destroyed during the French Revolution.

Further Reading: Hallam, Elizabeth M. *Capetian France, 987–1328.* London: Longman, 1980; Keen, Maurice. *The Laws of War in the Late Middle*

Ages. Toronto: University of Toronto Press, 1965; Lewis, P. S. *Later Medieval France: The Polity.* London: Macmillan, 1980.

ORLÉANS, DUKE OF. *See* CHARLES, DUKE OF ORLÉANS; LOUIS, DUKE OF ORLÉANS

ORLÉANS, SIEGE OF (1428–1429)

Perhaps the most studied and written-about military operation of the HUNDRED YEARS WAR, the English siege of Orléans, the chief dauphinist town on the Loire, ran from 12 October 1428 to 8 May 1429. Inspired by the most unorthodox of military leaders, JOAN OF ARC, a teenage girl who wore ARMOR and claimed to be sent by heaven to save France, the French relief of the city turned the tide of the war. Although it would take another twenty-four years to drive the English from France, Joan's victory at Orléans restored the prestige of the VALOIS monarchy and imbued its cause with the aura of divine approval, thereby demoralizing the English, who after Orléans found themselves largely on the defensive.

On 1 July 1428, Thomas MONTAGU, earl of Salisbury, landed in France with a force of about three thousand. The earl marched to PARIS, where, in consultation with JOHN, DUKE OF BEDFORD, and other English leaders, the decision was made to capture Orléans, thereby securing the Loire and threatening the heartland of dauphinist France. Although it was a breach of CHIVALRY to attack the possessions of a captive— CHARLES, DUKE OF ORLÉANS, had been an English prisoner since AGINCOURT in 1415— the operation was approved because taking the city might at last convince the French that the Valois cause was lost. In August,

A modern view of Orléans showing the bridge across the Loire that was the scene of much fighting during the English siege of the town in 1428–29. *Erich Lessing/Art Resource, New York.*

Salisbury isolated Orléans by systematically capturing other Loire towns, including Meung, Jargeau, and Beaugency. On 12 October, the earl, commanding a force of perhaps five thousand, including men hired from PHILIP THE GOOD, duke of BURGUNDY, encamped around Orléans. Although he lacked sufficient troops to completely encircle the city, which was large, high-walled, well-supplied, and defended by seventy-one guns and fifty-four hundred men commanded by

235

John, the Bastard of Orléans, brother of the captive duke (*see* JOHN, COUNT OF DUNOIS AND LONGUEVILLE [1402–1468]), Salisbury began an immediate bombardment. Within days, the English seized the Tourelles, a stone fortress that protected the far end of the bridge connecting the city to the south bank of the Loire. On about 24 October, Salisbury, while reconnoitering the city from an upper window of the Tourelles, was struck by metal fragments blasted from the fortress walls by French ARTILLERY. With much of his jaw and lower face gone, the earl died on 3 November.

The death of Salisbury stalled the English assault, for William de la POLE, earl of Suffolk, who now assumed command, was a more cautious leader. He moved most of the army into winter quarters in nearby towns, leaving only a token force before Orléans and thus enabling the French to bring more troops and supplies into the city. In December, John TALBOT and Thomas SCALES, Lord Scales, arrived at Orléans to assume joint command with Suffolk, while Sir William Glasdale took charge of the Tourelles. On 12 February, the failure of a French attempt to intercept an English supply convoy at the Battle of the HERRINGS severely damaged the city's morale. The besiegers also constructed a number of boulevards—low earthwork defenses—around the city, including a particularly strong one, known as the boulevard of the Augustins, before the Tourelles. These defenses seemed to indicate an English willingness to starve the city into surrender and a belief, shared by many in the increasingly demoralized town, that no relief attempt would be made by the dauphin. However, in early March, Joan of Arc came to the dauphin at Chinon, where she told him that God had sent her to relieve Orléans and see him crowned. Encouraged by the Maid, the dauphin began assembling a large relief force at Blois.

On 29 April, Joan entered Orléans from the east, bypassing the English Saint Loup boulevard without incident, an achievement later ascribed to a miracle worked by Joan,

although a diversionary attack on the boulevard by the garrison probably ensured her entry. Over the next four days, Joan vehemently urged an immediate attack on the English, while the Bastard, believing himself unready for such an assault, refused to do so; on 1 May, he left for Blois to gather more troops. Joan, meanwhile, in an apparent attempt to provoke the enemy into attacking, spoke to the English across the lines, demanding that they withdraw in obedience to God's will and receiving in return many insults. Upon the Bastard's return on 4 May, the French attacked and captured the Saint Loup boulevard. On 5 May, the French occupied the recently abandoned boulevard of Saint Jean le Blanc, and on 6 May, the French, in a furious assault led by Joan, captured the boulevard of the Augustins, thus pinning the English in the Tourelles between the city and the relieving force. On 7 May, despite the Bastard's desire to rest his men, the French assaulted the Tourelles at Joan's insistence. When Joan refused to leave the field after being wounded in the shoulder by an arrow, the French, who had been making little headway, were inspired by her courage and eventually carried the fortification. Glasdale, who had personally mocked Joan as a "whore of the ARMAGNACS" (DeVries, 75), was slain with most of his men.

Next day, 8 May, the English abandoned their remaining boulevards and ordered themselves for battle. The French sallied forth to meet them, but Joan, unwilling to fight on Sunday, urged them not to attack, but only to defend themselves from enemy assaults. Despite rumors that Sir John FASTOLF was approaching with reinforcements, the English had apparently lost faith in their boulevard defenses. When the French did not attack, they marched away, with Suffolk withdrawing to Jargeau and Talbot and Scales to Meung. News of the Maid's victory overjoyed the dauphinists and profoundly shocked the English. In June, Joan accompanied another French army that during a weeklong campaign culminating at PATAY, cleared the Loire of English garrisons (*see* LOIRE CAMPAIGN) and allowed the dauphin to march to Rheims and be crowned as CHARLES VII on 17 July.

Further Reading: Burne, Alfred H. *The Agincourt War*. Ware, England: Wordsworth Editions Ltd., 1999; DeVries, Kelly. *Joan of Arc: A Military Leader*. Stroud, England: Sutton Publishing, 2003.

P

PAPACY AND THE HUNDRED YEARS WAR

Although a supranational institution of wide influence, the papacy was hampered in its efforts to prevent or end the HUNDRED YEARS WAR by its perceived lack of impartiality. From 1305 to 1378, the papacy was viewed as being subservient to the French Crown, and from 1378 to 1417 effective papal mediation was rendered impossible by the "Great Schism," a disputed papal succession that resulted in several lines of popes competing with one another for the support of national rulers and thereby aggravating rather than healing the political divisions of the Hundred Years War. While most popes of the war period took seriously their duty to bring peace to Europe, and most of the peace conferences and truce talks of the fourteenth century had some papal involvement, no settlement was ever achieved largely because the English and French Crowns did not want one and because the papacy lacked sufficient influence to impose one.

The so-called "Babylonian Captivity" of the papacy began in 1305 with the election of Bertrand de Got, archbishop of BORDEAUX, a Gascon, who, as a subject of the French Crown and a vassal of the PLANTAGENET king-dukes of AQUITAINE, seemed a good choice to heal the rifts created by the bitter quarrel between PHILIP IV and the late pope, Boniface VIII (r. 1294–1303). Choosing the name Clement V (r. 1305–14), the new pope was persuaded by the French king to avoid the political turmoil of Rome and base his papacy in Avignon, a town in the Rhône valley that was then just outside the borders of France. For the next seventy-three years, a string of French-born popes, supported by a largely French cardinalate, presided over the Church from Avignon.

Jacques Fournier, who as Benedict XII (r. 1334–42) was pope at the start of the war in the 1330s, undertook strenuous but unavailing efforts to prevent the outbreak of hostilities. Although it suited English purposes to denounce the French-born pope as biased, Benedict failed not because he was pro-French, but because EDWARD III and PHILIP VI were fundamentally unwilling to reach a settlement. Pierre Roger, who was elected pope in 1342 as CLEMENT VI (r. 1342–52), brokered the Truce of MALESTROIT in 1343 and sponsored the AVIGNON PEACE CONFERENCE of 1344, by which he sought to bring the warring parties to terms. Again the talks failed largely because neither monarch truly wanted peace and because Clement's former position as chancellor of France allowed Edward to plausibly dismiss him as a VALOIS puppet. Although Clement genuinely sought peace, he, like Benedict, took a conservative rather than a pro-French view of the dispute over Aquitaine; that is, Edward III was seen as a feudal vassal challenging the authority of his legitimate overlord, who was a solemnly anointed king. In this context, it was hard for the Avignon popes to give serious consideration to Edward's claim to the French throne, which none of them ever recognized. Thus, all Anglo-French negotiations sponsored by the Avignon popes ended in failure, including the 1352–54 talks arranged by Étienne Aubert, who was pope as Innocent VI (r. 1352–62), and the 1375–77 BRUGES PEACE CONFERENCE sponsored by Pierre Roger de Beaufort, the nephew of Clement VI and pope as Gregory XI (r. 1370–78).

Papal influence declined steadily as the war progressed. In England, Edward III confiscated the property of French monastic houses on grounds of national security and PARLIAMENT enacted the statutes of Praemunire (1353, 1393) and Provisors (1351, 1390) to elicit more papal cooperation with the Crown, especially on ecclesiastical appointments. Blatant pro-French actions, such as the refusal of Guillaume de Grimoard, pope as Urban V (r. 1362–70), to permit a marriage between Edward's son, EDMUND OF LANGLEY, duke of York, and MARGUERITE, the daughter of LOUIS DE MALE, count of Flanders, while at the same time encouraging her marriage to CHARLES V's brother, PHILIP THE BOLD, duke of BURGUNDY, further eroded English respect for papal authority. In both kingdoms, monarchs taxed the clergy without papal sanction and exercised significant influence over the functioning of national churches.

In 1376, despite the protests of Charles V, Gregory XI returned the papacy to Rome. On his death two years later, the Roman mob forced the election of an Italian, Bartolomeo Prignano, who took the name Urban VI (r. 1378–89). Convinced by French cardinals that Urban's election was invalid, Charles V backed their election of one of their own, Robert of Geneva, as Pope Clement VII (r. 1378–94), an action that led to the creation of two competing lines of popes—one backed by the French and Scottish Crowns and headquartered in Avignon, and one backed by the English Crown and most of Europe and headquartered in Rome. This division, which ended any hope of papal war mediation, became even worse in 1409, when the Council of Pisa deposed the current Roman and Avignon popes and elected as their successor Pietro Philarghi as Pope Alexander V (r. 1409–10). Although France and England, for once in agreement, accepted Alexander, the deposed popes each retained the loyalty of other states, thus leaving the Church with three popes.

In 1416, Holy Roman Emperor Sigismund convened the Council of Constance in an effort to end the schism; however, all efforts in this direction were bedeviled by the ongoing Anglo-French hostility and by the intensifying FRENCH CIVIL WAR, as English delegates quarreled with French, and ARMAGNAC delegates argued with BURGUNDIANS. To end the papal divisions, Sigismund tried to secure the cooperation of the Houses of Valois and LANCASTER. He received a cold reception in PARIS, which he visited only six months after the Battle of AGINCOURT, but he was warmly welcomed to LONDON by HENRY V, who eventually persuaded him to sign the anti-French Treaty of CANTERBURY.

In 1417, the Council of Constance effectively ended the schism by securing the resignation or deposition of the various antipopes and electing Oddo Colonna as Pope Martin V (r. 1417–31). Headquartered in Rome, the new pope won the allegiance of most of Europe, including both England and France. However, his efforts to restore papal authority took precedence over war mediation, in which he was in any case tainted in English eyes by his refusal to accept the Treaty of TROYES in 1420. In 1434, his successor, Gabriele Condulmaro, who took the name Eugenius IV (r. 1431–47), officially recognized CHARLES VII as rightful king of France, thus limiting his effectiveness as a mediator at the Congress of ARRAS in 1435, where was made the last significant papal attempt to broker a settlement of the Hundred Years War.

Further Reading: Curry, Anne. *The Hundred Years War*. 2nd ed. Houndmills, England: Palgrave Macmillan, 2003; Mollat, G. *The Popes at Avignon, 1305–1378: The "Babylonian Captivity" of the Medieval Church*. New York: Harper and Row, 1965; Renouard, Yves. *The Avignon Papacy: The Popes in Exile, 1305–1403*. New York: Barnes and Noble, 1994.

PARIS

Paris during the HUNDRED YEARS WAR was the largest and wealthiest city in France, as well as the center of royal government.

Although not always the residence of the king and his court, it was the administrative and judicial heart of the kingdom, being the seat of the Chambre des Comptes, the central auditing office, and the PARLEMENT, the central law court. The city's cultural and economic dominance were guaranteed by the University of Paris, the most influential European university of the Middle Ages, and the rise within the city of great merchant families, who by the fourteenth century held important positions in royal government and finance. As a result of this preeminence, Paris played a key role in the history of the Anglo-French war, especially during the 1350s, when the city rose against royal authority, and the early fifteenth century, when Paris was under English occupation.

Paris arose from Celtic and Roman settlements on an island in the River Seine, later known as the Île-de-la-Cité, and its adjoining banks, later known, because of the river's many twists, as the Right and Left Banks (when facing downstream). The Roman city, called Lutetia, became known as Paris, from a local Celtic tribe, the Parisi, in the late fourth century. Under the early Capetian kings, Paris became the center of royal government, the expansion of which, especially after Louis VI took up residence in Paris after 1130, fueled the city's growth. The kings of the House of CAPET found the city's location ideal for checking the aspirations of regional dynasties, such as the Angevin and ultimately English royal House of PLANTAGENET to the west and the House of Champagne to the east. Under the kings of the twelfth and thirteenth centuries, Paris experienced unprecedented growth, both in population and wealth, with the university achieving corporate independence by the early thirteenth century. Louis IX reorganized the city's administration in 1261, creating the offices of *prévôt* to exercise royal authority within Paris, and *prévôt des marchands* to lead the merchant community. By the end of the thirteenth century, Paris was the acknowledged seat of the national capital, and Parisians, who dominated the royal bureaucracy, strongly supported the extension of royal authority.

At the start of the war in the fourteenth century, the city's population is estimated to have exceeded eighty thousand, with perhaps a quarter of that number being students. As the royal administration grew in size and competence, great lords, both lay and spiritual, found it increasingly important to be resident in the city, while important corporate bodies, such as towns and monasteries, found it necessary to maintain representatives in Paris. The bourgeoisie of Paris, increasingly dominated by families of great wealth, grew in economic strength and political sophistication.

The city's relations with the VALOIS kings fluctuated. Like his Capetian predecessors, PHILIP VI maintained an itinerant court, spending more time in royal manors than in the city, but JOHN II was frequently in residence at the royal palace on the western end of the Île-de-la-Cité and CHARLES V also spent much time in the capital, although his preferred residences were on the Right Bank, the Louvre, or the Hôtel de Saint-Pol. The latter was also a favorite residence of CHARLES VI, whose illness precluded much travel outside the city. However, CHARLES VII spent little time in Paris. Forced to flee a BURGUNDIAN mob in 1418, Charles did not return to Paris until the city was retaken from the English in 1436, and even thereafter spent more time at his Loire residences.

During the early fourteenth century, royal fiscal policy, especially the Crown's frequent manipulation of the currency, strained the city's once close collaboration with the king. Both PHILIP IV and PHILIP V met fierce opposition from the city, with the latter's advisors even debating the possibility of moving the capital to Orléans. Although the city suffered severely during the BLACK DEATH of the late 1340s, Paris continued to expand outside the walls built by Philip II in the early thirteenth century. In 1356, the *prévôt des marchands,* Étienne MARCEL, who was a member of one of the city's great merchant families, began construction of a new wall, which was continued by Charles

V. In the aftermath of John II's capture at POITIERS, Marcel led a revolutionary movement that drove the dauphin from the city. Demanding governmental reform, Marcel split his party by supporting the JACQUERIE in 1358, an action that allowed the dauphin to regain support in the city and led to Marcel's murder by a Paris mob. Another Parisian uprising, the *Maillotins*, erupted in 1382, when the city resisted the imposition of new royal taxes that bore heavily on urban populations. The government of Charles VI responded by crushing the rebellion and abolishing the office of *prévôt des marchands*.

During the FRENCH CIVIL WAR, the city supported JOHN THE FEARLESS, duke of BURGUNDY, who won over the bourgeoisie and the university by posing as a reformer. In April 1413, Burgundy, in an effort to maintain his dominance, incited the butchers of Paris to rise in favor of reform. Known as the CABOCHIENS, for their leader, Simon Caboche, the rebels plunged the city into a three-month reign of terror and forced the decree of a massive reform ordinance. The ARMAGNACS crushed the uprising when they entered Paris in September following Burgundy's flight. For the next five years, the city, suffering intermittent Burgundian sieges, was controlled by an Armagnac regime increasingly dominated by BERNARD, COUNT OF ARMAGNAC, who maintained order through his ruthless Gascon bands. After retaking the city in May 1418, the Burgundians slaughtered their rivals, killing the count and forcing the dauphin to flee. In 1420, conclusion of the Treaty of TROYES, which recognized HENRY V as heir to the French throne, brought the city under Anglo-Burgundian control, and for the next sixteen years Paris was the capital of the Lancastrian domains, while dauphinist southern France was administered from the dauphin's strongholds below the Loire. Although dissolution of the ANGLO-BURGUNDIAN ALLIANCE at the Congress of ARRAS in 1435 allowed Charles VII to regain Paris in 1436, it took until the end of the war in the 1450s for the city to regain its former political and economic dominance.

Further Reading: Butler, Raymond R. *Is Paris Lost? The English Occupation, 1422–1436*. Staplehurst, England: Spellmount, 2003; Couperie, Pierre. *Paris through the Ages*. New York: Braziller, 1968; Jones, Colin. *Paris: Biography of a City*. London: Allen Lane, 2004; Velay, Philippe. *From Lutetia to Paris: The Island and the Two Banks*. Paris: CNRS, 1992.

PARIS, TREATY OF (1259)

Concluded on 13 October 1259, the Treaty of Paris was a personal agreement between Louis IX (St. Louis) of France and Henry III of England regarding the feudal status of all French territories claimed by the English king. By making the king of England a vassal of the king of France, the treaty created an ultimately untenable relationship between two sovereign monarchs and their kingdoms. In the 1330s, the increasingly severe political and legal strains arising from this relationship became a root cause of the HUNDRED YEARS WAR.

Under Henry II and his sons, England had controlled a vast continental domain encompassing most of western France. In 1202, Philip II (Augustus), acting in his capacity as King John's feudal overlord, summoned John to the French court to answer an appeal launched against him by certain of his vassals in Poitou. When John failed to appear, Philip declared John's lands forfeit and by 1204 had seized NORMANDY, Maine, Anjou, and Touraine, leaving John with only Poitou (until 1224) and AQUITAINE. Thereafter, the two kings and their successors remained technically at war, with the kings of England still claiming the lost northern provinces and the kings of France still upholding the confiscation of Aquitaine.

By the 1250s, both monarchs had good reasons for wanting to stabilize their relationship. Henry III, embroiled with his barons and entangled in a scheme to make his brother ruler of Sicily, needed the friendship and military assistance of the French king. Although Louis was sincerely desirous of peace between the two kingdoms and their royal families, he also wanted to formalize a relationship that recognized him as the feudal overlord of the king of England. Negotiations between the two parties began in 1257 and a treaty was completed in May 1258, although settlement of various details delayed ratification until October 1259.

The main clauses of the treaty called for Henry to surrender his claims to Normandy, Maine, Anjou, Touraine, and Poitou, and for Louis to confirm PLANTAGENET possession of Aquitaine, which was to be restored to its 1204 extent by the surrender of various territories held by Louis or members of his family. Because of the complexity of landholding in the ceded areas, the clauses governing the transfer were complicated and soon became the cause of endless controversy. Henry was also to become a peer of France and to perform liege homage to Louis for all his holdings in France, including GASCONY, which, the English later argued, was an allod (i.e., a territory held in absolute ownership) and never held of the French king. Because liege homage implied a personal subordination to one's lord, performance of this rite, which was due on every change of duke or monarch, caused much friction. However, because he was eager for the five hundred knights Louis agreed to fund, Henry performed such homage in the garden of the royal palace in PARIS on 4 December 1259.

Although the treaty brought peace for several generations, it contained within it the seeds of the Hundred Years War. As a vassal of the king of France, the king-duke of Aquitaine suffered constant interference in the administration of his duchy. Any vassal who was unhappy with the king-duke's lordship could appeal to the PARLEMENT in Paris. If the king of France summoned the duke of Aquitaine to support him in a foreign war, as was his feudal right, the duke might find himself compelled to fight a ruler with whom he had an alliance as king of England, a circumstance that threatened his freedom of action in English foreign policy. Thus, EDWARD III eventually went to war with France to end his feudal subservience to a fellow monarch and to win full sovereignty in his French lands.

Further Reading: Curry, Anne. *The Hundred Years War*. 2nd ed. Houndmills, England: Palgrave Macmillan, 2003; Vale, Malcolm. *The Origins of the Hundred Years War*. Oxford: Clarendon Press, 2000.

PARLEMENT OF PARIS

Headquartered in PARIS, the Parlement was the central law court of the French monarchy. The Parlement received and tried appeals from lower royal courts and from seigniorial courts in the great fiefs and APPANAGE territories. Devoted to the interests of the French Crown and to the extension of royal authority throughout the realm, the personnel of the Parlement often used their authority to interfere with local administration, a practice that was particularly resented in the duchy of AQUITAINE, where jurisdictional conflict between the French Crown and the English king-dukes was an important factor in the coming and continuance of the HUNDRED YEARS WAR.

As the royal domain grew in the twelfth and thirteenth centuries, the great nobles and clerics, as well as towns and members of the lesser nobility, began to resort to the king's courts for more timely and impartial justice. By 1250, the court ceased to travel with the king and was permanently located in the royal palace on the Île-de-la-Cité in Paris, where it gradually developed a professional staff of clerical and lay officers trained in the law. The Parlement's central role in the dispensation of royal justice was cemented by Louis IX's decision to permit the court to hear appeals from the bailiwicks (*bailliages*) and seneschalcies (*sénéchaussées*), the main administrative districts of the royal domain. By the fourteenth century, most of the court's work involved appeals rather than cases of original jurisdiction. Philip III issued the court's first rules of operation in 1278, and its basic organization and procedures were solidified in the half century prior to the Hundred Years War.

The Parlement eventually comprised three departments. The original Parlement was the Grand'Chambre or Chamber of Pleas, which heard great cases of state and cases involving the death penalty or corporal punishment. It oversaw the other departments and issued the *arrêt*, or final decree that settled all cases. The Chambre des Requêtes heard petitions from anyone wishing to initiate a suit in the Parlement. If a petition was accepted, a commission was sent to the locality from which the suit originated to gather evidence. If, upon reviewing this material, the masters of the Grand'Chambre decided the investigation had been properly conducted, the case went to the Chambre des Enquêtes, where the written evidence was analyzed and conclusions drawn. The litigants never appeared before the Chamber. Final decision in the case was rendered by the masters of the Grand'Chambre, who issued the *arrêt* settling the matter.

The appeals that led to the various confiscations of PLANTAGENET Aquitaine, including the actions initiating the ANGLO-FRENCH WAR OF 1294–1303, the War of SAINT-SARDOS, and the Hundred Years War, all originated with and were decided by the Parlement. The APPEAL OF THE GASCON LORDS, which overturned the Treaty of BRÉTIGNY, was secretly lodged with the Parlement in May 1368. When EDWARD, THE BLACK PRINCE, refused a summons to appear before the court to answer the appeal, the Parlement pronounced him contumacious on 2 May 1369 and the formal confiscation of Aquitaine, which restarted the war, was decreed in the following November. After 1380, and especially after the onset of the FRENCH CIVIL WAR in the 1410s, the Parlement underwent frequent purges, as each new regime, whether MARMOUSET, BURGUNDIAN, or ARMAGNAC, sought to fill the court with its supporters. In 1420, the Parlement, now under Anglo-Burgundian control, formally registered, or approved, the Treaty of TROYES making HENRY V heir to CHARLES VI. In January 1421, the Parlement formally declared the dauphin, who had refused a summons to appear, incapable of succession and banished from the realm. The dauphin, in consequence, established his own Parlement in Bourges to supervise the administration of justice in the dauphinist portions of the kingdom, while the Paris Parlement continued to function for the Anglo-Burgundian realm. In 1435, when the Paris Parlement declared its 1421 decision banishing the dauphin illegal, PHILIP THE GOOD, duke of BURGUNDY, used the reversal as a pretext for abandoning the ANGLO-BURGUNDIAN ALLIANCE at the Congress of ARRAS. After regaining the capital in 1436, CHARLES VII merged the two bodies, abolishing the Bourges Parlement and gradually purging the Paris Parlement of its most pro-Burgundian and pro-English personnel.

Further Reading: Allmand, Christopher. *The Hundred Years War*. Cambridge: Cambridge University Press, 1988; Curry, Anne. *The Hundred Years War*. 2nd ed. Houndmills, England: Palgrave Macmillan, 2003; Shennan, J. H. *The Parlement of Paris*. Stroud, England: Sutton Publishing, 1998.

PARLIAMENT

Parliament was the supreme legislative and judicial assembly of medieval England. During the course of the HUNDRED YEARS WAR, Parliament, largely through the increasing royal need for money to fund the war, gradually acquired a variety of important rights and functions, including the approval of TAXATION, the right of petition and redress, and the power to impeach royal ministers.

The principle that the king could only obtain new taxes through the consent of his people in Parliament evolved in the 1290s out of EDWARD I's unprecedented need for taxation to conduct his wars in SCOTLAND and France (*see* ANGLO-FRENCH WAR OF 1294–1303). After 1337, the even greater financial needs of EDWARD III led to further parliamentary attempts to control royal finances. In early 1340, Parliament granted new taxation only on condition that royal tax-collectors be made responsible to it and that all taxes granted be spent only on the war. In the following spring, during the CRISIS OF 1340–1341, Parliament intervened in the dispute between the king and his chief minister, John STRATFORD, archbishop of

Canterbury, to protest attempts by Edward's supporters to prevent the archbishop from attending the assembly's sessions. Desperately in need of funds, Edward reluctantly assented to a series of parliamentary petitions that declared no peer could be arrested, tried, or imprisoned except in full Parliament; a public audit should be conducted of royal finances; and all high officers of state should be appointed in Parliament. Although Edward later annulled these measures, important precedents, such as no taxation without redress of grievances, had been set.

Despite this dispute, Edward's relations with Parliament were usually good. During the reign, the Lords, which comprised 21 bishops, 25 great abbots, and about 40–50 temporal peers, and the Commons, which comprised 2 knights from each of the 37 shires and about 180 burgesses from towns authorized to elect them, ceased to meet together. In the 1340s, the lower clergy ceased to sit with the Commons and instead sent representatives to Convocation, the legislative assembly of the English Church. These changes caused the knights of the shire to begin identifying more closely with the townsmen than with the nobility. Knights of the shire were selected in the county courts under the supervision of the sheriff, while burgesses were elected according to procedures laid down in each town's charter, which often restricted voting to small groups (*see* TOWNS AND THE HUNDRED YEARS WAR). By the 1370s, service in Parliament was seen as an honor and many gentlemen sought re-election to county positions or stood for election as town representatives. In 1406, Parliament enacted the first legislation regulating parliamentary elections and in 1430 it restricted the vote to freeholders with land worth at least 40 shillings per year. In 1445, election as shire MP (i.e., member of Parliament) was restricted to gentry with sufficient wealth to support the rank of knight. Although Parliament met, on average, once a year, some years, such as 1332 with four meetings, saw multiple sessions. Called and dismissed by the king, who generally gave sheriffs three to eight weeks' notice of a session, Parliament sat usually for five or six weeks at time, although some sessions lasted only one week while others ran for over twenty weeks. Most wartime Parliaments met at the palace of Westminster, just outside LONDON, although the king could have Parliament meet anywhere in the kingdom, and sessions in York, Carlisle, and other northern towns were common during campaigns in Scotland.

Reacting to military defeat and government weakness, the so-called Good Parliament of 1376 evolved the procedures of impeachment, whereby the Commons brought charges against corrupt and incompetent ministers who were then tried by the Lords. Among those impeached were the royal chamberlain, William Latimer, and the king's rapacious mistress, Alice Perrers. The impeachment movement was led by Sir Peter de la Mare, who became the first speaker of the Commons. Although de la Mare led the opposition in 1376, the office of speaker was later usually held by agents of the Crown who supervised debate and the passage of legislation in the government's interest.

RICHARD II had generally poor relations with his Parliaments, particularly the Merciless Parliament of 1388, which was dominated by the Appellants led by THOMAS OF WOODSTOCK, duke of Gloucester, who impeached, exiled, and executed many of the king's favorites. In 1399, acting upon the precedent set during the removal of EDWARD II in 1327, Parliament increased its influence by sanctioning Richard's deposition in favor of his cousin, HENRY IV. Except for the reign of HENRY V, when the king's deft management of Parliament procured the increased taxation needed to fund renewed war, the political position of the House of LANCASTER under Henry IV, who was a usurper, and HENRY VI, who was mentally unstable, was weak, and Parliament gained definite control over the granting of taxation in the fifteenth century. In 1407, for instance, Henry IV recognized the principle that all money bills had to originate in the Commons, and, later in the century, Parliament began granting new kings the right of collecting customs duties for life. The fifteenth century also saw parliamentary statute recognized as legally superior to the common law and able also to interfere with the canon law and the liberties of the Church. MPs also acquired various privileges, including immunity from arrest during sessions, although attempts to secure complete freedom of speech were strongly resisted by the Crown. Nonetheless, by the 1450s, Parliament, thanks to the financial and political needs of the Anglo-French war, had evolved much of its modern organization and procedure.

Further Reading: Butt, Ronald. *A History of Parliament: The Middle Ages.* London: Constable, 1989; Harriss, G. L. *King, Parliament and Public Finance in Medieval England to 1369.* Oxford: Clarendon Press, 1975; Richardson, H. G., and G. O. Sayles. *The English Parliament in the Middle Ages.* London: Hambledon Press, 1981; Sayles, G. O. *The King's Parliament of England.* New York: Norton, 1974.

PATAY, BATTLE OF (1429)

Fought on 18 June 1429, the French victory at Patay, a village located about ten miles northwest of Orléans, was the culminating engagement of the LOIRE CAMPAIGN, which was inspired and led by JOAN OF ARC. Seeking to complete the second part of her divine mission, the crowning of the dauphin, the Maid was anxious to open the road to Rheims, the traditional coronation site, by clearing the Loire of English garrisons.

Having broken the siege of ORLÉANS in early May, the reinforced dauphinist army, now commanded by JOHN, DUKE OF ALENÇON, proceeded, on 10 June, against he English-held towns in the Loire Valley. Driven by the Maid's insistence on quick action, the French captured Jargeau and then laid siege to Beaugency and Meung. On the morning of 18 June, an English relief force, jointly commanded by John TALBOT, Lord Talbot, and Sir John FASTOLF, was preparing to assault the bridge at Meung when news arrived of the fall of Beaugency. Facing the possibility of being caught between the Meung besiegers

and those of Beaugency, the English withdrew northward toward Janville. Unwilling to brook any delay, Joan told the French commanders, who led a force of between six and eight thousand men, to pursue their retreating enemies and bring them to battle.

A four-hour march brought the English near Patay around midday, when the rearguard informed Fastolf, who seems to have been in overall command, that the French were advancing rapidly. Fastolf decided to deploy his army, which may have numbered almost five thousand, in the traditional defensive formation that had won AGINCOURT and so many other HUNDRED YEARS WAR battles. Ordering his vanguard, supply train, and ARTILLERY into the woods on his flank, Fastolf sent Talbot and about five hundred mounted ARCHERS forward to delay the French while the army made its preparations. Unaware of Talbot's men, the French vanguard might have ridden into an ambush had it not been for a frightened stag, which leapt from the woods in front of the French and veered toward Patay and Talbot's concealed men, who, being startled, cried out. Thus alerted to the English presence, the French cavalry, which was commanded by Étienne de VIGNOLLES (known as ''La Hire'') and Poton de XANTRAILLES, crashed into Talbot's surprised men and drove them back onto Fastolf's line, which was not yet ready to receive an attack.

Between the confused flight of Talbot's archers and the atypically rapid onset of the French attack, Fastolf's force was quickly overwhelmed. The English army disintegrated, with many slain and many captured, including, among the latter, Talbot and Thomas SCALES, Lord Scales. Rallying a small force of archers, Fastolf escaped to Corbeil, where, next day, he personally informed JOHN, DUKE OF BEDFORD, of the defeat. According to one source, the duke angrily blamed Fastolf for the disaster and summarily stripped him of his GARTER. Joan, arriving on the field with the French rearguard, did not strike a blow, but it was her determination and stern demand for speed that had won the day. Although Patay temporarily strengthened the ANGLO-BURGUNDIAN ALLI-ANCE by compelling Duke PHILIP THE GOOD to help reinforce PARIS against possible attack, the French successes in the Loire Valley allowed the dauphin, accompanied by Joan, to march to Rheims and there be crowned king as CHARLES VII.

Further Reading: Burne, Alfred H. *The Agincourt War.* Ware, England: Wordsworth Editions Ltd., 1999; DeVries, Kelly. *Joan of Arc: A Military Leader.* Stroud, England: Sutton Publishing, 2003.

PÂTIS

Pâtis, or "RANSOMS of the country," were regular payments in cash or kind demanded by garrison commanders of the people in their district. An English innovation that arose in BRITTANY during the 1340s, *pâtis* replaced the disorganized thievery by which small English garrisons had initially sustained themselves with a more systematic protection scheme by which local communities paid their garrisons to leave them alone or to defend them from outside raiders. By the 1350s, the system was extended beyond Brittany to other English-controlled areas of France and in the 1360s was taken up on a less formal basis by the *ROUTIERS* that ravaged wide areas of the country.

Every garrison carefully staked out its ransom territory, demanding that all villages within marching distance pay a stated assessment in cash, food, wine, building supplies, or labor. Late or refused payments were extracted by force, and resistance often meant arbitrary executions and burned or plundered property. Assessment had to be carefully calculated so that the garrison could get maximum payment without precipitating an uprising or causing the peasants to flee their villages. Travelers through the district were also forced to pay for safe-conducts or to pass through tollgates and roadblocks. Profits from *pâtis* were pooled for the use of the whole garrison, although cuts were taken by the garrison commander and, theoretically, by the king. In many areas, however, the main benefit to the Crown was not in cash paid but in relief from the burden of supporting garrisons.

By the 1350s, payments became more systematic and more onerous as local garrisons and commanders became more interested in enriching themselves than in conducting the war. By engendering great hatred of the garrison, the practice often destroyed local support for the English cause and created serious political problems for EDWARD III. When CHARLES OF BLOIS, the French-backed claimant in the BRETON CIVIL WAR, besieged LA ROCHE-DERRIEN in 1347, enraged local peasants joined him, eager to attack the English garrison with sticks and stones.

The collecting of *pâtis* also had a more insidious effect. It tended to free commanders of small or isolated castles from the control of royal officers. Although loosely acknowledging the authority of the English Crown, these garrison commanders, who had often captured their fortresses on their own initiative, considered themselves local conquerors who were entitled to collect *pâtis* as their rightful spoils of war. As a result, the conduct of the war in Brittany and elsewhere often passed beyond the effective control of the king and his chief lieutenants. Nonetheless, *pâtis* continued to be collected and in 1361, as the mutual cession of territory called for by the Treaty of BRÉTIGNY began, Edward III demanded that English garrison commanders be paid all arrears of *pâtis* due to them before relinquishing their strongholds.

Further Reading: Seward, Desmond. *The Hundred Years War.* New York: Penguin, 1999; Sumption, Jonathan. *The Hundred Years War.* Vol. 2, *Trial by Fire.* Philadelphia: University of Pennsylvania Press, 2001.

PEASANTS' REVOLT OF 1381

A consequence of the profound socio-economic changes fostered by war and plague, the Peasants' Revolt of 1381 was the most dangerous English rebellion of the fourteenth century. Although its immediate cause was the imposition by PARLIAMENT of burdensome taxes designed to finance renewal of the HUNDRED YEARS WAR, its long-term cause was a social policy designed to protect the economic position of landlords by restricting the economic opportunities of peasants. While the rebellion itself was a failure, especially in terms of its most idealistic goal, the abolition of class distinctions, it marked the start of a gradual process whereby serfdom disappeared from English society.

By significantly reducing the number of agricultural laborers, the first visitation of the BLACK DEATH in the late 1340s significantly increased the demand for agricultural labor. With landlords now competing for scarce workers, wages rose and peasant mobility increased. Seeking to regain their economic advantage, noble and gentle landholders used their control of Parliament to pursue a restrictive labor policy. In 1349, EDWARD III promulgated a royal ordinance that froze wages and prices at preplague levels and fined serfs who left their lord's manor. In 1351, the first postplague Parliament fortified the king's decree with the Statute of Laborers, which increased fines and established special commissions in each county to enforce the new labor restrictions. Through these measures, labor regulation became a national rather than a local concern. Although there was scattered resistance to enforcement of these acts in the 1350s, the kind of class-driven violence that France had experienced in 1358 with the *JACQUERIE* did not appear in England until 1381, when new TAXATION aggravated peasant anger over labor restrictions. In February 1377, Parliament passed a new poll tax to be levied at the rate of one shilling per head. A second tax, enacted in April 1379 to help fund a proposed *CHEVAUCHÉE* by THOMAS OF WOODSTOCK, duke of Gloucester, was assessed at a graduated rate, but the poll tax of November 1380, which ignited the Peasants' Revolt, used a flat rate of 3 shillings a head, triple the 1377 assessment.

In the climactic moment of the Peasants' Revolt of 1381, William Walworth, the lord mayor of London, slays rebel leader Wat Tyler in the presence of Richard II. *Art Resource, New York.*

Evasion of the third tax was immediate and widespread. The 1370s had witnessed the loss of much of AQUITAINE, costly and fruitless campaigns, and French raids on English coasts. Tired of a war that cost them much and promised them little, peasants already frustrated with wage restrictions were unwilling to silently suffer the government's imposition of further economic hardship. On 30 May 1381, irate peasants in Essex drove out royal commissioners sent to investigate instances of tax evasion. Between 1 and 4 June, antitax disturbances erupted across Essex and Kent. By 10 June, the disorders turned violent, with rebels attacking tax collectors and destroying the property of local tax officials. In Essex, for instance, the rebels fell upon the Hospital of the Knights of St. John, the master of which was Robert Hales, who, as treasurer, was closely associated with the tax. The speed with which bands of local rebels coalesced into larger groups suggests a certain degree of organization and cooperation. Choosing as their leader Wat Tyler, an obscure figure who may once have fought in France, the rebels advanced on LONDON on 11 June, the day RICHARD II arrived in the capital from Windsor. On 12 June, as the king took shelter in the Tower of London, rebels sacked Lambeth Palace, the home of Archbishop Simon Sudbury, the chancellor of England, and then met with representatives of the city of London at Blackheath. Harangued by the radical preacher John Ball, who is best known for the rhyming couplet, "When Adam delved and Eve span / Who was then a gentleman?" the rebels crossed London Bridge and entered the city on 13 June. After breaking open Fleet and Newgate Prisons, destroying legal records at the Temple, and burning Savoy Palace, the London residence of Richard's unpopular uncle, JOHN OF GAUNT, duke of Lancaster, the rebels met the king at Greenwich, where the talks, which Richard conducted from his barge, came to naught.

On 14 June, after a night of riotous disorder in the city, the fourteen-year-old king met with the Essex rebels at Mile End, where he agreed to their demand for the abolition of serfdom. After receiving charters of freedom hastily drafted by royal clerks, many of the Essex men returned home. However, while the Mile End meeting was occurring, Tyler and some of the Kentish rebels stormed the Tower, where they seized and beheaded Sudbury, Hales, and John Legge, another royal official considered responsible for the poll tax. On 15 June, Richard met Tyler and the Kentish insurgents at Smithfield. Greeting the king with inappropriate familiarity, Tyler made a series of radical demands that included confiscation and redistribution of Church property and abolition of most bishoprics and secular lordships. In essence, Tyler wished to erase all social and ecclesiastical distinctions below the king. When Richard responded by asking why the rebels did not go home, Tyler grew angry and drew his dagger. The accounts of what happened next are confused and contradictory, but at some point the mayor of London, Sir William Walworth,

who was attending the king, struck Tyler, who was then stabbed repeatedly by one of the king's squires. With great presence of mind, Richard rode toward the rebels, among whom were many ARCHERS, and urged them to meet him at Clerkenwell, thus drawing them away from London and giving Walworth and Sir Robert KNOLLES time to gather loyal troops, including Londoners alienated by rebel looting. By evening, Tyler had been beheaded and order had been restored to the city.

Although smaller insurrections erupted elsewhere throughout the summer, the death of Tyler was the effective end of the uprising. On 2 July, while royal troops hunted down rebel leaders, Richard cancelled all charters of manumission issued on 14 June. On 15 July, John Ball was executed in St. Albans. Arrests and executions continued until August, when the king ordered their end. In November, Parliament granted a general pardon to all offenders. Despite the grave threat they had posed to the established order in June, by the end of the year, most rebels had again been reduced to serfdom.

Further Reading: Dobson, R.B., ed. *The Peasants' Revolt of 1381.* 2nd ed. London: Macmillan, 1983; Dunn, Alastair. *The Great Rising of 1381.* Charleston: Tempus Publishing, 2002; Hilton, R. H. *Bond Men Made Free: Medieval Peasant Movements and the English Rising of 1381.* New York: Viking, 1973; Hilton, R. H., and T. H. Ashton, eds. *The English Rising of 1381.* Cambridge: Cambridge University Press, 1984; Oman, Charles. *The Great Revolt of 1381.* Reprint, New York: Greenwood, 1969.

PÉRIGUEUX, PROCESS OF. *See* PROCESS

PHILIP IV, KING OF FRANCE (1268–1314) Known as *le Bel*, "the Fair," Philip IV was the son of Philip III and the grandson of Louis IX (St. Louis). During his reign, Philip expanded the authority of the House of CAPET within France and influenced the course of ecclesiastical and secular affairs throughout Western Europe. By vigorously exercising his overlordship in AQUITAINE, Philip initiated the ANGLO-FRENCH WAR OF

1294–1303, the first conflict between the two kingdoms since the Treaty of PARIS and a precursor of the HUNDRED YEARS WAR.

Philip married Jeanne of Champagne and Navarre in 1284, and succeeded his father as king in October 1285, having become heir to the throne on the death of his older brother in 1276. Devoted to the memory of his grandfather, whose achievements he sought to emulate, Philip persuaded the pope to canonize Louis in 1297. Committed to protecting the legitimate rights of the Capetian Crown, Philip, in May 1294, confiscated the duchy of Aquitaine after its duke, EDWARD I of England, refused a summons to appear at the French court. Although the summons was precipitated by a number of clashes between French and Gascon sailors (see GASCONY), the incidents were part of a long series of jurisdictional disputes arising out of the king-duke's feudal subordination to the French Crown. Believing that Edward sought to evade French overlordship, and perhaps desirous of extinguishing English rule in Aquitaine, Philip ordered his brother, Charles of Valois, to invade the duchy. Settled in 1303, the war resulted in no change in the status of Aquitaine, but had momentous consequences for Philip and France. It plunged France into war with FLANDERS, a recent ally of Edward I; embroiled Philip in a bitter quarrel with Pope Boniface VIII; and resulted, as part of its settlement, in a marriage between Philip's daughter Isabella (see ISABELLA, QUEEN OF ENGLAND [c. 1292–1358]) and Prince Edward (see EDWARD II), which gave Philip's PLANTAGENET grandson, EDWARD III, a claim to the French Crown.

Although eventually settled in Philip's favor, the Flemish war produced a humiliating French defeat at Courtrai in 1302. The quarrel with Boniface began with the pope's refusal to sanction royal TAXATION of the clergy to fund the Anglo-French war and then evolved into a dispute regarding the nature and limits of papal jurisdiction over secular affairs. A man of uncompromising orthodoxy and rigid morality, Philip charged the pope with heresy and im-

morality and ordered his minister, Guillaume de Nogaret, to bring Boniface to trial before a Church council. After Boniface died as a result of the violence offered him by Nogaret's men, Philip established French dominance of the papacy by persuading Clement V, a Gascon elected pope in 1305, to abandon Rome and establish the papal court at Avignon, thereby initiating the seventy-year period of papal history known as the "Babylonian captivity." Again alleging heresy and immorality, Philip also destroyed the Knights Templar, seizing their assets in 1307 and ruthlessly suppressing that order of crusaders in 1311.

In 1314, in another example of the king's stern morality, Philip threw doubt on the legitimacy of his own grandchildren by publicly charging two of his daughters-in-law with adultery. The scandal resulted in the imprisonment of the women and the execution of their alleged lovers. Philip's last years also saw formation of numerous leagues of discontented subjects protesting royal manipulation of the coinage and the suppression of local rights and customs. Philip died in November 1314 in the midst of these protests, and was succeeded by the eldest of his three sons, LOUIS X. When Louis died in 1316, his daughters were passed over in favor of his brother PHILIP V, whose own daughters were set aside at his death in 1322 in favor of his brother CHARLES IV. Charles's death without male heirs in 1328 brought the Crown to the first VALOIS king, PHILIP VI.

Further Reading: Brown, Elizabeth A. R. *The Monarchy of Capetian France and Royal Ceremonial.* London: Variorum, 1991; Brown, Elizabeth A. R. *Politics and Institutions in Capetian France.* London: Variorum, 1991; Strayer, Joseph R. *The Reign of Philip the Fair.* Princeton, NJ: Princeton University Press, 1980.

PHILIP V, KING OF FRANCE
(c. 1290–1322)

Known as *le Long*, "the Tall," Philip V was the second son of PHILIP IV and Jeanne of Navarre. By ignoring the rights of his niece, the only surviving child of his elder brother LOUIS X, Philip forced establishment of the precedent, later accepted as a rule of law, that women could not succeed to the throne of France. In 1328, this principle was extended to bar males, such as EDWARD III of England, from inheriting the Crown through a woman.

Philip became count of BURGUNDY in January 1307 upon his marriage to Jeanne, daughter of the previous count. Made count of Poitiers in 1311, Philip had his APPANAGE enlarged by his brother in 1315. When Louis died in June 1316, he left a four-year-old daughter, Jeanne, whose legitimacy had been called into question by the alleged adultery of her late mother, and a pregnant second wife. On 16 July, Philip secured the regency by outmaneuvering the other candidates—his uncle, Charles of Valois, and Jeanne's uncle, Eudes of Burgundy. Although the queen gave birth to a son, John I, on 13 November, the child died five days later.

By unknown means, Philip then induced Jeanne's most vocal champions—Valois and Philip's younger brother, Charles of La Marche—to support his accession, even though most of the nobility refused to attend his coronation at Rheims on 9 January 1317. To secure his shaky hold on the throne, Philip asked an assembly of notables, summoned to PARIS on 2 February, to confirm his accession. Unable to oppose an anointed king, the assembly legitimized Philip's usurpation and swept aside Jeanne's claim by declaring that women could not inherit the Crown of France.

Philip proved to be a strong and popular king. He instituted a series of reforms in national and local administration, pacified the leagues of discontented subjects that had disrupted the reign of Louis X, attempted to reform the coinage, and ended the ongoing hostilities in FLANDERS. EDWARD II of England, who was married to Philip's sister Isabella (see ISABELLA, QUEEN OF ENGLAND [c. 1292–1358]), had avoided paying homage for AQUITAINE to Louis X and continued to delay the ceremony after Philip's accession. In June 1319, Edward sent a deputation to swear homage on his behalf, but Philip

found this insufficient and threatened to retain the county of Ponthieu, an English possession seized by Louis in an Anglo-French trade dispute, if Edward did not personally render homage. This Edward finally did at Amiens in June 1320.

Philip died on 2 January 1322. Ironically, the declaration barring women from the throne that had confirmed Philip's accession denied the Crown to his four daughters—his only son having died in February 1317. Philip's younger brother, Charles of La Marche (see CHARLES IV), succeeded to the throne without opposition. See also SALIC LAW OF SUCCESSION.

Further Reading: Brown, Elizabeth A. R. *The Monarchy of Capetian France and Royal Ceremonial.* London: Variorum, 1991; Brown, Elizabeth A. R. *Politics and Institutions in Capetian France.* London: Variorum, 1991; Strayer, Joseph R. *Reign of Philip the Fair.* Princeton, NJ: Princeton University Press, 1980.

PHILIP VI, KING OF FRANCE (1293–1350)

The son of Charles, count of Valois, and the nephew and cousin of the last four Capetian kings of France, Philip VI was the first French ruler of the House of VALOIS. In the 1330s, Philip's growing dispute with EDWARD III over sovereignty in the PLANTAGENET fief of AQUITAINE and his attempts to thwart English ambitions in SCOTLAND led to the outbreak of the HUNDRED YEARS WAR.

As a youth, Philip of Valois had little expectation of ascending the throne; his uncle, PHILIP IV, had several sons and the House of CAPET had not failed of heirs since attaining the throne in the tenth century. However, Philip's eldest cousin, LOUIS X, and Louis's posthumous son, John I, both died in 1316. Louis's brother set aside his nieces to become king as PHILIP V, but then died himself in 1322, leaving his own daughters to be displaced by Philip IV's last son, CHARLES IV. On the death of his father in 1325, Philip of Valois, besides inheriting a substantial APPANAGE comprising the counties of Valois, Maine, and Anjou, became heir presumptive to his childless cousin. Upon the death of

Charles IV on 1 February 1328, the French nobility, ignoring a claim to the throne put forward by fifteen-year-old Edward III of England, a grandson of Philip IV through his mother Isabella (*see* ISABELLA, QUEEN OF ENGLAND [c. 1292–1358]), named Philip regent with the understanding that he would become king if Charles's pregnant queen gave birth to a daughter, which she did on 1 April. Crowned on 29 May, Philip VI, who later proved to be a poor military leader, started his reign with a major military victory, crushing, at the behest of his vassal, LOUIS DE NEVERS, count of FLANDERS, an army of Flemish rebels at Cassel on 23 August.

Not trained for kingship, Philip had little direct experience of government and tended to distrust courtiers and bureaucrats, preferring to govern secretively through family members and favored advisors. Although a serious man who worked hard at governing, Philip lacked political judgment and, as the chronicler Jean FROISSART declared, ''was always ready to accept advice from fools'' (Sumption, 108). The circumstances of his accession also left him with a more limited authority than that exercised by his predecessors, who did not owe their throne to the acquiescence of the nobility. The presence of possible rival candidates to the throne, such as Edward III, and another descendant of Philip IV through the female line, CHARLES THE BAD, king of Navarre, gave any disgruntled nobleman attractive alternatives to Philip. Later in the reign, many members of the nobility of NORMANDY and northwestern France intrigued with Navarre, while Philip's failure to rule in their favor on succession disputes in Artois and BRITTANY, led ROBERT OF ARTOIS and John de MONTFORT to ally themselves with Edward III.

Although Edward did homage to Philip for Aquitaine on 6 June 1329, ongoing jurisdictional disputes in the duchy strained Anglo-French relations in the 1330s. While Philip strengthened ties with Edward's opponents in Scotland, the English king constructed an ANTI-FRENCH COALITION among the princes of the Low Countries and Ger-

many. On 24 May 1337, Philip, having earlier proclaimed the ARRIÈRE-BAN throughout France, ordered the confiscation of Aquitaine, thereby officially initiating the Hundred Years War. During the early campaigns of the war, such as at Buirenfosse during the THIÉRACHE CAMPAIGN in 1339 and at the siege of TOURNAI in 1340, Philip frustrated his opponent and many of his own nobles by refusing battle. However, a new rebellion in Flanders in 1339 allowed Edward to construct an ANGLO-FLEMISH ALLIANCE that prompted him to lay formal claim to the Crown of France on 6 February 1340. In June, the English won a major naval victory at SLUYS, and in 1341 the commencement of the BRETON CIVIL WAR, initiated in part by Philip's decision to recognize his nephew, CHARLES OF BLOIS, as duke of Brittany, gave Edward a new front against France. Despite his acceptance of the papal-mediated Truce of MALESTROIT in 1343, Philip, like Edward, was uninterested in a negotiated settlement of the Aquitinian dispute; in 1345, the AVIGNON PEACE CONFERENCE hosted by Pope CLEMENT VI collapsed and war resumed.

During the last years of the reign, as the king grew tired and obese, the French military position deteriorated rapidly. In 1345, English victories at AUBEROCHE and BERGERAC cemented Plantagenet gains in Aquitaine, and, in August 1346, a large French army personally commanded by Philip suffered a disastrous defeat at CRÉCY. In June 1347, the English gained the upper hand in Brittany by capturing Blois at the Battle of LA ROCHE-DERRIEN, and in August, a yearlong siege that Philip was powerless to break ended with the fall of CALAIS. By the time the BLACK DEATH descended on France in 1348, temporarily ending the war and claiming the life of Philip's queen, Jeanne of BURGUNDY, the French war effort was in disarray. Stung by defeat at Crécy, the French nobility were angry and divided, while the Estates-General, convening in PARIS in late 1347, demanded significant governmental reforms before voting new war TAXATION. Discredited and heavily in debt, Philip died on 22 August 1350; he was succeeded by his son, JOHN II. *See also* CALAIS, SIEGE OF; ESTATES, GENERAL AND PROVINCIAL.

Further Reading: Perroy, Edouard. *The Hundred Years War.* Trans. W. B. Wells. New York: Capricorn Books, 1965; Sumption, Jonathan. *The Hundred Years War.* Vol. 1, *Trial by Battle.* Philadelphia: University of Pennsylvania Press, 1999.

PHILIPPA OF HAINAULT, QUEEN OF ENGLAND (c. 1314–1369)

Philippa, one of four daughters of William, count of Holland and Hainault, was the wife of EDWARD III. Although she took little direct part in English politics, her marriage to Edward significantly influenced the course of the HUNDRED YEARS WAR by making possible a series of important political and personal connections between England and the Low Countries.

Philippa met Edward, then Prince of Wales, in 1326, when he came to Hainault with his mother, Queen Isabella (*see* ISABELLA, QUEEN OF ENGLAND [c. 1292–1358]), who was seeking allies against her estranged husband, EDWARD II. The betrothal of Edward and Philippa, which was negotiated during the visit, suited both the prince and his mother—the former finding himself attracted to Philippa over her sisters, and the latter obtaining, as the bride's dowry, the men and money she needed to invade England and depose her husband. The young couple—he was fifteen and she about thirteen—was married in York on 30 January 1328, although Philippa's coronation did not occur until 4 March 1330, only three months before the birth of her first child, EDWARD, the future Black Prince. Philippa eventually bore her husband seven sons and five daughters, thus magnificently fulfilling the first duty of a medieval queen and significantly enhancing the possibilities of Edward's marriage DIPLOMACY.

Besides vital assistance in bringing about his early accession—Philippa's uncle, John of Hainault, was coleader of Isabella's invasion force—the alliance with Hainault provided Edward III with a secure base on France's northeastern frontier in the 1330s. Philippa's family connections also gave Edward important continental allies, such as the German emperor Ludwig of Bavaria and the marquis of Juliers, both of whom joined Edward's ANTI-FRENCH COALITION in the late 1330s. Edward was also able to make extensive territorial claims on Philippa's behalf, including to Zeeland on her brother's death in 1345 and to Holland on her nephew's death in the 1360s. Beyond high politics, Philippa's marriage brought many able knights from Hainault into the English camp, most notably Walter MAUNY. Philippa also drew important nonmilitary men to England; both JEAN LE BEL and Jean FROISSART, two of the most important chroniclers of the war in the fourteenth century, were from Hainault. The former came to England with his patron, John of Hainault, and the latter enjoyed the patronage of the queen herself. The unknown herald of Sir John CHANDOS who wrote a life of the Black Prince was also a Hainaulter.

Philippa accompanied the king on many military campaigns. She was with him in SCOTLAND in the 1330s; in the Low Countries from 1338 to 1342, when she was for a time a hostage to Edward's debtors; at the siege of CALAIS in 1347, when her intercession saved the town's leaders from execution; and at the naval battle of WINCHELSEA in 1350, which she witnessed from the shore. She also shared Edward's taste for CHIVALRY, presiding over tournaments and several times attending ceremonies of the Order of the GARTER. A pious and compassionate woman, Philippa also had an interest in education, being, for instance, patron and namesake of Queen's College, Oxford. Although her influence with the king waned when her attendant, Alice Perrers, became Edward's mistress in the 1360s, Philippa, who was apparently not beautiful and rather plump in later years, held her husband's affection until her death on 15 August 1369.

Further Reading: Hardy, B. C. *Philippa of Hainault and Her Times.* London, 1910; Packe, Michael. *King Edward III.* Ed. L. C. B. Seaman. London: Routledge and Kegan Paul, 1983.

PHILIP THE BOLD, DUKE OF BURGUNDY (1342–1404)

By combining the French APPANAGE of BURGUNDY with control of FLANDERS and various other provinces in the Low Countries and northern France, Philip the Bold, first VALOIS duke of Burgundy, laid the foundations of the Burgundian state that so powerfully shaped the course of the HUNDRED YEARS WAR in the fifteenth century. The fourth son of JOHN II and youngest brother of CHARLES V, Burgundy dominated the minority government of his nephew CHARLES VI and thus was instrumental in initiating the political feud that led eventually to the FRENCH CIVIL WAR.

In 1356, Philip, then only fourteen, fought beside his father at the Battle of POITIERS, where both were captured by the English. Released with the king after the conclusion of the Treaty of BRÉTIGNY in 1360, Philip was created duke of Touraine, a title that he surrendered in 1363 when his father made him duke of Burgundy and premier peer of the realm. Charles V confirmed his brother's titles in 1364 when he made Burgundy the key figure in his plan to forestall the creation of a powerful English appanage in Flanders and the Low Countries. Charles persuaded the pope to forbid a proposed marriage between EDMUND OF LANGLEY, earl of Cambridge and son of EDWARD III, and MARGUERITE, daughter and heir of LOUIS DE MALE, count of Flanders. In York's stead, Charles offered Burgundy, who, after two years of Anglo-Flemish negotiations, married Marguerite in 1369. Although Burgundy signed a secret undertaking to return, upon his assumption of power in Flanders, the territories demanded of the Crown by Louis de Male in the marriage treaty, Burgundy also promised his father-in-law that he would never do so, and thus retained all upon Louis's death.

In the 1380s, Burgundy significantly expanded his territorial holdings in the Low Countries and northeastern France. In 1382, on the death of his wife's grandmother—a daughter of PHILIP V—Burgundy gained control of Artois and Franche-Comté; in 1384, upon the death of his father-in-law, he became count of Flanders; and in 1390, he and his wife became coheirs to the duchy of Brabant. In 1385, he made possible the eventual incorporation of Holland, Zeeland, and Hainault into the Burgundian state by marrying two of his children into the Wittelsbach family.

Upon the accession of eleven-year-old Charles VI in 1380, Burgundy led the opposition to establishment of a regency under his eldest surviving brother, LOUIS, DUKE OF ANJOU, and thus came himself to dominate the royal government, which he did not hesitate to employ in his own interests. In 1382, he used his control of the council to authorize French intervention in Flanders, which had been in rebellion against Burgundy's father-in-law since 1379. A royal army defeated the rebels and killed their pro-English leader, Philip van ARTEVELDE, at Roosebeke in November. In 1388, Burgundy secured the services of another royal army to aid him in his quarrel with the duke of Guelders, and both Burgundy and his brother, JOHN, DUKE OF BERRY, drew liberally upon the royal revenues to support various of their personal projects.

In 1388, the MARMOUSETS, a group of former servants of Charles V who sought to end the uncles' exploitation of the Crown's resources, convinced the king to dismiss Burgundy and Berry. Supported by the king's brother, LOUIS, DUKE OF ORLÉANS, who resented his exclusion from power under the uncles, the Marmousets governed until August 1392, when the onset of Charles's mental illness allowed Burgundy to resume control of the royal administration. Although increasingly challenged at court by Orléans, who became a formidable rival after 1400, Burgundy continued to exercise significant influence until his death on 27 April 1404, when his title, lands, and political standing were inherited by his eldest son, JOHN THE FEARLESS, count of Nevers.

Further Reading: Palmer, J. J. N. *England, France, and Christendom, 1377–99.* Chapel Hill: University of North Carolina Press, 1972; Vaughan, Richard. *Philip the Bold: The Formation* *of the Burgundian State.* Woodbridge, England: Boydell Press, 2002.

PHILIP THE GOOD, DUKE OF BURGUNDY (1396–1467)

As the greatest nobleman of France and the dominant prince of the Low Countries, Philip the Good, the third VALOIS duke of BURGUNDY, played a major role in the Lancastrian phase of the HUNDRED YEARS WAR. During Philip's 47-year reign, the principality of Burgundy achieved effective autonomy and reached the height of its power, prestige, and prosperity. During the last decades of the Anglo-French war, Philip exploited the French Crown's weakness and the English Crown's need for military support to strengthen and enlarge the Burgundian state.

The son of JOHN THE FEARLESS, the leader of the BURGUNDIAN faction during the FRENCH CIVIL WAR, Philip succeeded his father as duke of Burgundy and count of FLANDERS in September 1419, when John was murdered by ARMAGNAC partisans of the dauphin at the MONTEREAU CONFERENCE. Convinced of the dauphin's complicity in the murder, Philip abandoned all attempts to make peace and instead allied himself with HENRY V through the 1420 Treaty of TROYES. Although the treaty made Henry heir to CHARLES VI and regent of France, the ANGLO-BURGUNDIAN ALLIANCE it created allowed Philip to consolidate his holdings in France and expand his territories in the Low Countries. In April 1423, Burgundy signed the Treaty of AMIENS, a tripartite alliance with JOHN, DUKE OF BEDFORD, who was now regent in France for his infant nephew HENRY VI, and JOHN V, duke of BRITTANY. Sealed by Bedford's marriage to Burgundy's sister ANNE, the treaty confirmed the signatories' acceptance of Henry's right to the French throne. However, the tenuous nature of Burgundy's commitment to the House of LANCASTER was demonstrated by the secret agreement he immediately signed with Brittany whereby the dukes agreed to remain allies should either one choose to reconcile with the dauphin.

In the 1420s, Burgundy provided only minimal military assistance to the Lancastrian war effort, preferring to focus his efforts on transforming Burgundy from a French APPANAGE to an independent state. By the early 1440s, Burgundy, who was a skilled diplomat and clever politician, had doubled his holdings, acquiring, through conquest or marriage, the provinces of Namur, Brabant, Luxembourg, Holland, Zeeland, and Hainault. In 1424–25, Burgundy's interest in the latter three provinces was challenged by HUMPHREY, DUKE OF GLOUCESTER, younger uncle of Henry VI. Gloucester's marriage to Jacqueline, countess of Holland, Zeeland, and Hainault, who had fled to England to escape the husband Burgundy had chosen for her, led the couple to invade Hainault, where clashes with Burgundian forces nearly wrecked the Anglo-Burgundian connection. Only Bedford's intervention and Gloucester's subsequent abandonment of his wife's cause saved the alliance. In May 1430, shortly after his forces captured her at Compiègne, Burgundy visited JOAN OF ARC in the tent where she was being held. Several months later, the duke handed her over to the English, who executed her in 1431.

When Anne, duchess of Bedford, died in 1432, the loss of her personal mediation caused relations between Philip and Bedford to deteriorate. By 1435, Burgundy had come to believe that he could exercise more influence over the weak and indolent dauphin, now king as CHARLES VII, than he could over the strong-willed Bedford. Although the duke despised Charles, growing dissatisfaction in PARIS with the Anglo-Burgundian regime threatened to weaken the duke's popularity there, and led him to explore the possibility of a reconciliation. In September, at the Congress of ARRAS, Burgundy made peace with Charles, who agreed to exempt the duke from paying homage for his French fiefs for his lifetime, to confirm all territorial concessions made to Burgundy by the English, and to send a representative to make humble apology on the king's behalf for the murder at Montereau.

Although the agreement humiliated Charles, it allowed him to retake Paris, reform his army and administration, and eventually expel the English (*see* CHARLES VII, MILITARY REFORMS OF).

Burgundy played no role in the last campaigns of the Hundred Years War, and instead tried unsuccessfully to convince Emperor Frederick III to recognize him as king of an independent Burgundian state. By 1453, Burgundy faced a revived Valois monarchy no longer menaced by the English. In 1456, Burgundy gave asylum to Charles's rebellious son, the dauphin, Louis, but the duke's influence in Paris waned and his principality remained essentially a Franco-Imperial appanage that lacked the cohesion to long survive the growing power of France. The model of late medieval CHIVALRY, Burgundy instituted the Order of the Golden Fleece in 1430 and established an elaborate court ceremonial that was eventually copied by many European rulers, including Edward IV of England. Philip died on 15 June 1467 and was succeeded by his son Charles the Bold, whose death in battle without male heirs in 1477 saw much of French Burgundy eventually reabsorbed by the Valois monarchy.

Further Reading: Cartellieri, Otto. *The Court of Burgundy: Studies in the History of Civilization.* New York: Askell House, 1970; Vaughan, Richard. *Philip the Good: The Apogee of Burgundy.* Woodbridge, England: Boydell Press, 2002.

PLANTAGENET, HOUSE OF

The name "Plantagenet" has been used by historians since the seventeenth century to refer to the English royal family that descended from Henry II (r. 1154–89), and that ruled England from 1154 to 1485. The Plantagenets were a French dynasty descended from the counts of Anjou and the dukes of NORMANDY. During the HUNDRED YEARS WAR, five Plantagenet kings—EDWARD III, RICHARD II, HENRY IV, HENRY V, and HENRY VI, the last three from the Lancastrian branch of the family—contended with the House of VALOIS for control of western France and possession of the French Crown.

The word "Plantagenet" originated as a nickname for Henry II's father, Geoffrey, Count of Anjou (d. 1151). Although the exact meaning of the name is unknown, it was suggested in the nineteenth century that it derived from Geoffrey's habit of wearing a sprig of broom (*Planta genista*) in his helm or cap. Other less widely accepted explanations claim that Geoffrey had a fondness for hunting among the broom or that Geoffrey planted broom as cover to improve his hunting. The name Plantagenet was never used by Henry II or his successors or applied to them by contemporaries; it was first adopted as a surname in the late 1440s by RICHARD, DUKE OF YORK, head of the Yorkist branch of the family, who probably assumed it to emphasize his direct descent from Henry II and so illustrate the superiority of his claim to the Crown over that of his political rivals.

In the mid-twelfth century, Henry II won the English Crown and inherited or otherwise acquired most of western France. Through his mother, the daughter of Henry I and granddaughter of William the Conqueror, he became king of England in 1154. Through his father, he received Normandy as a grant in 1150 and Anjou as an inheritance in 1151; through his marriage to Eleanor of AQUITAINE, he acquired that duchy in 1152; and through his son's marriage to the daughter of the deposed duke of BRITTANY, he acquired control of that duchy in 1166. Although technically a vassal of the House of CAPET, Henry in practice exercised a largely independent authority throughout his French domains. In 1204, Henry's son John lost most of these territories to Philip II Augustus of France. By the 1220s, only a portion of Aquitaine, the coastal region of GASCONY around BORDEAUX, remained under Plantagenet control. In 1259, John's son, Henry III, concluded the Treaty of PARIS with Philip's grandson, Louis IX (St. Louis), agreeing to renounce his claims to the lost provinces in return for formal recognition as duke of an enlarged Aquitaine. By making the king of England a vassal of the king of France, a feudal relationship that later Plantagenet kings found incompatible with their status as a sovereign monarch, the treaty initiated the long dispute over Aquitaine that in large part led to the Hundred Years War.

Henry III's son, EDWARD I, fought a war with France over the issue in the 1290s (*see* ANGLO-FRENCH WAR OF 1293–1303) and Edward's son, EDWARD II, fought another in the 1320s (*see* SAINT-SARDOS, WAR OF). Edward III, a grandson of PHILIP IV through his mother Isabella (*see* ISABELLA, QUEEN OF ENGLAND [c. 1292–1358]), added a new dimension to the dispute by claiming the French Crown, an action that promised an end to the quarrel over Aquitaine by making Edward his own overlord. He was unable to remove the Valois from the throne; however, in 1360, thanks to victories at CRÉCY and POITIERS, Edward won full sovereignty over an enlarged Aquitaine through the Treaty of BRÉTIGNY. The Valois regained most of this territory under CHARLES V, but then nearly lost the whole kingdom to Edward's great-grandson, Henry V, who in 1420 won recognition as heir to the French throne through the Treaty of TROYES. Henry's premature death and a military resurgence under CHARLES VII permitted the Valois to finally expel the Plantagenets from France in 1453.

In the later 1450s, the dynasty was torn apart by a succession dispute between the Lancastrian and Yorkist branches of the family. Henry VI, third king of the House of LANCASTER, held the throne in the 1450s because his grandfather, Henry IV, had deposed his cousin Richard II in 1399, thereby breaking the natural line of succession. The resulting civil war, known as the Wars of the Roses, ended in 1485, when the last Plantagenet king, Richard III, was defeated and killed by Henry VII, first king of the House of Tudor.

Further Reading: Fowler, Kenneth. *The Age of Plantagenet and Valois: The Struggle for Supremacy, 1328–1498*. New York: G. P. Putnam's Sons, 1967; Harvey, John. *The Plantagenets*. 3rd ed. London: Severn House, 1976.

POITIERS, BATTLE OF (1356)

Fought on 19 September 1356 near Poitiers, the capital of the southwestern county of Poitou, the Battle of Poitiers, like the battles of CRÉCY and AGINCOURT, was an unexpected English victory that had devastating consequences for France. By concluding with the capture of JOHN II, the battle thrust France into a period of severe political and social upheaval that threatened the continuance of VALOIS rule and led eventually to the Treaty of BRÉTIGNY and French acceptance of PLANTAGENET sovereignty in AQUITAINE.

To follow up his successful CHEVAUCHÉE OF 1355, which had severely damaged the economy of southern France, EDWARD, THE BLACK PRINCE, prepared in early 1356 for another raid in force from GASCONY, this time northward toward the Loire Valley. In June, HENRY OF GROSMONT, duke of Lancaster, landed in NORMANDY, where he led a CHEVAUCHÉE designed to draw French attention away from the prince's campaign, and to relieve pressure on the partisans of CHARLES THE BAD, king of Navarre, a potential English ally recently imprisoned by John. Although Lancaster avoided battle, his activities held John in the north, while the prince, after leaving BERGERAC on 4 August, marched northeast through central France. Leading an Anglo-Gascon force of about six thousand, the prince reached Tours on 7 September. On 11 September, after an unsuccessful assault on the town, the prince learned that John had crossed the Loire at the head of a large army and was now only ten miles from the English. Fearful of being caught between the royal army and the recently strengthened garrison of Tours, the prince withdrew immediately toward BORDEAUX.

By 17 September, the French army, which contained about eleven thousand men, had passed west of the English line of march and was in position to block any retreat into Gascony. On 18 September, the prince took up a strong defensive position on a hill about five miles southeast of Poitiers near the village of Nouaillé. That night, papal agents, whom the prince suspected of being pro-French, attempted to negotiate a truce. Exhausted, outnumbered, and short of supplies, the English were not eager to fight, but the French king, sensing his enemy's weakness, was unwilling to make any concessions that the prince could accept, and talks collapsed next morning.

The prince deployed his men in one line, with Thomas BEAUCHAMP, earl of Warwick, holding the left; William Montagu, earl of Salisbury; the right; and the prince himself in command of the center. About four hundred of the prince's two thousand ARCHERS acted as a reserve. Protected by hills, vines, and hedges, the English were difficult to reach, and Jean de Clermont, one of the French marshals, proposed that the French not attack until hunger and thirst forced the prince to abandon his prepared position, although this suggestion was derided as cowardice. However, because of the difficult terrain, the French, perhaps at the suggestion of William Douglas, Lord Douglas, leader of a sizable Scottish contingent, decided to abandon their centuries-old tradition of fighting from horseback. As a result, the entire army dismounted except for a force of about five hundred heavily armored knights, who were placed in front of the three parallel battle lines into which John divided his army. The first line was commanded by the dauphin (*see* CHARLES V) and Doug-

John II surrenders to the English to end the Battle of Poitiers, 1356. *Giraudon/Art Resource, New York.*

las; the second by the king's brother, Philip, duke of Orléans; and the third, consisting of two thousand picked men, by the king himself.

Realizing the seriousness of their situation, the prince and his commanders decided to begin a retreat while maintaining line of battle. When Clermont and Arnoul d'AUDREHEM, the French marshals in command of the cavalry, noticed movement on the English left, they launched immediate assaults on the archers holding each wing of the enemy force. Although English arrows proved relatively ineffective against the

heavily armored horses, both attacks failed because the difficult ground caused the horsemen to bunch up, thus blunting the force of their charge and exposing their more vulnerable flanks to the archers. The first French battle line followed the cavalry, suffering casualties from archer fire when it pushed through gaps in the hedgerow but otherwise reaching the English line in good order. After two hours of desperate hand-to-hand combat, the French retreated. Likely acting on the king's orders, the dauphin's knights escorted him from the field. Upon seeing his nephew withdraw, Orléans, perhaps thinking a general retreat had begun, also withdrew, taking the second French division with him. Left alone to face an English army that now outnumbered him, John attacked with the third division. Because of the unusual length of the battle and the prince's strict orders against breaking formation, the English archers were now almost out of arrows, allowing John's men to reach the English line with few casualties.

Although the French were fresh, while their opponents had been fighting for three hours, English morale was high. As the archers abandoned their longbows to fall upon the enemy with swords and knives, Jean de GRAILLY, the captal de Buch, led a mounted force of sixty men-at-arms and a hundred archers around the French army. Raising the standard of St. George as a signal, the captal attacked the French rear, thereby causing sufficient confusion to allow the prince to remount some of his knights and send a second cavalry charge led by Sir James AUDLEY crashing into the French front. The dismounted French line broke into small groups, with many men being shot down by English archers as they tried to flee the field. As John fought bravely on, the battle degenerated into an unseemly scramble for prisoners and RANSOMS. Some men were captured several times when their original captors, upon claiming a token of surrender, ran off to find other prisoners. When John and his son, PHILIP THE BOLD, eventually submitted, they were roughly handled by a crowd of men eager for a share of the royal ransom. The king was eventually rescued by Warwick, who conveyed him to the prince.

Because his men were more experienced at fighting on foot and his commanders better able to control the movements of their men, the prince had won a brilliant triumph. The English took about three thousand prisoners, including, besides the king and his son, Audrehem; Jean, count of Eu; the archbishop of Sens, and most of John's political and military advisors. The eventual ransoms were enormous. Not including John's ransom, the prisoners taken at Poitiers are estimated to have enriched their captors by almost £300,000, over three times what the English had spent on the previous year's campaign. Most of the important prisoners were bought by the prince and EDWARD III, with the captal de Buch receiving almost £5,000 for one of his captives. Among the twenty-five hundred French dead were Clermont; Pierre, duke of Bourbon; and Geoffrey de Charny, who had borne the OR-IFLAMME. In England, the sheer magnitude of the victory seemed a clear sign that God favored the Plantagenet cause, while in France, the shock of defeat bred social anarchy and political revolution, and made an eventual settlement on terms favorable to the English seem almost inevitable.

Further Reading: Barber, Richard. *Edward, Prince of Wales and Aquitaine.* New York: Charles Scribner's Sons, 1978; Burne, Alfred H. *The Crécy War.* Ware, England: Wordsworth Editions Ltd., 1999; Hewitt, Herbert J. *The Black Prince's Expeditions of 1355–1357.* Manchester: Manchester University Press, 1958; Sumption, Jonathan. *The Hundred Years War.* Vol. 2, *Trial by Fire.* Philadelphia: University of Pennsylvania Press, 2001.

POLE, MICHAEL DE LA, EARL OF SUFFOLK. *See* RICHARD II

POLE, SIR WILLIAM DE LA (d. 1366)

William de la Pole, a Yorkshire merchant and moneylender, rose to prominence by financing the military campaigns of EDWARD III. Pole's financial activities during the HUNDRED YEARS WAR led to perpetuation of a royal tax on wool exports and to the displacement of free trade in wool by large merchant monopolies.

Between 1327 and 1330, William and his brother Richard (d. 1345), wine merchants in the Yorkshire port of Kingston upon Hull, loaned the king over £13,000. The brothers financed these loans by borrowing from other merchants who were unwilling to lend to the king directly, but who trusted the Poles. During the early 1330s, while serving as mayor of Kingston upon Hull, William used the profits of his highly successful wool trade to provide loans and buy arms for Edward's campaigns in SCOTLAND. In

1337, Pole devised a scheme for funding the French war with wool exports. With LONDON merchant Reginald Conduit, Pole headed a syndicate that was given a monopoly on English wool exports and the power to require wool growers to sell on credit. The syndicate planned to ship thirty thousand sacks of wool each year to Dordrecht in the Low Countries and to advance the Crown £200,000 on the sale of the wool. When some of Pole's associates abused their power of compulsory purchase and smuggled some of the wool on their own account, royal officials, in dire need of funds to pay the king's allies, collapsed the scheme by confiscating the wool already collected in Dordrecht. The Crown issued the so-called DORDRECHT BONDS to the syndicate, which then agreed that the government should dispose of the wool as it saw fit, but the failure of the plan left the Crown impoverished and severely hampered the English war effort.

In 1338 and 1339, Pole, acting alone, loaned the king over £100,000, and was rewarded with reluctant sales of royal estates and elevation to the rank of banneret. Angered by the failure of the wool syndicate and by Pole's success at obtaining repayment, Edward ordered Pole's arrest on 30 November 1340. Charged with smuggling wool and punished with confiscation of his property—particularly the former royal estates—Pole was released in May 1342 when the king again had need of his services. In 1343, Pole organized a new company that was given control of the royal customs, which it used as security to raise new loans for the Crown. Pole withdrew from the company in 1345, but his successors financed the CRÉCY campaign and the siege of CALAIS before going bankrupt in the economic downturn that followed the BLACK DEATH in 1348–49.

Although Pole avoided any responsibility for the company's debts, the extended period of truce in the early 1350s (see CALAIS, TRUCE OF) improved the king's finances and allowed him to renew the charge of smuggling against Pole, who only escaped complete ruin by forgiving all outstanding royal debts and renouncing all claims to lands

purchased from the Crown. Pole was thus still a wealthy man when he died on 21 June 1366. Thanks to Pole's financial services to the Crown, his family entered the English peerage, his son Michael de la Pole becoming earl of Suffolk in 1385, his great-grandson William de la POLE, duke of Suffolk, serving as Henry VI's chief minister in the 1440s, and his great-great-great-grandson John de la Pole, earl of Lincoln, being recognized as heir to the throne in 1485. *See also* CRISIS OF 1340–41.

Further Reading: Fryde, E. B. *William de la Pole, Merchant and King's Banker.* London: Hambledon and London, 2003; Horrox, Rosemary. *The de la Poles of Hull.* Beverley, England: East Yorkshire Local History Society, 1983.

POLE, WILLIAM DE LA, DUKE OF SUFFOLK (1396–1450)

William de la Pole, duke of Suffolk, was one of the English commanders at the siege of ORLÉANS in 1429 and chief minister of HENRY VI in the 1440s. In the latter capacity, Suffolk was responsible for implementing the king's unpopular peace policy and, through the rapacity of his faction, for the royal financial difficulties that made peace with France necessary.

William was the great-grandson of William de la POLE, the Hull merchant who financed EDWARD III's early campaigns. His father, Michael de la Pole, the second earl of Suffolk, died at the siege of HARFLEUR in September 1415, and his elder brother, Michael, the third earl, was killed some weeks later at AGINCOURT, making William the fourth earl of Suffolk. The earl went to France in 1417, serving with HUMPHREY, DUKE OF GLOUCESTER, in NORMANDY and with HENRY V at the siege of ROUEN. In May 1419, Suffolk was appointed admiral of Normandy, his first significant command, and in 1420 he joined the king at the siege of MELUN. The earl became a member of the Order of the GARTER in 1421. After the king's death in 1422, Suffolk became one of the chief noble lieutenants of the regent, JOHN, DUKE OF BEDFORD, and compiled a competent, if not distinguished record, serving frequently under such veteran commanders as Thomas, MONTAGU, earl of Salisbury, and Richard BEAUCHAMP, earl of Warwick.

In October 1428, upon the death of Salisbury, Suffolk assumed leadership of the English forces besieging Orléans; however, in December, overall command of the siege went to John TALBOT. When the French under JOAN OF ARC and John, the Bastard of Orléans (see JOHN, COUNT OF DUNOIS AND LONGUEVILLE), lifted the siege in May 1429, Suffolk withdrew to Jargeau with part of the English army. On 12 June, during the French LOIRE CAMPAIGN, Suffolk surrendered Jargeau and was taken prisoner; forced to sell land to meet his RANSOM, the earl was released in the spring of 1430. In the following autumn, he married Alice Chaucer, the widowed countess of Salisbury, who was a kinswoman of Cardinal Henry BEAUFORT, a leading member of the regency council, and the granddaughter of the poet Geoffrey Chaucer.

In about 1433, Suffolk left France to pursue a political career in England. As a protégé of Beaufort, he supported the conclusion of peace with France, a policy that put him at odds with Gloucester, who led the war party. By the early 1440s, Suffolk had established himself as leader of a group of younger courtiers who exercised increasing influence over Henry VI. In 1444, Suffolk negotiated the Truce of TOURS with CHARLES VII and arranged Henry's marriage to the French king's kinswoman, MARGARET OF ANJOU, who became the earl's political ally after her coronation in 1445. The deaths of Gloucester and Beaufort in 1447 left Suffolk in control of the royal government and brought him a series of important offices and promotions, including appointments as lord admiral (1447) and governor of CALAIS (1448) and elevation to a dukedom (1448).

Although Suffolk and his supporters made enemies by using their influence with the king to enrich themselves and exclude others from power, it was military defeat that toppled the duke's administration. In 1448, the government ceded Maine to the French; although the highly unpopular surrender was the king's idea, it was Suffolk, as chief minister, who was blamed (see MAINE, SURRENDER OF). In 1449, the ill-considered English seizure of FOUGÉRES in BRITTANY provoked a French attack on Normandy, which, after a weak defense by Suffolk's protégé, Edmund BEAUFORT, duke of Somerset, fell in 1450 (see NORMAN CAMPAIGN [1449–1450]). The loss of Normandy created a public outcry against Suffolk, who was impeached by PARLIAMENT in February 1450. The Commons charged the duke with corruption, extortion, and treason, alleging that he had used diplomatic missions to France as opportunities to plot Henry's overthrow. On 17 March, the king intervened, dismissing the treason charge but declaring Suffolk's guilt on the others and ordering him banished for five years. Suffolk took ship for the Low Countries on 30 April, but was intercepted by an English privateer, the *Nicholas of the Tower*, which was probably acting on orders of his political enemies, particularly RICHARD, DUKE OF YORK, who blamed Suffolk for their exclusion from office. Suffolk was beheaded by his captors on 2 May, and his body was thrown ashore at Dover.

Further Reading: Griffiths, Ralph A. *The Reign of King Henry VI*. Berkeley: University of California Press, 1981; Harriss, G. L. *Cardinal Beaufort: A Study of Lancastrian Ascendancy and Decline*. Oxford: Clarendon Press, 1988; Watts, John. *Henry VI and the Politics of Kingship*. Cambridge: Cambridge University Press, 1996; Wolffe, Bertram. *Henry VI*. London: Eyre Methuen, 1981.

PONTOISE, PEACE OF. *See* FRENCH CIVIL WAR

PONTOISE, SIEGE OF (1441)
Situated on the Oise about twenty miles northwest of PARIS along the main road from ROUEN, the town and bridge of Pontoise offered the nearest river crossing and most direct northern approach to the capital. The ultimate success of the French siege of Pontoise, which ran intermittently from June to September 1441, freed Paris from the threat

of English assault, opened NORMANDY to the threat of French assault, and demonstrated the growing importance of ARTILLERY in SIEGE WARFARE.

Following the termination of the ANGLO-BURGUNDIAN ALLIANCE at the Congress of ARRAS in 1435, Pontoise reverted to its VA-LOIS allegiance, forcing John TALBOT to recapture the town by stealth on 13 February 1437. A group of Talbot's soldiers entered Pontoise from the south disguised as peasants, while a scaling party, dressed in white to blend into the snowy landscape, approached the walls from the north. At the appointed time, the former opened the gates to Talbot, while the latter swarmed over the walls, thus capturing the town before the garrison could strike a blow.

CHARLES VII's recapture of Pontoise in 1441 was a much longer and more difficult undertaking, with a French historian later describing the campaign as "a veritable siege of Troy" (Burne, 293). The French invested the city on 6 June with a force of about five thousand commanded by Constable Arthur de Richemont (see ARTHUR III) and including such leading French captains as Étienne de VIGNOLLES ("LA HIRE") and Poton de XAINTRAILLES. Unable to approach the city until the English had been cleared from the bridge, the French brought up their artillery, which, under the skillful direction of Jean BUREAU, weakened the barbican so that it could be carried by storm. Bureau's guns were then transported across the river, where they began bombarding the town. On about 16 June, as Talbot approached with a small relief force, the constable, acting on orders from the king, who was traveling with the army, reluctantly withdrew behind his defenses, thus allowing Talbot to resupply the garrison before drawing off. A short time later, Talbot reappeared with a new supply train, which again carried into Pontoise without hindrance from the French.

Heartened by the French king's unwillingness to give battle, an English army of perhaps three thousand, this time commanded by RICHARD, DUKE OF YORK, the Lancastrian lieutenant in France, approached Pontoise in mid-July. After a complicated two-week campaign during which the French crossed and recrossed various rivers to escape York, the siege was broken and Charles, having narrowly avoided capture, was back in Paris. Although he had relieved Pontoise, York was desperately short of supplies and could not remain in the field; by mid-August, he was back in Rouen. Charles, perhaps stung by whispered charges of cowardice arising from his tortuous efforts to avoid battle, ordered the reinvestment of Pontoise, which was again under bombardment by 16 August, when Talbot tried again to resupply the garrison. This time, the constable advanced against him, forcing Talbot to wheel around the northern flank and punch through the French siege lines where they had earlier been weakened to meet the English advance. Although Talbot resupplied the garrison again on 6 September, Bureau's guns continued battering the walls. By 16 September, the French had taken most of the suburbs, and, on 19 September, a simultaneous assault at various points along the weakened wall forced the capitulation of the garrison. About five hundred English soldiers were slain in the fighting, while John, Lord Clinton, the garrison commander, was put to RANSOM with most of his officers.

Further Reading: Burne, Alfred H. *The Agincourt War*. Ware, England: Wordsworth Editions Ltd., 1999.

PONTVALLAIN, BATTLE OF. *See* GUE-SCLIN, BERTRAND DU; KNOLLES, SIR ROBERT

PRAGUERIE. *See* CHARLES VII

PROCESS

"Process" is the term used for a series of Anglo-French commissions that met in the early fourteenth century to discuss and settle the many disputes arising between the two Crowns over the duchy of AQUITAINE. By failing to resolve the fundamental issue of sovereignty in Aquitaine, these processes contributed to the coming of the HUNDRED YEARS WAR.

In 1259, the Treaty of PARIS created a feudal relationship between the kings of France and England, making the latter vassals of the former by recognizing the English monarch's possession of Aquitaine. Thereafter, successive English rulers, accustomed to exercising unfettered authority in their own kingdom, grew increasingly unwilling to accept their feudal subordination to the king of France in their continental possessions, especially since French monarchs made frequent use of their overlordship to interfere in their vassal's administration of his own duchy. Both sides had cause for complaint. French royal officials often ignored the king-duke's jurisdiction, usurped the authority of his officers, and encouraged his Gascon subjects to appeal against his policies to PARIS. English administrators often hindered French officials in the performance of their legitimate duties and forcibly prevented Gascons from appealing the king-duke's decisions.

In June 1303, the ANGLO-FRENCH WAR OF 1294–1303, which had proved financially ruinous for both Crowns, was officially ended with the restoration of Aquitaine to PLANTAGENET control. Three years later, in an effort to avoid another war, PHILIP IV and EDWARD II finally put into practice a principle first enunciated in a 1285 statute of the Westminster PARLIAMENT, which called for creation of ad hoc Anglo-French commissions empowered to adjudicate disputes arising over local rights and duties not formally falling under the appellate jurisdiction of the French Crown. The first such commission, the Process of Montreuil, met from 1306 to 1311; the second, the Process of Périgueux, from 1311 to 1316. Both bodies had a sizable Gascon membership, and both mainly discussed compensation issues arising from property confiscated or other losses suffered during the late war. Neither conference led to a settlement largely because the French viewed the process as a lawsuit between unequals. With the French Crown acting as both accuser and judge, the English

came to believe that the real French policy was not amicable settlement, but the ultimate extinction of the king-duke's authority in Aquitaine through a slow but incessant process of administrative encroachment.

Further war was avoided until 1323 because Philip IV and his two elder sons, LOUIS X and PHILIP V, were too distracted by discontent in France and turmoil in FLANDERS to contemplate a new conflict with Edward II. However, CHARLES IV took a harder line toward Aquitaine, and the so-called War of SAINT-SARDOS (1323–25) resulted in another confiscation of the duchy, which lasted until 1329, when both thrones had new occupants—PHILIP VI in France and EDWARD III in England. To settle compensation issues arising from the new war, the kings created the Process of Agen, which sat from 1331 to 1334 and was no more successful than its predecessors. Three years after this third process collapsed in mutual recrimination, Philip again confiscated Aquitaine, thus initiating the Hundred Years War. *See also* GASCONY.

Further Reading: Cuttino, G. C. "The Process of Agen." *Speculum* 19 (1944): 161–78; Vale, Malcolm. *The Origins of the Hundred Years War.* Oxford: Clarendon Press, 2000.

PROPAGANDA AND WAR PUBLICITY

Because of its length, cost, and consequences to civilian populations, the HUNDRED YEARS WAR required that royal governments manage the expectations and secure the support of their people. Although the term "propaganda" did not come into use until the nineteenth century, it aptly describes the variety of activities in which the VALOIS and PLANTAGENET monarchies engaged to promote the involvement of their subjects in the ongoing war.

At the highest level, kings in both countries called upon scholars and legal experts to marshal evidence and devise arguments upholding the positions of each royal house. Although the resulting tracts and treatises were legalistic and pedantic works of Latin scholarship meant only for a learned and limited audience, they provided broad underpinnings for the royal claims upon which the war was being fought. Based on appeals to history, or at least to a particular view of history, these documents justified the war on legal and moral grounds. In England, such works carefully laid out the Plantagenet and Lancastrian claims to the French Crown, and, in France, they refuted English (and later Burgundian) claims by attempting to prove that the Valois were the true descendants of the Frankish kings.

Simpler messages were used to appeal to the uneducated and unsophisticated, who needed to be made aware of war events, particularly military successes. In 1346, Londoners organized processions celebrating EDWARD III's victory at CRÉCY and witnessed DAVID II of SCOTLAND, recently captured at NEVILLE'S CROSS, being paraded through the streets to the Tower. In May 1357, even grander celebrations welcomed EDWARD, THE BLACK PRINCE, as he entered the capital accompanied by his royal prisoner, JOHN II. In October 1416, on the first anniversary of AGINCOURT, HENRY V ordered public commemorations of that battle, and, in 1450, CHARLES VII ordered the issuance of a medal to similarly commemorate the recent English expulsion from NORMANDY.

Victories could also be profitably employed by the Church, which was frequently called upon to support the war effort by assuring subjects that God was on their side. Nothing conferred God's endorsement of a cause like victory on the battlefield, as English bishops and priests repeatedly emphasized in sermons preached after victories like Crécy and POITIERS. And if God fought for England, as seemed the case in the mid-fourteenth century, was it not then right for Englishmen to do the same? Of course, God could use war to punish as well as to honor, and throughout the conflict people in both countries were frequently exhorted to pray for good fortune in battle. In the English diocese of Lincoln, the government requested special prayers for war-related intentions on more than fifty occasions during the war. In an age that believed strongly in the efficacy of prayer and in divine intervention in human

affairs, praying for the success of the national cause was a powerful weapon.

Beyond boosting morale and commitment, the Church also kept people informed of war events. In the 1420s, the English nailed verses and illustrated genealogies tracing HENRY VI's claim to the French throne to the doors of Norman churches, which thus served as community bulletin boards for educating illiterate parishioners about the legitimacy of the House of LANCASTER. Priests were also active agents in the dissemination of war news, reading from the pulpit letters and reports sent from the battlefield by kings and commanders. Newsletters from the front, such as those dispatched by Edward III after Crécy and the Black Prince after NÁJERA, are so plentiful for the fourteenth century that they have been described as a "rudimentary publicity system... used for spreading military news" (Prince, 417), and the Church was the primary network through which this system operated.

War news and information was also distributed by literary writers—chroniclers, poets, and political commentators—who lauded national heroes and denigrated the enemy. In the fourteenth century, the ballads of Eustache Deschamps expressed the sense of French NATIONAL CONSCIOUSNESS that was growing out of the war, while, in the fifteenth century, the unknown composer of the "Agincourt Carol" captured English pride in Henry V. As the war progressed, the literary conventions of CHIVALRY, which called for one to honor and respect a worthy opponent, gave way to abuse, slander, and ridicule of the national enemy. French writers proclaimed that the English had tails, were arrogant and overbearing, and (particularly after the deposition of RICHARD II) delighted in killing their kings. In the fifteenth century, the French referred to the English as "godons," from "God-damn," a phase in wide use among English soldiers. English writers characterized the French as stubborn, effeminate, deceitful, and unable to see that God was against them. By thus condemning and stereotyping the enemy, propaganda literature played an important role in developing a sense of national consciousness in both countries during the course of the war.

Further Reading: Allmand, Christopher. *The Hundred Years War*. Cambridge: Cambridge University Press, 1988; Curry, Anne. *The Hundred Years War*. 2nd ed. Houndmills, England: Palgrave Macmillan, 2003; Maddicott, J. R. "The County Community and the Making of Public Opinion in Fourteenth-Century England." *Transactions of the Royal Historical Society*, 5th ser., 28 (1978): 34–35, 38; Prince, A. E. "A Letter of Edward, the Black Prince, Describing the Battle of Najera in 1367." *English Historical Review* 41 (1926): 415–18.

R

RANSOM

Medieval military convention recognized men taken in battle as the private property of their captors, not as prisoners of the state. Anyone who captured another man on the battlefield was entitled to detain his prisoner as long as he wished, to contract with him to receive an agreed-upon ransom for his release, or to mortgage or sell his ransom to the Crown or anyone else willing to pay a good price. During the HUNDRED YEARS WAR, prisoners were thus valuable and sought-after prizes of war, and the personal pursuit of high-ranking and wealthy captives was sometimes undertaken with greater energy and enthusiasm than the pursuit of military objectives.

Although custom dictated that ransoms should be reasonable, the actual practice during the Hundred Years War was to demand the highest possible ransom that the prisoner, when aided by friends, family, and tenants, could afford. In some instances, meeting one's ransom required the sale of land, which, particularly in the later stages of the war or the most ravaged regions of the country, did not always sell well or quickly. A noble family might thus be ruined by the need to pay ransom, as happened to the Burgundian lord William de Châteauvillain, who turned to his landed relatives to guarantee payment of the 20,000 saluts owed to his French captors in 1430. Sometimes prisoners had to call upon their king for assistance in paying ransom. HENRY VI contributed 1,500 livres for the ransom of Sir John Handford in 1444 and PHILIP VI assisted knights, who, having paid their ransoms, could not afford to remount or rearm

themselves. However, kings were often so hard pressed to fund the ongoing war that they were unable to help men burdened with high ransoms. Many of the French knights taken by the English in 1345 at BERGERAC and AUBEROCHE, two early battles that clearly demonstrated the financial benefits of ransoming captives, found themselves shunned by royal officials to whom they applied for assistance. Other captives of Auberoche, such as John de Galard, lord of Limeuil, took service with the English Crown in lieu of a ransom he could not pay. As the war gradually strengthened national feelings in both realms, such men often found themselves accused of treason by their former comrades.

A few men made great fortunes out of ransoms. HENRY OF GROSMONT, duke of Lancaster, realized almost £70,000 from the ransoms of Bergerac and Auberoche, sufficient for him to magnificently rebuild Savoy Palace outside LONDON. Sir Walter MAUNY grew rich on the ransoms received from a series of noble prisoners taken in FLANDERS and BRITTANY in the 1330s and 1340s. As the war continued, a substantial market in ransoms developed, driven in part by the royal practice of buying the ransoms of high-ranking prisoners, and by the actions of men who speculated in the purchase of ransoms. Among the latter was Sir John Cornwall, who in 1423 purchased the ransoms of the lords of Gaucourt and Estouteville and of John, duke of Bourbon, all of whom had been captives since 1415. Another such dealer in ransoms was Sir Walter Hungerford, who rebuilt his castle in Somerset with the ransoms of eight prisoners brought back from AGINCOURT. As to royal purchase of ransoms, EDWARD III paid Sir Thomas DAGWORTH £3,500 for the ransom of CHARLES OF BLOIS, the French-backed claimant to the duchy of Brittany, who was captured at LA ROCHE-DERRIEN in 1347, and HENRY V paid Sir John Cornwall a high price for the count of Vendôme, who was taken at Agincourt. Kings also rewarded their favorite lieutenants by purchasing their prisoners for significant sums, such as the 1,000 marks Edward III gave Mauny for John Crabbe, a military engineer seized in SCOTLAND. In the fifteenth century, CHARLES VII did something similar in France, granting estates in Poitou to his favorite, George de la Trémoïlle, to compensate him for an uncollectible ransom.

The most famous ransoms of the war were those Edward III demanded for the release of DAVID II of Scotland, taken at NEVILLE'S CROSS in 1346, and JOHN II of France, captured at POITIERS in 1356. The circumstances of John's capture illustrate how highly prized ransoms had become. Surrounded by enemies, John was called upon to surrender, but only did so when assured that his captor was a knight. Immediately upon handing over his gauntlet as a token of surrender, the king was seized by a band of Gascons, whose members struggled with one another to grab hold of John and thereby stake their claim to a portion of his ransom. More alarmed by this situation than by combat, John was rescued by the intervention of Thomas BEAUCHAMP, earl of Warwick, who respectfully led the king to EDWARD, THE BLACK PRINCE. The ransoms of both kings—100,000 marks for David and 3 million écus for John—severely strained the resources and political stability of their countries. However, in both cases, the process of collecting ransom, being conducted in communities throughout each realm, promoted the development of stronger national identities. *See also* NATIONAL CONSCIOUSNESS, GROWTH OF; PROPAGANDA AND WAR PUBLICITY.

Further Reading: Allmand, Christopher. *The Hundred Years War.* Cambridge: Cambridge Uni-

versity Press, 1988; Sumption, Jonathan. *The Hundred Years War.* Vol. 1, *Trial by Battle.* Philadelphia: University of Pennsylvania Press, 1999.

RHEIMS CAMPAIGN (1359–1360)

The last campaign commanded by EDWARD III and one of the largest English expeditions of the HUNDRED YEARS WAR, the Rheims Campaign, which lasted from October 1359 to April 1360, was an attempt to force the French to conclude peace on English terms. Although JOHN II was a captive in LONDON, and the government of Dauphin Charles (*see* CHARLES V) was hampered by internal unrest and financial weakness, the English campaign failed to achieve its original purpose, largely due to the dauphin's strategy of refusing battle. This tactic turned the expedition into a series of fruitless sieges and frustrating marches by an army struggling to keep itself fed and supplied.

With the failure of the Second Treaty of LONDON in March 1359, Edward recruited his largest army to date, a force numbering almost twelve thousand. The expedition's objective was the city of Rheims, the traditional coronation site of French kings, where Edward planned to have himself solemnly crowned king of France. As an anointed French monarch, Edward hoped to overthrow the VALOIS regime or, failing that, to increase pressure on the dauphin to make significant territorial concessions to end the war and regain his father's freedom. Joined by troops raised in Hainault by Walter MAUNY, the English fleet of eleven hundred ships landed at CALAIS on 28 October 1359. On 4 November, the English marched out of Calais in three columns; the king commanded the main force, which marched north through Artois, while EDWARD, THE BLACK PRINCE, led the southern wing through the Somme Valley and HENRY OF GROSMONT, duke of Lancaster, followed a middle route. Due to the size of the force and the lateness of the year, supply was a problem from the start and largely dictated the line of march, with each column proceeding on a broad front so as to draw provisions from the widest possible area.

The French withdrew into walled towns and made no attempt to hinder the English columns as they marched by. The weather proved a more dangerous enemy; a cold and rainy November made roads impassable and rivers unfordable, and the English columns briefly lost contact as food and fodder grew scarce. Edward reached Rheims on 4 December, and his army quickly surrounded the town, whose garrison was well supplied behind its high walls. When an attempt to storm the walls failed, the English began a winter siege; however, the supply situation soon grew critical, forcing Edward to withdraw on 11 January 1360.

With no settled plan except to keep his army in being, Edward moved toward BUR-GUNDY, where, on 10 March, the Burgundians agreed to the Treaty of Guillon, whereby they paid Edward 200,000 florins to spare the duchy. Meanwhile, bands of French partisans harassed the English columns, killing or capturing the unwary, including the writer Geoffrey Chaucer, who was put to RANSOM. In late March, with the weather finally improving, Edward made for PARIS. Although he probably did not expect to take the capital—even his army was insufficient for that—Edward did hope to force the dauphin to come to terms. Negotiations commenced, but, time being on their side, the French rejected Edward's territorial demands, which still reflected the Treaty of London. Unable to feed his army, Edward withdrew from Paris on 12 April. The next day, Monday 13 April, disaster struck the English. The weather, which had been unseasonably mild, turned suddenly cold, with sleet and rain followed by a hard freeze; so many sick and hungry men and horses died of exposure that the day became known among the English as "Black Monday."

The tragedy convinced Edward to moderate his demands and obtain the best settlement possible. He therefore sent messages to Paris signaling his willingness to treat on French terms. On 1 May, a peace conference opened at Brétigny, a village near Chartres.

By 3 May, the main provisions of the Treaty of BRÉTIGNY were agreed. Upon hearing that the dauphin had assented to the treaty on 10 May, the English marched quickly north, with Edward embarking from Honfleur on 19 May and the rest of the army proceeding to Calais, where the men took ship shortly thereafter.

Further Reading: Burne, Alfred H. *The Crécy War.* Ware, England: Wordsworth Editions Ltd., 1999; Sumption, Jonathan. *The Hundred Years War.* Vol. 2, *Trial by Fire.* Philadelphia: University of Pennsylvania Press, 2001.

RICHARD, DUKE OF YORK (1411–1460)

Richard, third duke of York, succeeded JOHN, DUKE OF BEDFORD, as HENRY VI's lieutenant in France, thereby assuming responsibility for conduct of the HUNDRED YEARS WAR. In 1460, York, after years in opposition, laid claim to the Crown, thus initiating the Wars of the Roses and precipitating his death in battle. With his son's subsequent seizure of the throne, the duke became the immediate ancestor of the royal House of York, which ruled England until 1485.

Richard was the only son of Richard, earl of Cambridge, who was executed for treason by HENRY V in 1415, and Anne Mortimer, who died shortly after her son's birth. He was descended from EDWARD III through both his parents. Cambridge was the son of Edward's fourth son, EDMUND OF LANGLEY, duke of York, and Anne was a great-granddaughter of Edward's second son, Lionel, duke of Clarence. Thus, through his mother, Richard had a claim to the PLANTAGENET throne that was technically superior to that of the House of LANCASTER, which derived from Edward's third son, JOHN OF GAUNT, duke of Lancaster. Richard was only four when the death of his paternal uncle at the Battle of AGINCOURT made him duke of York, and only fourteen when the death of his maternal uncle made him earl of March and heir to the Mortimer claim to the throne, which had lain dormant since HENRY IV deposed RICHARD II in 1399. To ensure York's loyalty to the Lancastrian regime, the government arranged his early marriage—he was perhaps fifteen—to Cecily Neville, the daughter of Ralph Neville, earl of Westmorland, a staunch Lancastrian. Knighted in 1426, York resided at court from 1428 and in 1430 attended Henry VI's coronation in PARIS. By 1434, the duke was in full possession of his patrimony and thus the wealthiest peer of the realm.

Elected to the Order of the GARTER in 1433, York received his first military command in May 1436, when the king, anxious to see "some great prince of our blood" (Johnson, 226) in command in France, named York to the French lieutenancy. Other than the king's surviving paternal uncle, HUMPHREY, DUKE OF GLOUCESTER, there was no one else who fit this description. By the time York reached HARFLEUR in early June, Paris had fallen to CHARLES VII, but the duke, working with John TALBOT, Lord Talbot, who had actual command of the armies, stemmed the French advance and ensured the safety of NORMANDY. In 1437, York, frustrated with the government's inadequate funding of his troops, asked leave to return home. The government, perhaps equally frustrated with York's lackluster performance as lieutenant, replaced the duke with Richard BEAUCHAMP, earl of Warwick. However, the earl's death in April 1439 precipitated a competition for the office between the war faction led by Gloucester, who offered himself as lieutenant, and the peace faction led by Cardinal Henry BEAUFORT, bishop of Winchester, who suggested his nephew, John BEAUFORT, earl of Somerset. Since he was not closely attached to either faction, York again emerged as the best candidate for the office.

Reappointed in July 1440, York demanded and received greater authority—he was given all Bedford's former powers—and better funding—he was promised £20,000 per year for his men. Arriving in Normandy in June 1441, York temporarily lifted the siege of PONTOISE, but otherwise undertook no further military effort. This inactivity allowed Cardinal Beaufort to win a major command for Somerset, whose ultimately unsuccessful 1443 campaign stripped York

of men, money, and authority. Although the government mollified the duke by paying the arrears of his wages and granting him an APPANAGE in southern Normandy, it did not reappoint him. The French lieutenancy went to Edmund BEAUFORT, the new earl of Somerset, in 1446. York was instead named lieutenant of Ireland, where he arrived in June 1449. While the Irish lieutenancy is often portrayed as political banishment arranged by Henry's chief minister William de la POLE, duke of Suffolk, who viewed York as an opponent of the government's peace policy, there is no indication that York openly opposed either the Truce of TOURS or even the English surrender of Maine.

Nonetheless, in 1450, following suppression of JACK CADE'S REBELLION and the murder of Suffolk, York returned from Ireland a determined opponent of the Suffolk-Somerset faction, whose members he denounced as traitors responsible for the loss of Normandy and the bankruptcy of the Crown. Fearing Beaufort ambitions, he tried unsuccessfully to have his position as heir apparent confirmed. In 1452, he led an abortive uprising aimed at removing Somerset from office. After 1453, York and his noble allies were increasingly at odds with Queen MARGARET OF ANJOU, who feared that York intended to displace her infant son as Henry's heir. With the onset of the king's mental illness in 1453, York twice served as protector, his second protectorate in 1455 being occasioned by victory over a royalist army at St. Albans, where the duke's chief rivals, including Somerset, were slain. In 1460, York laid claim to the Crown, but PARLIAMENT, being unwilling to depose Henry, imposed a settlement naming York Henry's heir. This arrangement precipitated civil war, and on 30 December 1460, York was slain at the Battle of Wakefield. However, in March 1461, York's eldest son seized the throne as Edward IV. *See also* MAINE, SURRENDER OF.

Further Reading: Johnson, P. A. *Duke Richard of York, 1411–1460.* Oxford: Clarendon Press, 1988.

RICHARD II, KING OF ENGLAND
(1367–1400)

The eighth king of the House OF PLANTAG-ENET, Richard II was the grandson and successor of EDWARD III. Like the reign of his deposed great-grandfather, EDWARD II, Richard's reign, which also ended in deposition, was characterized by ongoing conflict with the nobility. This strife arose in part from Richard's absolutist tendencies and in part from his determined pursuit of peace with France. Although eventually successful in concluding a truce with the VALOIS, Richard's efforts to end the HUNDRED YEARS WAR foundered on the opposition of his magnates and the unwillingness of the French to sign any agreement leaving French territory in English hands.

Born in BORDEAUX, the second son of ED-WARD, THE BLACK PRINCE, Richard became his father's heir upon the death of his elder brother, Edward of Angoulême, in 1371. He became heir to the English throne on his father's death in June 1376 and king of England at the age of ten in June 1377. Richard's minority government was directed by a council of nobles dominated by the king's eldest living uncle, JOHN OF GAUNT, duke of Lancaster, who was himself not a member of that body. Although the French under CHARLES V had largely erased the territorial gains achieved by Edward III, the council continued the war, imposing, through PARLIAMENT, a series of unpopular poll taxes designed to fund new campaigns. This high war TAXATION caused the most serious English rebellion of the fourteenth century, the PEASANTS' REVOLT OF 1381. Although only fourteen, Richard distinguished himself by courageously meeting the rebels on several occasions. From 1381 to 1386, Richard ruled through a group of favorites that included his tutor, Simon Burley; his chancellor, Michael de la Pole, earl of Suffolk; and his chamberlain, Robert de Vere, earl of Oxford. Richard's lack of enthusiasm for war, the growing influence of his favorites, and the extravagance of his court, caused the formation of a baronial opposition that initially included Lancaster. When

a plot to kill the duke was uncovered in 1385, Lancaster came armed to court to confront Richard, but was soon reconciled to his nephew by the intervention of the king's mother, Joan of Kent.

In 1386, Lancaster left for Spain, leaving behind a political vacuum that was filled by his younger brother, THOMAS OF WOODSTOCK, duke of Gloucester. In the so-called Wonderful Parliament of 1386, Gloucester and his allies—Richard Fitzalan, earl of Arundel, and Thomas Beauchamp, earl of Warwick—forced the king to dismiss his councilors and accept the tutelage of a council of nobles. In 1387, Richard attempted to have the originators of the noble council declared traitors, an act that forced Gloucester and his colleagues, who now included Thomas Mowbray, earl of Nottingham, and Lancaster's son, Henry, earl of Derby, to take arms and appeal (i.e., accuse) the king's supporters of treason. After defeating Oxford at Radcot Bridge on 20 December, the opposition lords, now known as the Lords Appellant, forced Richard to summon the Merciless Parliament, which was so named because it decreed the banishment or death of Richard's closest advisors. Dominated by Gloucester, the Appellant government continued the war. Although Arundel had won a naval victory at CADZAND in March 1387, lack of funds forced the Appellants to open peace talks that eventually resulted in the Truce of LEULINGHEN. In May 1389, one month before the truce was concluded, Richard, now twenty-two, used the imminent return of Lancaster to declare himself of full age and resume control of the government.

His Spanish ambitions satisfied, Lancaster, whom Richard made duke of AQUITAINE in 1390, now supported the king's peace policy. Sent to France in 1392 as the king's peace envoy, the duke failed to secure a permanent settlement, but did achieve successive extensions of the truce. Following the death of his queen, Anne of Bohemia, in 1394, Richard extended his peace effort by negotiating a match for himself with eight-year-old Isabella, the eldest daughter of CHARLES VI (see ISABELLA, QUEEN OF ENGLAND

[1388–1409]). Concluded in 1396, the marriage was accompanied by a 28-year truce that promised to end the war for a generation. The political stability of the years after 1390 ended in 1397 when the king struck down his old opponents. After arresting Gloucester, Arundel, and Warwick, Richard had all three condemned for treason in Parliament. Gloucester died mysteriously while in captivity in CALAIS, while Arundel was executed and Warwick imprisoned for life. Contemporary English chronicles, mostly written after Richard's deposition, ascribed the king's action to a thirst for vengeance, while more sympathetic French chronicles claimed that Gloucester and his companions, angered by the restoration of Brest to Duke JOHN IV of BRITTANY, were hatching a new plot against the king. Whatever the truth, Richard used the cessation of hostilities with France to consolidate his position in England, where he acted in an increasingly high-handed manner. Making frequent use of forced loans and other highly questionable means of raising revenue, Richard persuaded Parliament to rescind the acts of the Merciless Parliament and to compel all future peers to swear to uphold the acts of the current session.

In September 1398, a quarrel erupted between the two junior appellants, Nottingham (now duke of Norfolk) and Derby (now duke of Hereford). Norfolk, fearing that Richard would move against them, told Hereford so, but then denied it when Hereford told the king. Richard settled the matter by banishing both men. Upon Lancaster's death in February 1399, Richard confiscated the Lancastrian estates and made Hereford's banishment permanent. When Hereford landed in July, while the king was on campaign in Ireland, the nobility rallied around the duke. Captured in August, the childless king was brought to the Tower of London, where, on 29 September, he resigned the Crown, probably under compulsion, to his cousin. Hereford now took the throne as HENRY IV, first king of the House of LANCASTER. Richard was imprisoned in Ponte-

fract Castle, where he died around 14 February 1400. Precipitated by a plot hatched by Richard's supporters, the ex-king's death, whether the result of violence or starvation, was likely ordered by his supplanter.

Further Reading: Goodman, Anthony. *The Loyal Conspiracy: The Lords Appellant under Richard II*. London: Routledge and Kegan Paul, 1971; Palmer, J. J. N. *England, France, and Christendom, 1377–99*. Chapel Hill: University of North Carolina Press, 1972; Saul, Nigel. *Richard II*. New Haven, CT: Yale University Press, 1997; Tuck, Anthony. *Richard II and the English Nobility*. London: Edward Arnold, 1973.

ROBERT OF ARTOIS (1287–1342)

A kinsman of PHILIP VI, Robert of Artois, through a longstanding dispute over the County of Artois, fell into disfavor and was banished from France. Coming eventually to England, Robert became a confidant of EDWARD III and thereby influenced the course of events during the early years of the HUNDRED YEARS WAR.

Robert was a descendant of Louis VIII of France and the grandson of Robert II, count of Artois. Although his father was dead, Robert did not succeed his grandfather as count upon the latter's death in 1302. The inheritance customs of the county vested the succession in Robert's aunt, Mahaut, who maintained her control of Artois despite two legal challenges and endless intrigues initiated by her nephew. In 1330, after the deaths of his aunt and her daughter, Robert again laid formal claim to the county. As a close friend and advisor of his brother-in-law, Philip VI, Robert had good hopes of success. However, because his chief rival, Mahaut's granddaughter Jeanne, was married to Eudes, duke of BURGUNDY, a powerful magnate who was also the queen's brother, a formidable court faction developed in opposition to Robert. In December 1330, when the documents Robert had submitted in behalf of his claims were discovered to be forgeries, the king withdrew his favor and allowed a criminal prosecution to proceed. Unwilling to stand trial, Robert fled the court. In April 1332, when suspicions

Robert of Artois (far left) addresses an enthroned Edward III in this illustration from Jean Froissart's *Chronicles*. *Erich Lessing/Art Resource, New York.*

campaign in SCOTLAND and received numerous gifts of money and land. Although he seems to have genuinely liked Robert, Edward saw the exile primarily as a useful instrument for harassing Philip. Robert's claims of connections and influence in France and the Low Countries were exaggerated, but his growing influence in England infuriated Philip, who formally demanded Robert's extradition in December 1336. When Edward did not comply, Philip, in April 1337, used Edward's sheltering of his "mortal enemy" (Sumption, 184) as a principal reason for confiscating the Duchy of AQUITAINE, the act usually taken as the start of the Hundred Years War.

In the fourteenth century, Robert was also widely credited with convincing Edward to declare himself king of France. Although Robert's actual involvement in this decision was probably slight, a poem entitled *The Vow of the Heron*, which was written within months of Edward's announcement in 1340, claimed that Robert shamed the king into claiming the French Crown by serving him a roast heron, "the most timid of birds for the most cowardly of kings" (Sumption, 292), who had allowed another to usurp his rightful inheritance. With the start of war, Robert participated in the early English campaigns in the Low Countries, where Edward's efforts to seize Artois on Robert's behalf foundered on the objections of England's allies and a total lack of support from within the county. A poor general, Robert led an Anglo-Flemish army to defeat at the battle of SAINT-OMER in July 1340 and was slain while leading the English fleet in an unsuccessful attack on the Breton town of Vannes in November 1342. Despised in his own country, Robert of Artois was buried in LONDON.

were raised concerning his involvement in Mahaut's death, Robert was formally banished from the realm and deprived of all his possessions. Obsessed with the succession to Artois, Robert plotted rebellion and threatened to destroy the royal family by sorcery, thereby transforming Philip into an implacable enemy who detained Robert's family and sought by all means to secure his capture.

After various wanderings, Robert arrived in disguise in England in 1334. Edward granted Robert's request for asylum, but otherwise gave him no assistance in his quarrel with Philip. However, by 1336, Robert, who was a skilled courtier with a martial flair, was in high favor at the English court. He accompanied the king on

Further Reading: Sumption, Jonathan. *The Hundred Years War.* Vol. 1, *Trial by Battle.* Philadelphia: University of Pennsylvania Press,

1999; Wood, Charles T. *The French Apanages and the Capetian Monarchy, 1224–1328.* Cambridge, MA: Harvard University Press, 1966.

ROBERT OF BAUDRICOURT. *See* JOAN OF ARC

ROOSEBEKE, BATTLE OF. *See* FLANDERS; LOUIS DE MALE, COUNT OF FLANDERS

ROUEN, SIEGE OF (1418–1419)

The successful siege of Rouen, the capital of NORMANDY, cemented HENRY V's conquest of the duchy and brought the English within striking distance of PARIS. Distracted by the ongoing civil war between the BURGUNDIANS and ARMAGNACS, the French failed to relieve the city, thereby strengthening both Henry's determination to win the French Crown and the French willingness to negotiate a settlement.

On the night of 29 July 1418, Henry, having severed the river link between Rouen and Paris, arrived outside the Norman capital. The city was large and strong, being encircled by five miles of walls boasting sixty towers with plentiful ARTILLERY and six stout barbicans (i.e., fortified gateways). Flanked on the southwest by the Seine, the town was elsewhere protected by a wide and unusually deep ditch well laid with wolf-traps. Expecting a siege, the citizens had destroyed all structures outside the walls to deny cover to the enemy and had carried all available food and supplies inside the city, thus forcing Henry to provision his men from England via the Seine. A bank of earth had been piled up inside the walls to strengthen them against artillery bombardment and a garrison of four thousand men commanded by the experienced Guy le Bouteiller and ably assisted by citizens armed with crossbows defended the walls.

But time was on Henry's side. The city was soon cut off from any hope of reinforcement or supply by four fortified camps occupied by an army numbering nearly twice the garrison and soon reinforced by forty-five hundred additional troops, including fifteen hundred Irish kern, led by the king's brother,

HUMPHREY, DUKE OF GLOUCESTER. With Rouen sheltering thousands of refugees who had fled the fighting in Lower Normandy, Henry waited for starvation to win him the city. Despite rumors that a relieving army was near, JOHN THE FEARLESS, duke of BURGUNDY, who had just driven the Armagnacs from Paris, was in no position to help Rouen; he therefore advised the citizens to look to their own defenses.

By October, the defenders were eating horseflesh and by December rats, mice, and dogs. With too many mouths to feed, the garrison drove out the poor and the infirm, leaving almost twelve thousand people to spend winter in the surrounding ditch because Henry refused them passage through the English lines. Thousands died of cold and starvation both inside and outside the city, and on New Year's Eve, Bouteiller asked for talks. After ten days of negotiation, the defenders agreed to surrender the city at noon on 19 January 1419 if help did not arrive by then. In return for agreeing to take no arms against the English for a year, the garrison was allowed to march out without its weapons. The citizens were assured of their homes and property if they paid an indemnity of 300,000 gold crowns and took an oath of allegiance to Henry. When no relief arrived, the city surrendered as agreed and, on 20 January, Henry entered Rouen, where he remained for two months, repairing the city's defenses and organizing the administration of Normandy. Rouen now became the main English base in northern France, from which Henry could threaten Paris and launch new campaigns to the south. *See also* FRENCH CIVIL WAR.

Further Reading: Perroy, Edouard. *The Hundred Years War.* Trans. W. B. Wells. New York: Capricorn Books, 1965; Seward, Desmond. *The Hundred Years War.* New York: Penguin, 1999.

ROUTIERS

Routiers were unemployed soldiers who organized themselves into "free companies," or *routes*, for the purpose of supporting themselves by theft, pillage, and extortion.

Composed of and led by men of many different nationalities, *routier* bands appeared in France during the intervals of peace that punctuated the HUNDRED YEARS WAR, but were a particularly serious problem throughout the period 1357–69, following the Battle of POITIERS and conclusion of the Treaty of BRÉTIGNY, and in the years 1436–44, following collapse of the ANGLO-BURGUNDIAN ALLIANCE at the Congress of ARRAS. In both instances, the establishment of a regular, salaried French army to employ the best of the *routiers* and destroy the rest, along with acceptance of regular peacetime TAXATION to support that army, led to the eventual elimination of the *routier* menace.

The end of formal hostilities after conclusion of a truce or treaty left many veteran soldiers without employment. Unwilling to return to lives of poverty or serfdom, many of these men banded together and used their military training to live off the countryside, robbing, looting, killing, and torturing to obtain supplies and valuables. *Routier* companies could be formidable military organizations, with formal command structures and a regular staff of secretaries and *butiniers*, the officers who collected and distributed shares of booty. Some companies, such as the infamous *bande blanche* (white company) of Arnaud de CERVOLE, a famous *routier* leader known as "the Archpriest," had their own distinctive uniforms. Many of the *routiers* of the 1360s had served under EDWARD, THE BLACK PRINCE, but the companies comprised men of all armies and many countries, including Bretons, Spaniards, Germans, Frenchmen, and Englishmen. However, the majority were Gascons and thus subjects of the PLANTAGENET king-duke of AQUITAINE, and many famous *routier* captains were Englishmen, such as Sir John HAWKWOOD, Sir Hugh CALVELEY, Sir Robert KNOLLES, and Sir John Cresswell, facts that help explain why the French referred to all *routiers*, of whatever nationality, as *Anglais*, "English."

In the 1360s, the GREAT COMPANY, a constantly reforming army of *routier* bands, devastated southern France and Provence, seizing towns and castles to serve as bases from which to systematically pillage a particular area until it had been bled white. Another *routier* army, the so-called *Tard-Venus* (Latecomers), pillaged the region around Lyons, while a force led by the infamous Gascon captain, Seguin de BADEFOL, invaded BURGUNDY in eastern France. Employing such English innovations as the CHEVAUCHÉE and the PÂTIS, these *routier* armies extracted RANSOMS from towns and provinces, which, like the pope in Avignon, paid them to go away. In 1362, the Great Company even defeated a French royal army at the Battle of BRIGNAIS.

While local governments bribed *routiers* to go elsewhere, rulers such as CHARLES V and the Black Prince attempted to solve the problem by finding the companies other employment. The French constable, Bertrand du GUESCLIN, himself a former *routier* leader, attempted to gather companies for service against the Turks in Hungary. When this failed, he took a *routier* army to Castile in 1365 to help Henry of Trastámare overthrow Pedro I. In 1367, the Black Prince intervened with his own largely *routier* force to restore Pedro at the Battle of NÁJERA. However, when the CASTILIAN WAR OF SUCCESSION ended with Pedro's death in 1369, large numbers of *routiers* flowed back into Aquitaine and Languedoc. The first successful anti-*routier* effort occurred in Champagne in 1359, when local nobles and royal officers defeated a *routier* force at NOGENT-SUR-SEINE. The taxes levied in the last years of JOHN II's reign and the military reorganization that these funds allowed under Charles V created the professional French army that in the 1370s defeated both the English and the *routiers*.

In the 1410s, the outbreak of the FRENCH CIVIL WAR and HENRY V's renewal of the Hundred Years War initiated a new wave of brigandage. Known now as *écorcheurs* (flayers), *routiers* under such leaders as Rodrigo de Villandrando, a Castilian who had taken service under both PHILIP THE GOOD, duke of Burgundy, and CHARLES VII, and Étienne de VIGNOLLES, a dauphinist captain and companion of JOAN OF ARC, wasted northern and eastern France, particularly after the Franco-Burgundian peace of 1435. Although an attempt to interest the companies in an expedition against the Swiss in 1444 was only partly successful, the military reforms initiated by Charles VII during the Truce of TOURS in the 1440s created a regularly paid professional army that again defeated both the English and the *routiers*. *See also* CHARLES VII, MILITARY REFORMS OF.

Further Reading: Seward, Desmond. *The Hundred Years War*. New York: Penguin, 1999; Sumption, Jonathan. *The Hundred Years War*. Vol. 2, *Trial by Fire*. Philadelphia: University of Pennsylvania Press, 2001; Wright, Nicholas A. R. "'Pillagers' and 'Brigands' in the Hundred Years War." *Journal of Medieval History* 9 (1983): 15–25.

ROUVRAY, BATTLE OF. *See* HERRINGS, BATTLE OF THE

S

SAINTES, BATTLE OF (1351)

Fought on 1 April 1351 near the town of Saintes in the province of Saintonge, the Battle of Saintes resulted from an English attempt to provision the besieged garrison at Saint-Jean-d'Angély. Although an English victory, the battle, which is notable for the French commander's adoption of the English tactic of fighting on foot, failed to resupply the garrison and did not significantly alter the military situation in southwestern France.

Upon his accession in August 1350, JOHN II, ignoring his father's recent agreement to extend the Truce of CALAIS, prepared to launch a campaign against the English garrisons in Saintonge. By February 1351, several thousand men led by Guy de Nesle and his deputy Arnoul d'AUDREHEM arrived before the town of Saint-Jean-d'Angély, which was held by one of the largest English garrisons in France, a force of almost six hundred men. However, the garrison's winter stores were nearly exhausted and the town's walls were old and in disrepair. The French quickly surrounded the town and by late March had cut and fortified the main roads leading south into English GASCONY. On 31 March, the French commanders learned of the approach of a relieving force of several hundred men led by Sir John Cheverston, the seneschal of Gascony and Arnaud-Amanieu, son of the lord of ALBRET. Although too weak to break the siege, Cheverston and Albret planned to punch through the French lines and bring their large supply train to the relief of the garrison.

Leaving troops to maintain the siege, Guy de Nesle marched through the night to intercept the English, which he did next morning about three miles outside Saintes. The English dismounted and formed their usual line of battle, the horses being led to the rear; Guy de Nesle, abandoning the French proclivity for cavalry charges, which had proven so unsuccessful at CRÉCY and elsewhere, ordered most of his men to dismount as well. Except for small bodies of cavalry on each wing, the French then deployed on foot along a stretch of high ground. Although the details are uncertain, the ensuing battle was a short, sharp encounter that resulted in complete victory for the English. At some point, either just before or after the French attacked the English line, a force of several hundred men derived from the nearby English garrisons of Taillebourg and Tonnay-Charente assailed the French from the rear, thereby ensuring their defeat.

Over six hundred French knights were killed or captured, the latter including both commanders. Although a glorious triumph rich in RANSOMS, Saintes left Cheverston unable to break through to Saint-Jean-d'Angély, which was partially resupplied a few days later by a small force led by the commander of the Taillebourg garrison. Cheverston withdrew to BORDEAUX and John II quickly ransomed Guy de Nesle and reinforced the army around Saint-Jean-d'Angély, which fell to the French on 31 August.

Further Reading: Burne, Alfred H. *The Crécy War.* Ware, England: Wordsworth Editions Ltd., 1999; Sumption, Jonathan. *The Hundred Years War.*

Vol. 2, *Trial by Fire*. Philadelphia: University of Pennsylvania Press, 2001.

SAINT-MAUR, TREATY OF. *See* FRENCH CIVIL WAR

SAINT-POL DE LÉON, BATTLE OF. *See* DAGWORTH, SIR THOMAS

SAINT-OMER, BATTLE OF (1340)

Fought on 26 July 1340 outside the town of Saint-Omer in western Artois, the Battle of Saint-Omer resulted in the destruction of an Anglo-Flemish army and thereby contributed to the collapse of EDWARD III's ANGLO-FLEMISH ALLIANCE.

Following his victory at the Battle of SLUYS, Edward met James van ARTEVELDE and other Flemish leaders to devise a strategy for the summer's campaign in northern France. Fearful that a large French army then massing in Artois would overrun FLANDERS while their forces invaded France, the allied leaders agreed to field two armies. The first, commanded by the king himself, was to besiege the French town of TOURNAI. Because the second was to seize the town of Saint-Omer in Artois, Edward gave command of it to ROBERT OF ARTOIS, who claimed a large following within the county. With a force of a thousand English ARCHERS under Sir Thomas Oughtred and almost fifteen thousand infantry drawn from the towns of Flanders, Robert had a sizable, if inexperienced and ill-disciplined, army.

Nervous about the huge army PHILIP VI was gathering in Arras, Robert's Flemings worried about their homes and families; they saw little benefit to themselves in invading Artois and little evidence of support for Robert in the county. As a result, the allied army conducted a slow, disorganized advance that allowed John, count of Armagnac, to reinforce the Saint-Omer garrison. Commanded by Eudes, duke of BURGUNDY, who currently controlled Artois, the garrison now numbered several thousand men. On 26 July, Robert, faced with the possibility of being caught between the garrison and the approaching French army,

deployed his troops behind defensive works and sought to draw the garrison into battle. Burgundy, as ordered by Philip, refused combat, but, after hours of inactivity, a contingent of garrison troops charged, without orders, out the southeastern gate. Repulsed by the Flemings in their front, they retreated, only to charge again when their adversaries foolishly abandoned their defenses and pursued them to the town walls. Seeing this battle develop, Burgundy and Armagnac led their mounted retinues, almost a thousand men, into the fight.

Armagnac rounded the enemy's left flank and charged into the Flemish ranks. Thrown back with heavy losses, the Flemings fled to the rear, creating panic among the troops guarding the Anglo-Flemish encampment. By driving them into the River Aa, the French slew almost eight thousand Flemings. Meanwhile, Burgundy rode against his foe's right flank, where Robert commanded the English archers and the men of Bruges. Before the duke could attack, Robert's men charged and overwhelmed their enemy. However, Robert never made effective use of his archers, while the archers on the walls allowed Burgundy and most of his men to safely reenter the town. The battle now presented the odd spectacle of Armagnac's victorious men marching back to town along one side of the Arras road while Robert's victorious contingents marched back to their encampment along the other side. Too exhausted to resume the fighting, each force reached its destination with little hindrance from the other. Robert's jubilation dissolved when he found his camp deserted and the bodies of his men scattered across a wide area. The remaining Flemish troops immediately fled the field, forcing Robert and the English to follow; they arrived eventually at Edward's lines around Tournai.

The Battle of Saint-Omer disrupted the Anglo-Flemish alliance by exposing both Flanders and the army at Tournai to French attack. Within days, the leaders of the Flemish towns, including van Artevelde's opponents in Ghent, asked Philip for peace terms. Abandoned by his allies and deeply in debt, Edward reluctantly lifted the siege of Tournai and negotiated the Truce of Es-PLECHIN in September.

Further Reading: Lucas, Henry Stephen. *The Low Countries and the Hundred Years' War, 1326–1347.* Ann Arbor: University of Michigan Press, 1929; Sumption, Jonathan. *The Hundred Years War.* Vol. 1, *Trial by Battle.* Philadelphia: University of Pennsylvania Press, 1991.

SAINT-SARDOS, WAR OF (1323–1325)

Lasting from October 1323 to September 1325, the War of Saint-Sardos was the last Anglo-French conflict before the HUNDRED YEARS WAR. Ignited by a local dispute in AQUITAINE, the War of Saint-Sardos, like the ANGLO-FRENCH WAR OF 1294–1303, arose from tensions inherent in the feudal relationship created by the Treaty of PARIS between the king of France and the English king-duke of Aquitaine. The continued holding of French territory by the English king was as intolerable to the French Crown as continued French interference in the government of Aquitaine was to the English Crown. In its course and causes, the War of Saint-Sardos foreshadowed the Hundred Years War, and in its outcome and aftermath, it set the stage for the subsequent conflict.

Saint-Sardos was a village in the Agenais, a province belonging to PLANTAGENET Aquitaine. Because the local Benedictine priory was a daughter-house of the Abbey of Sarlat, which was outside the duke's authority, the abbot petitioned the PARLEMENT in PARIS to declare Saint-Sardos exempt from ducal jurisdiction. The question had been discussed at the PROCESS of Périgueux in 1311, but no action was taken until December 1322, when the Parlement declared for the abbot. This decision allowed the French Crown to authorize construction of a new royal *BASTIDE* in Saint-Sardos, an action that local landowners believed would draw settlers from their estates and local townsmen feared would harm their trade. On the night of 15 October 1323, just after a French sergeant arrived in Saint-Sardos to take possession of the site for the Crown, a local landowner, Raymond-Bernard, lord of the castle of Montpezat, burned the village and hanged the sergeant.

Although EDWARD II's protestation that he knew nothing about the attack was accepted, CHARLES IV summoned Ralph Basset, the English seneschal of GASCONY; Raymond-Bernard; and other ducal officials to appear before him. When Edward recalled Basset and none of the others appeared, Charles ordered that Montpezat be seized, an intrusion upon ducal jurisdiction that Edward met by ordering Raymond-Bernard to defend the castle. Unprepared for war and distracted by domestic concerns, Edward dispatched his brother, Edmund, earl of Kent, to negotiate with Charles. At the French court, anti-English feeling was running high, and Charles gave every indication of intending to expel the Plantagenets from Gascony. He demanded that Kent immediately agree to surrender both Montpezat and the contumacious officials, which the earl did on 10 June 1324. Kent also promised that Edward would come to France and pay homage for Aquitaine on 1 July. On about 24 June, when it became clear that Edward would not come, Charles authorized confiscation of the duchy.

In August, the king's uncle, Charles of VALOIS, invaded Aquitaine. When Kent surrendered La Reole on 22 September, after concluding a six-month truce, only BORDEAUX, Bayonne, and a few other strongholds held out for Edward. Although the French continued to make preparations for the final conquest of the duchy, Charles signaled his willingness to negotiate by suggesting that his sister Isabella, Edward's wife (*see* ISABELLA, QUEEN OF ENGLAND [c. 1292–1358]), act as mediator. Arriving in France in March 1325, Isabella won an extension of the truce, but could obtain no softening of the French terms, which demanded that Edward surrender the territories conquered by Valois until all outstanding disputes were settled, and that he temporarily surrender the rest of the duchy until such time as he had performed homage for it. Forced to accept the first demand, Edward modified the second by granting

Aquitaine to his son, Prince Edward, who officially ended the war by personally paying homage to Charles on 24 September.

Although the agreement ended the war, it humiliated Edward and discredited his already unpopular government, which Isabella, in possession of the prince and backed by English dissidents at the French court, overthrew in 1326. The deposition of Edward II in 1327 and the death of Charles IV without male heirs in 1328 then transformed the situation by placing Aquitaine in the possession of EDWARD III, an English king with a legitimate claim to the French throne.

Further Reading: Chaplais, Pierre. *The War of Saint-Sardos (1323–1325): Gascon Correspondence and Diplomatic Documents.* London: Royal Historical Society, 1954; Sumption, Jonathan. *The Hundred Years War.* Vol. 1, *Trial by Battle.* Philadelphia: University of Pennsylvania Press, 1991; Vale, Malcolm. *The Origins of the Hundred Years War.* Oxford: Clarendon Press, 2000.

SALIC LAW OF SUCCESSION

The Salic Law of Succession is a purported provision of the *Lex Salica*, a body of laws promulgated for the Salian Franks by the Frankish kings of the sixth and seventh centuries. The succession law supposedly bars women from inheriting property and thus from succeeding to the throne or transmitting a claim to the throne to their male descendants. The Salic Law of Succession is often described as the justification given for rejecting EDWARD III's claim to the French throne in 1328; however, no such law was mentioned at the time. In fact, the Salic Law of Succession, or rather the principle it represents, was not fully developed until the mid-fifteenth century when it became a means of defending the VALOIS throne against both English and Burgundian claims.

Beginning in 1316, the French royal house of CAPET, after more than three hundred years of unbroken father-to-son succession, experienced three succession crises within a twelve-year period. The death of LOUIS X, and five months later of his infant son John I, raised the possibility of a woman succeeding

to the throne. Louis left a seven-year-old daughter, Jeanne, as well as two adult brothers, the elder of whom, Philip, count of Poitiers, had acted as regent in the months following Louis's death. Because the problem had never arisen before, there existed no outright ban on female succession. What's more, women had long inherited noble fiefs in France and had succeeded to thrones in other kingdoms, such as Navarre, which was ruled by a cadet branch of the Capetian dynasty. The question was settled not by reference to Salic law, but by the political support Philip commanded, by Jeanne's youth, and by widespread acceptance of the notion that women were unfit to rule a kingdom. The regent was crowned as PHILIP V in January 1317.

To further justify his rule, Philip convened an assembly of notables that declared women unable to succeed to the throne of France. With this precedent established, there was no controversy when Philip died in 1322 and was succeeded by his brother CHARLES IV rather than by one of his five daughters. However, when Charles died without sons in 1328, the question was not the position of his daughters, but of his nephew, Edward III of England, who was the son of Charles's sister, Isabella (*see* ISABELLA, QUEEN OF ENGLAND [c. 1292–1358]). Edward was nearer in blood to the last Capetian kings than was his main rival, Philip, count of Valois, who was Charles's cousin. However, Philip's descent from the Capetian kings came through an unbroken male line, while Edward's depended on his mother. The question then was this: If a woman could not inherit the throne, could she transmit a claim to it to her male heirs? Again, the issue was settled by practical considerations rather than by appeal to Salic law. Philip was thirty-five, descended in the male line, and thoroughly French; he had also acted as regent while the kingdom waited to see if Charles's pregnant queen had a son (a daughter was born in April). To the French nobility, Edward, despite his French blood and peerage, was a foreign ruler. He was also only fifteen and his accession would give real power in France to his mother, whose role in the deposition of her husband, EDWARD II, did not recommend her. Little consideration was therefore given to Edward's claim and Valois was crowned as PHILIP VI.

The earliest reference to the Salic Law as bearing on the royal succession dates to 1358, when the chronicler Richard Lescot wrote of it to the council of JOHN II, who was then a prisoner in England. However, significant efforts to elucidate the Salic Law of Succession did not occur until the fifteenth century, when various treatises used Salic Law to attack HENRY V's claim to the French throne; to denounce the 1420 Treaty of TROYES, which made Henry heir to the throne; and to refute Burgundian claims to the French regency. In the 1450s, CHARLES VII, now secure on his throne, ordered a search of royal archives for documents upon which to base a *Grand traité* that formally declared invalid all claims to the French Crown that did not, like the Valois claim, descend through the unbroken male line. The Salic Law of Succession was thus manufactured in the fifteenth century and retroactively applied to the early fourteenth-century succession crises that helped precipitate the HUNDRED YEARS WAR.

Further Reading: Potter, J. "The Development and Significance of the Salic Law of the French." *English Historical Review* 52 (1937): 235–53; Taylor, C. "Edward III and the Plantagenet Claim to the French Throne." In *The Age of Edward III*, ed. J. S. Bothwell. Woodbridge, England: York Medieval Press, 2002.

SALISBURY, EARL OF. *See* MONTAGU, THOMAS, EARL OF SALISBURY; MONTAGU, WILLIAM, EARL OF SALISBURY

SCALES, THOMAS, LORD SCALES
(c. 1399–1460)

Co-commander of the English army at the siege of ORLÉANS in 1429, Thomas Scales, Lord Scales, served the House of LANCASTER in France for almost thirty years.

The younger son of Robert Scales, Lord Scales, Thomas inherited the family title in July 1419 on the death without children of his elder brother Robert. Scales went to France in about 1420. Following the English victory at VERNEUIL in August 1424, JOHN, DUKE OF BEDFORD, regent of France, placed Scales and Sir John FASTOLF in charge of Lancastrian operations in Maine. Admitted to the Order of the GARTER in 1425, Scales joined the besieging army at Orléans in December 1428, when he assumed joint command of the operation with William de la POLE, earl of Suffolk, and John TALBOT. After the city was relieved by JOAN OF ARC in May 1429, Scales withdrew with Talbot to Meung and then, after joining a relief force under Fastolf, was captured by the French at PATAY on 18 June. Freed by the spring of 1430, Scales attended HENRY VI when the king came to France in 1431 for his coronation. Named captain-general of western NORMANDY and steward of the entire duchy in 1435, Scales was also appointed to the captaincies of various important Norman strongholds, such as Domfront and Cherbourg. In 1440, the king rewarded Scales for his services with an annuity of £100.

Although the Truce of TOURS ended hostilities for five years beginning in 1444, Scales remained in France for most of the decade, during which he made significant loans to the impecunious royal government. Despite a close association with RICHARD, DUKE OF YORK, during the duke's French lieutenancy—Scales stood godfather to York's eldest son (the future Edward IV) in 1442—Scales's domestic political affiliations were with York's opponent, Suffolk, who was chief minister to Henry VI in the later 1440s. When Scales returned from France in 1449, he became a prominent supporter of the Suffolk regime. In 1450, Scales was charged with suppressing JACK CADE'S REBELLION; given command at the Tower of London, he helped loyal Londoners defend London Bridge against rebel assaults on the night of 5–6 July.

Acting in the Suffolk interest, Scales became an important figure in East Anglian politics in the 1450s. By the outbreak of the Wars of the Roses in 1459, Scales was closely associated with Queen MARGARET OF ANJOU and the anti-Yorkist court party. In June 1460, he attempted to hold LONDON against the Yorkists, but was forced to withdraw to the Tower when the city authorities opened the gates to York's ally, Richard Neville, earl of Warwick. With Robert Hungerford, Lord Hungerford, Scales stood siege in the Tower until the Yorkists' capture of the king at Northampton on 10 July made his position untenable. On 19 July, he slipped out of the Tower, but was captured and killed by London boatman in retaliation for his destructive bombardment of the city during the Tower siege. His body lay naked on the Southwark shore until his godson, now earl of March, gave it honorable burial.

Further Reading: Griffiths, Ralph A. *The Reign of King Henry VI*. Berkeley: University of California Press, 1981; Pollard, A. J. *John Talbot and the War in France, 1427–1453*. London: Royal Historical Society, 1983; Watts, John. *Henry VI and the Politics of Kingship*. Cambridge: Cambridge University Press, 1996.

SCOTLAND

The status of the kingdom of Scotland constituted a key issue throughout the HUNDRED YEARS WAR. While seeking to overturn VALOIS overlordship in AQUITAINE, the PLANTAGENET kings of England sought also to secure their own overlordship in Scotland. The possibility that PHILIP VI would help the Scots resist English ambitions toward their kingdom was an important immediate cause of the war. The effective use that both France and Scotland made of one another in threatening England allowed the FRANCO-SCOTTISH ALLIANCE of the 1290s to persist throughout the war, and, on occasion, turned Scotland into a major theater of Anglo-French conflict.

Anglo-Scottish relations were largely peaceful until the 1290s, when a Scottish succession dispute allowed EDWARD I to pursue his ambition of ruling all Britain. Having recently brought Wales under his authority, he sought to do the same in Scotland. At the request of the Scots, Edward presided over the court that decided the succession question in favor of John Balliol. However, the new king's authority was immediately undermined by Edward, who demanded that Balliol and his nobles perform military service in Aquitaine (*see* ANGLO-FRENCH WAR OF 1294–1303), and by the Bruces, Balliol's chief rivals, who continued to contest the court's decision. Balliol soon found himself at war with both Edward and the Bruces. In October 1295, a council of nobles acting in Balliol's stead concluded an alliance with France, a compact that, through repeated renewals, lasted into the sixteenth century and became known in Scotland as the "Auld Alliance." Unable to defeat his enemies, Balliol surrendered the kingdom to Edward in 1296, when many Scottish nobles renounced the French alliance and swore homage to the English king. However, a Scottish independence movement quickly emerged under William Wallace and others, who paved the way for Robert Bruce to be crowned king as Robert I in March 1306. The death of Edward I in 1307 and the military incompetence of EDWARD II allowed Robert to gradually expel the English from most of Scotland, especially following a decisive victory at Bannockburn in 1314. Although the pope placed Scotland under interdict at Edward's request, the Scots in 1320 issued the Declaration of Arbroath, declaring their intention to continue resisting English domination. In 1326, Robert renewed the French alliance.

In 1328, the government of Queen Isabella and her lover, Roger Mortimer, earl of March, was forced to accept Scottish independence in the unpopular Treaty of Northampton (*see* Isabella, Queen of England [c. 1292–1358]). However, the death of Robert I in 1329 and EDWARD III's overthrow of his mother's regime in the following year revived the Anglo-Scottish wars. With his victory at HALIDON HILL in 1333, Edward forced DAVID II, Robert's nine-year-old successor, to flee to France. The arrival of his Scottish ally persuaded Philip VI to demand that any Anglo-French settlement in Aquitaine also include the Scots. This requirement scuttled a proposed agreement and outraged Edward, who considered Scotland a purely English matter. When the Anglo-French conflict erupted in 1337, Edward declared French intervention in Scotland a major justification for his decision to go to war. Aided by the English preoccupation with France, the Scots, who proved themselves well able to maintain their independence without either a resident king or French troops, gradually drove out the English, allowing David to return in 1341. In 1346, David, upon hearing news of CRÉCY, invaded England in support of his ally. Defeated and captured at NEVILLE'S CROSS in October, David remained a prisoner until 1357, when he was released upon agreeing to a RANSOM of 100,000 marks. Having also agreed to cease fighting the English until the huge sum was paid in full, David in effect accepted an indefinite truce that limited active Scottish participation in the Anglo-French war for the rest of the century.

Upon his accession in 1371, Robert II, first king of the House of Stewart, renewed the French alliance, as did his son, Robert III, shortly after his accession in 1390. Anglo-Scottish hostilities continued in the form of constant cross-border raids and contrary allegiances in the matter of the great papal schism, with Scotland recognizing Clement VII and England Urban VI (see PAPACY AND THE HUNDRED YEARS WAR). In 1406, internal disorder forced Robert III to send his young son and heir, James, to France, although the boy was captured by the English while crossing the Channel. Upon Robert's death shortly thereafter, his brother, Robert, duke of Albany, assumed the regency on behalf of his imprisoned nephew. After HENRY V invaded France in 1415, the Albany regime allowed more frequent border raiding to increase pressure on England in Henry's absence. In 1419, the Scots responded to a plea from the dauphin for military assistance, and a large army was dispatched under John STEWART, earl of Buchan, who won a major victory at BAUGÉ in 1421. Rewarded with appointment as constable of France, Buchan persuaded other Scots to join French service, including Archibald DOUGLAS, earl of Douglas, who landed with an army of sixty-five hundred in 1424. Although Buchan, Douglas, and most of their men were slain at VERNEUIL in August 1424, many individual Scottish knights continued to serve CHARLES VII. Released in 1424 for a payment of 60,000 marks, James I renewed the French alliance in 1428 and agreed to dispatch a new army to the Continent in return for the county of Saintonge and the marriage of his daughter to Charles VII's son. James's murder in 1437 and internal disorder during the minority of his son, James II, prevented the Scots from playing a major role in the final campaigns of the Hundred Years War, although the Scots renewed the French alliance in 1448.

Further Reading: Curry, Anne. *The Hundred Years War.* 2nd ed. Houndmills, England: Palgrave Macmillan, 2003; Laidlaw, James, ed. *The Auld Alliance: France and Scotland Over 700 Years.* Edinburgh: University of Edinburgh, 1999; Nicholson, Ranald. *Scotland: The Later Middle Ages.* New York: Barnes and Noble, 1974; Wood, Stephen. *The Auld Alliance, Scotland and France: The Military Connection.* Edinburgh: Mainstream, 1989.

SEINE, BATTLE OF THE (1416)

Fought on 15 August 1416 in the mouth of the Seine Estuary near HARFLEUR, the Battle of the Seine was one of the largest naval encounters of the war. The English victory broke the French blockade of Harfleur and helped HENRY V achieve mastery of the seas, a necessary prelude to the conquest of NORMANDY.

Although Henry sought to make Harfleur as secure a base as CALAIS, the cross-Channel distance to the former was four times that of the latter and maintaining local control of the seas proved beyond the abilities of

English naval power. Despite his victories in the battles of VALMONT in March, Thomas BEAUFORT, earl of Dorset and commander of the Harfleur garrison, was in a desperate position by late spring. Blockaded by land and sea, Dorset wrote pleading letters to England describing the privations of his men. Deeply engaged in the discussions that led to conclusion of the Treaty of CANTERBURY with Sigismund, the Holy Roman emperor, Henry deputed the relief of Harfleur to his brother, JOHN, DUKE OF BEDFORD.

Bedford spent the early summer collecting ships and seamen at Southampton and Winchelsea and by early August had a fleet of perhaps a hundred vessels. After overcoming logistical delays and foul winds that allowed the enemy to harry the English coast, Bedford set sail on 14 August with a fair wind that put him in the Seine Estuary by nightfall. Dawn revealed a French fleet of perhaps 150 ships commanded by Guillaume de Montenay anchored in midstream before Harfleur. Besides numbers, the French had the advantage of possessing eight Genoese carracks, which were larger, higher, and more powerful than anything in the English fleet. The Genoese were the best sailors in Europe, and from the higher decks of their warships could rain missiles of all kinds down upon the English. However, with the French in an irregular massed formation, Bedford bore down on them at full sail, and the sandbars and close quarters of the estuary allowed the maneuverability of the smaller English vessels to outweigh the mass and height of the Genoese ships. With the element of luck also playing a part, the English prevailed after a long fight—the sources say seven hours—capturing three Genoese carracks and driving another aground. CASUALTIES were heavy in both fleets, with the English losing some twenty ships and their crews.

With the enemy fleet dispersed, half the remaining English ships made for Harfleur and the relief of the starving garrison, while the rest conveyed Bedford, who was wounded during the fight, back to England. Upon hearing of the victory, Henry, having that day concluded his treaty with Sigismund, rode with his new ally to Canterbury Cathedral to hear *Te Deum* sung. *See also* NAVAL WARFARE.

Further Reading: Allmand, Christopher. *Henry V.* New Haven, CT: Yale University Press, 1997; Burne, Alfred H. *The Agincourt War.* Ware, England: Wordsworth Editions Ltd., 1999.

SHAKESPEARE AND THE HUNDRED YEARS WAR

The Elizabethan playwright William Shakespeare used the HUNDRED YEARS WAR as the backdrop for several of his English history plays, particularly *Henry V* and *1 Henry VI*. Although these plays depict historical scenes and figures, Shakespeare compresses chronologies, distorts personalities, and fictionalizes events for dramatic effect, making the plays inaccurate history but realistic illustrations of sixteenth-century perceptions of the Anglo-French conflict.

Shakespeare deals only with the final phase of the war, from HENRY V's invasion of France in 1415 to the loss of Henry's gains during the reign of his son, HENRY VI, in the 1430s and 1440s. *Henry V* is the last play of the "major" tetralogy (i.e., four-play series), which also includes *Richard II* and *1* and *2 Henry IV*. With the "minor" tetralogy, comprising *1, 2,* and *3 Henry VI* and *Richard III*, these plays constitute Shakespeare's dramatic rendering of fifteenth-century English dynastic history from the deposition of RICHARD II in 1399 to the destruction of Richard III in 1485. The plays examine the nature of power and the devastating consequences of ambition for power, using the suffering of both the Hundred Years War and the Wars of the Roses as the manifestation of those consequences.

Written in 1599, *Henry V* contains in its title character one of the most dominating figures in the Shakespearean canon. The play has traditionally been read as a patriotic tribute to England's greatest hero-king, who crushed the ancient national enemy and brought England to unprecedented heights of international power and respect. As such, the play was well-suited to the tense period of Anglo-Spanish hostilities during the late Elizabethan years, and has since enjoyed renewed popularity during every national crisis. However, in the twentieth century, *Henry V* was more often read from an anti-heroic perspective that saw the king as a cold, ruthlessly ambitious hypocrite who used religion to justify a terrible war waged largely for his own benefit. However his personality is construed, and both views are valid, Henry is the dominating subject of the play. Evidence indicates that the powerful comic figure of Sir John Falstaff, a central character in *1* and *2 Henry IV*, was excised from *Henry V* so as to prevent any detraction from the play's central concern, the nature of the king's character and motivations.

Beginning with a disparagement of SALIC LAW, by which the French seek to deny Henry's just claim to their throne, the play presents Henry as a devout and thoughtful monarch who contrasts sharply with the French, who are depicted as vain, foolish, and deceitful. At the siege of HARFLEUR, in act 1, scene 3, Henry delivers one of the most inspirational speeches in English literature, crying "Once more into the breach, dear friends," to identify himself with his men as he exhorts them to new effort, and ending with the battle cry "God for Harry! England and St. George!" to assert God's support for his cause. In act 3, scene 4, as the English prepare for the Battle of AGINCOURT, Henry utters the most famous and moving of Shakespeare's patriotic speeches, the "Saint Crispin's Day Speech," in which the king tells his outnumbered men that "We few, we happy few, we band of brothers" will be remembered forever for the deeds done on Crispin's day. Counteracting this heroic image are various scenes depicting the king as cold, brutal, and hypocritical. In act 1, scene 2, Falstaff's friends lament his offstage death, which they attribute to Henry's harsh rejection of his former friend in *2 Henry IV*— "The king hath killed his heart." The king also makes horrifying, unchristian threats to the French ambassadors, promising death to "many a thousand . . . yet ungotten and un-

born" (1.2), and to the defenders of Harfleur, whose resistance will be punished with "naked infants spitted upon pikes" (3.3). On several occasions, Henry presents himself as the instrument of God's will, but his words leave little doubt that divine will coincides with the king's desire to conquer France for the House of LANCASTER. In the final scenes depicting Henry's courtship of CATHERINE OF VALOIS, the king's plain-speaking can be read as the bluff charm of a soldier wooing his love or as the false humility of a victorious king claiming his prize.

Written in early 1590, *1 Henry VI* runs from the 1422 funeral of Henry V to the 1445 marriage of Henry VI and MARGARET OF ANJOU, who is depicted as a scheming Frenchwoman, although Shakespeare, for dramatic effect, rearranges the order of events and compresses decades into a quick succession of scenes. For instance, the death of John TALBOT, which actually occurred in 1453 at the Battle of CASTILLON, is quickly followed in the play by the execution of Joan la Pucelle (JOAN OF ARC, known as *la pucelle*, "the maiden"), which actually occurred in 1431, and then by Henry VI's wedding. French victories are seen as the consequence of rivalries among the English nobility, a foreshadowing of the Wars of the Roses, which is the backdrop of the remaining plays of the minor tetralogy. The entire play projects a vicious anti-French bias, particularly toward Joan, who is depicted as a witch and whore and whose successes are ascribed to trickery and deceit. So virulent is the play's Francophobia that eighteenth- and nineteenth-century commentators denied Shakespeare's authorship, believing the great playwright incapable of such feelings. However, the play's treatment of Joan and her countrymen is an accurate depiction of both fifteenth- and sixteenth-century English views of the traditional French enemy, and probably reflects both the sources Shakespeare used and his ready acceptance of their historical soundness.

Further Reading: Boyce, Charles. *Shakespeare A to Z.* New York: Bantam Doubleday Dell, 1990; Norwich, John Julius. *Shakespeare's Kings.* New

This depiction of the French siege of the castle of Jean de Derval shows Bertrand du Guesclin on a white horse to the right and Louis, duke of Anjou, Charles V's lieutenant in Languedoc, standing before his tent to the left. *Erich Lessing/ Art Resource, New York.*

York: Scribner, 1999; Saccio, Peter. *Shakespeare's English Kings*. 2nd ed. Oxford: Oxford University Press, 2000.

SHEPHERD, BATTLE OF THE. *See* XAIN-TRAILLES, POTON DE

SHREWSBURY, EARL OF. *See* TALBOT, JOHN, EARL OF SHREWSBURY

SIEGE WARFARE

A siege is a military blockade or investment of a fortified castle or town undertaken to compel its surrender. Some of the most important engagements of the HUNDRED YEARS

WAR, such as those at CALAIS in 1346–47, ROUEN in 1418–19, ORLÉANS in 1429, and PONTOISE in 1441, were sieges, as were the main encounters of such major expeditions as the RHEIMS CAMPAIGN of 1359–60, the English NORMAN CAMPAIGN OF 1417–1419, and the French NORMAN CAMPAIGN OF 1449–1450. Sieges occurred more frequently than major battles, especially in GASCONY between 1340 and 1380 and in BRITTANY during the BRETON CIVIL WAR. Sieges often had more momentous results than pitched battles; for instance, EDWARD III derived more lasting gains from the successful siege of Calais than from the Battle of CRÉCY, while HENRY V won NORMANDY through successful siege warfare rather than at the Battle of AGINCOURT.

Since the Welsh and the Irish had few large castles, and Robert I of SCOTLAND destroyed castles taken from the enemy, thus reducing the importance of sieges in the Anglo-Scottish wars, the English, at the start of the war in the 1330s, had no particular advantage over the French in siege warfare. This explains in part the early English reliance on CHEVAUCHÉES, since such campaigns bypassed castles and towns to focus on destruction of the countryside. The widespread devastation caused by Edward III's THIÉRACHE CAMPAIGN in 1339 or EDWARD, THE BLACK PRINCE's CHEVAUCHÉE OF 1355 would have been impossible for an army encumbered with heavy siege equipment. An army meant for siege operations had different requirements from one intended to raid or fight battles. Cavalry, the elite wing of any army, was of little use in sieges, which is one reason that the focus of military preparation was usually on battles, not siege warfare. Weight of numbers also had less importance, since a relatively small but well-supplied garrison behind strong walls might hold off a much larger force indefinitely. As to ARCHERS, fortifications negated the great advantage of the longbow—its rate of fire. For attacking or defending a castle, the crossbow, with its accuracy and power, was the superior weapon. Sieges also required much specialized expertise—such as mining walls, solving problems of sanitation, establishing and maintaining food supplies, building and employing siege weapons, or siting and firing ARTILLERY.

Although kings employed military engineers to conduct siege operations, such as Brother Robert of Ulm, who built siege engines in Scotland for EDWARD I, the status of such men, who were technical experts, not military professionals, was far lower than that of knights. The engineers built and employed the equipment required to breech town or castle walls. The largest were the great siege towers known as belfries, which had been used since Roman times. Some were stationary structures that allowed besiegers to overlook walls, while others could be wheeled up to walls to allow besiegers to launch an assault. Many kinds of siege engines were used to fling stones or incendiary material into besieged castles. Known under various names, such as mangonels and *petraria*, these devices were of various types, such as leather slings or wooden torsion machines. In the thirteenth century, employment of massive counterweights led to development of the trebuchet, which could launch far larger projectiles with greater accuracy than could manually operated machines. Springalds were essentially large crossbows on wheels that fired huge quarrels. Battering rams broke down doors and gates and "cats" or "sows" were movable structures that shielded attackers or men undermining walls. Besides these large devices, a besieging army also required scaling ladders, ropes, picks, shields, and tools of various kinds.

The development of artillery gradually transferred the advantage in sieges from defenders to attackers. After 1417, campaigns involved more sieges than pitched battles, and the increasingly effective employment of more and larger guns, such as

those directed from the 1430s by CHARLES VII's master gunner, Jean BUREAU, led to the successful conclusion of most siege operations. A full-scale siege was a complex operation, involving the encirclement and blockade of a town or fortress. The aim was to starve the garrison into surrendering, although efforts were usually made to achieve a quicker conclusion by using siege engines to batter down walls or set a castle alight, or by tunneling under walls. In 1370 at LIMOGES, the Black Prince's miners shored up their tunnel with wooden braces that were then set on fire, causing the walls above to collapse and allowing the attackers to overrun the town. Attempts were also made to take castles by stealth. During the Thiérache Campaign, Thomas BEAUCHAMP, earl of Warwick, bribed the commander of the French garrison at Baupaume to surrender his fortress, but, before it could be implemented, the plan was discovered and Warwick arrived to find the commander's mutilated body hanging from the walls. In 1349, the French promised an enormous bribe to an Italian mercenary in Calais, who agreed to open a gate to a French party on New Year's Eve; however, Edward III learned of the plot and went himself with a party that included Sir Walter MAUNY and the Black Prince to surprise the French and foil their plan.

Because sieges could be extended affairs, they developed a set of recognized conventions for their proper conduct. The siege formally began upon the firing of the first shot from a siege engine or gun. A siege conducted by the king himself was more serious than one directed by a subordinate, a distinction recognized by INDENTURE pay rates. Indentures could also lay out the terms by which a commander could negotiate a surrender of his master's fortress. Rules as to pillage of a captured town depended on whether the surrender was by negotiated agreement or assault. Often a garrison agreed to surrender if not relieved by a certain date, as occurred at Rouen in 1419 when JOHN THE FEARLESS, duke of BURGUNDY, failed to come to the town's assistance. The fate of the garrison of a captured fortress also depended on the terms arranged. The defenders of some castles marched away under safe-conducts arranged with their besiegers, but the leading citizens of Calais appeared before Edward III with halters about their necks, their lives and goods forfeit because of their protracted resistance, while the defenders of MEAUX were executed or imprisoned by an angry Henry V.

Sieges could be horrific experiences, with hunger and unsanitary conditions affecting besiegers as well as besieged. At HARFLEUR in 1415, dysentery killed more people both within and without the town than did the actual fighting. In 1419, the people of Rouen were reduced to eating dogs and rats. When the poor of Rouen were expelled to save food, Henry V refused them passage through his lines; most died of starvation or exposure in a ditch outside the walls. At Meaux in 1422, conditions were as bad in the English siege lines as they were within the town, and the long winter operation is believed to have undermined the health of Henry V, who succumbed to dysentery three months later. *See also* BATTLE, NATURE OF; TOWNS AND THE HUNDRED YEARS WAR.

Further Reading: Allmand, Christopher. *The Hundred Years War*. Cambridge: Cambridge University Press, 1988; Curry, Anne, and Michael Hughes, eds. *Arms, Armies and Fortifications in the Hundred Years War*. Woodbridge, England: Boydell Press, 1994; Prestwich, Michael. *Armies and Warfare in the Middle Ages: The English Experience*. New Haven, CT: Yale University Press, 1996.

SIGISMUND, HOLY ROMAN EMPEROR.
See CANTERBURY, TREATY OF

SLUYS, BATTLE OF (1340)
The Battle of Sluys was the largest naval encounter and first major battle of the HUNDRED YEARS WAR. Fought on 24 June 1340 at the mouth of the River Zwin near the Flemish port of Sluys, the battle dispelled the threat of French landings in England and inaugurated a period of English initiative in FLANDERS and northern France.

In the late 1330s, French fleets controlled the Channel and Bay of Biscay, raiding English ports, threatening invasions of England or SCOTLAND, and disrupting communications with GASCONY. Although English counter-raids destroyed eighteen French galleys at Boulogne in January 1340, PHILIP VI soon managed to assemble a fleet of almost two hundred ships at Sluys, where it lay poised to intercept any English force. Commanded by Nicholas Béhuchet and Hugh Quiéret, the French fleet also contained Castilian and Genoese squadrons; the Castilians were French allies and the Genoese were paid mercenaries led by an experienced naval captain named Barbanera.

With considerable difficulty, EDWARD III assembled a fleet of about a hundred ships at the Suffolk port of Orwell, from which he set sail on 22 June. On route, he was met by fifty vessels of the northern fleet under Sir Robert Morley, who joined William de BOHUN, earl of Northampton, and Sir Walter MAUNY as the king's chief lieutenants. Consisting mainly of cogs, small shallow-draft merchant vessels best suited for transporting troops and supplies, the fleet carried an army that Jean FROISSART likely overestimated at four thousand men-at-arms and twelve thousand archers. After putting ashore spies who reported that the number of masts at Sluys was "like a great wood" (Seward, 43), Edward divided his fleet into three squadrons, with every group of three ships consisting of two filled with ARCHERS flanking one filled with men-at-arms. A fourth squadron carrying only archers acted as the reserve.

With the tide and wind in their favor and the sun at their backs, the English sailed into the tightly clustered French fleet at about noon on 24 June. What ensued was essentially a land battle fought across the decks of ships. After grappling an enemy vessel, the English longbowmen raked it with arrows before men-at-arms boarded to engage its crew in hand-to-hand combat. The English quickly recaptured the *Christopher* and the *Edward*, two royal vessels recently taken by the French, but also suffered the loss, through ARTILLERY fire, of a cog carrying various noblewomen sailing to join Queen PHILIPPA in Flanders. Slowly, and with heavy losses, the English advanced across decks, eventually sinking or capturing all enemy vessels except twenty-four ships of the rear squadron, which escaped under cover of darkness. Wounded in the leg, Edward ordered the execution of the French admirals, with Béhuchet being hung from the yardarm of the *Thomas*, the royal flagship.

Although a major victory that boosted English morale and allowed Edward to land an army in Flanders, it did not give the king command of the Channel or immediately improve English fortunes on land. The campaign of 1340 ended in failure at TOURNAI in September with conclusion of the Truce of ESPLECHIN. In 1342, French raiders sacked Plymouth. Nonetheless, Sluys generated enthusiasm for the war among the English, who took the victory as a sign that God favored the PLANTAGENET cause.

Further Reading: Burne, Alfred H. *The Crécy War*. Ware, England: Wordsworth Editions Ltd., 1999; Seward, Desmond. *The Hundred Years War*. New York: Penguin, 1999; Sumption, Jonathan. *The Hundred Years War*. Vol. 1, *Trial by Battle*. Philadelphia: University of Pennsylvania Press, 1991.

SOMERSET, DUKE OF. *See* BEAUFORT, EDMUND, DUKE OF SOMERSET; BEAUFORT, JOHN, DUKE OF SOMERSET

STAFFORD, EARL OF. *See* STAFFORD, RALPH, EARL OF STAFFORD

STAFFORD, RALPH, EARL OF STAFFORD (1301–1372)

A friend and captain of EDWARD III, and lord lieutenant of AQUITAINE, Ralph Stafford, earl of Stafford, is an example of an English commander who earned wealth and title

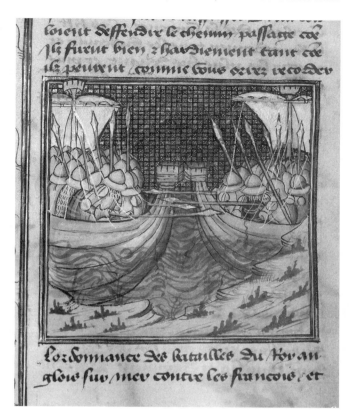

An illustration from the *Chronicles* of Jean Froissart depicting the naval Battle of Sluys, 1340. *Erich Lessing/Art Resource, New York.*

through military service in the HUNDRED YEARS WAR.

The eldest son of Edmund Stafford, who had served EDWARD I in SCOTLAND, Ralph succeeded to his father's estates by 1323, and began his career in royal service at Edward III's accession in January 1327, when he was made a knight-banneret. In 1330, Stafford joined the group of young courtiers who helped the king overthrow the regime of his mother, Queen Isabella, and her lover, Roger Mortimer, earl of March (*see* ISABELLA, QUEEN OF ENGLAND [c. 1292–1358]). Stafford fought in the Scottish campaigns of the 1330s, particularly distinguishing himself at the Battle of Dupplin Moor in 1332. For this service, Stafford, like his father before him, was recognized as a peer and summoned to

PARLIAMENT in November 1336 as Lord Stafford.

Stafford accompanied the king to France in 1338 and fought at the naval Battle of SLUYS in 1340. He was among the most prominent of the king's supporters during the political CRISIS OF 1340–41 and was twice sent to Archbishop John STRATFORD to press that cleric to submit to the Crown. In April 1341, Stafford led a group of king's men who unsuccessfully attempted to prevent Stratford from attending Parliament. In 1342, Stafford sailed to BRITTANY as a lieutenant under William de BOHUN, earl of Northampton. Stafford fought at MORLAIX on 30 September, but later in the autumn was captured at the siege of Vannes. Freed as part of a prisoner exchange, Stafford helped negotiate the Truce of MALESTROIT in January 1343 and in May was a member of the English embassy sent to defend Edward's claim to the French Crown before Pope CLEMENT VI.

In 1345, Stafford was appointed seneschal of GASCONY, where, as one of the chief lieutenants of HENRY OF GROSMONT, duke of Lancaster, he fought at BERGERAC and AUBEROCHE. In 1346, he captured AIGUILLON, where he was later besieged by John, duke of Normandy (see JOHN II). However, Stafford apparently escaped from Aiguillon before the duke raised the siege on 20 August, for the English captain fought with the king's army at CRÉCY in northern France on 26 August. Although reappointed seneschal of Gascony in October, Stafford did not return to the duchy, but took part in the siege of CALAIS, which ended in August 1347. After participating in negotiations that led to the Truce of CALAIS, Stafford returned to England where, among other rewards and favors, he became a founding member of the Order of the GARTER. In September 1348, Stafford entered into an INDENTURE with the king whereby he agreed to serve Edward for life with a retinue of sixty men-at-arms in return for an annuity of £600. In 1350, he fought with the king and EDWARD, THE BLACK PRINCE, at the naval battle of WINCHELSEA.

On 5 March 1351, Edward elevated Stafford to an earldom, awarded him an annuity of 1,000 marks to support that dignity, and appointed him lieutenant of Aquitaine. The earl fought a successful campaign in 1353, which brought him a number of rich RANSOMS, but thereafter made little headway against the French commander, John, count of Armagnac, and was replaced as lieutenant by the prince in 1355. Stafford accompanied the king on the RHEIMS CAMPAIGN in 1359 and participated in talks that culminated in the Treaty of BRÉTIGNY in May 1360. In 1361, Stafford accompanied the king's son, Lionel, earl of Ulster, to Ireland in an attempt to revive the PLANTAGENET lordship in that island. Although Jean FROISSART wrote that Stafford returned to France when war resumed in 1369, his age and ill health make that unlikely. He died at Tonbridge Castle in Kent on 31 August 1372.

Further Reading: Rawcliffe, Carole. *The Staffords: Earls of Stafford and Dukes of Buckingham, 1394–1521.* Cambridge: Cambridge University Press, 1978; Sumption, Jonathan. *The Hundred Years War.* Vol. 2, *Trial by Fire.* Philadelphia: University of Pennsylvania Press, 2001; Vale, Malcolm. *English Gascony, 1399–1453.* London: Oxford University Press, 1970.

STAR, ORDER OF THE

Founded by JOHN II of France in November 1351, the Order of the Star was a chivalric company of French knights designed to rival EDWARD III's Order of the GARTER. More lavish and political in conception than the English order, the Order of the Star was a royal attempt to reinvigorate noble morale after the disastrous Battle of CRÉCY and to rekindle support for the VALOIS Crown and enthusiasm for the HUNDRED YEARS WAR.

Formally titled the Company of Knights of Notre-Dame de la Noble-Maison, the Order of the Star was officially inaugurated at a magnificent ceremony held on 6 January 1352 at the royal manor of Saint-Ouen near PARIS. The charter endowing the order harked back to the reign of Louis IX, the supposed golden age of French CHIVALRY, when French knights were famous throughout Europe for their courage, strength, and honor, and for their dedication to royal service. The charter lamented the degeneration of this ideal by characterizing contemporary French knights as leading lives of idleness and selfish excess. To remedy this situation, John ordained creation of an elite order of five hundred knights sworn to serve him alone, to advise him to the best of their ability, and to fight for him until killed or captured. Failure to fulfill this last requirement, which was a direct response to the recriminations that followed Crécy, meant disgrace and expulsion from the order. Exemplary performance on the battlefield meant special recognition at the next annual chapter banquet to be held each August on the Feast of the Assumption.

The inaugural ceremony appears to have been rather sparsely attended, a lack of enthusiasm that may have stemmed from anger over the king's recent execution of Raoul, count of Eu and constable of France, or from dissatisfaction with the cost of the event, especially in light of the financial burdens recently placed on the nobility by an unsuccessful war and the BLACK DEATH. At the ceremony, members ate off gold plate and wore fur-trimmed robes of red and white as they processed though a chapter house decorated with specially made tapestries. Beyond this, the prestige of the order suffered an immediate blow. On the day of the ceremony, while the captain of the castle was attending the festivities, John Dancaster, an English soldier of fortune, ignored the Truce of CALAIS and surprised the fortress of Guines, one of the chief French strongholds on the march of Calais. This event, coupled with noble indifference and the members' strict adherence to the vow of no retreat—eighty-nine knights of the Star died at MAURON the following August—doomed the order. In October 1352, the king acknowledged this failure by issuing an ordinance that transformed the order from a political-chivalric institution to a confraternity for common worship.

Further Reading: Keen, Maurice. *Chivalry.* New Haven, CT: Yale University Press, 1984;

Painter, Sidney. *French Chivalry: Chivalric Ideas and Practices.* Ithaca, NY: Cornell University Press, 1940; Sumption, Jonathan. *The Hundred Years War.* Vol. 2, *Trial by Fire.* Philadelphia: University of Pennsylvania Press, 2001.

STEWART, JOHN, EARL OF BUCHAN (c. 1380–1424)

One of the most famous and successful Scottish warriors to fight for the dauphin (*see* CHARLES VII) in the fifteenth century, John Stewart, tenth earl of Buchan, was constable of France and victor of the Battle of BAUGÉ.

Stewart was the second son of Robert Stewart, duke of Albany, the brother of Robert III. Inheriting the earldom of Buchan from his younger brother in 1405, Albany granted it to his son John, who, owing to a lack of land to support the title, was not called earl until May 1412. Even though his earldom was technically one of the most important in northern SCOTLAND, Buchan never exercised much influence in the region nor held all the lands attached to the title. In his early years, Buchan was largely a pawn to his father's ambition to rule Scotland in place of his brother, who was an invalid given to bouts of depression. In 1402, the English captured Murdoch, earl of Fife, Buchan's elder half brother, at Homildon Hill, thus forcing Albany to groom Buchan as his political heir. Buchan began appearing regularly at court after 1406, when he also received appointment as chamberlain, an office long held by his father. In about 1410, Albany married his son to Elizabeth, the daughter of Archibald DOUGLAS, fourth earl of Douglas, a match that transformed Buchan's career, removing him from Scottish politics and involving him in the HUNDRED YEARS WAR.

In 1419, Buchan, thanks to his connection with Douglas and his father's exercise of the Scottish regency, was appointed joint commander, with Douglas's son, of a Scottish army sent to France to assist the dauphinists. Except for occasional diplomatic and recruiting missions to Scotland, Buchan was to spend the rest of his life in France serving the dauphin. On 22 March 1421, Buchan led the Franco-Scottish force that defeated and slew HENRY V's brother, THOMAS, DUKE OF CLARENCE, at Baugé. The earl was well rewarded for his victory, receiving the French constableship, the lands of the lordship of Châtillon-sur-Indre, and the services of a personal astrologer. Now a major dauphinist commander, Buchan scored a series of small successes in 1421–22, but his campaign in northern France in early 1423 failed due to a growing unwillingness among the French to follow a foreign constable.

Returning to Scotland, where his brother was now duke of Albany and regent for the captive James I, Buchan induced Douglas to enter French service. With HENRY VI's government threatening to release James, who was believed to be pro-English, the earl also concluded an agreement with his brother whereby the duke likely agreed to safeguard Buchan's lands in return for the earl's willingness to use the Scottish army in France to intervene in Scotland on Albany's behalf. This agreement was never implemented, for Buchan and Douglas were slain at VERNEUIL in August 1424. Although a disaster for the Albany interest in Scotland and a cause of lamentation at the dauphin's court, Buchan's death caused little mourning elsewhere in France, where the Scots were much disliked.

Further Reading: Bonner, E. "Scotland's 'Auld Alliance' with France, 1295–1560." *History* 84 (1999): 5–30; Laidlaw, James, ed. *The Auld Alliance: France and Scotland over 700 Years.* Edinburgh: University of Edinburgh, 1999; Wood, Stephen. *The Auld Alliance, Scotland and France: The Military Connection.* Edinburgh, Mainstream, 1989.

STRATEGY AND TACTICS

Strategy is the overall plan or policy employed by a military command to effectively defeat the enemy, while tactics involve the disposition and maneuvering of military forces in combat. Because of its length and the varying political, economic, and military conditions that applied during its several phases, the HUNDRED YEARS WAR witnessed important shifts in military strategy, while its course and outcome were affected by important tactical innovations.

The initial English strategy was the CHEVAUCHÉE, a swift destructive raid in force designed to cripple both morale and the ability to make war, thereby forcing the French to give battle or make peace on English terms. Fire was the main English weapon during the THIÉRACHE CAMPAIGN of 1339, when EDWARD III's men so devastated the Cambrésis that a year later papal officials distributing a special grant to relieve suffering reported that over 174 parishes had been virtually annihilated. The English estimated that during the campaign they burned or destroyed 2,118 villages and castles. During the *CHEVAUCHÉE OF* 1355, EDWARD, THE BLACK PRINCE, reportedly destroyed eleven large cities and thirty-seven hundred villages across southern France. Various other *chevauchées* in NORMANDY, BRITTANY, and GASCONY ravaged the countryside, where crops, except for vineyards and orchards, might recover quickly, but the loss of livestock, windmills, and other buildings was more devastating, leaving a local community without the resources either to rebuild or to contribute to the French war effort. By 1360, the scale of destruction and depopulation in rural France was horrific, with the depredations of *ROUTIERS* and the *JACQUERIE* rebels only adding to the damage done by the English.

Early in the war, the French strategy under PHILIP VI had been to avoid battle. Without a victory, maintaining both a field army and his grand ANTI-FRENCH COALITION proved beyond the resources of Edward III, whose campaigns in 1339 and 1340 were, despite the damage they caused, costly failures. Over the next two decades, Philip and his son JOHN II reversed this strategy, a decision that resulted in crushing defeats at CRÉCY in 1346 and POITIERS in 1356. However, in 1359, the future CHARLES V resumed the policy of avoiding battle, and thereby helped ensure the failure of Edward III's RHEIMS CAMPAIGN, a grand *chevauchée* designed to capture Rheims and have Edward crowned king of France. Believing that the English could not economically sustain such campaigns, Charles was less willing than his father to conclude the BRÉTIGNY agreement. With the renewal of war in 1369, the English continued the strategy of raiding and pillaging, but found it to be less effective. The French refused to fight, the English could no longer live off a countryside they had devastated, French towns and castles were better walled and fortified, the English themselves had to defend CALAIS and Brittany, and the campaigns became more expensive and less rewarding. Following the failure of the great CHEVAUCHÉE OF 1373 led by JOHN OF GAUNT, duke of Lancaster, the English largely abandoned the strategy of raid and pillage.

With the renewal of the war under HENRY V, English strategy changed. Henry's aim was to conquer castles and towns by means of SIEGE WARFARE, thus the AGINCOURT campaign of 1415 began with the siege of HARFLEUR, while the NORMAN CAMPAIGN of 1417–19 was a series of sieges culminating in the capture of ROUEN. Although several major battles were fought in the 1420s, such as CRAVANT in 1423 and VERNEUIL in 1424, most major campaigns of the fifteenth century involved sieges, such as MELUN in 1420, MEAUX in 1422, ORLÉANS in 1429, and PONTOISE in 1441. The NORMAN CAMPAIGN of 1449–50, which reconquered Normandy for CHARLES VII, comprised a series of sieges marked by Jean BUREAU's skillful handling of the French ARTILLERY. Even the last battle of the war in 1453 resulted from an unsuccessful attempt by John TALBOT, earl of Shrewsbury, to break the French siege of CASTILLON.

The great tactical innovation of the war was the English defensive formation that used dismounted cavalry in combination with ARCHERS. Although the exact disposition of English troops in this formation, especially at major battles like Crécy, is much debated by historians, this tactical deployment was largely responsible for numerous English victories, including, besides Crécy, MORLAIX, Poitiers, and Agincourt. The French made various attempts to counter this formation, including a flank attack on ROBERT OF ARTOIS's Flemish infantry at SAINT-OMER in 1340, a mounted charge on the archers by a large cavalry reserve at MAURON in 1352, and dismounted cavalry at Poitiers in 1356. Although these tactics had varying degrees of success, the French learned that chivalrous mounted charges, like those thrown repeatedly at the English lines at Crécy, spelled disaster against the new English formations. This lesson was momentarily forgotten at Agincourt in 1415, but the war of sieges that developed in the fifteenth century reduced the effectiveness of English archers and revealed the power of French artillery, which, by the 1440s, gave the French the tactical advantage the longbow had earlier given the English. *See also* CHIVALRY; HUNDRED YEARS WAR, PHASES OF.

Further Reading: Bennett, Matthew. "The Development of Battle Tactics in the Hundred Years War." In *Arms, Armies and Fortifications in the Hundred Years War*, ed. Anne Curry and Michael Hughes, 1–20. Woodbridge, England: Boydell Press, 1994; Prestwich, Michael. *Armies and Warfare in the Middle Ages: The English Experience.* New Haven, CT: Yale University Press, 1996.

STRATFORD, JOHN, ARCHBISHOP OF CANTERBURY (c. 1275–1348)

John Stratford, archbishop of Canterbury, was a senior royal councilor who served as both chancellor of England and president of the royal council. During the CRISIS OF 1340–1341, the most serious political upheaval of EDWARD III's reign, Stratford became the focus of the king's anger at what he believed was the failure of his ministers to faithfully support his foreign and military policies. Stratford's vigorous and reasoned defense of himself and his actions led to reaffirmation of the right of peers to be tried only in PARLIAMENT and to eventual royal acceptance of Parliament's right to consent to all TAXATION.

Born probably in Stratford upon Avon, Stratford studied at Oxford, where he earned a doctorate of civil law in 1312. By the early 1320s, he was dean of the Court of Arches and held various benefices in Lichfield, Lincoln, and York. In 1320, Stratford accompanied EDWARD II to Amiens, where the king rendered homage to PHILIP V for AQUITAINE. From 1321 to 1323, Stratford served mainly as English representative at the papal court in Avignon, where, in June 1323, Pope John XXII, acting contrary to the royal will, named him bishop of Winchester. After a period of disfavor, Stratford was again employed on diplomatic missions. In 1324, he negotiated with CHARLES IV over Aquitaine and in 1325, after accompanying Prince Edward to France, he tried un-successfully to persuade Queen Isabella to return to England (see ISABELLA, QUEEN OF ENGLAND [c. 1292–1358]).

When the queen landed in England in September 1326 to depose her husband, Stratford joined her. In January 1327, he was a member of the delegation sent to convince Edward II to abdicate and on 1 February he assisted at the coronation of Edward III. Although dispatched on other diplomatic missions, Stratford's increasing association with Henry, earl of Lancaster, cost him the favor of the queen and her lover, Roger Mortimer, earl of March. On 28 November 1330, a month after Edward III overthrew his mother and March, the king appointed Stratford chancellor; in November 1333, Edward also named him archbishop of Canterbury. Stratford retained the chancellorship until 1334, but later served twice more in that office, from June 1335 to March 1337 and again from December 1339 to April 1340. In 1338, Stratford traveled to the Continent, where he conducted talks with the French, oversaw intelligence efforts in the Low Countries, and acted as guarantor to the king's creditors.

On 30 November 1340, Edward, angry that lack of resources had thwarted his recent campaigns and forced him to conclude the Truce of ESPLECHIN, demanded that Stratford, then president of the council, appear before him to account for his actions. Stratford refused, insisting that he would submit himself only to the judgment of Parliament. When other ministers were arrested, and the archbishop's brother, Robert, was dismissed as chancellor, Stratford, fearing for his life, went to Canterbury Cathedral, where, on 29 December, the feast of the murdered archbishop Thomas Becket, he excommunicated several royal officers for publicly denouncing him as a traitor. In February 1341, the king published his attack on Stratford's administration, a wide-ranging and angry indictment that the archbishop derided as a *libellus famosus* (infamous libel). In March, the archbishop issued his *Excusaciones*, a detailed and dispassionate rebuttal of the king's charges.

Unwilling to go to extremes with an archbishop who appeared willing to court martyrdom, Edward soon realized the ineffectiveness of his methods. On 3 May 1341, following an intercession on Stratford's behalf by a delegation of lords and bishops, the king readmitted the archbishop to his favor, although he never again appointed Stratford to office. The archbishop died on 23 August 1348.

Further Reading: Haines, Roy M. *Archbishop John Stratford, Political Revolutionary and Champion of the Liberties of the English Church, c. 1275/80–1348.* Toronto: Pontifical Institute of Mediaeval Studies, 1986; Ormrod, W. M. *The Reign of Edward III: Crown and Political Society in England, 1327–1377.* New Haven, CT: Yale University Press, 1990; Waugh, Scott L. *England in the Reign of Edward III.* Cambridge: Cambridge University Press, 1991.

SUFFOLK, DUKE OF. *See* POLE, WILLIAM DE LA, DUKE OF SUFFOLK

T

TACTICS. *See* Strategy and Tactics

TALBOT, JOHN, EARL OF SHREWSBURY (c. 1384–1453)

John Talbot, earl of Shrewsbury, was the most feared and famous English commander in France during the last two decades of the Hundred Years War.

Born into a prominent Shropshire family, Talbot fought in Henry IV's campaigns in Wales, being present at the sieges of Aberystwyth and Harlech between 1407 and 1409. Under Henry V, he served as lieutenant of Ireland from 1414 to 1416 and again in 1418–19. His first service in France was during the Norman Campaign of 1417–19. He fought intermittently on the Continent during the 1420s, participating in the sieges of Melun and Meaux but also returning to Wales in 1422 to suppress disorders in the marches. He became Lord Furnivall by right of his wife in 1409 and Lord Talbot on the death of his elder brother in 1421. A quarrelsome man who willingly resorted to violence to defend his rights or honor, Talbot was briefly imprisoned in 1413, possibly as a result of his role in a bitter dispute with Thomas Fitzalan, earl of Arundel. He also maintained a long-running feud with the Ormond family in Ireland and involved himself, on his second wife's behalf, in the ongoing Berkeley-Lisle feud.

The best-known phase of his military career began in 1428, when Talbot succeeded Thomas Montagu, earl of Salisbury, as commander of the English forces at the siege of Orléans. Inspired by Joan of Arc, the French broke the siege in May 1429 and Talbot was subsequently defeated and captured at the Battle of Patay in June. After payment of a heavy ransom, Talbot was released in 1433. He fought briefly under Philip the Good, duke of Burgundy, and then served as chief military commander for a succession of English lords lieutenant in France. Brave and daring, he excelled at surprise attacks and won such a fearsome reputation among the French that mothers frightened their children into obedience by telling then Talbot would take them if they misbehaved. Credited with many bold exploits in the increasingly futile defense of Normandy, Talbot received numerous rewards and honors; he was made count of Clermont in 1434, marshal of France in 1436, constable of France in 1442, and constable of Ireland in 1446. A Knight of the Garter since 1425, Talbot was created earl of Shrewsbury by Henry VI in 1442.

After the fall of Gascony in 1451, Shrewsbury, although almost seventy, was the obvious choice to command the expeditionary force sent to retake the province in 1452. Although Shrewsbury's initial success in recapturing Bordeaux enhanced his reputation, Charles VII dispatched three armies to the province, and the subsequent campaign revealed how out of step the earl was with current military tactics and technology. In July 1453, Shrewsbury led his army to ruin with a suicidal charge against massed French artillery at the Battle of Castillon. With the earl and his son John dead on the field, the battle marked the end of English Gascony and of the Hundred Years War. To commemorate Shrewsbury's death, the French raised the Church of Notre-Dame-de-Talbot near the spot where he fell.

Further Reading: Pollard, A. J. *John Talbot and the War in France, 1427–1453*. London: Royal Historical Society, 1983.

TARD-VENUS. *See* ROUTIERS

TAX REVOLT OF 1382. *See* TAXATION AND WAR FINANCE

TAXATION AND WAR FINANCE

The length and scope of the HUNDRED YEARS WAR caused military expenditure to rise dramatically in both kingdoms. By the fifteenth century, the war accounted for between one-half and two-thirds of the funds collected and disbursed by the Crowns of France and England. The need to find and tap new sources of revenue also caused a significant expansion in the size and activities of both royal governments.

As a feudal overlord, the king of France could collect payments known as *aides* from his vassals on specific occasions, such as the knighting of the king's eldest son, and in lieu of military service. During the thirteenth century, the term *aide* was also used for occasional levies imposed, usually for military purposes, on subjects who were not royal vassals. With the ANGLO-FRENCH WAR OF 1294–1303, the Crown's need for greater revenue led PHILIP IV to demand new *aides* with controversial frequency. After the 1330s, *aides* became virtually synonymous with war subsidies and commonly took the form of indirect taxes levied irregularly on the sale of various commodities. In March 1341, PHILIP VI regularized collection of an indirect tax on salt known as the *gabelle*. The king ordered that salt henceforth be stored in royal warehouses and then sold for the Crown's profit by officials known as *gabelliers*. Hostility to the tax caused Philip to cancel it in 1347 in return for grants of war subsidies. In December 1355, the Estates-General, reacting to JOHN II's highly unpopular attempts to raise war funds by manipulating the currency, reauthorized the *gabelle* as one of several new indirect taxes, but resistance again caused its cancellation. However, in 1358–59, the *gabelle* reappeared in PARIS and Languedoc.

In December 1360, John II, in need of substantial sums to pay his RANSOM, reestablished three regular indirect taxes, including the *gabelle* and impositions on wine and various other commodities. These levies were in effect feudal *aides* imposed upon the entire kingdom. Until 1367, the *gabelle* was a 20 percent ad valorem tax, but then was changed to a surcharge of 24 francs per muid of salt. The tax on wine grew during the war from 8 percent of retail sales to 25 percent; and the third levy was a general value-added tax on the specified items. Unaccustomed to indirect taxes, Languedoc negotiated in 1362 for permission to pay these levies in a lump sum, the collection of which was apportioned among communities in the region. Known in the 1360s as *aides pour la délivrance*, and as "aids for the war" after resumption of the conflict in 1369, these taxes were collected until the middle of the FRENCH CIVIL WAR in 1417, when they were cancelled by the unpopular ARMAGNAC regime. Thereafter, the dauphinist government obtained irregular grants of new *aides* from the Estates-General until 1436, when that assembly restored the *aides* and *gabelle* as regular and permanent features of royal taxation.

In December 1363, John II secured a hearth tax, known as a *fouage*, from the Estates of Languedoil. Assessed on the basis of households, the *fouage* was usually paid by towns in an agreed-upon lump sum that was raised in any manner the locality chose to employ. When imposed as a direct tax, it was usually an assessment on the value of real property within the district, exclusive of ecclesiastical lands. The average payment was 3 francs per household, but the *fouage* had a graduated rate of 1 to 9 francs according to wealth. Although the *fouage* funded the reformed army that reconquered AQUITAINE after 1369, CHARLES V cancelled the tax on his deathbed in September 1380, an action that caused resistance to the payment of all royal taxes to increase sharply. In March 1381, the minority government of CHARLES VI secured a new *fouage* to run for one year from the Estates of Languedoil, but only on condition that the assembly controlled its collection and use. When further promises of reform produced no new taxes, nor lessened taxpayer resistance to the collection of existing levies, tax revolts erupted in Paris (the *Maillotins*), NORMANDY (the *Hérelle*), and elsewhere in northern France. These revolts were eventually suppressed and the government thereafter began imposing irregular direct taxes that were similar to the *fouage*, but known as *tailles*. Intermittent imposition of these levies ended in 1439, when CHARLES VII secured a permanent annual *taille* from the Estates-General, which also authorized the Crown to annually adjust the amount of the tax.

In the fourteenth century, claims by the nobility to exemption from taxation were largely denied. However, when the nobility, in the persons of the royal uncles, JOHN, DUKE OF BERRY, and PHILIP THE BOLD, duke of BURGUNDY, controlled the government during Charles VI's minority, the Crown issued ordinances exempting the nobility, upon certain conditions, from payment of the *taille* (1388) and *aides* (1393). By the mid-fifteenth century, the conditions of exemption were so broad as to effectively free most nobles from taxation. Taxation of the clergy was a contentious issue from the reign of Philip IV, when the king violently opposed Pope Boniface VIII's refusal to permit kings to tax their clergy without papal consent. Boniface eventually allowed the French Crown discretionary power to tax the clergy for defense of the realm, a right that the French-dominated Avignon popes interpreted broadly. The Crown also extracted other sums from the Church by leaving benefices vacant and appropriating their incomes.

In England, the wars of EDWARD I had established the right of PARLIAMENT to consent to the imposition of taxation. In 1336, EDWARD III convinced Parliament to grant him a subsidy on wool in addition to the customs duties that the Crown had collected on the import and export of various commodities since the 1270s. Although ostensibly a war tax, this subsidy was regularly voted by Parliament after 1355, including

during the years of peace that followed conclusion of the Treaty of BRÉTIGNY in 1360. Another indirect tax created by war needs was tunnage and poundage, a duty first imposed in 1345 on each barrel (tun) of wine and each pound of various other goods. In 1398, Parliament voted RICHARD II the right to collect customs duties for life, and then made the same grant to HENRY V in 1415 and HENRY VI in 1453.

The most common form of direct taxation in England was a levy on movable property. By the fourteenth century, the normal assessment was a fifteenth of the value of such property in rural areas and a tenth in towns and on royal lands. In 1334, tenths and fifteenths began to be levied on communities rather than individuals, and by the end of the century the assessments had become fixed sums rather than accurate current valuations of movable property, a situation the government tolerated because of the ease of collecting such sums and the difficulties of undertaking a new valuation. In 1371, the government imposed a flat levy on each English parish, but the results were disappointing, and in 1377 Parliament granted a poll tax assessed at a flat rate on everyone over the age of fourteen, save for beggars. A second poll tax assessed at a variable rate according to wealth was passed in 1379 and a third using a flat rate that promised a higher return than tenths and fifteenths was imposed in 1380. The last poll tax was widely evaded and became a direct cause of the PEASANTS' REVOLT OF 1381. In the fifteenth century, Parliament returned to the standard subsidies, sometimes granting several at a time, as in 1404 when HENRY IV received two tenths and fifteenths. In Henry VI's reign, Parliament tried various land taxes, and in 1435 and 1449 war emergencies led to another innovation, a graduated income tax.

Early in his reign, Edward III, needing huge sums to pay the subsidies promised to members of his ANTI-FRENCH COALITION, borrowed heavily both from LONDON merchants and Italian bankers. The English merchant William de la POLE was instrumental in arranging loans for the Crown, and was the initiator of a scheme to manipulate the wool trade, which ultimately failed and resulted in the Crown's issuance of the DORDRECHT BONDS. The government also continued to collect various feudal aids and assessments and to impose taxes on the clergy, which was routine practice in England by the start of the war. After the 1340s, the clergy met regularly in Convocation, which body eventually won the right to assent to clerical taxes in the same way Parliament spoke for the king's temporal subjects. The clergy also paid subsidies based on the tenth and fifteenth and were subject to such other levies as poll taxes. *See also* ESTATES, GENERAL AND PROVINCIAL; PAPACY AND THE HUNDRED YEARS WAR; TOWNS AND THE HUNDRED YEARS WAR.

Further Reading: Harriss, G. L. *King, Parliament and Public Finance in Medieval England to 1369.* Oxford: Clarendon Press, 1975; Henneman, John Bell. *Royal Taxation in Fourteenth-Century France: The Captivity and Ransom of John II.* Philadelphia: Royal Philosophical Society, 1976; Henneman, John Bell. *Royal Taxation in Fourteenth-Century France: The Development of War Financing, 1322–1356.* Princeton, NJ: Princeton University Press, 1971; Prestwich, Michael. *The Three Edwards: War and State in England, 1272–1377.* 2nd ed. London: Routledge, 2003.

THIÉRACHE CAMPAIGN (1339)

Conducted in or near the Thiérache region along France's northeastern frontier, the campaign of September–October 1339 was the first major campaign of the HUNDRED YEARS WAR and the first significant English incursion into the VALOIS realm. The campaign saw little fighting, as PHILIP VI, aware that EDWARD III lacked the resources to maintain an army in the field for long, refused battle. The campaign was thus characterized not by combat, but by Edward's inability to effectively exploit the ANTI-FRENCH COALITION he had so painfully constructed, and by the unprecedented suffering visited on French peasants by Edward's scorched earth policy.

The campaign began on 20 September 1339, when Edward, accompanied by most of his allies from Germany and the Low Countries, marched south from Valenciennes in Hainault toward the town of Cambrai, where the bishop, although an Imperial vassal, refused Edward passage into France. The allied army invested the town, while parties led by Walter MAUNY; HENRY OF GROSMONT, earl of Derby; and other English captains stormed local castles and ravaged the entire Cambrésis, which, according to Edward, his men "burned... for the whole of the following week so that the whole territory was laid waste and quite stripped of corn, cattle, and everything else" (Sumption, 281). While the surrounding countryside went up in flames, Cambrai, defended by a strong French garrison, held out. By the end of September, Edward was in a difficult position; he could not capture Cambrai and he could not provoke the French to battle. Since his allies were clamoring for payment of their subsidies, and Edward had no money to pay them, he needed to win a battle before his army disintegrated. Except to avoid the perception of timidity, Philip had no need to fight; dissention among Edward's allies and hunger among his troops would soon force him to withdraw.

In early October, Edward's brother-in-law, William, count of Hainault, abandoned the anti-French alliance, leaving to join Philip at Compiègne, where the French had amassed an army of over twenty thousand men. Although the count's uncle and most of the nobility of Hainault stayed with Edward, the defection increased the other allies' reluctance to invade France. However, on 9 October, with Cambrai untaken, the allied army crossed the French frontier. Edward's force numbered over ten thousand men, but less than half were English, so it was imperative that Edward engage and defeat the enemy before further defections weakened his army. Moving in a wide arc so as to maximize damage, the army moved unopposed through the countryside, burning everything in its path. The English were so thorough in their destruction that a year later the region was still devastated, with most villages abandoned and most fields uncultivated. Strongpoints were attacked and taken wherever possible, but the army needed to keep moving to supply itself and Edward had no siege equipment, so many were simply bypassed (see SIEGE WARFARE). Sweeping into Picardy, the army, on 14 October, passed within a mile of the new French position at Péronne. Although his spies told him the French were preparing to fight, Edward, fearing that French garrisons in his rear might intercept his line of retreat, withdrew to the east.

Hearing of the English withdrawal, Philip, angry that the English had learned his plans, issued a formal challenge for the two armies to meet in battle on about 21 October "at a place uncramped by rivers, walls, or earthworks" (Sumption, 285). Edward accepted, but, seeking more favorable ground, moved north into the Thiérache, stopping on 21 October in the open fields between La Capelle and La Flamengrie. The French halted next day near the village of Buirenfosse, about four miles to the southwest. Convinced that the French meant to attack on 23 October, Edward dismounted his men and placed them in three lines behind a deep ditch, with ARCHERS arrayed on each flank. Although completely new to his allies, this deployment had defeated the Scots at HALIDON HILL and seven years later was to devastate the French at CRÉCY. However, next morning, the French, who had stood all night in line of battle, retreated and began to entrench, Philip having decided not to assault the strong English position. By widening the rift between Edward and his allies, delay might defeat the English as effectively as battle. Since there was no question of attacking a superior force in an entrenched position, Edward's allies declared the campaign a moral victory and quickly decamped. However, Edward, who withdrew to Brabant, knew that the Thiérache Campaign had failed.

Further Reading: Perroy, Edouard. *The Hundred Years War.* Trans. W. B. Wells. New York: Capricorn Books, 1965; Sumption, Jonathan. *The Hundred Years War.* Vol. 1, *Trial by Battle.* Philadelphia: University of Pennsylvania Press, 1999.

THIRTY, COMBAT OF THE. *See* COMBAT OF THE THIRTY

THOMAS, DUKE OF CLARENCE (1389–1421)

Thomas, duke of Clarence, was the second son of HENRY IV and the brother and heir of HENRY V. Although an experienced soldier, Clarence was also a reckless commander, whose rash disregard of his captains' advice led to his death and to the temporary discomfiture of the English cause.

Born on 29 September 1389, Thomas was knighted and became steward of England in October 1399, shortly after his father deposed RICHARD II. In July 1401, the king appointed Thomas lord lieutenant of Ireland, a post he held until 1413, although he spent barely a third of that period in Dublin. Thomas also acquired military experience in WALES, where he served in Glamorgan in 1405, and at CALAIS, where he was captain of the fortress of Guines. In June 1410, Thomas and his younger brother JOHN, future duke of Bedford, were involved in serious disorders in LONDON, riots that may have formed the basis for stories of youthful misbehavior later attributed by William Shakespeare and others to Thomas's elder brother, Prince Henry.

By 1411, the prince's assumption of the government during the illness of their father created tension between Thomas and his older brother, who had opposed Thomas's marriage to Margaret, widow of their uncle, John Beaufort, earl of Somerset. With the government controlled by the prince and his allies, Thomas was also angered by council criticism of the fitful attention he paid to his duties in Ireland. However, the real source of trouble between the brothers stemmed from the prince's dispute with his father, who suspected his eldest son of being overeager for power and disagreed with him over French policy. Thomas supported his father's decision to conclude the Treaty of BOURGES with the ARMAGNAC faction in the FRENCH CIVIL WAR, while the prince favored alliance with the BURGUNDIANS. On 9 July 1412, Henry IV created Thomas duke of

Clarence and gave him command of the expeditionary force sent to France under the treaty. Clarence was also made lieutenant of Aquitaine, an appointment that slighted the prince, who had been duke of Aquitaine since 1399. Collapse of the Armagnacs dissolved the treaty and turned Clarence's campaign into a CHEVAUCHÉE that ended with the duke and his captains extracting a large ransom from the French before withdrawing to BORDEAUX.

Clarence returned to England upon his brother's accession in March 1413. Now heir to the throne, the duke became Henry V's loyal servant. Although the two brothers were never close, their former ill will faded away. Clarence became constable of England and presided over the commission that condemned the Southampton Plot conspirators in 1415. In that same year, the duke supplied 240 men-at-arms and 720 ARCHERS for the army Henry embarked for France. Clarence served at the siege of HARFLEUR, but fell ill and missed the Battle of AGINCOURT. One of the chief English commanders during the conquest of NORMANDY, he was instrumental in the capture of Caen in 1417, of Pont-de-l'Arche in 1418, and of ROUEN and Pontoise in 1419. He was also present when Henry ratified the Treaty of TROYES in 1420.

Upon his return to England in February 1421, Henry named Clarence king's lieutenant in France. Clarence, who was anxious to atone for his absence at Agincourt, rashly allowed himself to be drawn into battle at BAUGÉ before his archers could gather. The duke and most of his captains were slain, their bodies being retrieved only with difficulty by Thomas MONTAGU, earl of Salisbury, whose skill in stabilizing the military situation over the following weeks prevented Clarence's foolhardiness from overthrowing the entire English position in Normandy. After the duke's burial, rumors claimed, most improbably, that had Clarence lived, Henry would have executed his brother for failing to obey orders.

Further Reading: Allmand, Christopher. *Henry V.* New Haven, CT: Yale University Press, 1997;

Seward, Desmond. *Henry V as War Lord.* New York: Penguin Books, 2002.

THOMAS OF WOODSTOCK, DUKE OF GLOUCESTER (1355–1397)

Thomas of Woodstock, duke of Gloucester, was the fifth surviving son of EDWARD III and PHILIPPA OF HAINAULT. Twenty-five years younger than his eldest brother, EDWARD, THE BLACK PRINCE, Gloucester came of age in the reign of his nephew RICHARD II, with whom he was frequently at odds over the conduct of the HUNDRED YEARS WAR.

Knighted by his father in April 1377, Thomas was created earl of Buckingham by his nephew in the following July. To maintain his new estate, Buckingham was given an income of £1,000 a year, which was derived from the revenues of alien priories. Because these foreign houses were only in the possession of the Crown because of the war, the earl had a vested interest in the continuation of hostilities with France. Buckingham saw his first military action in a series of naval engagements with the Castilian fleet in the summer and autumn of 1377. In 1380, Buckingham commanded the last great English CHEVAUCHÉE of the fourteenth century, leading a force of five thousand that raided from CALAIS into BRITTANY. In 1381, he helped suppress the PEASANTS' REVOLT and in 1384 he was joint commander with his brother, JOHN OF GAUNT, duke of Lancaster, of an unsuccessful expedition into SCOTLAND. Although created duke of Gloucester in 1385, Thomas's income was still heavily dependent on royal annuities, which were not always regularly paid. As a result, the duke, an overbearing and ambitious man, believed himself insufficiently endowed in lands and offices for a king's son, especially in light of the rewards being given to such royal favorites as Robert de Vere, earl of Oxford.

In 1386, Lancaster, who had a restraining influence on his brother, left England to pursue his wife's claim to the Castilian Crown. Gloucester now assumed leadership of those nobles who opposed Richard's pursuit of peace with France. In the so-called

Wonderful PARLIAMENT of 1386, Gloucester and his chief allies, Richard Fitzalan, earl of Arundel, and Thomas Beauchamp, earl of Warwick, forced the dismissal of Richard's ministers and won appointment of a governing commission of which Gloucester was a member. The commission ended Richard's peace overtures to France and prepared to renew the war. In 1387, when Richard sought to undo the acts of the 1386 Parliament, Gloucester led an armed revolt against the king. In 1387, Gloucester, Arundel, Warwick, and others, calling themselves the Lords Appellant, met a new Parliament—known as the Merciless Parliament—to appeal (accuse) the king's ministers and favorites of treason. All those appealed were either banished or executed.

In 1387, the Appellant regime resumed the war, winning a naval victory at CADZAND, but failing to incite a pro-English uprising in FLANDERS and failing also to stem a Scottish invasion. By 1388, Gloucester was more receptive to a cessation of hostilities, and the regime entered into talks that led to conclusion of the Truce of LEULINGHEN in June 1389, shortly after Richard resumed control of the government. Through Lancaster's mediation, Gloucester was reconciled to his nephew, and in 1393 the two dukes led the English delegation to the Anglo-French peace talks at Leulinghen. Gloucester, however, remained opposed to the royal peace policy and to the king's marriage to Isabella of VALOIS (see ISABELLA, QUEEN OF ENGLAND [1388–1409]), which sealed a 28-year extension of the truce in 1396.

On 10 July 1397, the king suddenly arrested Gloucester, who was imprisoned at Calais, where he was likely murdered on the king's orders. The duke's death was announced in September, when Gloucester and the other leading Appellants were appealed of treason before Parliament. Although Gloucester was officially condemned for his actions in 1387, rumors suggested that the duke, opposed to the peace, and particularly to the clause calling for the English surrender of Brest, was arrested for devising a new plot to depose the king and resume the war.

Further Reading: Goodman, Anthony. *The Loyal Conspiracy: The Lords Appellant under Richard II*. London: Routledge and Kegan Paul, 1971; Palmer, J. J. N. *England, France, and Christendom, 1377–99*. Chapel Hill: University of North Carolina Press, 1972; Saul, Nigel. *Richard II*. New Haven, CT: Yale University Press, 1997; Tuck, Anthony. *Richard II and the English Nobility*. London: Edward Arnold, 1973.

TOURNAI, SIEGE OF (1340)

The two-month siege of Tournai, the focus of the English campaign of 1340, was meant to establish a PLANTAGENET bridgehead in northern France. However, the siege failed and resulted in an unwanted truce that demonstrated the financial inability of the English Crown to support a policy of paying for allies, and led to a serious political confrontation between EDWARD III and his subjects.

Having, through great diplomatic effort and prodigious expense, crafted an ANTI-FRENCH COALITION consisting of England and various states in Germany and the Low Countries, Edward sought to use the resulting army to carry the HUNDRED YEARS WAR into the French royal domain. Seeking to wound VALOIS honor by seizing an important town and thereby force the French to fight a pitched battle, Edward chose to invest Tournai, an industrial center on the River Scheldt that was readily accessible to his forces gathering in FLANDERS. Edward's naval victory at SLUYS in June allowed him to land an English army of about two thousand men—mainly ARCHERS—in Flanders, where the revolutionary government of the province, directed by James van ARTEVELDE, was hastily gathering forces to support the coming campaign. The allies decided on a two-pronged attack. ROBERT OF ARTOIS led a force of a thousand English archers and ten thousand Flemings into Artois, while the king, with the bulk of the allied army, besieged Tournai. However, this plan went awry when the French defeated Robert at SAINT-OMER on 26 July, five days before Edward began operations at Tournai.

Although the allied army was large, including, besides the English and the Flemings, contingents under the count of Hainault, the dukes of Brabant and Guelders, and the Margrave of Juliers, the French had almost six thousand men in Tournai. Strongly fortified, the city was difficult to assault, so the allies settled down around the town in hopes that treachery or famine would deliver it to them, or that their ARTILLERY could collapse a section of wall. Raiding parties devastated the surrounding countryside trying to provoke PHILIP VI, who was approaching with a large army, into engaging the allies. However, Philip refused to be drawn and the siege showed no signs of progress, while many allied soldiers began to complain of Edward's failure to deliver their promised pay. Money expected from England had not arrived and the king was paying 20 percent interest on loans to feed his troops. With time against them, the allies changed tack on 26 August and launched an assault on the walls. Conducted only by the English and the Flemings, it failed. Angry at the inactivity of the Germans and Brabanters, van Artevelde accused the duke of Brabant of cowardice. With much difficulty, Edward persuaded the duke to stay with the army, but the Brabanters, fighting only for pay, had no enthusiasm for the English cause. Edward knew that his allies would abandon him if he did not quickly take the city or win a battle.

On 7 September, Philip reached Bouvines, ten miles west of Tournai. Deploying between the city and the enemy, the allies launched several small attacks on the French lines on 8 September, but these were beaten back and Philip refused a general engagement. Declaring themselves unwilling to fight without being paid, several English allies began to negotiate with Philip on their own account. Realizing that he had no alternative, Edward overrode his own disappointment, and the protestations of van Artevelde and Robert of Artois, and consented to talks, which began in the nearby village of Esplechin on 23 September. Two days later, the kings signed the Truce of

ESPLECHIN, which halted the war until June 1341 and allowed all parties to keep whatever they held at the moment. While these terms worked to Edward's advantage in SCOTLAND and AQUITAINE, they only emphasized his failure in northern France. Believing that he had been forced into a shameful truce by the failure of his ministers in LONDON to support him financially, an angry Edward returned to England in November and precipitated the most serious political crisis of his reign (see CRISIS OF 1340–1341). See also SIEGE WARFARE.

Further Reading: Sumption, Jonathan. *The Hundred Years War*. Vol. 1, *Trial by Battle*. Philadelphia: University of Pennsylvania Press, 1991.

TOURS, TRUCE OF (1444)

The Truce of Tours, a two-year cessation of hostilities negotiated between France and England in May 1444, was the first diplomatic agreement between the two realms since the Treaty of TROYES in 1420. Although providing a much needed respite for the faltering English war effort, and forging a marriage link between the rival monarchs, the truce also allowed the French to forestall any renewal of the ANGLO-BURGUNDIAN ALLIANCE and to strengthen their armies for a final assault on GASCONY and NORMANDY.

By 1444, both parties were willing to talk. The loss of PARIS and other towns in the late 1430s, and the failure of the campaign led by John BEAUFORT, duke of Somerset, in 1443, fed a growing war weariness in England and discredited the war party led by HENRY VI's uncle, HUMPHREY, DUKE OF GLOUCESTER. Encouraged by the king, who was now in his early twenties, the peace party led by Cardinal Henry BEAUFORT, bishop of Winchester, and William de la POLE, earl of Suffolk, signaled its receptiveness to any diplomatic overtures from France. Although he had the military initiative, CHARLES VII also welcomed peace. Charles hoped to diplomatically isolate BURGUNDY, preventing Duke PHILIP THE GOOD from aiding the English and the English from supporting the duke. Charles also needed a respite to carry out military reforms required to strengthen his armies for eventual showdowns with both England and Burgundy.

Although it is unclear which side initiated discussions, by January 1444 the English council decided to open talks with Charles, and on 1 February dispatched Suffolk to France. Negotiations for a permanent peace quickly bogged down when the French refused any concessions. The English therefore accepted a truce running until 1 April 1446 and agreed to a marriage between their king and MARGARET OF ANJOU, a niece of Charles VII, who was unwilling to marry one his own daughters to Henry and thereby give the Lancastrians yet another possible claim to the French Crown. On 24 May 1444, with Suffolk acting as proxy, fifteen-year-old Margaret was formally betrothed to Henry at Tours.

Extended eventually until 1449, the Truce of Tours temporarily halted the fighting and opened a period of Anglo-French diplomacy. Although the English offered to relinquish Henry's claim to the French Crown in return for full sovereignty in Normandy, Charles rejected the proposal and pushed instead for the English surrender of Maine. Personally inclined toward peace and now under the influence of his new wife, Henry secretly agreed to this in December 1445. Although English officers in Maine refused to relinquish control until March 1448, Henry's apparent willingness to make further concessions in the face of either military or diplomatic pressure convinced Charles to renew the war. In June 1449, after charging the English with breaking the truce by sacking the Breton town of FOUGÈRES, Charles launched a campaign in Normandy that led to French reconquest of the duchy in 1450. *See also* CHARLES VII, MILITARY REFORMS OF; MAINE, SURRENDER OF; NORMAN CAMPAIGN (1449–1450).

Further Reading: Allmand, Christopher. *The Hundred Years War.* Cambridge: Cambridge University Press, 1988; Griffiths, Ralph A. *The Reign of Henry VI.* Berkeley: University of California Press, 1981.

TOWNS AND THE HUNDRED YEARS WAR

The HUNDRED YEARS WAR created enormous economic problems for towns in both France and England. In the former, the effects were more direct—towns could be burned, plundered, and depopulated by military action. In the latter, the effects were usually more indirect—towns could be thrown into severe economic decline by wartime disruption of trade and commerce.

At the start of the war, many French towns had no walls, and so were defenseless before the devastating English CHEVAUCHÉES, swift campaigns designed to maximize destruction of enemy resources. In the THIÉR-ACHE CAMPAIGN of 1339 and the operations surrounding the siege of TOURNAI in 1340, the English not only burned many towns and villages, but also desolated the surrounding countryside that fed and supplied them. The scope of the destruction was so great that Cardinal Bertrand de Montfavence fainted when an English official took him to the top of a convent tower at night and showed him the countryside red with flames for miles in all directions.

Even towns with defensive walls were adversely affected as frightened refugees from the surrounding area crowded into the town, many to stay for years as beggars because they had no homes to return to. During the fourteenth century, many French towns sunk a large portion of their civic resources into wall construction and maintenance. ROUEN spent a quarter of its municipal budget in this fashion. However, strong walls acted as magnets drawing both more refugees from the war-ravaged countryside and armies intent not on raiding, but on siege and conquest. Rouen twice stood siege in the fifteenth century. The town surrendered to HENRY V in January 1419 after a horrendous siege of seven months, and again to CHARLES VII after a six-week siege in 1449. In southern France, the CHE-VAUCHÉE OF 1355 led by EDWARD, THE BLACK PRINCE, caused tremendous destruction across a wide area and included the devastation of eleven sizable towns.

Already more susceptible than the countryside to the ravages of the BLACK DEATH, towns under siege or simply swollen with refugees were always in danger from disease, such as the outbreak of dysentery that killed both besiegers and besieged during the English investment of HARFLEUR in 1415. Even if they did not stand siege, towns could be seriously harmed by enemy action in the countryside that supported them. PARIS, for instance, counted upon the ports of NORMANDY for fish and upon a wide region around the capital for grain and other foodstuffs. When the forces of Charles VII captured Chartres, some fifty miles from Paris, in 1432, bread prices in the capital rose sharply. The resulting dissatisfaction with the Anglo-Burgundian administration was one reason that PHILIP THE GOOD, duke of BURGUNDY, decided to abandon the ANGLO-BURGUNDIAN ALLIANCE three years later at the Congress of ARRAS. Desolating the region upon which a town drew for its food was considered the surest way to take the town itself.

The war's damaging effect on trade harmed many ports on both sides of the English Channel. The trade of Caen in Normandy fell by more than half between the start of the war and the early fifteenth century; there was some revival during the period of English occupation when Normandy was not a battle zone, but the French reconquest in 1449–50 caused another downturn. The needs of war also disrupted commerce. The huge French fleet destroyed by the English at SLUYS in 1340 was drawn from most of the ports of FLANDERS and northwestern France, and the loss of so many vessels and so much of the shipping season seriously harmed the economy of the whole region. In England, a few ports felt the effects of war directly. Winchelsea in Sussex never recovered from a devastating French raid in 1380, and Melcombe Regis in Dorset, once a major shipping center, was in rapid decline in the early fifteenth century after twice being burned by the French

during the reigns of EDWARD III and RICHARD II. LONDON continued to prosper during the war, although costs rose as merchants in both countries had to spend more for larger crews and to recoup losses to pirates and enemy naval activity, such as the English capture of a huge French wine fleet at CADZAND in 1387. Other English towns, such as Bristol, had to gradually diversify their trade. As the war in GASCONY caused severe fluctuations in the wine trade with BORDEAUX, Bristol increased its trade with Spain and became more involved in fishing expeditions to Iceland. By the time the Gascon wine trade collapsed following the English defeat at CASTILLON in 1453, Bristol had already focused its economic activity elsewhere. *See also* NAVAL WARFARE; NORMAN CAMPAIGN (1417–1419); NORMAN CAMPAIGN (1449–1450); SIEGE WARFARE.

Further Reading: Allmand, Christopher. *The Hundred Years War.* Cambridge: Cambridge University Press, 1988; Curry, Anne. *The Hundred Years War.* 2nd ed. Houndmills, England: Palgrave Macmillan, 2003.

TROYES, TREATY OF (1420)

Concluded in May 1420 at Troyes, a town on the Seine in northeastern France, the Treaty of Troyes was a historic Anglo-French accord whereby HENRY V of England became regent and heir to the throne of France. By creating the prospect of a dual monarchy within the English House of PLANTAGENET, the treaty promised an end to both the Hundred Years War and the FRENCH CIVIL WAR.

In the spring of 1418, JOHN THE FEARLESS, duke of BURGUNDY, recaptured PARIS, driving out Dauphin Charles (*see* CHARLES VII) and his Armagnac supporters and regaining custody of CHARLES VI. Since the English victory at AGINCOURT in 1415, the civil war between BURGUNDIANS and ARMAGNACS had divided the French nobility and allowed Henry to conquer NORMANDY. In September 1419, during a meeting at MONTEREAU to discuss reconciliation, the dauphin's men murdered Duke John, thereby thrusting PHILIP THE GOOD, the new duke of Burgundy, into firm alliance with England and allowing Henry to denounce the dauphin as unfit to inherit the Crown of France.

On 2 December, after a month of negotiations with the English, Philip announced his willingness to recognize Henry as Charles's rightful heir. Although ambivalent about the prospect of English rule, Philip found it preferable to acknowledging his father's murderer as king. In January 1420, Henry dispatched representatives to the French court in Troyes and authorized them to draft a formal agreement. This document was ready by early May, when all parties agreed to meet in Troyes to ratify the treaty.

Largely dictated by Henry, the terms of the agreement called for his marriage to Charles's daughter, CATHERINE OF VALOIS, whom Henry took without a dowry; his recognition as Charles's heir in place of the dauphin, who was thereby disinherited; and his exercise of the French regency until Charles's death. The treaty envisaged a union of Crowns, a dual monarchy, not a union of kingdoms. France and England would retain separate administrations, laws, and institutions, but the dispute over the French Crown and over the status of English territories in France would be resolved—the king of England and his heirs would rule all.

On 20 May, Philip met Henry outside Troyes and conducted him to a meeting with Charles, his wife Queen ISABEAU, and their daughter Catherine. Next day, Henry arrived at St. Peter's Cathedral in Troyes with a party of about four hundred. Isabeau and Philip, acting as deputies for Charles, who was too ill to attend, led a French party of similar size. The text of the treaty was read at the high altar, each party giving assent thereto, and the seals of each king were affixed to the document, with Henry employing the seal EDWARD III had used to ratify the Treaty of BRÉTIGNY sixty years earlier. Led by Philip, the nobles present swore to uphold the treaty (i.e., to recognize Henry as heir to the throne) and to obey Henry as regent. Peace between the two realms was then officially proclaimed in both French and English. Next, Henry and Catherine were solemnly betrothed, with the wedding ceremony following on 2 June at the Church of St. John in Troyes.

The treaty was widely if not enthusiastically accepted in Paris and most of the English and Burgundian regions of northern France, where war weariness and economic distress made the conclusion of peace, on whatever terms, a welcome prospect. However, in most of the realm south of the Loire, loyalty to the dauphin was equally widespread, if often equally unenthusiastic, and the treaty was repudiated there as a settlement forced upon a captive king. How well the treaty would have worked is hard to say, for, to everyone's surprise, Henry predeceased his father-in-law, dying at the end of August 1422. When Charles VI died in the following October, the Treaty of Troyes made a nine-month-old infant, HENRY VI, ruler of both kingdoms, a circumstance that reinvigorated both the war and the dauphin's cause.

Further Reading: Allmand, Christopher. *Henry V*. New Haven, CT: Yale University Press, 1997; Perroy, Edouard. *The Hundred Years War*. Trans. W. B. Wells. New York: Capricorn Books, 1965.

URBAN V. *See* Papacy and the Hundred Years War

URBAN VI. *See* Papacy and the Hundred Years War

V

VALMONT, BATTLE OF (1416)

The Battle of Valmont encompassed a series of encounters fought in early March 1416 along the English army's line of retreat through the region northeast of HARFLEUR in NORMANDY. The battles illustrate the vital importance of Harfleur to HENRY V's operations in Normandy and the continuing harm done to the French military effort by the incompetence and overconfidence of its leaders.

On 9 March, Thomas BEAUFORT, earl of Dorset, commander of the English garrison at Harfleur, led about eleven hundred men on a three-day foraging expedition into the countryside northeast of the town. Blockaded by land and sea, the Harfleur garrison was in desperate need of supplies. All went well until the raiders turned for home, when they encountered a large French army near Valmont, some twenty miles from Harfleur. Commanded by BERNARD, COUNT OF AR-MAGNAC and constable of France, this army numbered almost four thousand. Dorset dismounted his men, sending the horses to the rear, and hastily formed a long thin line to protect his flanks. Although their charges pierced the English line in several places, the French knights, instead of turning to attack their foes in the rear, charged the grooms tending the horses and fell to looting the English baggage. This action gave Dorset the time he needed to reform his men in a nearby garden, which was protected by hedges and a ditch. With his enemy now deployed in a strong massed formation that faced out in all directions, Armagnac broke off the attack and commenced negotiations. Although Dorset was eager to reach an

agreement, the constable's terms proved unacceptable and the talks ended without result.

Under cover of darkness, Dorset's men slipped away that night, marching west and south until they reached the shelter of a wood at Les Loges, just east of Etretat. Upon discovering that the English were gone, Armagnac dispatched a force under Marshal Louis de Loigny to find the enemy and bar his path to Harfleur until the constable arrived. After lying quiet all day, Dorset set out again at nightfall, reaching the sea near Etretat and then marching south along the coast, where his seaward flank was secure. At dawn, with the Seine estuary in view, and Harfleur just beyond, the English were spotted from the cliffs by the marshal's men, who, seeing their enemy strung out along the shore, charged down the slopes. The haste with which the charge was launched and the steepness of the incline threw the French assault into complete disorder and allowed the English to form up and cut their attackers to pieces. Dorset's men were still looting the dead when Armagnac arrived. Without hesitating, the English rearmed and charged up the slope, so surprising Armagnac's column that it broke and fled eastward, where the Harfleur garrison, alerted by the sounds of battle, rode out to strike the flank of the fleeing army.

Although the Valmont battles boosted English morale and gained Harfleur a much needed respite, Armagnac, currently the dominant figure in the French government, was determined to retake the city. The French therefore tightened the blockade and the garrison was in dire straits until JOHN,

DUKE OF BEDFORD, relieved the city in August 1416 after his victory at the Battle of the SEINE.

Further Reading: Burne, Alfred H. *The Agincourt War.* Ware, England: Wordsworth Editions Ltd., 1999; Jacob, E. F. *The Fifteenth Century, 1399–1485.* Oxford: Oxford University Press, 1993.

VALOGNES, TREATY OF. *See* CHARLES THE BAD, KING OF NAVARRE

VALOIS, HOUSE OF

A cadet branch of the House of CAPET, the House of VALOIS was the ruling dynasty of France from 1328 to 1589. During the HUNDRED YEARS WAR, the first five Valois kings—PHILIP VI, JOHN II, CHARLES V, CHARLES VI, and CHARLES VII—contended with the English royal Houses of PLANTAGENET and LANCASTER for control of western France and for possession of the French Crown itself. Despite decades of political instability and military defeat, the Valois had by the mid-fifteenth century secured their Crown, expelled their English rivals, and expanded the scope of their authority and the size of their realm.

The family descended from Charles, count of Valois, the second son of Philip III (r. 1270–85) and younger brother of PHILIP IV. On his death in 1314, Philip IV left three sons. The eldest, LOUIS X, died in 1316, leaving, after the death of his posthumous son, John I, only daughters, whose claim to the throne was set aside by their paternal uncle PHILIP V. At a great council summoned by the new king in 1317, the French nobility declared that females could not inherit the Crown. When Philip died in 1322, this principle excluded his daughters from the throne in favor of his younger brother CHARLES IV. When Charles died without male heirs in 1328, the direct Capetian line ended, precipitating the first succession crisis since 987. Because Valois had died in 1325, the next heir in the male line was his son, Philip. However, Charles IV's closest male heir was not his Valois cousin, but his nephew, EDWARD III of England, the son of his sister Isabella (*see* ISABELLA, QUEEN OF

ENGLAND [c. 1292–1358]). Because Edward was only fifteen, a foreign ruler, and dominated by his strong-willed mother, the French nobility accepted the principle that a woman could not transmit a claim to the throne to her male heirs. Valois, a mature French nobleman with political and military experience, was thus crowned king of France as Philip VI.

Despite the decision of 1328, Edward III's claim to the Crown and that of another Valois cousin in the female line, CHARLES THE BAD, king of Navarre, attracted the allegiance of discontented nobles and provinces, especially after Philip's 1337 confiscation of Plantagenet AQUITAINE led to war between the two kingdoms. By 1340, with ROBERT OF ARTOIS, the frustrated claimant to that county; John de MONTFORT, the unsuccessful claimant to the duchy of BRITTANY; and James van ARTEVELDE, the leader of rebellion in FLANDERS, allied with him, Edward formally claimed the French Crown. Philip's reign ended in 1350, four years after a disastrous defeat at CRÉCY, and that of his son, John II, ended in 1364 with the king in captivity and his kingdom dismembered by the Treaty of BRÉTIGNY, which recognized Plantagenet sovereignty in Aquitaine.

Valois fortunes revived under Charles V, who, by his death in 1380, had strengthened royal authority and regained lost territory. However, under Charles VI, a victim of chronic mental illness, the Valois Crown was nearly destroyed by FRENCH CIVIL WAR, the rise of an independent APPANAGE in BURGUNDY, and the military success of HENRY V, who in 1420 had himself recognized as heir to the French throne in the Treaty of TROYES. Although both Henry V and Charles VI died in 1422, leaving only the infant HENRY VI as heir to the two thrones, Charles's disinherited son required the intercession of JOAN OF ARC to finally be crowned as Charles VII in 1429, and decades of political maturation and military and political reform to expel the English for good in 1453. It was Charles's son and grandson, Louis XI and Charles VIII, who finally extended the dynasty's authority into Burgundy and Brittany and bequeathed to their sixteenth-century successors a state in which Valois power was unchallenged.

Further Reading: Famiglietti, Richard. *Royal Intrigue: Crisis at the Court of Charles VI, 1392–1420.* New York: AMS Press, 1986; Fowler, Kenneth. *The Age of Plantagenet and Valois: The Struggle for Supremacy, 1328–1498.* New York: G. P. Putnam's Sons, 1967; Lewis, Peter S. *Later Medieval France: The Polity.* London: Macmillan, 1968.

VERNEUIL, BATTLE OF (1424)

Often known as the "second AGINCOURT," the Battle of Verneuil occurred on 17 August 1424 outside the town of Verneuil on the Norman-Angevin border. Fought between an English army led by JOHN, DUKE OF BEDFORD, regent of France, and a larger Franco-Scottish force commanded by Jean de Harcourt, count of Aumâle, Verneuil was an overwhelming English victory that effectively destroyed the dauphinist field army and virtually eliminated the Scots as a significant military presence for the rest of the war.

Determined to carry the war into dauphinist Maine and Anjou, Bedford, in the early summer of 1424, collected a force of more than ten thousand by combining troops recently arrived from England with men drawn from the garrisons and mobile reserves of NORMANDY and northern France. Leaving ROUEN on 11 August, the duke marched south to Ivry, which was then under siege by William de la POLE, earl of Suffolk. At almost the same time, a force of almost fifteen thousand, comprising a contingent of Scots, the levies of southern France, and mercenaries hired in Italy, marched north from Le Mans with the intention of driving the English from Normandy. When advance elements of these armies made contact near Ivry on 13 August, the leaders of the allied force, which was under the overall command of Aumâle, held a contentious council of war in which the senior French commanders overruled the Scots and resolved to avoid battle. The army would instead concentrate on retaking En-

glish-held towns along the Norman border. This decision led, on 14 August, to the capitulation of Ivry to the English and of Verneuil to the French.

Apprised of the situation by Suffolk, who had been shadowing the allied force, Bedford marched for Verneuil on 16 August. Pressed by the Scots leaders, Archibald DOUGLAS, earl of Douglas, and John STEWART, earl of Buchan, who, according to one French source, were fanatically determined to engage the hated English, the allied leaders reversed their earlier decision and deployed for battle in the plain north of Verneuil on 17 August. Seeing the enemy arrayed for combat, with the French on the allied left and sixty-five hundred Scots on the right, Bedford, who commanded the English right while Thomas MONTAGU, earl of Salisbury, led the left, drew up his nine thousand (garrisons having been left at Ivry and elsewhere) in the traditional English formation with men-at-arms in the center and ARCHERS on the flanks. Except for small detachments of cavalry on the allied flanks and two thousand mounted bowmen held in reserve in the English rear, all the men on the field were dismounted.

The two armies faced each other for some time without any movement, a pause that allowed Douglas to inform Bedford that the Scots neither expected nor would give quarter. A about four o'clock, Bedford sent his men forward. On the English right, the French cavalry swept down on the archers before the latter could set their traditional barrier of sharpened stakes. Although this action exposed it to flank attack, Bedford's division drove forward and engaged the French men-at-arms in their front. The French cavalry drove into the English rear where they were quickly engaged and driven off by Bedford's mobile reserve. Meanwhile, the duke's division, after almost an hour of some of the most intense combat of the war, broke the French line and pursued it toward the town ditch, into which many men, including Aumâle, were driven and drowned. On the allied right, the Italian cavalry flanked Salisbury's line and overran the English baggage park, which they proceeded to plunder until dispersed by the English reserve. That force, having already broken the French cavalry, was now moving to reinforce the English left where Salisbury was hard pressed by the Scots. In a fortunate convergence, Bedford's men reformed after their pursuit of Aumâle's division and pitched into the Scots' rear at about the same time the English reserve hit the Scots' flank. Surrounded and fighting valiantly, the Scots were slaughtered almost to the man.

In a letter written two days later, Bedford put the allied dead at more than seventy-two hundred. Scottish losses were catastrophic, including Douglas, Buchan, and more than fifty men of rank. While the loss of nearly a thousand was costly for the English, who suffered chronic manpower shortages, Verneuil rewarded the sacrifice by leaving dauphinist France open to attack. *See also* SCOTLAND.

Further Reading: Burne, Alfred H. *The Agincourt War.* Ware, England: Wordsworth Editions Ltd., 1999; Williams, E. Carleton. *My Lord of Bedford, 1389–1435.* London: Longmans, 1963.

VIGNOLLES, ÉTIENNE DE (c. 1390–1443)

Known as "La Hire" (Anger) for his fierce temper, Étienne de Vignolles was a military companion of JOAN OF ARC and one of the most able French captains of the fifteenth century. Although a mercenary leader whose raids were often launched on his own account, his most constant allegiance was to CHARLES VII and his daring exploits and association with Joan made him a French national hero, whose likeness still survives as the jack in a traditional French deck of playing cards.

Born in GASCONY, La Hire began his military career under BERNARD, COUNT OF ARMAGNAC, leader of the ARMAGNAC faction during the FRENCH CIVIL WAR. In about 1418, La Hire and his frequent companion, Poton de XAINTRAILLES, entered the service of the dauphin, for whom they seized the castle of Coucy. The two then campaigned in Lorraine, where they fought for a time in the pay of the cardinal of Bar. La Hire fought

again for the dauphin at BAUGÉ in 1421 and at VERNEUIL in 1424, and then joined the remaining dauphinist garrisons in Champagne, where he was captured by the English when they overran the county after Verneuil. Free by the summer of 1427, La Hire joined John, Bastard of Orléans (*see* JOHN, COUNT OF DUNOIS AND LONGUEVILLE), in the successful relief of MONTARGIS. In 1428, he briefly seized Le Mans, and by the end of the year had joined his band of mercenaries with the besieged garrison of ORLÉANS, from which he and the Bastard led a series of unsuccessful sorties against the English. In February 1429, La Hire and Xaintrailles supported the French retreat from the Battle of the HERRINGS; in late April, La Hire rode to Blois with the Bastard to join the army of Joan of Arc.

According to the *Journal of the Siege of Orléans*, La Hire, a rough and experienced soldier, became a loyal supporter of the Maid, accepting her military advice and even refraining from swearing in her presence. He played a leading role in the relief of Orléans in May and in the subsequent campaign to clear the Loire of English garrisons, being leader of the dauphinist van at the campaign's culminating victory at PATAY on 18 June. He took part in the Maid's abortive attack on PARIS in September and, using Joan's tactics of frontal assault, captured Chateau-Gaillard in 1430. However, by Joan's death in May 1431, the English had retaken the fortress and captured La Hire.

Ransomed by Charles VII, who had named him bailiff of Vermandois in 1429, La Hire resumed his military career. In 1435, La Hire and Xantrailles led a raid into BURGUNDY that temporarily disrupted the peace conference at ARRAS. In January 1436, the two captains invaded NORMANDY, reaching the gates of ROUEN, which they hoped would be opened to them by sympathizers within the walls. When this failed to occur, they withdrew to Ry, where they were defeated in a sharp skirmish by John TALBOT. Thereafter, La Hire participated in the capture of PONTOISE in 1440, undertook an unsuccessful relief of HARFLEUR in 1441, and assisted

CHARLES, DUKE OF ORLÉANS, at the siege of La Réole in 1442. La Hire died at Montauban in 1443 of a fever contracted at La Réole. *See also* LOIRE CAMPAIGN; RANSOM.

Further Reading: DeVries, Kelly. *Joan of Arc: A Military Leader*. Stroud, England: Sutton Publishing, 2003; Pernoud, Régine, and Marie-Véronique Clin. *Joan of Arc*. Trans. Jeremy Duquesnay Adams. New York: St. Martin's Press, 1999.

THE VOW OF THE HERON. *See* ROBERT OF ARTOIS

W

WALES, PRINCE OF. *See* EDWARD, THE BLACK PRINCE; EDWARD I; EDWARD II; EDWARD III; HENRY V

WAR OF THE TWO JOANS. *See* BRETON CIVIL WAR

WARWICK, EARL OF. *See* BEAUCHAMP, RICHARD, EARL OF WARWICK; BEAUCHAMP, THOMAS, EARL OF WARWICK

WEAPONRY. *See* ARMOR AND NONMISSILE WEAPONRY

WHITE COMPANY. *See* ROUTIERS

WINCHELSEA, BATTLE OF (1350)

Fought on 29 August 1350 in the English Channel within sight of the English port of Winchelsea, the naval battle of Winchelsea (also known as Les-Espagnols-sur-Mer) was a result of EDWARD III's attempt to clear the Channel of Castilian raiders. Although the bloody encounter was an English victory, the Castilian fleet remained in existence, and the threat to English shipping and cross-Channel communications was not eliminated.

Despite being included as French allies in the June 1350 extension of the Truce of CALAIS, the seamen of Castile felt no obligation to honor an undertaking of PHILIP VI of France. Accordingly, a Castilian fleet of about forty vessels, operating out of Sluys and other Flemish bases and carrying a large contingent of Flemish adventurers, launched attacks on English shipping throughout the summer of 1350. To end this threat to his vital lines of communication and supply, Edward

assembled a fleet of almost fifty vessels at Sandwich. With the king commanding from his cog *Thomas*, the English fleet set sail on 28 August. Among those commanding squadrons were the king's eldest son, EDWARD, THE BLACK PRINCE; HENRY OF GROSMONT, duke of Lancaster; and Thomas BEAUCHAMP, earl of Warwick. JOHN OF GAUNT, Edward's ten-year-old third son, was with his father, while John CHANDOS accompanied Prince Edward.

On the evening of 29 August, the English fleet intercepted a southbound Castilian squadron of about twenty-four vessels off Dungeness. Although the English had the advantage of numbers, the Castilian vessels were larger, stronger, and higher, allowing their crews to sweep the crowded English decks with crossbow bolts and catapult missiles. Lacking ARTILLERY, the only way to engage an enemy at sea was to grapple his vessel with hooks and chains and send boarding parties of men-at-arms to fight an approximation of a land battle on the ship's decks. This the English did, taking heavy casualties until they were close enough to board, when the advantage turned to them. By nightfall, at least seventeen Castilian vessels had been taken, with most of their crews slain and thrown into the sea—few onboard being deemed worthy of capture and RANSOM. English losses in both ships and men were high. With the prince's ship sunk and the *Thomas* severely damaged, both the king and his son were forced to transfer their flags to captured vessels.

Although Winchelsea was an impressive naval victory, many Castilian ships either escaped or avoided the battle and continued, in concert with French vessels, to prey upon

English shipping. The Castilians might have been reduced in numbers, but their mere presence in the Channel disrupted trade and, by the end of the year, forced the English to organize a convoy system, which was costly in men, money, and time, to protect merchant fleets crossing the Channel. *See also* NAVAL WARFARE.

Further Reading: Burne, Alfred H. *The Crécy War*. Ware, England: Wordsworth Editions Ltd., 1999; Sumption, Jonathan. *The Hundred Years War.*

Vol. 2, *Trial by Fire*. Philadelphia: University of Pennsylvania Press, 2001.

WINCHESTER, BISHOP OF. *See* BEAUFORT, HENRY, CARDINAL-BISHOP OF WINCHESTER

WINDSOR, TREATY OF. *See* LONDON, FIRST TREATY OF

WONDERFUL PARLIAMENT. *See* RICHARD II

X

XAINTRAILLES, POTON DE (1400–1461)

Like his frequent associate Étienne de VIG-NOLLES, Poton de Xaintrailles (or Saintrailles) was a famous mercenary captain who supported the dauphinist cause and fought alongside JOAN OF ARC. Although for much of his career a leader of the *écorcheur* bands that pillaged northern France, Xaintrailles rose eventually in royal service to become Viscount Bruillois and marshal of France.

In 1418, Xaintrailles and Vignoles, known as "La Hire," seized the castle of Courcy for Dauphin Charles (*see* CHARLES VII), but in 1421 both men were captured by the Burgundians at Mons-en-Vimeau and put to RANSOM. In 1424, Xaintrailles was in the Low Countries in the service of PHILIP THE GOOD, duke of BURGUNDY. By 1429, he was back in the dauphinist camp, having joined La Hire and other captains at the siege of ORLÉANS. He participated in the Battle of the HERRINGS in February, in Joan of Arc's relief of Orléans in May, and in the Maid's LOIRE CAMPAIGN in June, during which he and La Hire led the French van at the Battle of PATAY. On 11 August 1431, during an unsuccessful dauphinist attempt to ambush JOHN, DUKE OF BEDFORD, Richard BEAUCHAMP, earl of Warwick, captured Xaintrailles at the Battle of the Shepherd, which was so named because the English also captured there a French shepherd boy who claimed to be a divinely ordained successor to Joan of Arc. Carried to ROUEN, Xaintrailles received treatment very different from that recently accorded the Maid; the captive took his meals with Warwick and was even presented to HENRY VI when the boy-king passed through on his way to his French coronation in PARIS.

Exchanged for John TALBOT, a French captive since Patay, Xaintrailles, although receiving a royal appointment as bailiff of Bourges, resumed his mercenary career, joining La Hire on a raid into Burgundy that disrupted the peace conference at ARRAS in 1435 and helping suppress a peasant revolt in NORMANDY in 1436. On his raids, Xaintrailles acquired so much wealth in booty and ransoms that the king cited him by name when he ordered the *ROUTIER* bands of Normandy to cease their attacks. In 1444, Xaintrailles accompanied Dauphin Louis (the future Louis XI) on his campaign against the Swiss, but used the expedition as a further opportunity to pillage on his own account. However, following conclusion of the Truce of TOURS in 1444, Xaintrailles recommitted himself to royal service and became a leader of the new standing army created by the king during the cessation of hostilities (*see* CHARLES VII, MILITARY REFORMS OF). Becoming royal master of horse, Xaintrailles played an active role in the reconquest of Normandy and was allowed to carry the ceremonial sword *Joyeuse* before the king on his triumphal entry into Rouen in November 1449. He was named governor of Falaise in 1450 and took part in the reconquest of GASCONY in 1452–53. Appointed marshal of France in 1454, Xaintrailles became governor of Guienne (the former English AQUITAINE) in 1458. Xaintrailles died in BORDEAUX on 7 October 1461.

Further Reading: DeVries, Kelly. *Joan of Arc: A Military Leader.* Stroud, England: Sutton Publishing, 2003; Pernoud, Régine, and Marie-Véronique Clin. *Joan of Arc.* Trans. Jeremy Duquesnay Adams. New York: St. Martin's Press, 1999.

YORK, DUKE OF. *See* EDMUND OF LANGLEY, DUKE OF YORK; RICHARD, DUKE OF YORK

Appendix 1: Genealogies

Dukes of Brittany

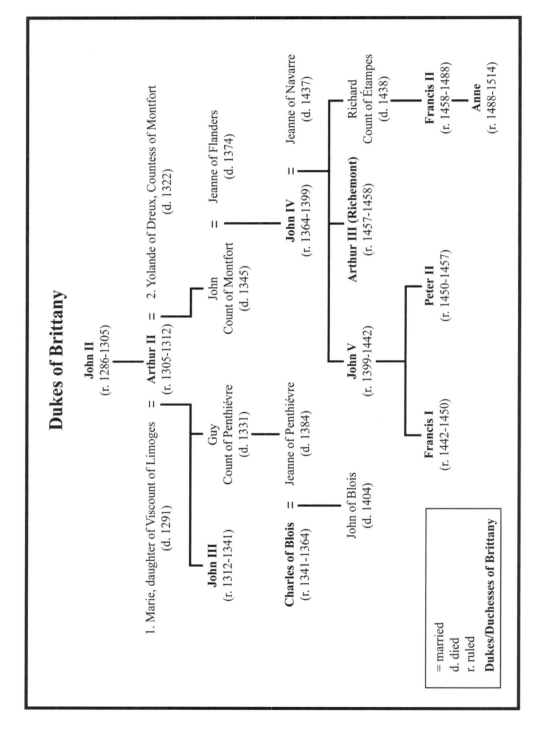

John II
(r. 1286-1305)

Arthur II = 2. Yolande of Dreux, Countess of Montfort
(r. 1305-1312)   (d. 1322)

1. Marie, daughter of Viscount of Limoges
(d. 1291)

John
Count of Montfort
(d. 1345)

Jeanne of Flanders
(d. 1374)

John IV = Jeanne of Navarre
(r. 1364-1399)   (d. 1437)

Richard
Count of Étampes
(d. 1438)

Arthur III (Richemont)
(r. 1457-1458)

Francis II
(r. 1458-1488)

Anne
(r. 1488-1514)

John III
(r. 1312-1341)

Guy
Count of Penthiévre
(d. 1331)

Jeanne of Penthiévre
(d. 1384)

Charles of Blois =
(r. 1341-1364)

John of Blois
(d. 1404)

John V
(r. 1399-1442)

Peter II
(r. 1450-1457)

Francis I
(r. 1442-1450)

= married
d. died
r. ruled
Dukes/Duchesses of Brittany

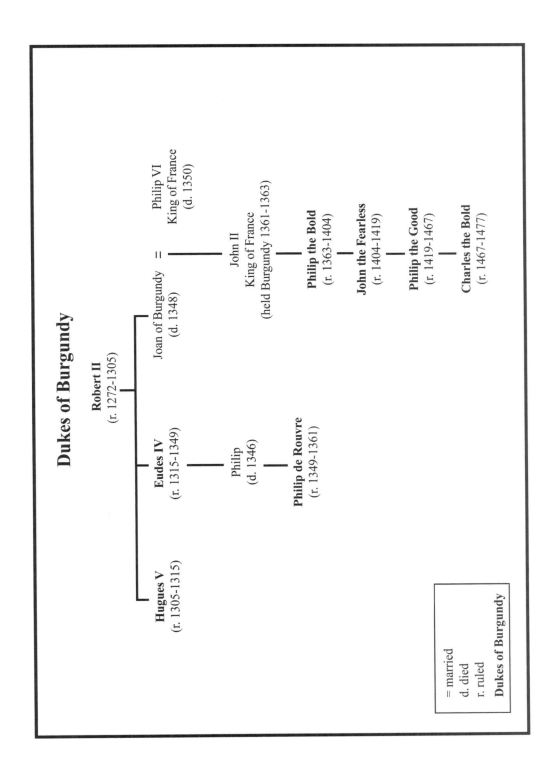

Dukes of Burgundy

Robert II
(r. 1272–1305)

Hugues V
(r. 1305–1315)

Eudes IV
(r. 1315–1349)

Joan of Burgundy
(d. 1348)
=
Philip VI
King of France
(d. 1350)

Philip
(d. 1346)

Philip de Rouvre
(r. 1349–1361)

John II
King of France
(held Burgundy 1361–1363)

Philip the Bold
(r. 1363–1404)

John the Fearless
(r. 1404–1419)

Philip the Good
(r. 1419–1467)

Charles the Bold
(r. 1467–1477)

= married
d. died
r. ruled
Dukes of Burgundy

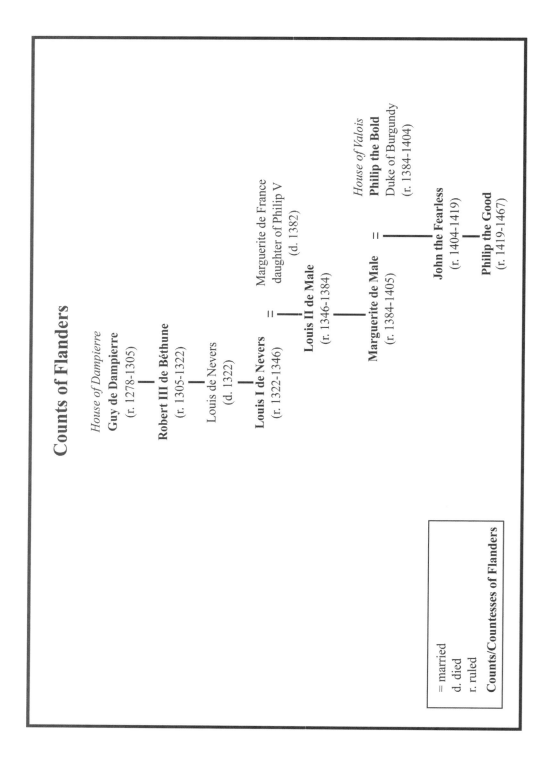

Counts of Flanders

House of Dampierre
Guy de Dampierre
(r. 1278-1305)

Robert III de Béthune
(r. 1305-1322)

Louis de Nevers
(d. 1322)

Louis I de Nevers
(r. 1322-1346)

Louis II de Male = Marguerite de France
(r. 1346-1384)   daughter of Philip V
                  (d. 1382)

Marguerite de Male = *House of Valois*
(r. 1384-1405)   **Philip the Bold**
                     Duke of Burgundy
                     (r. 1384-1404)

John the Fearless
(r. 1404-1419)

Philip the Good
(r. 1419-1467)

= married
d. died
r. ruled
Counts/Countesses of Flanders

316

French Royal Succession in the Early Fourteenth Century

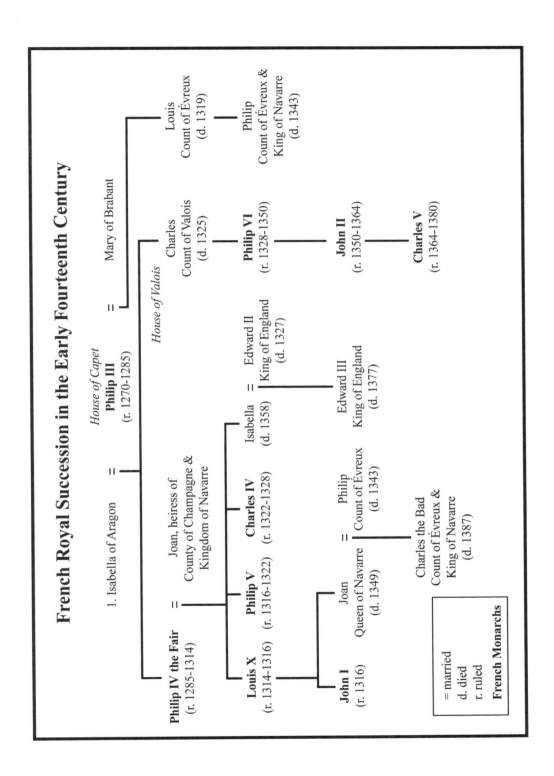

House of Lancaster and Beaufort Family

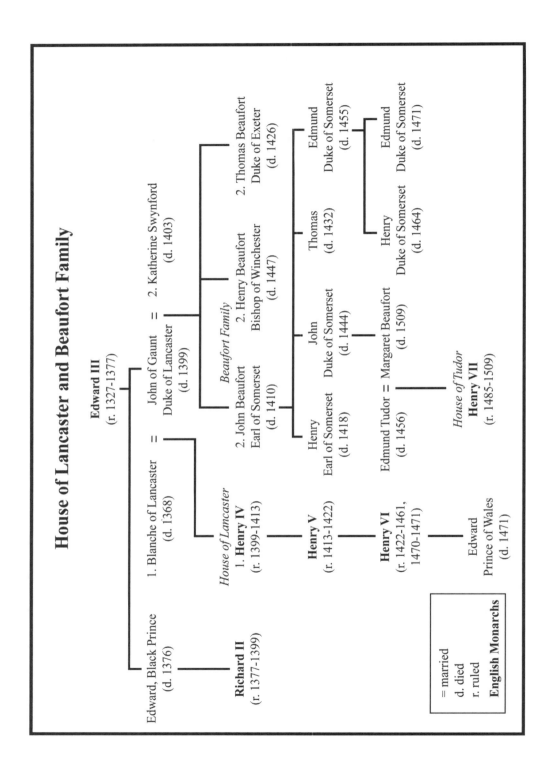

Edward III (r. 1327-1377)

Edward, Black Prince (d. 1376)

John of Gaunt Duke of Lancaster (d. 1399) = 1. Blanche of Lancaster (d. 1368)

John of Gaunt Duke of Lancaster (d. 1399) = 2. Katherine Swynford (d. 1403)

House of Lancaster

Richard II (r. 1377-1399)

1. **Henry IV** (r. 1399-1413)

Henry V (r. 1413-1422)

Henry VI (r. 1422-1461, 1470-1471)

Edward Prince of Wales (d. 1471)

Beaufort Family

2. John Beaufort Earl of Somerset (d. 1410)

2. Henry Beaufort Bishop of Winchester (d. 1447)

2. Thomas Beaufort Duke of Exeter (d. 1426)

Henry Earl of Somerset (d. 1418)

John Duke of Somerset (d. 1444)

Thomas (d. 1432)

Edmund Duke of Somerset (d. 1455)

Edmund Tudor (d. 1456) = Margaret Beaufort (d. 1509)

Henry Duke of Somerset (d. 1464)

Edmund Duke of Somerset (d. 1471)

House of Tudor
Henry VII (r. 1485-1509)

= married
d. died
r. ruled
English Monarchs

House of Plantagenet

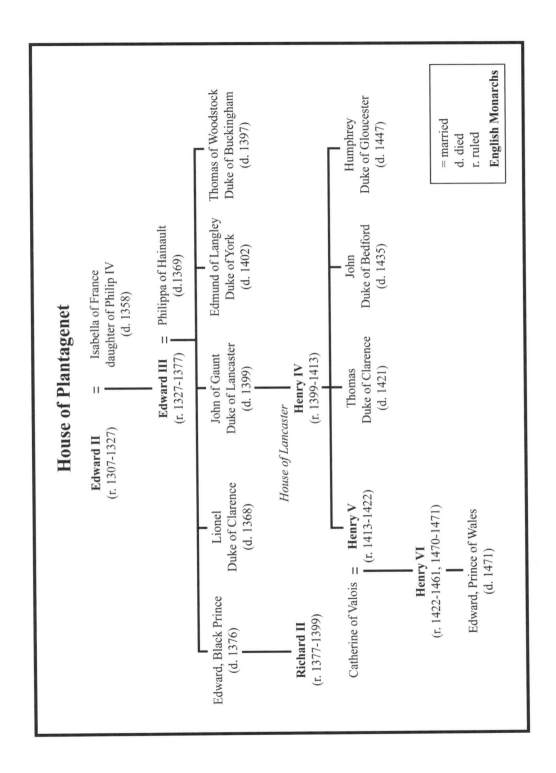

Edward II
(r. 1307-1327)

=

Isabella of France
daughter of Philip IV
(d. 1358)

Edward III
(r. 1327-1377)

=

Philippa of Hainault
(d.1369)

Edward, Black Prince
(d. 1376)

Lionel
Duke of Clarence
(d. 1368)

John of Gaunt
Duke of Lancaster
(d. 1399)

Edmund of Langley
Duke of York
(d. 1402)

Thomas of Woodstock
Duke of Buckingham
(d. 1397)

Richard II
(r. 1377-1399)

House of Lancaster

Henry IV
(r. 1399-1413)

Thomas
Duke of Clarence
(d. 1421)

John
Duke of Bedford
(d. 1435)

Humphrey
Duke of Gloucester
(d. 1447)

Catherine of Valois

=

Henry V
(r. 1413-1422)

Henry VI
(r. 1422-1461, 1470-1471)

Edward, Prince of Wales
(d. 1471)

= married
d. died
r. ruled
English Monarchs

319

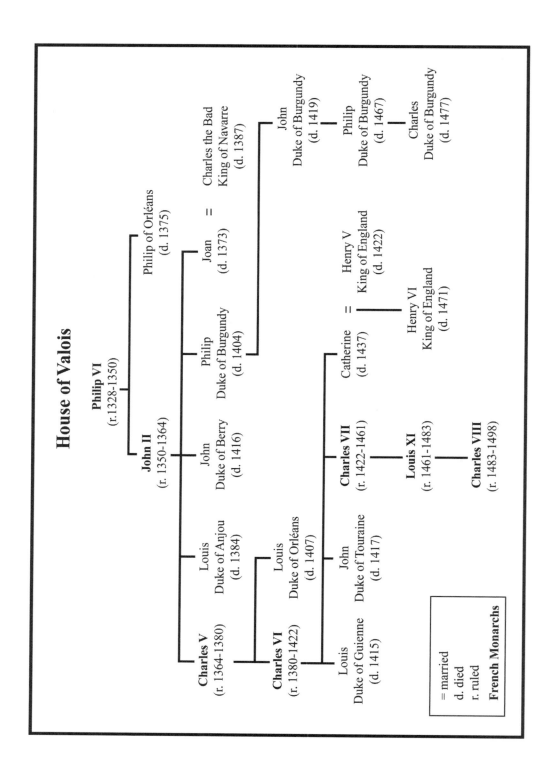

House of Valois

Philip VI
(r. 1328–1350)

Philip of Orléans
(d. 1375)

John II
(r. 1350–1364)

John
Duke of Berry
(d. 1416)

Philip
Duke of Burgundy
(d. 1404)

Joan = Charles the Bad
(d. 1373)   King of Navarre
(d. 1387)

John
Duke of Burgundy
(d. 1419)

Philip
Duke of Burgundy
(d. 1467)

Charles
Duke of Burgundy
(d. 1477)

Louis
Duke of Anjou
(d. 1384)

Louis
Duke of Orléans
(d. 1407)

John
Duke of Touraine
(d. 1417)

Louis
Duke of Guienne
(d. 1415)

Charles V
(r. 1364–1380)

Charles VI
(r. 1380–1422)

Charles VII
(r. 1422–1461)

Catherine = Henry V
(d. 1437)   King of England
(d. 1422)

Henry VI
King of England
(d. 1471)

Louis XI
(r. 1461–1483)

Charles VIII
(r. 1483–1498)

= married
d. died
r. ruled
French Monarchs

320

Appendix 2: Chronological Listing of Major Battles, Sieges, and Campaigns

Although the various phases of the Hundred Years War encompassed innumerable battles, sieges, sacks, skirmishes, assaults, ambushes, combats, and campaigns, only the largest, most important, or best known of these military actions are listed below. Naval battles and encounters occurring outside France or a French fief are so noted.

Action	Date
Halidon Hill, Battle of (Scotland)	19 July 1333
Thiérache Campaign	20 September–24 October 1339
Sluys, Battle of (naval)	24 June 1340
Tournai, Siege of	18 July–25 September 1340
Saint-Omer, Battle of	26 July 1340
Morlaix, Battle of	30 September 1342
Bergerac, Capture of	late August 1345
Auberoche, Battle of	21 October 1345
Aiguillon, Siege of	1 April–20 August 1346
Crécy, Battle of	26 August 1346
Neville's Cross, Battle of (Scotland)	17 October 1346
Calais, Siege of	4 September 1346–3 August 1347
La Roche-Derrien, Battle of	20 June 1347
Winchelsea, Battle of (naval)[1]	29 August 1350
Combat (Battle) of the Thirty	26 March 1351
Saintes, Battle of	1 April 1351
Mauron, Battle of	14 August 1352
Chevauchée of 1355	5 October–9 December 1355
Poitiers, Battle of	19 September 1356
Nogent-sur-Seine, Battle of	23 June 1359
Rheims Campaign	4 November 1359–10 May 1360
Brignais, Battle of	6 April 1362
Cocherel, Battle of	16 May 1364
Auray, Battle of	29 September 1364
Nájera, Battle of (Castile)[2]	3 April 1367
Limoges, Sack of	19 September 1370
La Rochelle, Battle of (naval)	23 June 1372
Chevauchée of 1373	August 1373–January 1374
Cadzand, Battle of (naval)[3]	24 March 1387
Harfleur, Siege of	18 August–22 September 1415
Agincourt, Battle of	25 October 1415
Valmont, Battle of	March 1416
Seine, Battle of the (naval)	15 August 1416

Norman Campaign (English)[4]	1 August 1417–19 January 1419
Rouen, Siege of[5]	29 July 1418–19 January 1419
Fresnay, Battle of	3 March 1420
Melun, Siege of	9 July–18 November 1420
Baugé, Battle of	22 March 1421
Meaux, Siege of	6 October 1421–2 May 1422
Cravant, Battle of	31 July 1423
Verneuil, Battle of	17 August 1424
Montargis, Siege of	15 July–5 September 1427
Orléans, Siege of	12 October 1428–8 May 1429
Herrings, Battle of the[6]	12 February 1429
Loire Campaign[7]	10–18 June 1429
Patay, Battle of[8]	18 June 1429
Pontoise, Siege of	6 June–19 September 1441
Fougères, Sack of	24 March 1449
Norman Campaign (French)[9]	12 August 1449–12 August 1450
Formigny, Battle of	15 April 1450
Castillon, Battle of	17 July 1453

1. Also known as the Battle of Les-Espagnols-sur-Mer.
2. Also known as the Battle of Navarrette.
3. Also known as the Battle of Margate.
4. The campaign effectively ended with the fall of Rouen on 19 January 1419, although a few Norman castles held out for several months more.
5. The capitulation of Rouen effectively ended Henry V's Norman Campaign.
6. Also known as the Battle of Rouvray.
7. Concludes with the Battle of Patay on 18 June 1429.
8. Battle is final action of the French Loire Campaign.
9. Concludes with the fall of Cherbourg on 12 August 1450.

Appendix 3: European Monarchs and Rulers, 1250s–1450s

Below are listings of the rulers of the most important kingdoms and states of Western Europe in the fourteenth and fifteenth centuries, including Aragon, Burgundy, Castile, England, Flanders, France, the Holy Roman Empire, Navarre, Portugal, and Scotland.

ARAGON

HOUSE OF CATALONIA
Jaime I (1213–76)
Pedro III (1276–85)
Alfonso III (1285–91)
Jaime II (1219–1327)
Alfonso IV (1327–36)
Pedro IV (1336–87)
Juan I (1387–95)
Martin the Humane (1395–1410)

HOUSE OF TRASTÁMARE
Fernando I (1412–16)
Alfonso V (1416–58)

BURGUNDY

CAPETIAN LINE OF DUKES
Hugues IV (1218–72)
Robert II (1272–1305)
Hugues V (1305–15)
Eudes IV (1315–49)
Philip de Rouvre (1349–61)

VALOIS LINE OF DUKES[1]
Philip the Bold (1363–1404)
John the Fearless (1404–19)
Philip the Good (1419–67)

CASTILE

HOUSE OF BURGUNDY
Alfonso X (1252–84)
Sancho IV 1284–95
Fernando IV (1295–1312)
Alfonso XI (1312–50)
Pedro the Cruel (1350–69)

HOUSE OF TRASTÁMARE
Henry II (1369–79)
John I (1379–90)
Henry III (1390–1406)
John II (1406–54)

ENGLAND

HOUSE OF PLANTAGENET
Henry III (1216–72)
Edward I (1272–1307)
Edward II (1307–27)
Edward III (1327–77)
Richard II (1377–99)

HOUSE OF LANCASTER
Henry IV (1399–1413)
Henry V (1413–22)
Henry VI (1422–61, 1470–71)[1]

---

1. When Duke Philip de Rouvre died childless in 1361, the duchy reverted to the French Crown; John II established the Valois line of dukes by granting Burgundy to his youngest son Philip in 1363.

---

1. During the English Wars of the Roses, Henry VI was deposed by his Yorkist cousin, Edward IV, in 1461, briefly restored to the throne in 1470, and then deposed again (and eventually murdered) in 1471.

FLANDERS
DAMPIERRE LINE OF COUNTS
Guy de Dampierre (1278–1305)
Robert III de Béthune (1305–22)
Louis I de Nevers (1322–46)
Louis II de Mâle (1346–84)

VALOIS LINE OF COUNTS[1]
Philip the Bold (1384–1404)
John the Fearless (1404–19)
Philip the Good (1419–67)

---

1. Louis de Mâle was succeeded by his son-in-law, Philip the Bold, duke of Burgundy; Flanders was thereafter ruled by the Burgundian dukes.

FRANCE
HOUSE OF CAPET
Louis IX (St. Louis) (1226–70)
Philip III the Bold (1270–85)
Philip IV the Fair (1285–1314)
Louis X the Quarrelsome (1314–16)
John I (1316)
Philip V the Tall (1316–22)
Charles IV the Fair (1322–28)

HOUSE OF VALOIS
Philip VI (1328–50)
John II the Good (1350–64)
Charles V the Wise (1364–80)
Charles VI (1380–1422)
Charles VII (1422–61)

HOLY ROMAN EMPIRE (GERMANY)
HOUSE OF HABSBURG
Rudolf I (1273–91)

HOUSE OF NASSAU
Adolf (1292–98)

HOUSE OF HABSBURG
Albert I (1298–1308)

HOUSE OF LUXEMBOURG
Henry VII (1309–13)

HOUSE OF WITTELSBACH
Louis IV (1314–47)

HOUSE OF LUXEMBOURG
Charles IV (1347–78)
Wenceslaus (1378–1400)

HOUSE OF WITTELSBACH
Ruprech III (1400–10)

HOUSE OF LUXEMBOURG
Sigismund (1410–37)

HOUSE OF HABSBURG
Albert II (1438–39)
Frederick III (1440–93)

NAVARRE
HOUSE OF CHAMPAGNE
Thibault II (1253–70)
Henry I (1270–74)
Jeanne I (1274–1305) and Philip II [Philip IV of France] (1285–1314)[1]

HOUSE OF CAPET
Louis I [Louis X of France] (1314–16)
Philip II [Philip V of France] (1316–22)
Charles I [Charles IV of France] (1322–28)
Jeanne II (1328–49) and Philip III of Everux (1328–42)[2]

HOUSE OF EVREUX
Charles II the Bad (1349–87)
Charles III (1387–1425)
Blanca (1425–41) and John I of Trastámare [John II of Aragon] (1425–79)[3]

---

1. Jeanne I, the daughter of Henry I married Philip IV the Fair of France, who then ruled Navarre in right of his wife.
2. Jeanne II, daughter of Louis X of France, inherited Navarre on the death of her last Capetian uncle Charles IV in 1328; Jeanne thereafter ruled Navarre with her husband Philip of Evreux.[1]

PORTUGAL
HOUSE OF BURGUNDY
Afonso III (1248–79)
Dinis (1279–1325)
Afonso IV (1325–57)
Pedro (1357–67)
Fernando (1367–83)

HOUSE OF AVIS
João I (1385–1433)
Duarte (1433–38)
Afonso V (1438–81)

SCOTLAND

HOUSE OF DUNKELD
Alexander III (1249–86)
Margaret (1286–90)

INTERREGNUM (1290–92)

HOUSE OF BALLIOL
John (1292–96)

INTERREGNUM (1296–1306)

HOUSE OF BRUCE
Robert I (1306–29)
David II (1329–71)

HOUSE OF STEWART (STUART)
Robert II (1371–90)
Robert III (1390–1406)
James I (1406–37)
James II (1437–60)

Appendix 4: Popes, 1294–1455

Below is a listing of all popes and anti-popes who reigned between 1294 and 1455. An * denotes French pope, while a # denotes those now regarded as anti-popes.

ROMAN POPES
Boniface VIII (1294–1303)
Benedict XI (1303–4)

AVIGNON POPES
*Clement V (1305–14)
*John XXII (1316–34)
#Nicholas V (1328–30)[1]
*Benedict XII (1334–42)
*Clement VI (1342–52)
*Innocent VI (1352–62)
*Urban V (1362–70)
*Gregory XI (1370–78)

GREAT SCHISM

ROMAN LINE	*AVIGNON LINE*	*PISA LINE*
Urban VI (1378–89)	Clement VII (1378–94)	
Boniface IX (1389–1404)	Benedict XIII (1394–1417)[2]	Alexander V (1409–10)
Innocent VII (1404–6)	Clement VIII (1423–29)[3]	John XXIII (1410–15)[4]
Gregory XII (1406–15)[5]		

ROMAN POPES
Martin V (1417–31)
Eugenius IV (1431–47)
#Felix V (1439–49)[6]
Nicholas V (1447–55)

---

1. Crowned by Emperor Louis IV, who quarreled with John XXII and declared him deposed, Nicholas V was an Italian cleric whose authority was not recognized outside parts of Italy.
2. Deposed by the Council of Constance in 1415
3. Voluntarily abdicated in favor of Martin V in July 1429.
4. Deposed by the Council of Pisa in 1409 and the Council of Constance in 1415 and formally submitted to Martin V in 1419.
5. Deposed by the Council of Pisa in 1409, but formally resigned to the Council of Constance in July 1415.
6. Selected as pope by the Council of Basle in an irregular election, Felix V, the former Duke Amadeus VIII of Savoy, was never recognized beyond his own duchy and a few small Italian states; he abdicated in favor of Nicholas V in April 1449.

Appendix 5: Holders of Selected English, French, and Continental Titles of Nobility during the Hundred Years War

Listed below are the individuals who held the chief titles of nobility under the English and French Crowns, as well as among the principalities of the Low Countries, during the Hundred Years War. Although these men were the chief military and political figures in their respective realms, it is often difficult to know which particular member of a noble family is being discussed since they are usually referred to only by their titles. Note the frequent intermarriage between royal and noble families and the resulting consolidation of territories within families, particularly the accumulation of provinces in the Low Countries by the Valois dukes of Burgundy. Note also how many noblemen were slain or captured during major battles of the war.

ENGLISH NOBILITY

Bedford, Dukes of
John (1414–35), son of Henry IV; brother of Henry V
  title lapsed on duke's death

Clarence, Dukes of
Lionel (1362–68), son of Edward III; uncle of Richard II
  title lapsed on duke's death
Thomas (1412–21), son of Henry IV; brother of Henry V
  title lapsed on duke's death at Battle of Baugé

Exeter, Dukes of
John Holland (1397–1400)
  title forfeited upon duke's execution for treason by Henry IV
Thomas Beaufort (1416–26), half-brother of Henry IV
  title lapsed on duke's death
John Holland (1444–47)
  son of first Holland duke of Exeter; restored to father's title
Henry Holland (1447–75)
  succeeded father; title lapsed on duke's death

Gloucester, Dukes of
Thomas of Woodstock (1385–97), son of Edward III; uncle of Richard II
  title lapsed on duke's death; likely murdered by orders of Richard II
Humphrey (1414–47), son of Henry IV; brother of Henry V
  title lapsed on duke's death

Lancaster, Dukes of
Henry of Grosmont (1351–61), cousin of Edward III
  title lapsed on duke's death
John of Gaunt (1362–99), son of Edward III; uncle of Richard II
  granted father-in-law's title
Henry of Bolingbrook (1399), son of John of Gaunt, duke of Lancaster
  succeeded father; became king as Henry IV, 1399
Henry of Monmouth (1399–1413), son of Henry IV
  succeeded father; became king as Henry V and title merged with Crown, 1413

March, Earls of
Roger Mortimer (1328–30)
  title forfeited upon earl's execution for treason by Edward III

Roger Mortimer (1348–60)
  restored to grandfather's title
Edmund Mortimer (1360–81)
  succeeded father
Roger Mortimer (1381–98)
  succeeded father; named heir
  presumptive to Richard II
Edmund Mortimer (1398–1425)
  succeeded father; briefly heir
  presumptive to Richard II
Richard, duke of York (1425–60)
  succeeded uncle

Northampton, Earls of
William de Bohun (1337–60)
Humphrey de Bohun (1360–73)
  succeeded father; title lapsed on earl's
  death
Henry of Bolingbroke (1384–99), son of John
  of Gaunt, duke of Lancaster
    granted father-in-law's title; became
    king as Henry IV, 1399
Anne (1399–1438), daughter of Thomas
  of Woodstock, duke of Gloucester
    succeeded as countess through her
    mother, Eleanor de Bohun; title
    lapsed on countess's death

Princes of Wales
Edward (1301–7), son of Edward I
  became king as Edward II, 1307
Edward, the Black Prince (1330–76), son
  of Edward III; father of Richard II
    predeceased father, 1376
Richard of Bordeaux (1376–77), son of
  Edward, the Black Prince
    became king as Richard II, 1377
Henry of Monmouth (1399–1413), son
  of Henry IV
    became king as Henry V, 1413
Edward of Lancaster (1453–71), son
  of Henry VI
    predeceased father, 1471

Salisbury, Earls of
William Montagu (1337–44)
William Montagu (1344–97)
  succeeded father

John Montagu (1397–1400)
  succeeded uncle; title forfeited on earl's
  execution for treason by Henry IV,
  1400
Thomas Montagu (1421–28)
  restored to father's title
Richard Neville (1428–60)
  granted father-in-law's title by right
  of his wife, 1428

Shrewsbury, Earls of
John Talbot (1442–53)
  slain at Battle of Castillon, 1453
John Talbot (1453–60)
  succeeded father

Somerset, Dukes/Earls of
John Beaufort (1397–1409), half brother
  of Henry IV
    created earl of Somerset
Henry Beaufort (1409–19)
  succeeded father as earl of
  Somerset
John Beaufort (1419–44)
  succeeded brother as earl; created
  duke, 1443
Edmund Beaufort (1444–55)
  succeeded brother as earl; created
  duke, 1448

Suffolk, Dukes/Earls of
Robert de Ufford (1337–69)
  created earl of Suffolk
William de Ufford (1369–82)
  succeeded father as earl; title lapsed
  on earl's death
Michael de la Pole (1385–88)
  stripped of title by Lords Appellant,
  1388; died in exile, 1389
Michael de la Pole (1399–1415)
  restored to father's earldom by Henry IV;
  died at siege of Harfleur
Michael de la Pole (1415)
  succeeded father as earl; slain at Battle of
  Agincourt
William de la Pole (1415–50)
  succeeded brother as earl, 1415; created
  marquis, 1444; created duke, 1448;
    stripped of dukedom and banished,
    1450

Warwick, Earls of
Thomas Beauchamp (1315–69)
Thomas Beauchamp (1369–1401)
    succeeded father; stripped of title by
        Richard II, 1397–99; restored by
        Henry IV, 1399
Richard Beauchamp (1401–39)
    succeeded father
Henry Beauchamp (1439–45)
    succeeded father; created duke, 1444;
        title of duke lapsed on duke's death

York, Dukes of
Edmund of Langley (1384–1402), son
    of Edward III; uncle of Richard II
Edward (1402–15)
    slain at Battle of Agincourt; title forfeited
        through treason of duke's brother,
        Richard, earl of Cambridge, 1415
Richard (1425–60), son of Richard, earl
    of Cambridge
        restored to uncle's title

FRENCH AND CONTINENTAL NOBILITY
Albret, Lords of
Bernard-Aiz (1324–59)
Arnaud-Amanieu (1359–1401)
    succeeded father
Charles (1401–15)
    succeeded father; slain at Battle
        of Agincourt, 1415
Charles (1415–71)
    succeeded father

Alençon, Dukes/Counts of
Charles (1325–46), brother of Philip VI
    succeeded father as count; slain at Battle
        of Crécy
Charles (1346–61)
    succeeded father
Peter (1361–91)
    succeeded brother, who resigned county
        to enter Church, 1361
John (1391–1415)
    succeeded father as count; created
        duke, 1414; slain at Battle of
        Agincourt

John (1415–74)
    succeeded father as duke; captured at
        Battle of Verneuil, 1424; fought with
        Joan of Arc at Orléans, 1429;
        stripped of title by Charles VII,
        1474

Anjou, Dukes/Counts of
John (1332–50), son of Philip VI
    title lapsed at count's accession as
        John II
Louis (1356–84), son of John II
    created count, 1356; created duke, 1360
Louis (1384–1417)
    succeeded father as duke
Louis (1417–34)
    succeeded father
Réne (1434–80)
    succeeded brother

Armagnac, Counts of
John (1319–73)
    launched "Appeal of the Gascon Lords,"
        1368
John (1373–84)
    succeeded father
John (1384–91)
    succeeded father
Bernard (1391–1418)
    succeeded brother; leader of Armagnac
        faction during French civil war; slain by
        Burgundian mob in Paris
John (1418–50)
    succeeded father

Artois, Counts of
Jeanne, countess of Burgundy (1330–47)
    succeeded mother as countess
Eudes, duke of Burgundy (1330–47)
    ruled county by right of wife, Jeanne
Philip de Rouvre, duke of Burgundy
    (1347–61)
        succeeded grandmother
Margaret of France (1361–82)
    succeeded sister's grandson
Louis de Male, count of Flanders (1382–84)
    succeeded mother
Marguerite de Flanders (1384–1405)
    succeeded father

Philip the Bold, duke of Burgundy
  (1384–1404)
    ruled county by right of wife,
      Marguerite
John the Fearless, duke of Burgundy (1405–19)
  succeeded mother
Philip the Good, duke of Burgundy (1419–67)
  succeeded father

Berry, Dukes of
John (1360–1416), son of John II
Marie (1416–34)
  succeeded father as duchess of Berry;
    appanage reverted to the Crown on
      death of duchess

Bourbon, Dukes of
Louis (1327–42)
  created duke by Charles IV, 1327
Peter (1342–56)
  succeeded father; slain at Battle of Poitiers
Louis (1356–1410)
  succeeded father
John (1410–34)
  succeeded father; captured at Battle of
    Agincourt, 1415, and died in captivity
Charles (1434–56)
  succeeded father

Brabant, Duke of
John (1312–55)
Joan (1355–1404)
  succeeded father as duchess
Antoine (1404–15), son of Philip the Bold,
  duke of Burgundy
    succeeded aunt; among prisoners slain
      at Battle of Agincourt
John (1415–27)
  succeeded father
Philip (1427–30)
  succeeded brother
Philip the Good, duke of Burgundy (1430–67)
  succeeded cousin

Brittany, Duke of
John III (1312–41)
John de Montfort (1341)
  failed in bid to succeed his half brother,
    1341

Charles of Blois (1341–64)
  awarded duchy by his uncle, Philip VI;
    slain at Battle of Auray
John IV (1364–99), son of John de Montfort
  won duchy at Battle of Auray
John V (1399–1442)
  succeeded father
Francis I (1442–50)
  succeeded father
Peter II (1450–57)
  succeeded brother
Arthur III (1457–58)
  succeeded nephew

Burgundy, Duke of
Eudes IV (1315–49)
Philip de Rouvre (1349–61)
  succeeded grandfather
John II (1361–63)
  duchy reverted to Crown
Philip the Bold (1363–1404)
  created duke by his father, John II
John the Fearless (1404–19)
  succeeded father
Philip the Good 1419–67
  succeeded father

Dauphins of France
Charles (future Charles V) (1349–64), son
  of John II
Charles (future Charles VI) (1368–80), son
  of Charles V
Charles (1389), son of Charles VI
Charles (1392–1401), son of Charles VI
Louis, duke of Guienne (1401–15), son
  of Charles VI
John, duke of Touraine (1415–17), son of
  Charles VI
Charles (future Charles VII) (1417–22), son
  of Charles VI
Louis (future Louis XI) (1423–61), son
  of Charles VII

Flanders, Counts of
Robert de Béthune (1305–22)
Louis de Nevers (1322–46)
  succeeded grandfather; slain at Battle
    of Crécy
Louis de Male (1346–84)
  succeeded father

Marguerite de Flanders (1384–1405)
  succeeded father as countess of
    Flanders
Philip the Bold, duke of Burgundy
  (1384–1404)
    ruled county in wife's right
John the Fearless, Duke of Burgundy
  (1405–19)
    succeeded mother
Philip the Good, Duke of Burgundy
  (1419–67)
    succeeded father

Hainault, Counts of
William III (1304–37)
  married sister of Philip VI
William IV (1337–45), brother of Queen
  Philippa, wife of Edward III
    succeeded father
Margaret (1345–56), sister of Queen
  Philippa, wife of Edward III
    succeeded brother as countess
William V (1356–88)
  succeeded mother as count

Albrecht I (1388–1404)
  succeeded brother
William VI (1404–17)
  succeeded father
John III (1418–25)
  brother of William VI; disputed
    succession with niece
Jacqueline (1417–32)
  daughter of William VI; disputed
    succession with uncle; forced to yield
      county to duke of Burgundy, 1432
Philip the Good, duke of Burgundy
  (1432–67)

Orléans, Duke of
Philip (1344–75), son of Philip VI
  title lapsed upon duke's death
Louis (1392–1407), son of Charles V; brother
  of Charles VI
    murdered by agents of John the Fear-
      less, duke of Burgundy
Charles (1407–65)
  succeeded father; captured at Battle of
    Agincourt, 1415

Appendix 6: Constables and Marshals of France and England during the Hundred Years War

The offices of constable and marshal were hereditary in England, but not in France, where the holders of both offices, but especially the constables, were particularly active in military command during the Hundred Years War. In England, the office of Lord High Constable was attached to the earldom of Hereford in the early twelfth century and so remained in the Bohun family until it passed through them to the Staffords in the late fourteenth century. In 1521, the office passed to the Crown with the execution of Henry, duke of Buckingham, its last Stafford holder. Since then, constables have only been appointed for coronations. The office of Lord Marshal of England (known as Earl Marshal after 1397) passed by inheritance to the Mowbray dukes of Norfolk in the late fourteenth century.

CONSTABLES OF ENGLAND

John de Bohun, fifth earl of Hereford
(1321–35)
Humphrey de Bohun, sixth earl of Hereford
(1335–61)
Humphrey de Bohun, seventh earl of
Hereford (1361–72)
Thomas of Woodstock, duke of Gloucester
(1372–97)
    son of Edward III and son-in-law
    of seventh earl of Hereford
Humphrey, earl of Buckingham (1397–99)
    son of duke of Gloucester
Edmund Stafford, earl of Stafford (1399–1403)
    son-in-law of duke of Gloucester
Humphrey Stafford, duke of Buckingham
(1403–60)
    son of earl of Stafford

MARSHALS OF ENGLAND

Thomas of Brotherton, earl of Norfolk
(1315–38)
    half brother of Edward II
Margaret, duchess of Norfolk (1338–85)
    daughter of earl of Norfolk; only woman
    ever to hold the office
Thomas Mowbray, first duke of Norfolk
(1385–98)
    grandson of duchess of Norfolk

Thomas Holland, duke of Surrey (1398–99)
    appointed by Richard II after Norfolk's
    banishment
Ralph Neville, earl of Westmorland
(1400–1412)
    appointed by Henry IV after Surrey's
    rebellion
John Mowbray, second duke of Norfolk
(1412–32)
    son of first duke of Norfolk
John Mowbray, third duke of Norfolk
(1432–61)

CONSTABLES OF FRANCE

Gaucher de Chatillon (1307–29)
Raoul I of Brienne, count of Eu (1329–44)
Raoul II of Brienne, count of Eu (1344–50)
    English prisoner, 1346–50; executed for
    treason by John II, 1350
Charles of Spain (1350–54)
    murdered by Charles the Bad, king of
    Navarre, 1354
Jacques, count of La Marche (1354–56)
Walter VI of Brienne (1356)
    slain at the Battle of Poitiers, 1356
Robert Morean de Fiennes
(1356–70)
Bertrand du Guesclin (1370–80)
Olivier IV de Clisson (1380–92)

Philip of Artois, count of Eu
  (1392–97)
Louis, count of Sancerre (1397–1402)
Charles d'Albret (1403–11)
Valeran III of Luxembourg (1411–13)
Charles d'Albret (1413–15)
  slain at the Battle of Agincourt, 1415
Bernard VII, count of Armagnac
  (1415–18)
      murdered in Paris by a Burgundian
      mob, 1418
Charles, duke of Lorraine (1418–25)
John Stewart, earl of Buchan, (1421–24)
Arthur de Richemont (1425–58)
  became Arthur III, duke of
      Brittany, 1457

MARSHALS OF FRANCE
Appointed by Philip VI
Anseau de Joinville (1339–43)
Charles de Montmorency (1344–81)
Robert de Waurin (1344–60)
Guy de Nesle (1345–52)
Edouard de Beaujeau (1347–51)

Appointed by John II
Arnoul d'Audrehem (1351–70)
Rogues de Hangest (1352)

Jean de Clermont (1352–56)
  slain at the Battle of Poitiers, 1356
Jean de Boucicaut (1356–67)

Appointed by Charles V
Jean de Mauquenchy (1368–91)
Louis, count of Sancerre (1369–1402)

Appointed by Charles VI
Jean II de Boucicaut (1391–1421)
  captured at the Battle of Agincourt,
      1415
Jean de Rieux (1397–1417)
Pierre de Rieux (1417–39)
Claude de Beauvoir (1418–53)
Jean de Villiers de L'Isle-Adam (1418–37)
Jacques de Montberon (1418–22)
Gilbert Motier de la Fayette (1421–64)
Antoine de Vergy (1422–39)
Jean de la Baume (1422–35)

Appointed by Charles VII
Amaury de Séverac (1424–27)
Jean de Brosse (1426–33)
Gilles de Laval-Montmorency (1429–40)
André de Laval-Montmorency (1439–86)
Philippe de Culant (1441–54)
Poton de Xaintrailles (1454–61)

Appendix 7: Counties, Duchies, and Regions of Medieval France

Provided below are brief descriptions and histories for some of the largest and most important French counties, duchies, and regions mentioned in the entries. For Aquitaine, Brittany, Burgundy, Flanders, Gascony, and Normandy, see the individual entries for each in the main entry listing. Please also refer to the map of provinces on page li.

AGENAIS

Located in southwestern France between the rivers Dordogne and Garonne, the Agenais was a county of shifting and irregular boundaries centered on the town of Agen. Controlled by the dukes of Aquitaine since the ninth century, the Agenais passed with the duchy to the English Crown in the twelfth century. Richard I granted the Agenais to the count of Toulouse in 1196, and English claims to the country thereafter lapsed until 1259, when the Treaty of Paris restored Aquitaine to the English Crown and allowed Henry III to reassert a claim to the Agenais. Although returned to the Plantagenets in 1279, the county remained in dispute between the Crowns and from 1293 was administered by both French and English officials. The Agenais saw heavy fighting and suffered severe destruction during the first decades of the Hundred Years War. The Treaty of Brétigny restored the province to England in 1360, but the French regained the county for good in the campaign of 1370.

ANGOUMOIS

The Angoumois was a small county in west-central France bordered by Poitou on the north, Périgord on the south, the Limousin to the east, and Saintonge to the west. Its only sizable town was Angoulême on the Charent. The county was incorporated into the duchy of Aquitaine in the eleventh century and passed to the Plantagenets in the 1150s when Henry II of England married Eleanor, duchess of Aquitaine. In 1200, Henry's son John abducted and married Isabella, the heiress of the county, an action that initiated Capetian intervention and led by the 1220s to the French conquest of the Angoumois and most of the rest of the Plantagenet holdings in France. In 1314, the Angoumois was incorporated into the French royal domain, but in 1360 the Treaty of Brétigny included the county in Plantagenet Aquitaine. In the 1370s, the county was reconquered by the Valois.

ANJOU

Anjou was an important medieval principality located in west-central France and centered on the town of Angers, which stood at the confluence of the rivers Loire and Mayenne. In the early twelfth century, the county of Maine was permanently attached to Anjou through marriage. The English ruling House of Plantagenet descended from Count Geoffrey of Anjou, who married Matilda, the daughter of Henry I of England, in 1128. On Henry's death in 1135, Geoffrey made good his wife's claim to the duchy of Normandy, which he conquered in 1144, but England, after a long civil war, remained under the rule of Matilda's cousin, Stephen. On Geoffrey's death in 1151, his son Henry became count of Anjou and duke of Normandy, and, in 1152, upon his marriage to Eleanor of Aquitaine, ruler of that duchy. After 1154, when Henry succeeded Stephen as King Henry II of England, Anjou stood at the heart of an English continental empire that stretched across western France from Normandy to the Pyrenees.

Henry's son, King John, lost Anjou to the French in 1202 and John's son, Henry III, renounced English claims to the county in the Treaty of Paris in 1259. John II made Anjou the appanage of his second son, Louis, duke of Anjou. In the fifteenth century, Anjou was a key Anglo-French battleground, the Battle of Baugé being fought there in 1421. Although Maine and other parts of the duchy fell under English control in the late 1420s, most of this territory, save for Maine, was retaken by the Valois over the next decade. In 1445, Margaret, the daughter of Réne, duke of Anjou, married Henry VI of England. During negotiations for the match, the English king agreed to surrender Maine to Charles VII, who finally regained possession of that county in 1448.

ARMAGNAC

Armagnac, a county of southwestern France, was part of the early medieval duchy of Gascony and as such was incorporated into the duchy of Aquitaine in the 1050s. In the twelfth and thirteenth centuries, the counts of Armaganc were vassals of the Plantagenet king-dukes of Aquitaine, Count Bernard-Aiz V being especially noted for his service to Henry III in the 1240s. In the fourteenth century, the counts acquired significant new fiefs under French lordship, a circumstance that weakened their allegiance to the English Crown. In 1368, John, count of Armagnac, unhappy with taxes imposed by his overlord, Edward, the Black Prince, appealed to the Parlement against the prince in defiance of the Treaty of Brétigny, under which Armagnac was assigned to the sovereign Plantagenet principality of Aquitaine. This appeal of the Gascon lords restarted the Hundred Years War and ended Armagnac's connection with the English dynasty. During the French civil war in the 1410s, Bernard VII, count of Armagnac, became constable of France and leader of the Armagnac faction.

The county finally passed to the French Crown in 1589.

ARTOIS

An important cloth-producing county of northwestern France, Artois belonged to the counts of Flanders until 1180 when it came to the House of Capet through marriage. Louis VIII gave the county as an appanage to his son Robert, the younger brother of Louis IX. When Count Robert II died at the Battle of Courtrai in 1302, succession to the county was disputed between his daughter, Mahaut, countess of Burgundy, and his grandson, Robert of Artois. Philip IV decided in favor of Mahaut, but Robert continued to press his claim with each succeeding monarch, particularly Charles IV and Philip VI, with whom he was in high favor. However, because Mahaut's descendants had married Eudes, duke of Burgundy, and Louis de Nevers, count of Flanders, those two powerful noblemen prevailed upon Philip VI to again rule against Robert, who then fled to England where he recognized Edward III as king of France. In 1337, Philip cited Edward's support for Robert as one of his reasons for confiscating the duchy of Aquitaine.

In 1382, Louis de Male, count of Flanders, inherited Artois from his mother, a granddaughter of Mahaut. In 1384, Louis's death passed the county to his daughter Marguerite, duchess of Burgundy. At Marguerite's death in 1405, Artois was inherited by her son, John the Fearless, duke of Burgundy, and thus became part of the great Burgundian principality of the fifteenth century.

AUVERGNE

Auvergne was a large region of central France that in the late ninth century became part of the territory of the duke of Aquitaine. Neither the counts of Auvergne nor their feudal overlords, the dukes of Aquitaine, exercised a strong hold over the region, which from the tenth through the twelfth centuries witnessed continuous wars between various local lords. In the 1150s,

Auvergne, with the rest of Aquitaine, became part of the continental empire ruled by the English House of Plantagenet; however, in 1189, Henry II of England recognized the suzerainty of Philip II of France over the region. In 1225, Louis VIII granted Auvergne as a appanage to his son Alphonse of Poitiers, the younger brother of Louis IX. Under the 1360 Treaty of Brétigny, Auvergne was assigned to John II of France, who gave it as an appanage to his son John, duke of Berry.

BERRY

The region of central France lying south of the Loire and west of Burgundy, Berry came into the possession of the royal House of Capet in 1101. In 1137, Berry was granted to Eleanor of Aquitaine as a dowry upon her marriage to Louis VII of France. Upon the annulment of that marriage, Eleanor brought Berry to her new husband, Henry, count of Anjou, whom she married in 1152. When the count became Henry II of England in 1154, Berry became part of the Plantagenet empire in France. In 1200, Henry's son, King John, returned Berry to the Capetians, whose control of the region grew during the thirteenth century. In 1360, John II granted Berry as an appanage to his son John, who, as duke of Berry, used duchy revenues to finance his artistic collections. In 1411–12, Berry was a battleground of the French civil war, the duke being one of the leaders of the Armagnac faction. With Paris under Anglo-Burgundian control between 1418 and 1436, Bourges, the capital of Berry, was the seat of the Valois government under Charles VII, who was sometimes derisively known as the "King of Bourges." On the death of Duke John's daughter Marie in 1434, Berry was reattached to the French Crown.

BLOIS

A county in north-central France lying east of Anjou and southwest of Paris and Orléans, Blois was for a time in the Middle Ages dynastically linked with the counties of Champagne and Chartres. Centered on the Loire town of Blois, the county was po-litically important in the early twelfth century. In 1135, Stephen, the younger brother of Count Thibaut of Blois, succeeded his maternal uncle, Henry I, as king of England, but was himself followed on the throne by his cousin's son, Henry, count of Anjou. The English dynasty founded by Henry II was thus Angevin, not Bloisian, and Blois never became part of the Plantagenet empire in France. During the Hundred Years War, the counts of Blois supported the House of Valois. Count Guy I married a sister of Philip VI, who made his younger nephew, Charles of Blois, duke of Brittany in 1341. Charles was eventually slain at Auray in 1364, thus ending the Breton civil war. Charles's elder brother, Count Louis, died fighting for the French at Crécy in 1346. Count Guy II, who subsidized part of Jean Froissart's *Chronicles*, sold Blois to Charles VI's brother, Louis, duke of Orléans, in 1391, allowing Blois to be incorporated into the royal domain in the late fifteenth century.

BOURBON/BOURBONNAIS

The Bourbonnais was a lordship of central France lying southwest of Burgundy, southeast of Blois, north of Auvergne, and east of Poitou. Known for its wines, the Bourbonnais, centered on the town of Moulins, was a fief of the French Crown from at least the tenth century. In 1327, Charles IV of France traded his county of La Marche to Louis, lord of the Bourbonnais, for his county of Clermont. As part of this arrangement, Charles also created Louis duke of Bourbon. Now peers of France, the dukes of Bourbon frequently married their children into the royal House of Valois. Duke Louis's son married the sister of Philip VI, while his granddaughter married Charles V. Duke Louis II was thus an uncle of Charles VI and a prominent member of Charles's minority government. The Bourbonnais suffered severely from the depredations of *routiers* in the late fourteenth century, and from the weak government that resulted from the nineteen-year imprisonment of Duke John I following his capture at Agincourt in 1415. However, the duchy revived in the fifteenth century under John's son and grandson and by 1500 the Bourbon territories constituted the largest block of nonroyal lands in France. The duchy was finally confiscated by the Crown in the 1520s following the rebellion of the last duke.

BRABANT

Although lying entirely within the Holy Roman Empire, the duchy of Brabant, a Low Country principality that is today part of Belgium, was predominantly French-speaking. The lord of Brabant took the title of duke in 1086. Like Flanders, Brabant developed important cloth-making towns, such as Antwerp and Brussels, which were assimilated into the duchy in the early four-teenth century through a series of power-sharing arrangements with the duke. The dukes supported King John of England against Philip II of France in the early thir-teenth century, but after John's defeat at Bouvines in 1214, Brabant maintained a careful neutrality between England and France. In the late 1330s, Duke John III briefly reversed this policy by joining Ed-ward III's anti-French coalition; although after the breakup of that alliance in the early 1340s, he moved closer to France by marry-ing his daughter, Jeanne, into the pro-French House of Luxembourg. In 1390, John's daughter designated her niece, Marguerite of Flanders, as her heir. However, when Jeanne outlived her niece, the duchy passed to Antoine, a young son of Marguerite and her husband, Philip the Bold, duke of Bur-gundy. Brabant was incorporated into Bur-gundy in 1430 when Antoine's line failed.

CHAMPAGNE

Champagne was a large county lying east of Paris and bounded by the rivers Aisne, Marne, and Yonne. Occupying a flat, fertile plain, Champagne became one of the wealthiest and most powerful feudal terri-tories of medieval France. In the thirteenth century, the counts came increasingly under royal influence, with Count Thibaut V mar-rying a daughter of Louis IX and his granddaughter, Jeanne, becoming queen of France as the wife of Philip IV. Through her great-grandmother, Jeanne was also queen of Navarre. Control of Champagne passed to Jeanne's son, Louis X, who left it to his daughter Jeanne. However, Louis's brothers, Philip V and Charles IV, dispossessed their niece and Champagne was attached to the French Crown. The county was hard hit by the Black Death in the 1340s, the *Jacquerie* in the 1350s, and *routier* bands in the 1370s. Although the first *routier* incursions were repelled following the battle of Nogent-sur-Seine in 1359, the English caused much de-struction during the Rheims Campaign and English and Burgundian forces operated in the region in the 1420s, particularly during the sieges of Melun and Meaux. The county thus suffered a severe demographic and economic decline that was not reversed until the late fifteenth century.

DAUPHINÉ (VIENNOIS)

The rulers of the Dauphiné, a region of southeastern France lying east of the Rhône, north of Provence, and west of Italy, called themselves counts of Vienne until the late thirteenth century, when they took the title of dauphin for themselves and Dauphiné for their principality. In 1349, Humbert II sold the Dauphiné to Philip VI, who bestowed it as an appanage on his eldest grandson, the future Charles V, who thereby became the first royal holder of the title dauphin. Because acquisition of the Dauphiné rep-resented the first extension of French sov-ereignty beyond the Rhône, the title and the appanage were thereafter reserved for the heir to the throne.

HAINAULT

Hainault was a county in the Low Countries lying southeast of Flanders and entirely within the Holy Roman Empire. Bound in a dynastic union with the county of Holland since 1299, Hainault in the late 1320s began a close association with England due to the marriage of Philippa, daughter of Count William III, to the future Edward III. Ar-ranged by Edward's mother, Queen Isabella, the match gave her the men she needed to overthrow her husband, Edward II, in 1326. In the 1330s, many men from Hainault, such as the queen's uncle, John of Hainault; Sir Walter Mauny; and Jean le Bel, came to England to offer their services, both military and literary, to Edward III. Philippa's brother, Count William IV, joined Edward's anti-French coalition in the late 1330s, but he died in 1345 and Hainault thereafter moved outside the English orbit, despite Edward's attempts to push his wife's claims to the county. In 1417, the last count was succeeded by his daughter, Jacqueline, who in 1422 left her husband, the duke of Brabant, to marry Humphrey, duke of Gloucester, the brother of Henry V. Gloucester's military intervention in Hainault threatened the eventual Burgundian acquisition of the county and thus severely strained the Anglo-Burgundian alliance. However, Gloucester abandoned his wife and Philip the Good, duke of Burgundy, invaded the county, which was formally annexed to the Burgundian domain in 1433.

LANGUEDOC

In its broad linguistic sense, the term "Langue d'oc" referred to the southern third of France, roughly the provinces south of the River Dordogne in which the Occitan language was spoken. Politically, Languedoc referred to the block of provinces in extreme south-central France that in the early thirteenth century were the heartlands of Catharism, a heretical movement that was eradicated during the Albigensian Crusade of the 1210s by crusaders from northern France led by Simon de Montfort. In 1224, Montfort's descendents ceded their rights in the region to Louis VIII, who thus brought Languedoc under royal authority.

Languedoc suffered severe destruction during the Hundred Years War. Edward, the Black Prince, devastated the region during the *Chevauchée* of 1355, and *routiers* caused serious damage, particularly in Quercy, Rouergue, and the Agenais, in the 1360s and 1370s. The region suffered severe famines in 1335, 1351, and 1374–76, and economic collapse and high taxation pre-

cipitated a series of urban revolts across the region between 1378 and 1382. A revolt of the peasantry, known as the rebellion of the Tuchins, was not suppressed until 1384. Nonetheless, in the 1420s, support for the Crown revived along with the economy, and the region provided both men and money for the armies of Charles VII. The last great independent fiefs in the region, the counties of Armagnac and Foix, were incorporated into the Crown in 1589.

LANGUEDOIL

The term "Langue d'oïl" arose in the late Middle Ages to describe the region north of the linguistic frontier that divided those areas where Old French was spoken from those areas where Occitan was spoken. The frontier was defined roughly by the Dordogne River and the Cevennes Mountains in south-central France, with the Languedoil being the northern two-thirds of France, where people spoke Old French, and the Languedoc being the southern one-third, where the natives spoke Occitan. During the Hundred Years War, the French Crown based many administrative and fiscal divisions on these regions. The most important of these concerned the Estates-General, whose meetings occasionally comprised only representations from the Languedoil; historians usually refer to such assemblies as the Estates General of Languedoil.

LIMOUSIN

Comprising the northeastern portion of medieval Aquitaine, the Limousin was a large, thinly populated county in central France. Bounded by Poitou to the west, Auvergne to the east, Berry and La Marche to the north, and Quercy and Périgord to the south, the Limousin had only one sizable town, its capital, Limoges. From the late ninth century, the county was under the authority of the counts of Poitou and then the dukes of Aquitaine. When Henry II of England married Eleanor, duchess of Aquitaine, in the 1150s, the county passed to the Plantagenets, but was conquered by the Capetians in the early thirteenth century and incorporated into the royal domain. In 1360, the Treaty of Brétigny assigned the county to Edward III, but French encroachments into the area began in 1370, when Edward, the Black Prince, sacked Limoges in retaliation for the town's surrender to John, duke of Berry. The county came under Valois control during the 1370s.

LORRAINE

An Imperial duchy on the northeastern frontier of France, Lorraine centered around the bishoprics of Verdun, Metz, and Toul, and the town of Nancy. From the early thirteenth century, the duchy developed increasingly close ties to France, with the duke of Lorraine becoming a vassal of the count of Champagne for various territories. Part of the middle kingdom set up between the realms of the East and West Franks by the 843 Treaty of Verdun, Lorraine became a duchy in 925. Divided into Upper and Lower Lorraine in about 960, the latter became the Duchy of Brabant while the former came by the thirteenth century to be known simply as Lorraine. In the fourteenth and fifteenth centuries, Lorraine came under increasing pressure from the Valois dukes of Burgundy, who controlled large blocks of territory lying both north and south of the duchy. During the Lancastrian phase of the Hundred Years War, Lorraine's location made it a battleground between Anglo-Burgundian and dauphinist forces and the resulting turmoil gave impetus to the career of Joan of Arc, a native of Lorraine, who took as her mission the salvation of the dauphinist cause. After 1431, a succession dispute allowed the dukes of Burgundy to intervene in the duchy. In 1477, Charles the Bold, the last Valois duke of Burgundy, was killed in battle at Nancy. Lorraine was finally incorporated into the kingdom of France in the eighteenth century.

MAINE

Centered on the town of Le Mans, Maine, a county in west-central France, was strategically located between Normandy to the north and Anjou to the south. Long dominated by the counts of Anjou, who contended for paramount influence in the county with the dukes of Normandy, Maine became permanently attached to Anjou in the early twelfth century when Count Foulques V of Anjou married the heiress of Maine. The county became part of the Plantagenet empire in 1154 when the son of Geoffrey, the late count of Anjou, became king of England as Henry II. Henry's son King John lost Maine, Anjou, and most of the empire to the Capetians in the early thirteenth century. The English retook Maine in the 1420s, making it an important buffer between Lancastrian Normandy and the dauphinist lands to the south. In the 1440s, Henry VI, as part of his policy to seek a negotiated peace with France, promised to surrender Maine to Charles VII. Although implementation of this promise was delayed by resistance to it from within the English military establishment in France, the English finally evacuated Maine in 1448.

NAVARRE

A small kingdom straddling the frontiers of northeastern Spain and southwestern France, Navarre came into the French orbit in 1284, when Joanna, queen of Navarre, married the future Philip IV, who took guardianship of the kingdom upon Joanna's death in 1305. The Crowns of France and Navarre remained united during the reigns of Joanna's sons, Louis X, Philip V, and Charles IV, but separated upon Charles's death in 1328 when the Navarrese declared themselves independent and offered the throne to Louis X's daughter, Joanna II, who waived her claim to the French Crown. Ruling in conjunction with her husband, Philip, count of Evreux (d. 1343), Joanna passed the kingdom to her son Charles II (known in French history as Charles the Bad) in 1349. Ambitious for power in France, Charles intrigued against his father-in-law, John II, and engaged in full-scale civil war during the early months of Charles V's reign. When his forces were defeated by a royal army at Cocherel in 1364, Charles II withdrew to Navarre, where he was succeeded by his son Charles III in 1387. Ferdinand of Spain annexed Spanish Navarre in 1516, while the tiny French portion of the kingdom was incorporated into the French Crown in 1620, two decades after the last independent king of Navarre succeeded to the French throne as Henri IV.

PÉRIGORD

A county of southwestern France centered on the town of Périgueux, Périgord formed the northeastern frontier of the duchy of Aquitaine and thus passed to the House of Plantagenet in the 1150s when Eleanor, duchess of Aquitaine, married Henry II of England. After the collapse of the Plantagenet empire in the early thirteenth century, control of Périgord remained divided between French and English until the Treaty of Paris assigned the province to the latter in 1259, although Périgord remained much in contention between the two Crowns. The county saw heavy fighting and much destruction during the Edwardian phase of the Hundred Years War. In 1360, the Treaty of Brétigny gave Périgord to Edward III, but the area suffered much at the hands of *routiers* and in the 1370s Périgueux became the main base for Bertrand du Guesclin's reconquest of Plantagenet Aquitaine.

POITOU

A large county in west-central France, Poitou became part of the huge duchy of Aquitaine in the tenth century. Poitiers, the Poitevin capital, became the capital of the duchy and the center of a wealthy court known for its patronage of Occitan love poetry. Upon the marriage of Eleanor, duchess of Aquitaine, to the future Henry II of England in 1152, Poitou became part of the Plantagenet empire. The region was conquered by the Capetians in the early thirteenth century, and Henry III of England renounced his claim to it as part of the Treaty of Paris in 1259. In the fourteenth century, the region saw much fighting, especially the Battle of Poitiers in 1356, and much subsequent *routier* activity. The 1360 Treaty of Brétigny included most of Poitou

in Plantagenet Aquitaine, but the region was retaken by the Valois in the early 1370s and was part of the dauphinist heartland in the early fifteenth century.

PONTHIEU

The county of Ponthieu was a small lordship on the estuary of the Somme in northwestern France. Once part of Normandy, and thus also part of the Plantagenet empire in France in the twelfth century, Ponthieu contained the towns of Abbeville, Le Crotoy, and Montreuil. The county came back into English possession in 1279 when Edward I became count by right of his wife, Eleanor of Castile, who inherited it from her mother. The county remained in English hands throughout the first decades of the Hundred Years War, and was the site of the Battle of Crécy in 1346. In 1360, the Treaty of Brétigny confirmed Plantagenet possession of the county, but the armies of Charles V overran Ponthieu in 1369 at the start of the Caroline phase of the war. In 1372, Sir Robert Knolles led an English *chevauchée* into the county and burned Le Crotoy. In 1435, Charles VII offered the county to Philip the Good, duke of Burgundy, as part of the Franco-Burgundian reconciliation negotiated at the Congress of Arras.

PROVENCE

Although sometimes used to describe the entire southern third of France where the Occitan language was spoken, the term "Provence" more precisely defined the region of southeastern France lying between the Alps on the east, the Mediterranean on the south, and the Rhône River on the west. Part of the Holy Roman Empire, Provence in the twelfth century was disputed between the counts of Toulouse and Barcelona, who eventually divided control of the region. In 1246, the heiress of Provence married Charles of Anjou, the brother of Louis IX of France. The resulting Angevin dynasty ruled Provence until 1481, when Louis XI incorporated the region into the French kingdom. In the 1360s, Provence was devastated by the Great Company and by various other *routier* bands, and the Provençal economy did not revive until the fifteenth century.

QUERCY

Transected by the River Lot, Quercy was a large and important county of southwestern France. The Haut-Quercy region lay north of the Lot and included the towns of Gourdon, Figeac, and Martel, and the viscounty of Turenne. South of the Lot, the Bas-Quercy, which extended to the Garonne and the new town of Montauan, included the chief town of the county, Cahors. Despite pressure from the dukes of Aquitaine, who, from the twelfth century, were also kings of England, the counts of Toulouse held Quercy from the ninth century until 1249, when the county passed to Alphonse of Poitiers, brother of Louis IX of France. The Treaty of Paris gave the county to the Plantagenets, although the terms of the agreement were never fully implemented and Edward I returned Bas-Quercy to the Capetians in 1286. Despite being included in the Plantagenet duchy of Aquitaine created by the Treaty of Brétigy in 1360, Quercy remained in dispute throughout the war and was not finally cleared of English troops until 1443.

ROUERGUE

Lying east of Quercy, Rouergue was a large county of south-central France centered upon the town of Rodez and including, on the east, the viscounty of Millau. Originally under the authority of the counts of Toulouse, the Rouergue passed to Louis IX's brother, Alphonse of Poitiers, in the mid-thirteenth century. Thereafter, the county was attached to the Crown of France until the Treaty of Brétigny gave it to the Plantagenets in 1360. English administration ended in 1368 when the count of Armagnac, the chief magnate in the county, became a party to the Appeal of the Gascon Lords, thereby reviving the war and initiating the French conquest of Rouergue.

SAINTONGE

A seaboard county of western France lying north and west of the mouth of the Gironde, Saintonge became attached to the duchy of Aquitaine in the early Middle Ages. Extending from the Gironde on the south to Poitou on the north and the Limousin on the east, the region included the island of Oléron in the Bay of Biscay. Its chief town was the port of La Rochelle in the north. Saintonge passed, with the rest of Aquitaine, under Plantagenet control in the mid-twelfth century, when Henry II of England married Duchess Eleanor. Lost to the Plantagenets in the early thirteenth century, Saintonge was restored to English control by the 1360 Treaty of Brétigny. In 1372, following the English defeat at the naval battle of La Rochelle, the region fell to the Valois and was incorporated into the French Crown.

TOULOUSE

Toulouse, an important county in southern France, was centered on the town of Toulouse. Controlling the trade routes into Spain and Italy, the counts of Toulouse dominated much of Languedoc between the Rivers Rhône and Garonne in the eleventh and twelfth centuries. Implicated in the Cathar heresy, a movement that was destroyed by the Albigensian crusaders from northern France in the early thirteenth century, the counts of Toulouse lost influence and the county came eventually into the possession of Alphonse of Poitiers, the brother of Louis IX of France. From the 1270s, the region was under royal control, although the town of Toulouse enjoyed considerable autonomy. The region was particularly hard hit by the English *Chevauchée* of 1355, during which Edward, the Black Prince, destroyed many towns and villages in the county, and by the activities of *routiers* in the 1360s. In the 1420s, Toulouse was a center of dauphinist support.

TOURAINE

A duchy of west-central France, Touraine, a land of valleys, orchards, and vineyards, was centered around the town of Tours on the Loire. In the twelfth century, the counts of Blois ceded the region to the counts of

Anjou, who, upon becoming the Plantagenet kings of England in the 1150s, brought Touraine into the extensive Plantagenet empire in western France. Conquered by the Capetians in the early thirteenth century, Touraine was one of the provinces renounced by Henry III of England upon conclusion of the Treaty of Paris in 1259. The region became the southern frontier of France in 1360 when the Treaty of Brétigny created Plantagenet Aquitaine, although most of that principality had been reconquered by 1380. In the 1420s, Touraine was the center of the so-called ''kingdom of Bourges,'' the center of the dauphinist domains. In 1424, the dauphin (the future Charles VII) gave the duchy of Touraine as an appanage to Archibald Douglas, earl of Douglas, leader of a large Scottish force sent to aid the French. After Douglas's death at Verneuil in August 1424, the duchy returned to the Crown.

Appendix 8: Annotated Listing of Selected Sources for the Hundred Years War

Because of the war's length and scope, many fourteenth- and fifteenth-century chronicles and histories written in numerous languages and countries bear upon some aspect of the Hundred Years War. Listed below is only a small selection of the more well-known and readily available sources, primarily of English provenance, although a few of the most famous French and Burgundian works are also included. For the two best known contemporary chroniclers of the war—Jean Froissart and Jean le Bel—see the entries on each man included in the main listing. See also the entry on Christine de Pizan for her works of history, particularly her eulogistic biography of Charles V. Although not truly a source for the war, although he long was, and sometimes still is, taken for one, William Shakespeare and his view of the war as presented in the plays *Henry V* and *1 Henry VI* are discussed in the entry "Shakespeare and the Hundred Years War." For more detailed discussion of important English and French chronicles and histories of the war period, see Antonia Gransden, *Historical Writing in England*, vol. 2, *c. 1307 to the Early Sixteenth Century*; John Taylor, *English Historical Literature in the Fourteenth Century*; Charles L. Kingsford, *English Historical Literature in the Fifteenth Century*; and William W. Kibler and Grover A. Zinn, eds. *Medieval France: An Encyclopedia.*

ACTA BELLICOSA

The *Acta Bellicosa* is an important eyewitness account of the movements of the English army in the weeks before the Battle of Crécy, which occurred on 26 August 1346. Known also as the *Chronique Anonyme* and the Corpus Christi Fragment (being contained in MS 370 at Corpus Christi College, Cambridge), this Latin diary of the Crécy campaign was written by an anonymous member of Edward III's army. It is best known by its opening words, "*Acta Bellicosa.*" The single surviving copy of the diary is incomplete, and dates from the late fourteenth century. Although apparently meant to be an account of the entire campaign, the extant document describes the English campaign from the king's landing in Normandy on 12 July to 28 July, and then resumes on 11 August and continues until 20 August, when it breaks off in mid-sentence.

Printed Versions

Life and Campaigns of the Black Prince: From Contemporary Letters, Diaries and Chronicles, Including Chandos Herald's Life of the Black Prince. Edited and translated by Richard Barber. Woodbridge, England: Boydell, 1986. Reprints and translates the *Acta Bellicosa.*

Moisant, J. *Le Prince Noir en Aquitaine, 1355–6, 1362–70.* Paris, 1894. Reprints in Latin.

ANONIMALLE CHRONICLE

Written in French prose and covering the period from Brutus to the Peasants' Revolt in 1381, the *Anonimalle Chronicle* is believed to have been compiled by someone in the north of England, although this is uncertain. Until 1333, the chronicle is based on the French *Brut*, but thereafter the chronicler used an unknown Latin chronicle from London, newsletters, and some oral eyewitness accounts. The chronicle is particularly important because it is the only contemporary work to cover military events during the last years of Edward III. Patriotic and chivalric in tone, the chronicle is particularly valuable for the Battle of Poitiers, the movements of Edward III after conclusion of the Treaty of Brétigny, and the 1370 *chevauchée* of Sir Robert Knolles. The chronicler is critical of the Brétigny agreement because it meant the surrender of some hard-won towns and of Charles V, who is condemned for treachery in eventually repudiating the treaty. The chronicler also describes the growing disillusionment of the English military with its leadership in the 1370s, particularly during the Knolles expedition and the great *Chevauchée* of 1373 led by John of Gaunt, duke of Lancaster.

Printed Version
The Anonimalle Chronicle, 1333–1381. Edited by V. H. Galbraith. Manchester, 1927.

BASIN, THOMAS (1412–91). *HISTOIRE DE CHARLES VII*

Born probably at Caudebec in Normandy, Thomas Basin earned his master of arts at the University of Paris in 1429 and later studied law at Louvain and Pavia. He held various clerical positions in Lancastrian Normandy before becoming bishop of Lisieux in 1447. In August 1449, the bishop and representatives of the town surrendered Lisieux to John, count of Dunois, thus ending Basin's attachment to the English Crown. The bishop next became a servant of Charles VII and one of the instigators of the rehabilitation trial of Joan of Arc in the 1450s. He also later wrote a defense of Joan, entitled *Opinio et consilium super processu et condemnatione Johanne, dicte Puelle.* In 1464, Basin joined the League of the Public Weal, an uprising against Charles's son, Louis XI, who seized the bishop's temporalities and forced him to flee France. Named archbishop of Caesarea by the pope in 1474, Basin spent the rest of his life in exile, living for various lengths of time in Rome, Trier, and Utrecht, where he died in December 1491.

Written during his years of exile, and infused with the bitterness of that circumstance, Basin's *Histoire de Charles VII,* which was originally written in Latin, is often critical of Charles VII, especially during the king's later years. Nonetheless, the work contains much valuable information on the Anglo-French war, especially concerning its devastating effect upon the French people and countryside. Basin also provides much information on diplomatic relations, explaining, for instance, that Charles VII refused to offer one of his own daughters as a wife for Henry VI, fearing that the union might only strengthen Lancastrian claims to the French throne.

Printed Versions
Basin, Thomas. *Histoire de Charles VII.* Edited by C. Samaran. 2 vols. Paris: Société d'Edition ''Les Belles Lettres,'' 1933, 1944.
———. *Histoire des règnes de Charles VII et de Louis XI.* Edited by J. E. J. Quicherat. 4 vols. Paris, 1855–59.

BOUVIER, JACQUES [GILLES]. *CHRONIQUES DU ROI CHARLES VII.*

Jacques Bouvier, also known as the Berry Herald or Berry, Herault du Roy, wrote his chronicle of the reign of Charles VII in about 1455, although it was not finally published until 1661. The chronicle is an important source for the final French campaigns of the Anglo-French war. Berry Herald was also the continuator of the *Grandes Chroniques* for the period 1402 to 1422.

Printed Version
Bouvier, Jacques. *Chroniques du roi Charles VII.* Edited by Henri Courteault and Léonce Celier. Paris, 1979.

BRUT

The *Brut* was one of the most popular and best known English chronicles of the fourteenth century. The first version of the chronicle, running from the supposed founding of Britain by the legendary Brutus to the thirteenth century, was written in French prose in the early fourteenth century. In the middle of the century, a continuation of the chronicle, done in two versions, was undertaken. The short version ends just before the Battle of Halidon Hill in 1333, but the long version, which is the most relevant for the Hundred Years War, ends with the Battle of Halidon Hill itself. Some time between 1350 and 1380, this second version was translated into English and continued until the death of Edward III. The Brut is patriotic and chivalric in tone and the English translation seems meant to be read aloud to noble and gentle audiences. Like the *Croniques de London*, the *Brut* had a distinct bias in favor of the family of the earls of Lancaster, whose opposition to Edward II and to the regime of Queen Isabella and Roger Mortimer, earl of March, is much lauded. Despite the coverage of the Anglo-French war contained in the English continuation to 1377, the *Brut* is particularly valuable for its account of the Anglo-Scottish wars in the reigns of Edward II and Edward III.

Printed Version
The Brut or Chronicles of London. Edited by F. Brie.
    2 vols. London: Early English Text Society,
    1906–8.

CAGNY, PERCEVAL DE. *CHRONIQUES DES DUCS D'ALENÇON*.
Written in about 1436 by Perceval de Cagny, an eyewitness to the 1429 Loire Campaign led by John, duke of Alençon, and Joan of Arc, the *Chroniques des ducs d'Alençon* is the prime source for that campaign and for the military activities of Joan until her capture in May 1430.

Printed Version
Cagny, Perceval de. *Chroniques des ducs d'Alençon*.
    Edited by H. Moranville. Paris, 1902.

CANTERBURY CHRONICLE
Written by an unknown chronicler based at Christ Church in Canterbury, the Canterbury Chronicle contains much unique and important information on the Hundred Years War. Some the chronicler's information for the period from 1346 to 1367 appears to be based on what he himself witnessed, such as the welcome accorded the captive John II in London both on his first arrival in England in 1357 and upon his return in 1364. Other information was apparently gleaned from high-level sources at court with whom the

chronicler came into contact through the archbishop and through the location and importance of the Becket shrine at Canterbury, which drew important figures and forged connections with London, Dover, and Calais. Among the events depicted are the French attempt to surprise Calais at the end of 1349 and the negotiation of the First Treaty of London in 1358. The Canterbury chronicler also describes the composition of the French army at Poitiers in 1356, the casualties at Auray in 1364, the Anglo-Flemish negotiations for Edmund of Langley's marriage to Marguerite of Flanders in 1364, and the breaking of parole by Louis, duke of Anjou, in 1363.

Printed Versions
"Chronicle of Christ Church, Canterbury, 1346–
    1367." In *Chronica Johannis de Readinge et
    Anonymi Cantauriensis, 1346–1367*, ed. James
    Tait, 99–186. Manchester, 1914.

CHANDOS HERALD. *LA VIE DU PRINCE NOIR [LIFE OF THE BLACK PRINCE]*.
The unknown herald, or messenger and officer of arms, of Sir John Chandos is the author of *La Vie du Prince Noir*, a French verse biography of Edward, the Black Prince. Possibly, like Jean Froissart, a native of Valenciennes in Hainault, the herald entered Chandos's service in about 1360. The herald is mentioned twice in Froissart's chronicle—in 1366 in a description of Chandos's negotiations with the Great Company and in 1369 when the herald carried a message from Chandos to the prince. It is unlikely that the herald knew the prince personally, though he certainly met him in the service of Chandos, who is himself a secondary subject of the work.

Written in the late 1380s, about a decade after the prince's death, the *Life* is based upon the author's own experiences, the information of other eyewitnesses, and some newsletters and other contemporary documents. The herald praises both the prince and Chandos as models of chivalry, men of courage and honor who were always in the forefront of battle. Despite its eulogistic tone and the fact that it was written years after the death of both its subjects, the *Life* is an important source for the prince's career, providing numerous details unavailable in other works. The *Life* is particularly valuable for the campaign and battle of Nájera in 1367, for which the herald was an eyewitness.

Printed Versions
Chandos Herald. *La Vie du Prince Noir by Chandos Herald*. Edited by D. B. Tyson. Tübingen: M. Niemeyer, 1975.
———. *The Life of the Black Prince by the Herald of Sir John Chandos*. Edited by M. K. Pope and E. C. Lodge. Oxford: Clarendon Press, 1910.

CHARTIER, JEAN. *CHRONIQUE DE CHARLES VII.*
Jean Chartier was the brother of Alain Chartier, who was secretary to both Charles VI and Charles VII. The *Chronique* is particularly valuable for major events at the French court during the later stages of the Hundred Years War.

Printed Version
Chartier, Jean. *Chronique de Charles VII*. Edited by Auguste Vallet de Viriville. 3 vols. Paris, 1858.

CRONIQUES DE LONDON
Written perhaps by an officer of the city of London, where official documents were prepared in Norman French, this prose chronicle covers events between the years 1259 and 1343. A more likely reason for the unknown author's use of French is his reliance on the French *Brut* for his account of national events prior to 1333. Only after that date do the *Croniques* become an independent source for the Hundred Years War. The chronicle's independent coverage of London history begins in 1327, when the chronicler ceased to draw on two unidentified London chronicles for local events.

Despite its coverage of London, the chronicle after 1333 focuses mainly on the French wars of Edward III. Like Robert of Avesbury, the chronicler has a strong royalist bias, praising Edward III as brave and chivalrous and denouncing Philip VI as "a cow-

ard and a recreant knight." The chronicle is an important source for the naval battle of Sluys, the siege of Tournai, and the events surrounding the political crisis of 1340–41, which is described from the king's point of view.

Printed Version
Croniques de London. Edited by G. J. Aungier. London: Camden Society, 1844.

ELMHAM, THOMAS (d. c. 1420). *LIBER METRICUS DE HENRICO QUINTO [A BOOK IN VERSE ON HENRY THE FIFTH].*
A monk at Canterbury and then chaplain to Henry V, Thomas Elmham accompanied the king to France in 1415 and was present at the Battle of Agincourt. Although he has been suggested as the author of the *Gesta Henrici Quinti*, this now seems unlikely. He was also identified as the author of the *Vita et Gesta Henrici Quinti* by the eighteenth-century antiquary Thomas Hearne, but this attribution has now been proven incorrect and that work is now known as the Pseudo-Elmham. Elmham did write a Latin prose life of Henry V, which is now lost, and the *Liber*, a Latin verse life of the king. Down to 1416, the *Liber* is based on the *Gesta*, which ends in that year, and thereafter it is believed that the *Liber* largely follows Elmham's lost prose biography of the king. Although highly eulogistic and concentrating heavily on religious affairs, particularly Henry's suppression of Lollardy, Elmham's biography is a valuable source for the reign.

Printed Version
Elmham, Thomas. "Liber Metricus de Henrico Quinto." In *Memorials of Henry the Fifth*, ed. C. A. Cole, 79–106. London: Rolls Series, 1858.

GEOFFREY LE BAKER (d. c. 1360), CHRONICLER
In about 1341, Geoffrey le Baker, a secular clerk from Swinbrook in Oxfordshire, began writing a Latin chronicle that eventually covered the period from 1303 to the battle of Poitiers in 1356. An important source for the Edwardian phase of the Anglo-French

war, Baker's chronicle relies on soldiers' accounts, newsletters, casualty lists, campaign itineraries, and official documents. Baker had a flair for dramatic narrative, and never missed an opportunity to tell a good story, such as his rousing depiction of the single combat that occurred prior to the Battle of Halidon Hill between Robert de Benhall and a Scottish champion, whom Baker described as "a very Goliath."

Baker is also very much in the chivalric tradition of fourteenth-century chroniclers, providing, for instance, detailed accounts of the founding of the Order of the Garter and of the heroic death of Sir Thomas Dagworth. Like other English chroniclers of the period, he patriotically depicts Edward III and Edward, the Black Prince, as chivalrous leaders, while Philip VI (always referred to as Philip de Valois) is called a "pseudo-king" and denounced, like all Frenchmen, as arrogant and prideful. Baker's descriptions of battles and campaigns contain many unique details, with his itineraries for Edward III's army during the Crécy campaign in 1346 and the prince's great *chevauchée* in 1355 being particularly valuable.

Printed Version
Geoffrey le Baker. *Chronicon Galfridi le Baker de Swynebroke.* Edited by E. M. Thompson. Oxford, 1889.

GESTA HENRICI QUINTI [THE DEEDS OF HENRY THE FIFTH].
This Latin prose biography of Henry V was written by an anonymous author between November 1416 and July 1417, and covers Henry's reign from his accession in March 1413 to the end of 1416. Although written to promote the king's aggressive policy in France and to stimulate enthusiasm in England for the war, the *Gesta* is an important source for the first year of the fifteenth-century resumption of the Anglo-French war.

Printed Version
Gesta Henrici Quinti. Edited with an English translation by Frank Taylor and J. S. Roskell. Oxford: Oxford Medieval Texts, 1975.

GRANDES CHRONIQUES
The *Grandes Chroniques de France* constitute the official history of the realm of France as compiled at the Monastery of Saint-Denis near Paris from the year 1285. The chronicle is extremely valuable for events in France during the Hundred Years War, since it was written contemporaneously with the events it describes. A series of clerical continuators took the chronicle through the entire period of the war and provide a French royal perspective on important battles, campaigns, treaties, truces, and political and social movements. From the end of the thirteenth century to about 1350, the chronicle was compiled by a series of anonymous monks at Saint-Denis. From then until 1384, the chronicle was written by Pierre d'Orgemont, the chancellor of France. Juvenal des Ursins, the archbishop of Rheims, took the work up to 1402; the Berry Herald continued it to 1422; and Jean Chartier, a monk of Saint-Denis, carried it to the death of Charles VII in 1461.

Printed Version
Les grandes chroniques de France. Edited by Jules M. E. Viard. 10 vols. Paris: Société de l'Histoire de France, 1920–58.

GRAY, SIR THOMAS (d. c. 1370). SCALACHRONICA.
Sir Thomas Gray of Heton was the first English lay chronicler since Anglo-Saxon times to come from a knightly or noble family. A native of Northumberland, Gray took up his chronicle in part to record the deeds of his father, another Sir Thomas, in the Scottish wars of Edward I and Edward II. Gray accompanied William Montagu, earl of Salisbury, to France in 1338, and was appointed sheriff and constable of Norham in 1345. He fought at the Anglo-Scottish Battle of Neville's Cross in 1346 and was captured by the Scots and imprisoned in Edinburgh Castle from 1355 to 1359, the period during which he began his chronicle. Upon his release, Gray participated, as a member of the Black Prince's division, in Edward III's Rheims Campaign. He died a few years after

being named keeper of the Scottish marches in 1367.

The title of Gray's work, *Scalachronica*, refers to a scaling ladder, which was a Gray family emblem. The chronicle runs from the time of the early Britons to 1363, with much of the fourteenth-century material coming from the personal experiences of Gray and his father. Unfortunately, the annals for the Hundred Years War period are incomplete, with Gray's work for the years 1340 to 1355 surviving only in abstracts made of the now missing leaves by the sixteenth-century antiquary John Leland. The *Scalachronica* is particularly valuable for the hardships faced by the English (and Gray himself) during the Rheims Campaign, but also contains detailed descriptions of conditions in France in the late 1350s, including accounts of the *Jacquerie* and of the activities of English *routiers*.

Printed Versions
Gray, Sir Thomas. *Scalachronica*. Edited by J. Stevenson. Edinburgh: Maitland Club, 1836.
———. *The Scalachronica of Sir Thomas Gray*. Edited and translated by H. Maxwell. Glasgow, 1907.

JOHN OF READING (d. c. 1369), CHRONICLER

Beginning in about 1365, only a few years before his death, John of Reading, a monk of Westminster, continued the *Flores Historiarum* chronicle from the years between 1346 and 1367. Although John's Latin is poor and he apologizes in his preface for his "lack of education and skill," this chronicle is an important source for the Hundred Years War precisely because, being no scholar, John relied on documents and conversation with eyewitnesses, not other chronicles, to complete his work.

Although especially useful for events in London during the period, the chronicle also pays close attention to the Anglo-French wars, English success in which is patriotically ascribed to the wise and godly leadership of Edward III and Edward, the Black Prince. Particularly valuable are John's accounts of the 1367 campaign and battle of Nájera as well as events related to Westminster, such the 1346 and 1359 visits by Edward III, who stopped at the shrine to pray for the success of the forthcoming Crécy and Rheims Campaigns.

Printed Version
John of Reading. "Chronicle of John of Reading." In *Chronica Johannis de Readinge et Anonymi Cantauriensis, 1346–1367*, ed. James Tait, 187–227. Manchester, 1914.

LE JOURNAL D'UN BOURGEOIS DE PARIS

Written between 1405 and 1449 by a resident of Paris who is believed to have been a canon of Notre Dame, this diary is an important source for life in the French capital at the end of the Hundred Years War. Written in French, the *Journal* covers events in Paris relating to the French civil war, the citizens' reactions to Joan of Arc, and the English occupation.

Printed Versions
Bourgeois of Paris. *Journal d'un bourgeois de Paris, 1405–49*. Edited by A. Teutey. Paris, 1881.
Quicherat, Jules, ed. *Procès de condamnation et de rehabilitation de Jeanne d'Arc dite la Pucelle*. 5 vols. Paris: Société de l'histoire de France, 1841–49. Reprints the *Journal* in vol. 4, pp. 461–74.

JOURNAL DU SIÈGE D'ORLÉANS

The *Journal du Siège d'Orléans* is an important French source for the military career of Joan of Arc. Although organized in its present form around the year 1468, the *Journal* is based on a register of events that was compiled in the city of Orléans in 1429 during the siege and subsequent Loire Campaign. The *Journal* portrays Joan as a miraculous figure and fully accepts the divine origins of her mission. For example, after describing the defeat of the dauphinists at the Battle of the Herrings in February 1429, the *Journal* explains that Joan, who was then tending her flocks in Lorraine, came to know of the encounter through "grace divine," and that she used this miraculous knowledge to convince Robert de Baudricourt, the local dauphinist commander, to arrange for her to be sent to the dauphin. The *Journal* does not stop with the relief of Orléans and the Battle of Patay, but also describes Joan's activities during the march to Rheims, the coronation of Charles VII, and the abortive attack on Paris in September 1429.

Printed Versions

Charpentier, Paul, and Cuissard, Charles, eds. *Journal du siège d'Orléans, 1428–1429: augmenté de plusieurs documents notamment des comptes de ville, 1429–1431* Orléans: H. Herluison, 1896.

Quicherat, Jules, ed. *Procès de condamnation et de rehabilitation de Jeanne d'Arc dite la Pucelle.* 5 vols. Paris: Société de l'histoire de France, 1841–49. Reprints the *Journal* in vol. 4, pp. 95–202.

JUVENAL DES URSINS, JEAN (1388–1473). *HISTOIRE DE CHARLES VI.*

The son of Jean Jouvenal (1360–1431), a councilor to both Charles VI and Charles VII as well as chancellor to Louis, duke of Guienne, Jean Juvenal des Ursins (the family assumed the new name around 1410) was archbishop of Rheims from 1449 until his death. The *Histoire* is an important source for the reign of Charles VI and the French civil war, during which the author's father was a participant in several important events, including the quelling of the Cabochien uprising in 1413.

Printed Version

Juvenal des Ursins, Jean. *Histoire de Charles VI.* Edited by J. A. C. Buchon. Paris, 1836.

KNIGHTON, HENRY (d. c. 1396), CHRONICLER

An Augustinian canon at the Abbey of St. Mary of the Meadows in Leicester, Henry Knighton (or Knyghton) wrote a four-volume history of England that covers the period from 965 to 1366. When increasing blindness forced Knighton to give up the work, a fellow canon wrote a fifth volume that takes the history from the end of Edward III's reign to 1395. The last two volumes of Knighton's own work, which begin in 1337, are of great importance for their description of the effects of the war and the Black Death on fourteenth-century English society.

Printed Versions

Knighton, Henry. *Chronicon Henrici Knighton vel Cnitthon Monachi Leycestrensis.* Edited by J. R. Lumby. 2 vols. London: Rolls Series, 1889–95.
———. *Knighton's Chronicle, 1337–1396.* Edited by G. H. Martin. Oxford: Oxford University Press, 1995.

MONSTRELET, ENGUERRAND DE (c. 1395–1453), CHRONICLER

The chronicler Enguerrand de Monstrelet held various posts in the service of Philip the Good, duke of Burgundy, and his work thus displays a pro-Burgundian bias and a hostility to Charles VII. Viewing himself as a continuator of Jean Froissart, Monstrelet takes up his story in 1400, the year Froissart's chronicle ends, and continues it until May 1444. Although lacking the literary merit of Froissart, Monstrelet's chronicle was popular and influenced later fifteenth-century writers. Monstrelet was present at Burgundy's interview with the newly captured Joan of Arc in 1430, and he covers military events from a Burgundian perspective, although political developments in other countries and the great religious events of the day, such as the Councils of Pisa and Constance, are also covered. Unlike Froissart, Monstrelet does not display a great fondness for chivalric deeds and feats of arms.

Printed Version

Monstrelet, Enguerrand de. *Chronique.* Edited by L. Douét-d'Arcq. 6 vols. Paris, 1857–62.

MURIMUTH, ADAM (c. 1274–1347), CHRONICLER

Born into an Oxfordshire family, Adam Murimuth was a clerical diplomat who served Edward II in various causes at the papal curia in Avignon. He first appeared at the papal court in 1311 as proctor for Oxford University, but by 1314 was the king's representative in a case involving a recent royal appointment to the deanery of St. Paul's in London. In 1321–22, Murimuth was in Avignon seeking papal assent to a clerical aid (i.e., a royal demand for money from the English clergy) and in 1323 expressed to the pope Edward's opposition to the Scots' request for removal of the interdict imposed on their country. For his services, Murimuth received numerous ecclesiastical preferments, including a prebendary (a stipendiary position on the clerical staff of a cathedral) at Hereford Cathedral in 1320, prebendaries at St. Paul's in 1325 and 1328, and the rectory at Wraysbury in 1337.

Murimuth's brief Latin chronicle covers the last years of Edward II and the first decades of Edward III. Fiercely antipapal and anti-French, Murimuth is primarily interested in diplomacy, especially Anglo-papal relations; national politics; and the course of the Anglo-French war, which he traces to the English victory over the Scots at Neville's Cross in October 1346. He strongly approves of Edward III's claim to the French Crown, referring to Philip VI only as Philip de Valois, and he provides numerous descriptions of both large and small military engagements fought during the 1330s and 1340s. Although generally reliable with names and dates, Murimuth's style is spare and factual, displaying no talent for narrative.

Much of Murimuth's political information derives from contacts among the royal clerks, while his military descriptions rely heavily on newsletters; for example, he reprints part of the letter of Michael de Northburgh, a royal councilor, to describe the 1346 campaign. For the events of 1332–37, he draws upon the *Annales Paulini*, which was also being written at St. Paul's at the time Murimuth was working there. While strongly supportive of Edward III's war aims, Murimuth is often critical of the king's methods, condemning his failure to mount a campaign in 1339 and his financial manip-

ulations of the wool trade in an attempt to purchase allies in the Low Countries.

Printed Versions

Murimuth, Adam. *Adami Murimuthensis Chronica Sui Temporis: Nunc Primum per Decem Annos Aucta, (M.CCC.III.–M.CCC.XLVI.) cum Eorundem Continuatione (ad M.CCC.LXXX.) a Quodam Anonymo.* Edited by Thomas Hog. London: English Historical Society, 1846.

Murimuth, Adam, and Robert of Avesbury. *Adae Murimuth Continuatio Chronicarum. Robertus de Avesbury de Gestis Mirabilibus Regis Edwardi Tertii.* Edited by E. M. Thompson. London: Eyre and Spottiswoode, 1889.

PSEUDO-ELMHAM. *VITA ET GESTA HENRICI QUINTI [LIFE AND DEEDS OF HENRY THE FIFTH].*

Because it was once erroneously attributed to Thomas Elmham, this anonymous biography of Henry V is today known as the Pseudo-Elmham. The work exists in two recensions. The first was written at the command of Walter Hungerford, Lord Hungerford, an important military and political figure in Henry's reign who was likely the source for many of the details of the work, particularly those relating to the siege of Meaux and the king's death. The second, which was completed in about 1446, is dedicated to John Somerset, who was physician to Henry VI between 1428 and 1432. Both Hungerford and Somerset had connections to Humphrey, duke of Gloucester, the king's brother, and so the biography relies heavily, for events prior to 1420, on Titus Livius's *Vita Henrici Quinti*, which was produced at the duke's request to promote the duke's career and policies.

Printed Version

[Pseudo-Elmham]. *Thomae de Elmham Vita et Gesta Henrici Quinti.* Edited by Thomas Hearne. Oxford, 1727.

ROBERT OF AVESBURY (d. c. 1359), CHRONICLER

Little is known of the life of Robert of Avesbury beyond what can be gleaned from his chronicle and his will. The former states that he was registrar of the archbishop of Canterbury's court at Lambeth, and the latter, which was dated 27 January 1359 and entered into the court rolls three weeks later, indicates that he lived in London, was predeceased by his wife Milicent, and had two sons, William and John.

Focusing on military events during the first three decades of Edward III's reign, the Latin chronicle of Robert of Avesbury is an important source for the first campaigns of the Hundred Years War. In his preface, Avesbury declares his purpose to be recording the "wonderful deeds of the magnificent king of England, the Lord Edward the third after the Conquest, and of his nobles." Indeed, Avesbury is so biased in favor of Edward it seems likely that he wrote specifically to curry favor with the king. The chronicler strongly supports Edward's right to the Crown of France and to overlordship in both Scotland and Brittany, and he mentions all Edward's victories, which are patriotically ascribed to the intervention of Christ, "who is always on the side of justice." Avesbury depicts Edward as brave, virtuous, and generous, the model of knightly chivalry, while John II of France is condemned as an incestuous lecher capable of ravishing even nuns.

Despite its bias, Avesbury's chronicle is valuable because it reproduces many contemporary newsletters that are otherwise unknown. For instance, Avesbury is the only source for letters by Edward, the Black Prince, describing his great *chevauchée* across southern France in 1355. Avesbury also copies the *libellus famosus,* the accusations Edward leveled at Archbishop John Stratford during the Crisis of 1340–41, and the newsletter of Richard de Winkley, describing the Crécy campaign of 1346. Avesbury is also the only or most detailed source for various episodes that are likely derived from lost newsletters written by eyewitnesses. For example, his chronicle provides a detailed account of Edward's dramatic foiling of a French attempt to surprise Calais in late 1349—an episode much in accord with Avesbury's chivalrous depiction of the

king—and a description of an otherwise unknown proposal for Henry of Grosmont, duke of Lancaster, to lead an expedition to the aid of Charles the Bad, king of Navarre, in 1355.

Printed Version

Murimuth, Adam, and Robert of Avesbury. *Adae Murimuth Continuatio Chronicarum. Robertus de Avesbury de Gestis Mirabilibus Regis Edwardi Tertii.* Edited by E. M. Thompson. London: Eyre and Spottiswoode, 1889.

VITA HENRICI QUINTI [LIFE OF HENRY THE FIFTH] BY TITUS LIVIUS FRULOVISI.

Written by Titus Livius Frulovisi, a poet and literary client of Humphrey, duke of Gloucester, the brother of Henry V, the *Vita* traces Henry's life from his birth until his death in 1422. Born in Italy, Titus Livius joined Gloucester's household in about 1436. Seeking to strengthen his position in the regency government and to promote a more vigorous prosecution of the war, Gloucester asked Titus Livius to write a biography of Henry V mainly to describe the triumphs of his brother's reign and thereby encourage his nephew, Henry VI, to emulate his father's policies. The duke plays a prominent part in the *Vita*, with his roles at Agincourt and at the fall of Cherbourg being particularly noted.

Printed Version

Titi Livii Foro-Juliensis Vita Henrici Quinti. Edited by Thomas Hearne. Oxford, 1716.

WALSINGHAM, THOMAS (d. c. 1422), CHRONICLER

A monk of St. Albans Abbey in Hertfortshire, where he was in charge of the scriptorium, or writing room, Thomas Walsingham wrote several important chronicles that make him the main authority for events in England during the reigns of Richard II, Henry IV, and Henry V. His most important work, the *Historia Anglicana*, covers the period from 1272 to 1422, although the period prior to 1377 is drawn largely from earlier chronicles. Walsingham's *Chronicon*

Angliae covers the period 1328–88 and overlaps to some degree with the *Historia Anglicana*. Walsingham's other works are the *Gesta Abbatun Sancti Albani*, a history of the abbots of St. Albans to 1381, and the *Ypodigma Neustriae,* a history of the dukes of Normandy that was written in about 1419 to justify Henry V's conquest of the duchy.

Walsingham is particularly valuable for the events of Richard's reign, including the Peasants' Revolt of 1381 and the king's deposition in 1399. He is especially hostile to the king's uncle, John of Gaunt, duke of Lancaster, and to John Wycliffe and the Lollard movement.

Printed Versions

Walsingham, Thomas. *Chronicon Angliae, 1328–1388*. Edited by E. M. Thompson. London: Rolls Series, 1874.

———. *Gesta Abbatun Sancti Albani*. Edited by H. T. Riley. 3 vols. London: Rolls Series, 1867–69.

———. *Historia Anglicana*. Edited by H. T. Riley. 2 vols. London: Rolls Series, 1863–64.

———. *Ypodigma Neustriae a Thoma Walsingham*. Edited by H. T. Riley. London: Rolls Series, 1876.

WAVRIN, JEAN DE (1395–1475). *RECUEIL DES CRONIQUES ET ANCIENNES ISTOIRES DE LA GRANDE BRETAIGNE, À PRESENT NOMMÉ ENGLETERRE [A COLLECTION OF THE CHRONICLES AND ANCIENT HISTORIES OF GREAT BRITAIN, NOW CALLED ENGLAND]*

The illegitimate son of a Burgundian nobleman, Jean de Wavrin fought for the French at the Battle of Agincourt in 1415. Following creation of the Anglo-Burgundian alliance in 1420, he fought for the English in the 1420s and remained pro-English in sentiment even after the alliance ended in 1435. His work traces the history of England through 1469 and is an important source for both Anglo-Burgundian and Franco-Burgundian relations during the late decades of the war.

Printed Version

Wavrin, Jean de. *Recueil des croniques et anciennes istoires de la Grande Bretaigne, à present nommé Engleterre*. Edited by William Hardy. 5 vols. London: Rolls Series, 1864–91.

Bibliography

This bibliography is a highly selective listing of major books and articles relevant to the study of the Hundred Years War. It contains mainly works in English, although it concludes with a section offering a number of important French-language works.

GENERAL AND REFERENCE

Allmand, Christopher. *The Hundred Years War: England and France at War, c. 1300–c. 1450*. Cambridge: Cambridge University Press, 1988.

Bak, János M. *Medieval Narrative Sources: A Chronological Guide*. New York: Garland Publishing, 1987.

Boyce, Charles. *Shakespeare A to Z*. New York: Bantam Doubleday Dell, 1990.

Curry, Anne. *The Hundred Years War*. 2nd ed. London: Palgrave Macmillan, 2003.

Duby, Georges. *France in the Middle Ages, 987–1460*. Translated by Jules Vale. Oxford: Blackwell, 1997.

Fowler, Kenneth A. *The Age of Plantagenet and Valois*. Macclesfield, England: Bookthrift, 1980.

———, ed. *The Hundred Years War*. London: Macmillan, 1971.

Fritze, Ronald H., and William B. Robison, eds. *Historical Dictionary of Late Medieval England, 1272–1485*. Westport, CT: Greenwood Press, 2002.

Gransden, Antonia. *Historical Writing in England*. Vol. 2, *c. 1307 to the Early Sixteenth Century*. Ithaca, NY: Cornell University Press, 1982.

Griffiths, Ralph A., and Roger S. Thomas. *The Making of the Tudor Dynasty*. New York: St. Martin's Press, 1985.

Harriss, Gerald. *Shaping the Nation: England 1360–1461*. Oxford: Clarendon Press, 2005.

Hicks, Michael. *Who's Who in Late Medieval England (1272–1485)*. Who's Who in British History Series. London: Shepheard-Walwyn, 1991.

Hooper, Nicholas, and Matthew Bennett, eds. *Cambridge Illustrated Atlas of Warfare: The Middle Ages, 768–1487*. Cambridge: Cambridge University Press, 1996.

Jacob, E. F. *The Fifteenth Century, 1399–1485*. Oxford History of England. Oxford: Oxford University Press, 1993.

Keen, Maurice. *England in the Later Middle Ages*. London: Eyre Methuen, 1977.

Kelly, J. N. D. *The Oxford Dictionary of Popes*. Oxford: Oxford University Press, 1988.

Kibler, William W., and Grover A. Zinn, eds. *Medieval France: An Encyclopedia*. New York: Garland Publishing, 1995.

Kingsford, Charles L. *English Historical Literature in the Fifteenth Century*. Reprint, New York: Burt Franklin, 1962.

Lewis, Peter. *Later Medieval France: The Polity*. London: Macmillan, 1968.

Lloyd, Alan. *The Hundred Years War*. London: Hart-Davis, MacGibbon, 1977.

McBrien, Richard P. *Lives of the Popes*. New York: HarperCollins, 1997.

McKisack, May. *The Fourteenth Century, 1307–1399*. Oxford History of England. Oxford: Oxford University Press, 1991.

Neillands, Robin. *The Hundred Years War*. Rev. ed. London: Routledge, 2001.

Perroy, Edouard. *The Hundred Years War*. Translated by W. B. Wells. New York: Capricorn Books, 1965.

Rubin, Miri. *The Hollow Crown: A History of Britain in the Late Middle Ages*. New York: Penguin Books. 2005.

Seward, Desmond. *The Hundred Years War*. New York: Penguin, 1999.

Starks, Michael. *A Traveller's History of the Hundred Years War in France*. New York: Interlink Books, 2002.

Sumption, Jonathan. *The Hundred Years War*. Vol. 1, *Trial by Battle*. Philadelphia: University of Pennsylvania Press, 1991.

————. *The Hundred Years War.* Vol. 2, *Trial by Fire.* Philadelphia: University of Pennsylvania Press, 2001.

Taylor, John. *English Historical Literature in the Fourteenth Century.* Oxford: Clarendon Press, 1987.

Tuchman, Barbara W. *A Distant Mirror: The Calamitous 14th Century.* New York: Ballatine Books, 1978.

Villalon, L. J. Andred, and Donald J. Kagay, eds. *The Hundred Years War: A Wider Focus.* Boston: Brill, 2005.

Wagner, John A. *Encyclopedia of the Wars of the Roses.* Santa Barbara, CA: ABC-Clio, 2001.

SOURCES

Brie, F. W. D., ed. *The Brut.* 2 vols. O.s, 136. London: Early English Text Society, 1908.

Chandos Herald. *Life of the Black Prince by the Herald of Sir John Chandos.* Edited and translated by Mildred K. Pope and Eleanor C. Lodge. Oxford: Clarendon Press, 1910.

Froissart, Jean. *The Chronicle of Froissart.* Translated by Sir John Bourchier. 6 vols. London: D. Nutt, 1901–3.

————. *Chronicles.* Translated by Geoffrey Brereton. Rev. ed. Harmondsworth, England: Penguin, 1978.

————. *The Lyric Poems of Jean Froissart.* Edited by Robe Roy McGregor, Jr. Chapel Hill: University of North Carolina Press, 1975.

Kingsford, C. L., ed. *The First English Life of Henry the Fifth.* Oxford: Clarendon Press, 1911.

Stevenson, J., ed. *Scalacronica of Sir Thomas Gray.* Edinburgh: Maitland Club, 1836.

Taylor, Frank, and John S. Roskell, trans. *Gesta Henrici Quinti [The Deeds of Henry V].* Oxford: Clarendon Press, 1975.

Thomas, A. H., and I. D. Thornley, eds. *The Great Chronicle of London.* Reprint, Stroud, England: Alan Sutton, 1983.

Thompson, Peter Edmund, ed. and trans. *Contemporary Chronicles of the Hundred Years War: From the Works of Jean le Bel, Jean Froissart and Enguerrand de Monstrelet.* London: Folio Society, 1966.

Tyson, D. B., ed. *La Vie du Prince Noir by Chandos Herald.* Tübingen: M. Niemeyer, 1975.

Venette, Jean de. *Chronique.* Edited by Richard A. Newhall. Translated by Jean Birdsall. New York: Columbia University Press, 1953.

Waurin, Jean. *Recueil des croniques et anchiennes istories de la Grant Bretaigne, a present nomme Engleterre (A Collection of the Chronicles and Ancient Histories of Great Britain, Now Called England).* 5 vols. London: Longman, Green, Longman, Roberts, and Green, 1864–91.

BACKGROUND AND CAUSES

Brown, Elizabeth A. R. *The Monarchy of Capetian France and Royal Ceremonial.* London: Variorum, 1991.

————. *Politics and Institutions in Capetian France.* London: Variorum, 1991.

Chaplais, Pierre. *The War of Saint-Sardos (1323–1325): Gascon Correspondence and Diplomatic Documents.* London: Royal Historical Society, 1954.

Cuttino, George P. *English Diplomatic Administration, 1259–1339.* 2nd ed. Oxford: Clarendon Press, 1971.

Dunbabin, Jean. *France in the Making, 843–1180.* Oxford: Oxford University Press, 1985.

Fawtier, Robert. *The Capetian Kings of France: Monarchy and Nation (987–1328).* Translated by Lionel Butler and R. J. Adam. London: Macmillan, 1964.

Gillingham, John. *The Angevin Empire.* 2nd ed. London: Edward Arnold, 2001.

Hallam, Elizabeth. *Capetian France, 987–1328.* London: Longman, 1980.

Jordan, William Chester. *The French Monarchy and the Jews from Philip Augustus to the Last Capetians.* Philadelphia: University of Pennsylvania Press, 1989.

Lewis, Andrew. *Royal Succession in Capetian France.* Cambridge, MA: Harvard University Press, 1981.

Raban, Sandra. *England under Edward I and Edward II, 1259–1327.* Oxford: Blackwell, 2000.

Vale, M. G. A. *The Origins of the Hundred Years War: The Angevin Legacy, 1250–1340.* Oxford: Clarendon Press, 2000.

Wood, Charles T. *The French Apanages and the Capetian Monarchy, 1224–1328.* Cambridge, MA: Harvard University Press, 1966.

ARMIES, ARMOR, WEAPONRY, AND MILITARY TECHNOLOGY

Blair, Claude. *European Armor, Circa 1066 to Circa 1700.* London: Batsford, 1958.

Bradbury, Jim. *The Medieval Archer.* New York: St. Martin's Press, 1985.

DeVries, Kelly. *Medieval Military Technology.* Peterborough, Ontario: Broadview Press, 1992.

Featherstone, Donald. *The Bowman of England.* Barnsley, England: Pen and Sword Books, 2003.

Hardy, Robert. *Longbow: A Social and Military History*. 3rd ed. Sparkford, England: Patrick Stephens, 1992.

Martin, Paul. *Arms and Armour from the 9th to the 17th Century*. Translated by René North. Rutland, VT: Charles E. Tuttle, 1968.

Nicolle, David. *French Armies of the Hundred Years War*. Oxford: Osprey Publishing, 2004

Oakeshott, R. Ewart. *The Sword in the Age of Chivalry*. London: Lutterworth, 1964

Patrick, John Merton. *Artillery and Warfare during the Thirteenth and Fourteenth Centuries*. Logan: Utah State University Press, 1961.

MILITARY OPERATIONS, BATTLES, AND MEDIEVAL WARFARE

GENERAL WARFARE AND DIPLOMACY

Barnie, John. *War in Medieval English Society: Social Values and the Hundred Years War, 1337–99*. Ithaca, NY: Cornell University Press, 1974.

Chaplais, Pierre. *English Diplomatic Practice*. London: Her Majesty's Stationer's Office, 1975–82.

———. *Essays in Medieval Diplomacy and Administration*. London: Hambledon Press, 1981.

Contamine, Philippe. *War in the Middle Ages*. Translated by M. C. E. Jones. Oxford: Blackwell, 1987.

Curry, Anne, and Michael Hughes, eds. *Arms, Armies and Fortifications in the Hundred Years War*. Woodbridge, England: Boydell Press, 1999.

DeVries, Kelly. *Infantry Warfare in the Early Fourteenth Century: Discipline, Tactics and Technology*. Woodbridge, England: Boydell Press, 1996.

Dickinson, Jocelyne G. *The Congress of Arras: A Study in Medieval Diplomacy*. Oxford: Clarendon Press, 1955.

Ferguson, John. *English Diplomacy, 1422–1461*. Oxford: Clarendon Press, 1972.

Fowler, Kenneth A. *Medieval Mercenaries*. Vol. 1, *The Great Companies*. Oxford: Blackwell, 2001.

Jones, Michael, and Malcolm Vale, eds. *England and Her Neighbours, 1066–1453*. London: Hambledon Press, 1989.

Mallett, Michael. *Mercenaries and Their Master: Warfare in Renaissance Italy*. Totowa, NJ: Rowman and Littlefield, 1974.

Powicke, M. R. *Military Obligation in Medieval England*. Oxford: Oxford University Press, 1962.

Prestwich, Michael. *Armies and Warfare in the Middle Ages: The English Experience*. New Haven, CT: Yale University Press, 1996.

———. *The Three Edwards: War and State in England, 1272–1377*. 2nd ed. London: Routledge, 2003.

Rodger, N. A. M. *The Safeguard of the Sea: A Naval History of Britain, 660–1649*. London: HarperCollins, 1997.

EDWARDIAN WAR, 1330s–1360

Ayton, Andrew. *Knights and Warhorses: Military Service and the English Aristocracy under Edward III*. Woodbridge, England: Boydell Press, 1994.

Bessen. David M. *Coping with Treason: The Valois Experience, 1354–1360*. Ada: Ohio Northern University, 1986.

Bothwell, J. S., ed. *The Age of Edward III*. Woodbridge, England: Boydell and Brewer, 2001.

Burne, Alfred H. *The Crécy War*. Ware, England: Wordsworth Editions Ltd., 1999.

Green, D. *The Battle of Poitiers 1356*. Stroud, England: Sutton, 2002.

Hewitt, Herbert J. *The Black Prince's Expeditions of 1355–1357*. Manchester: Manchester University Press, 1958.

———. *The Organization of War under Edward III, 1338–62*. Manchester: Manchester University Press, 1966.

Rogers, Clifford J. *War Cruel and Sharp: English Strategy Under Edward III, 1327–1360*. Woodbridge, England: Boydell and Brewer, 2000.

———. *The Wars of Edward III*. Woodbridge, England: Boydell Press, 1999.

Waugh, Scott L. *England in the Reign of Edward III*. Cambridge: Cambridge University Press, 1991.

CAROLINE WAR, 1369–89

Goodman, Anthony. *The Loyal Conspiracy: The Lords Appellant under Richard II*. London: Routledge and Kegan Paul, 1971.

Palmer, J. J. N. *England, France and Christendom, 1377–99*. London: Routledge, 1972.

Russell, Peter E. *The English Intervention in Spain and Portugal in the Time of Edward III and Richard II*. Oxford: Clarendon Press, 1955.

Tuck, Anthony. *Richard II and the English Nobility*. London: Edward Arnold, 1973.

Wylie, James H. *The History of England under Henry IV*. 4 vols. London: Longmans, 1884–98.

LANCASTRIAN WAR, 1415–53

Burne, Alfred H. *The Agincourt War*. Ware, England: Wordsworth Editions Ltd., 1999.

Curry, Anne. *Agincourt: A New History*. Stroud, England: Tempus Publishing Limited, 2005.

———. *Agincourt 1415: Henry V, Sir Thomas Er- pingham and the Triumph of the English Archers.* Stroud, England: Tempus, 2000.

———. *The Battle of Agincourt: Sources and Inter- pretations.* Woodbridge, England: Boydell Press, 2000.

Famiglietti, Richard C. *Royal Intrigue: Crisis at the Court of Charles VI, 1392–1420.* New York: AMS Press, 1986.

Griffiths, Ralph A. *The Reign of Henry VI.* Berke- ley: University of California Press, 1981.

Hibbert, Christopher. *Agincourt.* London: Wind- rush Press, 2003.

Jacob, E. F. *Henry V and the Invasion of France.* New York: Macmillan, 1950.

Newhall, R. A. *The English Conquest of Nor- mandy, 1416–24.* New York: Russell and Russell, 1971.

———. *Muster and Review: A Problem of English Military Administration, 1420–1440.* Cambridge, MA: Harvard University Press, 1940.

Thompson, G. L. *Paris and Its People under English Rule: The Anglo-Burgundian Regime, 1420–1436.* Oxford: Clarendon Press, 1991.

Wylie, James H., and W. T. Waugh. *The Reign of Henry the Fifth.* 3 vols. Cambridge: Cambridge University Press, 1914–29.

SOCIAL, ECONOMIC, LEGAL, AND RELIGIOUS HISTORY

Allmand, Christopher, ed. *Society at War: The Experience of England and France during the Hundred Years War.* Woodbridge, England: Boydell Press, 1998.

Barber, Richard. *The Reign of Chivalry.* New York: St. Martin's Press, 1980.

Bisson, Thomas. *Assemblies and Representation in Languedoc in the Thirteenth Century.* Princeton, NJ: Princeton University Press, 1964.

Boulton, D'Arcy J. D. *The Knights of the Crown: The Monarchical Orders of Knighthood in Later Med- ieval Europe, 1325–1520.* Woodbridge, England: Boydell, 1987.

Collins, Hugh E. L. *The Order of the Garter, 1348–1461: Chivalry and Politics in Late Medieval England.* Oxford: Oxford University Press, 2000.

Crowder, C. M. D. *Unity, Heresy and Reform, 1378– 1460: The Conciliar Response to the Great Schism.* New York: St. Martin's Press, 1977.

Cuttler, Simon H. *The Law of Treason and Treason Trials in Later Medieval France.* Cambridge: Cambridge University Press, 1981.

Dobson, R. B., ed. *The Peasants' Revolt of 1381.* 2nd ed. London: Macmillan, 1983.

Dunn, Alastair. *The Great Rising of 1381.* Char- leston: Tempus Publishing, 2002.

Fox, John. *The Lyric Poetry of Charles d'Orléans.* Oxford: Clarendon Press, 1969.

Given-Wilson, Chris. *Chronicles: The Writing of History in Medieval England.* London: Ham- bledon and London, 2004.

Gottfried, Robert S. *The Black Death: Natural and Human Disaster in Medieval Europe.* New York: Free Press, 1985.

Harriss, G. L. *King, Parliament and Public Finance in England to 1369.* Oxford: Clarendon Press, 1975.

Harvey, I. M. W. *Jack Cade's Rebellion of 1450.* Oxford: Clarendon Press, 1991.

Henneman, John Bell. *Royal Taxation in Fourteenth Century France: The Captivity and Ransom of John II, 1356–1370.* Philadelphia: American Philo- sophical Society, 1976.

———. *Royal Taxation in Fourteenth Century France: The Development of War Financing, 1322– 1356.* Princeton, NJ: Princeton University Press, 1971.

Herlihy, David. *The Black Death and the Transfor- mation of the West.* Cambridge, MA: Harvard University Press, 1997.

Hilton, R. H. *Bond Men Made Free: Medieval Pea- sant Movements and the English Rising of 1381.* New York: Viking, 1973.

Hilton, R. H., and T. H. Ashton, eds. *The English Rising of 1381.* Cambridge: Cambridge Uni- versity Press, 1984.

Kaeuper, Richard W. *War, Justice and Public Order: England and France in the Later Middle Ages.* Oxford: Clarendon Press, 1988.

Keen, Maurice. *Chivalry.* New Haven, CT: Yale University Press, 1984.

———. *English Society in the Later Middle Ages, 1348–1500.* London: Penguin, 1990.

———. *The Laws of War in the Late Middle Ages.* London: Routledge and Kegan Paul, 1965.

Lloyd, T. H. *The English Wool Trade in the Middle Ages.* Cambridge: Cambridge University Press, 1977.

Major, J. Russell. *Representative Government in Early Modern France.* New Haven, CT: Yale University Press, 1980.

———. *Representative Institutions in Renaissance France, 1421–1559.* Madison: University of Wisconsin Press, 1960.

McFarlane, K. B. *Lancastrian Kings and Lollard Knights.* Oxford: Clarendon Press, 1998.

McNiven, Peter. *Heresy and Politics in the Reign of Henry IV: The Burning of John Badby.* Woodbridge, England: Boydell Press, 1987.

Meiss, Millard. *French Painting in the Time of Jean de Berry: The Late Fourteenth Century and the Patronage of the Duke.* 2 vols. London: Phaidon, 1969.

Mollat, G. *The Popes at Avignon, 1305–1378.* New York: Harper and Row, 1965.

Mollat, Michel, and Philippe Wolff. *The Popular Revolutions of the Late Middle Ages.* Translated by A. L. Lytton-Sells. London: Allen and Unwin, 1973.

Norwich, John Julius. *Shakespeare's Kings.* New York: Scribner, 1999.

Oakley, Francis. *The Western Church in the Later Middle Ages.* Ithaca, NY: Cornell University Press, 1979.

Oman, Charles. *The Great Revolt of 1381.* Reprint, New York: Greenwood, 1969.

Omrod, W. M., and P. G. Lindley, eds. *The Black Death in England.* Donington, England: Shaun Tyas, 2003.

Painter, Sidney. *French Chivalry: Chivalric Ideas and Practices.* Ithaca, NY: Cornell University Press, 1940.

Renouard, Yves. *The Avignon Papacy, 1305–1403.* Translated by Denis Bethell. Hamden, CT: Archon, 1970.

Saccio, Peter. *Shakespeare's English Kings.* 2nd ed. Oxford: Oxford University Press, 2000.

Steele, Robert, and Mabel Day. *The English Poems of Charles d'Orléans.* London: Oxford University Press, 1941.

Strayer, Joseph R., and Charles H. Taylor. *Studies in Early French Taxation.* Cambridge, MA: Harvard University Press, 1939.

Tuck, Anthony. *Crown and Nobility: England, 1272–1461.* 2nd ed. Oxford: Blackwell, 1999.

Twigg, Graham. *The Black Death: A Biological Reappraisal.* London: Batsford, 1984.

Tyrrell, Joseph M. *A History of the Estates of Poitou.* The Hague: Mouton, 1968.

Vale, Juliet. *Edward III and Chivalry: Chivalric Society and Its Context, 1270–1350.* Woodbridge, England: Boydell Press, 1982.

Vale, M. G. A. *War and Chivalry: Warfare and Aristocratic Culture in England, France, and Burgundy at the End of the Middle Ages.* Athens: University of Georgia Press, 1981.

Wright, Nicholas. *Knights and Peasants: The Hundred Years War in the French Countryside.* Woodbridge, England: Boydell Press, 2000.

Ziegler, Philip. *The Black Death.* New York: Harper and Row, 1971.

COUNTRY HISTORIES AND REGIONAL, PROVINCIAL, AND MUNICIPAL STUDIES

Allmand, Christopher. *Lancastrian Normandy: The History of a Medieval Occupation, 1415–50.* Oxford: Clarendon Press, 1986.

Baker, Timothy. *Medieval London.* New York: Praeger, 1970.

Bates, David, and Anne Curry, eds. *England and Normandy in the Middle Ages.* London: Hambledon, 1994.

Beresford, Maurice. *New Towns of the Middle Ages: Town Plantation in England, Wales, and Gascony.* New York: Praeger, 1967.

Blois, Guy. *The Crisis of Feudalism: Economy and Society in Eastern Normandy ca. 1300–1550.* Cambridge: Cambridge University Press, 1984.

Brown, Michael. *The Black Douglases: War and Lordship in Late Medieval Scotland, 1300–1455.* East Linton, Scotland: Tuckwell Press, 1998.

———. *The Wars of Scotland, 1214–1371.* Edinburgh: Edinburgh University Press, 2004.

Butler, Raymond R. *Is Paris Lost? The English Occupation, 1422–1436.* Staplehurst, England: Spellmount, 2003.

Butt, Ronald. *A History of Parliament: The Middle Ages.* London: Constable, 1989.

Carpenter, Christine. *Locality and Polity: A Study of Warwickshire Landed Society, 1401–1499.* Cambridge: Cambridge University Press, 1992.

Cartellieri, Otto. *The Court of Burgundy: Studies in the History of Civilization.* New York: Askell House, 1970.

Couperie, Pierre. *Paris through the Ages.* New York: Braziller, 1968.

Galliou, Patrick, and Michael C. E. Jones. *The Bretons.* Oxford: Blackwell, 1991.

Grant, Alexander. *Independence and Nationhood: Scotland, 1306–1469.* London: E. Arnold, 1984.

Harriss, G. L. *King, Parliament and Public Finance in Medieval England to 1369.* Oxford: Clarendon Press, 1975.

Hillgarth, J. N. *The Spanish Kingdoms, 1250–1516.* 2 vols. Oxford: Oxford University Press, 1976–78.

Inwood, Stephen. *A History of London.* New York: Carroll and Graf Publishers, 1998.

Jones, Colin. *Paris: Biography of a City.* London: Allen Lane, 2004.

Jones, Michael. *Between France and England: Politics, Power and Society in Late Medieval Brittany.*

Burlington, VT: Ashgate Publishing Company, 2003.

———. *The Creation of Brittany: A Late Medieval State*. London: Hambledon, 1988.

———. *Ducal Brittany, 1364–1399: Relations with England and France during the Reign of John IV*. Oxford: Clarendon Press, 1970.

Labarge, Margaret Wade. *Gascony, England's First Colony, 1204–1453*. London: Hamish Hamilton, 1980.

Laidlaw, James, ed. *The Auld Alliance: France and Scotland Over 700 Years*. Edinburgh: University of Edinburgh, 1999.

Lucas, Henry S. *The Low Countries and the Hundred Years War, 1326–47*. Reprint, Philadelphia: Porcupine Press, 1976.

Morgan, Philip. *War and Society in Medieval Cheshire 1277–1403*. London: Palgrave Macmillan, 1988.

Nicholas, David. *Town and Countryside: Social, Economic, and Political Tensions in Fourteenth-Century Flanders*. Bruges: De Tempel, 1971.

Nicholson, Ranald. *Edward III and the Scots: The Formative Years of a Military Career, 1327–1335*. London: Oxford University Press, 1965.

———. *Scotland: The Later Middle Ages*. New York: Barnes and Noble, 1974.

O'Callaghan, James F. *A History of Medieval Spain*. Ithaca, NY: Cornell University Press, 1992.

Prevenier, Walter, and Willem Blockmans. *The Burgundian Netherlands*. Cambridge: Cambridge University Press, 1985.

Richardson, H. G., and G. O. Sayles. *The English Parliament in the Middle Ages*. London: Hambledon Press, 1981.

Sayles, G. O. *The King's Parliament of England*. New York: Norton, 1974.

Shennan, J. H. *The Parlement of Paris*. Stroud, England: Sutton Publishing, 1998.

Sheppard, Francis. *London: A History*. Oxford: Oxford University Press, 1998.

Vale, Malcolm. *English Gascony 1399–1453: A Study of War, Government and Politics during the Later Stages of the Hundred Years' War*. Oxford: Clarendon Press, 1970.

Vaughan, Richard. *Valois Burgundy*. London: Archon, 1975.

Velay, Philippe. *From Lutetia to Paris: The Island and the Two Banks*. Paris: CNRS, 1992.

Williams, Gwyn A. *Medieval London from Commune to Capital*. London: Athlone, 1970.

Wood, Stephen. *The Auld Alliance, Scotland and France: The Military Connection*. Edinburgh: Mainstream, 1989.

BIOGRAPHIES

Ainsworth, Peter F. *Jean Froissart and the Fabric of History: Truth, Myth, and Fiction in the Chroniques*. Oxford: Clarendon Press, 1990.

Allmand, Christopher. *Henry V*. Berkeley: University of California Press, 1992.

Arn, Mary-Jo, ed. *Charles d'Orléans in England, 1415–1440*. Woodbridge, England: D. S. Brewer, 2000.

Barber, Richard. *Edward, Prince of Wales and Aquitaine: A Biography of the Black Prince*. New York: Charles Scribner's Sons, 1978.

Barstow, Anne Llewellyn. *Joan of Arc: Heretic, Mystic, Shaman*. Lewiston, ME: Edwin Mellen Press, 1986.

Bevan, Bryan. *Edward III: Monarch of Chivalry*. London: Rubicon Press, 1992.

Boardman, Stephen. *The Early Stewart Kings: Robert II and Robert III, 1371–1406*. East Linton, Scotland: Tuckwell Press, 1997.

Buchan, Alice. *Joan of Arc and the Recovery of France*. London: Hodder and Stoughton, 1948.

Carson, Patricia. *James van Artevelde: The Man from Ghent*. Ghent: Story, 1980.

Denieul-Cormier, Anne. *Wise and Foolish Kings: The First House of Valois, 1328–1498*. Garden City, NY: Doubleday and Company, 1980.

DeVries, Kelly. *Joan of Arc: A Military Leader*. Gloucester, England: Sutton Publishing, 2003.

Doherty, Paul. *Isabella and the Strange Death of Edward II*. New York: Carroll and Graf Publishers, 2003.

Fein, David A. *Charles d'Orléans*. Boston: Twayne Publishers, 1983.

Fowler, Kenneth A. *The King's Lieutenant: Henry of Grosmont, First Duke of Lancaster*. London: Elek Press, 1969.

Fraioli, Deborah A. *Joan of Arc and the Hundred Years War*. Westport, CT: Greenwood Press, 2005.

Fryde, E. B. *William de la Pole: Merchant and King's Banker*. London: Hambledon and London, 2003.

Fryde, Natalie. *The Tyranny and Fall of Edward II, 1321–1326*. Cambridge: Cambridge University Press, 1979.

Gies, Frances. *Joan of Arc: The Legend and the Reality*. New York: Harper and Row, 1981.

Goodman, Anthony. *John of Gaunt: The Exercise of Princely Power in Fourteenth-Century Europe*. London: Longman, 1992.

Goodrich, Norma Lorre. *Charles Duke of Orleans: Poet and Prince*. New York: Macmillan, 1963.

Griffiths, Ralph A. *The Reign of Henry VI*. Berkeley: University of California Press, 1981.

Haines, Roy M. *Archbishop John Stratford, Political Revolutionary and Champion of the Liberties of the English Church, c. 1275/80–1348*. Toronto: Pontifical Institute of Mediaeval Studies, 1986.

Hardy, B. C. *Philippa of Hainault and Her Times*. London: J. Long, 1910.

Harriss, G. L. *Cardinal Beaufort: A Study of Lancastrian Ascendency and Decline*. Oxford: Clarendon Press, 1988.

———, ed. *Henry V: The Practice of Kingship*. London: Oxford University Press, 1985.

Harvey, John. *The Black Prince and His Age*. London: Rowman and Littlefield, 1976.

———. *The Plantagenets*. 3rd ed. London: Severn House, 1976.

Horrox, Rosemary. *The de la Poles of Hull*. Beverley, England: East Yorkshire Local History Society, 1983.

Howard, Donald R. *Chaucer: His Life, His Works, His World*. New York: E. P. Dutton, 1987.

Hutchinson, Harold F. *Edward II: The Pliant King*. London: Eyre and Spottiswoode, 1971.

———. *The Hollow Crown: A Life of Richard II*. London: Eyre and Spottiswoode, 1961.

———. *King Henry V: A Biography*. New York: Dorset Press, 1967.

Johnson, P. A. *Duke Richard of York, 1411–1460*. Oxford: Clarendon Press, 1988.

Kay, F. George. *Lady of the Sun: The Life and Times of Alice Perrers*. London: Frederick Muller, 1966.

Kenny, Anthony. *Wyclif*. Oxford: Oxford University Press, 1985.

Kirby, J. L. *Henry IV of England*. London: Constable, 1970.

Labarge, Margaret Wade. *Henry V: The Cautious Conqueror*. London: Secker and Warburg, 1975.

Maddicott, J. R. *Thomas of Lancaster, 1307–1322: A Study in the Reign of Edward II*. London: Oxford University Press, 1970.

Maurer, Helen E. *Margaret of Anjou: Queenship and Power in Late Medieval England*. London: Boydell Press, 2003.

Michelet, Jules. *Joan of Arc*. Translated by Albert Guérard. Ann Arbor: University of Michigan Press, 1987.

Mortimer, Ian. *The Greatest Traitor: The Life of Sir Roger Mortimer, Ruler of England, 1327–1330*. London: Pimlico, 2004.

Nicholas, David. *The van Arteveldes of Ghent: The Varieties of Vendetta and the Hero in History*. Ithaca, NY: Cornell University Press, 1988.

Ormrod, W. M. *The Reign of Edward III*. New Haven, CT: Yale University Press, 1990.

Packe, Michael. *King Edward III*. Edited by L. C. B. Seaman. London: Routledge and Kegan Paul, 1983.

Palmer, J. J. N., ed. *Froissart: Historian*. Woodbridge, England: Boydell Press, 1981.

Pearsall, Derek. *The Life of Geoffrey Chaucer: A Critical Biography*. Oxford: Blackwell, 1992.

Penman, Michael A. *David II, 1329–71*. East Linton, Scotland: Tuckwell Press, 2004.

Pernoud, Régine. *Joan of Arc: By Herself and Her Witnesses*. Translated by Edward Hyams. London: Scarborough House, 1994.

Pernoud, Régine, and Marie-Véronique Clin. *Joan of Arc: Her Story*. Translated by Jeremy Duquesnay Adams. New York: St. Martin's Press, 1999.

Phillips, J. R. S. *Aymer de Valence, Earl of Pembroke, 1307–1324: Baronial Politics in the Reign of Edward II*. Oxford: Clarendon Press, 1972.

Pollard, A. J. *John Talbot and the War in France, 1427–1453*. London: Royal Historical Society, 1983.

Prestwich, Michael. *Edward I*. Berkeley: University of California Press, 1988.

Rawcliffe, Carole. *The Staffords: Earls of Stafford and Dukes of Buckingham, 1394–1521*. Cambridge: Cambridge University Press, 1978.

Richards, J. E. *Reinterpreting Christine de Pizan*. Athens: University of Georgia Press, 1991.

Richey, Stephen W. *Joan of Arc: The Warrior Saint*. Westport, CT: Praeger, 2003.

Saul, Nigel. *Richard II*. New Haven, CT: Yale University Press, 1997.

Sedgwick, Henry Dwight. *The Black Prince*. New York: Barnes and Noble Books, 1993.

Seward, Desmond. *Henry V: The Scourge of God*. New York: Viking, 1988.

Shears, Frederic Sidney. *Froissart: Chronicler and Poet*. London: Routledge, 1930.

Strayer, Joseph R. *The Reign of Philip the Fair*. Princeton, NJ: Princeton University Press, 1980.

Talbot, Hugh. *The English Achilles: An Account of the Life and Campaigns of John Talbot*. London: Chatto and Windus, 1981.

Vale, M. G. A. *Charles VII*. Berkeley: University of California Press, 1974.

Vaughan, Richard. *Charles the Bold: The Last Valois Duke of Burgundy*. Woodbridge, England: Boydell Press, 2002.

———. *John the Fearless: The Growth of Burgundian Power*. Woodbridge, England: Boydell Press, 2002.

———. *Philip the Bold: The Formation of the Burgundian State*. Woodbridge, England: Boydell Press, 2002.

———. *Philip the Good: The Apogee of Burgundy.* Woodbridge, England: Boydell Press, 2002.

Vernier, Richard. *The Flower of Chivalry: Bertrand du Guesclin and the Hundred Years War.* Woodbridge, England: Boydell Press, 2003.

Warner, Marina. *Joan of Arc: The Image of Female Heroism.* New York: Vintage Books, 1982.

Watts, John. *Henry VI and the Politics of Kingship.* Cambridge: Cambridge University Press, 1996.

Weir, Alison. *Queen Isabella: Treachery, Adultery, and Murder in Medieval England.* New York: Ballantine Books, 2005.

Wheeler, Bonnie, and Charles T. Woods, eds. *Fresh Verdicts on Joan of Arc.* London: Garland, 1996.

Willard, Charity C. *Christine de Pizan: Her Life and Works.* New York: Persea, 1984.

Williams, E. Carleton. *My Lord of Bedford, 1389–1435.* London: Longmans, 1963.

Wolffe, Bertram P. *Henry VI.* New Haven, CT: Yale University Press, 2001.

Wood, Diana. *Clement VI: The Pontificate and Ideas of an Avignon Pope.* Cambridge: Cambridge University Press, 1989.

ARTICLES

Alban, John R., and Christopher T. Allmand. "Spies and Spying in the Fourteenth Century." In *War, Literature and Politics in the Late Middle Ages,* ed. C. T. Allmand. Liverpool: Liverpool University Press, 1976.

Ayton, Andrew. "English Armies in the Fourteenth Century." In Curry and Hughes, *Arms, Armies and Fortifications,* 21–38.

Bennett, H. S. "Sir John Fastolf." In *Six Medieval Men and Women.* Cambridge: Cambridge University Press, 1955.

Bennett, Matthew. "The Development of Battle Tactics in the Hundred Years War." In Curry and Hughes, *Arms, Armies and Fortifications.* 1–20.

Bessen, David M. "The Jacquerie: Class War or Co-opted Rebellion?" *Journal of Medieval History* 11 (1985): 43–59.

Biggs, Douglas. "'A Wrong Whom Conscience and Kindred Bid Me to Right': A Reassessment of Edmund of Langley, Duke of York, and the Usurpation of Henry IV." *Albion* 26, no. 2 (1994): 253–72.

Bonner, E. "Scotland's 'Auld Alliance' with France, 1295–1560." *History* 84 (1999): 5–30.

Bridbury, A. R. "The Hundred Years War: Costs and Profits." In *Trade, Government and Economy in Pre-Industrial England,* ed. D. C. Coleman and A. H. John, 80–95. London: Weidenfeld and Nicolson, 1976.

Brown, Elizabeth A. R. "Customary Aids and Royal Policy under Philip VI of Valois." *Traditio* 30 (1974): 191–258.

———. "Kings Like Semi-Gods: The Case of Louis X of France." *Majestas* 1 (1993): 5–37.

———. "The Political Repercussions of Family Ties in the Early Fourteenth Century: The Marriage of Edward II of England and Isabelle of France." *Speculum* 63 (1988): 573–95.

Chaplais, Pierre. "English Arguments Concerning the Feudal Status of Aquitaine in the Fourteenth Century." *Bulletin of the Institute of Historical Research* 21 (1948): 203–13.

———. "The Making of the Treaty of Paris (1259) and the Royal Style." *English Historical Review* 67 (1952): 235–53.

Curry, Anne. "English Armies in the Fifteenth Century." In Curry and Hughes, *Arms, Armies and Fortifications,* 39–68.

Cuttino, George P. "Historical Revision: The Causes of the Hundred Years War." *Speculum* 31 (1956): 463–77.

———. "The Process of Agen." *Speculum* 19 (1944): 161–78.

DeVries, Kelly. "Hunger, Flemish Participation and the Flight of Philip VI: Contemporary Accounts of the Siege of Calais, 1346–47." *Studies in Medieval and Renaissance History* 12 (1991): 129–81.

Diverres, A. "Froissart's Travels in England and Wales." *Fifteenth-Century Studies* 15 (1989): 107–22.

Emery, Richard W. "The Black Death of 1348 in Perpignan." *Speculum* 42 (1967): 611–23.

Foley, V., G. Palmer, and W. Soedel. "The Crossbow." *Scientific American* 252 (1985): 104–10.

Fowler, Kenneth A. "Sir John Hawkwood and the English *Condottieri* in Trecento, Italy." *Renaissance Studies* 12 (1998): 131–48.

Friel, Ian. "Winds of Change? Ships and the Hundred Years War." In Curry and Hughes, *Arms, Armies and Fortifications,* 183–94.

Hardy, Robert. "The Longbow." In Curry and Hughes, *Arms, Armies and Fortifications,* 151–60.

Henneman, John Bell. "The Black Death and Royal Taxation in France, 1347–1351." *Speculum* 43 (1968): 405–28.

———. "The French Ransom Aids and Two Legal Traditions." *Studia Gratiana* 15 (1972): 615–29.

———. "The Military Class and the French Monarchy in the Middle Ages." *American Historical Review* 83 (1978): 946–65.

———. "Reassessing the Career of Olivier de Clisson, Constable of France." In *Law, Custom, and the Social Fabric in Medieval Europe*, ed. Bernard Bachrach and David Nicholas, 211–33. Kalamazoo, MI: Medieval Institute, 1990.

———. "Who Were the Marmousets?" *Medieval Prosopography* 5 (1984): 19–63.

Hughes, Michael. "The Fourteenth-Century Raids on Hampshire and the Isle of Wight." In Curry and Hughes, *Arms, Armies and Fortifications*, 121–44.

Hughes, Muriel J. "The Library of Philip the Bold and Margaret of Flanders, First Valois Duke and Duchess of Burgundy." *Journal of Medieval History* 4 (1978): 145–88.

Jones, Michael. "Edward III's Captains in Brittany." In *Between France and England: Politics, Power and Society in Late Medieval Brittany*. Burlington, VT: Ashgate Publishing Company, 2003, pp. 98–118.

———. "War and Fourteenth-Century France." In Curry and Hughes, *Arms, Armies and Fortifications*, 103–20.

Jones, M. K. "Somerset, York and the Wars of the Roses." *English Historical Review* 104 (1989).

Kenyon, John R. "Coastal Artillery Fortification in England in the Late Fourteenth and Early Fifteenth Centuries." In Curry and Hughes, *Arms, Armies and Fortifications*, 145–50.

Kicklighter, Joseph A. "French Jurisdictional Supremacy in Gascony: One Aspect of the Ducal Government's Response." *Journal of Medieval History* 7 (1979): 127–34.

Lachaud, Frédérique. "Armour and Military Dress in Thirteenth- and Early Fourteenth-Century England." In *Armies, Chivalry and Warfare in Medieval Britain and France*, ed. M. Strickland. Stamford, CT: Paul Watkins, 1998.

Le Patourel, J. "Edward III and the Kingdom of France." *History* 43 (1958): 173–89.

———. "The Origins of the War." In *Feudal Empires: Norman and Plantagenet*, ed. Michael Jones, 28–50. London: Hambledon Press, 1984.

———. "The Plantagenet Dominions." *History* 50 (1965): 289–308.

———. "The Treaty of Brétigny 1360." *Transactions of the Royal Historical Society*, 5th ser., 10 (1960).

Maddicott, J. R. "The County Community and the Making of Public Opinion in Fourteenth-Century England." *Transactions of the Royal Historical Society*, 5th ser., 28 (1978): 34–35, 38.

Massey, R. A. "The Land Settlement in Lancastrian Normandy." In *Property and Politics: Essays in Later Medieval English History*, ed. A. J. Pollard. Gloucester, England: Alan Sutton, 1984.

McFarlane, K. B. "The Investment of Sir John Fastolf's Profits of War." In *England in the Fifteenth Century*. London: Hambledon, 1981.

———. "War, the Economy and Social Change: England and the Hundred Years War." *Past and Present* 22 (1962): 3–13.

McKisack, May. "Edward III and the Historians." *History* 45 (1960): 2.

Morgan, D. A. L. "The Political After-Life of Edward III: The Apotheosis of a Warmonger." *English Historical Review* 112 (1997): 856–81.

Omrod, W. M. "The Domestic Response to the Hundred Years War." In Curry and Hughes, *Arms, Armies and Fortifications*, 83–102.

Palmer, J. J. N. "England, France, the Papacy and the Flemish Succession." *Journal of Medieval History* 2 (1976).

Phillpotts, C. J. "The Fate of the Truce of Paris, 1396–1415." *Journal of Medieval History* 24 (1998).

———. "John of Gaunt and English Policy towards France, 1389–95." *Journal of Medieval History* 16 (1990).

Postan, M. M. "The Costs of the Hundred Years War." *Past and Present* 27 (1964): 34–53.

———. "Some Social Consequences of the Hundred Years War." *Economic History Review* 12 (1942): 1–12.

Potter, J. "The Development and Significance of the Salic Law of the French." *English Historical Review* 52 (1937): 235–53.

Prince, A. E. "A Letter of Edward, the Black Prince, Describing the Battle of Najera in 1367." *English Historical Review* 41 (1926): 415–18.

Rogers, C. J. "Edward II and the Dialectics of Strategy, 1327–1360." *Transactions of the Royal Historical Society*, 6th ser., 4 (1994).

Sherborne, J. W. "The Battle of La Rochelle and the War at Sea, 1372–75." *Bulletin of the Institute of Historical Research* 42 (1969).

———. "The Hundred Year's War: The English Navy: Shipping and Manpower." *Past and Present* 37 (1967): 163–75.

———. "Indentured Retinues and English Expeditions to France, 1369–89." *English Historical Review* 79 (1964).

———. "John of Gaunt, Edward III's Retinue, and the French Campaign of 1369." In *Kings and Nobles in the Later Middle Ages*, ed. Ralph A. Griffiths and James Sherborne, 41–61. New York: St. Martin's Press, 1986.

Smith, A. "Litigation and Politics: Sir John Fastolf's Defence of His English Property." In *Property and Politics: Essays in Later Medieval History*, ed. A. J. Pollard. New York: St. Martin's, 1984.

Smith, Robert D. "Artillery and the Hundred Years War: Myth and Interpretation." In Curry and Hughes, *Arms, Armies and Fortifications*, 151–60.

Taylor, C. "Edward III and the Plantagenet Claim to the French Throne." In Bothwell, *Age of Edward II*.

Templeman, G. "Edward III and the Beginnings of the Hundred Years War." *Transactions of the Royal Historical Society*, 5th ser., 2 (1952).

Tuck, J. A. "Richard II and the Hundred Years War." In *Politics and Crisis in Fourteenth Century England*, ed. J. Taylor and W. Childs. Gloucester, England: Alan Sutton, 1990.

Tyson, Diana B. "Jean le Bel: Portrait of a Chronicler." *Journal of Medieval History* 12 (1986): 315–32.

Vale, M. G. A. "England, France and the Origins of the Hundred Years War." In Jones and Vale, *England and her Neighbours*, 199–216.

———. "The War in Aquitaine." In Curry and Hughes, *Arms, Armies and Fortifications*, 69–82.

Warner, Marina. "The Anglo-French Dual Monarchy and the House of Burgundy, 1420–1435: The Survival of an Alliance." *French History* 11 (1997).

Warner, M. W. "Chivalry in Action: Thomas Montague and the War in France, 1417–1428." *Nottingham Medieval Studies* 42 (1998): 146–73.

Wright, Nicholas A. R. " 'Pillagers' and 'Brigands' in the Hundred Years War." *Journal of Medieval History* 9 (1983): 15–25.

FRENCH-LANGUAGE WORKS

Austrand, Françoise. *Charles VI*. Paris: Fayard, 1986.

Avout, Jacques d'. *Le meurtre d'Étienne Marcel*. Paris: Gallimard, 1960.

Beaucourt, Gaston du Fresne de. *Histoire de Charles VII*. 4 vols. Paris: Librairie de la Société Bibliographique, 1881–91.

Biraben, Jean-Noel. *Les Hommes et la peste en France et dans les pays européens et méditerranéens*. 2 vols. Paris: Moulton, 1975–76.

Bonenfant, Paul. *Philippe le Bon*. Brussels: La Renaissance du Livre, 1955.

Borfonove, Georges. *Jean le bon et son temps*. Paris: Ramsay, 1980.

Boüard, Michel de, ed. *Histoire de la Normandie*. 2nd ed. Toulouse: Privat, 1987.

Buttin, François. *Du costume militaire au moyen âge et pendant la Renaissance*. Barcelone: La Academia, 1971.

Cazelles, Raymond. *Étienne Marcel: champion de l'unité française*. Paris: Tallandier, 1984.

———. *Société politique, noblesse et couronne sous Jean le Bon et Charles V*. Geneva: Droz, 1982.

———. *La société politique et la crise de la royauté sous Philippe de Valois*. Paris: Argences, 1958.

Cheruel, Adolphe. *Histoire de Rouen sous la domination anglaise*. Geneva: Slatkine-Magariotis, 1976.

Contamine, Philippe. *Guerre, état et société à la fin du moyen âge: études sur les armies des rois dr France 1337–1494*. Paris: Mouton, 1972.

———. *La guerre de cent ans*. Paris: PUF, 1968.

———. *L'oriflamme de Saint-Denis aux XIVe et Xve siècles*. Nancy: Université de Nancy II, Institut de Recherche Régionale, 1975.

Delachenal, Roland. *Histoire de Charles V*. 5 vols. Paris: Picard, 1909–31.

De Lombars, Michel. *Histoire de l'artillerie français*. Paris: Charles-Lavanzelle, 1984.

Delumeau, Jean, ed. *Histoire de la Bretagne*. Toulouse: Privat, 1969.

Déprez, E. *Les Preliminaries de le Guerre de cent ans: La Papauté, la France et l'Angleterre (1328–1342)*. Paris, 1902.

Descroix, Bernard. *Seguin de Badefol: "ce fils d'iniquité"—qui fit trembler Anse et la France entière*. Lyon: Société d'Archéologie du Beaujolais, 1986.

Deviosse, Jean. *Jean le Bon*. Paris: Fayard, 1985.

Dupuy, Micheline. *Bertrand du Guesclin: capitaine d'adventure, connétable de France*. Paris: Perrin, 1977.

Farrère, Claude. *Histoire de la marine française*. Paris: Flammarion, 1962.

Favier, Jean. *La guerre de cent ans*. Paris: Fayard, 1980.

———. *Philippe le Bel*. Paris: Fayard, 1987.

Froissart, Jean. *Les oeuvres de Froissart—Chroniques*. Edited by Joseph M. B. C. Kervyn de Lettenhove. 25 vols. Brussels: Devaux, 1867–73 (vols. 1–17); Brussels: Closson, 1874–77 (vols. 18–25).

Gardelles, Jacques. *Bordeaux cité médiévale*. Bordeaux: Horizon Chimérique, 1989.

Giquel. Yvonig. *Olivier de Clisson, connétable de France ou chef du parti Breton?* Paris: Picollec, 1981.

Guillemain, Bernard. *La cour pontificale d'Avignon (1309–1376): etude d'une société*. 2nd ed. Paris: Borccard, 1966.

Histoire de l'Aquitaine. Publiée sous la direction de Charles Higounet. Toulouse: Privat, 1971.

Jacob, Yves. *Bertrand du Guesclin, connétable de France.* Paris: Tallandier, 1992.

Jean le Bel. *Chronique.* Edited by Jules Viard and Eugène Déprez. 2 vols. Paris: Renouard, 1904–5.

Kerhervé, Jean. *L'état Breton aux 14e et 15e siècles: les ducs, l'argent et les homes.* 2 vols. Paris: Maloine, 1987,

Kimm, Heidrun. *Isabeau de Bavière, reine de France, 1370–1435.* Munich: Stadtarchiv München, 1969.

Lehoux, Françoise. *Jean de France, duc de Berri: sa vie, son action politique.* 4 vols. Paris: Picard, 1966–68.

Léon-Martin, Louis. *Dunois, le bâtard d'Orléans.* Paris: Colbert, 1943.

Lot, Ferdinand, and Robert Fawtier. *Histoire des institutions françaises au moyen âge.* 3 vols. Paris: Presses Universitaires de France, 1957–62.

Lucenet, Monique. *Les grandes pestes en France.* Paris: Aubier, 1985.

Mangis, Édouard. *Histoire du Parlement de Paris.* 3 vols. Paris: Picard, 1913–16.

Merouville, M. Caffin de. *Le beau Dunois et son temps.* Paris: Les Sept Couleurs, 1961.

Mollat, Michel. *Histoire de Rouen.* Toulouse: Privat, 1979.

Pernoud, Régine. *La liberation d'Orléans, 8 mai 1429.* Paris: Gallimard, 1969.

Rey, Maurice. *Le domaine du roi et les finances extraordinaires sous Charles VI, 1388–1413.* Paris: SEVPEN, 1965.

Richard, Jean. *Les ducs de Bourgogne et la formation du duché.* Paris Les Belles Lettres, 1954.

Trabut-Cussac, Jean-Paul. *L'administration anglaise en Gascogne sous Henri III et Edouard I de 1254 à 1307.* Geneva: Droz, 1972.

van Werveke, Hans. *Jacques van Artevelde.* Brussels: Renaissance du Livre, 1942.

Index

Boldface page references denote full entries, or, in the case of French provinces or major historical sources for the war, a separate description in either Appendix 7 or 8. The abbreviation (illus.) indicates a photograph, genealogy, or other illustration.

INDEX

About the Author

JOHN A. WAGNER has taught British and U.S. history at Phoenix College and at Arizona State University. He holds a B.A. from the University of Wisconsin-Oshkosh and an M.A. and Ph.D. from Arizona State University. He is the author of *The Devon Gentleman: The Life of Sir Peter Carew* (1998); the *Historical Dictionary of the Elizabethan World* (1999), which was a History Book Club Selection; the *Encyclopedia of the Wars of the Roses* (2001); and *Bosworth Field to Bloody Mary: An Encyclopedia of the Early Tudors* (2003). He is also a contributor to the *Historical Dictionary of Late Medieval England, 1272–1485* (2002), to *Women in the Middles Ages: An Encyclopedia* (2004), and to the *Encyclopedia of American Race Riots* (2006).

GALILEO

ALSO BY JAMES RESTON, JR.

To Defend, To Destroy (novel)
The Amnesty of John David Herndon
The Knock at Midnight (novel)
The Innocence of Joan Little
Sherman, the Peacemaker (play)
Our Father Who Art in Hell: The Life and Death of Rev. Jim Jones
Jonestown Express (play)
Sherman's March and Vietnam
The Lone Star: The Life of John Connally
Collision at Home Plate: The Lives of Pete Rose and Bart Giamatti

GALILEO

A
_____
Life

JAMES RESTON, JR.

HarperCollins*Publishers*

GALILEO. Copyright © 1994 by James Reston, Jr. All rights reserved. Printed in the United States of America. No part of this book may be used or reproduced in any manner whatsoever except in the case of brief quotations embodied in critical articles and reviews. For information address HarperCollins Publishers, Inc., 10 East 53rd Street, New York, NY 10022.

HarperCollins books may be purchased for educational, business, or sales promotional use. For information please write: Special Markets Department, HarperCollins Publishers, Inc., 10 East 53rd Street, New York, NY 10022.

FIRST EDITION

Designed by George J. McKeon

Library of Congress Cataloging-in-Publication Data
Reston, James, 1941–
  Galileo : a life / James Reston, Jr.
    p. cm.
  Includes index.
  ISBN 0-06-016378-X
  1. Galilei, Galileo, 1564–1642—Biography. 2. Astronomers—Italy—Biography. I. Title.
QB36.G2R27 1994
520'.92—dc20
[B]   93-29221

94 95 96 97 98 ❖/HC 10 9 8 7 6 5 4 3 2 1

For Edward Burlingame